Supreme Court Activism and Restraint

Supreme Court Activism and Restraint

Edited by
Stephen C. Halpern
Charles M. Lamb
State University of New York
at Buffalo

LexingtonBooks
D.C. Heath and Company
Lexington, Massachusetts
Toronto

Library of Congress Cataloging in Publication Data
Main entry under title:

Supreme Court activism and restraint.

Includes bibliographical references and index.
1. United States. Supreme Court—Addresses, essays, lectures. 2. Judicial process—United States—Addresses, essays, lectures. I. Halpern, Stephen C. II. Lamb, Charles M.

KF8742.A5S86	347.73'26	81–47764
ISBN 0–669–04855–0	347.30735	AACR2

Copyright © 1982 by D.C. Heath and Company

Published simultaneously in Canada

Printed in the United States of America

International Standard Book Number: 0–669–04855–0

Library of Congress Catalog Card Number: 81–47764

Contents

List of Figures

List of Tables

Preface

The purpose of this book is to bring together for the first time in one place a collection of original historical, normative, and behavioral essays on the exercise of activism and restraint by the U.S. Supreme Court. Judicial activism and restraint are central concepts for students in any discipline who study the Supreme Court. Therefore, this volume can be used by upper-division undergraduates and graduate and law students studying constitutional law, legal history and philosophy, and judicial process and behavior.

The book is designed to examine questions of Supreme Court activism and restraint by presenting a wide spectrum of views on the character and scope of the Supreme Court's power in the American political system. Rather than advancing one point of view, the book illuminates the fundamental issues in the debate over the Court's power by providing provocative and conflicting perspectives on those issues. In this way, the book poses and explores afresh the enduring questions that have long informed scholarly inquiry on the Court's function in our constitutional system.

Despite the central place that students of the Supreme Court must assign to the concepts of activism and restraint, it is surprising that no volume in print attempts to do what we have tried to accomplish in this book. The salience of the subject matter, the diversity of positions advanced, the presentation of material written specifically for this volume, and the inclusion of chapters written from historical, normative, and behavioral perspectives lead us to believe that this book fills a substantial gap in scholarly work on the Court. To be sure, Raoul Berger's *Government by Judiciary* (1977), Donald L. Horowitz's *The Courts and Social Policy* (1977), and Lino Graglia's *Disaster by Decree* (1976) address some of the issues on which our contributors focus. However, these books have a narrower scope than this volume, are uniformly critical of the Supreme Court's policymaking, and advance highly individual assessments of the Court's proper role. It should also be emphasized that the chapters in this book were completed in 1979 and 1980, and thus do not address questions and arguments presented in two important books published recently: Jesse H. Choper's *Judicial Review and the National Political Process* (1980) and John Hart Ely's *Democracy and Distrust* (1980).

Like any book of this scope and length, the editors have benefited from the cooperation and assistance of many people since the volume was first conceived in 1978. First, of course, we express our deep appreciation to the contributing authors whose efforts will ultimately determine the value of this volume. Second, several anonymous reviewers significantly contributed to the process of substantive revisions. Finally, we wish to thank Karen Finger for typing various versions of the chapters, Robert Wigton for his assistance in proofreading the manuscript, and Caitlin McCormick for her editorial suggestions.

Part I
Historical Perspectives

The concepts of activism and restraint bear directly on what is perhaps the central question that can be asked about the U.S. Supreme Court—what is the proper role and range of powers of the Court in our governmental system? This has been an enduring question for scholars of the judiciary throughout the Court's history. Indeed, in the past several years we have witnessed a flurry of controversial books and articles on the "Imperial Judiciary" or "Government by Judiciary" which have once again raised scholarly and public debate about the role of the Court.[1] Most of this literature suggests that the courts are reaching out and grabbing too much power in the American political system.[2]

The chapters in part I focus on historical issues, showing that the history of the Supreme Court has been an extraordinary one. Unquestionably, the Court has evolved into a unique governmental institution. This is true primarily because of the frequency and significance of the Court's intervention in major political, social, and economic issues throughout our nation's history. There was surely little prescience at this country's founding of the position and authority the Court was to claim and win for itself in our system. It is worth recalling that in their history of the Republic, Morison and Commager concluded that "the Constitution left this branch of the government [the federal judiciary] even more inchoate than the others."[3] Indeed, even a cursory examination of the Constitution provides striking evidence of the unspecified nature and formless character of the judicial power established in Article III. A comparison with the other branches is instructive.

Article I of the Constitution establishes the legislative branch. It discusses the nature of the powers of Congress in approximately 2,300 words. The description of Congress in Article I, Section 8, includes a lengthy and rather precise elaboration of the authority that the national legislature was intended to exercise. Article II of the Constitution creates the executive branch. It describes in roughly a thousand words the authority of the president and lists the numerous specific powers, as well as the more general responsibilities, granted to the chief executive.

In striking contrast to the constitutional provisions structuring the power of the Congress and the president, Article III, which establishes the federal judiciary, consists of less than four hundred words. It contains no listing or itemization of powers of the sort found in the Articles creating the judiciary's sister branches. While Article III, Section II, speaks directly to the jurisdiction of the federal court system, there is no attempt whatever to delineate the nature of the judicial power. In fact, Article III, Section I seems to take that question for granted by simply stipulating, without further explanation, that "[t]he judicial

1

Power of the United States, shall be vested in one supreme Court, and in such inferior Courts as the Congress may from time to time ordain and establish." The form and substance of that power receives little elaboration. In fact, the Court's most dramatic power, that of judicial review, is not explicitly recognized or authorized in the Constitution, but derives from the clever but refutable logic of Chief Justice Marshall in *Marbury* v. *Madison*.[4]

The constitutional omission regarding the distinctive nature of the judicial power is of critical importance in appreciating the historical development of the Supreme Court. To a greater degree than has been true of the other branches, the Court has determined for itself the dimensions of its role in American government. To be sure, there was an uncertain start as prominent political and legal figures refused to accept, or resigned, seats on the Court, because the institution lacked the prestige and authority of Congress and the presidency.[5] However, beginning with several major—most would say activist—decisions under the chief justiceship of John Marshall from 1801 through 1835,[6] the Court gradually established its place as a third coordinate branch of our national government. Few would disagree with Lawrence Friedman's assessment that the great chief justice "had a sure touch for institutional solidity."[7] The Marshall era transformed the Court into far more than an ordinary court of law: it became a powerful policymaking body, which asserted and won the authority to influence some of the most salient issues of our nation's formative years. It is perhaps not entirely coincidential, then, that near the end of the Marshall era de Tocqueville was moved to remark that "[s]carcely any political question arises in the United States that is not resolved, sooner or later, into a judicial question."[8]

And so it has been throughout the course of American history as constitutional law and American political history have become inextricably intertwined. Of course, some Courts have leaned more toward frequent and influential intervention into the political process, while others have been relatively quiescent. Carl B. Swisher characterized such oscillations thus: "[i]n some periods and situations the Court appeared . . . so cautious and so eager to avoid decision of constitutional questions as to be derelict in the performance of its duties. At other times it has stirred popular wrath and damaged its prestige by deciding questions beyond the scope of seeming necessity."[9] In this sense an understanding of Supreme Court activism and restraint is vital, for in large measure the Court's tendencies toward activism and restraint constitute the core of its history and its impact on American national development. These concepts or their equivalents have therefore been used for nearly two hundred years to describe and understand the work of the Court.

Part I is composed of five chapters that attempt generally to place some of the questions about activism and restraint in historical perspective. In the initial chapter, Charles M. Lamb analyzes the concept and practice of judicial restraint, thus providing an introduction to restraint by examining and critiquing its basic premises and its leading maxims. Lamb emphasizes the subjective, relative nature of the concept and asks whether we should not totally abandon the notion of restraint because of the perplexing problems and ambiguities associated with it. He concludes that, although the concept of restraint suffers from several weaknesses, scholars have yet to develop an acceptable substitute; hence, Lamb argues that it should not at present be abandoned. Lamb further contends that rigorous behavioral research holds out the prospect of clarifying some of the limitations of the label.

Marvin Schick, in chapter 2, argues that judicial activism is a dynamic concept that must be assessed in the context of the politics and history of a given era. During most of the Court's history, he says, there was comparatively little judicial activism. However, he maintains that within the last half-century virtually every Supreme Court has been activist. Schick believes that this is due not to the predilections of individual justices, but to changes in the Court's environment. The pool of potential litigants is broader now, and it is more organized, attentive, and politicized than ever before. The growing politicization of the Court's environment has significantly changed the range and nature of issues brought before the justices, according to Schick, and has altered the role of the high tribunal in our governmental structure.

In a judicial system based upon precedent, one would expect that a Court's formative years would leave an indelible imprint on future developments. In a provocative argument in chapter 3, however, Wallace Mendelson examines the work of the Marshall Court during the country's early years and reaches some unorthodox conclusions as to the legacy that the Court left for latter-day judicial activists. The chapter challenges the conventional wisdom that Marshall was the first and perhaps the greatest exemplar of judicial activism.[10] It is a serious misreading of our constitutional history and law, Mendelson argues, to see the seeds of contemporary judicial activism in the work of the great chief justice. Mendelson's chapter, along with those of several other authors in this volume, raises the bedeviling issue of how one can properly define and apply the labels of judicial activism and restraint.

In chapter 4, Daniel Novak continues that theme in his exploration of activism and restraint in the economic sphere. He finds that Supreme Court decisions on economic and property rights present a consistent pattern of activism throughout much of our history. As Novak sees it, almost from its inception the Court protected business freedom and defended property rights against encroachments by elected legislatures and executives. Novak examines the Court's intervention in these matters from the country's founding to the 1930s. The Court's economic activism reached its peak, of course, in the conflict over President Franklin Roosevelt's New Deal. That conflict ultimatley deflated the Court's economic activism and caused it to retreat from its prominent role in national economic policymaking.

In the fifth and final chapter of part I, Gregory A. Caldeira and Donald J. McCrone provide an overview of the Supreme Court's development by asking whether the Court has been more activist in modern times than it was in previous eras. The authors measure activism by tallying the number of instances per year from 1800 to 1973 in which the Supreme Court invalidated state or federal laws. Historical patterns are presented and analyzed. The authors conclude that there was no significant trend in judicial activism toward the state and federal legislatures before the Civil War. However, they see the Civil War as a watershed period: from the end of the war through 1973, their data show that there have been gradual, albeit irregular, increases in the number of federal and state statutes invalidated by the Court each year.

Notes

1. See, for example, Raoul Berger, *Government by Judiciary: The Transformation of the Fourteenth Amendment* (Cambridge: Harvard University Press, 1977); Archibald Cox, *The Role of the Supreme Court in American Government* (New York: Oxford University Press, 1976); John Charles Daly, Abram Chayes, Ira Glasser, Antonin Scalia, and Laurence Silberman, *An Imperial Judiciary: Fact or Myth?* (Washington: American Enterprise Institute for Public Policy Research, 1979); Ward E. Elliott, *The Rise of Guardian Democracy: The Supreme Court's Role in Voting Rights Disputes, 1845-1969* (Cambridge: Harvard University Press, 1974); Nathan Glazer, "Should Judges Administer Social Services?" *The Public Interest* 50 (Winter 1978): 64-80; Nathan Glazer, "Towards an Imperial Judiciary?," *The Public Interest* 41 (Fall 1975): 104-123; Lino A. Graglia, *Disaster by Decree: The Supreme Court's Decisions on Race and Schools* (Ithaca: Cornell University Press, 1976); Donald L. Horowitz, *The Courts and Social Policy* (Washington: The Brookings Institution, 1977). For a sampling of the earlier literature that also raises the specter of an "Imperial Judiciary" and urges judical restraint, see Alexander M. Bickel, *The Least Dangerous Branch: The Supreme Court at the Bar of Politics* (Indianapolis: Bobbs-Merrill, 1962); Alexander M. Bickel, *The Supreme Court and the Idea of Progress* (New York: Harper and Row, 1970); Louis B. Boudin, *Government by Judiciary* (New York: Goodwin, 1932); Learned Hand, *The Bill of Rights* (Cambridge: Harvard University Press, 1958); Philip B. Kurland, *Politics, the Constitution and the Warren Court* (Chicago: University of Chicago Press, 1970); Philip B. Kurland, "Foreword: 'Equal in Origin and Equal in Title to the Legislative and Executive Branches of Government,' " *Harvard Law Review* 78 (November 1964): 143-176; Henry M. Hart, "Foreword: The Time Chart of the Justices," *Harvard Law Review* 73 (November 1959): 84-125; Louis H. Pollock, "Racial Discrimination and Judicial Integrity: A Reply to Professor Wechsler," *University of Pennsylvania Law Review* 108 (November 1959): 1-34; Herbert Wechsler, "Toward Neutral Principles of Constitutional Law," *Harvard Law Review* 73 (November 1979): 1-35.

2. Daly et al., *An Imperial Judiciary*, p. 11.

3. Samuel Eliot Morrison and Henry Steele Commager, *The Growth of the American Republic* (New York: Oxford University Press, 1962), 1:322.

4. 1 Cranch 137 (1803).

5. See, for example, Robert G. McCloskey, *The American Supreme Court* (Chicago: University of Chicago Press, 1960), p. 31.

6. For examples see *Marbury v. Madison,* 1 Cranch 137 (1803); *Fletcher v. Peck,* 6 Cranch 87 (1810); *Martin v. Hunter's Lessee,* 1 Wheaton 304 (1816); *McCulloch v. Maryland,* 4 Wheaton 316 (1819); *Cohens v. Virginia,* 6 Wheaton 264 (1821); *Gibbons v. Ogden,* 9 Wheaton 1 (1824).

7. Lawrence M. Friedman, *A History of American Law* (New York: Simon and Schuster, 1973), p. 117.

8. Alexis de Tocqueville, *Democracy in America,* ed. Phillips Bradley (New York: Knopf, 1945), p. 280.

9. Carl Brent Swisher, *The Supreme Court in Modern Role,* rev. ed. (New York: New York University Press, 1965), p. 5.

10. It is interesting to point out that Mendelson, like most other scholars, has previously classified Marshall as an activist. See Wallace Mendelson, *Justices Black and Frankfurter: Conflict on the Court,* 2d ed. (Chicago: University of Chicago Press, 1966), p. 116.

1 Judicial Restraint on the Supreme Court

Charles M. Lamb

In an introductory chapter of this kind, one should first point out that judicial restraint on the U.S. Supreme Court is no ephemeral development. Indeed, it is practically as old as the nation itself. Principles and maxims of restraint have historically played a momentous role not only in judicial decision making but in national politics generally. Dissension existed among early American political leaders over the proper role of the Court and its interpretations of the law.[1] Similar conflicts have persisted to the present. As a case in point, the Burger Court's composition purportedly reflects the view that the justices should exercise restraint.[2] With the rare opportunity to appoint four new members to the Court, Richard Nixon stacked that institution with justices who generally disagreed with the Warren Court's liberal activist policymaking.[3] Therefore, within the recent past, the nation has witnessed a modern analogue to historical judicial and political disagreements over whether the Court should play a restrained or activist role in American democracy.

The Warren Court was atypical, however. Over the course of its history the United States Supreme Court has been primarily a Court of restraint—or at least of mild and infrequent activism. Major exceptions, of course, include not only several landmark decisions of the Warren Court, but also a number of decisions of the federally oriented activism of the Marshall Court and the conservative economic activism of the laissez faire Court between 1890 and 1936. Still, it is accurate to say that most of the decisions of even the Marshall, laissez faire, and Warren Courts were not truly activist. As Marvin Schick points out in chapter 2, popular notions about the activism of these Courts should be tempered by the fact that most of their decisions were neither highly controversial nor made sweeping new policy.

Although it will be shown that many members of the Court have not closely and consistently adhered to the maxims of restraint, the basic historical pattern of restraint has nevertheless been the norm that most justices have usually followed. As Henry Abraham has written, "there is a recognition of the overriding need for judicial self-restraint. Its acceptance plays an omnipresent and omnipotent part in the attitude of the nine members of the highest Court in the United States."[4] Abraham adds that "[n]o matter how the judicial record of

The author would like to express his appreciation to Henry J. Abraham, Stephen C. Halpern, Arthur S. Miller, Harold J. Spaeth, and Robert H. Stern for their valuable comments on an early draft of this chapter. However, of course, they do not share the responsibility for any shortcomings herein.

these nine individuals may appear on a chart or graph, no matter how predictable or unpredictable their position on certain issues may be . . . , they are fully aware of their role in, and responsibility to, the democratic body politic which they serve with such dedication."[5]

In introducing the uninitiated to the phrase "judicial restraint," one must stress that it embodies at least six fundamental notions: 1. that the justices abide by the intent of the framers of the Constitution and statutes, and that the justices not read their own personal preferences into the law; 2. that the justices pay deference to the legislative and executive branches of the federal and state governments by seldom overruling their policies, and then only on strictly "legal" grounds; 3. that the justices rely upon statutory rather than constitutional construction wherever possible; 4. that the justices accept for decision only "cases and controversies" where the litigants have standing to sue in live issues; and 5. that the justices neither issue advisory opinions nor 6. answer political questions. It should also be emphasized at the outset that there are significant differences in the ideas of activism and restraint on the one hand, and liberalism and conservatism on the other. One legacy of the Warren Court was for much of the public to equate judicial activism and judicial liberalism. Yet, while conservatives may tend to be practitioners of restraint, conservatives have also been activists in certain historical eras, and liberals have behaved in a restrained manner in others.

Judicial restraint is thus a belief system, a role concept, an ideal of how judges ought to function in a democratic society. When particularly outraged at activism by a Court majority, there is little that a restraint-oriented justice can do other than bargain with his colleagues to gain a more moderate policy statement, and if bargaining proves futile, to issue a separate concurrence or dissent. This has meant that different justices have frequently disagreed over the breadth and content of the Court's decisions, and that one justice's "law" may be another's "judicial legislation." As Justice Robert H. Jackson once observed, "[e]very Justice has been accused of legislating and every one has joined in that accusation of others. . . ."[6] Thus, while it is true that there have been long stretches of time when the Court was quite restrained and its opinions established relatively little new law, it is also true that many significant decisions have directly resulted from the eagerness of a majority coalition of Court members to answer particular questions from an activist standpoint. This has naturally led to overt expressions of conflicting perceptions of the Court's proper governmental role and to the development of principles and maxims in support of judicial restraint.

This chapter is mainly intended to serve as an introduction to judicial restraint and its practice, to clear up some of the confusion associated with the term, and thus to lay a foundation for later chapters. Specifically, the chapter has four purposes and four corresponding sections. The first section explains the premises underlying restraint. The second discusses maxims of restraint as reflected in leading opinions from throughout the Supreme Court's history. The third section assesses the relative and subjective nature of restraint by examining what students of the Court have concluded about decisions of the Burger era. However, while exploring these topics, the chapter also emphasizes some common inconsistencies relating to the notion of restraint. Specifically, an attempt is made to separate theory from practice and myth from reality. The term "restraint" may be meaningful, but it may in fact not be practiced. This emphasis leads to the concluding section which poses the question of whether judicial restraint should not be totally abandoned because of the perplexities associated with its common usage, and because it is often praised but not adhered to. Hence, this chapter is not written to advocate or defend restraint. Instead, it goes beyond simply describing the meaning and characteristics of this judicial doctrine by presenting an analysis, critique, and some opposing views that provide a more rounded picture of the role that restraint plays in the Supreme Court's decision-making process.

Basic Premises Underlying Restraint

To begin to understand judicial restraint, one is most likely to turn to the opinions of either Justice Oliver Wendell Holmes or Justice Felix Frankfurter. Although Holmes was a seminal spokesman for restraint, I am looking more carefully at Frankfurter's opinions because they are more contemporary, and because they seem to spell out more frequently and elaborately the restraintist view of the proper function of the Court in American government. Moreover, chapter 12, by Anthony Champagne and Stuart Nagel, clearly concludes that Frankfurter should be used as a prototype of restraint since, according to their statistics, Frankfurter more closely abided by this doctrine than did other great restrainters—Holmes, Louis D. Brandeis, and Harlan F. Stone.

Following in the doctrinal footsteps of Holmes three decades later, the principle of restraint was Justice Frankfurter's professional heart and soul. It was Frankfurter who repeatedly claimed that, regardless of his own personal views on an issue, he relied on his conception of the Court as an arbitrator of questions of *law*—not questions of politics or economics or social reform—in making decisions. It was Frankfurter who pushed the doctrine of restraint to its outer limits, even beyond those enunciated by Justice Holmes as a dissenting and critical member of the activist laissez faire Court. And it is Frankfurter's opinions that most clearly state the two major premises that serve as underpinnings of the restrainter's insistence on a limited role for the courts in our political system.

The first premise typically drawn upon to support restraint involves the assertion that judicial policymaking conflicts with the very essence of a democratic society. Judicial policymaking is said to defeat the purposes intended by the people's elected representatives and therefore to run counter to popular sentiment. Proponents of restraint, so the argument goes, should endeavor to stand aloof from political controversy. Some restrainers would even let social problems fester until such time as the political branches of government set them straight. In other words, advocates of restraint believe in a quiescent role for courts. They are reluctant to read their own personal predilections into the law, to judge the wisdom of legislation, or to rely on "government by judiciary." They hold dear the democratic decision-making process, the concept of a federal system of government, and the doctrine of separation of powers. They loathe judicial interference, even if justice and liberty are not forthcoming from the political process. It is the people's representatives who must be mainly relied upon as the guardians of rights in American democracy, and it is primarily the cumbersome give-and-take of the legislative process that allows the majority's will to be truly known.

In contrast, Supreme Court members have the luxury of lifetime appointments and, according to the argument, are thus not directly accountable to the public. To a supporter of restraint this suggests that the Supreme Court can act as an undemocratic, countermajoritarian, politically irresponsible, oligarchic body. As Justice Frankfurter counseled: "[t]he Court is not saved from being oligarchic because it professes to act in the service of humane ends. . . . Judges appointed for life whose decisions run counter to prevailing opinion cannot be voted out of office and supplanted by men of views more consonant with it."[7] Frankfurter added that judges "are even farther removed from democratic pressures by the fact that their deliberations are in secret and remain beyond disclosure. . . ."[8] Put somewhat differently, Frankfurter, speaking for the Court in *Rochin* v. *California,* observed that "[w]e may not draw on our merely personal and private notions and disregard the limits that bind judges in their judicial function."[9]

The same theme was elaborated upon by Justice Frankfurter in *West Virginia State School Board of Education* v. *Barnette,* which overturned the antilibertarian *Gobitis* decision.[10] Frankfurter wrote in dissent that:

> [a]s a member of this Court I am not justified in writing my private notions of policy into the Constitution, no matter how deeply I may cherish them or how mischievous I may deem their disregard. The duty of a judge who must decide which of two claims before the Court shall prevail, that of a State to enact and enforce laws within its general competence or that of an individual to refuse obedience because of the demands of his conscience, is not that of the ordinary person. It can never be emphasized too much that one's own opinion about the wisdom or evil of a law should be excluded altogether when one is doing one's duty on the bench. The only opinion of our own . . . that is material is our opinion whether legislators could in reason have enacted such a law.[11]

This outlook led Frankfurter to believe that the Court's revered position in the political system is chiefly based on public confidence which, as he contended in

Baker v. *Carr*, "must be nourished by the Court's complete detachment, in fact and in appearance, from political entanglements and by abstention from injecting itself into the clash of political forces in political settlements."[12]

Regardless of the assertions of Justice Frankfurter and other spokesmen for restraint, it must be recognized that their arguments are by no means self-evident propositions. Indeed, they may be rebutted quite persuasively. As Arthur S. Miller and Stephen C. Halpern make clear in chapters 7 and 9, for example, Frankfurter's premise that the Supreme Court is an undemocratic, oligarchic body does not fully distinguish it from the federal bureaucracy or even from Congress. Of course, the federal bureaucracy is certainly not an elected, responsive force in American government. And Supreme Court decisions do not necessarily undermine democratic rule more than do congressional decisions because legislative seats may not be equally apportioned, and because congressmen (especially United States Senators who have up to six years of discretionary decision making) may behave largely contrary to their constituents' wishes.[13] Congress also has a number of undemocratic features, such as filibusters in the Senate and the design of committee systems in both of its houses.[14] Therefore, even if one concedes that the Supreme Court is an undemocratic institution in terms of accountability and the way that it makes decisions, the Court still does not stand by itself as the only such institution in the American political fabric.

The existence of the Bill of Rights also is testimony to the fact that the form of government in the United States was never intended to be an absolute democracy based solely on majority will. As Justice Jackson has written, "[t]he very purpose of the Bill of Rights was to withdraw certain subjects from the vicissitudes of political controversy, to place them beyond the reach of majorities and officials and to establish them as legal principles to be applied by courts."[15] Additionally, as long as Supreme Court decisions are in essence democratic, the fact that the justices are appointed for life and the manner in which they make decisions should matter little. How can one contend that Warren Court activism was undemocratic, when its decisions extended civil rights, protected the rights of those accused of crime, upheld the rights guaranteed by the First Amendment, and required the reapportionment of federal, state, and local legislative districts? Clearly, the result of such decisions was highly democratic. Moreover, the Supreme Court has never long opposed what the mass of the American people wanted or what the Congress and the president have been determined to have.[16] The Court therefore cannot always be viewed as a deviant, undemocratic institution of government. Nor is it all-powerful. It is, as Alexander Hamilton said, the least dangerous branch.

Loren P. Beth has made another noteworthy point regarding the Court's power of judicial review. He believes that "[j]udicial review is democratic in the sense that it is accepted by most people, if in no other way. Such an institution can only survive so long as the general public and officialdom as well accept it, both in principle and in practice."[17] Beth correctly reminds us that the Supreme Court cannot force its decisions on the remainder of the political system without the system's acceptance. "Consequently, if the [Warren] Court 'gets away' with its . . . activist course in cases involving civil liberties, this would seem to be an indication that the general public (a) still respects and is willing to follow the Court and its power; and/or (b) acquiesces in the major line of court decision."[18] According to Beth, it is likely "that the American public (consciously or subconsciously) feels the need for some sort of 'constitutional guardian' despite our general attachment to majority rule."[19] In short, although the Court may make decisions in an undemocratic manner, virtually no one would seriously contend that the Court cannot or should not rely on the power of judicial review when it deems it necessary to do so. Judicial review cannot be said, then, to be inherently undemocratic in character.

The second premise in support of judicial restraint is that courts simply are not equipped to make wise policy, and therefore judicial policymaking can never effectively meet the broad range of pressing societal needs. Compared to a legislature, a court lacks the staff, financial resources, and power to hold hearings with multiple witnesses presenting myriad facts and points of view.

Once more stating the strongest case for restraint, Justice Frankfurter argued that "[c]ourts are not equipped to pursue the paths for discovering wise policy. A court is confined within the bounds of a particular record, and it cannot even shape the record. Only fragments of the social problem," contended Frankfurter, "are seen through the narrow windows of a litigation. Had we innate or acquired understanding of a social problem in its entirety, we would not have at our disposal adequate means for constructive solution."[20] The suggestion here is that even the best educated justices, the most superbly prepared amicus and Brandeis briefs, the availability of highly qualified law clerks to assist the justices, and the use of masters and experts would not approach the point whereby a justice could make wise decisions based upon an adequate amount of facts and data. A related argument was proffered by Frankfurter in the famous free-speech case of *Dennis* v. *United States,* where, in a concurring opinion, he admonished that courts "are not designed to be a good reflex of a democratic society. Their judgment is best informed, and therefore most dependable, within narrow limits. . . . History teaches," wrote Frankfurter, "that the independence of the judiciary is jeopardized when courts become embroiled in the passions of the day and assume primary responsibility in choosing between competing political, economic, and social pressures."[21] Again, such decisions should be made by elected officials.

But myth must be separated from reality. Frankfurter's comparison is a weak one at best. While federal and state legislatures typically do have larger staffs than the justices, legislators nevertheless cast hundreds of votes on bills each session upon which they have little or no personal knowledge. They frequently depend on the views of other congressmen with whom they usually agree, or party colleagues assigned to the committee that framed the legislation.

Hence, a legislator is frequently less informed on pending statutes than a justice is on pending cases. Also, it is the responsibility of each attorney appearing before the Supreme Court to bring all relevant information to the attention of the justices as it bears on a specific case. Thus, if the Court is uninformed on a case before it, the blame lies just as much on American lawyers as on the Court.

It is even more important to point out that the Frankfurtian premise that the Court is ill-equiped to make wise policy applies more accurately to complicated economic, tax, medical, antitrust, or technological questions. Questions of general social policy, such as desegregation, criminal justice, reapportionment, and school prayers, with which the Court often deals are quite another matter. They tend to be nontechnical. They require that policymakers, whether judicial, executive, or legislative, reach value judgments about the resolution of major social problems. Unlike more technical subjects, social policies touch all our lives. Judges are likewise influenced by social policies, but they are well educated and are not blind to various extrajudicial sources of information that affect their views toward policy questions.[22] Moreover, there are few hard-and-fast solutions to social problems; social scientists are the first to admit this. It stands to reason, then, that since social policy questions are resolved by authorities within the political system based upon their personal judgments, value judgments by members of the Supreme Court may be equally as sound as those of elected officials.

The need for the justices to make value judgments becomes even more crucial when elected officials cannot or will not resolve a policy problem because of its political sensitivity. Federal appellate court judges, especially those serving on the Supreme Court, constitute a legitimate political elite. They do and must act as regular participants in the political process by vindicating constitutional and statutory rights, instead of acting as the apolitical arbitrators of purely legal issues that the idea of restraint has historically indicated. Law and social policy are inevitably interrelated, and when other authorities within the political system reach a stalemate, policymaking responsibility passes to the Supreme Court in areas where the issues brought to Court meet requirements of jurisdiction and standing, and particularly where individual rights are at stake.[23] As Stephen L. Wasby contends, "[i] f the Court does not stress constitutional rights—with the positive effect on popular views such as judicial action can have—no other institution in our political system is likely to do so."[24] Arthur S. Miller has added that when governmental officials are held accountable against enduring constitutional values, that is the essence of democracy and not, as some critics charge, its antithesis.[25] Furthermore, the Court is particularly well situated to perform this function, for it operates in a largely insulated environment where it may dispassionately resolve issues where individual rights, often of unpopular groups or minorities, have been violated.

Nevertheless, Donald L. Horowitz has attempted to extend Justice Frankfurter's argument. In 1977, Horowitz maintained that "[j] udges do not choose their cases and so may often have to act on matters in which they lack complete confidence in their information base."[26] Stated more broadly, Horowitz insists that:

> As the debate over the democratic character of judicial review wanes, there is another set of issues in the offing. It relates not to legitimacy but to capacity, not to whether the courts *should* perform certain tasks but whether they *can* perform them competently.

> Of course, legitimacy and capacity are related. A court wholly without capacity may forfeit its claim to legitimacy. A court wholly without legitimacy will soon suffer from diminished capacity. The cases for and against judicial review have always rested in part on assessments of judicial capacity: on the one hand, the presumably superior ability of the courts "to build up a body of coherent and intelligible constitutional principle;" on the other, the presumably inferior ability of courts to make the political judgments on which exercises of the power of judicial review often turn.[27]

Horowitz, like Frankfurter, concludes that courts must exercise greater restraint because their fact-finding function is inadequate for determining social or legislative facts. More bluntly stated, in some cases judges are simply incapable or incompetent to make decisions because of limited staff and information.[28] It was apparently these two arguments—the oligarchic nature of the Court and the view that the Court is ill-equipped to make wise social policy—that led Justice Harlan F. Stone in 1936 to warn that "[w]hile unconstitutional exercise of power by the executive and legislative branches of the Government is subject to judicial restraint, the only check on our own exercise of power is our own sense of self-restraint. For the removal of unwise laws from the statute books appeal lies not to the courts but to the ballot and to the processes of democratic government."[29]

Maxims of Restraint

For the two reasons given above, Supreme Court justices have felt it necessary to establish basic ground rules concerning the exercise of judicial restraint. For the most part these ground rules are not required by Article III of the Constitution which addresses the federal judiciary. Rather, they have been imposed on the Court by its own members. These decision-making traits are commonly referred to as "maxims of judicial restraint."[30] Opinions of justices who have served throughout the history of the Court supply a multitude of illustrations. These maxims of restraint, in turn, provide a convenient framework for further defining judicial restraint and for identifying those justices who have contributed to, and at least in many instances abided by, those principles.

Some of the most elementary maxims of restraint, which also apply to the lower federal courts, are so widely known that they need be mentioned only briefly. One basic rule, derived from Article III, is that a "case or controversy" must be involved before the Supreme Court will accept an appeal. A case or controversy must include adverse litigants and interests, that is, be an actual controversy. The appeals of so-called friendly parties will be rejected, for there is no antagonistic assertion of rights. A "substantial federal question" must also be involved, and the Court, in the words of Justice Jackson, "has no self-starting capacity and must await the action of some litigant so aggrieved as to have a justiciable case."[31] Furthermore, the justices are supposed to decide only legal issues based on the specific record of the lower courts. Still another requirement is that parties coming before the Court must have standing. In other words, the parties must be directly affected by the law and be the appropriate ones to bring a case in view of the Court's own requirements for standing and jurisdiction. The Court, too, answers only "live" rather than moot legal questions, and all other possible legal remedies must be exhausted before the Court will accept a case for decision.

There are other maxims of restraint, all open to debate and criticism. I will focus on six of the most important, mentioned earlier in this chapter.

The foremost of the six is that justices must abide by the intentions of the framers of the law. This notion is derived from the fundamental ideas that the American political system is based on government of laws, not of men, that there shall be justice *under law* (not "justice" as the members of the Court happen to perceive it), and that there should be little room for a broad judicial construction of constitutional and statutory pronouncements. Dozens of examples could be provided regarding this maxim as stated by advocates of restraint. But more interestingly, activist justices pay lip service to it as well, although they observe the maxim most often when it fits their own purposes in a specific case. For instance, Justice George Sutherland was one of the more conservative activists on the laissez faire Court between 1922 and 1938. However, Sutherland warned in the Minnesota mortgage default case of *Home Building and Loan Association* v. *Blaisdell* that "[t]he whole aim of construction, as applied to a provision of the Constitution, is to discover the meaning, to ascertain and give effect to the intent, of its framers and the people who adopted it."[32] Three decades later Justice Arthur J. Goldberg, a leading member of the activist Warren Court majority, stressed the same point in *Bell* v. *Maryland.* Goldberg commented that "[o]ur sworn duty to construe the Constitution requires . . . that we read it to effectuate the intent and purposes of the Framers."[33]

What is usually glossed over, however, is the crucial question of how a Supreme Court justice can determine precisely what the framers intended in a document nearly two centuries old. This is no easy question, which is exactly why it is often avoided. Moreover, who were "the framers"? The thirty-nine men who signed the Constitution? The state legislators who ratified it? Even if we can agree on a category of identifiable persons who can be labeled "the framers," their intentions cannot always be ascertained. The limited contemporary documentation and the contradictory nature of such documentation as there is makes "the use of the intention of the Framers and of other community leaders of the time questionable."[34] Additionally, even where they can be ascertained, those intentions may run counter to the current needs of society. Assuming that the justices are capable of discovering and agreeing upon the framers' intent, this determination is still of little consequence if constitutional construction falls short of meeting societal needs—what Cardozo called the "welfare of society"[35] —that the legislative or executive branches do not or cannot adequately address. In other words, although the Supreme Court has no monopoly on constitutional interpretation, the justices must *help* to keep the Constitution in tune with the times.

In the strict sense, says John P. Roche, "the intention of the Framers is essentially irrelevant except to antiquarians and polemicists. . . ."[36] But if correct construction of the Constitution is what a justice ideally seeks, it still largely depends on the times, the issues in a case, and who is interpreting the Constitution. If the justices of the Supreme Court are to contribute to the growth of the law in an increasingly complex society, they must at times lay aside the rule that the framers' intentions must always prevail. Thus, Justice Holmes wrote in *Missouri* v. *Holland* that "when we are dealing with words that also are a constituent act, like the Constitution of the United States, we must realize that they have called into life a being the development of which could not have been foreseen completely by the most gifted of its begetters. . . . The case before us," continued Holmes, "must be considered in light of our whole experience, not merely in that of what was said a hundred years ago."[37] Or, in the words of Justice Stone, "the great constitutional guarantees and immunities of personal liberty and property, which give rise to the most perplexing questions of constitutional law and government, are but statements of standards to be applied by courts according to the circumstances and conditions which call for their application."[38]

Apostles of judicial restraint nevertheless have frequently gone out on a weak limb in their enthusiasm over construing the law as the framers intended. They have even argued that no judicial discretion can be exercised outside of simply applying the law as it is written! In 1824 Chief Justice John Marshall wrote that "[j]udicial power, as contradistinguished from the power of the law, has no existence. Courts are mere instruments of the law, and can will nothing."[39] The great chief justice added that "[w]hen they [the courts] are said to exercise a discretion, it is mere legal discretion, a discretion to be exercised in discerning the course prescribed by law; and when that is discerned, it is the duty of the court to follow it. Judicial power is never exercised," claimed Marshall, "for the purpose of giving effect to the will of the judge; always for the purpose of giving effect to the will of the legislature; or, in other words, to the will of the law."[40] The point here is not that John Marshall was a practitioner of restraint in all of his decisions, for plainly he was not in such famous cases as *Marbury* v. *Madison*,[41] *Fletcher* v. *Peck*,[42] *Cohens* v. *Virginia*,[43] and *Gibbons* v. *Ogden*.[44] Rather, the point is that even Marshall found it necessary at times to justify the placing of limitations on a judge's power and to support the maxim that the law be read strictly as written. In other words, Marshall alleged that the substance of landmark Court policies derived not from the personal will of a sitting justice, but instead from the commands of the Constitution itself. However, as Benjamin Cardozo has told us, the above statement by Marshall "can never be more than partly true. Marshall's own career is a conspicuous illustration of the fact that the ideal is beyond the reach of human faculties to attain."[45]

Equally as idealistic, yet praised as maxims of restraint, are some of the statements contained in the opinions of Chief Justice Roger B. Taney, Marshall's successor. The most obvious example comes from *Dred Scott* v. *Sandford*. On the brink of the Civil War, the Court held that slaves were not entitled to citizens' rights provided by the Constitution—even if they had resided in free territories before being forced to return to slave states. Chief Justice Taney's opinion maintained that the Constitution "speaks not only in the same words, but with the same meaning and intent with which it spoke when it came from the hands of its framers, and was voted on and adopted by the people of the United States."[46] Taney continued by asserting that "[a]ny other rule of construction would abrogate the judicial character of this court, and make it the mere reflex of the popular opinion or passion of the day."[47] Since the framers of the Constitution had not intended to extend constitutional rights to slaves, blacks could not claim the rights and privileges automatically conferred on all other citizens. Understandably, the *Dred Scott* ruling was reversed after the Civil War by the addition of the Fourteenth Amendment to the Constitution, but Taney's words still echo in the ears of some spokesmen of restraint.

Even more farfetched than the positions of Marshall and Taney on how judges should abide by the intent of the framers was the literalist interpretation of Justice Owen J. Roberts in the case of *United States* v. *Butler,* which found unconstitutional the Agricultural Adjustment Act passed by the New Deal Congress in 1933. In his often quoted *Butler* opinion, in which a majority of the Court joined, Justice Roberts simplistically wrote:

> There should be no misunderstanding as to the function of this court. . . . It is sometimes said that the court assumes a power to overrule or control the action of the people's representatives. This is a misconception. The Constitution is the supreme law of the land ordained and established by the people. All legislation must conform to the principles it lays down. When an act of Congress is appropriately challenged in the courts as not conforming to the constitutional mandate, the judicial branch of the Government has only one duty, to lay the article of the

Constitution which is invoked beside the statute which is challenged
and to decide whether the latter squares with the former. All the court
does, or can do, is to announce its considered judgment upon the question. The only power it has, if such it may be called, is the power of
judgment. This court neither approves nor condemns any legislative
policy. Its delicate and difficult office is to ascertain and declare
whether the legislation is in accordance with, or in contravention of,
the provisions of the Constitution; and, having done that, its duty
ends.[48]

Justice Roberts's support for a literal, restrained interpretation of the law is
ironic, for the *Butler* decision is a prime example of the use of judicial review to
uphold the conservative activism of the laissez faire Court. Roberts twisted the
idea of restraint in such a way as to arrive at an activist conclusion. His statement also comes strikingly close to Sir William Blackstone's old-fashioned view
that judges are "the depositories of the law; the living oracles who are bound by
an oath to decide according to the law of the land."[49] Roberts's expression thus
epitomizes what Dean Roscoe Pound earlier labeled "mechanical jurisprudence."[50] In the words of Alpheus T. Mason, Roberts "likened the judicial function of that of the grocer weighing the coffee or the dry goods clerk measuring
calico."[51]

Virtually any modern-day student of the judicial process will reject the
Roberts position hands down as running counter to any realistic model of
judicial decision making. Judicial decisions simply cannot, by any stretch of the
imagination, be made using Roberts's directive to lay "the article of the Constitution which is invoked beside the statute which is challenged and . . . decide
whether the latter squares with the former." If the meaning of the Constitution
was so clear, then a number of constitutional provisions would necessarily be
self-explanatory: "due process of law," "freedom of speech and press," "the
common defense and general welfare," "unreasonable searches and seizures,"
"cruel and unusual punishment," and "equal protection of the law." They are
not self-explanatory. As Justice William O. Douglas once put it, "matters of
constitutional interpretation are always open."[52] This means that from time to
time judges *must* read their own personal attitudes into the law, and there is a
huge body of literature clearly demonstrating this fact.[53]

The second of the six maxims, logically flowing from the positions taken by
Marshall, Taney, and Frankfurter—but not from that taken by Roberts—is the
maxim of restraint dictating that justices should be extremely reluctant to exercise the power of judicial review. This is apparent in Justice Frankfurter's
opinion in *American Communications Association* v. *Douds,* a leading anti-
Communist decision of the 1950s. "No one could believe more strongly than I
do," emphasized the dedicated Frankfurter, "that every rational indulgence
should be made in favor of the constitutionality of an enactment by Congress.
I deem it my duty to go to the farthest possible limits in so construing legislation

as to avoid a finding that Congress has exceeded the limits of its powers."[54] Moreover, according to Frankfurter, rather than exercise judicial review, courts should allow legislatures to correct their own mistakes wherever possible. Again arguing that the Supreme Court is a countermajoritarian body, Frankfurter advised that:

> Even where the social undesirability of a law may be convincingly urged, invalidation of the law by a court debilitates popular democratic government. Most laws dealing with economic and social problems are matters of trial and error. That which before trial appears to be demonstrably bad may belie prophecy in actual operation. It may not prove good, but it may prove innocuous. But even if a law is found wanting on trial, it is better that its defects should be demonstrated and removed than that the law should be aborted by judicial fiat. Such an assertion of judicial power defeats responsibility from those on whom in a democratic society it ultimately rests—the people.[55]

Justice Frankfurter at times assumed a similar position involving the exercise of federal judicial review in state cases. For example, Frankfurter agreed in *Bridges* v. *California* that "[w]e are not invested with jurisdiction to pass upon the expediency, wisdom or justice of the laws of the States as declared by their courts, but only to determine their conformity to the Federal Constitution and the paramount laws enacted pursuant to it." "Under the guise of interpreting the Constitution," he wrote, "we must take care that we do not import into the discussion our own personal views of what would be wise, just and fitting rules of government to be adopted by a free people and confound them with constitutional limitations."[56]

Related to the limited use of judicial review is the maxim of restraint directing justices to follow the rule of *stare decisis,* that is, that they abide by the Court's prior rulings. As Justice Roberts observed in *Smith* v. *Allwright,* decisions of the Supreme Court cannot fall "into the same class as a restricted railroad ticket, good for this day and train only."[57] But however central the rule of *stare decisis* is, it has been taken to surprising or illogical ends at times. For instance, Justice Stone once wrote that "the rule of *stare decisis* embodies a wise policy because it is often more important that a rule of law be settled than that it be settled right."[58] Additionally, if *stare decisis* is truly a maxim of restraint adhered to by the justices, the Court would rarely, if ever, have overruled itself— as it has, in well over a hundred decisions,[59] including the *Legal Tender Cases,*[60] *West Coast Hotel* v. *Parrish,*[61] *Erie Railroad Co.* v. *Tompkins,*[62] *Brown* v. *Board of Education,*[63] *Mapp* v. *Ohio,*[64] *Baker* v. *Carr,*[65] *Gideon* v. *Wainwright,*[66] and *Malloy* v. *Hogan.*[67] For this reason Glendon Schubert has flatly asserted that "for the justices of the United States Supreme Court, institutional *stare decisis* does not have even the status of customary norms. . . ."[68]

The third of these six maxims of restraint further stipulates that justices of the Supreme Court should avoid constitutional questions wherever possible. In

Ashwander v. *Tennessee Valley Authority,* for example, Justice Louis D. Brandeis instructed the Court to interpret and apply statutes whenever that option is available. Brandeis cautioned that "[t]he Court will not pass upon a constitutional question, although properly presented, if there is also present some other ground which the case may be disposed of. This rule has found varied application. Thus," wrote Brandeis, "if a case can be decided on either of two grounds, one involving a constitutional question, the other a question of statutory construction or general law, the Court will decide only the latter."[69]

Statutory construction is consequently said to be employed more frequently by the Supreme Court than is constitutional interpretation. Moreover, statutory construction is used when the language or intent of legislative enactments is nebulous, which is often. Frequently relying on extrinsic sources, such as congressional hearings and debates, and always demanding adherence to the meaning of the legislature's words, canons of construction supposedly guide the justices in applying provisions of statutes to litigation before the Court.[70] Particularly when legislative intent remains unclear after reference to extraneous materials, the restraint model encourages courts to employ these canons of construction in making decisions. These canons, however, do not permit a broad interpretation of statutory words, whereas activists are more likely to extend a statute's application to litigation within the law's "reason or spirit." It is also worthwhile to note that Justice Holmes viewed canons of construction as "axioms of experience," but Justice Frankfurter took the position that they "are not in any true sense rules of law."[71] Although helpful in guiding interpretation when intent cannot be determined, Frankfurter observed that canons of construction do not "save us [justices] from the anguish of judgment" because usually dual, conflicting canons exist.[72] Similarly, Karl Llewellyn complained that "[a]s in argument over points of case-law, the accepted convention [in statutory construction] still, unhappily, requires discussion as if only one single correct meaning could exist."[73]

According to the fourth maxim of restraint noted here, the justices are also supposed to decide only legal issues based on the specific record of the lower courts. This maxim contains two very questionable facets. First, of course, the Court inevitably answers social policy questions that constitute a hidden agenda within many legal issues. Certainly a large percentage of the Court's decisions affect various actors and institutions within its environment. Evidence suggests, however, that at times the Court disregards the lower court record. For instance, Richard Richardson and Kenneth Vines investigated labor and civil liberties cases decided by the Warren Court between 1964 and 1965. They found that in 48.7 percent of all cases the Court only mentioned the lower court's record in passing. Essentially, the lower court's logic was completely ignored. In 15.4 percent of the remaining cases, the Warren Court placed moderate reliance on the record of the lower court, but in only 35.9 percent did the Court extensively rely on the record.[74] Similar findings emerged from a study by Arthur S. Miller and

Jerome Barron that focused on the Supreme Court's treatment of the lower court record in three landmark decisions. They discovered that the Court paid virtually no attention to either the adjudicative facts or the legal reasoning stressed by the lower courts.[75] Justice Frankfurter thus overstated his case in declaring that the Supreme Court "is confined within the bounds of a particular record, and it cannot even shape that record."[76] That may be true most of the time, but certainly not all of it.

A fifth maxim of restraint was first established during George Washington's presidency and was elaborated in later Court decisions.[77] This maxim states that the Court will not issue advisory opinions, that is, the Court will not provide its opinion on abstract, hypothetical questions. Instead, an actual case or controversy must be officially brought to the Court. We know, however, that a number of justices have formally or informally broken this rule.[78] In all likelihood others have given advisory opinions but the fact has remained undetected. It is not uncommon for justices to furnish legal advice to presidents or members of Congress with whom they maintain strong friendships and personal ties. Hence, this maxim of restraint hardly constitutes a strict principle guiding the behavior of individual justices.

One final maxim deserves attention, the one that stipulates that the Court will not answer political questions, for these are properly resolved by the executive and legislative branches of government. The problem with this maxim is that the justices have from time to time hotly disagreed over what constitutes a political question. Indeed, "the definition of a political question can be expanded or contracted in accordion-like fashion to meet the exigencies of the times."[79] It is nevertheless generally accepted that there are at least three types of questions that the Court still deems "political": those dealing with whether or not a state has a "republican form of government," those involving foreign relations, and those concerning how a constitutional amendment is to be ratified.

The issue of reapportionment furnishes the best illustration of the shifting sands that underlie the political question doctrine. Until 1962, the Court refused to address the issue of extreme legislative malapportionment and adhered to the principles laid down in *Colegrove v. Green.*[80] In *Colegrove* the Court accepted Justice Frankfurter's admonition that it should not enter the "political thicket" in the reapportionment of congressional legislative districts, and ruled that it was the sole responsibility of the Congress to oversee state procedures for electing congressional members. Although some may assert that the Court departed from its *Colegrove* precedent in *Gomillion v. Lightfoot,*[81] concerning a related issue of redefining city boundaries so as to exclude blacks from voting in city elections, it in fact was not until *Baker v. Carr*[82] that the Court directly overruled the *Colegrove* precedent. The *Baker* case announced that federal courts have jurisdiction under the Fourteenth Amendment's equal protection clause in cases involving state legislative reapportionment and that such cases are justiciable in federal courts. After *Baker* the Warren Court continued to intervene regularly in what was formerly considered the political question of reapportion-ment.[83] By so doing the Court simultaneously acknowledged that all political questions may at some point become justiciable, and gave added support to the old notion that the Court is indeed a political branch of the federal government. In the words of Justice Holmes, the judicial concept of political questions is "little more than play on words."[84] This was indeed the principal lesson of *Baker* and its progeny. The fact that the Court prior to 1962 had viewed reap-portionment as a political question, but did not after that year, also illustrates the subjective, relative nature of judicial restraint.

The Relative, Subjective Nature of Judicial Restraint

Ideas such as judicial restraint—thought to be widely and popularly understood—are often exceedingly difficult to define, analyze, and apply precisely. Among those who have seriously embraced the idea of restraint, there apparently exists a consensus that judicial interpretation should not take on the stark character of legislation. But beyond that point agreement tends to decrease, for the meaning of restraint inevitably depends on the context in which it is being used, the time period in which it is used, and who is using it. Justices Brandeis and Stone, for example, were staunch advocates of restraint when the laissez faire Court was handing down conservative activist economic decisions. Yet the same justices, one might argue, might well have been supporters of liberal egalitarian activism had they served on the Warren Court during the 1950s and 1960s, for they were both liberals at heart. As Sheldon Goldman has explained, "Brandeis . . . and other liberals who later served on the Court were considerably more activist when it came to matters of civil liberties. . . . Had Justice Brandeis been on the Court in the 1960s and early 1970s, I would wager that he would have been found with modern liberal activists."[85]

This plainly suggests that judicial restraint is a relative, subjective phrase. It is relative because it varies from justice to justice over time. In some cases a particular justice may appear to be an advocate of restraint; in others he may not, may even be an activist, or may display in one opinion traits of both ac-tivism and restraint. And restraint is a subjective term—it cannot easily be satisfactorily defined; it is used in a variety of different contexts depending on who is applying it. Only on a few occasions, such as we shall see in part III, has judicial restraint been operationally defined and then measured in any scientific way.

To demonstrate these important distinctions by closely examining each major period of restraint on the Supreme Court would go beyond the scope of this book. Therefore, for purposes of illustration, this section will focus on the relative, subjective nature of certain Burger Court decisions as perceived by leading students of the Court. One would think that sufficient time has passed since Richard Nixon's first term in office to reach solid conclusions concerning the shift from Warren Court activism to Burger Court restraint. However, a survey of the literature demonstrates that there are significant differences of opinion on what kind of role the Burger Court has assumed. What we find is a series of opinions and testimonials concerning the Burger Court's alleged activism and restraint. Both the subjective, relative nature of the concepts and the unpredictable nature of the Burger Court seem to be clearly at work. So, let the experts speak for themselves.[86]

Writing in 1970, Philip Kurland noted even at that early date that "[c]ertainly the outlook of the Court has already been vastly changed by the substitution of Warren Burger for Earl Warren and Harry Blackmun for Abe Fortas."[87] Two years later Wallace Mendelson found that "[d]rastic changes came with a new Chief, and later a new Associate Justice."[88] Mendelson concluded that "President Nixon's campaign for 'strict construction' seems to have had some effect! . . . The great question now is this: Will the full Nixon Court keep these early counsels of restraint?"[89] During the same year Gerald Gunther commented that many Burger Court "'[r]etreats' were more typically refusals to extend Warren Court tendencies and narrow readings of Warren Court precedents: not firm strides to the rear but sidesteps and refusals to step forward. . . ."[90] Such legal sidestepping is of course frequently a cardinal trait of judicial restraint, and there seems little doubt that the Burger Court has, in Richard Funston's words, "exhibited a desire to transfer the burden of solving society's difficult problems from the judicial to the political process. The days when the Court would attempt to save us from ourselves may have ended."[91]

In 1974, Alpheus T. Mason observed that the Burger Court had not reversed the most crucial Warren Court decisions.[92] "The three major pillars in the Warren Court's constitutional edifice—Race Relations, Reapportionment, and Rule of Criminal Procedure—though somewhat eroded, are still virtually intact."[93] Stephen L. Wasby has expressed the view that the transition from the Warren to the Burger Court was characterized by its "playing a more limited role in the American political system."[94] Indeed, outside the area of criminal procedure, many students of the Court feel that there exists a high degree of continuity between the Warren and Burger Courts, which says essentially that the Burger Court has exercised restraint by neither overturning nor extending most Warren Court precedents. Thus, Funston argues that the Burger Court is leading the way toward a "revival of the 'passive virtues.' "[95] But even in criminal procedure, Funston, writing in 1977, remarked that "the record is mixed, with principles established by the Warren Court being broadened as well as qualified."[96] With respect to equal protection, Robert Steamer noted that Chief Justice Burger "and his flock have made changes in degree and not in kind," and that "in spite of the handwringing of civil rights activists, the contrast between the Burger and Warren Courts is not as sharp as they allege."[97] The trend toward New Federalism and decentralization of judicial decision making can also be viewed as one of restraint, whereby state courts are seen as taking on new responsibilities to protect individual rights. Thus, in 1978, Ellis Sandoz could generally conclude that the Burger Court "is clearly less prone to judicial intervention, less activist, less libertarian."[98]

Yet demonstrating the relative, subjective character of restraint, a number of scholars assert that in specific areas the Burger Court has *not* been exercising restraint but has been conservatively and selectively activist. In 1979, Jesse H. Choper, drawing upon numerous examples, demonstrated how the Burger Court has failed to follow the tenets of judicial restraint.[99] Jonathan D. Casper has also suggested that the Burger Court has not exercised restraint in reapportionment, obscenity, and criminal justice cases. Casper noted that Burger Court decisions in these areas "suggest modifications in policy to some extent congruent with the demands of [Warren] Court opponents."[100] In other words, the Burger Court has chipped away at certain Warren Court precedents—as many expected it would. Although judicial restraint normally refers to a Court's recognition of and deference to the law-making functions of the legislative branch, it also includes a Court's upholding its predecessor's decisions. Indeed, as explained earlier, the rule of *stare decisis* is fundamental to the philosophy of restraint. In this respect some have observed instances of activism on the part of the Burger Court that contrast sharply with Warren Court policy. Accordingly, former Justice Arthur J. Goldberg has argued that the Warren Court's activism in defense of individual rights was warranted, while Burger Court activism to overturn decisions of the Warren era are unjustified.[101]

With respect to criminal procedure, Leonard Levy has made the strongest case for the Burger Court being activist. Levy has particularly viewed Chief Justice Burger as a "conservative activist,"[102] as have Bob Woodward and Scott Armstrong in their book, *The Brethren.*[103] S. Sidney Ulmer similarly argues in chapter 13 of this book that activism lives in various Burger Court criminal procedure decisions. Archibald Cox notes that, in view of decisions such as those involving abortions,[104] "the new Justices are not restrained by a modest conception of the judicial function but will be activists when a statute offends their policy preferences."[105] Raoul Berger, among others, believes that in tossing out the traditional requirement for a twelve-member jury in *Williams* v. *Florida,*[106] the Burger Court was clearly functioning in an activist mode.[107] Donald Horowitz[108] interprets the Court's civil rights decisions in *Griggs* v. *Duke Power Company*[109] and *Lau* v. *Nichols*[110] as activist in nature. Various other commentators have pointed out a general retreat in civil rights.[111] Likewise, in the fields of labor law[112] and federal securities law,[113] other authors argue that the Burger Court is handing down activist decisions. Hence, after eight years of Burger Court decisions, Laurence H. Tribe noted that "[n]o great acumen is required to detect in recent decisions of the United States Supreme Court a retreat from the vigorous defense of liberty and equality."[114]

And so the debate continues. These illustrations could easily be multiplied to demonstrate the relative, subjective nature of judicial restraint. The overall conclusion must be that the Burger Court is far less predictable than the Warren Court. Some Burger Court decisions fit the restraint mold, while others reflect activism. At the same time, as Walter Murphy and C. Herman Pritchett have emphasized, the Supreme Court's decisions have been as political under the leadership of Warren Burger as they were under John Marshall, Charles Evans Hughes, and Earl Warren.[115] It thus seems obvious that in addition to the relative, subjective nature of judicial restraint, the Burger Court has acted and will continue to act as a political body. At times it will display restraint; at other times it will use its power of judicial review and discretionary interpretation to make policy in politically sensitive questions. There can be little doubt that the Burger Court is typical in this regard, and virtually any "restraint Court" will receive mixed receptions as to whether it is in fact a Court of restraint.

Should We Abandon the Concept of Restraint?

My purpose up to this point has been to introduce the reader to judicial restraint, and to separate myth from reality. Various weaknesses in the phrase have been deliberately highlighted. The preceding has indeed demonstrated that the label of restraint is confusing and ambiguous. This quite naturally leads to the question of whether the concept should be completely abandoned because it is such a perplexing label for describing specific cases, the role conceptions of individual justices, or decisional tendencies of the Court during a given historical period.

One could argue in favor of abandoning the concept of restraint on the basis of a number of points already raised. First, although most of the Court's decisions and history have been characterized by restraint rather than activism, the cornerstones underlying judicial restraint still remain debatable. Justice Frankfurter and others notwithstanding, the Supreme Court, as we have seen, is not unique in its oligarchic and undemocratic structure and decision-making procedures. Congress and the federal bureaucracy, in particular, have similar features. So do state governments. Nor is the Court so ill-equipped today in terms of information and staff that it cannot make wise policy in the vast majority of cases which it accepts for decision. And one does *not* have to be an advocate of activism to reach these conclusions.

Second, maxims of restraint are not as regularly adhered to by the justices as some observers seem to think they are. Despite disclaimers to the contrary, justices seldom strictly abide by the intent of the framers of the Constitution and statutes because intent is often indefinite or not discernible. Many justices have consequently read their personal, subjective preferences into the law out of necessity, as well as through their own choice. For many of the cases accepted for full-dress treatment, there is no law until the decision is made. Choices often must be made between principles of equal persuasiveness. Neither do the justices consistently observe the rule of *stare decisis;* they have overturned the Court's own precedents dozens and dozens of times. Similarly, the justices have on occasion issued a type of advisory opinion and answered political questions.

One might logically ask, what is wrong or culpable about all of this? Among other things, repeated appeals to maxims of restraint, which are not adhered to, perpetuate the mysticism that surrounds Supreme Court decision making from the lay person's standpoint. The myths associated with restraint give the public the false impression that the law is a fixed, objective phenomenon which the justices simply apply, somewhat mechanically, in cases appealed to them. The truth is otherwise. The law is fluid—it is an open-ended process. It has changed in contradictory, unpredictable, mysterious ways, depending on the needs of the times and the predilections of Court members. Demystification (or demythification) of the law and how it is made by the Supreme Court is a worthwhile goal, one which should be pursued with respect to the well educated and the general public alike. We need not worry that the Supreme Court might lose some of its prestige as a result. In a nation that calls itself democratic, it is preferable that citizens adjust to the realities of Supreme Court decision making than for them to be kept uninformed or misinformed. After all, the Court has survived books like *The Brethren* without noticeable diminution of prestige or power.[116]

Third, in applying the label of restraint to the Burger Court, it becomes plain that the term is so subjective and relative that even the foremost students of the Court sharply disagree over the extent to which it has exercised restraint. The concept is especially complicated by the fact that virtually all justices have lauded its virtues on numerous occasions, whether on the Burger Court or its predecessors. If authorities on the law and the judiciary differ widely concerning the degree to which the Burger Court has exercised restraint, what useful purpose does the term serve? And the same problem applies to other Courts and justices. As one illustration, John Marshall and his Court are typically described as activists in several landmark decisions, but Wallace Mendelson challenges such conventional wisdom in chapter 3 of this book. Such arguments could be extended to other Courts and other times.

Beyond this, one could argue that judicial restraint should be renounced because it has never been uniformly practiced or followed, case after case, by any Supreme Court justice. One could instead assert that the decisions of all justices have involved gradations of activism from exceedingly weak to dogmatically strong in different substantive areas. This is one of the lessons learned from Bradley C. Canon's contribution to this book. As Canon suggests, the frequency and magnitude of activism has varied throughout the Court's history and among different justices, but there has never been a justice who has always exercised restraint. Anthony Champagne and Stuart S. Nagel demonstrate in chapter 12 that Justice Frankfurter followed the tenets of restraint more than did other famous restraintist justices. But Frankfurter concurred with such activist decisions as *Brown* v. *Board of Education*,[117] *Cooper* v. *Aaron*,[118] *McCullom* v. *Board of Education*,[119] Watkins v. *United States*,[120] *Youngstown Sheet and Tube Company* v. *Sawyer*,[121] and *Zorach* v. *Clauson*,[122] while even writing the Court's majority opinion in other activist cases.[123] Moreover, voting behavior research by Harold J. Spaeth, involving eighty nonunanimous cases announced between the 1953 and 1960 Terms of the Warren Court, has demonstrated that Frankfurter was similarly not a restraint-oriented justice in litigation concerning federalism and the decisions of federal regulatory agencies.[124]

One could also criticize the use of a phrase consciously avoided here—that of judicial *self*-restraint. After a series of controversial activist decisions, the Court has often tended to assume a low profile. However, its members have done so, one might suggest, *not* because they feel a renewed responsibility to demonstrate restraint, but because they have consciously sought to avoid political attacks, a loss of esteem within the political system, and other adverse impacts of their decisions. In the most extreme instances, it is not inconceivable that a nonactivist posture could essentially be imposed upon the justices out of fear that the president would refuse to enforce the Court's policies or that Congress would reduce the Court's jurisdiction, pass legislation overruling the Court's statutory interpretations, or initiate constitutional amendments or impeachment proceedings. After John Marshall established the power of judicial review in *Marbury* v. *Madison*,[125] he never again exercised it in federal cases. One could speculate that the main reason was that Marshall, a cunning politician as well as a great chief justice, recognized that the other branches of the federal and state governments would vehemently oppose its repeated use.[126] And as Sheldon Goldman and Thomas P. Jahnige have commented with regard to the activist Hughes and Warren Courts, because of the loss of support from outside the Court, it "*had* to adjust its output if it was to retain its integrity as a system. Something had to give if the federal judicial system was to persist."[127] In these two historic periods the Courts changed directions because of vigorous political resistance to its policies—not because the individual justices believed it their personal duty to observe the tenets of restraint. Thus, the term judicial self-restraint appears in some cases to disguise the reasons for the rise and fall of the Court's decisional trends. The maxims of restraint that the Court has imposed upon itself have undoubtedly been observed by many justices on many occasions. Yet when the Court as a whole exercises restraint, individual support for those maxims does not totally account for the justices' behavior. Externally imposed political pressures must be recognized, and in many instances they explain the resumption of restraint more effectively than do the maxims of restraint themselves. Indeed, it is possible that some of the Court's maxims were judicial expressions flowing directly from the application of political pressures from its environment.

Finally, a case for abandonment of the term judicial restraint might be based on the simple notion that the Constitution's majestic generalities, such as the due process and equal protection clauses, should not and cannot be restrictively construed. With respect to this point Arthur S. Miller has written that the Constitution's undefinable constructs provide "outstanding example[s] of the purposive use of ambiguity which, in our governmental system, gives power to the judiciary to set national policy."[128] If this is an acceptable assumption, and I believe that it is, then a true restraintist interpretation of the Constitution's greatest generalities is not only impossible but highly undesirable—regardless of whether or not the justices "ought" to practice restraint. When the Supreme Court feels it is appropriate to make needed policy changes that the other branches of government refuse to make, the flexibility of these constitutional concepts is essential for governmental adaptation and transition. As John Marshall put it in *McCulloch* v. *Maryland,* the Constitution is "intended to endure for ages to come and, consequently, to be adapted to the various crises of human affairs."[129] So it has been in the past, and so it should remain in the future. The difficult questions, of course, are: how are we to know what changes are needed and when? What are the limits on the Court to mandate such changes? And what criteria, if any, govern those determinations? These are key questions that have understandably received little attention in the literature because of their inherent complexities and the value judgments that necessarily come into play in answering them.

I, for one, would urge the abandonment of the term judicial restraint for a combination of the above reasons—and there are surely others—were it not for two simple but crucial facts. First, we would remain in the uncomfortable position of not having developed a concept to replace it. Despite the opposition of justices and scholars alike to labels and "code words,"[130] they are essential. Although restraint has been an imprecise or even misleading tool for analysis as it has been frequently used in the past, and although many justices have not practiced the restraint that they preach, rejecting it without an adequate conceptual substitute would not resolve our fundamental need to be able to generalize about trends in Supreme Court policymaking. Instead, we would be left with a significant conceptual void. It has been, quite frankly, rather easy to criticize the principles and maxims of restraint; that is always the case with qualitative labels. The far more difficult challenge is to expand our horizons by creating an alternative concept to replace restraint. This must be part of our future agenda. Until then, perhaps all that we can do is to be especially precise in how we define and apply restraint, as the authors have attempted to do in parts I and II of this book. Some problems may also be solved if we become accustomed to speaking in terms of gradations of activism and restraint, as is suggested by Bradley C. Canon in chapter 15, rather than arbitrarily labeling a decision, a justice, or a Court as being black or white—either activist or restraintist.

A second reason for retaining restraint is because more than a glimmer of hope remains for its continued use, in spite of what I have just said. There is a strong possibility that rigorous analyses and applications of the term can clarify the confusion that often surrounds restraint. This becomes evident when one reads the contributions in parts I and II of this volume, and even more so when one considers the chapters in part III. Henry Abraham has taken the position that "not even the many and energetic modern apostles of the scientific method and behavioralism can help us draw [the] line" between activism and restraint.[131] With all due respect, I must dissent. The chapters in part III demonstrate that scholars can carefully operationalize and measure restraint (as well as activism) and thereby yield results of substantive and heuristic value. This all-to-rare accomplishment indicates that optimism is indeed appropriate for the continued use of judicial restraint as a descriptive or even explanatory term. There is a compelling need for additional behavioral research of this kind. Then, and possibly only then, will we be able to avoid the pitfalls that have been so clearly associated with the term restraint throughout the course of American history.

Notes

1. For examples from the eighteenth and nineteenth centuries see Alfred H. Kelly and Winfred A. Harbison, *The American Constitution: Its Origins and Development,* 5th ed. (New York: Norton, 1976), chaps. 8, 10, 13, *passim.*

2. But see the section on "The Relative, Subjective Nature of Judicial Restraint," in this chapter.

3. See, for example, James F. Simon, *In His Own Image: The Supreme Court in Richard Nixon's America* (New York: David McKay, 1973); Charles M. Lamb, "The Making of a Chief Justice: Warren Burger on Criminal Procedure, 1956-1969," *Cornell Law Review* 60 (June 1975):743-788.

4. Henry J. Abraham, *The Judicial Process: An Introductory Analysis of the Courts of the United States, England, and France,* 4th ed. (New York: Oxford University Press, 1980), p. 372.

5. Ibid.

6. Robert H. Jackson, *The Supreme Court in the American System of Government* (Cambridge: Harvard University Press, 1955), p. 80. It is interesting to note that even the most activist justices have acknowledged that the Supreme Court should not function as a "super-legislature." As Justice William O. Douglas wrote in *Griswold v. Connecticut:* "We do not sit as a super-legislature to determine the wisdom, need, and propriety of laws that touch economic problems, business affairs, or social conditions." 381 U.S. 479, 482 (1965). However, the justices have not always practiced what they preached, as is evident in *Griswold* itself.

7. *American Federation of Labor v. American Sash and Door Company,* 335 U.S. 538, 555–556 (1949).

8. Ibid., p. 556. For a similar version of this position see Alexander M. Bickel, *The Least Dangerous Branch: The Supreme Court at the Bar of Politics* (Indianapolis: Bobbs-Merrill, 1962), pp. 16–17; Learned Hand, *The Bill of Rights* (Cambridge: Harvard University Press, 1958), p. 11.

9. 342 U.S. 165, 170 (1952).

10. *Minersville School District v. Gobitis,* 310 U.S. 586 (1940).

11. 319 U.S. 624, 647 (1943).

12. 369 U.S. 186, 267 (1962). See also *Louisiana ex rel. Francis v. Resweber,* 329 U.S. 459, 470–471 (1947).

13. Craig R. Ducat, *Modes of Constitutional Interpretation* (St. Paul: West, 1978), p. 132, n. 35.

14. Ibid., p. 175.

15. *West Virginia Board of Education v. Barnette,* 319 U.S. 624, 638 (1942).

16. Arthur S. Miller, "Some Pervasive Myths About the United States Supreme Court," *St. Louis University Law Journal* 10 (Winter 1965):160. See also Richard Funston, "The Supreme Court and Critical Elections," *American Political Science Review* 69 (September 1975):795–811.

17. Loren P. Beth, "The Supreme Court and the Future of Judicial Review," *Political Science Quarterly* 76 (March 1961):22. See also Eugene V. Rostow, *The Sovereign Prerogative: The Supreme Court and the Quest for Law* (New Haven: Yale University Press, 1962), chap. 5.

18. Beth, "The Supreme Court and the Future of Judicial Review," p. 22.

19. Ibid.

20. *Sherrer v. Sherrer,* 334 U.S. 343, 365–366 (1948). See also Alexander M. Bickel, *The Supreme Court and the Idea of Progress* (New York: Harper and Row, 1970), p. 175.

21. 341 U.S. 494, 525 (1951).

22. See generally Sheldon Goldman and Thomas P. Jahnige, *The Federal Courts as a Political System,* 2d ed. (New York: Harper and Row, 1976), chap. 7; Charles M. Lamb, "Judicial Policy-Making and Information Flow to the Supreme Court," *Vanderbilt Law Review* 29 (January 1976):45–124.

23. Numerous authorities have expressed the belief that the Supreme Court is often justified in making policy where the other two branches of the federal government reach a stalemate. See, for example, Archibald Cox, *The Warren Court: Constitutional Decision as an Instrument of Reform* (Cambridge: Harvard University Press, 1968), pp. 117–118; Robert H. Jackson, *The Struggle for Judicial Supremacy: A Study of a Crisis in American Power Politics* (New York: Knopf, 1941), pp. 284–285; Alpheus Thomas Mason, "The Burger Court in Historical Perspective," *Political Science Quarterly* 89 (March 1974):34; J. Skelly Wright, "The Role of the Supreme Court in a Democratic Society— Judicial Activism or Restraint?," *Cornell Law Review* 54 (November 1968):6.

24. Stephen L. Wasby, *The Supreme Court in the Federal Judicial System* (New York: Holt, Rinehart and Winston, 1978), p. 22.

25. Arthur S. Miller, "For Judicial Activism," *New York Times,* November 11, 1979, section 4, p. 21.

26. Donald L. Horowitz, *The Courts and Social Policy* (Washington: The Brookings Institution, 1977), p. 66.

27. Ibid., p. 18.

28. Ibid., pp. 45-51. For a full critique of Horowitz's work see Charles M. Lamb, "Book Review of *The Courts and Social Policy*," *U.C.L.A. Law Review* 26 (October 1978):234-252. While the Court admittedly has limited staff, the justices often have access to more information than is normally recognized. See Lamb, "Judicial Policy-Making and Information Flow to the Supreme Court;" Arthur S. Miller and Jerome A. Barron, "The Supreme Court, the Adversary System, and the Flow of Information to the Justices: A Preliminary Inquiry," *Virginia Law Review* 61 (October 1975):1187-1245.

29. *United States v. Butler,* 297 U.S. 1, 78-79 (1936). Although Stone was an advocate of restraint in 1936 at the height of the laissez faire Court, it must be remembered that two years later he suggested the need for activism where First Amendment and minority rights are involved. See *United States v. Carolene Products Company,* 304 U.S. 144, 152-153, n. 4 (1938). As one might expect, Justice Frankfurter disagreed with this "preferred position" doctrine. See, for example, *West Virginia Board of Education v. Barnette,* 319 U.S. 624, 648 (1943).

30. See, for example, Abraham, *The Judicial Process,* pp. 372-400.

31. Jackson, *The Supreme Court in the American System of Government,* p. 24.

32. 290 U.S. 398, 453 (1934).

33. 378 U.S. 226, 288-289 (1964).

34. Miller, "Some Pervasive Myths About the United States Supreme Court," p. 166.

35. Benjamin N. Cardozo, *The Nature of the Judicial Process* (New Haven: Yale University Press, 1921), p. 67.

36. John P. Roche, "Judicial Self-Restraint," *American Political Science Review* 49 (September 1955), p. 763.

37. 252 U.S. 416, 433 (1920).

38. Harlan F. Stone, "The Common Law in the United States," *Harvard Law Review* 50 (November 1936):23.

39. *Osborn v. Bank of the United States,* 9 Wheaton 738, 866 (1824).

40. Ibid.

41. 1 Cranch 137 (1803).

42. 6 Cranch 87 (1810).

43. 6 Wheaton 264 (1821).

44. 9 Wheaton 1 (1824).

45. Cardozo, *The Nature of the Judicial Process,* p. 169.

46. 19 Howard 393, 426 (1857).

47. Ibid.

48. 297 U.S. 1, 62–63 (1936).

49. Sir William Blackstone, *Commentaries on the Laws of England,* quoted in *Courts, Judges, and Politics: An Introduction to the Judicial Process,* 3rd ed., ed. Walter F. Murphy and C. Herman Pritchett (New York: Random House, 1979), p. 4.

50. Roscoe Pound, "Mechanical Jurisprudence," *Columbia Law Review* 8 (December 1908):605–623.

51. Alpheus Thomas Mason, "Judicial Activism: Old and New," *Virginia Law Review* 55 (April 1969): 420.

52. *Glidden Company v. Zdanok,* 370 U.S. 530, 592 (1962).

53. See, for example, Glendon Schubert, *The Judicial Mind Revisited: Psychometric Analysis of Supreme Court Ideology* (New York: Oxford University Press, 1974); Sheldon Goldman, "Voting Behavior on the United States Courts of Appeals Revisited," *American Political Science Review* 69 (June 1975):491–506; Charles M. Lamb, "Exploring the Conservatism of Federal Appeals Court Judges," *Indiana Law Journal* 51 (Winter 1976):257–279; S. Sidney Ulmer, "Toward a Theory of Sub-Group Formation in the United States Supreme Court," *Journal of Politics* 27 (February 1965):133–153.

54. 339 U.S. 382, 421 (1950).

55. *American Federation of Labor v. American Sash and Door Company,* 335 U.S. 538, 553 (1949).

56. 314 U.S. 252, 281 (1941), quoting *Twining v. New Jersey,* 211 U.S. 78, 106–107 (1906).

57. 321 U.S. 649, 669 (1944).

58. *United States v. Underwriters Association,* 322 U.S. 533, 579 (1944).

59. The Library of Congress, *The Constitution of the United States of America: Analysis and Interpretation* (Washington, D.C.: Government Printing Office, 1964), pp. 1541–1551.

60. 158 U.S. 601 (1895).

61. 300 U.S. 379 (1937).

62. 304 U.S. 64 (1938).

63. 347 U.S. 483 (1954).

64. 367 U.S. 643 (1961).

65. 369 U.S. 186 (1962).

66. 372 U.S. 335 (1963).

67. 378 U.S. 52 (1964).

68. Glendon Schubert, *Judicial Policy Making: The Political Role of the Courts,* rev. ed. (Glenview, Ill.: Scott, Foresman, 1974), p. 33.

69. 297 U.S. 288, 346–348 (1936). A related notion advanced by Brandeis is that the Court should not pass on the wisdom of legislation, as opposed to its constitutionality. See *Jay Burns Baking Company v. Bryan,* 264 U.S. 504, 519–520 (1924).

70. For various canons of construction that theoretically guide statutory construction see Karl Llewellyn, *The Common Law Tradition: Deciding Appeals* (Boston: Little, Brown, 1960), pp. 521-535.

71. Felix Frankfurter, "Some Reflections on the Reading of Statutes," quoted in Murphy and Pritchett, *Courts, Judges, and Politics,* p. 542.

72. Ibid.

73. Llewellyn, *The Common Law Tradition,* p. 521.

74. Richard J. Richardson and Kenneth N. Vines, *The Politics of Federal Courts: Lower Courts in the United States* (Boston: Little, Brown, 1970), pp. 156-157.

75. Miller and Barron, "The Supreme Court, the Adversary System, and the Flow of Information to the Justices," pp. 1193-1194.

76. *Sherrer v. Sherrer,* 334 U.S. 343, 365 (1948).

77. The leading example is *Muskrat v. United States,* 219 U.S. 346 (1911).

78. For examples of formal and informal advisory opinions see Walter F. Murphy, *Elements of Judicial Strategy* (Chicago: University of Chicago Press, 1964), pp. 147-150; Murphy and Pritchett, *Courts, Judges, and Politics,* pp. 217-218, Wasby, *The Supreme Court in the Federal Judicial System,* pp. 112-113.

79. Roche, "Judicial Self-Restraint," p. 768.

80. 328 U.S. 549 (1946).

81. 364 U.S. 339 (1960).

82. 369 U.S. 186 (1962). Again dwelling on his theme that the Court is an undemocratic, oligarchic body, Justice Frankfurter argued that "[i]n a democratic society like ours, relief must come through an aroused popular conscience that sears the conscience of the people's representatives" (p. 270).

83. See *Gray v. Sanders,* 372 U.S. 368 (1963); *Wesberry v. Sanders,* 376 U.S. 1 (1964); *Reynolds v. Sims,* 377 U.S. 533 (1964); *Avery v. Midland County,* 390 U.S. 474 (1968). Like Frankfurter, Justice John Marshall Harlan was a determined restraintist and critic of the Warren Court's reapportionment decisions. In *Reynolds v. Sims* Harlan deplored the fact that the Court's one-man-one-vote standard was simply "a piece of political ideology" and that the Court should never take upon itself the authority to answer political questions. 377 U.S. 533, 590 (1964). Similarly, in *Avery v. Midland County* Harlan wrote: "I am frankly astonished at the ease with which the Court has proceeded to fasten upon the entire country at its lowest political levels the strong arm of the federal judiciary, let alone a particular political ideology which has been the subject of wide debate and differences from the beginning of our Nation." 390 U.S. 474, 490 (1968).

84. *Nixon v. Herndon,* 273 U.S. 536, 540 (1927).

85. Sheldon Goldman, "In Defense of Justice: Some Thoughts on Reading Professor Mendelson's 'Mr. Justice Douglas and Government by Judiciary,'" *Journal of Politics* 39 (February 1977):149, 150.

86. The remainder of this section is a revised version of Charles M. Lamb and Mitchell S. Lustig, "The Burger Court, Exclusionary Zoning, and the

Activist-Restraint Debate," *University of Pittsburgh Law Review* 40 (Winter 1979):169-174. Copyright 1979 by Charles M. Lamb and Mitchell S. Lustig; revised and reprinted with the permission of the authors.

87. Philip B. Kurland, *Politics, the Constitution and the Warren Court* (Chicago: University of Chicago Press, 1970), p. 49.

88. Wallace Mendelson, "From Warren to Burger: The Rise and Decline of Substantive Equal Protection," *American Political Science Review* 67 (December 1972):1228.

89. Ibid., p. 1233. Nevertheless, Mendelson views early Burger Court decisions as activist in the area of school desegregation. See ibid., p. 1232.

90. Gerald Gunther, "In Search of Evolving Doctrine on a Changing Court: A Model for a Newer Equal Protection," *Harvard Law Review* 86 (November 1972): 2.

91. Richard Y. Funston, *Constitutional Counter-Revolution? The Warren Court and the Burger Court: Judicial Policy Making in Modern America* (New York: Schenkman, 1977), p. 342.

92. Mason, "The Burger Court in Historical Perspective," p. 27.

93. Ibid., p. 35.

94. Stephen L. Wasby, *Continuity and Change: From the Warren Court to the Burger Court* (Pacific Palisades, Calif.: Goodyear, 1975), p. 206.

95. Funston, *Constitutional Counter-Revolution?*, p. 348, referring to Alexander M. Bickel's famous article, "The Passive Virtues," *Harvard Law Review* 75 (November 1961):40-79.

96. Funston, *Constitutional Counter-Revolution?*, p. 336.

97. Robert Steamer, "Contemporary Supreme Court Directions in Civil Liberties," *Political Science Quarterly* 92 (Fall 1977): 432, 442. However, Steamer suggests that the Burger Court has handed down some activists decisions. See ibid., p. 426.

98. Ellis Sandoz, *Conceived in Liberty: American Individual Rights Today* (North Scituate, Mass.: Duxbury, 1978), p. 79.

99. Jesse H. Choper, "The Burger Court: Misperceptions Regarding Judicial Restraint and Insensitivity to Individual Rights," *Syracuse Law Review* 30 (Summer 1979):771-774. Suggestions on the same theme can be found in a careful reading of Sheldon Goldman's "In Defense of Justice."

100. Jonathan D. Casper, "The Supreme Court and National Policy Making," *American Political Science Review* 70 (March 1976):59.

101. Arthur J. Goldberg, *Equal Justice: The Warren Court Era of the Supreme Court* (Evanston: Northwestern University Press, 1971), pp. 74-75.

102. Leonard W. Levy, *Against the Law: The Nixon Court and Criminal Justice* (New York: Harper Torchbooks, 1974), p. 20.

103. Bob Woodward and Scott Armstrong, *The Brethren: Inside the Supreme Court* (New York: Simon and Schuster, 1979), chap. 1 (the 1969 Term).

104. *Roe v. Wade,* 410 U.S. 113 (1973); *Doe v. Bolton,* 410 U.S. 179 (1973).

105. Archibald Cox, *The Role of the Supreme Court in American Government* (New York: Oxford University Press, 1976), p. 54.

106. 399 U.S. 78 (1970).

107. Raoul Berger, *Government by Judiciary: The Transformation of the Fourteenth Amendment* (Cambridge: Harvard University Press, 1977), chap. 22.

108. Horowitz, *The Courts and Social Policy,* pp. 13-17.

109. 401 U.S. 442 (1971).

110. 414 U.S. 563 (1974).

111. See, for example, Lucius J. Barker, "Black Americans and the Burger Court: Implications for the Political System," *Washington University Law Quarterly* (Fall 1973):747-777. Lamb and Lustig, "The Burger Court, Exclusionary Zoning, and the Activist-Restraint Debate," pp. 177-226.

112. Florian Bartosic, "The Supreme Court, 1974 Term: The Allocation of Power in Deciding Labor Law Policy," *Virginia Law Review* 62 (April 1976): 600.

113. Lewis D. Lowenfels, "Recent Supreme Court Decisions Under the Federal Securities Laws: The Pendulum Swings," *Georgetown Law Journal* 65 (April 1977):891-923.

114. Laurence H. Tribe, "Unraveling *National League of Cities:* The New Federalism and Affirmative Rights to Essential Government Services," *Harvard Law Review* 90 (April 1977):1065.

115. Murphy and Pritchett, *Courts, Judges, and Politics,* p. 3.

116. Woodward and Armstrong, *The Brethren.*

117. 347 U.S. 483 (1954).

118. 358 U.S. 1 (1958).

119. 333 U.S. 203 (1948).

120. 354 U.S. 178 (1957).

121. 343 U.S. 579 (1952).

122. 343 U.S. 306 (1952).

123. See, for example, *Rochin v. California,* 342 U.S. 165 (1952).

124. Harold J. Spaeth, "The Judicial Restraint of Mr. Justice Frankfurter—Myth or Reality," *Midwest Journal of Political Science* 8 (February 1964):22-38; Harold J. Spaeth, *Supreme Court Policy Making: Explanation and Prediction* (San Francisco: W.H. Freeman, 1979), pp. 78-80.

125. 1 Cranch 137 (1803).

126. The states did react accordingly to *Martiv v. Hunter's Lessee,* 1 Wheaton 304 (1816) and *Cohens v. Virginia,* 6 Wheaton 264 (1821). See Stephen L. Wasby, *The Impact of the United States Supreme Court: Some Perspectives* (Homewood, Ill.: Dorsey, 1970), pp. 198-199.

127. Goldman and Jahnige, *The Federal Courts as a Political System,* p. 11. (Goldman's and Jahnige's emphasis.)

128. Arthur S. Miller, "Statutory Language and the Purposive Use of Ambiguity," *Virginia Law Review* 42 (January 1956):32.

129. 4 Wheaton 316, 407 (1819).

130. See, for example, Hugo L. Black, *A Constitutional Faith* (New York: Knopf, 1968), pp. 15-22; Wallace Mendelson, "The Neobehavioral Approach to the Study of the Judicial Process: A Critique," *American Political Science Review* 57 (September 1963):593-603.

131. Henry J. Abraham, *The Judiciary: The Supreme Court in the Governmental Process,* 5th ed. (Boston: Allyn and Bacon, 1980), p. 196.

Judicial Activism on the Supreme Court

Marvin Schick

To borrow a bit from Richard Neustadt's much-admired study of presidential power,[1] nowadays all Supreme Courts are activist. The modern Supreme Court is a tribunal which uses its authority expansively and which decides cases that once upon a time (and not so long ago) were thought to be beyond the pale of judicial power.[2] The justices retain the freedom to avoid decisions which challenge the political branches. They also are not required to hear cases which they want to sweep under a jurisdictional carpet or to extend the law beyond the point where they find it. But they are not as free as they often are thought to be, and they cannot avoid social issues which Supreme Courts of yesteryear, including those that according to accepted canons were activist, would never have touched. Activism has triumphed, at least for now. And its triumph is all the more impressive because, apart from enduring scholarly and philosophical interest, the major practical function of the restraintist approach now is to curtail somewhat the rambunctiousness of activism. Activism is therefore partly tethered; heed must be paid to those who plead the cause of modesty.[3] Yet on the record of more than a generation, the inescapable conclusion is that activism can be slowed down, can be made more self-conscious—but no more than that.

Thus, if Hugo Black, once and perhaps still the idol of libertarian activists, were alive, he likely would have little trouble deciding that the Court presided over by Warren Burger, much criticized in certain quarters for curtailing Warren Court rulings and for sidestepping opportunities to make new law,[4] has been a good deal more activist than the Roosevelt Court on which he sat. When that Court invalidated a state program which offered released time in public school for religious instruction,[5] no less an authority than Edward S. Corwin wondered whether the Supreme Court was about to become a national school board.[6] These days, the Court, and the federal judiciary generally, regularly pokes around in the nooks and crannies of school administration,[7] not to mention prison administration,[8] welfare administration,[9] health and mental health administration,[10] and much else of the social and political structure which is thought to be deserving of a more exacting judicial scrutiny.

* * * * *

Although the Supreme Court has been distinctly activistic during most of the twentieth century, the lion's share of this judicial activism has occurred in the lower federal courts.[11] This is not surprising. It is inevitable in activist times that lower court judges do the nuts-and-bolts work of expanding the reach of judicial authority. A single ruling by the Supreme Court permitting judicial intervention in a new field serves as a signal to the bench and bar that additional litigation is acceptable. The Supreme Court thereby imparts legitimacy to actions by inferior courts which may themselves be a good deal more far-reaching that what the Court has pronounced and even more far-reaching than what it would accept should the actions come before it for review. For example, Burger Court decisions involving education, welfare policy, and prisons have contributed in this way to the prevailing climate of activism.

This labeling of the Burger Court as activist is paradoxical and probably controversial as well. Objection could come from the feisty Chief Justice and also from the small army of ideologically oriented critics who have had a field day lambasting him and the Court for scoring low on liberalism scales.[12] How can "strict constructionist" justices who were appointed by Richard Nixon to curtail the excesses of the Warren era be included in the ranks of activism? How can a Court which has snipped away at its predecessor's criminal law rulings, engaged in a small war with the press, and refused to review hundreds of appeals which raised interesting and at time important questions, be regarded as a kindred spirit of the Warren Court? How can it be anything but retrogressive?

The answer to these questions would require a review of Burger Court rulings, which is beyond my purpose here. So the controversy can continue. But the paradox must be explained, and the explanation lies in the reduced freedom the Supreme Court enjoys in controling what it does.

From its earliest days, much has been made of the fact that the justices decide whether to decide, a point brought home in President Washington's administration by the Supreme Court's refusal to render an advisory opinion.[13] Much of the restraintist–activist debate has been predicated on the assumption of judicial freedom and discretion. After all, if the Court must render an opinion whenever it is asked to do so, judicial disagreement would ordinarily be restricted to deciding what the law is or what it is supposed to be. There still would be ample room for disagreement along lines which often have set apart activists and restraintists, but the debate over judicial power which has been at the heart of the conflict between the two approaches would be muted.

Supreme Court justices do, in fact, have enormous jurisdictional latitude.[14] Custom and judicial practice, congressional statutes, and the Court's own rules have resulted in a vast framework of discretionary action. As everyone knows, the Court takes only a handful of the pleas for review presented to it.[15] Even major constitutional litigation can be turned aside "for want of a substantial federal question." What is more, for about a century the Court has had remarkable success in getting Congress to alleviate its caseload by expanding the domain of judicial discretion, a record which may well be extended soon should Congress accede to Chief Justice Burger's long-standing request to establish a national court of appeals.[16] Cases of original jurisdiction are by now a rare species, while certified questions have become a vanishing breed because the justices no longer want lower-court judges to pass the buck to them.

The concept of discretion is embedded in constitutional history, and it has been buttressed by the consensus that when the justices have rushed to judgment, more often than not they have made bad law. It is boilerplate constitutional law that Chief Justice Marshall did not have to invalidate section 13 of the Judiciary Act of 1789 in *Marbury* v. *Madison*,[17] that *Dred Scott* v. *Sandford*[18] was dangerous, that *Pollock* v. *Farmer's Home Loan Association*[19] (invalidating the graduated income tax) was mischievous, and that much of what the Supreme Court decided after the Civil War until the great turnabout of 1937 was the expression of conservative activists who were determined to restrict constitutional development.[20]

Until the last generation, at least, judicial discretion was given another boost in the strong preference among scholars for justices who preached the doctrine of restraint.[21] With some notable exceptions—good examples are John Marshall, for those who rank him among the activists, and Hugo Black for those who are able to ignore or reinterpret his final years—the most-admired justices have been those who were identified as restraintists.[22] This preference arose in an important way from an advantage enjoyed by the advocates of restraint. Statesmanlike appeals for modesty are, after all, much better copy within the legal profession than polemical calls for justices to use any means within their arsenal to achieve presumably desirable ends. The sins and excesses committed in the name of activism also have made it harder to be impressed by that school.

Attitudes have changed much since the advent of the Roosevelt Court, and the reputation of activism has greatly improved with the promotion of libertarian causes. However, the long-lasting esteem of judges who have spoken out against the use of judicial power has reinforced the view that judges have the freedom to decide whether to decide.

The text of Supreme Court opinions and the nature of the Court's adjudicative processes provide additional support for the common view that members of the Supreme Court control much of their destiny. Indeed, conventional wisdom has it that members of the Supreme Court are rarely required to take a stand or to exercise the full force of their authority. Justice Louis D. Brandeis's often-quoted concurring opinion in *Ashwander* v. *Tennessee Valley Authority*[23] is illustrative. There he spelled out how the Court has developed a "series of rules under which it has avoided passing upon a large part of all the constitutional questions pressed upon it for decision,"[24] the implication supposedly being that judicial limitations are mostly a matter of judicial discretion.

This implication permeates Supreme Court opinions, as well as scholarly analysis of them, resulting in a view of the Court which amounts to the proposition that the justices can do just about anything they please. If they decide not to decide or to use their power parsimoniously, it is their decision to do so and not a result compelled by forces over which they have little or no control. Each time the justices argue over the proper use of judicial authority, a frequent exercise each term, the message seems to be: we are the ones who determine. "The only check upon our own exercise of power is our own sense of self-restraint,"[25] said Justic Harlan Fiske Stone in his much-quoted attack on the conservative activists who were wreaking havoc on New Deal legislation. Either way, restraint or activism, was a matter of judicial choice.

Small wonder, then, that the activism of the Burger Court is puzzling. If the justices are free, Warren Burger and a majority of his colleagues should be able to turn back the clock to undo much of what was done in the 1960s by the Warren Court. They should be able to fulfill the expectations of the presidents who appointed them—expectations with which it seems they are in general agreement.

* * * * *

Justice Brandeis did not suggest in *Ashwander*[27] that the justices could avoid passing on all constitutional questions, and indeed they cannot. Judicial discretion, a cornerstone of the doctrine of judicial limitations, is itself limited. This means that the justices are not always free to choose whether to decide. Nor are they always completely free to determine how to decide. Decisions are influenced by doctrinal and ideological commitments, by elements of personal style, by relations with colleagues, by likes and dislikes, by intellectual interests and limitations, and by other factors that can be rightly said to be within the province of members of the Court.[28] Pressures and forces outside of the nearly sealed-off environment of their marble palace may also sway the justices and, even more, limit their freedom. That is why the restraintist and conservative-leaning Burger Court at times sounds more activist and libertarian than it is expected to sound.

Supreme Court justices are limited by past decisions and by past commitments. Adherence to the past is usually thought of as producing conservative results, which is the way lawyers have tended to understand *stare decisis.* What is being conserved or preserved, however, may be attitudes or actions which in an ideological sense are anything but conservative. After periods of intense judicial activism, *stare decisis* actually produced decisions which are no less than moderately activist. That is what occurred on the Supreme Court after the great period of laissez faire activism of 1880–1910 and what has happened in the aftermath of the Warren Court. In the earlier situation, fidelity to the doctrine of *stare decisis* led to conservative activism. In the case of the Burger Court, a commitment to the goal of continuity has restricted the justices' ability to depart from such controversial precedents in criminal law as *Mapp* v. *Ohio*[29] and *Miranda* v. *Arizona.*[30]

Actually, the past limits the justices in another way, this one less formal and legalistic. Political scientists recognize that presidents are limited by previous commitments made by themselves or by their predecessors. The same is true of the Supreme Court, although not so clearly or openly. By the time that President Eisenhower named Earl Warren as chief justice, there was no turning back or away from the issue of school desegregation, given the Supreme Court rulings in the previous fifteen years in cases involving segregation in higher education.[31]

Likewise, the options of the Burger Court were severely limited in the criminal cases by earlier decisions which held that most of the procedural rights of the first eight amendments were both fundamental and applicable to the states through the due process clause of the Fourteenth Amendment. What was the Supreme Court to do in the 1970s—defundamentalize certain rights? Was the Burger Court to say that states were no longer bound by the various provisions of the Bill of Rights? The clock could not be turned back. All that the Supreme Court has been able to do is to refuse to move the clock ahead, and this it has done by refusing to expand on precedents and by restricting the meaning, though not the applicability, of certain rights.

Generally, whenever the Supreme Court in an activist vein decides that a certain question is justiciable, all that a later Court can do is to rule on the merits. Thus, once the Warren Court entered the political thicket of legislative apportionment (and found that it was not as forbidding or treacherous as Justice Felix Frankfurter had warned),[32] as a practical matter there was no way for the Court to use jurisdictional grounds as an excuse for avoiding such questions.

As much as judicial discretion is limited by the past, the present environment in which the Court operates restricts even more the freedom of the justices. For all their discretionary jurisdiction, Supreme Court members exercise little control over the feeder processes which supply cases for their docket. Success in convincing Congress to expand the boundaries of discretion at the Supreme Court level has not been matched in influencing what Congress has done to stimulate activist-oriented litigation throughout the judicial system.[33] Nor has the Supreme Court been able to cool off activist impulses in the parts of the legal profession which promote constitutional litigation. Ultimately all of this activity in the lower federal courts affects what the Supreme Court is required to do. A torrent of activist decisions in the district courts and the courts of appeals at the very least generates requests for Supreme Court review. There must be some action by the Supreme Court, if only the perfunctory denial of review, which intended or not is a signal to the activist bench that they can continue to expand the role of courts and judges.

In a noteworthy book published shortly after his untimely death, Benjamin Twiss argued that the conservative judicial activism of the post–Civil War period was the product of the control over the legal profession by major bar organizations whose members were beholden to corporate and railroad interests.[34] In the Gilded Age and beyond, the Supreme Court was the captive of adherents of laissez faire capitalism.

Although the development has not received a great deal of attention, much the same has happened of late, though it has certainly not come from the same ideological camp. Since some time in the 1960s—probably from the time of the rising of the Great Society and its attendant concept of community action—there has been a strong air of activism about much of the legal profession, and this has created unavoidable involvement for the judiciary in what had previously been nonjudicial issues. From the encouragement of pro bono legal work to public interest law firms, from foundation-supported litigation to hundreds of private associations contemplating legal action to achieve their organizational goals, from federally funded legal services agencies to locally funded legal aid societies, hundreds of lawyers have been poised to launch constitutional attacks on just about every aspect and institution of American life. In line with Alexis de Tocqueville's great insight of nearly a century and a half ago, the mood of challenge to the character of society has been channeled into litigation.[35]

This mood has been abetted by Congress which, apart from providing the funds for legal activity, has significantly included in certain legislation invitations to interested parties to litigate. Furthermore, Congress has made provision for special recompense to public interest lawyers and to others who generate activist legal work.[36]

When one adds to all of this law review articles and other more or less learned importunings for legal remedies to felt social ills, what emerges is a legal profession as much gripped by a spirit of libertarian activism as the old laissez faire lawyerdom and judiciary were gripped by conservative activism.[37] As happened nearly a century ago, this activist spirit intimidates judges high and low. The surprise, perhaps, is not that the Burger Court or the judiciary has been so activist, but rather that there has been less activism than might be expected in light of the activist pressures generated by the feeder processes to the federal judiciary. Indeed, the Supreme Court emerges as consistently more restrained than the lower federal judiciary, particularly in the district courts, which testifies to the relative efficacy of the discretionary controls maintained at the Court.

At the federal district court and intermediate appellate court levels, activism has erupted in full force and has been yoked to the profound dislocations which have been occurring in the scheme of separation of power/checks and balances. The executive/bureaucratic-judicial relationship has undergone considerable extraconstitutional alteration as courts have undertaken administrative and oversight responsibilities. Donald L. Horowitz has analyzed this development in his book, *The Courts and Social Policy,* and he has sharply delineated the pitfalls in the judiciary's assumption of this new role.[38] What needs to be added to his analysis is a historical framework which links recent judicial administrative activities to prior actions. On the one hand, federal trial courts have always had essentially an administrative function in bankruptcy cases and in other litigation where referees have been appointed. But this oversight of commercial activity has been a far cry from the ongoing review of the operations of governmental bodies which Horowitz has studied. Closer conceptual affinity is found in the

1955 follow-up to the previous year's school desegregation decision in which the lower federal judiciary in the South was given the responsibility of monitoring compliance with the *Brown* ruling.[39]

The recent judicial supervision of a myriad of public institutions (schools, prisons, hospitals) is so different in degree from what was contemplated in the original school desegregation decisions, where lower federal judges were brought into the picture in line with the desire for "all deliberate speed," that it really also is different in kind. This seems to be a throwback to the nineteenth century when the jurisdiction of federal courts was as much a matter of equity as of law. The "new equity," as the practice may be termed, is not divorced from law but is strongly enmeshed in statutory and constitutional provisions. The current practice is to locate some constitutional provision—usually the broad and appealing expanses of due process and equal protection—and then to enlarge what the courts may do in enforcing rights located in these constitutional clauses by referring to the inequity implicit in permitting those responsible for the wrong to correct the situation without close judicial supervision. The new equity requires, for instance, that courts do more than invalidate overcrowded prison facilities. They must also fashion an administrative order (under the guise of a judicial decree) in which they spell out acceptable operating standards. This administrative order is apt to be as detailed as instructions emanating from prison officials. In other words, while judges do not have the fact-finding resources or nominal expertise of administrators, and while they certainly do not have operating personnel under their control, they increasingly find it convenient to act as if they manage full-fledged bureaucracies. They have the power to do so, but it is power unchecked by responsibility.[40]

While recent libertarian activism resembles the old laissez faire activism in the control which activist forces exert over judicial feeder processes, in an important sense there is a major distinction between the two periods. When the Court embraced Social Darwinism and struck down legislation aimed at regulating economic and social life, its impact was mostly negative. Further legislative initiatives were discouraged, and processes of social change were slowed down or aborted. Modern activism is generative, not prophylactic; the message sent out by the judiciary is one encouraging further action and social change. The judiciary itself has become a potent instrumentality for promoting and achieving change. Its relationship with the activist feeder processes which have been discussed is of the feedback variety. Forces which are important to the judicial environment spur litigation whose purpose it is to achieve change. To the extent that the Supreme Court accedes to those pressures, it signals forces that they are on the right track.

* * * * *

The present climate of superactivism thus dwarfs anything which the American judiciary has known and sets the context in which the Supreme Court operates. The Supreme Court is very much a prisoner of this environment, able to an extent to ward off campaigns for new horizons of judicial policymaking but hardly capable of being a restraintist Court or of turning back the clock. As the 1980s opened, a group of constitutional scholars considered "The Burger Court: Reflections on the First Decade."[41] Their general conclusion, as reported by the *New York Times* under the headline, "Burger-Led Court Surprises Experts," was that the Supreme Court under Chief Justice Warren Burger "has confounded expectations that it would retreat from either the activism or the principles espoused by the Court under Earl Warren."[42] As I have explained it here, Chief Justice Burger and his colleagues were limited not only by their predecessors. They also could not escape the lower federal judiciary, or the processes which feed cases to the Court, or the environment in which it operates.

It follows that the activist–restraintist debate which has been waged since the New Deal has been robbed of much of its relevance. This is so because of the inappropriate frame of reference which has served as a guidepost for constitutional scholars. As we contemplate a lower federal judiciary which, for instance, concocts a constitutional right for female reporters to enter the locker rooms of male athletes,[43] it is apparent that we do not have a libertarian activist judiciary in the Roosevelt Court sense of the term. We have instead a lower federal judiciary acting without restraint, without much of a sense that there are things that it cannot do. If labels must be used, this could serve as the key to identification: the Burger Court has been activist, while some lower federal courts have acted without restraint.

*　*　*　*　*

If nowadays all Supreme Courts are activist, it does not follow that all recent Courts act alike—that they all are located in roughly the same position along an activist–restraintist continuum. There are differences—major ones—and the question therefore is to ferret out the elements composing activism so that we may determine how activist courts presumably differ from one another.

In an important way the activist–restraint debate has been artificial, even contrived. It is a matter of finding convenient and easy-to-understand labels to help identify the justices, much the same way as "liberal" and "conservative" simplify the world of politics.[44] Nuances are lost in the shuffle. The in-betweens make life difficult, for they require discernment and maybe also wordy explanations which are not easy to follow. This is why Justice Black's final years have caused difficulty,[45] and why writers who should know better ignore his record on World War II prosecutions and Fourth Amendment appeals, why it often is convenient to neglect Justice Frankfurter's activism in freedom of religion and federal search-and-seizure cases,[46] and why Warren Burger has confounded the experts.[47]

The core element of judicial activism is the notion that judges should decide cases, not avoid them, and that judicial power should be used broadly, not parsimoniously. There are both jurisdictional and substantive aspects to this notion. On the jurisdictional side, activist judges are willing to take and decide cases which can be said to be at the periphery of justiciability. (Clearly, however, even the judges who are least concerned about jurisdictional limitations are occasionally constrained by judicial considerations.) They are ready to contract the conventional tools for avoiding decision, such as the concepts of standing, mootness, and the political questions doctrine.

The jurisdictional aspect of activism includes the view that the Supreme Court's discretionary authority should not be used promiscuously to prevent review of important appeals by the full Court. Whether via certiorari or on appeal, the court has enormous theoretical discretion in deciding what to hear. An activist Court is willing, even eager, to decide tough and/or novel questions, while in restraintist times such opportunities are far more likely to be foregone.[48] Yet the choices presented to the justices cannot always be stated so precisely. When the Supreme Court is perceived as distinctly tending toward self-restraint and the lower courts, as well, are not particularly activist, the justices are not likely to have to turn aside a large number of appeals which present unique opportunities for activist decisions. As has been suggested, in recent years the scope of Supreme Court discretion over its docket has been curtailed somewhat by the activist legal forces that comprise much of its environment and control the feeder processes to the Court. The results have been dialectical. While the Supreme Court has been compelled to hear appeals which the justices would just as soon have preferred to avoid, these activist forces, as they have operated in the lower federal judiciary and in some state courts as well, have produced a near torrent of petitions for Supreme Court review of novel and interesting questions. The Court has not had the resources of time, or intellectual and physical strength, to handle the great volume of important cases coming to it for review. This is why perhaps the best case that can be made for labeling the Burger Court as restraintist rests on the large number of appeals raising significant questions which it has turned aside. Substantive activism in the lower courts has thus produced an element of jurisdictional restraint in the Supreme Court.

Substantively, judicial review is the crux of activism, although there has been a remarkable tendency to overstate its role in the activist–restraint scheme of things and to neglect other elements. Because judicial action negating congressional legislation or a presidential decree has an awesome quality and because courts elsewhere do not have so potent an authority, judicial review has been treated as if it is coextensive with activism. But there is much more to the activist mood. Judicial review is not all that important, if only because it is used so sparingly.[49] In the entire Warren era, only a handful of rulings came down invalidating actions of the coordinate branches. Yet no one would deny that this was an activist period, a characterization which then must arise in some measure from judicial activity which was either short of or different from judicial review.

What the Warren Court did was to interpret constitutional rights expansively so as to enlarge the domain of personal freedoms. In the area of criminal law, both the most controversial and broadest field of Warren Court activism, judicial review, as such, was not a factor. Rather, all that the justices did was to interpret the Fourteenth Amendment's due process clause and some of the provisions of the Bill of Rights so as to increase the rights of persons accused of crime. In almost every criminal case the question facing the Court was whether the accused had received a fair trial, not whether the statute under which he was tried was valid.

Activist periods are marked by a significant expansion in the scope and volume of constitutional litigation and interpretation. But this is a phenomenon apart from (albeit related to) judicial review. Even more, statutory interpretation, the staple of Supreme Court activity in calm times, can be part of the activist arsenal.[50] In *Yates* v. *United States,*[51] the Warren Court left much of the Smith Act in shambles. The judicial eye may have been on the First Amendment, yet all the justices needed to do to achieve the desired result was to interpret the statue so as to make it unenforceable. Or, to give another example, in the cases in which the Court expanded the concept of conscientious objection,[52] principal reliance was on the language of the Selective Service Act, not on any constitutional provision.

This is not to say that if judicial review were discarded activism would endure. Judicial review is the most potent exercise of judicial power. It is the most extreme way by which an activist judiciary reaches intended results. However, it is not the only device of judicial power. In some instances—criminal law, for example—it is almost irrelevant.

* * * * *

This examination of the elements of judicial power and its use brings us closer to a differentiation between gradations of activist Courts and justices. Even in its most libertarian period the Roosevelt Court stuck pretty close to accepted jurisdictional standards, something which was not true of the Warren Court in the 1960s.[53] The Burger Court has been more restraintist in the jurisdictional sense than in the substance of the decisions it has rendered.[54]

Ultimately, however, an understanding of activism requires more than an analysis of judicial power. There are other elements, all of them linked to judicial power, yet distinct from it. A study of the Supreme Court in its most activist years (the post-Civil War, Roosevelt, and Warren Courts) suggests the following elements.

First, judicial activism in its fullest sense means more than the use of judicial power. Essentially, activism is the reliance on the judicial role to establish new law—really, to legislate. This is what the Court did after the Civil War, especially during the 1890s and in the early years of this century. Substantive due process was fashioned out of the Fourteenth Amendment, and the doctrines of laissez faire capitalism received the stamp of judicial approval. There were few, if any, clear precedents for the many rulings which are now universally criticized. To the contrary, in order to achieve what was desired, the Court at times warped or abandoned accepted doctrine, as when congressional efforts to bar the products of child labor were invalidated,[55] though legislation predicated on similar reasoning which regulated lottery tickets[56] and oleomargarine[57] was upheld.

The pre-1937 Supreme Court, on the other hand, was also activist, yet not in the same way that the Supreme Court of such justices as Field, Fuller, and Brewer were. Not one of the anti–New Deal decisions was without precedent. *United States* v. *Butler*[58] and *Carter* v. *Carter Coal*[59] were the direct progeny of *United States* v. *E.C. Knight Company.*[60] As unwarranted or as mischievous as these ruling were, in a judicial sense they were not as activist as the earlier pronouncements of the Court.

Second, it has been said that activist justices are result-oriented, a true enough point which must be treated with a modicum of caution. After all, the justices make decisions, and therefore they are in the business of bringing about results.[61] There is a crucial distinction, however, between a justice who wants to be on the winning side or to have his view prevail and a justice who is determined to bring about certain results, no matter what the nominal legal or judicial obstacles. What distinguishes the major activist Courts and justices and what marks them as distinctively result-oriented is the transparency of their efforts to fashion the law to meet their policy preferences. Three illustrations from the Warren Court are most telling.

Before the decision in *Brown* v. *Board of Education,*[62] the Court actively sought to figure out what history could teach about the attitude of the framers of the Fourteenth Amendment. In his opinion, Chief Justice Warren explicitly downplayed the historical question and instead relied on social psychology. A decade later, in *Wesberry* v. *Sanders,*[63] Justice Black for the majority discovered that "construed in its historical context," the simple prepositional phrase "by the people" of Article I of the Constitution means that in congressional elections the one-man-one-vote rule must apply—an historical interpretation which had eluded scholars and lawyers since 1787. Most notoriously, *Miranda* v. *Arizona*[64] discovered a right to counsel in the self-incrimination clause of the Fifth Amendment, a result made even more extraordinary by Earl Warren's incredible assertion that the ruling was supported by ample precedents.

These decisions may have been justified, as I think they were. The point is that the Court in each case fixed itself on a desired result and found whatever means were necessary to arrive there.

Third, nothing irked Justice Oliver Wendell Holmes more than the assertion that it was the job of justices to do justice. And nothing stamps the activists more

clearly than their insistence that there is (or should be) a judicial remedy for
social wrongs brought before the Court. The opinions of the great activist justices ring out with declarations of the judicial obligation to guard the Constitution, promote justice, abort evil, protect liberty, guarantee equality, and so on.
An illustration comes from the first Justice Harlan, perhaps the most activist
justice to ever sit on the Court. In *International Postal Supply Company* v.
Bruce,[65] Harlan wrote: "In my judgment it is not possible to conceive of any
case, arising under our system of constitutional government, in which courts
may not, in some effective mold, and properly, protect the rights of the citizen
against illegal aggression, and to that end, if need be, stay the hands of the
aggressor. . . ."[66]

What distinguishes the most activist Courts and justices is the use of some
philosophical system which, they say, directs the course of law and judicial
action. Law must be adapted by judicial means to the imperatives of one or
another philosophy, and the justices must do their duty. Reliance on natural law
philosophy was a familiar device of nineteenth-century judicial activists. In the
Taft Court, for all of its conservative impulses and actions, there is no sense of
overwhelming fidelity to a higher obligation. This was true, also, of the several
pre-1937 cases in which New Deal legislation was invalidated. The majority opinions in these cases did not convey any great care about preserving the institutions of laissez faire capitalism from an invasion by the onrushing welfare state.
It was only after the conservative activists were put to rout in the Supreme
Court revolution of 1937 and 1938 that they articulated a philosophy. The
activism of the turn-of-the-century Supreme Court and of the Warren Court is
another story. In these periods, justice and its corollaries were regularly invoked
by the Court using judicial power to make new law.

Fourth, allied with the articulation of a philosophy is the employment of a
style which itself can be labeled as activist. The great activists tend to preach,
to lecture their fellow judges or the public about good and evil, right and wrong.
Justices Field, the first Harlan, and Murphy were preachers on the bench, as
were Hugo Black and Earl Warren. They did not exercise restraint in language;
rather they engaged in rhetorical excesses, and they allowed no quarter to the
opposing viewpoint. They were often carried away by the position they were
advocating, and they exaggerated the case they had to make. This is why there is
such a pronounced tendency to dictum in the most activist opinions.

The absence of restraint in language characterized Justice Frankfurter's
most important utterances in support of judicial restraint. He lectured his colleagues and took great pains to justify his position, as, for instance, in his emotional dissent in *West Virginia State Board of Education* v. *Barnette*.[67] Philip
Elman, Frankfurter's law clerk when *Barnette* was decided, tried to dissuade him
from including a personal statement at the beginning of the dissent. Years later
Elman remarked that while Frankfurter "preached judicial disinterestedness," he
was perhaps the most frequent violator of that norm on the Court.[68] This is

what made him markedly different from Justice Holmes, and is the reason I believe that Frankfurter's faithfulness to the restraintist ideal was tarnished. Holmes, on the other hand, was the near-perfect restraintist judge. Not only did he use judicial power sparingly, but he also was not apologetic about his modesty. His opinions in *Buck* v. *Bell*[69] and *Meyer* v. *Nebraska*[70] are models of restraint in language.

* * * * *

These dimensions of activism afford further insight into the character of the Burger Court and help us to understand the paradox of activism in a Court which should behave differently.

A Supreme Court whose activism is self-generated, the product of firm doctrinal commitments held by a majority of its members, must be expected to behave in a significantly different way than an activist Court whose decisions are brought about in large measure by forces over which it has limited control. The former Court will be consistently activist, except, of course, for occasional decisions which deviate from the expected pattern. This activism will be manifested incrementally in decisions which go beyond previous rulings in extending the scope of judicial power and policymaking. It will also be evident in the Court's style. Activist opinions will not be wishy-washy but clear expressions of a philosophical or ideological commitment. The language will be preachy, with the justices insisting on the full correctness of their position. Little quarter will be given to opposite viewpoints or to the possibility that the justices, finite in their wisdom and limited in the resources needed to decide correctly, may be making the wrong choices. The desire to reach activist results will be apparent and paramount, and thus no concern will be expressed as to either internal inconsistencies in opinions or the adverse effect of the opinion on some other values or social goals. Expression will be passionate and full of conviction. There could be no doubt as to the activism of such a Court.

This is how it was with the Warren Court, not always, of course, but with more than enough frequency to establish a clear pattern of the nature of its activism. No one could sensibly claim that the Court during the 1960s was less than activist, a judgment which was expressed equally by Earl Warren's admirers and by his critics. There was enormous coherence in the style and substance of opinions.

The key distinction between the Warren Court or any Court whose activism is confident and self-generated and one whose activism is other-directed is in the ambivalence of the latter, an ambivalence which is far more likely to appear in the style and language of its opinions than in substantive law. As for its decisions, since the justices are acting in large measure because of forces in its environment over which it has limited control, it is not to be expected that they will be much different from rulings of an unambiguously and passionately activist

Court. There is no prospect of turning the clock back, of reversing activist rulings of an earlier Court. In fact, it is likely that the outside forces which command adherence to activist precedents may also possess the potency to achieve further advances in judicial activity through constant pressure on the ambivalent justices.

These forces cannot compel ambivalent justices to be enthusiastic or passionate about their activism. Nor can such justices be expected to adopt wholeheartedly the doctrines which are advocated by the energetic elements which are in the driver's seat. Activism of this sort is apt to be listless and prone to misinterpretation by those who emphasize style over substance. The language by which this activism is achieved is likely to be poorly synchronized with the results.

It is impossible to do more than guess how the Warren Court would have acted had its tenure extended into the 1970s. One would doubt, however, that the decisions would have been significantly more activist than they have been in the Burger Court. Burger Court activism flies not only in the face of expectations but also is counter to the general conservative trend in recent years in American life and politics. But it has been consistent with the attitude of much of the lower federal judiciary and other important components of the Supreme Court's environment.

Those who assert that the Burger Court has not been activist ignore the record of the past decade, a record that continues to be extended,[71] and they have much explaining to do. What they have going for them—and really little else—is the style of the Court. This style has been clinical and passionless and devoid of any strong sense of commitment. The activist rulings of the Burger Court are not preachy; they aren't even very confident of the correctness of the position which has prevailed. It is as if the justices in the majority have reluctantly concluded that an activist decision is required, though they would not have been upset had the other side won.

It may be that this lack of passion and the accompanying lack of philosophical or doctrinal exposition have given rise to the view that the Burger Court is a restraintist body. Even when they have upheld and expanded personal freedom, the justices seem not to care about civil rights and civil liberties. In an era when image counts at least as much as reality, it is not really surprising that the Court presided over by Warren Burger has often been called something that it is not.

Notes

1. Richard E. Neustadt, *Presidential Power: The Politics of Leadership With Reflections on Johnson and Nixon,* 2d ed. (New York: Wiley, 1976).

2. See, for example, Raoul Berger, *Government by Judiciary: The Transformation of the Fourteenth Amendment* (Cambridge: Harvard University Press,

1977); Lino A. Graglia, *Disaster by Decree: The Supreme Court's Decisions on Race and Schools* (Ithaca: Cornell University Press, 1976).

3. See Charles M. Lamb, "Judicial Restraint on the Supreme Court," chap. 1, this volume.

4. See, for example, Alpheus Thomas Mason, "The Burger Court in Historical Perspective," *Political Science Quarterly* 89 (March 1974):27–45; Laurence H. Tribe, "Unraveling *National League of Cities:* The New Federalism and Affirmative Rights to Essential Government Services," *Harvard Law Review* 90 (April 1977):1065–1104.

5. *McCollum v. Board of Education*, 333 U.S. 203 (1948).

6. Edward S. Corwin, "The Supreme Court as a National School Board," *Law and Contemporary Problems* 14 (Winter 1948):3. The question raised by Professor Corwin had been expressed by Justice Jackson in his concurring opinion in *McCollum* when he lamented the majority's willingness to pronounce a sweeping constitutional doctrine: "It seems to me that to do so is to allow zeal for our own ideas and what is good in public instruction to induce us to accept the role of a super board of education for every school district in the nation." 333 U.S. at 237.

7. *Goss v. Lopez*, 419 U.S. 565 (1975); *Cleveland Board of Education v. Lafleur*, 414 U.S. 632 (1974); *Tinker v. Des Moines Independent School District*, 393 U.S. 513 (1969).

8. *Wolff v. McDonnell*, 418 U.S. 539 (1974); *Procunier* v. *Martinez*, 416 U.S. 396 (1974); *Campbell v. McGruder*, 580 F.2d. 521 (C.A.D.C. 1978); *Bono v. Saxbe*, 462 F.Supp. 146 (E.D.Ill. 1978).

9. *United States Department of Agriculture v. Murry*, 413 U.S. 508 (1973), *Goldberg v. Kelly*, 397 U.S. 254 (1970); *Shapiro v. Thompson*, 394 U.S. 618 (1969); *Welfare Recipients v. King*, 474 F.Supp. 1374 (D. Mass. 1979); *Newman v. Alabama*, 349 F.Supp. 278 (M.D. Ala. 1972).

10. *Wyatt v. Stickney*, 344 F.Supp. 387 (M.D. Ala. 1972), affirmed in part in *Wyatt v. Aderholt*, 503 F.2d 1305 (5th Cir. 1974); *Evans v. Washington*, 439 F.Supp. 483 (D.C.D.C. 1978); *Welsch v. Likins*, 550 F.2d 1122 (8th Cir. 1977).

11. See, for example, Donald L. Horowitz, *The Courts and Social Policy* (Washington: The Brookings Institution, 1977); Nathan Glazer, "Should Judges Administer Social Services?" *The Public Interest* 50 (Winter 1978):64–80.

12. See, for example, Glendon Schubert, *Judicial Policy Making: The Political Role of the Courts*, rev. ed. (Glenview, Ill.: Scott, Foresman, 1974), p. 189.

13. The matter is discussed in *Muskrat v. United States*, 219 U.S. 346 (1911).

14. See Joseph Tanenhaus, Marvin Schick, Matthew Muraskin, and Daniel Rosen, "The Supreme Court's Certiorari Jurisdiction: Cue Theory," in *Judicial Decision-Making*, ed. Glendon Schubert (New York: Free Press, 1963), chap. 5; S. Sidney Ulmer, William Hintze, and Louise Kirklosky, "The Decision to Grant or Deny Certiorari: Further Consideration of Cue Theory," *Law and Society*

Review 6 (May 1972):637–643; S. Sidney Ulmer, "The Decision to Grant Certiorari as an Indicator of Decision 'On the Merits,'" *Polity* 4 (Summer 1972): 429–447.

15. See, for example, Sheldon Goldman and Thomas P. Jahnige, *The Federal Courts as a Political System,* 2d ed. (New York: Harper and Row, 1976), pp. 30–31.

16. Ibid.

17. 1 Cranch 137 (1803).

18. 19 Howard 393 (1857).

19. 158 U.S. 601 (1895).

20. See, for example, Loren P. Beth, *Politics, the Constitution and the Supreme Court* (New York: Harper and Row, 1962), pp. 111–130.

21. See the discussion in Alexander M. Bickel, *The Least Dangerous Branch: The Supreme Court at the Bar of Politics* (Indianapolis: Bobbs-Merrill, 1962), chap. 1.

22. See generally Henry J. Abraham, *The Judicial Process: An Introductory Analysis of the Courts of the United States, England, and France,* 4th ed. (New York: Oxford University Press, 1980), chap. 9.

23. 297 U.S. 288 (1936).

24. Ibid., p. 346.

25. *United States v. Butler,* 297 U.S. 1, 57 (1936).

26. This is by no means new. See Goldman and Jahnige, *The Federal Courts as a Political System,* p. 62; Harold J. Spaeth, *Supreme Court Policy-Making: Explanation and Prediction* (San Francisco: W.H. Freeman, 1979), pp. 102–105.

27. *Ashwander v. Tennessee Valley Authority,* 297 U.S. 288 (1936).

28. See, for example, Goldman and Jahnige, *The Federal Courts as a Political System,* chap. 5; Walter F. Murphy, *Elements of Judicial Strategy* (Chicago: University of Chicago Press, 1964).

29. 367 U.S. 643 (1961).

30. 384 U.S. 436 (1966).

31. *McLaurin v. Oklahoma State Regents for Higher Education,* 339 U.S. 637 (1950); *Sweatt v. Painter,* 339 U.S. 629 (1950); *Missouri ex rel. Gaines v. Canada,* 305 U.S. 337 (1938).

32. See Frankfurter's opinions in *Baker v. Carr,* 369 U.S. 186 1962, and *Colegrove v. Green,* 328 U.S. 549 (1946).

33. The following are several illustrations of congressional encouragement of litigation through provisions included in reform-oriented legislation: judicial review of the standards of the Department of Health, Education, and Welfare in occupational health and safety, *United States Code,* 29, section 665(f); civil remedies under the Freedom of Information Act, *United States Code,* 5, section 5529(g); civil remedies for damages resulting from illegal wiretaps, *United States Code,* 18, section 2520; and challenges to alleged age discrimination in federal programs, *United States Code,* 42, section 6105. Of course, numerous other

examples could be given, for much domestic legislation contains explicit language dealing with litigation.

34. Benjamin Twiss, *Lawyers and the Constitution: How Laissez Faire Came to the Supreme Court* (Princeton: Princeton University Press, 1942).

35. "Scarcely any political question arises in the United States that is not resolved, sooner or later, into a judicial question." Alexis de Tocqueville, *Democracy in America,* ed. Phillips Bradley (New York: Knopf, 1945), p. 280.

36. In addition to the examples given in note 33, the following statutes provide for payments to attorneys who bring certain forms of activist-oriented litigation: the Civil Rights Attorneys Fees Awards Act of 1976, *United States Code,* 42, section 1988; the Privacy Act of 1974, *United States Code,* 5, section 552a(g); and the Fair Housing Act of 1968, *United States Code,* 42, section, 3612(c).

37. There is some evidence, much of it concerning the activities of lawyers, of a new attitude toward activist litigation. Foundation support for public interest law has been curtailed, and Congress has placed some new restrictions on the use of federal legal services funds. But so far there does not seem to be a great deal of an impact on the lower federal judiciary and, in any case, recent developments do not alter the interpretation of the activism of the Burger Court.

38. Horowitz, *The Courts and Social Policy.*

39. *Brown v. Board of Education,* 349 U.S. 294 (1955).

40. See the cases cited in note 8.

41. *New York Times,* Jan. 6, 1980, p. 25.

42. Ibid.

43. *Ludke v. Kuhn,* 461 F.Supp. 86 (S.D.N.Y. 1978). This ruling may seem to be in conflict with the right to privacy which has been so highly revered by activist judges ever since *Griswold v. Connecticut,* 381 U.S. 479 (1965). The contradiction is unmistakable, yet also not difficult to explain. The way activism works, what counts the most is the judicial validation of the right asserted in each case. It matters little that the acceptance of a claim theoretically collides with another right that may be asserted in another case.

44. See Henry J. Abraham, *The Judiciary: The Supreme Court in the Governmental Process,* 5th ed. (Boston: Allyn and Bacon, 1980), pp. 196-198.

45. Compare Glendon Schubert, *The Constitutional Polity* (Boston: Boston University Press, 1970), pp. 118-129 to S. Sidney Ulmer, "The Longitudinal Behavior of Hugo LaFayette Black: Parabolic Support for Civil Liberties, 1937-1971," *Florida State University Law Review* 1 (Winter 1973):131-153.

46. See Lamb, "Judicial Restraint on the Supreme Court," chap. 1, this volume.

47. Ibid.

48. During the period of the Vinson Court, in particular, one of the interesting side questions in the long-running debate between Justices Black and Frankfurter was over the approach to certiorari jurisdiction. See especially

Justice Frankfurter's unique statement in *Maryland v. Baltimore Radio Show, Inc.*, 338 U.S. 912 (1950) in which he attempted to explain the implications of a denial of a petition for review. Certiorari jurisdiction was a major issue throughout the tenure of the Vinson Court, with the chief justice and a majority of the Court sharply rebuked for what was regarded as a failure to consider cases which merited review. The attack was led by Fowler Harper. See Fowler Harper and Alan S. Rosenthal, "What the Supreme Court Did Not Do in the 1949 Term—An Appraisal of Certiorari," *University of Pennsylvania Law Review* 99 (December 1950):293–325; Fowler Harper and Edwin D. Etherington, "What the Supreme Court Did Not Do During the 1950 Term," *University of Pennsylvania Law Review* 100 (December 1951):354–409; Fowler Harper and George C. Pratt, "What the Supreme Court Did Not Do during the 1951 Term," *University of Pennsylvania Law Review* 101 (January 1953):439–479. Chief Justice Vinson's position was given in a 1949 speech before the American Bar Association which appeared at 69 S. Ct. v.

49. See the Library of Congress, *The Constitution of the United States: Analysis and Interpretation* (Washington, D.C.: Government Printing Office, 1964), pp. 1541–1551. See also Gregory A. Caldeira and Donald J. McCrone, "Of Time and Judicial Activism: A Study of the U.S. Supreme Court, 1800–1973," chap. 5, this volume.

50. See, for example, Jonathan D. Casper, "The Supreme Court and National Policy Making," *American Political Science Review* 70 (March 1976): 56–57; Murphy, Elements of Judicial Strategy, chaps. 7, 9.

51. 354 U.S. 298 (1957).

52. *Welsh v. United States*, 398 U.S. 333 (1970); *United States v. Seeger*, 380 U.S. 163 (1965).

53. Contrast the Roosevelt Court's rulings in *Tileson v. Ullman*, 318 U.S. 44 (1943) involving Connecticut's anticontraceptive law and *Colegrove v. Green*, 328 U.S. 549 (1946) involving legislative apportionment with the Warren Court's decisions in *Griswold v. Connecticut*, 381 U.S. 479 (1965) and *Baker v. Carr*, 360 U.S. 186 (1962).

54. The Burger Court has done very little to disturb the jurisdictional restraints involving standing, mootness, and the political questions doctrine. But it has frequently used the equal protection and due process clauses to achieve activist results. On the jurisdictional side, two Burger Court actions are noteworthy. In *Sarnoff v. Schwartz*, 409 U.S. 929 (1972), certiorari was denied in a taxpayer's suit challenging expenditures in pursuit of the war in Vietnam. Justices Douglas and Brennan dissented, relying on the Warren Court holding in *Flast v. Cohen*, 392 U.S. 83 (1968). In *Sierra Club v. Morton*, 405 U.S. 727 (1972), the Burger Court held that an environmental group lacked standing to block the development of a ski resort and summer recreation area. There were separate dissents by Justices Douglas, Brennan, and Blackmun.

55. *Bailey v. Drexel Furniture Co.*, 259 U.S. 20 (1922); *Hammer v. Dagen-hart*, 247 U.S. 251 (1918).

56. *Champion v. Ames*, 188 U.S. 321 (1903).

57. *McCray v. United States*, 195 U.S. 27 (1904).

58. 297 U.S. 1 (1936).

59. 298 U.S. 238 (1936).

60. 156 U.S. 1 (1895).

61. There hardly has been a more result-oriented justice in the history of the Court than Felix Frankfurter, who consistently pressured colleagues to follow his lead. Considerable evidence of this is provided in Joseph P. Lash, *From The Diaries of Felix Frankfurter* (New York: Norton, 1975); and J. Woodford Howard, *Mr. Justice Murphy: A Political Biography* (Princeton: Princeton University Press, 1968). Justice Brandeis demonstrated how restraint itself could be used to influence judicial results. He would withdraw a written dissenting opinion if the majority would agree to accept modifications which he suggested. See Alexander M. Bickel, ed., *The Unpublished Dissenting Opinions of Mr. Justice Brandeis: The Supreme Court at Work* (Cambridge: Harvard University Press, 1957).

62. 347 U.S. 483 (1954).

63. 376 U.S. 1 (1964).

64. 384 U.S. 436 (1966).

65. 194 U.S. 601 (1904).

66. Ibid., p. 615.

67. 319 U.S. U.S. 624, 646–47 (1943).

68. Israel Shenker, "Friends of Felix Frankfurter Reminisce at Exhibit Honoring the Justice," *New York Times*, October 23, 1977, p. 34.

69. 274 U.S. 200 (1927).

70. 262 U.S. 390 (1923). The dissenting opinion of Justice Holmes in *Meyer* was published after *Bartels v. Iowa*, 262 U.S. 404, 412, (1927).

71. On successive days in the week preceding the writing of these lines, the Supreme Court decided that (1) an arrest warrant was needed by police before entering a home to make a routine arrest, and (2) local governments could be sued for civil rights violations committed unintentionally by their employees. See Linda Greenhouse, "Court Say Warrant is Needed at Homes for Routine Arrest," *New York Times*, April 16, 1980, p. 1; Linda Greenhouse, "High Court Limits Localities' Defense on Suits on Rights," *New York Times*, April 17, 1980, p. 1.

Was Chief Justice Marshall an Activist?

Wallace Mendelson

Rampant law making by the Warren Court antagonized many, indeed most, Americans, according to the Gallup polls.[1] It also attracted numerous outspoken admirers. Not a few of the latter undertook to justify Warrenism on the basis of a comparable aggressiveness they claimed to find in Chief Justice Marshall.[2] More accurately, perhaps, they did not find, but rather derived, it from the Progressive Historians whose views had germinated in the incredible era of laissez faire justice from the 1890s until 1937. As though bent upon proving that all history is contemporary history, the Progressives read back into Marshall's day the activism they saw in the judges of their own time. For them judicial review was at least suspect—a device that Marshall in an artful opinion[3] foisted upon the nation, and then used extravagantly for his own purposes; namely, to promote nationalism at the expense of local self-government, and property at the expense of human or personal rights. All this, if true, surely was what it was called: "Government by Judiciary."[4]

It has long been implicit in praise for the Warren Court that in principle nothing was wrong with government by the "nine old men." They erred, it seems, only in governing us unwisely. This we have on the high authority of Mr. Justice Douglas.[5] Similarly, learned professors—including Charles Black and Eugene Rostow—have recently insisted that judicial review and democracy go hand in hand. This in the face of *Dred Scott*,[6] the *Income Tax*,[7] *Sugar Trust*,[8] *Child Labor*[9] cases, *Plessy*,[10] *Lochner*,[11] and all the rest! Many seem to have forgotten that not very long ago the academic world was overwhelmingly skeptical of judicial supremacy, as it was then called. Learned professors in the 1920s and early 1930s found "the divine right of judges" (to use a then familiar term) entirely out of place in a nation dedicated to democracy and striving for its perfection. Obviously there are fashions in scholarship, as in hemlines.

The Progressive Historians, one wants to believe, would reject the Douglas-Rostow-Black vogue out of hand, for a basic premise of their stance was that government by judges is a poor substitute for government by the people. It is difficult for one who knew them well to believe they would find nothing wrong with elitist oligarchy, or dictatorship in general, provided it were in their view benevolent. Still for them as for some others much might depend upon whose sacred cow is gored.

What follows here is a suggestion that Chief Justice Marshall was not, as charged, an activist with respect to the powers of the federal courts, the sovereignty of the nation, or the claims of property.

Judicial Review

Regarding Federal Measures

Five years before John Marshall became a judge the Supreme Court exercised the power of judicial review in *Hylton* v. *United States*.[12] Each of the participating justices recognized explicitly that the issue before them was the constitutionality of a federal statute, and each explicitly based his opinion (upholding the act) on constitutional grounds. There was no fanfare of explanation or justification. The power of review was taken for granted. Only Mr. Justice Chase indicated doubt as to whether the Court "has the power to declare an act of Congress void. . . ." Four years later (well before *Marbury*) he observed in *Cooper* v. *Telfair* that "[i]t is, indeed, a general opinion, it is expressly admitted by all this bar, and some of the Judges have, individually, in the circuits, decided, that the Supreme Court can declare an act of Congress unconstitutional, and therefore invalid. . . ."[13]

What after all can the Constitution possibly mean in Article III that grants to the federal courts jurisdiction of cases "arising under this Constitution" (as well as under federal statutes and treaties), if it does not mean that such courts shall have power to pass upon the meaning of the Constitution with respect to measures challenged as unconstitutional? Article VI refers to the Constitution as "law." Are we to assume that this law somehow is not subject—as is law generally—to judicial interpretation and application? Article VI dubs the Constitution not only "law," but "supreme" law; though it gives Acts of Congress supremacy only when they are "made in pursuance" of the Constitution.[14] Read in conjunction with the Article III provision just quoted, does this not plainly authorize federal courts to decide in appropriate cases whether particular acts of Congress are "in pursuance of" the Constitution?

Obviously, the *Hylton* Court accepted the implication of these questions; namely, that what we have come to call judicial review is a constitutionally authorized power of the federal courts. On this point the pre-Marshall judges were not alone. In Section 25 of the Judiciary Act of 1789 the first Congress (including nearly a score of the Founding Fathers) explicitly authorized Supreme Court review of state decisions "where is drawn in question the validity of a treaty or statute . . . of the United States, and the decision is against their validity" (or where a state measure is questioned and upheld). Of course a state decision invalidating a federal law (or upholding a state law) may be found quite correct on review; state decisions on constitutional issues are not inevitably erroneous. Thus Congress went on to provide in Section 25 that all such state decisions "may be reexamined and reversed or affirmed by the Supreme Court. . . ." Obviously, Congress, in adopting this legislation twelve years before Marshall went to the bench, explicitly recognized the right of both the federal Supreme Court and state courts to declare national (as well as state) laws unconstitutional. How, then, can it be said that judicial review as such—whether with respect to state or federal measures—was an activist innovation of the Marshall Court?

Marbury v. *Madison*[15] simply followed congressional and judicial precedent. It was not a case of first instance with respect to judicial review; it did not entail the indispensable element of judicial activism; namely, innovation.

Early in the *Marbury* opinion there is extensive discussion which concludes that the plaintiff was entitled to what he requested, and that *mandamus* was a proper vehicle for getting it. This is said to be an abusive use of the judicial function, since, as the Court concluded, it lacked jurisdiction of the case. Exploration of those preliminary issues was perfectly compatible with a major principle of judicial restraint; namely, that before judges delve into a constitutional problem, they should make sure that there is no other basis for decision.

Finally, even if the fabrication, or usurpation, charge is valid with respect to *Marbury* (does any serious scholar now so insist?), what Marshall and his colleagues *held* bears no relation whatsoever to the blatant political function activist judges later undertook in the name of judicial review. The fact is the Marshall Court over a period of some thirty-four years vetoed only one congressional act—a very narrow technical one at that. What *Marbury* held after all is simply that Congress may not enlarge the original jurisdiction of the Supreme Court—a matter of little significance in the life and well-being of the Republic. To find in such a narrow holding anything comparable to, or precedent for, Warren Court activism is to make a vast mountain range out of an anthill.

As we shall see, Congress did not give general federal-question jurisdiction to federal courts until after the Civil War. It follows that, apart from Section 25, the only general occasion for judicial review in Marshall's day arose out of the diversity-of-citizenship jurisdiction, authorized in Section 11 of the 1789 Judiciary Act.[16] An activist Court presumably would have construed this jurisdiction broadly. Marshall's Court did the opposite, reading it strictly in three important cases.[17] Similarly one would not expect aggressive judges to repudiate federal jurisdiction of common-law crimes;[18] to take a narrow view of admiralty jurisdiction;[19] to construe strictly their own appellate authority;[20] or to hold the Bill of Rights inapplicable to the states.[21] Yet Marshall's Court—exercising what would now be called judicial restraint—did all of these things.

Before the Civil War only two federal laws suffered Court veto; the first in *Marbury,* the second in *Dred Scott* v. *Sandford.*[22] While the holding in the former was innocuous, that in the latter was a major disaster.

If antebellum judicial history was destined to inspire later Court attitudes, surely the *Dred Scott* catastrophe would have eclipsed *Marbury*. It must follow that neither had much effect upon judicial things to come; that the rampant activism which prevailed from the 1890s until 1937, and again in the 1960s, must have been sui generis springing from new sociopolitical conditions;[23] and that *Marbury* was influential, if at all, only as an excuse or rationalization.

Some may conclude that the Warren, and the laissez faire, justices had more in common with each other than either had with those who decided *Marbury* v. *Madison*.

Regarding State Measures

Several years before Marshall became a judge, the Supreme Court struck down a state law on constitutional grounds. That case—*Ware* v. *Hylton*[24]—held that a Virginia law discharging debts owed enemy aliens conflicted with a federal treaty and was thus void by virtue of Article VI of the Constitution. The latter provides that federal measures, including treaties, "shall be the supreme law of the land." Here too the power of judicial review was taken for granted.[25]

As we have seen, Article III of the Constitution gives federal courts jurisdiction of cases arising under the Constitution or other federal law. But with few exceptions nothing in federal law makes this jurisdiction an exclusive function of federal tribunals. State courts may and do decide such cases. Indeed it was not until 1875 that Congress gave federal trial courts a general jurisdiction to decide federal-law questions. Before then, such matters had to be heard initially by state judges (which is still the fashion in all other federal systems). Inevitably, then, Section 25 of the Judiciary Act of 1789 authorized Supreme Court review of state decisions challenged as not giving full effect to the Constitution, laws, or treaties of the United States. For example, when a state tribunal upheld a state law in the face of constitutional objection, the decision was (and still is) subject to Supreme Court review.

The reason and basis for Section 25 is clear. The Constitution in Article VI imposes upon state judges a duty to treat federal law as supreme, "anything in the constitution or laws of any state to the contrary notwithstanding." Section 25 was an effort to ensure via Supreme Court supervision that this obligation would be honored. Thus judicial review of state—as well as federal—measures was the creature of Congress, not of the Supreme Court. It was perceived and explicitly authorized by statue in accordance with Congressional understanding of the Constitution—and exercised by the Court—long before Marshall became a judge.

If "the Great Chief Justice" was an activist, support for that view must come not from his recognition of the power of review, but from how he used it in state-law cases. For it was in these that he made all of his famous constitutional pronouncements save that in *Marbury*.

National Sovereignty

The crux of the difficulty under the Articles of Confederation was that each state (per Article II) "retains its sovereignty." What little central authority there was—confined to foreign affairs, a postal system, coinage of money, and standard weights and measures—depended entirely upon the goodwill of the states. For the overall "government" had no way to enforce its policies, and only such funds as the constituent sovereignties were willing to contribute via "requisitions." The result, as the Founding Fathers saw it by 1787, was impending disaster. To them the tenuous confederation seemed about to break under the stress of a crushing debt, an empty treasury, and paralysis for lack of authority to raise taxes, regulate trade, enforce laws and treaties, or attain respect from foreign nations. Conflict among the states with respect to commerce and boundary disputes, state intrusions upon contractual and property interest, loose monetary practices, and finally Shay's Rebellion, convinced the Founders that the states had to be curbed; that sovereignty had to be transferred from the parts to the whole. George Washington put it succinctly in a letter to John Jay on August 1, 1786:

> Your sentiments, that our affairs are drawing rapidly to a crisis, accord with my own. What the event will be is also beyond the reach of my foresight. . . . I do not conceive we can exist long as a nation without having lodged somewhere a power which will pervade the whole Union in as energetic a manner, as the authority of the State Governments extends over the several States. . . . Requisitions are a perfect nullity, where thirteen sovereign, independent, disunited States are in the habit of discussing and refusing compliance with them at their option. Requisitions are actually little better than a jest and a byeword throughout the land. If you tell the Legislatures they have violated the treaty of peace and invaded the prerogatives of the Confederacy, they will laugh in your face. What then is to be done? Things cannot go on in the same train forever. It is much to be feared, as you observe, that the better kind of people, being disgusted with the circumstances, will have their minds prepared for any revolution whatever. We are apt to run from one extreme into another. To anticipate and prevent disastrous contingencies, would be the part of wisdom and patriotism.[26]

James Madison's explanation of the "Origin of the Constitutional Convention" (1835) describes the problem in some detail:

> At the date of the Convention, . . . the political condition of the U.S. could not but fill the public mind with gloom. . . . It was seen that the public debt . . . remained without any provision for its payment. The reiterated and elaborate efforts of Congress to procure from the States a more adequate payment had failed. The effect of the ordinary requisitions of Congress had only displayed the inefficiency of the authority making them. . . .
>
> The want of authority in Congress to regulate commerce had produced in foreign nations . . . a monopolizing policy injurious to the trade of the U.S., and destructive to their navigation. . . .

The same want of power over commerce led to an exercise of the power separately, by the States, which not only proved abortive, but engendered rival, conflicting and angry regulations. . . .

In certain cases the authority of the Confederacy was disregarded, as in violation not only of the treaty of peace, but of treaties with France and Holland. . . .

As a natural consequence of this distracted and disheartening condition of the union, the federal authority had ceased to be respected abroad. . . . At home it had lost all confidence and credit; the unstable and unjust career of the States had also forfeited the respect and confidence essential to order and good government. . . . [27]

Such views—justified or not—were the views of those who convened at Philadelphia in 1787 to devise "a more perfect union." There is said to have been only one states' righter among them. It was the overwhelming consensus that national authority had to be substantially enlarged (Constitution, Article I, Section 8) and made supreme vis-à-vis the states (Article VI); that the states' power to harm one another and the country as a whole must be severely cut down (Article I, Section 10, and Articles IV and VI); and that the old Congress (merely a meeting of the ambassadors of sovereign states) had to be replaced by a true government including a legislature, an executive, and a judiciary (Articles I, II, and III). This—the commitment of the Founding Fathers to national sovereignty—permeates the pronouncements of the Marshall Court.

Each of its great decisions in this context—*Martin* v. *Hunter's Lessee,*[28] *McCulloch* v. *Maryland,*[29] and *Gibbons* v. *Ogden*[30]—involved a state act which impinged upon national interests. In *Hunter,* Virginia's highest judges refused to honor a Supreme Court judgment. In *McCulloch* a state tax threatened operations of the Bank of the United States. In *Gibbons* a state-authorized steamboat "monopoly" hindered traffic in New York waters—a link in the trade route between the East Coast, the Midwest, and New Orleans via the Hudson River, the Erie Canal, the Great Lakes, and the Ohio and Mississippi rivers. In each case the Supreme Court removed the state impediment. To have done otherwise would have been a return to state sovereignty and the problems of the Confederation. As Felix Frankfurter observed, the Marshall Court "was on guard against every tendency to [treat] the new union as though it were the old confederation." Even Thomas Jefferson—hardly an ardent nationalist—agreed in principle, if a priori, that such measures could not stand. For in his view

the States should severally preserve their sovereignty in whatever concerns themselves alone, and that whatever may concern another State or any foreign nation, should be made a part of the federal sovereignty; . . . some peaceful means should be contrived [judicial review?] for the federal head to force compliance on the part of the states.[31]

The only question, then, in the cases just mentioned, was how to eliminate the offending measures. Each of them had been upheld by a state tribunal in the face of constitutional objections. This per Section 25 of the Judiciary Act brought the appellate jurisdiction of the Supreme Court into play.

Initially in *Hunter* the Court had struck down a Virginia confiscation act as a denial of the supremacy which Article VI of the Constitution gives to federal treaties. The problem was that Virginia's high court had refused to honor the Supreme Court's decision. The rationale for the refusal was that Virginia being a sovereign entity, there could be no appeal from the edict of its highest court. The issue was starkly presented: was it to be state or national sovereignty; were we a confederacy or a nation; did the Supremacy Clause of Article VI mean what it says? Let James Madison give the answer:

> The jurisdiction claimed for the Federal Judiciary [under Section 25] is truly the only defensive armor of the Federal Government, or rather for the Constitution and laws of the United States. Strip it of that armor and the door is wide open for nullification, anarchy and convulsion, unless twenty-four States, independent of the whole and of each other, should exhibit the miracle of a voluntary and unanimous performance of every injunction of the parchment compact.[32]

Mr. Justice Story, for a unanimous Court in *Hunter*—like the Great Chief Justice in *Cohens* v. *Virginia*[33]—spelled out the Madisonian view in constitutional terms:

> That the United States form, for many and for most important purposes, a single nation, has not yet been denied. In war, we are one people. In making peace, we are one people. In all commercial regulations, we are one and the same people. In many other respects, the American people are one; and the government which is alone capable of controlling and managing their interests in all these respects, is the government of the Union. It is their government, and in that character they have no other. America has chosen to be, in many respects, and to many purposes, a nation; and for all these purposes, her government is complete; to all these objects, it is competent. The people have declared that in the exercise of all powers given for these objects it is supreme. It can, then, in effecting these objects, legitimately control all individuals or governments within the American territory. The constitution and laws of a state, so far as they are repugnant to the Constitution and laws of the United States, are absolutely void. These states are constituent parts of the United States. They are members of one great empire—for some purposes sovereign, for some purposes subordinate.[34]

In a government so constituted, national review of state decisions on questions of national law was indispensable because

> Judges of equal learning and integrity, in different states, might differently interpret a statute, or a treaty of the United States, or even the constitution itself. If there were no revising authority to control these jarring and discordant judgments, and harmonize them into uniformity, the laws, the treaties, and the Constitution of the United States would be different in different states, and might, perhaps, never have precisely

the same construction, obligation, or efficacy, in any two states. The public mischiefs that would attend such a state of things would be truly deplorable; and it cannot be believed that they could have escaped the enlightened convention which formed the constitution. What, indeed, might then have been only prophecy, has now become fact, and the appellate jurisdiction must continue to be the only adequate remedy for such evils.[35]

Far from exercises in judicial activism, *Hunter* and *Cohens* involve no more than a literal application of the explicit terms of the Constitution and an act of Congress—an application completely compatible with their spirit as well. Though endlessly pressed in the antebellum era to strip down Article 25 jurisdiction, Congress steadfastly refused to do so.[36]

Gibbons presents more complex problems. It involved inter alia a claim that the New York steamboat monopoly was incompatible with the Commerce Clause itself. This entailed an inquiry into the meaning and scope of congressional authority to "regulate commerce . . . among the several States. . . ." Few would insist the meaning of this provision standing alone is obvious in the context of *Gibbons* v. *Ogden.* In that impasse Marshall for the Court sought help in an old principle of interpretation: the *Rule in Heydon's Case.*[37] As Marshall put it:

If from the imperfection of human language, there should be serious doubts respecting the extent of any given power, it is a well-settled rule that the objects for which it was given, especially when those objects are expressed in the instrument itself, should have great weight in the construction.[38]

A basic "object" of the Constitution was "to form a more perfect Union."[39] One of the most vexing imperfections of the old one was the problem of state interference with interstate commerce, and lack of national authority to do anything about it.[40] An expansive view of congressional power under the Commerce Clause was thus required if a more perfect union was to be achieved—that is, if we were to avoid a return to the trade barriers that were so familiar during the Confederation. Thus, following an ancient rule of construction, Marshall read the doubtful language of the Commerce Clause in the light of the well-known circumstances that produced it. The result was a broad view of the congressional commerce power, a view that has prevailed throughout our history except in that tragic era of judicial activism that ran from 1895 until 1937.[41] What the Marshall Court did in *Gibbons* was simply this: it resolved (a mainly linguistic) doubt in favor of Congress and the democratic process. This is a far cry indeed from activism. It would seem rather that to have minimized congressional authority, to have ignored the origins of the Commerce Clause—as the 1895-1936 Court did—would have been an abuse.

Counsel for the steamboat monopoly next argued that, even if the commerce power was to be read broadly, it should be treated as a concurrent power, that is, one available to the states as well as to Congress. In this view the New York law would stand (absent an incompatible federal regulation). On this point Marshall found no help in *Heydon's* rule. Quite obviously he was sympathetic to the argument that the commerce power was not concurrent, but exclusively national: "There is great force in this argument—and the court is not satisfied that it has been refuted."[42]

Still, given the magnitude of the consequences of a judgment either way, and the lack of *Heydon* clues, judicial restraint was called for. And so, anticipating one of the *Ashwander*[43] rules, "he avoided a critical constitutional issue by finding an alternative basis for decision; namely, a Supremacy Clause conflict between the New York steamboat law and an act of Congress. The result was to postpone a crucial question of constitutional law that might more wisely be settled with the benefit of further experience under our new federal system of government. Meanwhile the ball was in the congressional court. For *Gibbons* left Congress free to alter, if it chose, the measure found to be in conflict with the New York law. What was this, if not judicial restraint? Only Mr. Justice Johnson was prepared to accept the exclusive view. He, it will be recalled, was Jefferson's appointee and "representative" on the bench. Neither of these gentlemen could be deemed entirely unsympathetic to states' rights.

McCulloch v. *Maryland*[44] involved a state tax plainly and completely incompatible with the continued operation of the Bank of the United States (BUS) in Maryland. Thus the tax ran afoul of the Supremacy Clause, if congressional enactment of the bank law was "pursuant to the Constitution." The Marshall Court found that it was; that congressional authority to create it was implicit in, and incidental to, the powers expressly given to the national government. This was fully in accord with the view of "the father of the Constitution." "In . . . debate on the tenth amendment, Madison successfully resisted an attempt to insert one word, to make it say that powers not *expressly* delegated to the United States are reserved to the states or the people. No government, he contended, could be limited to express powers: 'There must necessarily be admitted powers by implication.' "[45]

Recall that BUS had been proposed initially by Alexander Hamilton, a member of the Constitutional Convention and an author of the *Federalist Papers.* It had been chartered by a Federalist Congress which included several of the Founding Fathers, and then approved by President Washington who had been president of the Constitutional Convention. In 1811 it was rechartered by a Republican Congress and approved by President Madison. Surely judges would have to be high-handed to override such impressive credentials—as Marshall's opinion of the Court suggests. But impressive credentials or not, how can judges rationally be charged with activism when they defer to Congress, when they leave major policy issues to the processes of democracy? It is noteworthy that a few years after the decision in *McCulloch,* BUS expired when Congress sustained President Jackson's veto of a recharter bill. The people had the first, and the people had the last, word on BUS. This is light-years away from government by judges as we came to know it beginning in the 1890s and again in the 1960s.

If in *Hunter, Gibbons,* and *McCulloch* the Marshall Court honored federal law and the national democratic process, in each of those cases *pari passu* it struck down a state measure and to that extent intruded upon state self-government. Marshall for the Court responded to this problem in *McCulloch* when counsel argued that, if a state tax on federal operations is invalid, then a federal tax on state operations must also fail:

> But the two cases are not on the same reason. The people of all the states have created the general government, and have conferred upon it the general power of taxation. The people of all the states, and the states themselves, are represented in Congress, and, by their representatives exercise this power. When they tax the chartered institutions of the states, they tax their constituents; and these taxes must be uniform. But, when a state taxes the operations of the government of the United States, it acts upon institutions created, not by their own constitutents, but by people over whom they claim no control. It acts upon the measures of a government created by others as well as themselves, for the benefit of others in common with themselves. The difference is that which always exists, and always must exist, between the action of the whole on a part, and the action of a part on the whole—between the laws of a government declared to be supreme, and those of a government which, when in opposition to those laws, is not supreme.[46]

As though supplementing these thoughts (they are the same as those that inform the Supremacy Clause itself), Marshall in reference to the national commerce power observed in *Gibbons:*

> If, as has always been understood, the sovereignty of Congress, though limited to specified objects, is plenary as to those objects, the power over commerce with foreign nations, and among the several States, is vested in Congress as absolutely as it would be in a single government, having in its constitution the same restrictions on the exercise of the power as are found in the Constitution of the Untied States. The wisdom and the discretion of Congress, their identity with the people, and the influence which their constitutents possess at elections, are, in this, as in many other instances . . . the sole restraints on which they have relied, to secure them from its abuse. They are the restraints on which the people must often rely solely, in all representative governments.[47]

Generations later Mr. Justice Holmes would say:

> I do not think the United States would come to an end if we lost our power to declare an Act of Congress void. I do think the Union would

be imperiled if we could not make the declaration as to the laws of the several States. For one in my place sees how often a local policy prevails with those who are not trained to national views and how often action is taken that embodies what the Commerce Clause was meant to end.[48]

Guided by the Founders, Marshall's nationalistic opinions laid the foundation for the American common market. They were not oblivious to state interests. In *Gibbons,* though Marshall favored the exclusive conception of the national commerce power, he left the issue open. Later in *Willson* v. *Blackbird Creek Marsh Co.*[49] he upheld "states' rights" in an interstate commerce setting. Delaware had authorized a dam across a small yet navigable stream thus hindering interstate commerce as had New York in *Gibbons.* Except for a difference in the importance of the two waterways as trade routes, the two cases seem quite alike. Yet the Court's judgments ran in opposite directions: the New York law was struck down, the Delaware law upheld. The one was treated as a regulation of commerce, the other as a police measure to protect local health and reclaim local land from a marsh infestation. Of course the difference in terminology is not decisive; a rose by any other name would smell as sweet. What Marshall must have been groping for (but lacked enough cases to spell out) was a dividing line between undue local interference with national interests, and state protection of legitimate local claims. How he might have solved the problem, if he had been given adequate opportunity for a rounded answer, we do not know. One supposes the difference in the outcome of the two cases is not unrelated to the fact that New York's law reflected the same self-seeking provincialism that had devastated the Confederation; the Delaware law did not. For it is one thing to seek a selfish local advantage simply by imposing burdens on outsiders, but quite another to cure local evils though at some cost to others. Especially is this so because (as Marshall recognized in *Gibbons*) the local problem which by hypothesis "concerns more states than one" may be regulated (preempted) by Congress, if it finds the local solution noisome from the national point of view. Similarly, in *Brown* v. *Maryland*[50] Marshall recognized that while the Constitution outlaws state duties on imports (Article I, Section 10), this does not mean that an imported item is forever immune from state taxation. At some point, he recognized, the import like local goods must be subject to state levys. Groping again, he tentatively drew a line via the original package doctrine. Marshall's was not a dogmatic nationalism, blind to local needs.

Property Interests

If, as charged, Marshall favored ownership interests, much might be said in extenuation of such a tendency. In his day property had not yet become suspect.

Das Kapital would not appear for years to come. Great disparities in wealth had not yet developed in this country. Most Americans owned a farm or had reasonable expectations of acquiring one. Rich and poor alike respected ownership, knowing that property was the key to personal and family well-being. Indeed in a poor, developing nation private property was a social security system protecting against the pitfalls of sickness, old age, widowhood, and orphanage. Especially for Thomas Jefferson—the lion of liberalism—property was indispensable to liberty. As he saw it, the widespread ownership of farms saved us from the misery and bitter class conflicts of the Old World. "When we get piled up upon one another in large cities, as in Europe, we shall become as corrupt as in Europe and go to eating one another as they do there."[51] The urban mobs of Paris, he thought, were in effect slaves because, being propertyless, they were dependent upon their "betters." As Brandeis would say later, "The necessitous man is not free." It was largely to ensure a continuing "Empire of Liberty" which comes with individual private ownership of farms that Jefferson—unconstitutionally, he thought—made the Louisiana Purchase.

According to Irving Brant—James Madison's inspired biographer—the great accomplishment of the Founding Fathers was that "[a] convention dominated by devotees of property rights was able to write a democratic Constitution. Save for two or three delegates, the whole convention desired to protect property . . . by the strength and form of the national government, and to strike down state laws designed to wipe out debt or impair financial contracts."[52] It follows from all this that, if Marshall was indeed especially sensitive to proprietary claims, he was in full accord with the temper of the American people of his day and with the outspoken purposes of those who gave us the Constitution. But do *Fletcher* v. *Peck*[53] and the *Dartmouth College* case[54]—endlessly cited to support the charge of property bias—in fact support it?

Fletcher arose when land speculators cheated the people of Georgia out of millions of acres of public land by bribing state legislators. When Georgia voters discovered this they compelled a new legislature to rescind the transaction. Meanwhile innocent buyers had acquired some of the land from the wrongdoers. They attacked the rescinding act as a violation of the Contract Clause.[55] Marshall, for the court, upheld the challenge. The effect was to sustain the property claims of the innocent buyers. The alternative would be to sustain the property claims of the innocent people of Georgia. Either way, the Court would be deciding proproperty—and also antiproperty. Either way, an innocent party would be hurt. There seems to have been no way to escape a decision upholding the plaintiff's, or the defendant's, ownership claim. One fails to see how *Fletcher* can be said to involve a property bias. Was there, however, bias of another sort in deciding for the ultimate buyers rather than for the initial owners? Far from arbitrary, the choice was informed by a long-settled (and still prevailing rule of Anglo-American equity jurisprudence. While a fraudulent purchaser takes a good title *at law,* it is subject to cancellation by a chancery decree. Thus in a clash between a cheating buyer and his innocent victim the latter prevails. But *Fletcher* involved a clash between the innocent victim and an equally innocent subsequent purchaser for value. As between the two guiltless parties the chancellor—finding the moral claim of the one no better than that of the other—does not intervene. The equities being balanced, he lets the chips fall as they may (the victim's recourse being an action for damages against the fraudulent party). In short Marshall and the Court read the Contract Clause in the light of a long familiar, time-tested rule of equity. If this be activism, it is not property biased, and it is not a brand similar to that of the Warren Court.

Critics press two allegations: The Contract Clause was not intended to apply to state contracts, nor to grants (as distinct from contracts). The fact is, the language of the clause literally covers *all* contracts in explicit terms. There is no hint of limitation in the written words of the Constitution, nor have critics revealed any discussion in the Constitutional Conventions or in the *Federalist* in support of an unwritten limitation. Had the Founders wanted to protect only private (as distinct from state) agreements, they need only have said so—as indeed the Continental Congress had just done in the Northwest Ordinance. (Earlier in England *An Agreement of The People* (1649) had undertaken to protect only *public* contractual obligations.) On August 28, 1787, Rufus King moved to insert the private-contract provision of the Northwest Ordinance into the Constitution. After brief discussion, it was rejected. Some two weeks later (September 14), at the suggestion of the Committee of Style, the Constitutional Convention adopted the present Contract Clause. We have no record of any here relevant discussion either in the Committee or in the Convention. Strictly all that we know of the *Convention's* intent, then, is that it was invited to adopt the private-contract approach and refused to do so. Shortly thereafter it adopted a similar provision which refers merely to contracts in general as distinct from *private* contracts per the Northwest Ordinance (and as distinct from *public* contracts per *An Agreement of The People*).

Surely this bespeaks rejection of one view in favor of another. Those who favor the apparently rejected position rely essentially on the proposition that the great contract problem of the time was a host of state debtor-relief laws which went far to obliterate private debtor obligations. This clearly was a major and notorious problem. Yet it is no basis for holding that related matters, though literally covered by the Contract Clause, are somehow excluded. After all, state negligence with respect to state obligations was hardly unknown! The Founders wrote broadly; we are urged to assume they thought narrowly, that they used unqualified language of principle to deal only with quite limited, easily definable specifics. The argument moreover leads to the proposition that the Contract Clause applies only in a debtor-relief context—a position seemingly without significant support in any quarter. Even if we knew absolutely that every one of the Framers individually intended their written words to apply only to private compacts, this would not justify adopting that view judicially. Those who ratified can hardly be said to have ratified something other than the words of the document itself.

The other anti-Marshall point—that grants are not contracts—entails an anachronism. Certainly today a grant and a contract are two quite different things. But in the late eighteenth century the term "contract" had far broader connotations than it does today, embracing not only executory, but executed, agreements as well.[56] Alexander Hamilton's view in his well-known pamphlet on the subject clearly anticipated the Court's position in *Fletcher*, as did the highest court of Massachusetts in *Darby* v. *Blake*.[57] The broad language of Madison's 44 *Federalist* also supports both the public-contracts and the grants aspect of *Fletcher*. Nowhere does it even dimly suggest the restrictive outlook.

It is worth noting that the land problem involved in *Fletcher* was so troublesome that President Jefferson appointed an investigatory commission—James Madison, Albert Gallatin, Levi Lincoln. The recommendations of that most distinguished body of Jeffersonians agreed with Marshall (though by a different route) that the innocent purchasers should prevail.[58]

The *Dartmouth* case involved these circumstances: a group of philanthropists agreed (contracted) that each in consideration of the donations of the others would contribute to a fund for the education of American Indians, among others. By their agreement the fund was to be administered by trustees selected in a prescribed manner. The British King approved and gave these arrangements legal sanction in a charter for Dartmouth College—whereupon the promised contributions were made. Later (after Independence) the State of New Hampshire tried by legislation to take over and govern the school contrary to the donors' agreements as set out in the charter. Marshall's Court blocked the effort via the Contract Clause. Viewed narrowly the trustees won the case, but they had no beneficial interest in the property. They won on behalf of the donor-philanthropists (presumably deceased) and generations of students. Were these really property interests—does the decision reveal a prejudice in favor of material wealth?

The traditional Progressive answer is that the *Dartmouth* decision was a crafty gambit purposefully designed to an ulterior purpose: protection of corporation charters from legislative interference. That it was highly successful is demonstrated, we are told, by the enormous growth of corporate enterprise thereafter. This is make-believe. Mr. Justice Story in *Dartmouth* pointed out that no state need grant irrevocable or nonamendable charters; that the power to alter, amend, or revoke may be reserved. In fact this became standard practice over the years after *Dartmouth*, and was not unknown before. Also the granting of corporation charters by special legislation (which was the real basis of abuse) gave way following the Jacksonian reform movement to general-law, standard-provision incorporation.

It is strange that those who charge Marshall with proproperty bias seem always to ignore his "antiproperty" decisions. *Gibbons,* for example, destroyed an enormously valuable ownership interest when it killed the New York steamboat charter.[59] How is *Gibbons* to be reconciled with *Fletcher* and *Dartmouth?* The two latter, one suggests, are not proproperty, but rather protransaction, cases. They mean that when the equities are not plainly imbalanced (there being no clearly overriding public interest, as in *Gibbons*), judges will not disturb the "contracts," or transactions by which men and women conduct their personal affairs—be they philantrhopists (*Dartmouth*) or land speculators and farmers (*Fletcher*).[60] An inclination toward unfettered human activity was deep in the temper of the times. It was apparently accepted as so natural, so inevitably right, as not even to rise to the level of awareness. Americans were on the make. They had escaped the Old World fetters: king, feudal aristocracy, and established church. They were the "new men." A vast spiritual, as well as geographic, frontier provoked ingenuity and initiative. The standard of living was low, but natural resources were great. This put a high premium on constructive, developmental human effort. That legal support for such interests came via the Contract Clause was not by chance. As Sir Henry Maine would later observe, the transition from medieval to modern civilization was a shift from "status to contract."[61] Under feudalism a person acquired a fixed social status by birth; all of his rights and duties were determined thereby. Thus if a man were born a serf, he and his descendents were serfs for life. Each status had reciprocal, or mutually supplementary, rights and duties—the serf, for example, provided the community's food; the military man its protection from marauders. With the decline of feudalism this reciprocal right–duty system faded away in favor of a network of voluntary contractual relationships. This was the "new freedom." This was how men—according to their talents rather than birth—made their way in life. And so in the new social milieu it was crucial that contractual arrangements be honored, and not lightly disturbed. This was the spirit that informed Marshall's construction of the Contract Clause. He recognized in *Dartmouth* that such a case probably "was not particularly in the view of the framers of the Constitution." What was immediately in their minds, he seemed to say, was the old problem of debtor-relief laws. Yet, as he noted, they used language far broader than would be required if they were concerned only with that familiar problem. Accordingly he saw no reason why the broad terms used should not be read as they were written—to cover the "rare case" of *Dartmouth.* This reasoning would apply also to the state-agreement aspect of *Fletcher.*[62]

It is revealing that the Progressive critique shifts ground according to the progressiveness of the case under discussion. Marshall is charged with activism in *Fletcher* and *Dartmouth* for not confining the Contract Clause to the debtor-relief problem which he and all others agreed was its prime target. In *Ogden* v. *Saunders*[63] he insisted (in dissent) on using it in this prime intended sense to kill a debtor-relief law. For this he is accused of being a "supreme conservative"—obviously because his progressive critics like the "liberal" Jacksonian relief law in question. If late in its day the Marshall Court—succumbing to Jacksonian fever—indulged in a bit of activism, the Chief Justice did not. Ironically the liberal tradition lampoons him for not following the minimum (debtor-relief) meaning in *Fletcher* and in *Dartmouth,* and for following it in *Saunders.* This of course indicates less about Marshall than about his critics.

It is not hardheartedness that led the framers (and Marshall) to outlaw state interference with debtor-creditor relationships. Experience under the Confederation convinced them such matters should be handled by the national government. That is why the bankruptcy power was given to Congress in Article I, Section 8 of the Constitution, and seemingly denied to the states in the Contract Clause.

Conclusion

There is substantial reason to believe—and some to doubt—that the Founding Fathers embraced the power of judicial review.[64] No matter, the "arising under" language of the Constitution plainly authorizes it. So at least the first Congress thought—and explicitly provided in Section 25 of the Judiciary Act of 1789. The pre-Marshall Court, obviously agreeing, exercised the power as a matter of course. Chief Justice Marshall and his colleagues, then, can hardly be said to have invented judicial review. Did they, however, abuse it, or use it in an activist manner? They struck down only one act of Congress in almost two generations—a narrow inconsequential measure of no general interest whatsoever. This does not constitute much of a case for abuse or activism. Nor does acquiescence in, and deferral to, all other congressional measures that came before the Court—certainly not, if activism is defined by the conduct of judges in the laissez faire and Warren eras.

All of the state measures that suffered veto because they clashed with extra-state interests (for example in *Gibbons, McCulloch, Hunter,* and *Brown*) reflected the same narrow state provincialism that had proven so costly during the Confederation—and which was indeed the chief reason for calling the Constitutional Convention. The Supremacy Clause and Section 25 were aimed specifically at curing that problem. To have upheld the state measures in question would have been to ignore the Constitution, congressional legislation, and the history that produced them. It would have constituted a return to state sovereignty and the old Confederation.

Fletcher and *Dartmouth,* which are said to show a proproperty bias in the Marshall Court were, as suggested, not proproperty but protransaction, that is, personal liberty, cases. It is significant that before *Fletcher*—the first of the contract cases—only four states had contract clauses in their constitutions. Thereafter, in the Marshall era, eight more states adopted them. So also did fourteen others in the next thirty years. In each instance save one the clause was included in the state's bill of rights. Obviously, the prohibition against contract impairment as interpreted by the Supreme Court was widely "viewed as one of those restrictions upon governmental power which serve to protect the most valuable rights of the citizen."[65]

Finally, modern activists can find no support or satisfaction in Marshall's vigorous self-restraint in the jurisdiction cases,[66] nor in his allegedly activist nationalism; for his opinions in that context merely reflect the outlook of those who produced the Constitution. In sum, he followed their basic design to create a system in which the parts could no longer emasculate the whole. To put it in more modern (economic) terms, he gave us what they wanted: a common market. Moreover, as *Blackbird, Brown,* and *Gibbons* make clear, he was far from dogmatic in his antiparochialism. *Gibbons* is particularly interesting because, while in that case Marshall was markedly nationalistic on the scope of the Commerce Clause, he was plainly nonnationalistic (despite his expressed personal inclination) on the exclusive-concurrent problem. The desideratum, it would seem, was not nationalism but the purpose (or nonpurpose) of the Founders as deduced via *Heydon's* rule. Finding in that approach no clue to the Founders' design with respect to the exclusivity problem, Marshall and his colleagues exercised judicial restraint. That is, they decided the case on a less momentous ground, leaving the crucial issue for resolution in the light of such further wisdom as additional experience and discussion might provide.

It was not Marshall who set precedent for Warren Court imperialism; it was rather the laissez faire activists beginning in the 1890s. The father of that movement was Mr. Justice Field.[67] His son-in-law (so to speak) was Mr. Justice Black who passed the torch to the Warren Court activists[68] —and lived to regret it.[69]

Notes

1. "High Court Seen Losing Backers," *New York Times,* June 15, 1969, p. 43.

2. See Philip B. Kurland, *Politics, the Constitution and the Warren Court* (Chicago: University of Chicago Press, 1970), pp. 10–12.

3. *Marbury v. Madison,* 1 Cranch 137 (1803).

4. Louis B. Boudin, *Government by Judiciary* (New York: Goodwin, 1932).

5. *Poe v. Ullman,* 367 U.S. 496, 517–518 (1961).

6. *Dred Scott v. Sandford,* 19 Howard 393 (1857).

7. *United States v. E.C. Knight Co.,* 156 U.S. 1 (1895).

8. *Pollock v. Farmers' Loan & Trust Co.,* 158 U.S. 601 (1895).

9. *Hammer v. Dagenhart,* 247 U.S. 251 (1918).

10. *Plessy v. Ferguson,* 163 U.S. 537 (1896).

11. *Lochner v. New York,* 198 U.S. 45 (1905).

12. 3 Dallas 171 (1796).

13. 4 Dallas 14, 19 (1800).

14. "This Constitution, and the Laws of the United States which shall be made in Pursuance thereof; and all Treaties made, or which shall be made, under the Authority of the United States, shall be the supreme Law of the Land; and the Judges in every State shall be bound thereby, any Thing in the Constitution or Laws of any State to the Contrary notwithstanding."

15. 1 Cranch 137 (1803).

16. *Fletcher v. Peck,* 6 Cranch 87 (1810), was a diversity case.

17. *New Orleans v. Winter,* 1 Wheaton 91 (1816); *Bank of the United States v. Deveau,* 5 Cranch 61 (1809); *Hepburn v. Ellzey,* 2 Cranch 445 (1804).

18. *United States v. Hudson and Goodwin,* 7 Cranch 32 (1812).

19. To the surprise of the admiralty bar, *The Steamboat Thomas Jefferson,* 10 Wheaton 438 (1825), confined the admiralty jurisdiction of the federal courts to cases involving tidal waters. The Taney Court adopted a more expansive view in *Genesee Chief v. Fitzhugh,* 12 Howard 443 (1851).

20. *Durousseau v. United States,* 6 Cranch 307 (1810).

21. *Barron v. Baltimore,* 7 Peters 243 (1833).

22. 19 Howard 393 (1857).

23. Wallace Mendelson, "The Politics of Judicial Activism," *Emory Law Journal* 24 (Summer 1975):43-66.

24. 3 Dallas 199 (1796).

25. The Marshall Court explored the basis of review in such cases at length in *Martin v. Hunter's Lessee,* 1 Wheaton 304 (1816), and *Cohens v. Virginia,* 6 Wheaton 264 (1821), discussed below.

26. George Washington, *The Writings of George Washington,* ed. John Fitzpatrick (Washington, D.C.: Government Printing Office, 1938), 28:502-503.

27. James Madison, "Origin of the Constitutional Convention," 1835.

28. 1 Wheaton 304 (1816).

29. 4 Wheaton 316 (1819).

30. 9 Wheaton 1 (1824).

31. Jefferson to G. Wythe, 16 Sept. 1787.

32. Madison to J.C. Cabell, 1 April 1833.

33. 6 Wheaton 264 (1821).

34. Ibid., pp. 413-414.

35. *Martin v. Hunter's Lessee,* 1 Wheaton 304, 348 (1816).

36. Henry M. Hart, ed., *Henry M. Hart and Herbert Wechsler's The Federal Courts and the Federal System* (Mineola, N.Y.: Foundation Press, 1973), p. 455.

37. Heydon's Case, 3 Co. Rep. 7a, 76 Eng. Rep. 637 (Exch. 1854).

38. *Gibbons v. Ogden,* 9 Wheaton 1, 188-189 (1824).

39. Preamble to the Constitution.

40. See *Hughes v. Oklahoma,* 99 S. Ct. 1727, 1731 (1979).

41. Robert G. McCloskey, *The American Supreme Court* (Chicago: University of Chicago Press, 1960), pp. 144-150.

42. Madison also was inclined toward the exclusive view. See Max Farrand, ed., *The Records of the Federal Convention of 1787* (New Haven: Yale University Press, 1911), 2:625.

43. See the Brandeis opinion in *Ashwander v. Tennessee Valley Authority,* 297 U.S. 288, 346-348 (1936).

44. 4 Wheaton 316 (1819).

45. Irving Brant, "The Madison Heritage," in *The Great Rights,* ed. Edmund Cahn (New York: Macmillan, 1963), p. 34. As president, Madison approved the rechartering of BUS.

46. 4 Wheaton 316, 435-436 (1803).

47. 9 Wheaton 1, 197 (1824).

48. "Law and the Court" in Oliver Wendell Holmes, *Collected Legal Papers,* 295-296 (1920), quoted in Wallace Mendelson, *The Constitution and the Supreme Court* (New York: Dodd, Mead, 1959), p. 28.

49. 2 Peters 245 (1829).

50. 12 Peters 419 (1827).

51. Thomas Jefferson, *Notes on the State of Virginia* (New York: Harper and Row, 1964).

52. Irving Brant, *James Madison: Father of the Constitution, 1787-1800* (New York: Bobbs-Merrill, 1950), 3:45,61.

53. 6 Cranch 87 (1810).

54. 4 Wheaton 518 (1819).

55. U.S. Constitution, Article I, Section 10: "No State shall . . . pass any law . . . impairing the obligation of contracts. . . . "

56. As Dean Roscoe Pound has explained, "Contract was then used, and was used as late as Parsons on Contracts in 1853 to mean [what] might be called "legal transaction". . . . Not merely contract as we now understand it, but trust, will, conveyance, and grant of a franchise are included. . . . The writers on natural law considered that there was a natural legal duty not to derogate from one's grant. . . . This is the explanation of *Fletcher,* . . . and no doubt is what the [contract clause] meant to those who wrote it into the Constitution." ("The Charles River Bridge Case," *Massachusetts Law Quarterly* 27, no. 4, at pp. 19-20.)

57. 226 Mass. 618 (1799).

58. See C. Peter Magrath, *Yazoo: Law and Politics in the New Republic* (New York: Norton, 1966), pp. 35-37.

59. See also, for example, *Barron v. Baltimore,* 7 Peters 243 (1833), holding the Fifth Amendment does not require compensation for *state* construction of private property; *Providence Bank v. Billings,* 4 Peters 514 (1830), undermining valuable economic interests by strict construction of a public grant; and *Mason v. Haile,* 12 Wheaton 370 (1827), which diminished protection for creditors by upholding even retroactive abolition of imprisonment for debt.

60. *Gibbons* also promoted transactional freedom by destroying the steamboat monopoly.

61. Sir Henry Maine, *Ancient Law* (New York: Scribner, 1864), p. 165.

62. It is noteworthy that Alexander Hamilton, too, believed the Contract Clause applied to state as well as private-party agreements. See his brief with respect to the Yazoo claims, reproduced in Magrath, *Yazoo*.

63. 12 Wheaton 213 (1827).

64. Raoul Berger, *Congress v. The Supreme Court* (Cambridge: Harvard University Press, 1969).

65. Benjamin F. Wright, *The Contract Clause of the Constitution* (Cambridge: Harvard University Press, 1938), p. 61. See also ibid., pp. 60, 86–88.

66. See notes 17–21 and related text.

67. See Wallace Mendelson, "Mr. Justice Field and Laissez Faire," *Virginia Law Review* 36 (February 1950):45–58.

68. Wallace Mendelson, *Justices Black and Frankfurter: Conflict in the Court,* 2d ed. (Chicago: University of Chicago Press, 1966).

69. Ibid., pp. 132 ff. See also Mr. Justice Black's dissent in *Harper v. Virginia Board of Elections,* 383 U.S. 663 (1966).

Economic Activism
and Restraint

Daniel Novak

If one were to rely on the current spate of literature on judicial activism, one might conclude that such activity is a fairly recent phenomenon. Discussion tends to begin with an evaluation of the Warren Court, the due process revolution in criminal justice, civil rights, school prayer and so forth, and goes on to examine the propriety of judicial oversight of legislative reapportionment, racial balancing, busing and public school finances. It is, of course, not uncommon for such debates to concentrate upon the most recent and relevant examples of the genre, but this must not lead us to ignore the fact that the activism–restraint argument is as old as the Court itself.

This chapter will endeavor to place the controversy in its appropriate historical perspective, through an examination of the Supreme Court's posture in economic controversies. Such an analysis leads almost inexorably to the conclusion that the Court has been activist in this area from its early years straight through to the famous "switch-in-time" of the New Deal period. What have changed are the issues and areas of activist jurisprudence; the nature of the activity seems immutable.

There is one further variance between the debate over the Court's economic actions and the modern controversies—the descriptive terminology. No one accused John Marshall, or Rufus Peckham, of "activism"; terms such as "judicial usurpation of power," and "judicial aggressiveness" were the ones used at the time.

If the argument that the Court has always been activist is to stand, however, the terminology of today should be just as applicable to the past as to the present. These terms are somewhat ambiguous and vague by their nature, and exactly what constitutes "judicial self-restraint," for example, varies from one scholarly analysis to another. Most scholars would, I think, agree that one or more of the following could be combined to provide a reasonable definition:

judicial deference to the other branches of government, that is, an unwillingness to substitute the judgment of the Court for that of the elected representatives of the people;

a lack of result-orientation. The Court concerns itself with legal principles, not the social or economic effects of its decisions;

a respect for precedent or *stare decisis;* "let the decision stand," and aim at a system of "settled" and understood law;

avoidance of "political" questions which must be left to the democratic process as expressed through the electorate and its representatives.

Of these four, the most significant are undoubtedly judicial deference and lack of result-orientation, for these qualities are those the critics of the Court most often cite as being sadly lacking. In all these respects, however, the history of the Supreme Court in the economic area demonstrates that it has always been activist, and that evaluating that history using these modern terms does not challenge that conclusion. While evidence of economic activism is present from the earliest days of the Court, perhaps the best jumping-off place for this analysis begins with the father of constitutional law, John Marshall.

Marshall, Taney, and the Birth of Economic Activism

The Marshall Court began a period of judicial activism in the area of economic cases which continued through the New Deal. Before the advent of John Marshall, the Court had not been effective as a *Supreme* Court. It had, of course, already established the dominant concept of "vested rights" in a number of cases,[1] so that Marshall was not facing a tabula rasa. (Vested rights are interests which have been given legal sanction; that is, interests which are now protected by law. The basic right involved here is that of property.) It soon became clear, however, that *stare decisis* would not, in any case, have proved a great hindrance to the inventive and active mind which was to dominate the Court for so long a tenure. Through the use of a broad interpretation of the Constitution, and a concept of general principles of free government, the Marshall Court did battle with state legislatures whose views of vested rights were at variance with its. That is, it was consistently able to find cause by which state laws could be invalidated.

Perhaps the area of greatest activism may be found in examining the Court's interpretation of the Contract Clause. In *Fletcher* v. *Peck* (1810),[2] for example, Marshall upheld the rights of an "innocent third party" who had purchased land fraudulently acquired by grant from the legislature of Georgia,[3] despite the revocation of that action by the succeeding legislature. What is striking about the opinion is the nature of the rationale which Marshall gives for his decision. He is clearly unsure *why* the repealer was unconstitutional, but, by God, he knew that there was something wrong with it. Therefore, Marshall relied upon the ex post facto clause (which was clearly inapplicable by *Calder* v. *Bull*[4]), bills of attainder, the Contract Clause and "general principles . . . common to our free institutions"[5] to justify the decision the Court reached. In brief, we are given a shopping list of potential sins and are offered a choice, to mix a metaphor, of picking one from column A and two from column B. This extraordinary position was, it appears, not strong enough for the redoubtable First Dissenter,

Justice Johnson, who relied on general principles to a degree that he claimed they "will impose laws even on the deity."[6] As Arthur Miller has pointed out, the Court did not again attempt to place legal restraints upon God, but surely no Court will ever go further in its activism.[7] Clearly, the discovery of general principles of natural law, upon which previously obscured rights may be based, is the process of judicial decision making which underlies much activist endeavor. Marshall had to rely on such vague terms because of the insecurity of his legal ground; ex post facto and bill of attainder were clearly inapplicable; the Contract Clause had been thought to apply only to executory contracts, not those that had been fulfilled, nor had it been thought to cover public as well as private contracts.[8] Therefore, Marshall "invoked the principles of natural law for cosmic reinforcement."[9]

In *New Jersey* v. *Wilson* (1812),[10] the Court reiterated its position of the irretrievable nature of legislative activity. A tax immunity given to land which was owned and inhabited by Indians was removed by the state when the tribe sold the land—a seemingly rational conclusion to an initially rational and humane act. The Supreme Court, however, declared that the tax immunity attached to the land itself and was, therefore, irrevocable.

In *Terret* v. *Taylor* (1815),[11] Virginia, having recognized the title of the Church of Virginia to certain lands in 1776, revoked the title in the process of disestablishing the church some ten years later. (The land had not been granted by either the King or the legislature, it had simply recognized the claim of title.) Justice Story, bereft of a hook to hang his opinion on (there was no grant or contract) fell back upon the general principles of higher law. These cases may not seem significant in themselves, but they provided the basis for the invalidation of numerous legislative acts.[12]

Dartmouth College is too well known to require extensive explication here; it is enough to point out, as various observers have,[13] that Marshall's determination to defend corporate charters from state regulation led him to take a view of the Contract Clause that, in his own words, "was not in the mind of the Convention"[14] which promulgated it.

The broad strokes of Marshall's opinion regarding the Commerce Clause do nothing to challenge the activist image presented above. Commerce Clause issues are clearly different in emphasis—national supremacy rather than private rights provides the essential rationale. It is, of course, also true that this nationalism served much the same purpose as did the doctrine of vested rights, that is the protection of those private rights. At that time only the state governments were actually taking actions which threatened such interests; to deny their power to do so in the name of an unused potential power in the national government was as effective a deterrent as an outright denial that any such power existed. It is this actuality which enables one to "reconcile" *Gibbons,* for example, with the other "proproperty" cases cited above. (In this instance, I disagree with Professor Mendelson, who presents an effective argument to the contrary in chapter 3 of this volume. It is doubtless ironic, and perhaps faintly amusing, that in the end Marshall becomes a New Dealer, and that his opinions provide the basis for the vast government regulation of the economy of today. This does not, however, reflect the enduringly neutral nature of those opinions, but rather the vastly changed role of the federal government. In any case, decisions like *Gibbons* v. *Ogden*[15] or *Brown* v. *Maryland*[16] are examples of activism in their own right, without regard for any result-orientation. In *Brown,* the same result could have been reached by a far less sweeping attack on state authority. Marshall reached out to encompass as much of commerce as possible under the national umbrella; indeed, the dicta of his *Gibbons* opinion make it difficult to find any such animal as intrastate commerce at all. It has been persuasively argued that Marshall's paramount interest was to embellish the function of the Court as final arbiter in such questions.[17]

It should be noted that this general position has been challenged by Wallace Mendelson in this volume. I do not dispute his contentions with regard to the concept of judicial review, but, as is evident, I do take issue with the characterization of *Dartmouth College, Gibbons* and others. An argument from results has a continuing attraction, that is, the fact that the decisions cited did, over time, have the effects attributed to them. The effects on the parties in groundbreaking litigation is not the true measure of result-orientation unless one presumes that judges do not foresee the long-term results of their decisions. It is perhaps unfair to cite a fellow-contributor's positions to counter his present views; no opinion need be cast in concrete. On the other hand, it seems only rational to note that I found Wallace Mendelson's previous analysis (see notes 13 and 17) more persuasive than his current one.

In sum, I would contend that the major decisions of the Marshall Court in the economic realm present an image consistent with that which modern scholars have called judicial activism: a lack of deference to the popularly elected branches; a willingness to involve the Court in political questions (*Marbury*); the use of vague and sweeping doctrines which provide a basic formula by which the Court is freed to roam; and a result-orientation which is clear and indeed often stated openly. "The Constitution," in Marshall's words, "was intended to endure for ages and consequently to be adapted to the various crises of human affairs."[18] It is clear that the Supreme Court, under Marshall's or other appropriate (that is, conservative) tutelage, was to oversee and control this adaptation.

The Taney Court (and Chief Justice Taney in particular) has gained the reputation of a great restraintist Court. The Beards have argued that "Jacksonian judges . . . broke down the historic safeguards thrown around property rights by the letter of the Constitution and the jurisprudence of John Marshall. For practical purposes they declared the states to be sovereign."[19] Indeed, Mendelson seems almost to credit Taney with the creation of the concept of judicial self-restraint. Doubtless, at least by comparison with its predecessor, these characterizations are largely valid. The Taney Court was more deferential to state legislatures (and to states' rights generally) and it did mute some of the more outstanding examples of Marshallian activism. On the other hand, one need not be terribly restraintist to reject some of the excesses of the Marshall Court, just as one could remain quite conservative in one's economic views while still remaining far to the left of Marshall or Story.

Certainly, the first of the three renowned cases of the Taney Court's first year, *Charles River Bridge,*[20] gives every indication of great changes to come. The scope of the Contract Clause, the bulwark of vested rights, was significantly circumscribed in theory and the rhetoric of the opinion was striking in its deference to the representatives of the popular will. Although the Charles River Bridge Company had a reasonable claim than its contractual rights had been violated, the Taney Court argued that in grants to the public, nothing passes by implication. When the conflict was between the right of a business to operate and the right of the state to act for the general welfare, the balance must be shifted to the side of the state. Public grants were to be strictly interpreted, with the benefit of the doubt being given to the public. Little wonder, then, that when Story presented Marshall's "dissents from the grave" (that is, he said that Marshall had told him, before he died, that he agreed with the dissents[21]) conservatives everywhere threw up their hands in horror.[22] A caveat must be inserted here, however. In the midst of this "populist" rhetoric, Taney does get to the heart of the matter, which is: if the Court does not restrict the doctrine of implied contracts, "[t]he millions of property which have been invested in railroads and canals . . . will be put in jeopardy."[23] Twenty years later, in a similar contract case with a very different result, the Court was still concerned over the "millions of money in that state and millions upon millions of banking capital in other states [that] are to be affected by its judicial decision."[24] The Court, in short, took care of the millions and let the pennies take care of themselves. The nature of the economy was changing and the conflict was no longer necessarily between state power and vested rights, but rather between two different sets of private rights. When the old conflict was presented to it, the Taney Court was fairly consistent in opting for the vested right. In *Piqua Branch Bank* v. *Knoop* (1853),[25] for example, Ohio attempted to change its method of taxing banks. The charter, which provided for 6 percent of the profits to be taken in lieu of taxes, did not say that this was granted in perpetuity, a fact conceded by the Court. Obviously, one would be led to expect that the Court would apply the *Charles River Bridge* doctrine; instead the Court (though not Taney himself) chose to infer perpetuity and to reconfirm simultaneously Marshall's doctrines in *New Jersey* v. *Wilson.* When Ohio changed its constitution to accomplish the same result, the Court again said that a state may be bound by its legislature forever, and that the "people of a State could no more impair the obligations of contracts by means of a Constitution than by a statute. . . . The moral obligations never die."[26] We may well agree with Justice Catron's dissent in *Piqua,* that the *Charles River Bridge* protections of the public welfare were illusory. In *Gelpcke* v. *Dubuque* (1864)[27] the Court found a violation of the Contract Clause caused by the successful appeal of a judicial decision despite its own maxim that decisions of courts do not constitute laws. In sum, it is not surprising that Benjamin Wright should find the Contract Clause a stronger protection for property after the Taney Court than before.

Further, as the economy grew more complex, new areas arose wherein judicial activism could serve the cause of business. Most notably, we begin to see the growth of the interstate corporation, and the Taney Court was quick to rise to its defense. The Marshall Court was traditionally seen as probusiness and the Taney Court sympathetic to state control. In the final analysis, however, it was the latter which greatly enhanced the status of interstate corporate growth in a series of activist decisions. For example, the decision in *Bank of Augusta* v. *Earle*,[28] wherein "foreign" (that is, out-of-state) corporations could be barred completely by a state, but once permitted, were protected by interstate comity, was clearly a restraintist and deferential one, in theory. Its practical effect, however, as might have been expected by any beginning student of economics, was to give corporations an open season for interstate expansion. If *Earle* were restraintist in theory, in *Louisville R.R.* v. *Letson*[29] the Taney Court reversed Marshall's decision in the *U.S. Bank* v. *Deveaux*[30] and declared that corporations were citizens for the purpose of suing in diversity of citizenship cases in the federal court system.

Further, in *Swift* v. *Tyson*,[31] where a federal commercial common law was "discovered" by Justice Story (that is, a hitherto unsuspected power was found, hidden away in the spirit of the Constitution), the jurisdiction of the federal courts was extended into areas where even Congress was powerless, unbound by state court rulings even in matters of state law. *Swift* and *Letson* both served to make it easier to gain access to the friendly confines of the federal courts for corporations under duress in the state arena.

The one economic area in which the Taney Court was most inconsistent, that is, occasionally deferential, is to be found in cases relating to the Commerce Clause. Within the crazy quilt of Commerce Clause opinions there is a pattern to be discerned, if I may be permitted a metaphoric oxymoron. In many of the major cases (*New York* v. *Miln*,[32] the *Passenger Cases*,[33] and the *License Cases*[34]) the all-confounding question of slavery made its presence felt. The *Passenger Cases*, for example, which overtly dealt with the right of a state to impose a fee on out-of-state passengers, was in reality a reflection of this larger problem. There were nine separate opinions in a 5-4 decision, which seemed to be a close victory for states' rights. However, this seeming deference was a mask for the real question, which revolved around the basic policy preferences of the justices with regard to the slave trade. The reach of federal control over interstate commerce constituted a looming threat to the easy transportation of slaves. That the judges were concerned not with the case at issue, but with its implications for slavery, is made clear in their letters as well as the opinions.[35]

The culmination of this line of cases was reached in *Cooley* v. *Board of Port Wardens*.[36] Here the legacy of John Marshall is again seen, as the Court enunciated a selective "exclusivity" rule, whose mysteries could only be plumbed by federal courts. In Arthur Miller's words, "it fits with Marshall's nationalizing opinions, aids corporate growth, and, *again puts the Court in the forefront of articulating economic policy via constitutional interpretation.*"[37] That the Court, three days later, reversed a Marshall decision which had restricted the maritime jurisdiction of the federal courts to the tidewater, adding to that jurisdiction all public navigable lakes and rivers in the nation, was simply gilding the lily.[38]

It is hardly necessary to point out that the Taney Court must inevitable be seen as an activist Court—in economic policy, at least. *Swift* v. *Tyson* and *Gelpcke* v. *Dubuque* alone make that conclusion ineluctable. Certainly, it was generally less activist than the Marshall Court, but while deference to state sovereignty was more common, it was often made in name only. Marshall had made it easier for a result-oriented Court to follow precedent while protecting business growth; but where precedent failed, the Taney Court had little trouble in exercising a far-reaching creative instinct to serve the same purpose.

Before Laissez Faire

It is clear that the so-called laissez faire Court must be a main object of interest in any discussion of economic restraint and activism. The very idea of substantive due process, by itself, constitutes a radical advance in the activist capabilities of the judiciary, a quantum jump in judicial power which has provided the constitutional basis for oft-criticized actions of contemporary Courts. When this development is combined with the rather cavalier handling of Commerce Clause issues, that is, the totally contradictory stances taken when the reach of the clause was used to restrict unions rather than business, this period of Supreme Court history becomes the sine qua non of activism.

Some of the classic cases of the "entrepreneurial liberty" period are not as significant to this discussion as they would be in a paper purely emphasizing the probusiness, antilabor bias of the Court. The bias of the Court is, I think, undeniable, but this does not always presuppose a strongly activist position. For example, the *Debs*[39] case, an almost laughable travesty of judicial process, is simply a minor example of result-orientation when seen from a restraintist-activist point of view. The Court was simply ratifying the activities of the Attorney General and the executive. If it did so by unearthing a previously hidden national police power, it was essentially expanding the powers of other branches of the government. Thus, like *McCulloch* v. *Maryland, Debs* falls beyond the scope of this chapter.

Before the Robber Barons' "Great Barbecue"[40] was to be judicially sanctified, however, the Court went through a brief period of truly restraintist deference under Chief Justice Waite. The Contract Clause, home of the Vested Rights doctrine, had fallen into disrepute. First, the states had finally caught on to the basic loophole available to them, that is, the automatic inclusion, in all corporate charters, of a clause entitling the legislature to change the terms of the agreement. Story's opinion in *Dartmouth College* had made clear that this had always been a state option; state legislatures now began to use it. Of even greater significance was the Court's reliance upon a new doctrine of an inalienable police power and a reserved police power.

That is, the Waite Court shifted away from the *New Jersey* v. *Wilson* line of cases and concluded that the states could not barter away their powers in matters of public health and morals. In *Beer Co.* v. *Massachusetts*[41] the Court claimed an inalienable public health responsibility for the state, and in *Northwest Fertilizer Co.* v. *Hyde Park,*[42] although the state had reserved no power to amend the original charter, this same principle was relied upon. Given the nature of the businesses in these cases, one might be led to assume that for some reason, the public's sense of smell was somehow deserving of special judicial dispensation. The Court's new sense of deference to the legislature went further, however, for in *Ruggles* v. *Illinois*[43] a railroad charter conflict was resolved in favor of the state on the basis of reserved police powers, in *Spring Valley Water Co.* v. *Shottler*[44] a water company charter was similarly construed, and in *Stone* v. *Mississippi*[45] the state's power to regulate gambling was deemed inalienable.

Contemporaneously, the Court added a fresh definition of property which further buttressed the latitude of the states to regulate commerce. In *Munn.* v. *Illinois*[46] (one of the *Granger Cases*), Waite argued that property becomes "clothed with a public interest when used in a manner to make it of public consequence and affects the community at large."[47] If property is devoted to such usage, its owner, "in effect, grants to the public an interest in that use and must submit to be controlled by the public for the common good. . . . [It] cease[s] to be *juris privati* only."[48] If businesses disliked this submission, they were free to withdraw their property from such public usage, or "resort to the polls, not the courts."[49] Surely there could be no more restraintist or deferential position than this.[50]

This state of affairs was not to endure, however, for even as majorities in the Waite Court were establishing these doctrines, the foundations of the instrument of their destruction were being laid by a vocal and growing minority. This is not the place to trace the evolution of the concept of "substantive" due process in detail. A brief summary of its development will suffice.

The traditional view of due process, that it guaranteed a set of regularized procedures in the execution of the law, had been briefly challenged before the Civil War, most notably by the New York Court of Appeals in *Wynhammer* v. *New York*[51] and in an almost casual aside by Taney in *Dred Scott.*[52] When the idea that due process involved an examination of the substance of legislation was pressed on the Court by ex-Justice Campbell in the *Slaughterhouse Cases,* it received short shrift from the majority: "under no construction of that provision that we have ever seen, or that we deem admissible, can the restraint imposed . . . be held to be a deprivation of property within the meaning of that provision."[53] This new note did strike a responsive chord in the breasts of Justices Bradley and Swayne, however, and more was yet to come. In the *Granger Cases,* discussed above, counsel for the granaries and railroads argued a unique cojoining of vested rights and the new substantive due process, adding that if rates could be set, their reasonableness must be left to the judiciary. Only Justice Field formally accepted this notion, although even Waite gave a grudging nod to the possibility that some statutes may violate due process. In *Davidson* v. *New Orleans* (1878)[54] Justice Miller scolded counsel for continuing to use arguments so consistently rejected by the Court.

Within the space of eight years, however, Justice Waite himself was to formally accept the concept of substantive due process, albeit in dictum. In *Stone* v. *Farmers Loan and Trust*[55] the Court upheld the regulatory statute in question establishing a railroad commission, but announced that rates were subject to judicial scrutiny. Reasonableness of rates was not, as Waite had stated in *Munn,* to be left solely to the legislature, but was an appropriate subject for the courts to decide. In *Mugler* v. *Kansas* (1887)[56] and *Powell* v. *Penn* (1888)[57] the Court continued to uphold state legislation, but with the significant caveat that they were not to be "bound by mere pretense" and were under the obligation to look at the substance of things. Although the Court did invalidate a statute in the *Minnesota Commission Case* (1890),[58] partly on substantive due process grounds, the main objections were violations of procedural due process. Finally, in *Smythe* v. *Ames* (1898),[59] the doctrine reached its fruition, and a rate regulation was reversed on purely substantive grounds. It is noteworthy that in this case the Court provides us with a shopping list of potential criteria for use in determining judicial reasonableness of rates. The items listed were variable— that is, the Court could add, subtract, or select from them, at its pleasure, in order to determine a reasonable return on the "fair value" of the property.[60] The latitude thus achieved enabled the justices to exercise a vast power to impose their own policy preferences on the legislatures—it was judicial activism in its purest sense.

In fairness, it should be noted that the probusiness, antiregulation bias of the "laissez faire Court" presumed by the arguments just presented (and in the discussion that is to follow) has been challenged by a number of scholars. Pointedly, however, these challenges tend to concentrate on the results at which the Court was aiming, for example, that the protection of "competitive capitalism" was promoted, rather than the suppression of reform.[61] In other words, the nature of the bias of the Court has been challenged, and motivations other than the protection of business from governmental interference are ascribed to the justices. For example, Mary Cornelia Porter has argued that "substantive due process, as it pertained to state regulation of intrastate public utility rates, served as a surrogate for the [then] inapplicable Commerce Clause,"[62] that is, that the Court was attempting to establish a uniform national rule for the rates utilities might charge. Regardless of the validity of these positions (which cannot be covered here), they in no way affect the thesis that the Court was activist. They simply shift the focus of that activism.

The "Laissez Faire" Court

Before we leave the nineteenth century, however, we should take careful note of three major economic decisions. In 1895, a very good year for economic conservatives, the Supreme Court decided *In re Debs*,[63] *United States* v. *E.C. Knight*[64] *(*the *Sugar Trust Case)*, and *Pollock* v. *Farmers' Loan and Trust (*the *Income Tax Case)*.[65] The first of these, *Debs,* has been briefly discussed, as an example of result-oriented jurisprudence, which, while unearthing a hitherto wholly unsuspected national police power to protect the general welfare, was deferential in the sense that it was merely supportive of the activities of the executive.[66] Simple acquiescence in the behavior of elected officials or their agents (in this case, Attorney General Richard Olney), no matter how outrageous that behavior, or how strained the reasoning of the decision, does not constitute the sort of superactivism in which the Court was then almost routinely engaged in the economic realm. On the other hand, the *Income Tax Case* provided a sound example of just such activity. The Wilson-Gorman Act provided for a flat tax on incomes over $4,000. The government could call upon two major precedents to support its case. As far back as 1796, in *Hylton* v. *United States*,[67] the government had set up a case, in order that the nature of direct taxes could be defined by the Supreme Court. (This was significant because such taxes could only be levied among the states proportional to population.) The decision of the Court had been that only taxes on land and people were direct. This precedent had been reaffirmed in *Springer* v. *United States* (1881)[68] when the validity of a Civil War–time income tax had been upheld. Now, the Court dealt with the new tax in two successive decisions. In the first of these, Justice Fuller emphasized a connection between taxing land and taxing the income from land, and stated that there was no difference between the two. The taxes on the income from land fell into a special category, he contended, and were clearly unconstitutional.

When the case was reheard a month later, the Court, imitating the legendary worm which ate its own tail, declared that taxes on the income from land were indistinguishable from any other sort of income tax on property and all were unconstitutional. As the original decision was based on the unique character of income from land, and second on its lack of such character, it is little wonder that Mr. Dooley could remark that a stone wall to a layman is a triumphal arch to a lawyer. Of course, all of this was tangential to the real argument, which was made on other grounds. Joseph Choate, as attorney for the plaintiff, called the income tax "socialistic, communistic . . . populistic"; in essence, an attack on the established order by the populace which the Court had a duty to forestall.[69]

The last of the 1895 cases, *United States* v. *E.C. Knight,*[70] is the start of a long journey into never-never land—the application by the Court of the Sherman Antitrust Act. In this case, the Court denied the jurisdiction of Congress over the Sugar Trust on the grounds that manufacturing, by its nature, was not in interstate commerce, but was purely local (intrastate) in character. This conclusion was, perhaps, a startling statement on its own hook, but was even more absurd in this particular situation. The Sugar Trust had at least as great a monopoly over sales of sugar as it did over refining—more than 90 percent. The Court, in essence, wrote manufacturing out of the Commerce Clause (and the Sherman Act) on the grounds that such regulations must be left to the states. This solicitude for states' rights was spurious, of course, as it was clear that states could not control huge trusts on their own. In Corwin's terms, there was created a realm of "no government—a governmental vacuum, a political 'no man's land'."[71] (It should be recalled that in transportation, where the states did attempt to regulate, the Court had responded with substantive due process.)

It is true that the government won antitrust suits in *American Tobacco*[72] and *Standard Oil,*[73] but they were hollow victories indeed. The Sherman Act outlawed "every" restraint of trade, but the Supreme Court added a word to the statute—only "unreasonable" restraints of trade were barred. This was pure judicial legislation, for Congress never, despite considerable pressure, added the word "reasonable" to the Act (or to the Clayton Act that followed). It was argued that one could not draw the line between "good" and "bad" trusts—all must be barred. President Taft agreed, and added that courts could not make such decisions. (When serving as chief justice, Taft enforced the "rule or reason"; role perceptions were no empty terms for him.) The pyrrhic nature of the victories in *American Tobacco* and *Standard Oil* is made clear by the fact that following them, the government won no more. The great combinations were all "reasonable." The shoe machinery monopoly,[74] *U.S. Steel,*[75] and *International Harvester,*[76] were all found to be "good" trusts. The expansion of trusts after *E.C. Knight* was extraordinary, and after the insertion of "reason" into the Sherman Act, the new combines were reasonably safe from federal prosecution.

While the protection of the trusts through judicial legislation was striking in its own right, the Court provided even greater evidence of its activist tendencies in the areas in which it did apply the Sherman and Clayton Acts. Although the legislative history of the former indicated its purpose was to provide a tool for the repression of the great business combinations, the Supreme Court found it could serve another function; namely, the suppression of unions. While the Sherman Act was the basis of the injunction issued by the district court in the *Debs* case, the Supreme Court, as we have seen, did not rely upon it in its opinion. This omission was soon remedied. In *Loewe* v. *Lawlor*[77] the American Federation of Labor had listed a hat manufacturer on its boycott list. Although the lower courts refused *Loewe* an injunction, the Supreme Court heard the case. There were two main arguments for the union: first, that the Sherman Act did not apply to unions (almost unquestionably correct);[78] and second, even if the Act did apply it could not in this case, for neither the union nor the manufacturer was in interstate commerce. After all, the Supreme Court had itself asserted that manufacturing was local in character with only a vague and indirect effect on interstate commerce in the *Sugar Trust Case*. However, Chief Justice Fuller, for an unanimous Court, ruled that the Sherman Act did apply to unions; that a secondary boycott was a restraint of trade under the Act; and that the effect on interstate commerce was sufficient for jurisdiction—after all, *every* restraint of trade was covered.[79] This decision was rendered just one week after Justice Harlan, in *Adair* v. *United States*,[80] had proclaimed that the Commerce Clause did not cover labor relations, not even for railroad workers. (This, of course, dealt with a congressional attempt to *assist* those workers.) If the *Debs* injunction was a "gatling gun on paper," the *Loewe* case instituted a trend toward government by injunction.

In two major labor injunction cases, the Court did not rely on the Sherman Act but instead used common-law injunctions. In *Gompers* v. *Buck Stove & Range Co.* (1911)[81] Samuel Gompers was convicted of contempt for daring to write an editorial in the union newspaper against an injunction granted by a lower court. Noting parenthetically that calling an employer "unfair" is equivalent to force, the Supreme Court made clear that freedom of the press stops where it interferes with the right of business to be free from union boycotts. This concept was carried a step further in *Hitchman Coal & Coke* v. *Mitchell* (1917),[82] where the Court upheld an injunction preventing the United Mine Workers from using argument, persuasion or reason to convince any employees (or potential employees) to join the union. This truly breathtaking idea, of protecting the bulk of mankind (remember, all but sucklings and toddlers were potential employees in those days of unfettered child labor) from exposure to the besetting sin of reason, is on a par with Justice Johnson's contractual restraints upon God.

In response to cases like these (and particularly *Loewe* v. *Lawlor*), Congress tried to diffuse the tendency through passage of the Clayton Act, which seemed on its face to largely exclude unions from antitrust jurisdiction. A Court which had the capacity simultaneously to exclude most trusts and include unions in the previous Act, however, had no difficulty in summoning up the necessary legerdemain to pervert this new statute similarly. In the *Duplex Printing* case (1921)[83] the Court followed the *Loewe* precedent, and converted the Clayton Act into an antiunion instrument. Further, in *Bedford Stone Cutters' Association* (1927)[84] Justice Sutherland applied the Act to a secondary strike while conceding that the strike was local in character. He discovered that the motive was national; thus, the union could be restrained.

This litany of inconsistent absurdities is not intended to emphasize merely the biases of the Court, but rather its willingness to use, manipulate, and obscure the law to reach a desired result. For example, the Court could be equally inconsistent in segregation cases under the Commerce Clause; a state statute barring segregation on a railroad was held to encroach on congressional commerce powers; a statute enforcing it was held legitimate.[85] Such inconsistencies can always be explained away by reliance upon the mystique of the law—"only those trained in reason and the law" can understand what is being done. This myth is central to the Court's success, for without it, reasonable men would ally themselves with Mr. Bumble and conclude that the law is an ass.

Liberty of Contract

One further area of laissez faire activism must be examined: the development of the doctrine of liberty of contract. Once again, the Court engaged in pure judicial legislation, using "the legal imagination" to the full. The Fourteenth Amendment, which had been eviscerated of its original function (that of protecting the rights of the freed slaves in the South), had already been found to be a useful tool for the protection of business through the application of substantive due process to the regulation of rates. Now, a further expansion of that clause was engendered, attached to the word *liberty* in "life, liberty, or property." This new liberty was "liberty of contract;" that is, the freedom of an employee to engage in any sort of contract with his employer, without the interference of a paternalistic government. It was a response to the notion, then gaining popular acceptance, that the state had a positive duty to protect the health and safety of workers through the legislative regulation of such matters as hours, wages, and labor relations. Maximum hour laws at first received a judicial imprimatur in *Holden* v. *Hardy* (1898),[86] where miners were restricted by Utah law to an eight-hour day. This regulation was upheld on the grounds that mining was a sufficiently dangerous occupation to justify legislative action. This result was achieved despite the "liberty of contract" concept, but it was clearly a special case due to the nature of the employment. In *Lochner* v. *New York*,[87] however, a divided Court struck down a New York statute establishing a maximum ten-hour day, six-day week for bakers. The state had defended it as a health measure, but Justice Peckham, speaking for the majority, rejected this reasoning:

> There is, in our judgment, no reasonable foundation for holding this to be necessary or appropriate as a health law to safeguard the public health or the health of the individual who are following the trade of a baker. If this statute be valid, and if, therefore, a proper case is made out in which to deny the right of an individual, *sui juris*, an employer or employé, to make contracts for the labor of the latter under the protection of the provisions of the Federal Constitution, there would seem to be no length to which legislation of this nature might not go.[88]

In other words, the Court, in assessing the wisdom of the legislation, failed to agree with the state that bakers required special protection. There is none of the usual presumption of constitutionality. Property, as usual, held a "preferred position," wherein presumptive unconstitutionality is the rule, and the burden of proof is shifted to the state. (The preferred freedoms doctrine, in short, was by no means a radical departure from past precedent when presented in the *Carolene* footnote;[89] the change lay in the nature of the freedoms preferred.) Further, Peckham is pointedly defending the rights of the employee, as well as that of the employer; that is, a worker must be free to contract to work as many hours as he pleases. This is extraordinary judicial activism, for it explicitly derives from an interpretation of the word "liberty" undreamed of in the philosophy of the framers of the Fourteenth Amendment.

Despite the strictures of Justice Holmes, who argued for legislative "reasonableness," liberty of contract became the law of the land. (Harlan, White, and Day, who also dissented, did so on the grounds that there was a connection between hours of work and health considerations; they accepted the doctrine and simply disagreed on the value of the justificatory evidence presented by the state.) The Court had formally declared itself to be a superlegislature, as it had in rate regulation, and wise men took note of the fact. When Louis Brandeis successfully defended an Oregon statute establishing maximum hours for women,[90] he acted as if he were testifying before a legislative committee. The first "Brandeis Brief" was a compendium of fact: sociological, medical, economic, and psychological evidence of the need for special protection for women. He not only won his case; he received special mention for his efforts. The justices were clearly entranced by this approach. They wanted to be treated as legislators, and Brandeis obliged.

Liberty of contract had implications beyond maximum hour or minimum wage laws.[91] The most significant of these concerned the infamous "yellow-dog contract," wherein an employer extracts, as a condition of employment, a pledge not to join a union. Such contracts were extremely significant, not because they gave an employer a right to fire an employee for union activity; the employer already had both the power and the right to fire him for any reason whatsoever. Rather, if employers had yellow-dog provisos in their contracts, union organizers were subject to being charged with inducing workers to breach of contract, and were often enjoinable on those grounds. In fact, given the nature of the employer's freedom, one can question if yellow-dog contracts were true contracts at all: there was no "exchange of valuable considerations." The employer gives nothing, the worker is presumably paid for an acceptable performance of his tasks, but is forced to surrender his right to join a union for no considerations whatever. Regardless of this, yellow-dog contracts were held beyond the reach of congressional legislation barring them.[92] And in *Coppage* v. *Kansas*,[93] of state legislation which did the same, *Coppage* gives a fascinating glimpse into the mind of laissez faire justices. For example, Justice Pitney rejected the earlier reasoning of the Court on liberty of contract—that employer and employee stood upon an equal basis and must be free to fight out contract terms without state interference.

While Pitney observed that contractual freedom is as important to the worker as to his employer, he concludes that "there must and will be inequalities of fortune, and thus it naturally happens that parties negotiating about a contract are not equally hampered by circumstances."[94] In John Roche's words, this "amounts to the statement that a poor man's right to negotiate from weakness is as essential to him as the rich man's right to negotiate from strength ... that the winners in the battle of life had received some Divine afflatus."[95]

The entire line of liberty of contract cases stretches the meaning of the due process clause to an extraordinary limit, and they clearly represent activism of an extreme sort. This same Court could, on the other hand, ignore obvious violations of even procedural due process where they affected, for instance, the rights of criminal defendants, or the rights of minorities.[96] Due process of law means what the Supreme Court says it means, and this Court made clear where its preferences lay.

The Court and the New Deal

The New Deal period represented the last fling of economic activism by the Court, and it resulted in a direct conflict between the power of the judiciary and that of the major part of the elected officials of the nation. It did not appear as the last gasp of a fading economic and judicial philosophy; it had all the earmarks of Armageddon for the doctrine of judicial review. The legacy of the Populist and Progressive years, the idea of a positive role for the state in matters of economics, social welfare, and the like, was raised to a new standard as a response to the Great Depression. The new Administration, the new Congress, and many of the states were committed to this idea, and a vast new range of regulation was imposed upon the economy by legislation. Much of this activity was out of line with the basic principles which had guided the Court over the years. As a result, the nation was presented with the spectacle of the "nine old men" taking on all comers in a battle royal over the future course of the nation.

In the years from *Dred Scott* to 1935, the Court had struck down less than one act of Congress per year; now, in the space of seventeen months (January 1935 to May 1936) twelve congressional acts were declared unconstitutional. At least seven of these were important, and all were part of the New Deal Administrative strategy to combat the Depression. It is doubtless true that the program was not really working, but it nonetheless had the broad support of much of the country and its elected leaders. The Court's attack was, therefore, widely seen as judicial arrogance of the first water, and a direct challenge to the democratic process. Further, the tone of the Court majority, slim though it was, added to the turmoil, as the famed "Four Horsemen of the Apocalypse" (Butler, Van Devanter, McReynolds, and Sutherland) clearly considered the New Deal as heresy, not merely error. When the Court overturned Roosevelt's dismissal of a Federal Trade Commission member in *Humphrey's Executor* v. *United States*,[97] one would be led by the Court's opinion to suspect that President Roosevelt was acting on whim or caprice, indulging in the arbitrary actions of a Caligula at play. In fact, the President had acted upon a dictum produced in *Myers* v. *United States*,[98] a decision in which four of the then current members of the Court had participated, including the author of the *Humphrey's* opinion. If the Roosevelt Administration chose to paint the conflict as Court versus country, who could blame them?

The list of cases is long, but perhaps the most indicative may be found toward the end of the seventeen-month attack in *Carter* v. *Carter Coal Co.*[99] and *Morehead* v. *Tipaldo*.[100] The first dealt with a congressional statute, the second with a state act, and both were roughly treated by the Court. *Carter* involved the Bituminous Coal Act, the "little NIRA" for coal. In this area, the National Industrial Recovery Act *had* worked. Thus, after the whole of the NIRA had been declared unconstitutional in the *Schechter*[101] case, Congress had passed a specific act for the coal industry, eliminating the production code which has provided the Court's rationale for killing NIRA as a whole. The government had a strong case, perhaps the strongest of the New Deal. The company was clearly in interstate commerce, for all of its coal was being sold across state lines. The coal industry directly affected commerce in at least twenty-six states, and the labor provisions of the act were defensible because of the relationship between mining and interstate commerce. Indeed, the United Mine Workers had, just previously, been enjoined by the Court because of the effect of these labor problems on the economy of the nation.[102] Seven states had filed amicus briefs for the government, none had opposed, and the major coal companies had joined the union in supporting the legislation.

In striking down this apparently idyllic piece of legislation, Justice Sutherland fully revived the Sugar Trust doctrine of dual federalism and virtually denied the concept of national supremacy. He essentially reversed the *Shreveport*[103] doctrine which had, in theory at least, blurred the distinction between direct and indirect effects upon interstate commerce and had seemed to place most areas of commerce under the congressional aegis. Further, he attempted to prove that interstate commerce was not directly affected by strikes! The Court had denied federal control over production, as well as labor, save when the Sherman or Clayton Acts could be used to enjoin union activity.

Morehead v. *Tipaldo*[104] was perhaps the most telling of the New Deal cases. The bulk of the Court's activism had been exhausted upon the national government's regulatory legislation, and often the rationale for those decisions had been a professed solicitude for the sovereignty of the states. Timing may not be all, but it carried weight; and when a decision, following seventeen months of judicial vetoes on states' rights grounds, denied these very states the power to regulate labor relations, a bitter reaction was only to be expected.

New York had established a minimum wage for women, but it had paid careful heed to the strictures of the Court in *Adkins* v. *Children's Hospital.*[105] *Adkins* had hinged on the relationship of the fair value of the labor to the wage established. Since the statute in that case had not encompassed this relationship, it was deemed invalid. The New York statute suffered no such failing; the minimum wage set was to correspond to the fair value of the service performed. The majority, however, ignored this difference and declared the statute unconstitutional, using *Adkins* and *Lochner* as precedents. Although the *Carter* decision had just declared that labor and wages are local matters and reserved to the states, Justice Butler now went beyond *Adkins* and stated that the states have no power at all to establish minimum wages.

Morehead exposed the philosophy of the majority for what it was: a determined attempt to maintain "a twilight zone in which business management could operate free from *any* control"[106] This arbitrary application of doctrine to achieve a desired result was, of course, nothing new. We have seen the process go forward in a number of areas, from the application of antitrust law, to the use of the due process clause of the Fourteenth Amendment to aid business, while gutting it for the protection of civil rights for blacks. The difference, now, was that the Court majority faced a truly determined president and Congress, with overwhelming popular support. The ranks of the justices themselves were badly split: while Chief Justice Hughes dissented in *Morehead* because of the fair value provision, Stone, Cardozo, and Brandeis rejected the whole concept of liberty of contract. *Morehead* was the high-water mark of economic activism—a devastating ebb was on the horizon.

The Switch in Time: Recantation of the Creed

The remarkable retreat from the economic activism that had dominated the workings of the Supreme Court for most of its history was abrupt and total. Whether it resulted from the menace of Roosevelt's Court-packing plan, the overwhelming electoral victories of the New Deal in November, 1936, or some other factor, lies beyond the confines of this chapter. The fact remains, however, that within a two-week period, from March 29 to April 12, 1937, the Court reversed its pattern of economic activism, and did so without any change in membership. The whole panoply of doctrinal instruments—economic due process, liberty of contract, dual federalism, the local nature of manufacturing, direct or indirect effects on interstate commerce, all were abandoned in an orgy of reversal.

Liberty of contract was first to go, in *West Coast Hotel* v. *Parrish*[107] on March 29. *Morehead* was reversed in less than ten months, possibly a record recantation. The Court's pretense was that it had not been asked to consider the validity of the liberty of contract doctrine in that case; had it been asked, it would have reversed *Adkins* at that time. This evasion of the issue fooled no one. Indeed the New York statute was by far potentially easier to uphold than the Washington act in *West Coast Hotel*. As further evidence of the turnabout, the Court sustained, on the same day, two revised congressional measures whose principles it had earlier rejected.[108]

On April 12, the Court upheld the Wagner Act (which created a National Labor Relations Board, with power to determine collective bargaining units and fair labor practices, and to uphold the right of workers to bargain collectively), in a series of five decisions.[109] It continued to discard those doctrines which had been the heart of its capacity to impose its economic philosophy. These changes in doctrine were accompanied by a similar change in tone; deference was the keynote. In most economic matters, the Court was saying, only legislatures can decide; these were no longer appropriate subjects of judicial review.

It is difficult to call a process that rejects the precedents and philosophies of much of our judicial history as restraintist. The new concepts were surely deferential; but a total reversal of long-standing precedent and practice, in such a brief space of time, is surely activism in some sense. In fact, the dissenters from this "new" Court said as much. Justice Sutherland's dissent in *West Coast Hotel* demonstrates the difficulties of the terminology itself.

> It is urged that the question involved should now receive fresh consideration, among other reasons, because of "the economic conditions which have supervened;" but the meaning of the Constitution does not change with the ebb and flow of economic events. We frequently are told in more general words that the Constitution must be construed in the light of the present. If by that it is meant that the Constitution is made up of living words that apply to every new condition which they include, the statement is quite true. But to say, if that be intended, that the words of the Constitution mean today what they did not mean when written—that is, that they do not apply to a situation now to which they would have applied then—is to rob that instrument of the essential element which continues it in force as the people have made it until they, and not their official agents, have made it otherwise. . . .

> The judicial function is that of interpretation; it does not include the power of amendment under the guise of interpretation. To miss the point of difference between the two is to miss all that the phrase "supreme law of the land" stands for and to convert what was intended as inescapable and enduring mandates into mere moral reflections.[110]

As Sutherland draped the mantle of self-restraint about his shoulders, he was retrospectively doing so for the departed brethren who had created "liberty of contract", who had overseen the dismantling of the Fourteenth Amendment and the Sherman Act for their intended purposes; and who had recreated them in different guise (for equally different goals). If these precepts are those of restraint, where can activists be found? Of course, Sutherland is dealing from a different position; his opponents also claim to be practitioners of the fine art of judicial self-restraint. What is clear is that "activist" is a term of opprobrium, to be eschewed by all. As economic activism is discarded, new battle lines are drawn, as presaged by Sutherland; the conservative attack on the "liberal" Court was to be an attack couched in the same phrases as had been used by the liberals.

Conclusion

This history of economic activism serves to point out that the more things change, the more they remain the same. Current critiques of judicial activism parrot those of earlier Courts. The Warren Court was attacked for its tendency to ignore such things as the legislative mandate and "the will of the people." It was accused of "acting like a legislature" and basing its judgments on its own vision of what was "right" or "good" legislation. Assuming these charges to be true, the Warren Court did little more than follow precedent. It acted as its predecessors had done over the long history of the Supreme Court. What had changed was merely the subjects for which activism was invoked; the process remained unchanging.

Following "the switch in time that saved nine," the Court, with a changed membership, proceeded to remove itself from the business of business regulation. It accepted a restraintist role on economic issues and adopted the "liberal" position. This rejection of the "Basic Doctrine of American Constitutional Law," so beloved of political and economic conservatives, was accompanied by a new stance in other areas. The Court filled the vacuum by taking an interventionist, activist position in civil liberties and civil rights. This is, of course, another liberal position, and was anathema, in the circumstances, to the conservatives. Justice Frankfurter stands out as a true restraintist, and his position remained consistent—"let the legislatures alone"—on both economic and civil liberties questions. Most justices in history have been one-winged restraintists, in the sense that many politicians are one-winged doves or hawks.

The historical evidence, however, leads us to the firm conclusion that most of the Supreme Court membership has always been activist. In the economic realm, whatever standard of activism is applied, there can be little doubt of the outcome of the analysis. Even the Waite Court, which had been economically deferential for a time, was activist on civil rights in the same period—that is, it overturned or eviscerated the Civil Rights Acts and rendered the Fourteenth Amendment useless for the protection of the freed slaves of the South.

Judicial self-restraint tends to be present only when it suits the policy preferences of the justices or when they are trying to avoid a conflict with a determined president, Congress or an aroused public. Courts are called activist when they fail to take into account such factors, at which point activism is a term of opprobrium. That is to say—"whose ox is gored" remains the basic rule of constitutional interpretation and of critics of the Court. The basic restraint on the Court is the existence of opposing centers of political power—the same restraint which exists for every other political branch of government. The legalistic needlepoint often necessary to "explain" judicial inconsistencies in doctrine and application is most often a feeble substitute for the far simpler explanations that result from placing such decisions in historical, political, economic, or social context.

It should be made clear that this position does not require or even suggest that the Supreme Court sees itself as a superlegislature, removed from considerations of law. The mythology of the law is far too pervasive for that. It simply posits the idea that whatever rationales the justices use in their own minds, the evidence indicates that their actions consistently fit the role defined as activist.

From this perspective, however, the activist–restraintist debate seems to become an empty exercise. If, as contended, activism is a given for the Court, why discuss it at all? As a pure exercise in intellectual agility, it pales beside the doctrinal hairsplitting so beloved of legal academics. Of course, one could simply maintain that the Court has been acting improperly since its creation, and demand a reversal of these practices.[111] This would doubtless restore the validity of the debate, but seems both politically immature and impractical.

These difficulties are removed, however, if it is possible to distinguish economic activism from its libertarian counterpart. This is perhaps not the proper place for a full explication of such a process, and, doubtless, other contributors to this volume will undertake the task. It does seem appropriate, however, to define briefly the limits of such an argument. Essentially, the Court, when activist in civil liberties, is merely serving the only valid function of a nondemocratic institution in a democratic political system—the protection of minority rights against majority will (when the rights involved are essential to the democratic process). Civil liberties, broadly construed, constitute the fundamental rights necessary for the continued existence of democracy and cannot be left to the vagaries of majoritarianism. In general, economic issues, important as they may be, are not truly proper subjects for judicial review. If this is so, and the theory of constitutional democracy, if not that of free enterprise, seems to demand the distinction, the Supreme Court has what amounts to a mandate for libertarian activism and economic restraint. In Ronald Dworkin's words, "Constitutionalism—the theory that the majority must be restrained to protect individual rights—may be good or bad political theory, but the United States has adopted that theory, and to make the majority judge in its own cause seems inconsistent and unjust."[112]

Notes

1. See, for example, *Vanhorne's Lessee v. Dorrance,* 2 Dallas 304 (1795); *Ware v. Hylton,* 3 Dallas 199 (1796); *Chisholm v. Georgia,* 2 Dallas 419 (1793).

2. 6 Cranch 87 (1810).

3. The innocence of the party is in question, as it appears that the sale was made in order to establish the Court's jurisdiction under the diversity-of-citizenship aegis.

4. 3 Dallas 386 (1798). The Court held that the ex post facto clause applied only in criminal cases.

5. *Fletcher v. Peck,* 6 Cranch 87 (1810).

6. Ibid.

7. Arthur S. Miller, *The Supreme Court and American Capitalism* (New York: Free Press, 1968), p. 37.

8. When an executory contract has been executed, it is no longer a contract.

9. John P. Roche, *John Marshall: Major Opinions and Other Writings* (Indianapolis: Bobbs-Merrill, 1967), p. 83.

10. 7 Cranch 164 (1812).

11. 9 Cranch 43 (1815).

12. Some twenty-five state statutes were overturned on the basis of *New Jersey v. Wilson* alone. See Alfred H. Kelly and Winfred A. Harbison, *The American Constitution: Its Origins and Development,* 5th ed. (New York: Norton, 1976), p. 262.

13. *Dartmouth College v. Woodward,* 4 Wheaton 518 (1819). See, for example, Wallace Mendelson, *Capitalism, Democracy, and the Supreme Court* (New York: Appleton-Century-Crofts, 1960), p. 24.

14. *Dartmouth College v. Woodward,* 4 Wheaton 523.

15. 9 Wheaton 1 (1824).

16. 12 Wheaton 419 (1827).

17. Mendelson, *Capitalism, Democracy, and the Supreme Court,* p. 26.

18. *McCulloch v. Maryland,* 4 Wheaton 316 (1819).

19. Charles A. Beard and Mary R. Beard, *The Rise of American Civilization* (New York: Macmillan, 1940), p. 689.

20. *Proprietors of the Charles River Bridge v. Proprietors of the Warren Bridge,* 11 Peters 420 (1837).

21. See Story's dissent in *New York v. Miln,* 11 Peters 102 (1837) and in *Briscoe v. Bank of Kentucky,* 11 Peters 257 (1837).

22. Daniel Webster wrote, "Judge Story . . . thinks the Supreme Court is *gone* and I think so too . . ." and that "The decision of the Court will have completely overturned, in my opinion, a great provision of the Constitution [the

contract clause]." A Boston newspaper noted, "The vested rights class cry out bloody murder . . . [they] are maintaining radical and revolutionary doctrines." Quoted in Charles Warren, *The Supreme Court in United States History* (Boston: Little, Brown, 1926), 2: 10, nn. 25, 26.

23. *Proprietors of the Charles River Bridge v. Proprietors of the Warren Bridge,* 11 Peters 420 (1837).

24. *Dodge v. Woolsey,* 18 Howard 331 (1856).

25. 16 Howard 369 (1853).

26. *Dodge v. Woolsey,* 18 Howard 331 (1856).

27. 68 U.S. 220 (1864). This case also seems irreconcilable with Section 34 of the Judiciary Act. See Warren, *The Supreme Court in United States History,* p. 530.

28. 13 Peters 519 (1839).

29. 2 Howard 497 (1844).

30. 5 Cranch 61 (1809).

31. 16 Peters 1 (1842).

32. 11 Peters 102 (1837).

33. 7 Howard 283 (1849).

34. 5 Howard 504 (1847).

35. See, for example, Warren, *The Supreme Court in United States History,* 2:168-184.

36. 12 Howard 299 (1851).

37. Miller, *Supreme Court and American Capitalism,* pp. 47-48. (Emphasis added.)

38. *Genesee Chief v. Fitzhugh,* 12 Howard 443 (1851).

39. *In re Debs,* 158 U.S. 564 (1895).

40. The phrase in from Mendelson, *Capitalism, Democracy, and The Supreme Court,* p. 63.

41. 97 U.S. 25 (1878).

42. 97 U.S. 659 (1878). See also *Boyd v. Alabama,* 94 U.S. 645 (1877).

43. 108 U.S. 526 (1883).

44. 110 U.S. 347 (1884).

45. 101 U.S. 814 (1880).

46. 94 U.S. 113 (1877).

47. Ibid.

48. Ibid.

49. Ibid. Indeed, Professor Roche argues that the *Granger Cases* taken *en masse* undercut virtually any constitutional attack the corporations could raise against the state's police power. John P. Roche, "Entrepreneurial Liberty and the Fourteenth Amendment," *Labor History* 4 (Winter 1963):16.

50. A caveat is in order here; this is true only with regard to corporate power. The Waite Court was simultaneously highly activist in civil rights matters.

51. 13 N.Y. 378 (1856).

52. *Dred Scott v. Sandford,* 19 Howard 393 (1857).

53. 16 Wallace 36 (1873).

54. 96 U.S. 97 (1878).

55. 116 U.S. 307 (1886).

56. 123 U.S. 123 (1887).

57. 127 U.S. 678 (1888).

58. *Chicago, Milwaukee and St. Paul Railway Company v. Minnesota,* 134 U.S. 418 (1890).

59. 169 U.S. 466 (1898).

60. Ibid.

61. Frank R. Strong, "The Economic Philosophy of Lochner: Emergence, Embrasure and Emasculation," *Arizona Law Review* 15, no. 2 (1973):419.

62. Mary Cornelia Porter, "That Commerce Shall Be Free: A New Look at the Old Laissez-Faire Court," in *The Supreme Court Review* ed. Philip B. Kurland (Chicago: University of Chicago Press, 1976), p. 135.

63. 158 U.S. 564 (1895).

64. 156 U.S. 1 (1895).

65. 158 U.S. 601 (1895).

66. *Debs* did reverse, however, the doctrine established in *United States v. Hudson and Goodwin,* 7 Cranch 32 (1812), that the federal government had no power to impose punitive sanctions without statutory authority. See Roche, "Entrepreneurial Liberty and the Fourteenth Amendment."

67. 3 Dallas 171 (1796).

68. 102 U.S. 586 (1881).

69. Quoted in Arnold Paul, *The Conservative Crisis and the Rule of Law* (Ithaca: Cornell University Press, 1960), pp. 192-193.

70. 156 U.S. 1 (1895).

71. Edward S. Corwin, "Congress's Power to Prohibit Commerce," *Cornell Law Quarterly* 18 (July 1933):498. See also Robert H. Jackson, *The Struggle for Judicial Supremacy: A Study of a Crisis in American Power Politics* (New York: Vintage, 1941), chap. 2, *passim.*

72. *United States v. American Tobacco Co.,* 221 U.S. 106 (1911).

73. *Standard Oil Co. v. United States,* 221 U.S. 1 (1911).

74. *United States v. Winslow,* 227 U.S. 202 (1913).

75. *United States v. United States Steel Corp.,* 251 U.S. 417 (1920).

76. *International Harvester of New Jersey v. United States,* 214 F.2d 987 (1914), cert. denied, 248 U.S. 587 (1917).

77. 208 U.S. 274 (1908).

78. See, for example, Charles O. Gregory, *Labor and the Law* (New Yrok: Norton, 1946), pp. 205-217.

79. The case was sent to trial on the merits, and the union was fined a quarter of a million dollars. *Lawlor v. Loewe,* 235 U.S. 522 (1915).

80. 208 U.S. 161 (1908).

81. 221 U.S. 418 (1911).

82. 245 U.S. 229 (1917).

83. *Duplex Printing Press Co. v. Deering*, 254 U.S. 443 (1921). The Clayton Act had, in Section 6, declared that the antitrust laws were not to be construed to forbid labor unions the lawful pursuit of their legitimate objectives. Section 20 of the same Act forbade the issuance of injunctions by U.S. courts in labor cases involving peaceful persuasion of others to strike or against primary boycotts. The definitions of the terms "legitimate," "lawful," and "peaceful" gave the Court the opening it needed.

84. *Bedford Cut Stone Company v. Bedford Journeyman's Stone Cutters' Association*, 274 U.S. 37 (1927).

85. *Hall v. DeCuir*, 95 U.S. (1877); *Chiles v. C. and O. Railway*, 218 U.S. 71 (1910).

86. 169 U.S. 366 (1898).

87. 198 U.S. 45 (1905).

88. Ibid., p. 58.

89. *United States v. Carolene Products Company*, 304 U.S. 144, 152–153, n. 4 (1938). This was a doctrine to the effect that any law restricting the democratic process is essentially subject to a reversal of the usual presumption of constitutionality. The burden is on the state to prove its reasonableness.

90. *Muller v. Oregon*, 208 U.S. 412 (1908).

91. In *Adkins v. Children's Hospital*, 216 U.S. 525 (1923), the Court declared that minimum wage laws were unconstitutional because they did not relate the value of labor to the minimum wage, as well as the standard liberty-of-contract reasoning. Justice Sutherland's opinion goes on to describe labor as a commodity to be bought and sold like any other, despite the Clayton Act's absolute prohibition of this idea, as well as previous decisions to this effect.

92. *Adair v. United States*, 208 U.S. 161 (1908), using the due process clause of the Fifth Amendment.

93. 236 U.S. 1 (1915).

94. Ibid., p. 17.

95. Roche, "Entrepreneurial Liberty and the Fourteenth Amendment," p. 86.

96. See, for example, *Frank v. Mangum*, 237 U.S. 309 (1915) and *Hodges v. United States*, 203 U.S. 1 (1906).

97. 295 U.S. 602 (1935).

98. 272 U.S. 52 (1926).

99. 298 U.S. 238 (1936).

100. 298 U.S. 587 (1936).

101. *Schechter v. United States*, 295 U.S. 495 (1935).

102. *Appalachian Coal Co. v. United States*, 288 U.S. 344 (1933).

103. *Shreveport Rate Cases*, 234 U.S. 342 (1914).

104. 298 U.S. 587 (1936).

105. 216 U.S. 525 (1923).

106. Benjamin F. Wright, *The Growth of American Constitutional Law* (Boston: Houghton Mifflin, 1942), p. 179. (Emphasis added.)

107. 300 U.S. 379 (1937).

108. *Wright v. Vinton Branch Bank,* 300 U.S. 440 (1937); *Virginia Railway Company v. System Federation No. 40,* 300 U.S. 515 (1937). These were cases dealing with the revised Farm Mortgage Act of 1935 and the Railway Labor Act as amended in 1934.

109. *National Labor Relations Board v. Jones and Laughlin Steel Corporation,* 301 U.S. 1 (1937); *N.L.R.B. v. Freuhauf Trailer Company,* 301 U.S. 49 (1937); *N.L.R.B. v. Freedman-Harry Marks Clothing Co.,* 301 U.S. 58 (1937); *Associated Press v. N.L.R.B.,* 301 U.S. 103 (1937); *Washington V. and M. Coach Company v. N.L.R.B.,* 301 U.S. 142 (1937).

110. *West Coast Hotel Company v. Parrish,* 300 U.S. 379, 402–404 (1937).

111. Raoul Berger, *Government by Judiciary: The Transformation of the Fourteenth Amendment* (Cambridge: Harvard University Press, 1977) comes close to such a position.

112. Ronald Dworkin, *Taking Rights Seriously* (Cambridge: Harvard University Press, 1977), p. 273.

5

Of Time and Judicial Activism: A Study of the U.S. Supreme Court, 1800-1973

Gregory A. Caldeira and
Donald J. McCrone

Introduction

Each generation the Supreme Court comes under fire from certain sectors of the polity—for actions it has taken, for moves it has not made; and sometimes critics lambaste the Court for doing too much.[1] For the last twenty years or so, commentator after commentator—from journalism, politics, law, and academia—has criticized the Supreme Court for immersing itself too deeply in the fabric of American politics and society—for practicing the art of judicial activism.[2] This criticism, once the province of right-wingers and segregationists, now flows from the pens of quite respectable authorities—indeed, from members of the establishment. The Court, Nathan Glazer charges, is more powerful and authoritarian than ever in our history.[3] Even so loyal and aggressive a sponsor as Arthur Miller quite candidly states that "the Justices of the Supreme Court of the United States . . . have become deeply immersed in the travail of society; they are 'activist' as never before in American history."[4]

Thus, most commentators—regardless of ideological persuasion—seem to agree that the modern Supreme Court is, in some fashion or other, practicing judicial activism, however defined, more than it has before. But, for all of the books and articles this debate has generated, few scholars have bothered to do much in the way of systematic empirical inquiry into the issues raised. From historians, political scientists, and lawyers, we have countless works that discuss, in literary fashion, the development of the Supreme Court as it has participated in the struggle for power and policy in the arenas of American politics and society during the first two centuries of the Republic.[5] For instance, Robert McCloskey's elegant *The American Supreme Court*[6] presents a division of judicial history into three critical periods of development; and, of course, scholars of constitutional politics have always used the tenures of chief justices

We appreciate the help of the Department of Political Science and of the Laboratory for Political Research, both of the University of Iowa, in the preparation of this manuscript. Discussions with Andrew T. Cowart, G.R. Boynton and John Alford proved very helpful at certain stages. Thomas Yantek, now of the State University of New York at Stony Brook, performed some of the statistical analyses. We have used the Econometric Software Package at the University of Iowa in carrying out our analyses.

as means of demarcating eras of activity on the Court. Robert Dahl, speaking of the Court's role as a national policymaker and its connections with other governmental institutions, has argued that the Court is never very far out of line with the policy preferences that dominate in the congressional process. He concludes that the Court could not oppose for too long "major alternatives sought by the lawmaking majority."[7] Dahl's investigation differed from earlier ones—aside from its subtle argument—in the sense that it relied upon quantitative analysis. Some years later Jonathan Casper contended that Dahl's conclusion had several difficulties—first, it ignored statutory interpretation and the nullification of state statutes, "a good deal of what the Court in fact contributes to national policymaking;" second, "it did not place enough emphasis on those cases in which the Court succeeded in delaying policies for periods of up to 25 years;" and, third, its conception of influence as a zero-sum proposition misleads one about the actual impact of the Supreme Court.[8] Yet other scholars, also using data on the Court's declarations of federal statutes as unconstitutional over time, have argued about whether periods of partisan realignment coincide with or precipitate periods of intense judicial activism on the Supreme Court.[9] Our purpose here is to examine patterns, discontinuities, trends, and cycles in the incidence of the Supreme Court's activism toward the federal and state legislatures—as measured by the number of cases in a particular year in which the justices invalidated an enactment—over the period 1800 through 1973.

The works we have discussed raise, but do not go very far toward answering, a number of fundamental questions about the Supreme Court and judicial activism. First and most important, has the Supreme Court's activism manifested patterns, that is, has it been a nonrandom occurrence? Second, has the activism of the Court, over time, increased in a linear fashion, that is, is there a trend toward greater judicial activism? Third, has the Court's activism, as certain scholars suggest,[10] exhibited discontinuities, periods of marked increase or decrease, in response to cataclysmic events, such as wars, or more normal shocks, such as congressional actions? Fourth, does the Court's activism demonstrate periodicity—are there distinctive cycles in which the Court alternates periods of activism and acquiescence—quite apart from long-term growth? Fifth, if activism on the Court does occur in cyclical patterns, does this periodicity appear to be deterministic or nondeterministic—are these cycles regular? Sixth, does the amplitude, the sharpness of the swing from activism to acquiescence and back again, of cycles of judicial activism grow over time?

We have so far delayed tackling an important issue in the study of judicial activism. Scholars, in discussing judicial activism, have not often made clear the object of the Court's actions.[11] Quite clearly, we think, the Supreme Court can attempt to influence or alter the behavior of several sets of actors—federal, state, and local governments—through declaring their enactments contrary to the Constitution of the United States. One can well imagine that the Court might be considerably more deferential toward the enactments of Congress than it is toward those of state legislatures. For, after all, the Constitution—although vague on the issue of judicial review of federal laws—contains a rather unambiguous statement of the supremacy of the federal Constitution, laws, and treaties—all of which clearly indicates the subordination of the states. Thus, keeping this important institutional distinction in mind, we pose a seventh interrogatory: has the pattern of the Supreme Court's activism toward the states differed from that toward Congress? Put more simply, does judicial activism toward the state and federal legislatures seem to coincide? Is judicial activism a generalized phenomenon or one directed at particular targets at particular times?

These, then, are among the most important queries we shall address here. We shall also take the liberty of engaging in some educated speculations about the relationships between the trends, cycles, and discontinuities in judicial activism and the matrix of political, social, and economic forces within which the Supreme Court must operate.

The next section sets out four models of the process of change in the level of judicial activism toward the state and federal legislatures over the first two centuries of United States history. Later we shall explore a number of problems of conceptualization, estimation, and measurement error in the study of judicial activism.

Four Models of Political Change

The Supreme Court, as the American Republic got under way, did not show much promise of being the institution it is now—one that exercises considerable political power, or, in John Marshall's words, "comes home in its effects to every man's fireside . . . passes on his property, his reputation, his life, his all."[12] For one thing, most of the framers had underestimated its importance—as Hamilton said, it is "the least dangerous branch" of government.[13] And, of course, it is a commonplace that the failure of the framers of the Constitution to make a clear grant of judicial review to the Court placed it under severe constraints from the beginning. Until the era of the great Chief Justice John Marshall, a seat on the Supreme Court was hardly the sort of place a man of action or abilities would seek. The Court heard few cases, and those were for the most part trivial. Each justice was required, in fulfillment of his duties, to "ride circuit"—a task that was always grueling and that could, at times, be fatal. Refusing nomination to the Court as chief justice in December 1800, former Chief Justice John Jay wrote President Adams: "I left the bench perfectly convinced that under a system so defective it [the Court] would not obtain the energy, weight, and dignity which was essential to its affording due support to the national government; nor acquire the public confidence and respect which, as the last resort of justice in the nation, it should possess."[14]

Thus for many years the Supreme Court remained a political eunuch. Under the aegises of Chief Justices Marshall and Taney, however, the Court began to build up, in gradual fashion, power and prestige; soon it became a political force with which to contend. But one must recall that, so far as the use of its power to declare statutes invalid, the Court was quite dormant before the Civil War. For instance, the Court during this period declared only two federal statutes unconstitutional—in *Marbury* v. *Madison* and *Dred Scott* v. *Sandford.* The Court was, without doubt, reticent toward the state legislatures for a number of reasons, but surely the delicacy of the balance between nation and state must have given it considerable pause. After the Civil War, however, the Supreme Court faced a situation much more hospitable to the active use of judicial power. "For one thing," McCloskey says, "the nation-state problem had changed its nature drastically."[15] Justices no longer feared "that centrifugal forces would tear the nation apart. . . ."[16] The end of the Civil War signaled the existence of, in Chief Justice Chase's phrase, "an indestructible Union, composed of indestructible states. . . ."[17] Emboldened by a successful conclusion to the war, the members of the Court could evaluate a state law with the confidence that invalidating it would not have destabilizing effects on the polity. Second, the end of the Civil War unleashed capitalism and industrialization—forces that raised bundles of new legal questions, which of course permitted substantial room for judicial activism. Third, the increasing "nationalization" of political, economic, and social forces necessitated a similar uniformity in the structure of the legal order—a situation that behooved the Court to bring the states into line.[18] Fourth, the national government began to expand the scope of its activities, and it was natural that critics should call into question the constitutionality of some of these actions. Those challenges permitted the Supreme Court to exercise its naysaying power over Congress. Fifth, the new amendments to the Constitution provided opportunities for the justices to interpret new and wonderfully vague clauses, in the face of new circumstances, in ways that might assert the Court's power over the enactments of state legislatures.

Thus, we argue, the Supreme Court's activism began after the Civil War. This statement implies that, before the Civil War, the Court's forays into the realms of judicial activism were, in essence, random fluctuations. For us, the Civil War is the watershed in the development of the Court's use of judicial review to declare state and federal enactments invalid.[19] It marks the solidification, or, in Nelson Polsby's sense of the word, "institutionalization," of the Court's power to negate actions of the legislative departments.[20] We conceptualize the Civil War, then, as a discrete, or very near-discrete, historical event or shock to the constitutional order that might well have or not have changed the level of the Court's activism in certain fundamental modes. The empirical question, then, is: what are the actual effects of an historical shock such as the Civil War on the activism of the Supreme Court toward the state and federal legislatures? The political outcome of such a cataclysm is not, in our view, at all unambiguous; for one can conceive of a number of different results, each of them representing very subtle variations in the effects of the war. Numerous outcomes spring to mind, but here we formulate four of the most important and probable alternative models of the Civil War's effects on judicial activism.

Now it is entirely possible that the Civil War did not induce any increase or decrease in the amount of activism on the Supreme Court, as figure 5-1a shows. There the x-axis represents time (T); the y-axis, the number of cases in which the Court has declared a statute unconstitutional in a particular year; and W, the Civil War. In that figure, we operate on the assumption that judicial activism was growing in a more or less linear fashion—quite apart from any inpetus the Civil

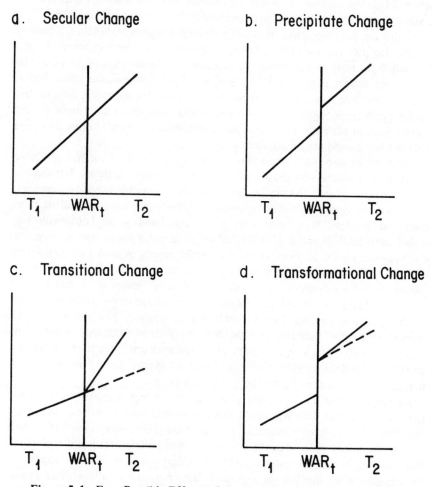

a. Secular Change

b. Precipitate Change

c. Transitional Change

d. Transformational Change

T_1 WAR$_t$ T_2

Figure 5-1. Four Possible Effects of the Civil War on Judicial Activism

War might have provided. To argue, then, that the Civil War caused or facilitated an increase of the Court's journeys into the realms of judicial activism would be fallacious. That pattern instead represents long-term, persistent change, and no abrupt change as the result of the war. The Court's activism could well have been a function of such forces as industrialization, capitalism, and so on—if one assumes that these forces were not themselves accelerated by the war. This first model, then, we call a *secular change* in judicial activism. The equation for this model is as follows:

$$JA_t = b_0 + b_1 T_1 + b_2 T_2 + b_3 \, WAR_t + e_t \qquad (5.1)$$

where JA_t is the number of cases in a particular year in which the Court declares a statute unconstitutional; T_1 is a counter for the time trend before 1865; T_2 is a counter for the time trend from 1865 through the present; WAR_t is a dummy variable for pre- and post-1865; and e_t is an error term. The coefficients b_0, b_1, b_2, and b_3 consist of parameters to be estimated. Under conditions of secular change, we expect that $b_1 > 0$, $b_2 > 0$, and $b_3 \leqslant 0$—significant trends before and after the war, but no effect from the war itself. Furthermore, because this model predicts no significant alteration in the continuous movement toward greater judicial activism, $b_1 \simeq b_2$—the coefficients for trends before and after the Civil War should not be different.

One might also, with equal plausibility, argue that the Civil War produced a very abrupt increase in the overall level of the Court's activism, but did not permanently accelerate the rate of that phenomenon—and figure 5-1b represents this situation. Social, political, economic, military controversies—all of them results of the Civil War—might have gotten translated, as de Tocqueville suggested, into legal disputes. That limited set of disputes might find its way into the Supreme Court, an eventuality that could permit or lead to a temporary burst of judicial activism. It would not, however, alter the basic pace of the growth of the incidence of the Court's asserting its power to declare statutes unconstitutional. The Court, after a momentary change of tempo, would return to the groove it had occupied before the conflagration. This second model—*precipitate change*—indicates that $b_1 > 0$, $b_2 > 0$, $b_3 > 0$—that trends exist prior to and after the war, and, perhaps more important, that the Civil War has an effect on judicial activism. But, in addition, we expect that b_1 is equal to b_2—that the trends before and after the war do not differ.

Change in the level of judicial activism need not materialize overnight. Events such as the Civil War could produce greater judicial activism but might take hold at a much more measured pace than the second model implies. In such a case, one would observe few if any instances of judicial activism that the Civil War spawned in a direct fashion; rather, the Court would increase, or accelerate, its activities after the war in a gradual fashion as the result of more fundamental changes in structure wrought by the conflict—and, among these, are the

Thirteenth, Fourteenth, and Fifteenth Amendments. Figure 5-1c shows such a pattern—no short-term change but a new degree of movement toward greater activism—*transitional change*. Thus, from the third model we draw the predictions that $b_1 > 0$, $b_2 > 0$, and $b_3 \leqslant 0$—that trends exist before and after the Civil War and that the war has no linear effect on judicial activism—so far, the predictions garnered from the first model, *secular change*. Here, however, we expect that $b_1 \leqslant b_2$—that the slope of the trend after the war will be larger than that before the conflict.

And, of course, the Civil War could have yielded both short-term and long-run increases in the level of judicial activism. Thus, as in the second model, disputes from the war might have generated a short-run increase in the Court's activism; but, in addition, as in the third model, here fundamental changes in social, political, or economic conditions the war has caused or coincided with result in long-term increases in the level of judicial activism. There is, then, an increase in the pace or rate as well as in the level of judicial activism, shown in figure 5-1d. From this model of *transformational change*, we deduce that $b_1 > 0$, $b_2 > 0$, and $b_3 > 0$—that trends exist before and after the war, and that the Civil War does indeed increase the incidence of judicial activism. Further, we see from this fourth model that $b_1 < b_2$—that the rate of judicial activism increases after the Civil War.

Having set out these four models of political change in some detail, we now turn to a discussion of a number of conceptual and methodological problems.

Problems of Conceptualization, Estimation, and Measurement Error

To operationalize the concept of "judicial activism," we have used a pair of very straightforward indicators—the numbers of cases in which the Supreme Court has invalidated a state or federal legislative enactment in a particular year from 1800 through 1973. Scholars do not always agree on these matters—that is, whether the Court has struck down a statute—but we have relied upon the numbers provided in a source generally considered quite accurate, The Library of Congress's *The Constitution of the United States: Analysis and Interpretation*,[21] compiled originally under the editorship of Edward S. Corwin and brought up to date in 1974.

Quite clearly, we think, "judicial activism," or for that matter governmental activism, is a concept on whose meaning few scholars, commentators, lawyers, or politicians would agree. Does one define activism as the sheer amount of actions —opinions, orders, cases filed and decided—that the Supreme Court generates? Should one monitor qualitative changes in the nature of judicial activism—for, as Donald Horowitz argues, "it is no longer approximately accurate to say that the courts exercise only a veto. What is asked and what is awarded is often the doing of something, not just the stopping of something"?[22] Should one map out changes in the range or scope of policymaking activities that the Supreme Court pursues now than it did not earlier?[23] To evaluate the Court as more or less active, must one determine the length of periods of activism—that is, must judicial action occur consistently over a sustained length of time for the Supreme Court to fall under the rubric of judicial activism? Must the Supreme Court, for one to consider it activist in asserting its power, dominate other political institutions? The contention of some critics is that the Court has not only become more activist than it once was but also more active than competing centers of power in American politics.[24]

To begin with, we concede the subtleties of the concept of judicial activism. Judicial activism, because so many commentators have discussed it without precision, has taken on considerable undesirable intellectual baggage. But quite apart from abuse of the term, judicial activism, in the real world, manifests itself in a multitude of forms, some of which we have mentioned here. In an ideal world we would create indicators of judicial activism that reflect all of the facets of this complex phenomenon. But here we have chosen a very simple quantitative indicator—the number of assertions of the Court's power to declare laws invalid. That indicator commends itself to us because, first, it certainly represents one of the more extreme forms of judicial activism and so one of the most interesting; second, it is a statistic around which a considerable consensus regarding its accuracy has formed—although, as we have stated, some disagree about details; and third, it is quite readily available over a long period of time. This statistic, then, measures judicial activism in the sense of the incidence of judicial negations of the will of legislative majorities. We make no claim that it does any more than that. Queries about the increasing scope of judicial policymaking, qualitative change from negative to affirmative judicial activism, and the relative activism of the Supreme Court and coordinate private and public institutions—all of these remain fascinating issues, but are far beyond the scope of this particular study.

Two more details need mentioning. First, we have used as our unit of analysis the case rather than the statute for reasons of convenience; but our analyses indicate that, regardless of the unit, the results are the same. Second, we have chosen to focus on state and federal statutes and exclude municipal ordinances. That strategy is, we think, a wise one because inclusion of ordinances complicates—needlessly, in our view—analysis and exposition. And, of course, as a matter of law, municipalities are creatures of the state government.

To answer the interrogatories posed earlier, we have relied upon three sets of statistical tools. First of all, to estimate the effects of the Civil War on the phenomenon of judicial activism, we have used an interrupted time-series (ITS) design.[25] That design conceptualizes the Civil War as a "treatment" in a quasi experiment that nature has very kindly provided. To estimate the models, then, one uses ordinary least-squares regression. Now, of course, in a time series of the sort under examination here considerable autocorrelation is present. We have adjusted the estimated coefficients based upon the magnitude of *rho*, an estimate of the degree of serial correlation obtained with the Hildreth-Lu procedure.[26] Second, we have used spectral analysis as a means of discovering whether cycles of judicial activism occur in a deterministic fashion.[27] Third, following standard operating procedures of economists, we have used moving averages as a way of smoothing our data.[28] And we have used standard tests of statistical significance, at the .05 level, as a convenient way of evaluating the regression coefficients.

Having discussed some of the more problematic methodological and conceptual issues this research raises, we proceed to our estimations of the effects of the Civil War on judicial activism on the Court—first, toward Congress; and second, toward the state legislatures.

Findings

Congress, Judicial Activism, and the Civil War

Figure 5-2 presents the number of cases in which the Supreme Court has declared federal statutes unconstitutional from 1800 through 1973. It takes but a glance at this graph—or prior knowledge that only two federal statutes fell before the Court's judgment prior to the Civil War—to suggest that the Supreme Court engaged in no systematic patterns of activism before 1865. Estimating the effects through ordinary least-squares, we have:

$$\text{FED}_t = .0430 - .0004\, T_1 + .0104\, T_2 + .3690\, \text{WAR}_t$$
$$\quad\ \ (.17)\quad (-.05)\quad (3.41)\quad\ \ (1.17)$$
$$R^2 = .22 \quad D.W. = 1.29$$
$$F = 15.5 \quad N = 174 \tag{5.2}$$

where FED_t is the number of cases in which the Court struck down federal statutes in a particular year; the t-ratios are inside the parentheses below the relevant coefficient; R^2 is the coefficient of multiple determination; $D.W.$ is the Durbin-Watson statistic; F is the overall F-ratio for the equation; and N is the number of observations. Quite clearly, then, the Court's activism toward the American Congress before the Civil War occurred on an episodic, nonsystematic basis, for no trend emerges. Furthermore, the end of the Civil War does not have the effect of inducing a significant short-run increase in the incidence of judicial activism toward Congress. But we do observe a significant increase in the trend toward greater activism after the war. Thus, as we expected, the Civil War is indeed the watershed in the growth of judicial activism, at least toward Congress. After Appomattox, the Court, at least in its behavior toward Congress, arrived as an institution—exercising its ultimate power on a regular basis. That

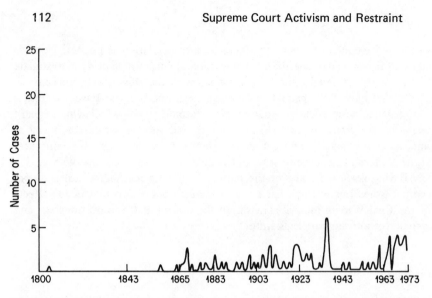

Figure 5-2. Federal Statutes: The Number of Judicial Decisions Declaring a Law
        Unconstitutional

much said, we must caution that the acceleration of the growth of judicial
activism in postbellum America was hardly what one could call rapid; the
Supreme Court has, over the last century, increased the number of cases in
which it has invalidated federal statutes only .0104 cases each term, a figure that
yields an increase of one more case each ninety-six years. This is certainly
eloquent testimony to the glacial pace that often characterizes American law and
politics.

Congress and Cycles of Judicial Activism?

Quite apart from trends, does judicial activism toward the American Congress
occur in cycles—that is, is there periodicity in these data? If cycles do occur, do
these phenomena happen in a deterministic or nondeterministic pattern? Figure
5-3 displays a seven-year moving average of the detrended series of the incidence
of judicial activism toward Congress. Simple visual inspection of these data
indicates that the Supreme Court's periods of aggressiveness toward Congress
have not occurred on a very regular basis. To test the notion that cycles of
judicial activism occur in a deterministic fashion, we have fitted a sine curve to
these data, and the results confirm what the figure very strongly suggests—little
regularity. That much said, it does appear that there are peaks and valleys in
cycles of judicial activism toward Congress. Quite as clearly, with each succeeding cycle, oscillations have grown more extreme, swings from aggressiveness to

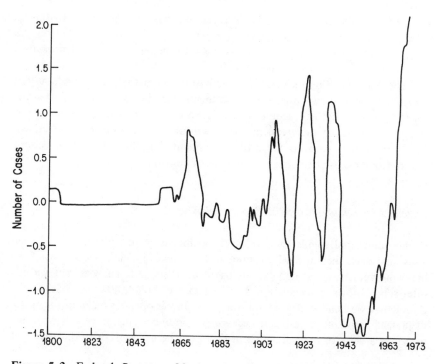

Figure 5-3. Federal Statutes: Moving Average of Residuals from Detrended Time Series

acquiescence and back again have become sharper and sharper. These data show five distinct periods of judicial activism toward Congress—during the late 1860s; during the administration of Theodore Roosevelt; after World War I; during the 1920s and 1930s; and during the 1960s, a cycle that has not yet begun its decline. During each of these periods, of course, the Supreme Court attacked very different kinds of federal legislative action. Under Chief Justice Chase, the Court found wanting Congress's enactments on legal tender; under White, on labor relations; under White, Taft, and Hughes, economic regulation; and under Warren, political expression and the rights of the accused.

It appears as if cycles of judicial activism have become more and more extreme; but we also know that during this time a more general pattern or trend toward growth has occurred. Thus we need to know whether peaks and valleys have become more extreme, quite apart from overall growth. There is, in nature and certainly in social, political, and economic activities, a tendency for most phenomena to increase in incidence over time. That each successive cycle of judicial activism toward the American Congress should be more extreme could well convince commentators on the Court that it is "getting out of hand", and this pattern could explain much of the recent worries about judicial activism. To correct, then, for the natural growth, we have relativized the residuals from the detrended series of the Court's actions toward Congress. Figure 5-4 presents a seven-year moving average of these numbers.

The Supreme Court's periods of activism toward Congress, after one has relativized them, show rather clearly no increase in the swing or oscillation between aggressiveness and acquiescence. These cycles of judicial activism are in fact proportional to the trend in the growth of that activism. We have no evidence, then, that supports the critics' argument that the Court, in its actions toward Congress, is increasingly getting out of control.

Judicial Activism and Congress: Some Explanations

Having uncovered trends and cycles in the incidence of activism toward Congress, one must then ask: what causes such bursts of judicial aggressiveness? We have not yet arrived at conclusions based on systematic analysis, but we can offer some informed speculation. In doing so, we should, however, state at the outset that we believe that no uniform set of forces operates on all of the cycles of judicial activism; there is not necessarily one underlying process that permits or causes a wave of judicial activism. From our earlier analysis of the effects of

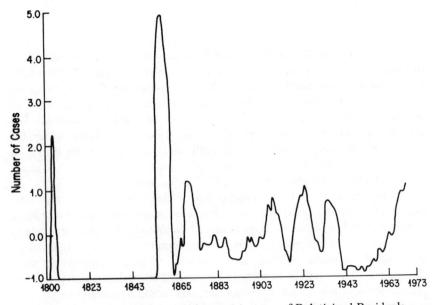

Figure 5-4. Federal Statutes: Moving Average of Relativized Residuals

the Civil War, we know that it did a great deal to spur on the Court's initial period of activism toward Congress. It is also clear that both of the world wars preceded periods of considerable judicial activism—perhaps as a result of Congress's excesses in these war efforts, but more probably because each unleashed tremendous social, political, and economic energies. For instance, one can argue very plausibly that the participation of blacks in World War II, which led to their increased mobilization in a variety of ways, began a process that ended with the Court's taking notice of them. And, of course, such economic phenomena as industrialization, depression, and the rise of corporations must have had some influence on the Court's activism during the earlier, pre-Warren periods. Perhaps the most persistent proposition, in the sense that scholars offer it over and over again, about judicial activism toward Congress is that it occurs as the result of partisan realignments, a time during which the majorities on the Court and in the Congress and the polity are not in tune.[29] Now the standard periods of critical realignments of the party system are the years around the elections of 1800, 1836, 1860, 1896, 1932, and perhaps 1968.[30] So, in the post–Civil War era, partisan realignment cannot account for at least two cycles of judicial activism (1920–1924, 1908–1912); and in two periods, the late 1860s and early 1930s, partisan realignment and spurts of judicial activism toward Congress occurred at virtually the same time, so one could hardly argue that one led to the other. Part of the problem in testing such a proposition is that critical realigning periods differ from each other in so many important ways. For instance, the election of 1896 was in fact a reaffirmation or strengthening of the Grand Old Party's hold on power. Thus majorities on the Court and in Congress did not get out of synchronization with each other because one party controled both institutions for quite a long time. The data here suggest, then, that partisan realignment is perhaps a sufficient, but not a necessary, condition for a period of judicial activism toward Congress. We share the skepticism of Paul Beck and Bradley Canon and S. Sidney Ulmer that there is a straightforward relationship between partisan realignment and periods of activism toward congressional enactments.[31]

State Legislatures, Judicial Activism, and the Civil War

We have discussed in some detail the trends, cycles, and discontinuities in patterns of the Court's activism toward the American Congress. That Congress is a coordinate branch of government, can increase or decrease the Court's appellate jurisdiction or membership, and has closer ties to the mass public and so more legitimacy—all of these things must retard the degree of the Court's aggressiveness toward the federal legislature. But state legislatures are clearly subordinate, in a constitutional as well as a political sense, and have no control over either the Court's docket or membership. Furthermore, the framers, as we have mentioned, stated that the "Constitution, and the Laws of the United States . . . , shall be the supreme Law of the Land; and the Judges in every State shall be bound thereby, any Thing in the Constitution or Laws of any State to the Contrary notwithstanding." And as we have also argued, the Civil War strengthened this edict and the Court's position vis-à-vis the states.

Figure 5-5 presents, on an annual basis for the years 1800 through 1973, the number of cases in which the Supreme Court has declared state statutes to be contrary to the Constitution of the United States. We observe considerable growth over time in the incidence of judicial activism toward the states. And, just as clearly, the Court has declared many, many more state than federal statutes unconstitutional. That is, in part, because the state legislatures produce so many more laws than does the Congress. One could argue that the increase in the number of "targets," that is, number of states, over time can account for, or at least confuse the analysis of patterns of judicial activism toward the states. At the very least, one could argue that it makes comparisons of judicial activism toward the state legislatures and Congress inappropriate. To alleviate these problems in part, we have taken the straightforward step of standardizing each of the observations in figure 5-5 for the number of states in the Union at the

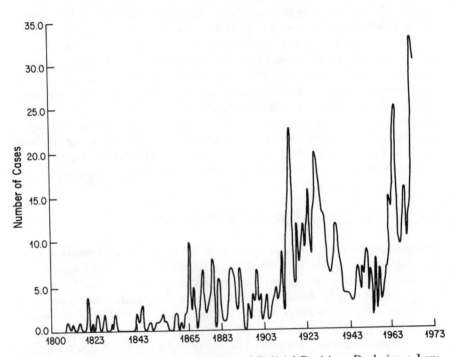

Figure 5-5. State Statutes: The Number of Judicial Decisions Declaring a Law Unconstitutional

time of the judicial action. These numbers then appear in figure 5-6. With a few exceptions, the number of states has had no effect on the incidence of the Supreme Court's activism toward the state legislatures.

Visual inspection of these data suggests that the Court did not engage, in a systematic fashion, in activism toward the states before the Civil War. For the effects of the Civil War on judicial activism, ordinary least-squares yields the following estimates:

$$\text{STATE}_t = .3810 + .0081\ T_1 + .0994\ T_2 + 1.8591\ \text{WAR}_t$$
$$(.34)\quad (.26)\qquad (7.38)\qquad (1.33)$$
$$R^2 = .48\qquad D.W. = .75$$
$$F = 51.0\qquad N = 174$$

where STATE_t is the number of cases in which the Court invalidated a state statute in a particular year, and the remaining notation is the same as before. Before the Civil War, then, the Court's activism toward the states occurred haphazardly—although, if we compare the t-ratios for the trend before the war

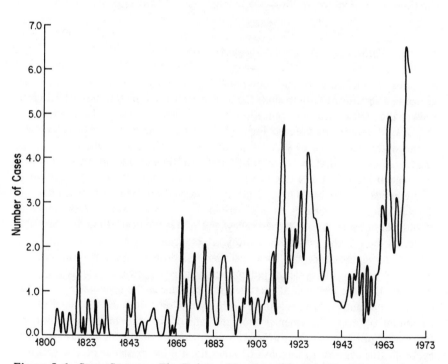

Figure 5-6. State Statutes: The Relative Number of Judicial Decisions Declaring a Law Unconstitutional

for the federal and state statutes, more pattern and less randomness characterizes the Court's actions toward the states. Thus before the Civil War the Supreme Court struck down state statutes from time to time but did not do so often enough to indicate that such activism had become institutionalized. The short-term effect of the war on judicial activism approaches but falls short of standard levels of statistical significance. So in our judgment the Civil War did not lead to a short-term increase in the level of judicial activism toward the states. But after the Civil War, the Supreme Court's activism toward the states manifested considerable and significant growth. We find that the end of the Civil War constituted the beginning of systematic patterns of judicial activism toward the states—just as it had for the Court's actions toward Congress. Change came over the longer haul rather than over the short run. For each ten years since the end of the Civil War, the Court has declared state statutes unconstitutional in one more case—a rate of growth in activism ten times faster than that toward Congress. Thus judicial activism toward the states has grown at a fairly sharp clip. The Court is, as we expected, more likely to strike down state than federal laws; and after 1865 it has done so at a much faster rate. Quite apart from magnitude, however, the same model of political change fits the effects of the Civil War on the Court's activism toward both the federal and state legislatures.

State Legislatures and Cycles of Judicial Activism?

We have established that the Supreme Court's activism toward the states has grown in a significant fashion since the end of the Civil War. Has judicial activism toward the states occurred cyclically? If it has, then do these cycles happen in a regular or deterministic fashion? Figure 5-7 presents a seven-year moving average of the detrended series of judicial actions toward the state legislatures. It indicates, of course, that cycles of judicial activism toward the states do not occur on a regular basis. Fitting a sine curve to these data demonstrates the irregularities of the cycles of activism. Quite as clearly, however, the Court's activism toward the states does evidence a cyclical or periodic component. Each successive period of judicial activism has a deeper valley and a steeper peak. In earlier periods, especially before the twentieth century, fluctuations are smaller—swings from activism to acquiescence and back again are less pronounced. Since the turn of the century, swings in cycles of judicial activism have grown sharper. It is tempting to look at the patterns of the twentieth century as the beginnings of a more or less deterministic process—that, on a regular schedule, the Supreme Court has bursts of energy in which it trims the sails of the state legislatures. But we think it is appropriate to be cautious about such statements, for we have too few cycles in this century to establish with confidence the existence of a deterministic process. This figure does show two periods of incredible judicial activism—from about 1912 through the middle of the 1920s and from the middle 1950s

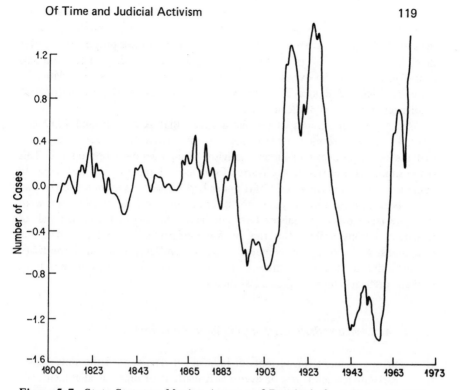

Figure 5-7. State Statutes: Moving Average of Residuals from Detrended Time Series

through 1973. During that first cycle, under the leadership of chief justices White and Taft, a very conservative Court struck down statute after statute from state legislatures on matters such as labor relations and the regulation of business enterprise. During the latter period, under Chief Justice Warren and later Burger, the Court invalidated state enactments that discriminated on the basis of "suspect" classifications; that infringed upon freedom of expression, association, or religion; and that violated minimum standards of proper criminal procedure. That the latter burst of judicial hyperactivism toward the states had not, as of the early 1970s, yet subsided and was still on the rise must alarm the critics of the Supreme Court.

Earlier, we demonstrated that judicial activism grows over time—apart from the cyclical component. Even after the series has been detrended, an upward trend might remain in the cycles. That the amplitude of cycles of judicial activism is getting larger and larger over time might lead one to conclude that the Court is getting "out of hand"—when in fact what is happening is that the Court, because it has moved to a higher level of activism, has more room for variation. The question, then, is: has the amplitude of cycles of judicial activism toward the state legislatures increased or are these cycles more or less proportionate over time? To correct for a rise in the general level, we have divided the residuals from figure 5-7 by the overall trend—a procedure that yields a set of relativized numbers. Figure 5-8 arrays a seven-year moving average of these detrended, relativized indicators of judicial activism.

Apart from the bursts of judicial activism that peaked around 1912 and 1924, the cycles are more or less proportionate. There is little evidence, then, that the swings in cycles of judicial activism have grown more pronounced. This figure should give critics of the Warren Court considerable reason for pause. In numerical terms, the Supreme Court under Earl Warren was no more active than it had been in most earlier cycles. For sheer quantity of judicial activism toward the state legislatures, the laissez faire and Taft Courts—which fought a pair of rearguard actions against the rise of the modern welfare state—remain the champions. To be sure, the members of the Warren Court were judicial activists, but their sins, at least in quantitative terms, were no greater than those of most of their forebears and a good deal less than some.

Judicial Activism and State Legislatures: Some Explanations

How can one account for patterns of judicial activism toward the state legislatures? Partisan realignments, or even reaffirmations of previous alignments, do not, it seems to us, go far toward explaining cycles of judicial activism directed at the states. The greatest sprees of judicial activism happened before—not during or after—a realignment of partisan forces. So, although we cannot reject out of hand the idea that partisan change results in judicial activism, we must for now render the Scottish juror's verdict—"not proved." Much of the problem of demonstrating this connection comes from the overly simplistic statements that scholars have made about it. Thus a relationship might well exist, but, to show it, one would have to make a very clear specification of the conditions under which it would be present.

The increasing complexities of modern business, economic palpitations, state legislatures' attempts to cope with those and other problems, and the White and Taft Courts' unwillingness to tolerate such regulation led to the periods of the most extensive judicial activism toward the state legislatures. Increasing crime, concern for procedural safeguards, and lack of uniformity across states, in part, must have animated the Warren Court. Each of these periods of judicial activism ended in the "nationalization," in Stokes's sense of the word, of some element of the American politico-legal order.[32] Thus, we would argue, one of the primary functions of these periods of judicial activism toward the states is the imposition of a minimum national standard on the states. For, as Justice Holmes once speculated, "the United States would not come to an end if we [the Court] lost our power to declare an Act of

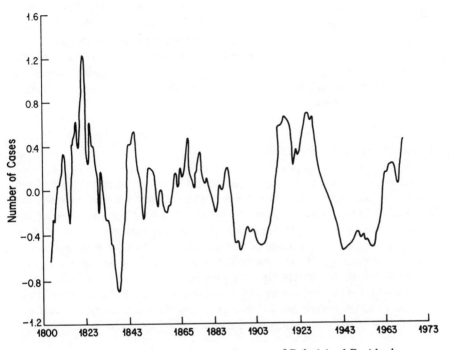

Figure 5-8. State Statutes: Moving Average of Relativized Residuals

Congress void. . . . I do think the Union would be imperilled if we could not make that declaration as to the laws of the several states."[33]

Congress, State Legislatures, and Judicial Activism

One last set of queries remains. Does the incidence of judicial activism toward the state and federal legislatures coincide? Have these two phenomena shared growth, or a trend upward, or have they grown in different patterns? Do cycles of judicial activism toward Congress and the state legislatures occur at more or less the same time? In other words, when the Court pursues a policy of activism toward one level of governance, does it do so with the other?

First of all, the overall pattern of growth of judicial activism toward state and federal legislatures shows a very high correlation—because, of course, both increase after the Civil War. For both sorts of judicial activism, as we have seen, the Civil War marks the real beginnings. Second, after detrending the two series, we do not observe significant relationships between cycles of judicial activism toward the states and Congress. In several cases—the late 1860s and the 1870s, the middle 1920s, and the late 1950s and the 1960s—the Court did take on the state legislatures and Congress at the same time. For the Taft and Warren Courts, these two-front wars proved very costly. Perhaps the moral to extract here is that the Court can practice judicial activism to its heart's content—if it is willing to aim its actions at one level of government at a time. In any event, quite apart from a shared upward trend, the Supreme Court's activism toward the state legislatures and Congress seem to be very separate.

Summary and Concluding Remarks

We return to the issue that began our inquiries: is the Supreme Court of the modern period more active than it was in earlier times? We have discussed the complex, multidimensional nature of judicial activism. Has the scope of the Court's decisions increased? Has the sheer amount of activities—opinions, decisions,—increased? Have periods of judicial activism become more persistent? Has the Court arrogated unto itself more issues or problems than have Congress, the president, or the states? Here we provide answers to one narrowly drawn interrogatory: does the Supreme Court do more now, in the sense of the number of cases in which it invalidates a state or federal statute, than it did in previous eras? On the basis of our results, we make the following arguments.

There is no significant trend in judicial activism toward the federal or state legislatures before the Civil War.

The Civil War did not lead to a short-term increase in judicial activism toward the state and federal legislatures.

After the Civil War, judicial activism toward the state and federal legislatures showed a significant but gradual growth.

Apart from a general trend toward a higher level of activism, the Supreme Court's activism toward the state and federal legislatures evidences considerable cyclicalities.

These cycles, however pronounced, are not regular.

The absolute size of the cycles has in fact increased over time.

The relative amplitude of the cycles has not grown as time has passed.

Aside from sharing a general trend toward greater judicial activism, the Supreme Court's behaviors toward the state and federal legislatures seem to be quite independent of each other.

"The Supreme Court isn't what it used to be," C. Herman Pritchett reminds us, "and what's more, it never was,"[34] for change as well as stability characterizes the behavior of this institution. To evaluate the Court and its incumbents, one needs to keep in mind that no set of justices operates in a vacuum. We need to place the behavior of the Supreme Court at any particular time in the context of previous events. For instance, the Supreme Court under Earl Warren appears to have invalidated state statutes at an incredible rate—until, of course, one recalls that under the leadership of White and Taft, the Court was equally aggressive toward the state legislatures. Furthermore, the Court's actions toward state legislatures under Warren appeared even more offensive than it might have, on average, because the Warren Court followed a period of extreme judicial acquiescence vis-à-vis the states after the departure of the nine old men—so, although the Court did not do more than it had before, it upset a lot of people because it reached a high peak of judicial activism in such a short period of time.

We have discussed some alternative explanations of the phenomenon of judicial activism toward Congress and the state legislatures. Political, social, and economic change, we believe, interacts with—sometimes preceding, sometimes following, sometimes occurring simultaneously—changes in patterns of judicial activism. The trick, of course, is the ferreting out and specification of these relationships—a task that is far beyond the scope of this study and is the topic of a future one. We do believe that a cycle of judicial activism, once begun, has, in a certain sense, a life of its own. Once the institutional forces of the Court have moved forward, a certain political or legal logic takes over. The Supreme Court, in our view, begins a period of judicial activism through creating uncertainty, litigants seek clarification, the justices attempt to clarify or perhaps increase confusion, and the process continues until certainty returns and the Court becomes less active after a time. Political, social, and economic change govern the beginning, end, perigee, and apogee of cycles of judicial activism— but cannot change the general outlines of this stubborn institutional pattern.[35]

Notes

1. For some indication that periods of criticism recur see Stuart S. Nagel, *The Legal Process from a Behavioral Perspective* (Homewood, Ill.: Dorsey, 1969), pp. 245–279; Sheldon Goldman and Thomas P. Jahnige, *The Federal Courts as a Political System,* 2d ed., (New York: Harper and Row, 1976), pp. 272–278; Alpheus Thomas Mason, "Judicial Activism: Old and New," *Virginia Law Review* 55 (April 1969):385–426. In the 1920s and 1930s liberal scholars criticized the Supreme Court's negation of state and federal legislative attempts at the regulation of economic activities. See, for instance, Thomas Reed Powell, "The Logic and Rhetoric of Constitutional Law," *Journal of Philosophy, Psychology, and Scientific Method* 15 (November 1918):645–658; Thomas Reed Powell, *Vagaries and Varieties in Constitutional Interpretation* (New York: Columbia University Press, 1956); Edward S. Corwin, *The Twilight of the*

Supreme Court (New Haven: Yale University Press, 1934); Louis B. Boudin, *Government By Judiciary* (New York: Godwin, 1932).

2. For the most recent work see Raoul Berger, *Government by Judiciary: The Transformation of the Fourteenth Amendment* (Cambridge: Harvard University Press, 1977); Archibald Cox, *The Role of the Supreme Court in American Government* (New York: Oxford University Press, 1976); Nathan Glazer, "Towards an Imperial Judiciary?" *The Public Interest* 40 (Fall 1975):104-123; Nathan Glazer, "Should Judges Administer Social Services?" *The Public Interest* 50 (Winter 1978):64-80; Lino A. Graglia, *Disaster by Decree: The Supreme Court's Decisions on Race and Schools* (Ithaca: Cornell University Press, 1976); Ward E. Elliott, *The Rise of Guardian Democracy: The Supreme Court's Role in Voting Rights Disputes, 1845-1969* (Cambridge: Harvard University Press, 1974); Alexander M. Bickel, *The Morality of Consent* (New Haven: Yale University Press, 1975); Alexander M. Bickel, *The Supreme Court and the Idea of Progress* (New York: Harper and Row, 1970); Donald L. Horowitz, *The Courts and Social Policy* (Washington: The Brookings Institution, 1977); Philip B. Kurland, *Politics, the Constitution and the Warren Court* (Chicago: University of Chicago Press, 1970). For a recent symposium see John Charles Daly, Abram Chayes, Ira Glasser, Antonin Scalia, and Laurence Silberman, *An Imperial Judiciary: Fact or Myth?* (Washington: American Enterprise Institute for Public Policy Research, 1979).

3. Glazer, "Towards an Imperial Judiciary?"

4. Arthur S. Miller, "Judicial Activism and American Constitutionalism: Some Notes and Reflections," in *Nomos XX: Constitutionalism,* ed. J. Roland Pennock and John W. Chapman (New York: New York University Press, 1979), p. 334.

5. Charles Warren, *The Supreme Court in United States History* (Boston: Little, Brown, 1926); Charles Grove Haines, *The American Doctrine of Judicial Supremacy* (Berkeley: University of California Press, 1932); Charles Grove Haines and Foster Sherwood, *The Role of the Supreme Court in American Government and Politics, 1835-1864* (Berkeley: University of California Press, 1957); Charles Grove Haines, *The Role of the Supreme Court in American Government and Politics, 1789-1835* (Berkeley: University of California Press, 1944); Charles Fairman, *History of the Supreme Court of the United States: Reconstruction and Reunion, 1864-88* (New York: Macmillan, 1971); Julius Goebel, *History of the Supreme Court of the United States: Antecedents and Beginnings to 1801* (New York: Macmillan, 1971); Carl Brent Swisher, *History of the Supreme Court of the United States: The Taney Period* (New York: Macmillan, 1974); Paul L. Murphy, *The Constitution in Crisis Times, 1918-1969* (New York: Harper and Row, 1972); William F. Swindler, *Court and Constitution in the 20th Century—The Old Legality, 1889-1932* (Indianapolis: Bobbs-Merrill, 1969); William F. Swindler, *Court and Constitution in the 20th Century—The New Legality, 1932-1968* (Indianapolis: Bobbs-Merrill, 1970).

6. Robert G. McCloskey, *The American Supreme Court* (Chicago: University of Chicago Press, 1960).

7. Robert A. Dahl, "Decision-Making in a Democracy: The Supreme Court as a National Policy Maker," *Journal of Public Law* 6 (Fall 1957):279-295.

8. Jonathan D. Casper, "The Supreme Court and National Policy Making," *American Political Science Review* 70 (March 1976):50-63.

9. See David W. Adamany, "Legitimacy, Realigning Elections, and the Supreme Court," *Wisconsin Law Review,* no. 3 (1973):790-846; Richard Funston, "The Supreme Court and Critical Elections," *American Political Science Review* 69 (September 1975):795-811; Bradley C. Canon and S. Sidney Ulmer, "The Supreme Court and Critical Elections: A Dissent," *American Political Science Review* 70 (December 1976):1215-1218; Paul Allen Beck, "Critical Elections and the Supreme Court: Putting the Cart Before the Horse," *American Political Science Review* 70 (September 1976):930-932. Some earlier speculation about the relationship between partisan change and judicial behavior appears in at least two places: Wallace Mendelson, "Judicial Review and Party Politics," *Vanderbilt Law Review* 12 (March 1959):447-457; John P. Roche, *Courts and Rights* (New York: Random House, 1961), pp. 22-24, 46.

10. McCloskey, *The American Supreme Court;* Adamany, "Legitimacy, Realigning Elections, and the Supreme Court."

11. But see Casper, "The Supreme Court and National Policy Making," p. 57.

12. Remarks of Chief Justice John Marshall at the Virginia Constitutional Convention of 1829-1830, quoted in Robert K. Faulkner, *The Jurisprudence of John Marshall* (Princeton: Princeton University Press, 1968), p. 70.

13. Jacob E. Cooke, ed., *The Federalist* (New York: Meridian, 1961), no. 78, p. 522.

14. Leonard Baker, *John Marshall: A Life in Law* (New York: Macmillan, 1974), p. 332.

15. McCloskey, *The American Supreme Court,* p. 101.

16. Ibid., p. 102.

17. *Texas v. White,* 7 Wallace 700, 725 (1869).

18. On the "nationalization" of political forces see Donald E. Stokes, "Parties and the Nationalization of Electoral Forces," in *The American Party Systems: Stages of Political Development,* ed. William Nisbet Chambers and Walter Dean Burnham (New York: Oxford University Press, 1967), pp. 182-202; E.E. Schattschneider, *The Semi-Sovereign People: A Realist's View of Democracy in America* (New York: Holt, Rinehart and Winston, 1960), chap. 5; Douglas R. Rose, "National and State Forces in State Politics: The Implications of Multi-Level Policy Analysis," *American Political Science Review* 67 (December 1973):1162-1173.

19. For related arguments see McCloskey, *The American Supreme Court;* Harold M. Hyman, *A More Perfect Union: The Impact of the Civil War and*

Reconstruction on the Constitution (New York: Knopf, 1973), chap. 14; Alfred H. Kelley and Winfred A. Harbison, *The American Constitution: Its Origins and Development,* 5th ed. (New York: Norton, 1976), p. 420; Haines and Sherwood, *The Role of the Supreme Court in American Government and Politics,* p. 518. For a bit different but still related argument see Warren, *The Supreme Court in United States History* 2: chaps. 35-36.

20. Nelson W. Polsby, "The Institutionalization of the U.S. House of Representatives," *American Political Science Review* 62 (March 1968):144-168.

21. The Library of Congress, *The Constitution of the United States: Analysis and Interpretation* (Washington, D.C.: Government Printing Office, 1974).

22. Horowitz, *The Courts and Social Policy,* p. 6. For a summary of views on this question see Stephen C. Halpern, chapter 9, this volume.

23. For a discussion see Halpern, ibid.

24. For example, see Glazer, "Towards an Imperial Judiciary?"

25. See Thomas D. Cook and Donald T. Campbell, "The Design and Conduct of Quasi-Experiments and True Experiments in Field Settings," in *The Handbook of Industrial and Organizational Psychology,* ed. Marvin D. Dunnette (Chicago: Rand-McNally, 1976), pp. 223-326; Donald T. Campbell and Thomas D. Cook, *The Design and Analysis of Quasi-Experiments for Field Settings* (Chicago: Rand-McNally, 1978).

26. G. Hildreth and J.Y. Lu, "Demand Relations with Autocorrelated Disturbances" (Technical Bulletin 276, Agriculture Experiment Station, Michigan State University, 1960).

27. See Jan Kmenta, *Elements of Econometrics* (New York: Macmillan, 1971); Robert S. Pindyck and Daniel L. Rubinfeld, *Econometric Models and Economic Forecasts* (New York: McGraw-Hill, 1976); John Johnston, *Econometric Methods,* 2d ed. (New York: McGraw-Hill, 1972).

28. K.A. Yeomans, *Statistics for the Social Scientist* (London: Penguin, 1969), chap. 1, *passim.*

29. For examples see Adamany, "Legitimacy, Realigning Elections, and the Supreme Court"; Funston, "The Supreme Court and Critical Elections"; Canon and Ulmer, "The Supreme Court and Critical Elections"; Mendelson, "Judicial Review and Party Politics."

30. To be sure, students of critical elections do not agree on the occurrence or exact date of a partisan alignment, realignment, or affirmation. For discussions see Chambers and Burnham, *The American Party Systems;* James L. Sundquist, *Dynamics of the Party System: Alignment and Realignment of Political Parties in the United States* (Washington: The Brookings Institution, 1973); Charles Sellers, "The Equilibrium Cycle in Two-Party Politics," *Public Opinion Quarterly* 29 (Spring 1965):16-37; Thomas P. Jahnige, "Critical Elections and Social Change: Towards a Dynamic Explanation of National Party Competition in the United States," *Polity* 3 (June 1971):465-500.

31. Beck, "Critical Elections and The Supreme Court"; Canon and Ulmer, "The Supreme Court and Critical Elections."

32. Stokes, "Parties and the Nationalization of Electoral Forces."

33. Oliver Wendell Holmes, Jr., *Collected Legal Papers* (New York: Harcourt, 1920), pp. 295-296.

34. C. Herman Pritchett, quoted in Walter F. Murphy, Joseph Tanenhaus, and Daniel Kastner, *Public Evaluations of Constitutional Courts: Alternative Explanations* (Beverly Hills: Sage, 1973), p. 29.

35. See Gregory A. Caldeira, "The United States Supreme Court and Criminal Cases: Alternative Models of Agenda-Building" *British Journal of Political Science* (forthcoming, 1982); and Thomas Likens, "Agenda Setting by the Court: Systematic Processes or Noise?" (Paper presented at the Annual Meeting of the American Political Science Association, Washington, D.C., 1979), for a similar pattern, over time, on decisions to deny or grant petitions for certiorari.

Part II
Normative Perspectives

Since the early days of the Republic there has been extended debate over the proper role of the U.S. Supreme Court in the American political system.[1] The debate long turned on the nature of constitutional interpretation or, more specifically, the extent to which discretion in constitutional interpretation enabled the justices to legislate as to the requirements and meanings of the basic charter.[2] Scholarly consensus seems to have been reached on part of this question. Even so ardent an advocate of judicial restraint as Felix Frankfurter explicitly conceded the inevitability of individual discretion in constitutional adjucation. Frankfurter once observed:

> The words of the Constitution are so unrestricted by their intrinsic meaning or by their history or by tradition or by prior decisions that they leave the individual Justice free, if indeed they do not compel him, to gather meaning not from reading the Constitution but from reading life . . . [M]embers of the Court are frequently admonished by their associates not to read their economic and social viewpoints into the neutral language of the Constitution. But the process of constitutional interpretation compels the translation of policy into judgment.[3]

That the justices of the Supreme Court make law is now something of an open secret. Yet as Paul Freund has reminded us, that is only the beginning of sophistication.[4] The more central question for the modern Court is not whether it legislates but what is the constitutionally proper and politically feasible range of its power to establish national public policy. This issue speaks to the very basis and scope of the modern Court's authority in our system of government.

Each generation of scholars seems destined to rekindle and reconsider the debate over the appropriate scope of the Court's authority from the vantage point of its own historical position. There is no analogue to the normative debate over the proper role of the Supreme Court in the literature treating either of the other two branches of the federal government. While questions about proper institutional role have obviously been posed about other political bodies and branches, that concern has not assumed the continuing and transcendent importance that it has in connection with the Court. Historically, there has been far less conflict, both scholarly and political, about the appropriate range of power of the Court's coordinate branches. The Court's undemocratic structure has no doubt fueled the conflict about its place in our governmental system. "We have to worry more about an imperial judiciary than we do about an imperial presidency or an imperial Congress," Lawrence Silberman recently observed,

129

because we "can throw the rascals out of the executive branch or the Congress; we cannot throw them out of the judiciary."[5]

This consideration has often made the justices of the Supreme Court more self-conscious and perhaps less self-confident in the exercise of their power than may be generally true of office holders in the other branches. Indeed, the voluminous debate over the appropriate function and functioning of the Court indirectly reflects this, for one of the richest veins of that literature has been mined by the writings of the Supreme Court justices themselves.[6] It is rare to find publications by presidents, members of Congress, or bureaucrats that examine in a scholarly and introspective fashion the appropriate range and limits of their power. By contrast, Supreme Court justices have conducted just such intellectual soul-searching, often in a formal, public way in off-the-bench writings as well as Court opinions.

This unusual judicial tradition has nourished communication and contact between justices and those in the academy writing about the work of the Court.[7] Consequently, scholars of the Court may well have a more influential impact on the justices than do students of the other branches on the objects of their study. Edwin S. Corwin recognized that special relationship when he observed that "[i]f judges make law, so do [legal and political] commentators."[8] It is, of course, our hope that the chapters in part II of this book will continue that tradition and contribute further to the unusual partnership between scholars and judges.

As the following chapters will make clear, forceful and persuasive arguments can be made for both activism and restraint. To a degree, both logic and history bear out portions of the argument each side typically advances. For instance, advocates of restraint have good philosophical grounding to argue, as they do, that in making constitutional interpretations the justices must bind themselves to the specific intentions of those who framed the relevant constitutional provision.[9] An apostle of activism, on the other hand, can quite reasonably assert, as did John Marshall in *McCulloch v. Maryland*, that the Constitution must be a living, flexible document designed to endure to meet the needs of future generations.[10] In fact, because much scholarship on the Court has been part of the longstanding debate over activism and restraint, commentators advancing opposing positions have occasionally manifested a degree of inflexibility and partisanship perhaps more appropriate to the legal brief than to scholarly inquiry.

Chapter 6 was written by Lino A. Graglia, a major contributor to the "Imperial Judiciary" literature.[11] Graglia presents a case for judicial restraint— or, if one prefers, a case against activism. He observes that during the past twenty-five years a nation founded on principles of decentralized, representative self-government has been increasingly the captive of unelected, lifetime judges initiating policies for which there is little popular support. Purporting to exercise the power of judicial review, Supreme Court justices, as Graglia sees it, have become the final decision makers in many areas of national social policy, but most notably in school desegregation. Accordingly, the author contends that we now have government by Platonic Guardians or Philosopher-Kings. Graglia essentially presents an argument for the supremacy of democratic controls rather than domination by the Supreme Court.

Countering Graglia's position, Arthur S. Miller makes a case for a strong and assertive Supreme Court. Indeed, his chapter is especially provocative because the kind of Court that Miller envisions would exercise far greater power than even the most assertive Courts in our history. Miller contends that the Court is as democratic as Congress or the bureaucracy, even though, as he views it, the Court acts as a faculty of political theory in deciding controversial public issues. The author also maintains that a breakdown in pluralism in the American political order is obvious. He foresees a much stronger and more authoritarian American government. In that context, Miller argues that a powerful Supreme Court will be essential to counterbalance and moderate the initiatives of the other branches.

The following chapter, by Henry J. Abraham, addresses the question of whether one can draw an intellectually consistent and convincing line between Supreme Court activism and restraint. Abraham straddles the extreme positions advanced by Graglia and Miller. Essentially he asserts that one can successfully draw such a line. In so doing, the justices must be ever aware, he admonishes, that their basic role is to say yes or, more dramatically, no as to the constitutionality of the actions of the other branches of government. Abraham maintains that in providing that answer, the justices must look to both the letter and spirit of the constitutional text. Nonetheless, when interpreting the spirit of the text Abraham believes that the justices must resolutely shun prescriptive policy making and abide by the traditional maxims of restraint, even though they must occasionally rely on their ultimate power of judicial review.

Since 1975, several influential scholars have advanced the proposition that the Court has become excessively powerful in our governmental system. They warn, to use the characterization first advanced by Nathan Glazer, that we now have an Imperial Judiciary.[12] In chapter 9 Stephen C. Halpern advances a dissenting view. He examines leading works in the Imperial Judiciary literature and concludes that these authors' critiques are typically flawed because they derive from a narrow sweep of vision. As Halpern sees it, their error is that they look only at the development of the Court's power and function. Halpern insists that we must assess the nature and evolution of the Court's role in the context of the comparative historical development of other major national political institutions and of American national government generally.

Finally, in chapter 10, Joan Roelofs presents a stimulating Marxist critique of the activism of the Warren Court. She analyzes decisions in the areas of racial discrimination, civil liberties, criminal justice, and reapportionment. In her concluding section, the author contends that reforms initiated by the Warren Court majority impeded radical change and channelled legal reform in a direction consonant with the interests of corporate capitalism. In this sense Warren Court activism, according to Roelofs, must be seen as having had a conservative impact that produced only marginal reforms. The more significant and enduring legacy of the Warren years, the author suggests, is that they helped to better reconcile and rationalize the control of the elites that dominate American life.

Notes

1. The issues in this debate are discussed by numerous scholars. See, for example, Chalres L. Black, Jr., *The People and the Court: Judicial Review in a Democracy* (New York: Macmillan, 1960); Alfred H. Kelly and Winfred A. Harbison, *The American Constitution: Its Origins and Development,* 5th ed. (New York: Norton, 1976).

2. Compare, for example, Alexander M. Bickel, *The Supreme Court and the Idea of Progress* (New York: Harper and Row, 1970) to J. Skelly Wright, "Professor Bickel, the Scholarly Tradition, and the Supreme Court," *Harvard Law Review,* 84 (February 1971): 769–805. Also compare Herbert Wechsler, "Toward Neutral Principles of Constitutional Law," *Harvard Law Reveiw,* 73 (November 1959): 1–35 to Arthur S. Miller and Ronald F. Howell, "The Myth of Neutrality in Constitutional Adjudication," *University of Chicago Law Review,* 27 (Summer 1960): 661–695.

3. Alpheus Thomas Mason, *The Supreme Court from Taft to Warren* (Baton Rouge: Louisiana State University Press, 1955), p. 15, quoting Felix Frankfurter.

4. Paul Freund, *On Understanding the Supreme Court* (Boston: Little, Brown, 1951), p. 3.

5. John Charles Daly, Abram Chayes, Ira Glasser, Antonin Scalia, and Lawrence Silberman, *An Imperial Judiciary: Fact or Myth?* (Washington: American Enterprise Institute, 1979), p. 23.

6. There is a large body of literature by Supreme Court justices, either written before they were appointed to the Court, while they served on it, or after leaving it. See Hugo L. Black, *A Constitutional Faith* (New York: Knofp, 1968); William O. Douglas, *An Almanac of Liberty* (Garden City, N.Y.: Doubleday, 1954); William O. Douglas, *The Right of the People* (New York: Pyramid, 1958); Abe Fortas, *Concerning Dissent and Civil Disobedience* (New York: Signet, 1968); Arthur J. Goldberg, *Equal Justice: The Warren Era of the Supreme Court* (Evanston, Ill.: Northwestern University Press, 1971); Charles Evans Hughes, *The Supreme Court of the United States* (New York: Columbia University Press, 1928); Robert H. Jackson, *The Struggle for Judicial Supremacy: A Study of Crisis in American Power Politics* (New York: Knopf, 1941); Robert H. Jackson, *The Supreme Court in the American System of Government*

(Cambridge: Harvard University Press, 1955).

7. See Chester A. Newland, "Legal Periodicals and the United States Supreme Court," *Midwest Journal of Political Science*, 3, no. 1 (1959): 58–74. See also Walter F. Murphy, *Elements of Judicial Strategy* (Chicago: University of Chicago Press, 1964), pp. 128–129.

8. Alpheus Thomas Mason and William M. Beaney, *American Constitutional Law: Introductory Essays and Selected Cases*, 6th ed. Englewood Cliffs: Prentice-Hall, 1978), p. xi, quoting Edwin S. Corwin.

9. Obvious examples are Raoul Berger, *Government by Judiciary: The Transformation of the Fourteenth Amendment* (Cambridge: Harvard University Press, 1977); William W. Crosskey, *Politics and the Constitution in the History of the United States* (Chicago: University of Chicago Press, 1953).

10. 4 Wheaton 316, 415 (1819).

11. Lino A. Graglia, *Disaster by Decree: The Supreme Court's Decisions on Race and Schools* (Ithaca, N.Y.: Cornell University Press, 1976).

12. Nathan Glazer, "Towards an Imperial Judiciary?" *The Public Interest*, 40 (Fall 1975): 104–123. See also the works cited in the introduction to Part I, n. 1.

In Defense of Judicial Restraint

Lino A. Graglia

All peoples have pious fictions and sacrosanct expressions which make free thought and honest speech seem improper. This is true even among people noted for their progress in science and technology. . . . Men who dare to call the Emperor naked when he has no clothes have been pointing out that time-honored national dogmas in regard to our constitutional system are full of logical fallacies and historical errors. It is therefore the business of scholars or those engaged in weighing evidence to examine these issues critically, regardless of the fact that for doing so they may be called unpatriotic by ignorant men in popularly influential positions.

—Morris Raphael Cohen, *The Faith of a Liberal*

American judges have, almost from the beginning, assumed and exercised a degree of power unique in the history of government. Over the past quarter century, this power has been so expanded, the judges have taken from the democratic political process and assumed final say over so many fundamental issues of the nature of the American polity, culture, and civilization, that it is no longer an exaggeration to say that we now have a system of government by unelected judges holding office for life. If tyranny describes government in which the governors are not regularly subject to the control of the governed, this system qualifies for the description. That this extraordinary system should have developed in a nation founded on the revolutionary principle that the people are capable of governing themselves and need not be governed by an elite, and founded on a Constitution that does not grant such power to judges, makes the situation not only all the more remarkable but ironic as well.

The Power of Our Judges

That we are in fact now ruled by our judges would not seem open to dispute. Apart from the conduct of foreign affairs, where our judges have not generally chosen to intervene directly (though some judges have been willing to intervene),[1] nearly all major changes in American society during the last quarter century—many of which can be described as revolutionary and many of which are not favored by a majority of the American people—have been brought about by our judges. To mention only a few of the more prominent examples, our judges have written a detailed legal code regarding the practice of abortion, almost totally depriving the states of the power they formerly possessed to protect prenatal life and effectively establishing a uniform nationwide policy of abortion on demand.[2] Our judges have determined that the nation's public school systems should be "racially balanced" even though this requires the exclusion of children from their neighborhood schools and their transportation to more distant schools on the basis of their race.[3] Despite the fact that this policy requires the practice of racial discrimination by government, constitutes a massive infringement of individual liberty, typically serves to increase rather than decrease racial separation and animosity in the schools and elsewhere, and contributes to the financial plight of many of our public school systems and cities, it is regularly implemented across the nation.

By severely limiting the ability of all levels of government, federal, state, and local, to regulate the sale and distribution of pornographic materials[4] and contraceptives,[5] our judges have successfully defied traditional concepts of sexual morality and the need for social channeling of the sexual impulse and restraints on its commercial exploitation. They have also invalidated traditional legal distinctions between legitimacy and illegitimacy in procreation.[6] Similarly, our judges have rejected traditional concepts of the value of inculcating and rewarding patriotism by disallowing prohibitions on desecration of the American flag[7] and by forbidding the government to exclude members of groups advocating the government's violent overthrow from teaching and other official positions.[8] Our judges have also rejected traditional concepts of the value of peace, quiet, and order in public places by invalidating most restraints on public demonstrations and solicitations, antivagrancy laws, and laws restricting the public use of indecent language.[9] Thus, an American town may not, for example, protect the survivors of Nazi concentration camps by prohibiting a march in their neighborhoods by self-proclaimed Nazis advocating further genocide, and a state may not prohibit the parading of vulgarity through a state courthouse.[10] Neither the states nor the federal government, our judges have ruled, may accommodate the desire of many parents to have their children educated in religious schools by allowing part of the taxes they pay to be used in aid of such schools; nor do our judges permit school authorities to make provision for voluntary prayer or devotional Bible reading in public schools.[11]

Most important, perhaps, in terms of the possibility of maintaining a civilized society by protecting personal security is the revolution worked by our judges in the enforcement of the criminal law. Apparently influenced by the theory, popular in the 1960s, that punishment is rarely merited or useful, our judges have created impediments to the investigation, prosecution, and punishment of crime such as are known to no other legal system. They have created, for example, ever more grounds for the exclusion of relevant evidence and for reversal of convictions;[12] they have created seemingly endless opportunities for further appeals of convictions—permitting, for example, criminal defendants who have exhausted all appeals in a state court system to begin again, in effect, in the federal court system, with all costs to be paid from public funds should the defendant's funds prove insufficient.[13] The effect has been to increase the time, expense, and difficulty of attempting to enforce the criminal law to the point of making the attempt often seem futile. A totally realistic outside observer, a Soviet espionage agent, succinctly stated the result:

> In England, now that the war is over and espionage trials take place in open court, persons detected in espionage on behalf of the Soviet Union are instructed by whichever of our organizations it is which has been using them to plead guilty and to admit to the police their participation in the particular crime of which they are accused, and nothing more. In the United States such persons are at present instructed to proceed in precisely the opposite way and deny everything. This is a compliment to England. . . . In the United States, where legal proceedings are likely to be prolonged and confused, and all sorts of considerations may prevent the truth from appearing, it is worthwhile putting up a plea of not guilty, no matter how absurd this may be in view of the real facts.[14]

The Myth that Our Judges' Power Is Derived from and Limited by the Constitution

The list of basic policy decisions made and imposed on the country by our judges in recent years could be extended indefinitely, but the foregoing surely sufficiently demonstrates that our judges do in fact govern many of the most important aspects of American life. The question to be considered here is not the merits or demerits of the particular policy decisions our judges have made, but the even more basic question of how it came to be, in a country supposedly dedicated to self-government, that these decisions were made by judges rather than by the elected representatives of the people, and were made, typically, in defiance of and by overruling the policy decisions of those elected representatives. What is the source of this power? Most important, what are the actual limits, if any, of this power today? What is it that our judges *cannot* now do?

Surprising as it may seem in a secular and scientific age, the power of our judges is based entirely on a myth, on the successful inculcation and exploitation of a fiction. Like the clothes of the naked emperor in the fable, the power of our judges depends on a failure of perception, an inability or unwillingness to see the obvious truth. The myth is that in making their extraordinary decisions our judges do no more than enforce the Constitution, that the policy choices involved are not those of the judges but those of the framers of the Constitution. Our judges, the myth has it, do not make, but only apply and are bound by the law (the preestablished, authoritative rules set forth in the Constitution), and it is this that makes them "judges," properly so called, rather than legislators, and this that makes what they do consistent with constitutional self-government. As the Supreme Court put it in a classic statement of the myth:

> When an act of Congress is appropriately challenged in the courts as not conforming to the constitutional mandate, the judicial branch of the Government has only one duty—to lay the article of the Constitution which is invoked beside the statute which is challenged and to decide whether the latter squares with the former. All the court does, or can do, is to announce its considered judgment upon the question.[15]

No justice of the Supreme Court and no other judge has ever had the temerity to suggest that he is authorized to substitute his views of public policy for those of elected legislators, that he may reject legislative choices on the ground that he considers them unwise or unenlightened. The claim invariably is, instead, that the rejected legislative choice is *unconstitutional,* that it is prohibited by some provision of the Constitution. This would certainly be too obvious to require statement, except for the fact that it is so obvious that it has apparently long been forgotten. For if it is not forgotten, if the judges' claim to having found inconsistencies with the Constitution is observed and taken seriously, it can also be observed in almost all cases that such claims are false. As Felix Frankfurter, later a justice of the Supreme Court, once pointed out to President Roosevelt: "People have been taught to believe that when the Supreme Court speaks it is not they who speak but the Constitution, whereas, of course, in so many vital cases it is *they* who speak and *not* the Constitution. And I verily believe that this is what the country needs most to understand."[16] This is still what the country needs most to understand, for nothing more than this understanding is necessary to return the government of the country to the hands of its people.

By far the most important thing to be understood about constitutional law is that it has almost nothing to do with the Constitution. In almost every "constitutional" case actually brought to the courts for decision, the Constitution is simply irrelevant to the decision reached except that it provides the peculiar phrases—usually "due process" or "equal protection"—used by the judges to state their ultimate conclusions when they disagree with the public policy choices made by others. If this is surprising or even shocking, it certainly is not because it is either a new or a profound insight or because it is difficult to demonstrate. As long ago as 1717, Bishop Hoadly pointed out to King George I that "Whoever hath an absolute authority to interpret any written or spoken laws, it is he who is truly the lawgiver, to all intents and purposes, and not the person who first spoke or wrote them."[17] The power—even if not the theoretical legal authority—of the Supreme Court to "interpret" the Constitution is for all practical purposes absolute. As Charles Evans Hughes, later a chief justice of the Supreme Court, stated in 1907, "We are under a Constitution, but the

Constitution is what the judges say it is."[18] Which is to say the we are under the judges, and this is surely even more true today than it was in 1907.

Thomas Reed Powell, the leading constitutional law scholar of his time, pointed out in 1918 that so "few of the questions of constitutional law are answered by any specific language in the Constitution" that "there is something fictitious in calling the work of the courts a work of interpretation."[19] Powell, indeed, often began his classes in constitutional law at Harvard by advising his students not to read the Constitution, as it would only confuse their understanding of the subject. Karl Llewellyn, one of the greatest legal scholars in our history and a man even less subject to illusion than Powell, wrote in 1934:

> Men limp along for years or decades with an outworn, performance-baffling framework of their thought, until some child, inadequately taught to "see," cries out that the king in question has no clothes. . . . The king in question here is our Constitution. The framework of orthodox constitutional theory consists of a number of propositions which to a new Adam or the well-known sudden visitor from Mars would seem appalling. Indeed, save for the blinders of familiarity, they would appall the thinking man of here and now.

Among these propositions, Llewellyn listed "the notion that the primary source of information as to what our Constitution comes to, is the language of a certain Document of 1789" and its amendments, and "the notion that rulings of the Supreme Court on constitutional points *interpret* or *apply,* seldom do more than *merely* interpret or apply, this Document as Amended." The usefulness of this constitutional theory for judges, he pointed out, is that it "offers a refuge from responsibility," a means of "escape from answering in public for their manner of deciding issues."[20]

Llewellyn found it "a bit amusing" that the power to decide constitutional issues "derives in no slightest manner from the words of the Document on which the judges purport to rest the decisions which they make. . . ." Llewellyn goes on to argue that the Court arrogated to itself the authority to be the ultimate arbiter of the meaning of the constitutional text and no one has seriously contested its title to that territory. "Occupation—and assiduous cultivation," he notes, "produce title under any one of a number of theories."[21]

That the Constitution is not the source of the decisions the judges make in its name can be easily shown. The Supreme Court's decisions on race and the schools, for example, provide almost the equivalent of a scientific experiment on the question. There was a time when "the Constitution," according to the judges, *permitted* the assignment of children to school on the basis of race in order to keep the races apart.[22] There then came a time when "the Constitution" *prohibited* racial assignment.[23] Finally, there came a time when "the Constitution" *required* racial assignment for the purpose of increasing racial mixing.[24] In all of this time the Constitution was not changed in any relevant respect, and each of the decisions reaching these conflicting results purported to interpret and apply the same constitutional provision. In an intellectually respectable discipline, the possibility of reaching conflicting results on the basis of a single theory is taken as proof that the theory is invalid, but in constitutional law, as in astrology, this presents no serious difficulty.

To take another example from the same area of the law, in *Brown* v. *Board of Education*,[25] the second of the decisions just referred to, the Supreme Court decided that the states may not require school racial segregation. The basis for this decision, supposedly, was that school racial segregation denied blacks "the equal protection of the laws" contrary to the Fourteenth Amendment.[26] The Court held this, it may be noted in passing, despite the fact that the Fourteenth Amendment, far from prohibiting separate schools for blacks, did not, as the need to adopt the Fifteenth Amendment shows,[27] even prohibit the states from denying blacks the right to vote; despite the further fact that the same Congress that proposed the Fourteenth Amendment also provided for segregated schools in the District of Columbia;[28] and finally, despite the fact that school racial segregation was earlier held constitutional by a unanimous Supreme Court that included such respected constitutional authorities as Justices Holmes, Brandeis, and Stone.[29]

On the same day as the *Brown* decision the Court also decided *Bolling* v. *Sharpe*,[30] involving a challenge to school racial segregation in the District of Columbia. The Fourteenth Amendment, by its terms, applies only to the states; the District of Columbia, of course, is subject only to the federal government, and the Constitution contains no "equal protection" clause applicable to the federal government. The absence of the supposed constitutional basis for *Brown*, however, made not the slightest difference in the result the Court reached in *Bolling*. School racial segregation in the District of Columbia was also found to violate the Constitution, only now it was said to be prohibited by the "due process" clause of the Fifth Amendment,[31] which does apply to the federal government. To believe that this decision was based on the Constitution, it is necessary to believe that the Fifth Amendment, adopted in 1791 as part of a Constitution repeatedly recognizing and protecting slavery (as, for example, in the provision that slaves were not to gain freedom by escaping to a nonslave state),[32] was meant to prohibit school racial segregation.

"In view of our decision [in *Brown*] that the Constitution prohibits the states from maintaining racially segregated public schools," Chief Justice Earl Warren explained for the Court in *Bolling*, "it would be unthinkable that the same Constitution would impose a lesser duty on the Federal Government." The Constitution, however, is full of provisions that apply only to the states or only to the federal government; Section 10 of Article I, for example, contains three paragraphs of restrictions that explicitly apply only to the states. Again, this is reasoning that would not be acceptable or permissible in an intellectually respectable discipline; it is reasoning permissible only for judges and other practitioners of mythological arts; it is "reasoning" for the purpose of defying reason. Our judges, after all, are all lawyers; and the schooling of lawyers is largely a process of training in the evasion of reason, in the skill of weakening resistance to the illogical and incredible. A good lawyer is one who can, like the White Queen, believe, or at least cause others to believe, "six impossible things before breakfast." Other examples of this skill are the decisions of the Court that virtually eliminated capital punishment as unconstitutional in the face of a Constitution that explicitly and repeatedly recognizes the taking of life as punishment for crime.[33]

The enormous range and variety of matters our judges have found to be covered by the Constitution easily create an impression of a voluminous and detailed document. The Constitution, however, is very short—six or seven thousand words usually printed on less than twenty booksize pages—and the vast majority of its provisions have not given rise to any significant number of constitutional decisions. Most constitutional decisions today are concerned with imposing limitations or requirements on the states, and virtually all of these decisions purport to be based on a single constitutional provision, one sentence in the Fourteenth Amendment, and indeed, on four words in that sentence: "due process" and "equal protection." The judges have in effect made of these four words a second Constitution, which is a very different and in many ways a vastly more important, Constitution than the one that came from the hands of the framers. By divorcing those words from their historic meaning and purpose— "due process" was essentially meant to guarantee a certain method of trial, and "equal protection" was essentially meant to guarantee certain basic civil rights to blacks, such as the right to own property and make contracts, to sue in the courts, and to be subject to the same punishment for crime as whites[34]—and thus making them almost totally meaningless, our judges have been able to find in these words whatever the judges choose to put into them.

The judges thus made of the power of judicial review—a power Karl Llewellyn could not find in the Constitution—the power to impose their policy choices on the country without even the most general of limitations or standards. They thereby gave themselves carte blanche to govern on whatever matters they saw fit, permitting the policy choices made through the political process to prevail only so long as the judges, like the military in some other countries, find those choices agreeable. It may be possible to argue that government by judges is a good form of government, preferable to democracy, but it should not be possible to argue, as defenders of judicial review nonetheless do—usually with heavy resort to mysticism—that our judges do not govern, that they merely "interpret" and apply a written Constitution.

The Myth that Our Judges' Power Is Limited by
Moral or Legal Principles

If not the Constitution, what, if anything, does limit the power of our judges? One answer often given is that our judges, surprising as it may seem in light of all they have done, are without "real" power because they control "neither the purse nor the sword." The force and effectiveness of their decisions depend, therefore, the argument goes, on the judges' "moral authority," on their special ability to discover and articulate "fundamental American values and principles," even if those values and principles are not necessarily to be found in the Constitution, and to serve as the "conscience of the nation." Judges are seen as akin to highly respected and influential educators or spiritual leaders. This argument is no less mythical or mystical, however, than the argument that the judges merely interpret the Constitution. The essential difference between judges and teachers or preachers is, of course, that the views of the latter are not regularly enforced by the coercive power of government.[35]

While it is true that our judges do not "control the sword" in that they do not ordinarily directly command the military, they can and do effectively command those who command the military. Even the orders of a five-star general are effective only insofar as they are regularly enforced by others and ultimately by those who hold the weapons, and the orders of our judges are regularly enforced. President Jackson reportedly refused to order enforcement of a Supreme Court decision with the statement, "[Chief Justice] John Marshall made the decision, let him enforce it."[36] President Lincoln simply ignored an order of Chief Justice Taney that a wartime prisoner be released.[37] No such examples can be found, however, in more recent times. President Eisenhower disagreed with the *Brown* decision, but nonetheless ordered the use of troops in Little Rock to enforce it.[38] Surely, no clearer illustration of the reality of the power of judges today can be given than the fact that their orders requiring the transportation of tens of thousands of school children and the expenditure of millions of dollars in order to attempt to create school "racial balance,"which, even if achievable, is not known to serve any good purpose,[39] are nonetheless docilely obeyed almost everywhere. The few attempts at popular resistance, as in Boston, are put down by whatever force may be necessary.

Similarly, although our judges do not in theory possess "the power of the purse," the power to tax and spend, they nonetheless can and do issue orders requiring enormous expenditures, and their orders are regularly obeyed. Judges have, for example, ordered the remaking of prison systems and mental institutions, often specifying down to the smallest detail the facilities and services to be provided regardless of cost.[40] Court-ordered "desegregation" has involved the expenditure of hundreds of millions or perhaps even billions of dollars nationwide, not only for the acquisition and operation of buses but, more important, for the closing of usable school facilities and the construction of new facilities in attempts to minimize the amount of busing that would otherwise have been required.[41] It is hardly even true that our judges cannot levy taxes, for they now have successfully assumed the power to order that taxes be levied.[42]

The claim that the power of our judges is based on their "moral authority" or on a peculiar ability to discern and define "fundamental values and principles"[43] is either meaningless—mere mystical obfuscation—or incredible. Defenders of judicial review seem to forget that judges are not moral philosophers or persons selected because of unusual erudition or depth of ethical insight. They are lawyers who do not cease being lawyers by donning a robe, and the study and practice of law is hardly a process to be recommended for acquiring moral acuteness and fastidiousness. It would be difficult indeed to demonstrate from our history that our judges have been worthier exponents of values or ideals than our political leaders.[44] More important, the solution of a difficult problem of social choice does not depend on an ability to discern the fundamental value or principle involved. A problem is difficult not because a single basic value or principle is involved, but because more than one such value or principle is involved which cannot all be fully served at the same time. As Justice Oliver Wendell Holmes, one of the very few judges in our history who could claim the title of philosopher, pointed out, "All rights tend to declare themselves absolute to their logical extreme. Yet all in fact are limited by the neighborhood of principles of policy which are other than those on which the particular right is founded, and which become strong enough to hold their own when a certain point is reached."[45]

Freedom of speech, for example, is of extremely high value in a democracy and is properly considered a fundamental right, but that cannot mean that no restraint is permissible, that anything can be said anywhere at any time. There are other interests, such as public peace and good order, protection against slander, and the prevention of perjury, that are also extremely valuable and that must at some point be considered strong enough to hold their own; but there is no fundamental principle that tells us where that point is or should be located. To take another example, there is no fundamental principle that gives us the "correct" resolution of the conflicting interests involved in the problem of the extent to which government should accommodate the desire of some parents for prayer in the schools or for the education of their children in sectarian schools. These problems are not peculiar to the United States. They arise in many countries but what is peculiar to the United States is that we allow them to be answered by judges who have no special competence to do so and who have no basis for answering them except their personal biases. These questions are not answerable merely by logic or by factual knowledge any more than they are answerable by examination of the Constitution, which is why they should be answered by the collective will, wishes, and wisdom of the people, rather than by majority vote of a committee of lawyers or by any panel of "experts."

Far from being based on any supposed moral authority, the power of our judges can more accurately be said to be based on their relative freedom from the moral—as well as political—restraints applicable to other wielders of governmental power in a democracy. Indeed, because our judges are not constitutionally authorized to declare and put into effect their personal policy views, but are required to claim, as they invariably do, that they are merely enforcing the Constitution, the practice of judicial review is inherently inconsistent with openness and candor. To support their findings of unconstitutionality, judges are in effect required to demonstrate what cannot be demonstrated, and wide departures from ordinary standards of accurate statement and rational argument are the inevitable result. Especially in attempting to justify their decisions working basic social changes, judges typically write opinions that, as in *Bolling* v. *Sharpe,* can make no claim to intellectual coherence or respectability. Far from being exemplars of integrity and trustworthiness, our judges in fact pursue their ideological objectives by practices—misstatement of fact, patently fallacious reasoning, misreading of applicable statutes—that would rightly be considered intolerable if engaged in by other officials of government.

An understanding of the behavior of judges, and therefore of the nature and source of constitutional law, cannot be gained from generalities or abstract discussion, but only from detailed examination of the actual performance of judges in particular areas of constitutional law. Nothing serves this purpose better than examination of the Supreme Court's decisions on race and the schools.[46] By these decisions the Court converted *Brown's* prohibition of school racial segregation—a prohibition of racial discrimination by government—into a requirement of school racial integration—a requirement of racial discrimination by government—without admitting, and by always denying, that a change in the law had been made. Because a constitutional requirement of racial discrimination could not be justified, the Court continuously insisted, despite what it required in fact, that the only requirement continued to be compliance with *Brown.*

"[T]he fundamental principle" of *Brown,* the Court said, is "that racial discrimination in public schools is unconstitutional."[47] "[T]he Constitution of the United States, in its present form," the Court stated in *Bolling* v. *Sharpe,* decided with *Brown,* "forbids, so far as civil and political rights are concerned, discrimination by the General Government or by the States against any citizen because of his race."[48] The Court thereafter prohibited all racial discrimination by government, not just discrimination in education, by simply referring to *Brown.*[49] Although the Court—without precedent or legal justification—did not require immediate compliance with *Brown* or even set a definite limit on the time for compliance, but allowed the states to proceed "with all deliberate speed," Congress's enactment of the 1964 Civil Rights Act, which adopted the *Brown* prohibition of all racial discrimination by government, quickly brought to an end the assignment of children to schools according to race. The ending of racial discrimination in assignment of children to schools, as required by *Brown,* did not, however, result in the end of all school racial separation. Because of the existence of areas of residential racial concentration, the nonracial assignment of children to schools according to neighborhood often meant that school racial separation, though no longer complete or required by law, would continue to exist. This result proved deeply unsatisfying to many judges and others who had fought so long, so hard, and so successfully for the ending of racial discrimination by government, and the late 1960s and early 1970s were a time when all things seemed possible—especially to judges—given sufficient government coercion. In 1968, therefore, in *Green* v. *New Kent County*,[50] the Supreme Court, urged on by the Civil Rights Commission, the Department of Health, Education, and Welfare, and others, decided to move from *Brown's* prohibition of segregation to a very different and vastly more ambitious requirement of integration.

A requirement of integration, however, is a requirement of racial discrimination by government, a return to assignment according to race—though now to compel increased racial mixing instead of to compel complete separation—and that, everyone thought, had been prohibited by *Brown* and by the 1964 Civil Rights Act. Compulsory integration, a legal requirement of racial discrimination to increase racial mixing, is logically distinguishable from compulsory segregation, a legal requirement of racial discrimination to separate the races; and, the Constitution being what the Court says it is, the Court could have, in theory, announced that, although "the Constitution" prohibits the latter, it requires the former. Had the Court done this, its policy choice could certainly have been questioned on its merits, but at least the Court would have stated its requirement openly. But the power of even the Supreme Court is, of course, not absolute. As a practical matter, the Court could not, after years of emphatic insistence that all racial discrimination by government is constitutionally prohibited, suddenly announce in 1968 that some racial discrimination by government was now constitutionally required.

The Court, however, was determined to require integration and was unwilling to let this difficulty stand in its way. It therefore determined to achieve by deception what it could not achieve openly: to compel integration in fact, but to deny that it was doing so and claim that it was only continuing to enforce *Brown's* prohibition of segregation. Instead of openly stating that the Constitution simply requires school racial integration, the Court in *Green* required integration by what it ordered done, but stated that the requirement continued to be only "desegregation," as had been required by *Brown*. Although no distinction between "separation" and "segregation" (and, therefore, between a legal requirement of "integration" and a legal requirement of "desegregation") is ordinarily observed in common usage, the distinction is crucial to understanding the constitutional law of race and the schools.

The Court's insistence in *Green* and all later cases that the constitutional requirement is only "desegregation," that is, compliance with *Brown's* prohibition of all official racial discrimination, and not integration as such, that is, the ending of all school racial separation however caused, was essential to the Court's successful imposition of a requirement of integration in fact. First, it appeared in 1968 that a constitutional requirement of "desegregation" would necessarily be applicable only in the South, where there had been or was segregation; a simple requirement of integration would be applicable nationwide, to the racial separation that existed in the schools of the North and West as well as in the schools of the South. This served to minimize national attention and concern: it appeared that the Court was simply continuing to combat racial discrimination in the South; and the South, in the view of the North at the time, undoubtedly deserved whatever the Court was proposing to do to it. The effect was that of a divide-and-conquer strategy. The North's turn to be "desegregated" would eventually come, but only after the courts had done their worst in the South and the North could no longer look to it for sympathy and help—and even then it would come for only one city at a time in the North, since the requirement would not apply until findings of "segregation" and not merely of separation were made in each case.

Second, by purporting to require only "desegregation," the Court was able to deny that any significant change in the law had taken place and to claim that it was merely continuing to enforce *Brown's* prohibition of segregation and all official racial discrimination, which had by 1968 received almost universal acceptance. Third, by the same token, the Court was able to obviate all need to explain or justify compulsory integration either in terms of the Constitution or in terms of some good to be achieved. To this day the Court has not said one word about what it expects compulsory integration to accomplish in the way of improved education, improved race relations, or anything else; the Court simply continues to insist that it does *not* require integration as such, but only "desegregation," in compliance with *Brown.*

Fourth, by purporting to require only "desegregation," the Court made it appear that it required only what was required in any event by the 1964 Civil Rights Act, and thus was able to mask the fact that its actual requirement of integration is precisely what the Act explicitly and repeatedly states it does *not* require. The Act does indeed require desegregation, but, unlike the Court, it requires desegregation in fact as well as in name. The Act provides that "'[d]esegregation' means the assignment of students to public schools and within such schools without regard to their race," and, to prevent any possible misunderstanding, it repeats that "'desegregation' shall not mean the assignment of students to public schools in order to overcome racial imbalance." In a further manifestation of caution (insisted on by representatives of the South), the Act also states, "Nothing herein shall empower any official or court of the United States to issue any order seeking to achieve a racial balance in any school by requiring the transportation of pupils or students from one school to another. . . . " Finally, the Act states that "[n]othing in this title shall prohibit classification and assignment for reasons other than race. . . . "[51] Assignment of students "without regard to their race" is precisely the opposite of what "desegregation" means as actually applied by the Court.

The only difficulty with the Court's claim that it required only desegregation (and not integration as such) is that it was inconsistent—as each succeeding case made more clear—with what the Court required in fact. The integrity, trustworthiness, and moral authority of our judges may be judged by the Supreme Court's performance in the two most important of these cases: *Swann* v. *Charlotte-Mecklenburg*,[52] decided in 1971, the Court's first busing decision, and *Keyes* v. *School District No. 1, Denver*,[53] decided in 1973, which extended compulsory integration and busing outside the South. In *Swann* the Court, insisting as always that the requirement was only "desegregation," stated that its objective was to ensure that "school authorities exclude no pupil of a racial minority from any school, directly or indirectly, on account of race."

By prohibiting the assignment of children to neighborhood schools, however, when racial imbalance would result, what the Court ordered in fact was precisely the exclusion of pupils, minority as well as majority, from schools on account of their race. The Court imposed a requirement of racial exclusion with no other explanation than that all racial exclusion is prohibited, an "explanation" available only to a decision maker subject to no review.

Similarly, the Court stated in *Swann* that the purpose of the busing ordered was "to accomplish the transfer of Negro students out of formerly segregated Negro schools and transfer of White students to formerly all-Negro schools." In fact, however, most of the busing ordered did not involve "'formerly segregated Negro schools," but was for the purpose of transferring white students to, and black students from, schools that either had never been segregated—having been built after segregation had ended in Charlotte-Mecklenburg—or that had been white segregated schools which had become predominantly black as a result of the recent rapid growth in the black population.[54] As Justice Lewis Powell pointed out in his separate opinion in *Keyes*, the busing ordered in *Swann* could not be justified as desegregation because the school racial separation that existed in Charlotte-Mecklenburg in 1971 "did *not* result from historic, state-imposed *de jure* segregation" but resulted from residential patterns such as exist in all cities, including those that had never required segregation.[55]

The Court further stated in *Swann* that the busing ordered was justified because of district court findings, approved by the court of appeals, that "a dual [unconstitutionally segregated] school system had been maintained by the school authorities at least until 1969" and that "the school board had totally defaulted in its acknowledged duty to come forward with an acceptable ["desegregation"] plan of its own."

The fact, available to anyone taking the trouble to read the lower court opinions, is that no such findings were made. First, the dual school system ended in Charlotte-Mecklenburg no later than 1965; the district court so found at that time, and this finding was affirmed by the court of appeals in 1966.[56] Second, the district judge, unlike the Supreme Court, ingenuously stated that he ordered busing in Charlotte-Mecklenburg, not because the school board had failed to comply with *Brown*, but because "the rules of the game ha[d] changed," and because he believed that under the new rules, integration was required to improve black academic performance.[57] The Supreme Court, simply ignoring the district judge's actual basis of decision, said not a word about improving black educational performance. Third, far from finding that the school board had "totally defaulted," the district judge praised the board for its good faith and for maintaining an excellent school system;[58] and far from approving any such finding, the court of appeals was so complimentary to the board that two dissenting judges on the court criticized the majority for "implying that the actions of this Board had been exemplary."[59]

Finally, and surely the most reprehensible, is the Court's treatment in *Swann* of the 1964 Civil Rights Act. The Act defines "desegregation" as meaning the assignment of students to schools "without regard to their race" and as not meaning assignment "to overcome racial imbalance." Assignment according to race in order to overcome racial imbalance is exactly what the Supreme Court nonetheless ordered in *Swann*. The Court disposed of the Act with the statement that the Act's definition of "desegregation" was applicable only to the "*de facto* segregation*" of the North and was not applicable in the South where school racial separation had been explicitly required by law. This interpretation of the Act can most charitably be described as totally without basis in either the Act or its legislative history. The fact is that the Act's repeated insistence that it was meant to preclude all use of race in the assignment of children to schools was inserted at the insistence of representatives of the South for the purpose of protecting the school systems of the South.[60] Far from seeing a need in 1964 to prevent the Act from being misread as compelling integration in the North, Congress was of the view that no such integration requirement was possible, even if desired, because all racial discrimination in school assignment had been prohibited by *Brown*. As Senator Hubert Humphrey, the Senate floor manager and leading proponent of the Act, stated:

> [W]hile the Constitution prohibits segregation, it does not require integration. The busing of children to achieve racial balance would be an act to effect the integration of schools. In fact, if the bill were to compel it, it would be a violation, because it would be handling the matter on the basis of race and we would be transporting children because of race.[61]

The *Keyes* decision is an even clearer example of the Court's ability and willingness to misstate fact and defy logic. If, as the Court continued to state, the requirement was only to "desegregate," how, one might wonder, could it be applied to Denver, where segregation had always been prohibited by the Colorado constitution, and which had been in advance of even the federal government in prohibiting racial discrimination? As difficult as it is to believe, Denver was required to "desegregate" its schools, not because it had ever segregated them, but because it had made exceptional voluntary efforts to increase integration. In brief, after adopting a series of measures to increase school racial integration by such things as redrawing school attendance boundaries and the placement of new schools, the Denver school board decided to take the ultimate step of requiring busing to create majority-white schools in the heavily black Park Hill section of northeast Denver. This was going too far even for the people of Denver, who thereupon elected a new school board which rescinded the busing plan before it could be put into effect. On suit by proponents of the plan, the district court held the rescission unconstitutional. It found that the adoption and rescission of the plan converted the predominantly black schools of Park Hill from a status of constitutional "*de facto* segregation" to a status of unconstitutional "*de jure* segregation." According to the judge, steps to increase integration, even though not constitutionally required, may not, once voluntarily undertaken, constitutionally be discontinued. Because the rescinded plan was to apply to only Park Hill, however, and not to Denver's other predominantly black area, "the core area," the district judge held that the all-black or nearly all-black schools of that area had not become unconstitutionally (*"de jure"*) segregated and remained only "*de facto* segregated."[62]

The Supreme Court allowed plaintiffs to appeal the district judge's finding of no unconstitutional segregation in the core area, but did not allow the school board to appeal his finding of unconstitutional segregation in Park Hill. It was thus able to ignore the actual basis of the district judge's decision and to proceed on the assumption, plainly contrary to fact, that the district judge had found acts of racial discrimination by the board in Park Hill. The Court then held that the district judge could have found unconstitutional segregation in the core area, as well as in Park Hill, on the basis of either or both of two "presumptions." First, having supposedly found racially discriminatory acts by the board in Park Hill, the district judge should have presumed that the predominantly black schools in the core area were the result of other racially discriminatory acts by the board in that area. Second, the judge should have presumed that the schools in the core area were predominantly black as a result of the discriminatory acts by the board supposedly found in Park Hill. On the basis of these presumptions, the Court held, the district judge could order racial balance by busing in every school in Denver—"all-out desegregation"—which is what the district judge then did.

The factual and logical defects in the reasoning by which the Court ordered busing in Denver in the guise of enforcing *Brown* include: (1) the district judge had *not* found racial discrimination, and therefore unconstitutional segregation, in Park Hill except, as he explicitly stated, on the basis of his paradoxical rescission theory, which the Supreme Court did not accept and which, in a later case,[63] it held to be erroneous; (2) even if the board had committed acts of racial discrimination in Park Hill, those acts could not possibly have caused the

racial concentration in the core area schools, as those schools had become predominantly black long before the supposed discriminatory acts by the board in
Park Hill; (3) far from having racially discriminated to increase school racial
separation, the board had voluntarily done all it could to increase integration
and was in constitutional difficulty only because of those efforts; (4) there could
be no doubt, in any event, that the existence of predominantly black schools in
Denver—in both the core area and in Park Hill—was simply the result of the existence of black residential concentration, for which the board was not responsible
and over which it had no control.

All of this would have been unnecessary if the Court had been willing to
state simply and openly that the Constitution requires racially integrated or
"balanced" schools; it was necessary only because the Court wished to impose
that requirement in fact, but wished also to pretend, for reasons of political
prudence, that it was doing no more than requiring desegregation to enforce the
Brown prohibition of racial discrimination. It is clearly not the Court's "moral
authority," ability to define "fundamental values," or devotion to principle, but
its lack of moral scruples in pursuing its ends, that has made its busing orders
possible.

Other Theoretical Limits on the Power of Judges

Written Opinions

Swann and *Keyes* also illustrate how little merit there is to the argument made
by defenders of judicial review that the power of judges is restrained by a supposed requirement that they write opinions explaining and justifying their decisions in terms of legal principles. The fact is that Supreme Court justices, at least,
are not required to explain and justify their decisions any more than they choose
to do so. Furthermore, the convention that judges write opinions in their more
important cases obviously imposes no restraint on the judges if they are able and
willing, as in *Swann* and *Keyes,* to ignore and misrepresent the facts of the cases
before them and to assert the illogical or the impossible. Just as the Constitution
is what the Court says it is, a sufficient explanation of a decision is also what the
Court says it is. The rulings of judges are not any less effective or enforceable
when, as in *Swann* and *Keyes,* the accompanying opinions are based on grossly
inaccurate statements of fact and patently invalid reasoning. As the unusually
candid and able Justice Robert Jackson once pointed out, "We are not final because we are infallible, but we are infallible only because we are final."[64]

Constitutional Amendment

Many other factors are cited by defenders of judicial review as restraints on the
power of judges and, therefore as means of reconciling judicial power, at least to

some extent, with democracy. Most of these potential restraints unfortunately turn out on inspection to be more theoretical than real. The most obvious potential restraint is the possibility of adopting a constitutional amendment overturning an objectionable judicial decision or even, perhaps, abolishing judicial review itself. Surely, the argument goes, our judges must realize that they cannot go too far in defying the popular will, lest the people finally rise up and effectively curb their power by constitutional amendment. Given the extent to which the judges have in fact successfully and repeatedly defied the popular will, however, it is not easy to see what might constitute "going too far" in this context. If the Supreme Court's busing decisions, for example, which are opposed by an overwhelming majority of the people, bitterly resented by almost everyone they directly affect, and massively injurious to the social fabric—and much the same could be said of such other decisions as those undermining the enforcement of criminal law or those prohibiting exclusion of Communist party members from public school teaching[65] and even defense plant jobs[66]—do not go "too far," "too far" must be remote indeed.

The Constitution makes the amending process extremely difficult: the proposal of amendments requires the consent of two-thirds of both houses of Congress or an application to Congress by the legislatures of two-thirds of the states, and adoption requires ratification by the legislatures of three-quarters of the states. The amending process itself, therefore, is extremely undemocratic. This is not surprising in a document that is designed to create a fairly permanent structure of national government with limited powers, that does not expressly contemplate judicial review, and that contains very few restraints on the power of the people to govern themselves and to make basic social policy choices through their state governments. As indicated above, however, the situation drastically changed with the adoption of the Fourteenth Amendment and the Supreme Court's making of that Amendment an unlimited grant to itself of public policy-making power. The possibility of controling judicial power by constitutional amendment is made all the more unlikely by the scripturelike reverence with which the Constitution is regarded by all portions of the political spectrum and by the argument, invariably made in opposition to proposed amendments, that we should not "tinker with the Constitution." This argument simply ignores the fact that the Court "tinkers with the Constitution" whenever it sits, and amounts to a recommendation of total abdication of legislative power by elected representatives.

We should indeed be extremely reluctant to amend the Constitution to change the structure of government the Constitution created, or even to settle particular issues of public policy more or less permanently and nationwide; but we should have no reluctance to adopt amendments that merely deny judicial assertions of authority to settle those issues. For example, it would be one thing, and antidemocratic, to adopt a constitutional amendment resolving the abortion issue, one way or another, nationally—thereby taking from the people of the states the power to resolve it in different ways at different times. It would be a very different and prodemocratic thing to adopt an amendment rejecting our judges' assertion that they are authorized to resolve the issue.

Not more than four constitutional amendments have been adopted in response to judicial decisions, and not more than one or two of these can be seen as a successful assertion of popular sovereignty over judicial power. The clearest such case is the adoption of the Eleventh Amendment in 1798, overruling a Supreme Court decision that permitted private suits against the states. The fate of the Eleventh Amendment, however, illustrates a further limitation on the effectiveness of an amendment as a restraint on judicial power: once they become part of the Constitution, amendments, too, mean what the Supreme Court says they mean. The Supreme Court has virtually repealed the Eleventh Amendment by simply adopting the fiction that a suit against state officials for acts performed in their official capacity (the only way in which a state can act) is not necessarily a suit against the state, and therefore is not barred by the Eleventh Amendment.[67]

It is usually said that the Fourteenth Amendment, adopted in 1868, overruled the Supreme Court's *Dred Scott*[68] decision that Congress was without power to prevent the extension of slavery to new areas; but it might more realistically be said that the Civil War overruled that decision. The Sixteenth Amendment, adopted in 1913, overruled a Supreme Court decision invalidating a federal income tax, but the Court was by then probably prepared to overrule that decision itself. Finally, the Twenty-sixth Amendment overruled a Court decision that invalidated a federal statute insofar as the Amendment prohibited the states from denying the right to vote to persons eighteen years of age or over. However, the Court had itself created an impossible situation by upholding the same statute insofar as it required the states to permit voting by eighteen-year-olds in elections for federal office.[69]

Justice Felix Frankfurter, during his many years on the Court, was noted for his frequently expressed view that judges should exercise self-restraint lest they finally be found to have gone "too far"; Justice William Douglas, during his even more years on the Court, was noted for the opposite view. Experience proves that Justice Douglas was right: The judges have nothing to fear from constitutional amendment, and they know it.[70]

"Case or Controversy"

Another supposed limitation on the power of judges is that they can do no more than decide actual "cases or controversies" brought to them by others and can initiate nothing themselves. Even Justice Douglas could not simply get out of bed in the morning and ask what evil remained in the world for him to correct that day; he had to wait for someone to challenge the alleged evil in the form of a lawsuit. He rarely had to wait very long, however. As de Tocqueville noted early in the nineteenth century, few questions of social policy did not, even then, in this peculiarly legalistic and litigious country, get brought to the Supreme Court for decision in the guise of a constitutional question.[71] Tocqueville's observation became even more accurate in this century with the creation of professional litigating institutions, such as the NAACP Legal Defense Fund and the American Civil Liberties Union, which seek to implement through the courts policy views they could never implement through the ballot box. It is probably only a small exaggeration to say that there is no policy so inconsistent with the possibility of a harmonious society that some such organization has not urged or considered urging its adoption by some judge.

Legislative Control of Jurisdiction

A potentially important and valuable means for limiting judicial power is the power of Congress, explicitly granted in the Constitution, to limit the appellate jurisdiction of the Supreme Court. The Constitution provides that the Supreme Court can exercise appellate jurisdiction only "with such Exceptions, and under such Regulations as the Congress shall make,"[72] and all other federal courts exist only by virtue of federal statute. It would seem therefore that Congress could, by ordinary statute, limit or eliminate most of the Supreme Court's power and all lower federal court power. A major difficulty, however, is that the constitutionality of any such statute would be for the courts themselves to decide, and they can be expected to give it a most hostile reception. There is also the very serious practical difficulty that Congress is most anxious to retain unweakened federal courts for the purpose of having uniform nationwide enforcement of the ever-increasing body of federal law. In any event, all of the many proposals to limit the Supreme Court's power by this means have failed of adoption, with the single exception of a relatively minor statute enacted during Reconstruction.[73]

Impeachment

Theoretically, judges can be removed from office by impeachment. The grounds for impeachment, Representative Gerald Ford said in urging the impeachment of Justice Douglas, are what Congress says they are, which is true—except, of course, that the judges may say otherwise. Again, the purely theoretical nature of this restraint is indicated by the fact that it has never successfully been employed. No Supreme Court justice has ever been impeached and convicted, and the very few impeachments of lower federal court judges have been only for violation of criminal laws or for demonstrated physical or mental incapacity. President Jefferson sought to impeach Supreme Court Justice Samuel Chase for abuse of his judicial office and as a first step to breaking the stranglehold the Federalists, who had been defeated at the polls, still maintained over the judiciary. Jefferson's effort to obtain the required two-thirds vote of the Senate failed, after a trial presided over by Chief Justice John Marshall. Jefferson concluded that the threat of impeachment of judges is a "farce," and "not even a scare-crow."[74] There is no legal or constitutional reason that judges cannot or should not be impeached for demonstrable usurpations of legislative power or blatant bad faith in performance of the judicial function, but the failure of the effort to impeach even Justice Douglas, probably the most radical and unjudicial member of the Supreme Court in our history, seems to demonstrate conclusively that the threat of impeachment remains "not even a scare-crow." Judges have simply been too successful in inculcating the myth that an attack on them is an attack on the Constitution.

Appointment of Judges

Presidents, of course, appoint federal judges, with the advice and consent of the Senate, and attempt thereby to affect what courts do. Indeed, there may be no better reason today for participating in the election of presidents and senators than the hope of affecting the selection of the judges who will make the law. The hope, however, is a slim one. Presidents have been notoriously unsuccessful in changing the course of judicial decision through their appointments, and have frequently been bitterly disappointed in the performance of their appointees, who, after acquisition of lifetime tenure and acclimation to the exhilaration of power, often seem to become different persons.[75] Nothing better illustrates this than the fact that President Nixon, who made the curbing of judicial power a major part of his program, and who was exceptionally fortunate in having four Supreme Court appointments to make during his first term, nonetheless produced a Court that gave us the busing and abortion decisions, two of the most extraordinary assertions of judicial power in our history.

President Franklin Roosevelt, less fortunate than President Nixon in this regard, made no appointments in his first term. He therefore sought to prevent the Court from invalidating his New Deal program by attempting to have Congress create additional seats on the Court to which he could then appoint presumably sympathetic justices. The aura of sanctity surrounding the Court, however—it is not in vain that the justices wear robes and sit in a temple—was such that President Roosevelt, riding a wave of unprecedented popularity and enjoying the almost total acquiescence of Congress in his program, met his first defeat. Although his proposal was of unquestionable constitutionality—in our history the number of Supreme Court seats has varied between six and ten—it was rejected by Congress as an "utterly injurious abandonment of constitutional principle." Although it was an extremely mild attempt, in a time of desperation, to prevent the frustration of an urgent and overwhelming popular will by five or six men, it was denounced by Congress as "violat[ing] every sacred tradition of American democracy."[76] Jefferson and Madison would have been amazed to learn what "American democracy" had come to mean.

Judicial Review and Democracy

The central problem of government is the reconciliation of order and freedom. In the phrase of Justice Benjamin Cardozo, the need is for "a scheme of ordered liberty." Creation and maintenance of an effective and productive society—a society in which life is other than, as Hobbes put it, "nasty, brutish, and short"— requires, unfortunately, a structure of legalized coercion, the granting to some individuals of power over the behavior of others. The problem is to create a structure of government that grants the power needed for the common good and yet confines its exercise to this need. The beginning of wisdom is acceptance of the fact that no structure of government can be devised that will guarantee that governmental power will not be misused. All government is government of men and not of laws, because laws do not enforce themselves; and all men are subject to mistake and the temptation to serve immediate self-interest. Democracy—self-government—certainly provides no such guarantee, and thus is born the search for limits on or alternatives to democracy, for governors better, wiser, and more trustworthy than ourselves. History and an understanding of human nature indicate that the search is futile, that our best hope is to take our chances with one another. All that can be said for democracy, Winston Churchill once pointed out, it that it is better than its alternatives—but that is all that can be said for most things.

Judicial review is generally defended as a structural device to limit the power of government in the interest of the individual. All it does or can do, however, is limit the power of legislators by transferring power to judges, who are also officials of government. The question is, therefore, what reason is there to trust judges, who are not subject to the restraints of the ballot, more than legislators, who are subject to that restraint? All arguments for judicial review are based on distrust of democracy, on the belief that "someone somewhere must oversee and protect the people from themselves . . . the classic line of antidemocrats from time immemorial."[77] To the extent that judges have the power to govern and to make basic policy decisions, elected representatives of the people do not.

To say that judicial review and democracy are necessarily inconsistent is not, however, to say that they are mutually exclusive; both are matters of degree and therefore can exist together in almost any mix. A system is democratic to the degree that public policy decisions are subject to popular control, and is a system of government by judges to the degree that such decisions are made by judges and the judges are removed from popular control. To be opposed to judicial review as it now exists is not necessarily to be opposed to all judicial review. Only a small degree of distrust of democracy is required to favor a system of judicial review in which judges are authorized to invalidate the acts of elected representatives pursuant to fairly definite and specific constitutional provisions, and in which the judges' decisions can be more or less readily overturned by constitutional amendment or by legislation reaffirming the validity of the invalidated act; but an almost total distrust of democracy is required to favor the system of judicial review that has now developed in this country.

Changed Meaning of "Judicial Review"

It is often said in favor of judicial review, in an appeal to sound conservative instincts, that it has been with us from the beginning. This is in a sense true; but "judicial review" has meant very different things at different times, and it is only in very recent times that it has meant anything like the degree of power our judges now possess.[78] Surely the first thing to be noted about judicial review, the power of judges to invalidate the acts of other government officials on the basis of the Constitution, is, as Karl Llewellyn noted, that it is not itself explicitly provided for in the Constitution. It is simply not credible that the framers of a charter of representative self-government could have meant to grant judges the power of final decision on questions of public policy—a power with no precedent in the history of government—without setting it forth in unmistakable terms. Furthermore, the Constitution is on its face unsuited as a basis for judicial review: its many generalities are entirely appropriate as guides to legislators and the electorate, but they are entirely inappropriate for enforcement by judges as a legal code.

An ill-defined power of judicial review was obliquely referred to by some delegates to the Constitutional Convention and was discussed during the ratification debates; but even these remarks clearly contemplated no more than a power to refuse to enforce legislation that is in unmistakable conflict with a specific constitutional provision—a power the exercise of which would require no more than the ability to read and understand English. Delegate Elbridge Gerry, for example, thought that such a power would not enable judges to pass on "the policy of public measures," and Alexander Hamilton thought that judges would be able to "take no active resolution whatever."[79] The continuing debate on the intent of the framers on this issue is, therefore, quite beside the point for present purposes; whatever the framers intended regarding judicial review, they clearly did not intend judges to have policymaking power.

The power of judicial review had a most inauspicious beginning. The authority of judges to question the constitutional validity of duly enacted legislation and to declare invalid legislation found to be inconsistent with the Constitution was first asserted and exercised by the Supreme Court in 1803 in the famous case of *Marbury* v. *Madison.*[80] It was asserted on the basis of arguments that almost everyone now agrees are themselves invalid.[81] It was argued, for instance, that it would be absurd to have a written Constitution without such judicial authority, when in fact many nations had written constitutions and none recognized such an authority. Although Marshall's arguments for judicial review have been shown to be invalid or insufficient, the power of judicial review continues to exist, causing the decision to be compared to the grinning Cheshire cat that gradually disappeared until only the grin remained.[82]

Whatever the validity of Marshall's arguments in *Marbury* for the power of judicial review, his examples of its possible applications indicate a power of extremely limited scope. Marshall gave as examples of laws the Court could hold unconstitutional a law permitting conviction for treason on the basis of the testimony of one witness despite the explicit constitutional requirement of "the Testimony of two Witnesses,"[83] and a law taxing exports from a state despite the specific constitutional provision that "No Tax or Duty shall be laid on Articles exported from any State."[84] Such a power of judicial review, limited to judicial enforcement of definite, specific constitutional provisions, would constitute only a very limited intrusion on democracy, the intrusion inherent in any constitutional provision that restrains the policy choices of a current majority. It would not involve policymaking by judges, and there would be almost no occasion for its exercise because such laws are almost never enacted. Elected representatives, as well as judges, are members of this society, and the great majority of them, at least, are no less devoted than judges to its basic principles and values.

It may be noted in passing that Marshall reached his conclusion that the statutory provision supposedly involved in *Marbury* was unconstitutional by first finding in the statute something that was not there, and then finding a logical inconsistency with the Constitution that did not exist.[85] He was careful to do this in a case in which his ultimate decision would be for the defendant Madison, that is, for the Jefferson administration then in power, thereby avoiding the need to issue any order against the administration, which, as he knew, Jefferson would almost surely have ignored. As the eminent philosopher Morris Raphael Cohen put it, "Possibly the clearest instance of the logical and historical absurdity of a decision declaring an act of Congress unconstitutional was the case of *Marbury* v. *Madison,* which lawyers have, for over a century, worshiped with blind piety."[86] Marshall never again undertook to invalidate federal legislation during his remaining thirty-two years as chief justice. There is no serious dispute today that the *Marbury* decision was no more than a political maneuver by members of the defeated party to retain through the courts an influence they had lost at the polls.

The power asserted by the Court in *Marbury* in 1803 was not exercised again by the Court to invalidate federal legislation for over fifty years, until

1857, when, in the infamous *Dred Scott* decision,[87] the Court held that Congress was without authority to legislate on the slavery issue, and thereby helped bring on the Civil War. During this period the power was exercised against state legislation in only a small number of cases, and then usually only to prevent state intrusion on federal legislative power. After the Civil War, the power was exercised in the almost equally infamous *Civil Rights Cases*[88] of 1883, in which the Court held that Congress was without power to prohibit racial discrimination by railroads, inns, and other places of public accommodation.

The power began to assume something like its present form in the late nineteenth century and the first decades of the twentieth, when the Court discovered in the "due process" clauses of the Fourteenth and Fifth Amendments authority to invalidate state and federal legislation (primarily regulations of economic and business affairs) that it considered unreasonable. The Court invalidated minimum wage and maximum hour legislation, price controls, legislation protecting labor unions, and legislation restricting child labor.[89] This era in the history of judicial review, which ended in the late 1930s, is now almost uniformly deplored by constitutional scholars; virtually now all agree that the Court had no constitutional basis for doing what it did. This conclusion is undoubtedly correct, despite the fact that the interests the Court was then favoring—state autonomy, ownership of private property, freedom of contract—are not without protection in the Constitution. Most of the Court's major decisions of the past twenty-five years, which most of the same scholars now undertake to justify, have even less basis in the Constitution.

The modern era of judicial review began with *Brown v. Board of Education* in 1954. The race issue has always been America's most intractable, and the politics of race have been the most aberrational. If undemocratic, revolutionary, anticonstitutional means can ever be justified in this country as a means of resolving an issue, they surely can be on this issue. The Court's previous efforts on the issue, however, as in *Dred Scott* and the *Civil Rights Cases,* gave little ground for confidence that further intervention was likely to be of help. What is unfortunate is not that the Court decided *Brown* as it did, but, as prior history showed, that it was permitted and expected to decide such an issue. Assuming that the issue was to be decided by the Court, the best justification for *Brown* is that a decision the other way, refusing to prohibit segregation, would not simply have left the status quo undisturbed. It would have been seen, mistakenly but inevitably, as constitutional, and even moral, approval of segregation; and it would, therefore, have been a victory for the forces of racial discrimination that by 1954 were everywhere else being defeated.

As a result of Hitler and World War II, racism had lost all defensibility and respectability, and racial discrimination was gradually being eliminated in American life. President Truman, for example, had ended segregation in the armed forces; the federal government had ceased requiring or encouraging segregation in federally subsidized housing; and Jackie Robinson had broken the color line in the national sport.[90] The Court, therefore, could and did base the *Brown* decision on the clear, simple principle that government may not deal with any individual on the basis of his race, which, even if not a constitutional principle, was one that few could very much longer openly or persuasively dispute. Indeed, it is hardly possible to disapprove of the *Brown* decision except on the ground of the great danger inherent in having a decision of such magnitude made by a group so removed from popular control, a danger that subsequent events have shown to be all too real.

That the Court issued the *Brown* decision with great trepidation and caution is shown by the facts that it did not demand immediate compliance or even set a definite time for compliance and that the Court thereafter withdrew from the field for ten years. It is possible to argue, indeed, considering that racial discrimination was already crumbling on all fronts, that the end of segregation and all other racial discrimination by government would not have been much longer delayed if the Court had not decided *Brown*. The eventual triumph of the *Brown* decision, after its principle received the support of Congress in the 1964 Civil Rights Act, worked a basic change, however, in the perception of the role and power of judges in our system of government. As Alexander Bickel stated a decade ago:

> *Brown* v. *Board of Education* was the beginning. Subsequently, the Court declared Bible reading and all other religious exercises in public schools unconstitutional; it ordered the reapportionment of the national House of Representatives, of both houses of state legislatures, and of local government bodies on a one-man, one-vote basis; it reformed numerous aspects of state and federal criminal procedure, significantly enhancing the rights of the accused, . . . and it laid down a whole set of new rules governing . . . , in effect, the conduct of police throughout the country toward persons arrested on suspicion of crime.
>
> The Court also—needless to say, this listing is not comprehensive—enlarged its own jurisdiction to hear cases challenging federal expenditures . . . and introduced a striking degree of permissiveness into the regulation—what is left of it—by state and federal authorities of material alleged to be obscene. In addition, the Court limited the power of state and federal government to forbid the use of birth-control devices, to restrict travel, to expatriate naturalized or native-born citizens, to deny employment to persons whose associations are deemed subversive, and to apply the laws of libel.[91]

In short, the prime importance of *Brown* is that it gave a new meaning to judicial review. If the Court could bring about this revolution, it came to be thought by judges and others, what revolutions could it not bring about? What need was there for proponents of basic social change to undergo the delays and uncertainties of the democratic political process? Judges came to be seen as forces for moral enlightenment and engines of progress, whose public policy choices were obviously much to be preferred to those of mere politicians beholden to a multitude of private interests. Whatever might be said for judicial review prior to *Brown*—and it had on the whole almost surely been more harmful than helpful[92]—it took on a very different meaning with *Brown*. The enhanced status, prestige, and self-esteem of the judges enabled them to withdraw any social issue from the political process and settle it according to their own views. The possibility of an effective external restraint on the judges had been largely removed, and there was no longer any recognition of a need for self-restraint.

Sources of Support for Judicial Review

How can so massive a negation of democracy, so total a transferral of lawmaking power to judges be permitted to continue in a nation supposedly still devoted to the principles of self-government? Can it be that we as a nation have in fact lost faith in self-government—that is, in ourselves and in one another—and now prefer to be governed by unelected officials holding office for life? Even if this is so, of course, it does not make our present system democratic, any more than a monarchy would be democratic if the king-for-life was once elected by the people or appointed by persons who were themselves elected. Can it really be, after all the judges have done, that the people are still fooled by the myth that the judges do no more than interpret the Constitution? The question is a difficult one, but it remains a fact that the defenders of judicial review and the judges themselves still very rarely attempt to defend government by judges on its own merits,[93] but continue to insist, instead, regardless of how untenable the insistence has become, that all our judges have done and do is in some sense— often an extremely mystical one—derived from the Constitution. There can be little doubt that most Americans, under the influence of this constant insistence, do continue to hold quasi-theological beliefs concerning the Constitution and the nature and source of constitutional law. Most undoubtedly believe the judges can and do make mistakes in "interpreting the Constitution." The judges and their defenders have succeeded, however, in preventing general recognition of the facts that no question of constitutional interpretation—or, for that matter, of discovering fundamental values or principles—is involved in most constitutional decisions, and that these decisions have no basis other than the policy preferences of the judges, the policy preferences, ultimately, of a majority of the nine lawyers who constitute the Supreme Court.

Much of the strength of judicial review derives from the support it receives from academics and other intellectuals. It is easy enough for academics, particularly "social scientists," and other professional thinkers to believe that social policy would be better made if left in their hands rather than in the hands of "the masses." They believe that unelected judges, who are also graduate school products and live primarily in a world of words, are more likely to be similar to themselves in outlook, or at least more subject to their influence, than is the ordinary citizen or the persons he is likely to choose at elections.[94] The more the judges base their decisions on the latest sociological theory, as they have increasingly been doing since *Brown,* the more important are the sociologists. Constitutional law professors, a fraternity of the most ardent and effective supporters of judicial review and protectors of judges from adverse political action, gain even more directly by having constitutional law continue to be the nation's most important subject. Much of the course of judicial decision over the last twenty-five years can be seen as a triumph of intellectual, doctrinaire ideology over such "simple-minded" notions, values, and traditions of the ordinary citizen as that there is such a thing as obscenity, that religion and patriotism are good, that parents should control the lives of their children, that crime is deterred by and deserves punishment, and that men (and women) are not in fact equal in talent and initiative.

The strength of judicial review undoubtedly also derives in part from the undying but forlorn human hope of somehow relieving ourselves of the difficulties and uncertainties of decision making on basic questions of public policy by finding persons of exceptional wisdom and goodness to whom the responsibility can be entrusted. No more should be necessary to curb the present-day power of judicial review than the realization that we have not found such persons in our judges. As the *Swann* and *Keyes* decisions show, for example, Lord Acton's dictum that power corrupts applies no less to judges than to others. Power corrupts, not because it changes good intentions to bad—the intentions of our judges have been and are of the best—but because it distorts perspective, creates an illusion of unlimited personal wisdom and goodness, and instills a conviction that the moral and legal restraints properly applied to others do not apply to oneself. As Thomas Jefferson, our most fervent believer in democracy, constantly insisted, "Our judges are as honest as other men, and not more so. They have, with others, the same passions for party, for power, and the privilege of their corps . . . and their power is the more dangerous as they are in office for life, and not responsible, as the other functionaries are, to the elective control."[95] And as the prescient de Tocqueville warned more than a century ago:

> The President, who exercises a limited power, may err without causing great mischief in the state. Congress may decide amiss without destroying the Union, because the electoral body in which Congress originated may cause it to retract its decision by changing its members. But if the Supreme Court is ever composed of imprudent or bad men, the Union may be plunged into anarchy or civil war.[96]

Means of Improving the Present System

If it is a system of government by philosopher-kings—such as Plato favored—that we in fact now want, we should, at the very least, seek a more effective and appropriate method of achieving it than the present method of judicial review. Most obviously, we should improve the method of selecting our philosophers. We should not confine our search for persons of unusual wisdom, goodness, and intellectual attainment to the products of law schools and law offices, for that produces only lawyer-kings. Next, we should provide our philosopher-kings with whatever personnel, equipment, and other resources that may be helpful to the performance of their task. We should allow them, for example, to conduct or commission such studies or experiments as may provide data relevant to the issues they must decide; we should permit and encourage their open communication with other philosophers or other relevant experts; and we should give them full control over the order in which issues should be considered and decided. We should not, as at present, confine their source of information almost exclusively to the presentations made by two lawyers or teams of lawyers, each with a strong personal interest in a diametrically opposed result and each skilled more in methods of rhetoric than in methods of analysis.

Most important, we should not require or permit our philosopher-kings to pretend to be doing something they are not, such as "interpreting the Constitution." To require this is to require an activity and provide a spectacle no more useful or enobling than to require them to pretend to read the entrails of birds. The need to engage in this pretense, if taken at all seriously, as it sometimes is by some judges, can lead to bizarre results favored by no one, such as requiring the busing of children for "racial balance"—the real purpose of which is to create majority white schools—in a school district that is already majority black.[97] Abandonment of the pretense would allow and encourage the philosophers to identify and consider, openly and realistically, the actual conflicting interests that give rise to the issues to be decided and to state the real grounds for their decisions in terms that may persuade others to accept those decisions and that may prove helpful to later philosophers in deciding similar issues.

One may hope, of course, that a system of rule by philosopher-kings is not, however, what the people of this country now want and that, once it is seen for what it is, the clandestine form of that system we have now achieved through judicial review will be eliminated or limited rather than improved. One may hope that we will return to a faith in self-government, to a recognition that our best hope for freedom, security, and prosperity lies not in government by lawyer-judges pretending to mine the words "due process" and "equal protection," but in acceptance of the fact that we are in each other's hands.

Notes

1. See, for example, Justice William Douglas's dissenting opinions in *Holmes v. United States,* 391 U.S. 936 (1968); *Hart v. United States,* 391 U.S. 956 (1968); *McArthur v. Clifford,* 393 U.S. 1002 (1968).

2. *Roe v. Wade,* 410 U.S. 113 (1973); *Doe v. Bolton,* 410 U.S. 179 (1973).

3. *Swann v. Charlotte-Mecklenburg Board of Education,* 402 U.S. 1 (1971).

4. For example, *Memoirs v. Massachusetts,* 383 U.S. 413 (1966); *Stanley v. Georgia,* 394 U.S. 557 (1969); *Miller v. California,* 413 U.S. 15 (1973); *Jenkins v. Georgia,* 418 U.S. 153 (1974).

5. *Griswold v. Connecticut,* 381 U.S. 479 (1965); *Eisenstadt v. Baird,* 405 U.S. 438 (1972).

6. For example, *Levy v. Louisiana,* 391 U.S. 68 (1968); *Trimble v. Gordon,* 430 U.S. 762 (1977).

7. For example, *Street v. New York,* 394 U.S. 576 (1969); *Spence v. Washington,* 418 U.S. 405 (1974).

8. For example, *Baggett v. Bullitt,* 377 U.S. 360 (1964); *Keyishian v. Board of Regents,* 384 U.S. 589 (1967).

9. For example, *Gregory v. Chicago,* 394 U.S. 111 (1969) (demonstrations); *Papachristou v. City of Jacksonville,* 405 U.S. 156 (1972) (vagrancy); *Rosenfeld v. New Jersey,* 408 U.S. 901 (1972) (indecent language).

10. *National Socialist Party v. Skokie,* 432 U.S. 43 (1977) (Nazis); *Cohen v. California,* 403 U.S. 15 (1971) (vulgarity).

11. For example, *Committee for Public Education v. Nyquist,* 413 U.S. 756 (1973) (financial aid); *Engle v. Vitale,* 370 U.S. 421 (1962) (prayer); *Abington School District v. Cohen,* 374 U.S. 203 (1963) (Bible reading).

12. For example, *Brewer v. Williams,* 430 U.S. 387 (1977).

13. For example, *Fay v. Noia,* 372 U.S. 391 (1963) (begin again); *Douglas v. California,* 372 U.S. 353 (1963) (costs of appeal); *Gideon v. Wainwright,* 372 U.S. 385 (1963) (attorney's fees).

14. Rebecca West, *The New Meaning of Treason,* as quoted in Allen Weinstein, *Perjury* (New York: Knopf, 1978), p. 159.

15. *United States v. Butler,* 297 U.S. 1 (1936).

16. Max Freedman, *Roosevelt and Frankfurter* (Boston: Little, Brown, 1967), p. 383.

17. As quoted in William B. Lockhart, Yale Kamisar, and Jesse H. Choper, *Constitutional Law,* 4th ed. (St. Paul: West, 1975), p. 1.

18. Ibid., p. 7.

19. Thomas Powell, "The Logic and Rhetoric of Constitutional Law," *Journal of Philosophy* 15 (November 1918):648–649.

20. Karl N. Llewellyn, "The Constitution as an Institution," *Columbia Law Review* 34 (January 1934): pp. 3–4.

21. Ibid., pp. 4–5.

22. *Cumming v. Richmond County Board of Education,* 175 U.S. 528 (1899).

23. *Brown v. Board of Education,* 347 U.S. 483 (1954).

24. *Green v. County School Board of New Kent County,* 391 U.S. 430 (1968).

25. 347 U.S. 483 (1954).

26. "No State shall . . . deny to any person within its jurisdiction the equal protection of the laws." U.S. Constitution, Amendment XIV.

27. "The right of citizens of the Unived States to vote shall not be denied or abridged by the United States or by any State on account of race, color or previous condition of servitude." U.S. Constitution, Amendment XV.

28. See Lino Graglia, *Disaster by Decree: The Supreme Court's Decisions on Race and Schools* (Ithaca: Cornell University Press, 1976), p. 21.

29. *Gong Lum. v. Rice,* 275 U.S. 78 (1927).

30. 347 U.S. 497 (1954).

31. "No person shall . . . be deprived of life, liberty, or property, without due process of law." U.S. Constitution, Amendment V.

32. U.S. Constitution, Article IV, Section 2.

33. For example, *Furman v. Georgia,* 408 U.S. 238 (1972); U.S. Constitution, Amendment V ("capital" crime, "jeopardy of life," "deprived of life"), Amendment XIV ("deprived of life").

34. See Raoul Berger, *Government by Judiciary: The Transformation of the Fourteenth Amendment* (Cambridge: Harvard University Press, 1977), pp. 166-220.

35. See Clifton McCleskey, "Judicial Review in a Democracy: A Dissenting Opinion," *Houston Law Review* 3 (Fall 1966):359, a concise and devastating rebuttal of standard rationalizations for judicial review.

36. Quoted in Herbert Jacob, *Justice in America: Courts, Lawyers, and the Judicial Process,* 2d ed. (Boston: Little, Brown, 1972), p. 214.

37. See Walter F. Murphy, *Elements of Judicial Strategy* (Chicago: University of Chicago Press, 1964), p. 27.

38. See *Cooper v. Aaron,* 358 U.S. 1 (1958).

39. See Graglia, *Disaster by Decree,* chap. 11.

40. See Donald L. Horowitz, *The Courts and Social Policy* (Washington: The Brookings Institution, 1977); Nathan Glazer, "Should Judges Administer Social Services?" *The Public Interest* 50 (Winter 1978):64-80.

41. See Graglia, *Disaster by Decree,* pp. 264-265.

42. *Griffin v. County School Board of Prince Georges County,* 377 U.S. 218 (1964).

43. See, for example, Alexander M. Bickel, *The Least Dangerous Branch: The Supreme Court at the Bar of Politics* (Indianapolis: Bobbs-Merrill, 1962), p. 109: The Supreme Court "is charged with the evolution and application of society's fundamental principles." But see Alexander M. Bickel, *The Supreme Court and the Idea of Progress,* (New York: Harper and Row, 1970), and John Hart Ely, "Foreword: On Discovering Fundamental Values," *Harvard Law Review* 92 (November 1978):pp. 5-55.

44. McCleskey, "Judicial Review in a Democracy," p. 360.

45. *Hudson County Water Co. v. McCarter,* 209 U.S. 349, 355 (1908).

46. For a fully detailed discussion of each of these decisions from *Brown* to 1974, see Graglia, *Disaster by Decree.*

47. 349 U.S. 294 (1955) (decision on the decree).

48. 347 U.S. 497 (1954).

49. See, for example, *Mayor of Baltimore v. Dawson,* 350 U.S. 877 (1955) (beaches); *Gayle v. Browder* 352 U.S. 903 (1956) (buses).

50. 391 U.S. 430 (1968).

51. 42 U.S.C. sections 2.2000(b), 2000c-6(A), 2000c-9.

52. 402 U.S. 1 (1971).

53. 413 U.S. 189 (1973).

54. See Graglia, *Disaster by Decree,* pp. 125-126.

55. 413 U.S. 222-223.

56. 243 F.Supp. 667 (W.D.N.C., 1965), affirmed 369 F.2d 29 (4th Cir. 1966).

57. 300 F.Supp. 1360 (1969).

58. Ibid., p. 1372.

59. 431 F. 2d 138, 154, Note 9.

60. See Graglia, *Disaster by Decree,* pp. 46-52.

61. *Congressional Record* 110 (June 4, 1964), p. 12717.

62. 313 F. Supp. 61, 75 (D. Colo. 1970).

63. *Dayton Board of Education v. Brinkman,* 433 U.S. 406 (1977).

64. *Brown v. Allen,* 244 U.S. 443, 540 (1933) (concurring opinion).

65. For example, *Keyishian v. Board of Regents,* 385 U.S. 589 (1967).

66. *United States v. Robel,* 389 U.S. 258 (1967).

67. *Ex parte Young,* 209 U.S. 123 (1908).

68. *Dred Scott v. Sandford,* 19 Howard 393 (1857).

69. *Oregon v. Mitchell,* 400 U.S. 112 (1970).

70. See Ely, "On Discovering Fundamental Values," pp. 21-22.

71. Alexis de Tocqueville, *Democracy in America,* ed. Phillips Bradley (New York: Knopf, 1945), p. 280.

72. U.S. Constitution, Article III, Section 2.

73. *Ex parte McCardle,* 7 Wallace 506 (1869).

74. Quoted in Gerald Gunther and Noel T. Dowling, *Constitutional Law,* 8th ed. (Mineola, N.Y.: Foundation Press, 1970), p. 13.

75. See Ely, "On Discovering Fundamental Values."

76. Senate Judiciary Committee Report, June 14, 1937, quoted in Gunther and Dowling, *Constitutional Law,* p. 170.

77. McCleskey, "Judicial Review in a Democracy," p. 359.

78. See William Nelson, "Changing Conceptions of Judicial Review: The Evolution of Constitutional Theory in the United States, 1790-1860," *University of Pennsylvania Law Review* 120 (June 1972):1166-1185.

79. Max Farrand, *Records of the Constitutional Convention of 1787,* (New Haven: Yale University Press, 1911); Alexander Hamilton, James Madison, John Jay, *The Federalist,* ed. Jacob Cooke (Middletown, Conn.: Wesleyan University Press, 1961), No. 78 (Hamilton).

80. 1 Cranch 137 (1803).

81. See, for example, William Van Alstyne, "A Critical Guide to *Marbury v. Madison,*" *Duke Law Journal* (January 1969):1–47; Morris R. Cohen, *The Faith of a Liberal* (New York: Holt, 1946), pp. 182–186.

82. See, for example, Bickel, *The Least Dangerous Branch,* chap. 1.

83. U.S. Constitution, Article III, Section 2.

84. U.S. Constitution, Article I, Section 9.

85. See, for example, Van Alstyne, "A Critical Guide to *Marbury v. Madison;*" and Cohen, *The Faith of a Liberal,* pp. 178–181.

86. Cohen, *The Faith of a Liberal,* p. 178.

87. *Dred Scott v. Sandford,* 19 Howard 393 (1857).

88. 109 U.S. 3 (1883).

89. See Lockhart et al., *Constitutional Law,* pp. 527–529.

90. See, for example, Richard Bardolph, *The Civil Rights Record* (New York: Crowell, 1970), part 5.

91. Bickel, *The Supreme Court and the Idea of Progress,* pp. 7–8 (citations omitted).

92. See Cohen, *The Faith of a Liberal,* p. 186.

93. But see Arthur S. Miller, "In Defense of Judicial Activism," chap. 7, this volume.

94. See Ely, "On Discovering Fundamental Values," p. 17.

95. Jefferson to William C. Jarvis, September 28, 1820.

96. Tocqueville, *Democracy in América.*

97. *Milliken v. Bradley,* 418 U.S. 717 (1974); see Graglia, *Disaster by Decree,* chap. 10.

7 In Defense of Judicial Activism

Arthur S. Miller

" 'Judicial activism' is a slippery term"—Robert G. McCloskey[1]

Introduction

Is there a case to be made for judicial activism? No answer can come until the term is defined.[2] Of course it is slippery, as Robert McCloskey said, but it does have some meaning. To him one of its aspects was "the Supreme Court's propensity to intervene in the governing process."[3] Under that definition, obviously in need of greater specificity, the answer is a definite yes: judicial activism is not only defensible, it may be indispensable to the American system of constitutionalism. "The two fundamental correlative elements of constitutionalism . . . ," Charles McIlwain said, "are the legal limits to arbitrary power and a complete political responsibility of government to the governed."[4]

Without the Supreme Court, McIlwain's two elements would be impossible— not that the ideal is reached; quite the contrary. American constitutionalism has always been characterized by a gap between pretense and reality. There is no reason to suppose that will change. In Woodrow Wilson's words, the Constitution "in operation" always varies, in greater or lesser degree, from the Constitution of the books.[5] Arbitrary power and lack of responsibility are at least endemic, and perhaps pandemic, in American governance.

The remainder of this chapter has three parts. The first part counters the case *against* activism. Here it will be suggested that critics dislike the results more than they care to admit, all commentators being "result-oriented." The second part analyzes the breakdown of pluralism in the American political order, with the consequence that there is no official body other than the Supreme Court that can define national values. Finally, the role of the Supreme Court in the era of the Constitution of Control is examined.

First, some preliminary observations are desirable to clear away some underbrush:

1. The Constitution is a politico-legal palimpsest. The men of 1787 were brilliant subversives who at once effected a structural change in American

---

This chapter, written in 1980, is an extension of a previous article: Arthur S. Miller, "Judicial Activism and American Constitutionalism: Some Notes and Reflections," in *NOMOS XX: Constitutionalism*, ed. J. Roland Pennock and John W. Chapman (New York: New York University Press, 1979), pp. 333–376.

government and delegated to later generations the task of keeping the Constitution current. Those delegates have had to move far and wide to update the fundamental law, which was ratified at about the time that science and technology began to effect basic alterations in the social milieu in which it had to operate. The consequence is clear enough: today's Constitution is related to the Document of 1787 only in metaphorical ways.

2. The United States is now moving into its *fourth* constitution. The first was the Articles of Confederation, which were considered by some, but not all, to be inadequate to the need. The Document of 1787 established the Constitution of Quasi-Limitations—the one the popular wisdom calls the Constitution of Limitations—that existed from 1789 to 1937. That second constitution is the parchment upon which succeeding fundamental laws are inscribed. It still exists (as a palimpsest). (It is here called one of quasi-limitations because, despite judicial adherence at times to laissez faire principles, government under it was always precisely as strong as conditions required. Government in the United States has always been relative to circumstances.) It is of passing interest to note three assessments by Englishmen of the original Constitution: Macauley called it "all sail and no anchor;" Gladstone thought it the most wonderful work ever struck off at a given time by men; and Lord Acton said that "weighed in the scales of Liberalism," it was "a monstrous fraud."[6]

The third Constitution was created, without the midwifery of amendment or convention, when the Supreme Court constitutionalized the New Deal in the 1930s—first in *Nebbia* and *Blaisdell* and then in *Parrish* and the famous Volume 301 of the U.S. Reports (containing *Jones & Laughlin* and the *Social Security Cases*).[7] That development was promptly labeled by Edward S. Corwin the Constitution of Powers—and that it was, insofar as the Court upheld intervention by the state into socioeconomic matters which for fifty years had largely been forbidden territory for legislatures. The justices found new principles in the Constitution because the *zeitgeist* had been altered. To save "the system," they began to permit massive regulation of the economy. That regulation soon became more ostensible than real when the businessman gave up on the Court as the protector of his liberties.

The second Constitution overlaid the third; another thin cover is now coming—a fourth fundamental law, the Constitution of Control. The nation is rapidly moving into an era when crisis government is becoming the norm.[8] That this will mean major changes in time-honored doctrine, or at least in the practices of the "living" Constitution, cannot be doubted. The beginnings are already evident. Under the Constitution of Control, increasingly authoritarian government will become routine—as Arnold Toynbee predicted in 1975.[9] This development will call for extraordinary, even heroic, measures from the justices, a call that may not be heeded save in form or facade.

3. Anglo-American law was, until the end of the nineteenth century, largely made by judges. Legislatures are latter-day instrumentalities, which in turn have been supplanted in large part by administrative agencies.

4. Constitutional interpretation is distinctly *not* a judicial monopoly. A form of politico-legal reductionism has led scholars to concentrate upon the Supreme Court. But surely such statutes as the Sherman Antitrust Act, the Full Employment Act of 1946, and the Civil Rights Act of 1964 are constitutional in nature; they are more important than most amendments. The president, too, makes constitutional decisions—as, for example, in the development of the principle of raison d'etat since the beginnings of the Republic.[10] And the "private" governments of the nation are also able to make decisions of constitutional dimension; they are, in Gianfranco Poggi's terminology, "quasipolities"—"a constitutional and legal system of their own, effectively preserved from interference and control by properly political, state organs."[11] (This is an area where more, much more, judicial activism is required.)

5. The Supreme Court routinely creates law when making constitutional decisions. Furthermore, by often employing the so-called "balancing test," it reads relative policy standards into what could be rigid commands. This technique, which is a product of the pragmatic temper regnant, has become overt in the past forty years. Use of it permits the ancient document to be altered in fact—but without change in its terms. Constitutional law, in sum, has joined politics in becoming avowedly relative to circumstances. The Rule of Law has, as a consequence, become in large part the Rule of Barter Economics.

6. The Court is not a superlegal-aid bureau. The cases chosen for full consideration on the merits (about 150 each term) are taken for reasons that transcend the immediate litigants.

7. Since *Cooper* v. *Aaron* (1958),[12] the justices seek at times to promulgate norms of general applicability. They attempt—not always but in some outstanding cases—to state "the law of the land" rather than "the law of the case." This means that the Court at times does not legislate interstitially, as Holmes maintained, but makes law wholesale. Even when the justices rule only on the facts and issues of a case, the wide publicity and national attention accorded the Court is subtly transforming the law of the case into a more general norm.[13]

8. Even so, the actual power of the justices to alter human behavior is still an unanswered question—in the short as well as the long run. The Court apparently cannot long be out of step with the dominant political forces of the nation. That means that the *zeitgeist*, rather than "the law," determines the course of Supreme Court decision making. The *zeitgeist* tends to reflect configurations of actual political power at any given time.

9. The Constitution is always in a state of "becoming," always being brought up to date to meet the successive exigencies faced by the American people.

10. Finally, trying to divine the intentions of those who drafted the Constitution and using those intentions (if found) as the main, perhaps sole, criterion of decision making is a puerile type of filiopietistic antiquarianism. The task of constitutional interpretation is far more difficult.

Who Decides? Who Should Decide?

Each generation of Americans writes its own Constitution.[14] It is fatuous to think otherwise. The questions thus become: Who should do the writing? By what criteria? Attacks on judicial activism are on two grounds—that judicial statement of constitutive norms is "undemocratic" and that the judges do not write "principled" opinions. The literature, of course, is enormous; it is both contemporaneous and ancient. From as far back as Chief Justice John Marshall's opinion in *Marbury* (1803), running through splenetic attacks on the Court by such people as Judge Spencer Roane and Thomas Jefferson to Louis Boudin's *Government by Judiciary* (1932) and Raoul Berger's *Government by Judiciary* (1977), a consistent thread of harsh criticism of the justices is evident.[15] Some of the assaults can be summarily dismissed; others, however, emanate from thoughtful observers; their complaints merit attention.

I think the thoughtful critics are wrong—dead wrong—in both of their criticisms. They have asked the wrong questions, and thus could not possibly have produced correct answers. "No answer is what the wrong question begets,"[16] Alexander Bickel maintained. That is not quite correct: the wrong questions beget wrong, not no, answers.

The Court and "Democracy"

"All laws, written, and unwritten," Thomas Hobbes maintained in 1651, "have need of interpretation."[17] So they do, particularly when they are deliberately couched in nebulous terms. Who, then, is to interpret them? The answer is easy for the Constitution: officials in each branch not only do so but do so routinely. Each time Congress enacts a statute and each time the president performs one of his constitutional responsibilities an assumption is made that the action is valid under the Constitution. That interpretation may be tacit: Congress, for example, seldom expressly asks whether its statutes are constitutionally valid.

And, as Bishop Hoadly said in his Sermon to the King in 1717, he who interprets is the true lawmaker. The point is that most constitutional interpretation is routine, is accomplished by judges and politicians and bureaucrats alike, and is usually final. The problem posed by judicial activism comes in that minuscule number of governmental decisions in which officers within the three branches (or officers in the federal judiciary and those in state and local governments) differ in their interpretations and the resulting disputes wind up in court. How, then, does the Supreme Court act in those few conflicts? According to the *Harvard Law Review*, during the 1977 Term the justices decided 135 cases on the merits. Of those, 59 were "constitutional" and 76 were listed as "other." In cases in which the government was a party, 61 were decided for the government and 51 against.[18] Can that be called judicial activism? McCloskey has shown that in only eight years of the 1948-1968 period did the government lose more cases than it won, and then only by small margins. The same pattern continues. The ineluctable conclusion is that it is not the *quantity* of decisions that leads to criticism of judicial "activism," but *what* is decided (the substantive issues, regardless of number). The point is significant: under any of the familiar definitions of democracy, the branches that allegedly represent the people usually prevail.

Most commentators, on and off the bench, who attack activism for being undemocratic do so either without vouchsafing a definition of democracy or assume, as if it were self-evident, that Congress and legislatures generally are democratic.[19] That is a comfortable position, no doubt, but it adds little to anyone's understanding of important governmental institutions. It does not comport with reality.

That the Supreme Court is an oligarchic institution is beyond debate. But attempts to reconcile or attack the Court's decisions—minute in number but often huge in prominence—as jibing or not jibing with democratic theory are based on two untenable assumptions: that *democracy* has a commonly accepted meaning and that other organs of government are democratic under that definition. Neither assumption holds water.

George Orwell once said that the word *democracy* has "several meanings which cannot be reconciled with one another." Not only was there no agreed definition, but the attempt to make one is resisted from all sides. Surely that is accurate: there are at least two-hundred definitions of the term.[20] In many respects, as Bernard Crick has observed, to call any government democratic "is always a misleading piece of propaganda."[21] But the word is used, even though it is emotion-charged, and it behooves those who assert that judicial review is or is not consonant with democratic theory to do more than make the flat assertion or the unverified assumption that elected bodies are democratic. At the very least, they should set out their theory of democracy and evaluate whether the American governmental system comports with it.

No useful purpose is served by calling the Supreme Court undemocratic unless Congress, the president, and state governments can accurately be called democratic. Surely we have learned enough about the shortcomings (and the positive side) of those institutions to know that it is idle, even mischievous, to call them democratic. Congress exists mainly to put the decisions of pressure groups and the experts into statutory form. It does not represent "the people;" it represents groups. Indeed, "the people" does not exist as such; it is not a monolith. The president, too, may speak in terms of the national or public interest, but he has to operate strictly within the limitations of the political order (the system of pluralism). As for state and local governments, no evidence need be adduced to buttress the proposition that they usually exemplify Michels's "iron law of oligarchy."

Rather than asking the wrong question—is the Court democratic?—the problem is one of fulfilling the Madisonian prescription: the tasks of government are to control the people and oblige it to control itself.[22] A tension has always existed between the ideal of popular sovereignty and the institution of judicial review. But if one asks how government can be obliged to control itself, the answer must come not from a sense, or even a spirit, of self-restraint by the avowedly political branches of government, but by some institution external to them. In other words, if the Supreme Court and judicial review did not exist, they—or something similar—would have to be invented. Politicians do not police themselves. Nor does the electorate.

It matters little if that external organ is oligarchic. Probably it is better that way. Surely election of Supreme Court justices would not improve the situation (and likely would make it worse); nor would recall of justices serve any useful purpose. And it does not really matter that the Court's decisions are not "reasoned" in ways that some Ivy League professors and other votaries in the cult of Frankfurter worship would approve. What does matter, and matter a great deal, is that the external organ—the Court—speak with authority, make sociologically wise decisions, and that its personnel have the competence to do so. On these questions, one should not be sanguine. The justices do have some authority, and thus some power, although how much appears to vary with the issues being decided. Whether its decisions are sociologically wise and whether the justices (and the adversary system) are up to the need is another problem, much more difficult to assay and answer. Wisdom and sociological competence in the legal profession are noteworthy for their rarity.

How can there be "legal limits to arbitrary power" unless some institution is available to call halt—to cry *haro!*[23]—when legislatures and others are alleged to have exceeded the limits of their lawful authority? That, in brief, is the present role of the Court. I do not maintain that it is very successful in that endeavor; indeed, it is not. No court, or system of courts, can hope to monitor the millions of decisions routinely made by other governmental entities. The Supreme Court can try to make some of those decisions nonarbitrary, but at best it issues decrees and must depend upon the bona fides of those in the political branches to make them effective. Having neither purse nor sword nor enforcement power of its own, the Court must tread warily when it enters the thickets of politics, as it routinely does in constitutional cases. No one should think that the justices or a purportedly powerful judge like Frank Johnson in Alabama can make that much difference. It is a sobering lesson that Johnson's decrees in the mental hospital and prison cases are still not translated into compliance. And the brave promise of *Brown* v. *Board of Education* is rapidly being dissipated.[24]

In lawyers' language, legal limits to "arbitrary power" means due process of law. But it is "procedural" rather than "substantive" due process about which McIlwain spoke. The problem with procedural due process lies in its underlying assumptions—that the goals or ends of society are settled and all that remains is to sort out the details. Perhaps that is why Daniel Bell can define constitutionalism as "the common respect for the framework of law, and the acceptance of outcomes under due process."[25] The difficulty, however, is that in the contentious areas of constitutional decision making, societal ends or goals are not settled. Those substantive goals are the issue, the subject of dispute, rather than ways to attain them.

What can the Court do when social ends are not commonly accepted? Here, some statements of the late Alexander Bickel seem pertinent. The Court, he said, is "an institution charged with the evolution and application of society's fundamental principles:" its task is "to define values and proclaim principles."[26] Bickel, of course, was a, perhaps *the*, leading academic exponent of judicial self-restraint, a mindset that must have been strongly influenced by his mentor, Justice Felix Frankfurter. So he argued for the passive virtues—for a Court, that is, that adhered to "the morality of process," which to him was "the highest morality." That position conflicts with the need to define values. Process-morality is a Burkean concept, one in which the rules of the game favor those who win. Bickel was concerned with methodology, not with conflicting value choices, and was not consistent in his judicial philosophy.

Methodology is not enough. Any polity must have some way—some instrumentality—to articulate values and principles. In the American system, the president cannot because he is the victim of the shortcomings of pluralism. Pluralism assumes common values, something that does not exist in the United States. The United States is not (not yet, at least) a theocracy, so no religious leader can define those values. What else do Americans have? The answer is clear: The Supreme Court, which in constitutional matters sits as an authoritative (at times) faculty of political theory and of social ethics. The Court may not be democratic, under any definition, but it can at times hold the feet of the allegedly democratic officers to the fire of the enduring values of American constitutionalism. It can tell politicans that someone is watching them. The justices, in sum, can act as a national conscience for a populace whose reach has always exceeded its grasp. Let no one pretend, however, that they are very good in that role.

The Court and "Sovereign Reason"

All judges are "result-oriented;" so, too, are all commentators upon the work of the judiciary.[27] There is no possible way to separate ends and means in either judgment of litigants or judgment of judges. We all carry our "can't helps" around with us. Try as one might to be invincibly disinterested, the human mind is not up to that need. The requirement, accordingly, is for judges and commentators alike to face their valuations—as Gunnar Myrdal has long advocated.[28] Most commentary on the Court is seriously flawed in two respects—a refusal to inquire into the social and economic philosophies of the justices and an accompanying failure to indicate the writer's own values.

Those shortcomings become manifest when the critics of the justices belabor them for not writing "principled" opinions. Prompted by the shade of Felix Frankfurter, the Ivy League School of Judicial Criticism is particularly shrill in its demands that the justices shape up and write better opinions.[29] To them, Reason (note the capital R) is the life of the law; and the Court has sullied its image of an impartial tribunal far above the sweaty mob. By ignoring history, including the history of the judiciary, and by failing to take cognizance of the nature of human knowledge and thought, these critics ask for the impossible. Ends and means cannot be separated. Those who belabor the *procedure* of adjudication—which is essentially what the demand for Sovereign Reason entails—must also be considered to dislike the *substance* of decisions (the results reached). Put another way, critics of judicial activism are (tacitly) "result-oriented."

Reason is distinctly not an end in itself. Nor can it be. Law is not a homeless, wandering ghost; it is a human institution created and implemented by humans, with a consequent panoply of human shortcomings. Those who plump for Reason as the life of the law fail to consider that law, as all human institutions, is a slender reed that reflects not Sovereign Reason but the power relationships of society at any given time. Surely Emerson was correct when he observed that law is "only a memorandum;" it is not something external to the pulls and tugs of the political process. Any sociologist of law knows that the State and its legal system are closely entwined.

Any first-year law student of middling competence can dissect almost any Supreme Court opinion and reveal flaws in reasoning. The law reviews provide ample testimony to buttress that proposition; they are a surfeit of tedious explications of why a justice was correct but for the wrong reasons or incorrect for no reason at all. What passes for scholarship in legal periodicals tends to be dreary analyses of appellate court opinions, usually badly written and larded with mountains of footnotes. They are, in short, a monument to the prevailing ideology of lawyers and many political scientists—"legalism,"[30] which is essentially a form of latter-day scholasticism.

Emphasis in law schools on the bastardized form of logic called legal reasoning has ascertainable consequences for the legal profession, one of which is of present relevance: the propensity of judges to make their opinions look like law journal articles. Almost all judges who issue written opinions are graduates of some law school and almost all judges are now assisted by young law clerks mint-fresh from law school (and the law reviews). These small bureaucracies produce opinions, some of which are read by law students (and all of which now end in the dusty stacks of law libraries). As a result, a well-structured opinion—one that reads well—is, to many, the *ne plus ultra* of the art of judging. Felicity with language thus becomes a substitute for justice (the just result). An opinion by Justice John M. Harlan the younger, for example, is valued for its structure, without regard for the result. Why judicial methodology should be so applauded is difficult to perceive—unless those who criticize badly written opinions are hiding their dislike of the decisions. No one, to be sure, advocates opinions that do not opine. Nor should one. The end of the law, however, is justice, not mellifluity in language.

Judges strive to make their opinions appear to be models of rationality, a habit of self-delusion that also deludes others. The law has only a putative rationality. The really important aspect of judicial opinions is the major premise—the inarticulate assumption—that judges bring to the case.[31] Opinions in multimember appellate courts, particularly the Supreme Court, are negotiated documents, the product of a process of bargaining, often intense bargaining. Rather than striving to jibe with Reason (however defined, and it never is in the literature about the Supreme Court), the opinion ofttimes strikes a common denominator that will maximize votes of colleagues.[32]

That should be obvious, and, indeed, it is conceded by most knowledgeable observers. The concession, however, is only superficial. There seems to be an inexhaustible need to demand that the ideal be achieved by judges; or, if not achieved, at least avidly pursued. "Courts," Chief Justice John Marshall once said, "are mere instruments of the law, and can will nothing."[33] That is a laudable sentiment—a pleasant goal—but it requires the neglect of or failure to recognize some hard facts about the human mind. Rationality, however defined, is at best only one characteristic of the thought processes of humans—and not necessarily the dominant one.

Judges, rather than being omnicompetent, as a rule display mind-habits depressingly characteristic of lawyers. Lawyers tend to be narrow-minded legal mechanics—technocrats with one goal: client interest. That makes the "profession" one of hired guns—urbane "hit men" in buttoned-down collars and vested suits. When lawyers become judges, they often carry with them the thought patterns carefully nurtured in law school and cultivated in the practice—adherence to "legalism," that mind-set that considers the law to be "there," a discrete entity separate and apart from politics and economics.[34] Only occasionally does a judge transcend the limitations of his past. For every Skelly Wright or Frank Johnson there are at least a baker's dozen of federal judges such as Roger Robb and George Hart.

There should be little wonder that Reason is considered to be the life of the law, and even less wonder that lawyer-judges do not display that quality of mind demanded by the Ivy League School of Judicial Criticism. Their entire training and work before ascending to the bench is the antithesis of taking the large view, of seeing problems whole, of being broad-gauged. Wedded to the adversary system—to verbalized trials by combat—judges use the words and techniques of Reason, but for ends often unstated. An idol of the Ivy League School is

Justice Felix Frankfurter—the most overrated judge in this century and perhaps in American history, a judge whose opinions opine only because of a widespread myopia that prevents seeing them as often-mistaken political documents dressed up in lawyers' language. Why Frankfurter is so revered is difficult for any cool-minded observer to assay. He did one good thing—helping to get unanimity in *Brown* v. *Board of Education*—but in the main was an apologist for executive power and a person whose ideas of that process that is due were on the odd side.

Emphatically, I am not advocating arbitrary decisions. Far from it. My purpose is simply to note the obvious—that there is at least a hint, and perhaps more, of fiat (or arbitrariness) in every decision by the Supreme Court. Is it not better to call, as does Ray Forrester, for "truth in judging"[35] than to devote excessive time to worrying about the reasoning, or lack of it, by the justices? Critics of the Court tend to hide their objections to the results—the decisions—behind an impenetrable fog of legalistic verbiage about the opinions. In the real world, it is the results that count—who wins or loses. As Leonard Levy once ruefully observed, "the public cares about results and has little patience for reasons."[36] So it is. Criticisms of reasoning or an alleged lack of it are fatally flawed because of an almost complete failure to analyze either the concept of Reason itself or the results of Supreme Court decisions—who wins or loses—in terms of a polity that likes to call itself democratic. Decisions, as Frankfurter once noted in language that his votaries should ponder, can be logically arbitrary but sociologically nonarbitrary.

Summary

Two facts about the Court are beyond dispute: it is indeed an oligarchic institution and the opinions of the justices have never been characterized by Reason (as demanded by the Frankfurterites). It is idle, and serves no useful purpose, to attempt to make the Court fit any theory of democracy; and it is even more idle not to acknowledge that an element of fiat exemplifies the operations of the justices. Seldom are major premises stated (and if they are, we are asked to accept them on faith); and never are predilections openly avowed. Judges try to hide their biases; they like the appearance of open-mindedness. (An open mind, to be sure, may be an empty mind.) If that means that there is more than a hint of arbitrariness in Supreme Court practices, so be it. I do not believe that it can be avoided.

How, then, can one justify judicial activism? The answer is relatively simple: any polity requires a consensus about the values important to the populace. This consensus can come without conscious thought; some things are widely believed because they are taken for granted. If this be so in most matters there would be little need for constitutional adjudication and, indeed, there would be almost none. In this sense an important aspect of any polity is what people take for granted—the assumptions, tacit or otherwise, they make. But tacit consensuses simply do not exist in a rapidly changing society such as the United States. So the values—the consensus—must be externally and explicitly articulated. In a secular society that once trumpeted that God is dead, this means that some central symbol of authority and wisdom must be substituted for the Deity. That, then, is the role of the Court and the justification for judicial activism. There is no one else to do the job—no person, not even the president, no established church, no recognized moral leader. That is an awesome responsibility thrust upon men whose main claim to eminence has usually been that they either knew or were brought to the attention of a president. Of course they stumble, for they too are mortal men; but even in stumbling they help form the national consensus.

The arguments of the critics of judicial activism fall of their own weight. Critics often hide their values, as Judge Skelly Wright has said, behind a fog of discussion about judicial method. As Wright observed, the "fundamental dispute [is] over the good society."[37] On this level the critics have little or nothing to offer—little more than to assume without evidence that the political process is up to the needs of modern America. That blind adherence to politics clouds a basic fact: the system of pluralism has either broken down or is rapidly breaking down. It fails partially because it provides no spokesman for the public (or national) interest—for the national consensus. The Supreme Court, because of the consequent vacuum, is a leader in a vital national seminar that leads to the formulation of values for the American people. Leaders are necessary, if for no other reason than that stated by the Grand Inquisitor: people require miracle, mystery, and authority[38]—precisely what they get from the justices (in small part, at least).

The Desuetude of Pluralism

The case against the critics of activism can be stated more positively. Here I develop a basic reason *for* activism, necessarily iterating and expanding some ideas broached earlier.

Pluralism is the operative ideology of American politics (and political scientists). It is a pluralism of semiautonomous groups, some of which have taken over the substance of sovereignty. In a form of Adam Smith economics writ large and translated into politics, pluralism assumes that out of the clash of interest groups consensuses will emerge, each one roughly, but not permanently, identified as being in the "public" or "national" interest. Historically, the system worked; the nation waxed large and strong. But that was true even though it was less a system than a historical accident: "The extraordinary affluence of the United States has been produced by a set of fortuitous, nonreplicable, and nonsustainable factors."[39]

That era is ending, in T.S. Eliot's well-known words, not with a bang but with a whimper. Politico-legal mechanisms that were adequate in the past are at least obsolescent and perhaps obsolete, simply because the social milieu has changed so radically. A "culture of narcissism" has been created—a fancy name for the "me generation."[40] The politics of selfishness has taken over. Never has there been a greater need for an authoritative spokesman for national values; and never has that task been so demanding. The Supreme Court seems to be groping toward fulfilling that role. A felt need creates a response. The vacuum of moral and ethical leadership had to be filled—by someone, by some institution. As with all human institutions, the Court is an imperfect instrument; but if it lives up to its promise (and perhaps the expectations of the American populace) it then can help the nation navigate the stormy seas ahead.

The justices have no real opposition in that task, not even the president. Were one to take the assumptions about American democracy seriously, then the president, as the sole official elected (albeit indirectly) by all of the people, would be in the best position to fulfill the need of moral and ethical leadership. In some rather small respects he can do so; the chief executive is the high priest of the civil religion (nationalism) of a secular society.[41] At the moment he can attempt to set national goals. But it is increasingly obvious that he, as well as other elected officials, is the prisoner of the shortcomings of pluralism—of what Theodore Lowi called "interest-group liberalism."[42] The "textbook presidency" exists only in the textbooks.[43] The president is confined both by the built-in constitutional roadblocks of separation of power and by the interplay of decentralized interest groups. Those groups are able to influence, even control, many congressional decisions and to "regulate the regulators." The bureaucracy, as a consequence, is a congeries of fiefdoms headed by persons often outwardly—that is, in legal theory—responsible to the president, but which in fact are basically autonomous, feudal-like entities. The president negotiates with, rather than dominates, these baronies. His power of command, even with aid of the institutionalized presidency, is diminished to an often unsuccessful "power" to persuade. In this process, the public or national interest is often confused with—is in fact conterminous with—the interests of those groups with the greatest political clout.

That is not the theory of pluralism; rather, it is the consequence. Pluralism is not supposed to work that way. Supposedly the public interest is produced "by an invisible hand." But that is not so. It is a parlous situation indeed, one that cries out for sweeping reform. Sweeping reform, however, is precisely what is *not* possible under the American system of constitutionalism. The most that has been possible, and the most that seems possible now and in the future, is "incrementalism"—a series of ad hoc adjustments often, perhaps usually, made after a problem has become a crisis and there is no possibility of rational resolution.

Pluralism thus leaves a political and moral vacuum in national norm-setting (or goal-setting). Bargaining among groups is the overriding desideratum of policy, which in turn means that the lowest common denominator controls. The Supreme Court, more by happenstance than by design, appears to be seeking to fill that vacuum. In so doing, the justices draw upon their own consciences[44] to set standards that become the conscience of the American people, articulating values toward which the nine men believe the people should strive. The nine, to be sure, often disagree—but about details, not about whether the Court should set ethical and moral standards. It is a role for which there is no *vade mecum,* no road map or compass to steer by. The 102 persons who have sat upon the Court have had perforce to make up the rules as they went along, rules both of their own operations and the rules of moral and ethical conduct (stated as juristic principles of politics).

One must cut through a mass of penny-ante cases with which the justices should not be (but are) concerned to find a core of decisions in which they identify and define values. These few cases are dredged up from the detritus of the political process; they involve issues that under that process cannot be—at least, are not—settled by the workings of the political system. Pluralism, that is, provides no answers for these social problems. The issues are, of course, highly political, yet not "political questions" in the Article III sense. The justices state norms, using "reasoned" fiat couched in language with which lawyers are familiar and thus comfortable. Often they go outside the borders of the adversary system in doing so—in, that is, informing themselves about the nature of the *social* conflict that *individuals* (natural and artificial) bring before them.[45]

Since 1803 the process has been developed. The justices had to sail uncharted seas, feeling their way between rocks upon which they might have foundered. At times they have erred, as in the *Dred Scott* decision, but not fatally. By making the justices keenly aware of the limitations of the art of the possible, the self-inflicted wounds the Court has suffered have, through time, served to strengthen rather than weaken it. The consequence is that today the justices are seen, and accepted, as authoritative spokesmen for national values. Elementary beginnings of the process are detectable in the nineteenth century; but it is only since the end of the era of American innocence (around World War I) that the Court has moved, slowly at first but then with increasing speed, to be a modern version of the Delphic oracle. In the authority, and the opacity of its pronouncements, it resembles that institution of ancient Greece.

The modern Court began in the late 1930s. A series of permissive decisions, in which expansive new powers were found in ancient constitutional language, led to the so-called "constitutional revolution" of the thirties and forties. The Constitution of Quasi-Limitations became one of Powers. But that episode merely constitutionalized political pluralism. The formal law enunciated by the Court reflected the group basis of politics. *Jones & Laughlin*[46] is, of course, the key case, the one in which the Court agreed with the president and Congress that the public interest would be served by the interplay at the bargaining table between management and labor. Not that the justices wrote their decision in those words; rather, they in that case, and in *Parrish*,[47] rewrote the interstate commerce and due process clauses to reflect political reality. A salutary lesson had been learned: The justices may influence the formation of the *zeitgeist*, but they cannot for long withstand the brute force of public opinion. Their ability to state norms, in other words, is limited by an evaluation of what the people (speaking generally) will tolerate. The Court as national conscience must by some means plumb the collective conscience of the populace; but it can also help make the conscience conscious. Not an easy task, that, as they learned when in the forties, fifties, and sixties the justices sought and found their new and modern role as Delphic oracle.

To constitutionalize political pluralism is one thing; that merely involved self-abnegation, stepping aside and letting the politicians have free rein. But it is quite another thing to state affirmative norms of what other governmental officers must do (as distinguished from what they cannot do or what they may do). The discovery that the Constitution contained certain positive duties came late in American history.[48] Not before the 1940s was a conception of legally concretized decency slowly read into the fundamental law, wittingly or un-wittingly, by nine middle-aged or elderly men who sought to give those who could not—at least, did not—win in the political process the benefit of fuller participation in the American community.

A slight beginning was made in 1938 in the *Missouri Law School* case,[49] where the Court held that a black who wanted to attend Missouri's lily-white law school could not be prevented from doing so even though the state was willing to pay his expenses at some law school in another state. That crack in the wall of indecency in treatment of blacks was soon widened. In retrospect, *Screws* and *Classic*[50] seem to be unavoidable decisions, but they were not then so considered. Nor was *Allwright*[51] the linchpin of several "white primary" cases. *Shelley* v. *Kraemer*[52] finally recognized what should have been obvious to all except the willfully blind—that judicial action was state action within the terms of the Fourteenth Amendment. An immensely important decision, *Shelley* sits as a time bomb in the *United States Reports* awaiting the time when five justices will recognize its full implication—that private action, too, can be state action once the machinery of government is triggered. The need is manifest in the area of the activities of those artificial persons called corporations.

The movement toward decency—toward stating affirmative principles of morality—peaked in *Brown* and *Baker*, *Miranda* and *Roe*.[53] By design or by happenstance or possibly because the justices had insight into a system of absolute values, some segments of American society unable to benefit from the pluralistic political process found a champion in a handful of lawyers. Strange, very strange, one might say, particularly when one scrutinizes the legal profession.

But perhaps not so strange if John Griffith is correct: "[T]he judiciary in any modern industrial society, however composed, under whatever economic system, is an essential part of the system of government and . . . its function may be described as underpinning the stability of that system and as protecting that system from attack by resisting attempts to change it."[54] Not all attempts, to be sure, but those minimally necessary to stifle discontent. That means that the Supreme Court is, in part at least, a safety valve.

The Court as safety valve may best be discerned in precisely those decisions singled out by Raoul Berger for slashing opprobrium: *Brown* v. *Board of Education* and *Baker* v. *Carr*.[55] Even Frankfurter knew that long bottled-up fires of discontent would soon explode; hence, he was instrumental in getting the justices to achieve unanimity in *Brown*. He simply could not believe, on the other hand, that voters who were victims of the rotten borough systems of the several states were in the same position; hence, his cloudy crystal ball in *Baker. Brown,* its predecessors in racial cases and its progeny, signaled a revolution in the jurisprudence of the Court. Whether one agrees with Griffith that judges are establishment figures whose function is to stabilize the social order or with those who see the justices as self-appointed protectors of the disadvantaged, the tentative probes epitomized by *Brown* were soon extended to other areas. "Discrete and insular minorities" began to receive benefits long denied them.

To neoconservatives, such as Nathan Glazer, this meant that the justices had abandoned prudence.[56] That, however, can hardly be true. They saw a vital need, the political vacuum created by the failures of pluralism, and moved to fill it. The Court as safety valve, the Court as protector of minority interests, became in Adolf Berle's hyperbolic words "a revolutionary committee."[57] For the first time in American history, nonestablishment plaintiffs (and some defendants) found in the Court a haven for claims long denied by a polity that professed to give them. Not only blacks but diverse others began to "work within the system"—to use the judiciary as a target of pressure-group tactics, to ask judges to recognize rights and liberties that under the American myth had always been theirs.

Not everyone agreed, of course. Those who had prevailed in politics at times found *their* oxen being gored. And they didn't like it. The justices found themselves in the midst of controversy—over prayer in public schools, over reapportionment, over racial matters, over allegedly being soft on criminals, in short, for doing a job that needed to be done and for the doing of which no other person or institution existed. Some critics, of course, were from the lunatic fringe that has always characterized American society. Others, however, are thoughtful and deserve careful consideration.

One such is Judge Learned Hand, who cried *haro!* in his 1958 volume, *The Bill of Rights,* against the new role of the Court (of the judiciary generally, for lower court federal judges and some state judges were even more activist than the nine men headed by Chief Justice Earl Warren). Hand erred on two counts.

Technically, his mellifluous diatribe was wrong for calling the Court a group of "Platonic Guardians," for Plato spoke of "philosopher-kings." Plato's Guardians were not to be decision makers in his *Republic*. (This technical mistake by Hand has been uncritically accepted and repeated ad nauseam since Hand wrote.) Of much more importance was his error in thinking, however implicitly, that the political process was sufficient to the need. There he joined forces with Frankfurter, and no doubt would have agreed with the latter's splenetic asseverations in *Baker* that politicians should be asked to vote themselves out of office. Even a Supreme Court justice who had been a law professor should have known that politicians simply do not act that way.

Hand and Frankfurter are the patron saints in the hagiology of the Ivy League School of Judicial Criticism. Their votaries are many, their critics few. The chorus is led by a group of neoconservatives whose dirgelike wails fill the law journals and some of the magazines (such as *Commentary* and *The Public Interest*). They reject the call issued by Alexander M. Pekelis a generation ago for "systematic participation . . . of the judiciary in the travail of society."[58] They are content to belong to or try to join the "Society of Jobbists"—that "strange cult . . . which 'undertakes only those jobs which the members can do in proper workmanlike fashion' . . . . It demands right quality, better than the market will pass"[59] (not recognizing that a Jobbist may take on only minuscule tasks because his capabilities permit no more). If, as Jacob Landynski has asserted, "constitutional law is in large measure the nation's own deepest feelings writ large,"[60] this group of critics would either have those feelings submerged and not articulated or would have their own Whiggish, Burkean notions written into the fundamental law.

They may well prevail—sooner or later. The justices have not mastered their new role. One gets a sense that the nine men are floundering, without sail or rudder, as they seek to keep the Constitution current with new demands and new conditions. It is no accident that the Court took on that new role at precisely the time that the nation entered its Golden Age—the period of roughly 1945 to 1970 when economic growth was seemingly permanent, when the dollar was sovereign in international economics, when American military might spread the world over, when, in sum, all things seemed possible in this best of all possible worlds. It was the era of Pax Americana.

Richard Nixon was no doubt guilty of great crimes, both of omission and commission, but packing the Supreme Court with "strict constructionists" was not among them. He was entitled, as are all presidents, to nominate whomever he desired, although one may perhaps wish that he had found people of greater intellectual attainments. His appointees now dominate a neoconservative Court that is the direct result of Nixon's selections. Their decisions, however, are not always Nixonian. Certainly *Roe* is not, it being the most latitudinarian decision in recent memory. The Court now faces a time when the issues it considers increasingly involve a zero-sum game. *Bakke* and *Weber*, even *Rodriguez*,[61] are testimony to that. Some group (not some one person, as in criminal law cases) must lose in such cases, ineluctably, the socioeconomic process not being infinitely expandable. (Groups are the most important factors in many constitutional cases, even though litigation is usually brought in the names of individuals.)[62] The assumptions underlying the decisions in the constitutional revolution of the thirties and forties have now been shown to be faulty. Those decisions constitutionalized Keynesian economics as well as political pluralism. During the Golden Age, the Court could and did operate in ways that seemed to be making the dream of human equality a reality, not only in equal protection matters but also in due process and interstate commerce cases.

One should not fault the Nixon Court for perceiving, at least intuitively if not expressly, that the American cornucopia is being emptied; that the hard choices that were and are being made unavoidably mean that some group is going to lose. The movement toward equality, long ago perceived by Alexis de Tocqueville, is drawing to a close. The harsh fact about contemporary America is that people will have to "elevate their sights a little lower" as the age of frugality approaches.[63] It would be odd indeed if this were not reflected in Supreme Court opinions.

Even so, this should not portend a quietistic role for the Court. Rather, it argues for even more activism. The justices can make some choices, hard for officers in the political branches, that simply will have to be made as the Constitution of Control comes into existence. They can help ameliorate what is certain to be a rocky and rough passage ahead.

One such choice that should be made, and soon, would be to bring the disparate groups of decentralized social (and political) power under the ambit of the formal Constitution—the palimpsest drafted in 1787 and some twenty-six times amended. That change can be easily accomplished. All that is needed is the perception that those groups, such as the giant corporations, are private governments—as Arthur Bentley said, "governments through and through,"[64]—and that as such they clearly belong within the concept of "state" or governmental action.[65] This would not take a major leap in doctrine, for the Court has already done just that for political parties and (twice) for corporations.[66] (That one of the latter decisions has since been overruled merely reveals how blind to socioeconomic reality the Nixon Court can be at times.) The need is for much more judicial activism, in order to bring the units of neofeudalism under a measure of constitutional control. An Australian, Leicester Webb, has put the matter well:

> Since there is as yet no comprehensive and accepted theory of group-State relationships to guide legislators and since the association, individual and State are in constantly changing equilibrium, it may be that the harmonizing of these three elements, which Acton regarded as "the true aim of politics," is best carried out through the processes of a widely-competent judiciary.[67]

Further discussion is not presently needed. Suffice it only to say that a system of private governments has existed for some time, that it requires control beyond that of present statutes, and that, rather than being an instrument of statism run wild, constitutionalizing private governments would be a way in which the public interest could be furthered while still permitting maximum privateness in enterprise. It would, in sum, be a new form of private regulation for the public interest.[68] A system of government that has promoted, despite the charade of the antitrust laws, large enterprise and a Court that constitutionalized Keynesian economics and political pluralism, are now faced with the task of taming the social beasts thereby unleashed.[69] A more fundamental need is probably far beyond the capacity of the Supreme Court to accomplish—the devising of some means by which the elites of disparate social groups will take the public or national interest into consideration when making decisions. How can the most manifest of the shortcomings of pluralism be overcome? No ready answer is apparent. The Court can set a standard but must rely upon the goodwill of others, at all levels of government, to translate it into operational reality. American history gives no basis for optimism that any judicial attempt to alleviate pluralism's faults will succeed.

But try the justices should, even though their reach exceeds their grasp. The Supreme Court may be a poor example of Plato's philosopher-kings, but we have no substitute. It is time for the justices, openly and avowedly, to forget Bacon's admonition and to move on to greater goals. Said Bacon: "Judges ought to remember that their office is *jus dicere*, and not *jus dare;* to interpret law, and not to make law, or give law. Else it will be like the authority, claimed by the Church of Rome, which under pretext of exposition of Scripture, doth not stick to add or alter; and to pronounce that which they do not find; and but show of antiquity to introduce novelty."[70] Ray Forrester's call for "truth in judging" is more than a call that judges make "their office . . . *jus dare;*" it should also involve a call for making their office one of seeking and stating new norms that will adapt the Constitution "to meet changing conditions."[71] The Court should, in other words, be a leader. With life tenure and time for reflection, the justices are in a better position than politicians to erect standards toward which the nation could aspire.

That is a delicate task indeed, calling for a level of competence and wisdom that has not been particularly evident on the Court, today or in the past. This means that our philosopher-kings should be specially educated, as Plato advocated. They should also be specially selected. If, in other words, we are to have (as I think we should) a group of latter-day philosopher-kings, then at the very least more intelligent ways of identifying them should be developed.

Summary

Political pluralism as a self-correcting system is as mythical as the market of the classical economists. It does not exist. Pluralism "worked" in the past for two reasons: first, because of an ever-expanding economy, one that made—for a time, at least—the realization of the material demands of the populace possible; and second, because only one group dominated politics until the 1930s—the business corporation. Economic growth, however, is now over; or, if not over, badly slowed, as the nation enters the age of frugality. As it does so, serious deficiencies in time-honored constitutional institutions have become increasingly apparent. It is to this most pressing of all constitutional questions that we now turn. Our focus will be narrow—on the role of the Supreme Court in the era of the Constitution of Control—time and space not permitting more extensive exposition.[72]

The Court under the Constitution of Control

In one of his last opinions, Justice William O. Douglas said, "cases such as this one reflect festering sores in our society; and the American dream teaches that if one reaches high enough and persists there is a forum where justice is dispensed. I would lower the technical barriers and let the courts serve that ancient need."[73] That provides a partial theme for this section, which deals with a newly emergent layer on the ancient parchment that is the Constitution. It is called the Constitution of Control simply because the United States is now entering a time when more and more social controls are being and will be placed on individual behavior (both of natural and of artificial persons). A further statement of our partial theme comes from Ronald Downing:

> The fact that the courts are the principal forum for resolving so many political issues is indicative of serious default on the part of our legislative and executive institutions. So long as this default continues, and the courts are responsive to pleas for resolution of such issues, the judiciary (a most fragile institution in the halls of power politics) will continue to be buffeted by the full force of increasingly devastating political conflicts arising in the nation. . . .
>
> There appears to be little prospect that the legislative and executive processes can soon be transformed in such a way as to permit our political system to cope with society's deepest problems. . . .
>
> In short, while it is very doubtful that the courts can save the country, only they may be able to buy the time necessary for revitalization of our other institutions.[74]

They will do this in two ways: helping alleviate those "festering sores" about which Justice Douglas spoke and helping to make, as McIlwain said, the government more responsible to the governed.

First, however, what is the Constitution of Control? Writing in 1974, Senators Frank Church and Charles Mathias asserted that "emergency government has become the norm."[75] That is not really accurate—and somewhat less so since enactment of the National Emergencies Act of 1976.[76] Had they used the term "crisis government," they would have been closer to the mark. For that is the age Americans are now entering—a time when crisis government, and the attempted management of overlapping crises, has indeed become the norm.

The idea of crisis government has been discussed elsewhere.[77] It is enough now to state the implications of the incipient climacteric into which humankind is entering. It is a climacteric rather than a crisis, a coalescence of crises that have erupted in the past decade the world over. They come together to create a sea change in the way that the species Homo Sapiens confronts life on Spaceship Earth.

Government in the United States, despite ostensible adherence to laissez faire principles in the past, has always been relative to circumstances—precisely as strong as conditions required. The Constitution is not only a "fighting Constitution," as the Court once asserted, it is also a fundamental law that has been amenable to other crises in human affairs. Chief Justice John Marshall knew that long ago, when he set out in *McCulloch* v. *Maryland* the basic principle of constitutional interpretation adhered to before and since: it should never be forgotten that it is a constitution that is being expounded, a constitution designed to fit the various crises in human activity. The nation has moved a long way since Marshall wrote in 1819, so far that a critical question has become whether further adaptations can be made in interpretation of ancient language or whether a new Constitution should be written.

If it is assumed, as it should be, that there is no likelihood of a new fundamental law being drafted, then the role of the Supreme Court becomes critical, as the nation and its political officers grapple with coalescing crises. There can be little doubt that American government will become increasingly authoritarian. The age of parliamentary democracies is drawing to a close. The American Congress is the sole legislative body of any significant nation in the world today that still wields, ostensibly at least, considerable power. That will not last. No institution consisting of two committees, one of 100 and one of 435 members, can hope to be an effective instrument of governance in the modern world. As crises multiply, so too will executive power—both in the presidency itself and in the bureaucracy. This is truly the age of the bureaucratic state[78]—and there is no possibility that that trend will be reversed. "Caesarism"[79] is coming to America, and fast. The nation cannot, and will not, tolerate a weak executive; neither, for that matter, will Congress. Congress not only does not govern; it does not want to govern. True it is that some members, because they represent (in fact) important interest groups, do exercise some considerable political power. But the general rule is different: effective governing power lies at the other end of Pennsylvania Avenue.

Where, then, will the Supreme Court fit in a scheme of governance that is one of permanent crisis? The question asks much, and can only be summarily treated here. It is more easily asked than answered. .

We may begin with what the Court will *not* do. One thing seems certain: the justices will erect no barriers to what the political branches of government want to do in their attempts to meet the crises that are already apparent and others that are foreseeable. General policies will meet constitutional tests, as they have in the past. Specific actions may at time fail to pass muster, as, for example, when they are alleged to collide with other constitutional commands (procedural due process and equal protection mainly). What must be done will be done, sooner or later. The American people will not long tolerate elected officials who do not act in the face of obvious needs.

The meaning is clear. The justices will constitutionalize any effort to meet the burgeoning crises the nation faces.[80] Beyond that, they can try to assure that governmental actions, when taken, do not unduly encroach upon the liberties of Americans—civil liberties, not economic liberties. Here, again, the meaning is clear: The Court will continue to help build the permissive society, one in which human activities not deemed harmful to the State will not only be permitted; they will be subtly encouraged.

Another thing the justices cannot do is to make structural changes in the fundamental law. However much such changes may be needed, the Court's power to "say what the law is" does not extend to formal amendment of the Constitution. What it can do, and what it has routinely done, is to read new meanings into the litigable parts of the Constitution. It is conceivable that this could even extend to a thoroughgoing commitment to supranationalism. Such a commitment is in fact in process of being built—step by step, as the nation, through international agreement and otherwise, meshes its policies with others of like ideology. Politics follows economics; as business more and more has become multinational, so too have political arrangements. The Court has placed no barrier to the development—seen, for instance, in the International Monetary Fund, the North Atlantic Treaty Organization, and international commodity agreements. There is no reason to believe that the Court would not, were the situation to arise, approve American membership in the European Common Market or a move to make the American dollar a segment of the European Currency Units. A written constitution may not be infinitely expandable, but what politicians want, in the face of perceived need, can be accommodated within the ancient words. The initiative, however, must come from the political branches of government; the justices cannot *sua sponte,* or in the context of any conceivable litigation, mandate such an exponential leap in American policy.

The Court, then, can legitimize new public policies, some not yet foreseeable—and that it will doubtless do. It can also help to preserve the values of legally concretized decency that are embedded in the due process and equal protection clauses (and also in the Bill of Rights generally) and it can continue its attempts to bring "discrete and insular minorities" into the mainstream of American life. Constitutionalism need not die in the era of the Constitution of Control. This means that some of the more abrasive features of what likely will emerge—an increasingly authoritarian government—can be ameliorated.

Whether that will in fact occur will depend upon specific factors, including material shortages, the extent of which cannot now be forecast. Those shortages will occur, and will trigger governmental responses—sooner or later (probably sooner) and of varying intensities.[81]

That much seems fairly clear—as clear as it can be when one attempts to predict the future during an era of rapid social change. Beyond that, the view is foggy, but the need is manifest. It has already been stated—the notion that the Court can be a leader in helping to set national goals.

The Court as Delphic Oracle

Here I enter terra incognita; or almost so, for a few portents of this role of the justices have already appeared. Suggested above is the view that they are becoming a modern version of Plato's philosopher-kings. The argument is now advanced one step further.

The suggestion is for more—much more—judicial activism; but activism of a certain kind. Here, some analogy to another theological institution—the Roman Catholic Church—is meet. The Supreme Court, although hydra-headed, bears marked resemblances to the Pope. Both are infallible—by self-assertion. Both are "final" within their respective spheres. ("We are not final because we are infallible," Justice Robert H. Jackson once said, "but we are infallible only because we are final."[82]) Both operate in secrecy; and both wear robes. Each has its bureaucracy. Each speaks with authority, and thus fulfills one of the Grand Inquisitor's trio of human wants (miracle, mystery, and authority). Each says what the law is—canon law (often merging with the law of the State) for the Pope; the law of the Constitution for the justices. Each maintains that a sacred document is the source of wisdom and that pronouncements are mere interpretations. The Supreme Court, in sum, consists of nine men who are priests of the nation's civil religion (nationalism; constitutionalism).

For some time it has been apparent that American constitutional law should be concerned not only with what governments can and cannot do but also with what they must do if a democratic society is to survive. Some steps in that direction have been taken—a slowly emerging concept of constitutional duty is being formulated. The movement is far from full blown; it is more a tendency—a sporadic tendency—than a reality.[83] The Court at times has said what government officers must do—for example, in the reapportionment cases. Other judges, both federal and state, have done the same in other areas—for instance, the New Jersey Supreme Court in financing public schools and Judge Frank Johnson in the Alabama mental hospital and prison cases.[84]

Judges just tread warily along such paths. They must not only see wrongs that should be corrected; they must also be ready to develop new remedies. "Should judges administer social services?", Nathan Glazer plaintively, perhaps testily, asks.[85] The answer comes back, Yes, but only as a last resort, only when the other organs of government have failed to respond, only when the need is manifest and unfulfilled.

The decisions thus made, the norms thus stated, will not ipso facto be able definitively to resolve disputes. Courts do not have that much power. But what judges can do is to alter the mix of social affairs, to inject new factors into public dialogues about important issues. At times, as in reapportionment matters, they can tell legislatures to comply with the command of the Constitution or the Court will do it for them. At other times, as in *Robinson* v. *Cahill*,[86] they can threaten to close schools unless an income tax is enacted to pay for costs of education. They can set up administrative organs to monitor compliance with certain decisions (as in Judge Johnson's prison decision). And they can issue "norms of general applicability," as in *Cooper* v. *Aaron,* and thereby seek—and, in seeking, succeed—to bind people throughout the land, not merely the litigants before the bar of the Court.

They have, in short, enormous discretion if they choose to employ it. And all of that is done without federal judges running afoul of Article III requirements.[87] Not yet have any of these extraordinary remedial decisions been held to encompass nonjudicial functions contrary to the Constitution. Since judges, including justices of the Supreme Court, are the final arbiters of what a nonjudicial function is under the Constitution, there is no way short of constitutional amendment to stop this trend.

The question now is whether it can (and, indeed, whether it should) be taken a giant step further. Seen in even the brief time since, say, *Brown* v. *Board of Education* in 1954, the Court and judges generally have indeed come a long way. They have perceived vital social needs and attempted to fill them. Their successes should be applauded, if for no other reason than that they have afforded legislative and executive officials some time to revitalize themselves. Judges are not to be blamed for failures of those officials to move beyond yesteryear. They *can* be blamed for not going further—as, for example, in not constitutionalizing the giant corporations and other centers of decentralized power; or in not seeing some of the lingering (even growing) "festering sores" of racial discrimination (in *James* v. *Valtierra, Warth* v. *Seldin, Milliken* v. *Bradley,* and *Rodriguez*)[88] or for unduly deferring to local officials, as in *Rizzo, Paul,* and *National League of Cities;*[89] or for not finding justiciability, when obviously there was a "case" or "controversy," as in *Laird* and *Richardson.*[90] These failures mean, at the very least, that the oracle can err, and err quite badly; and suggest that before the Supreme Court goes further, before it takes another giant step, serious thought be given to its composition.

The words of the litigable parts of the Constitution are, in the words of Learned Hand, "empty vessels into which [a judge] can pour nearly anything he will."[91] The Court, furthermore, should not be equated with an ordinary court of law; it is, at the very least, "a very special kind of court." Legal training as a consequence is not up to the needs of constitutional interpretation, unless it can be shown (as it cannot in the law schools and legal practice) that law includes all social knowledge. There is, therefore, no essential requirement that Supreme Court justices have legal training or a legal background to decide constitutional cases. That education and professional practice may well be counterproductive to the type of constitutional decisions that the Court should issue. In a changing society the relations between government and governed are essentially political; that is, decided on the grounds of social policy; and it is only by an intellectually indefensible fiction that they can be called logical deductions from the written instrument that is the Constitution. Judges need an appreciation of social conditions and an accurate appraisal of the actual effects of conduct.

The Constitution is an appeal to the decency and wisdom of those with whom its interpretation rests. Learned Hand, in a famous passage, declared that "everything turns upon the spirit" as a judge approaches the questions before him.[92] If a judge is properly to perform his function, Hand maintained that he must be aware of changing social tensions which require new schemes of adaptation and societal organization.

The requirement, then, is not for an *elegantia juris,* for the construction of an internally consistent edifice of legal principles, but for making socially wise decisions. Lawyers have no special expertise for that; and it is past time that presidents (and the Senate) recognize that and name to the Court men and women who have not had the alleged "benefits" of legal education (which, seen objectively, is a form of brain damage). The Constitution, as Woodrow Wilson told us, is not a mere lawyers' document.

American freedoms depend upon more than adherence to procedural niceties (even though Justices Brandeis and Frankfurter would have had it otherwise). They are, finally, dependent upon the type of society in which the citizenry lives—a society that will attempt to further, and succeed in furthering, the ideal of human dignity. Legalistic niceties are only a part, and a very small part at that, of such a society. We, as a people, must affirmatively know what we want and then try to get it. We must, in other words, eschew "pragmatism" as a philosophy, and avowedly construct and promulgate an ideology.

It is here that a properly constituted Supreme Court can be of major assistance to a polity that is floundering on an uncharted sea. Given the will, the justices can state norms toward which the people should aspire, can call attention to sores, festering and otherwise, in the body politic, can, that is to say, formulate general pronouncements of what Felix Cohen once called "the Good."[93] I do not say what specific principles should be enunciated as part of the Good— save in the highest level abstraction: to further the cause of human dignity the planet over, insofar as American public policies can influence that end.

That, to be sure, would be activism compounded, activism taken a giant step further. We should not flinch at the idea. Rather, we should determine the root causes of social discontent, of which there are many, and then ask whether the oracle in the marble palace has anything to say.

Conclusion

Under the Constitution of Quasi-Limitations the Court legitimized the nationalization of public policy in the early years of the nineteenth century. Having done that, it invented the constitutional doctrine of *raison d'etat* in the Civil War. But it did not rest. Principles of Social Darwinism—that the economy ought to be ruled by a plutocracy, that poverty is both inevitable and at bottom the fault of the poor themselves, and that government should be limited in socioeconomic affairs to the position of a policeman or night watchman—were read into the Constitution for about fifty years (from 1886 to 1936). In this, the justices did not lead but were led; they reflected the dominant economic forces in the nation. In legal terms, it was the heyday of substantive (economic) due process.

When the layer of the Constitution of Powers was added, the Court read new economic and political theories into the fundamental law. It is not too much to assert that in so doing they, as with FDR, helped to save "the system." Capitalism (in whatever form) would not have survived without that change, which came without amendment and which by and large was approved by the people. The change came, however, during America's Golden Age. The justices did more than create the Constitution of Powers; they sought and found a new role as protector of individual rights and liberties in the age of collectivism (both public and private). Now a new age is dawning, requiring another posture of government and of the Court. Crisis government is becoming routine; the Constitution of Control is being born out of the coalescing crises—the climacteric—that mark the modern era.

Just as the Supreme Court shifted gears and took on a new role under the Constitution of Powers, so too will it have to assume another role (as well as retaining its older one) under the new Constitution. I have suggested above what might be, knowing full well that those who oppose present-day activism will be appalled beyond measure at such a suggestion. I realize also that the justices may pronounce but that no one will listen; or if they do listen, that few will try to comply. The call is not for a Council of Revision, such as was voted down in the 1787 Convention, but for a Council of State, one with power to make affirmative statements, to render "advisory opinions" to the populace, as well as to perform the time-honored functions of the highest tribunal in the land. The nettle should be grasped, and soon. "The quality of the judge's performance is at bottom an ethical responsibility," Paul Freund has observed.[94] The ethical responsibility of the justices in the age of the Constitution of Control is to transcend historical limitations, to see their job large and whole, and to provide necessary moral leadership to a populace that knows not where it is or where it is going. The developing consciousness of the country deserves an institution that can speak and act with miracle, mystery, and authority. That is the Supreme Court as modern Delphic oracle. Some well-known words of Alfred North Whitehead may show the need:

> It is the first step in sociological wisdom to recognize that the major advances in civilization are processes which all but wreck the societies in which they occur—like unto an arrow in the hand of a child. The art of free society consists first in the maintenance of the symbolic code; and secondly in fearlessness of revision, to secure that the code serves those purposes which satisfy an enlightened reason. Those societies which cannot combine reverence to their symbols with freedom of revision, must ultimately decay either from anarchy, or from the slow atrophy of a life stifled by useless shadows.[95]

So it is. And so the Supreme Court may be able to do (or help Americans to do): maintain the symbolic code (which is the ancient Constitution) while fearlessly revising it.

One should not be sanguine about the Court doing this. Wedded to the legal profession and its attendant ideology of legalism, it will take more courage and wisdom than has thus far been apparent. But the trend seems clear: the direction in which the justices may and should be moving is outlined above. This, to be sure, does not answer the question of which values the Court should define and articulate. The concept of human dignity requires much more specificity. My position, to repeat, is that there is no other institution in the United States that is in a better position to identify and promulgate the details of that concept.

Is there, then, a case to be made for judicial activism? The answer can only be a more-than-tentative yes. Poor and puny though it is, fraught with fiat and arbitrariness though it may be, Supreme Court activism is the one reed—the one frail reed—that enables Americans, at times but far from always, to rise above the petty tyrannies of everyday life and see the world whole. It can challenge Americans with principles of legally concretized decency. Surely the justices cannot be blamed if their appeals to the conscience of Americans meet little or no response.

The contents of the dialogue over the Supreme Court have by and large been established by the Ivy League School, those termed by Judge J. Skelly Wright to be "self-appointed scholastic mandarins."[96] That is unfortunate, mainly because the developing dialogue has served to cloud issues and questions that badly need examination—for example, whether the results the Court reaches are consonant with "the Good." The "ultimate test of the justices' work," Judge Wright maintains, "must be goodness"—not, as the Ivy League School would have it, whether the decisions of the Court are accepted by the cognoscenti. The mandarins display a naive belief in the effectiveness of pluralism as a political process, coupled with an insensitivity to the legitimate claims of the politically powerless. One of their number, the late Alexander Bickel, spoke of "the jockeying, the bargaining, the trading, the threatening and promising, the checking and the balancing" of the political process in glowing (but erroneous) terms.[97] Even mandarins should be able to see what, in L'il Abner's terms, "any fool kin plainly see," that pluralism rewards only the powerful. There is indeed a compelling case to be made for judicial activism—now and in the future.

Notes

1. Robert G. McCloskey, *The Modern Supreme Court* (Cambridge: Harvard University Press, 1972), p. 338.

2. See Arthur S. Miller, "Judicial Activism and American Constitutionalism: Some Notes and Reflections," in *NOMOS XX: Constitutionalism,* ed. J. Roland Pennock and John W. Chapman (New York: New York University Press, 1979) pp. 333–376. Two important books, published since the present essay was written in 1980, have not been considered: John Hart Ely, *Democracy and Distrust: A Theory of Judicial Review* (Cambridge: Harvard University Press, 1980), and Jesse Choper, *The Supreme Court and the National Political Process* (Chicago: University of Chicago Press, 1980).

3. McCloskey, *The Modern Supreme Court,* p. 338.

4. Charles H. McIlwain, *Constitutionalism: Ancient and Modern* (Ithaca: Cornell University Press, 1958), p. 146.

5. Woodrow Wilson, *Congressional Government: A Study in American Politics* (New York: Meridian, 1967).

6. Macauley's observation is quoted in Louis Henkin, *Foreign Affairs and the Constitution* (Mineola, N.Y.: Foundation Press, 1972), p. 271; Gladstone's statement may be found in Arthur S. Miller, *The Supreme Court: Myth and Reality* (Westport, Conn.: Greenwood Press, 1978), p. 8. Lord Acton's acid comment is found in his *Lectures on Modern History* (Gloucester, Mass.: Peter Smith, 1960). Acton went on to say that development of the principle of federalism produced a powerful, prosperous, intelligent, and free community—a classic example of thinking that legal mechanisms can control social conditions. That is an example of what Franz Neumann called "constitutional fetishism." Franz Neumann, *The Democratic and the Authoritarian State* (Glencoe, Ill.: The Free Press, 1957).

7. *Nebbia v. New York,* 291 U.S. 502 (1934); *Home Building and Loan Association v. Blaisdell,* 290 U.S. 398 (1934); *West Coast Hotel Co. v. Parrish,* 300 U.S. 379 (1937); *NLRB v. Jones and Laughlin Steel Corp.,* 301 U.S. 1 (1937); *Helvering v. Davis,* 301 U.S. 619 (1937); *Steward Machine Co. v Davis,* 301 U.S. 548 (1937).

8. For a preliminary discussion see Arthur S. Miller, "Constitutional Law: Crisis Government Becomes the Norm," *Ohio State Law Journal* 39, no. 1 (1979), pp. 736-751.

9. Said Toynbee: "In all developed countries, a new way of life—a severely regimented way—will have to be imposed by ruthless authoritarian government." *Christian Science Monitor,* Feb. 10, 1975, p. 5.

10. For a discussion, see Arthur S. Miller, *Democratic Dictatorship: The Emergent Constitution of Control* (Westport, Conn.: Greenwood Press, 1981).

11. Gianfranco Poggi, *The Development of the Modern State* (Stanford: Stanford University Press, 1978), p. 128.

12. 358 U.S. 1 (1958).

13. This area of the Court's work has received almost no scholarly attention. The difference is that between, say, *Marbury v. Madison,* 1 Cranch 137 (1803) and *Miranda v. Arizona,* 384 U.S. 436 (1966).

14. Strenuous efforts to reconcile present-day decisions by the Court with the original document usually end in verbal confusion. See, for example, John Hart Ely, "Foreword: On Discovering Fundamental Values," *Harvard Law Review* 92 (November 1978), pp. 5-55; Raoul Berger, *Government by Judiciary: The Transformation of the Fourteenth Amendment* (Cambridge: Harvard University Press, 1977). See also Arthur S. Miller, "The Elusive Search for Values in Constitutional Interpretation," *Hastings Constitutional Law Quarterly* 6 (Spring 1979):487-509.

15. *Marbury v. Madison,* 1 Cranch 137 (1803); Louis B. Boudin, *Government by Judiciary* (New York, Godwin, 1932); Berger, *Government by Judiciary.*

16. Alexander M. Bickel, *The Least Dangerous Branch: The Supreme Court at the Bar of Politics* (Indianapolis: Bobbs-Merrill, 1962), p. 103.

17. Thomas Hobbes, *Leviathan,* ed. Michael Oakeshott (New York: Macmillan, 1962), p. 205.

18. See "The Supreme Court, 1977 Term," *Harvard Law Review* 92 (November 1978):333-335. Subsequent surveys verify this point.

19. Professor Ely thinks the answer to the observation that legislatures are not democratic is to make them more democratic. But he does not vouchsafe any way to do that; or, indeed, does not proffer any definition of democracy. See Ely, "On Discovering Fundamental Values."

20. See Mostafa Rejai, *Democracy: The Contemporary Theories* (New York: Atherton, 1967).

21. Bernard R. Crick, "Introduction," Niccolo Machiavelli, *The Discourses,* ed. Bernard R. Crick (Harmondsworth, England: Penguin, 1970), p. 27.

22. Alexander Hamilton, James Madison, and John Jay, *The Federalist,* ed. Clinton Rossiter (New York: New American Library, 1961), No. 51.

23. As the late Adolf Berle pointed out, this cry was used in medieval times as "a recognized means of appeal to the conscience of feudal power." It is "probably one of the origins of the British law of equity." Adolf A. Berle, *The*

Twentieth-Century Capitalist Revolution (New York: Harcourt, Brace, 1954), p. 62. In other words, even the king was not exempt.

24. See Arthur S. Miller, "*Brown's* 25th: A Silver Lining Tarnished with Time," *District Lawyer* 3 (April/May, 1979):22-30. Aviam Soifer, "Complacency and Constitutional Law," *Ohio State Law Journal* 42 (1981):383-409.

25. Daniel Bell, "The End of American Exceptionalism," *The Public Interest* 41 (Fall 1975):193-224.

26. Bickel, *The Least Dangerous Branch,* p. 109. Bickel evidently changed his mind toward the end of his life. See Alexander M. Bickel, *The Supreme Court and the Idea of Progress* (New York: Harper and Row, 1970). Judge J. Skelly Wright took this book apart with aplomb in "Professor Bickel, The Scholarly Tradition, and the Supreme Court," *Harvard Law Review* 84 (February 1971):769-805.

27. See Arthur S. Miller, "The Myth of Objectivity in Legal Research and Writing," *Catholic University Law Review* 18, no. 3 (1969):290-307. On judges, see J. Braxton Craven, Jr., "Paean to Pragmatism," *North Carolina Law Review* 50 (June 1972):977-1015.

28. See, for example, Gunnar Myrdal, *The Political Element in the Development of Economic Theory* (London: Routledge and Kegan Paul, 1953).

29. See Philip B. Kurland, "Foreword: 'Equal in Origin and Equal in Title to the Legislative and Executive Branches of the Government,'" *Harvard Law Review* 78 (November 1964):143-176. For a discussion of Frankfurter's influence, see H.N. Hirsch, *The Enigma of Felix Frankfurter* (New York: Basic Books, 1981).

30. See Judith N. Shklar, *Legalism* (Cambridge: Harvard University Press, 1964).

31. See Miller, *The Supreme Court,* chap. 5. See also Hans A. Linde, "Judges, Critics, and the Realist Tradition," *Yale Law Journal* 82 (December 1972):227-256. Linde writes: "However useful it is to recognize that the law emerges from what judges do, it does not serve well as a source of premises for what judges should do." (p. 252).

32. See Walter F. Murphy, *Elements of Judicial Strategy* (Chicago: University of Chicago Press, 1964).

33. *Osborn v. Bank of the United States,* 22 U.S. 738 (1824).

34. The best discussion is in Shklar, *Legalism.*

35. William Ray Forrester, "Are We Ready for Truth in Judging?," *American Bar Association Journal* 63 (September 1977):1212-1216.

36. Leonard W. Levy, *Against the Law: The Nixon Court and Criminal Justice* (New York: Harper Torchbooks, 1974), xiv.

37. Wright, "Professor Bickel, the Scholarly Tradition, and the Supreme Court," p. 803.

38. The legend of the Grand Inquisitor may be found in Fyodor Dostoevsky's novel, *The Brothers Karamazov,* ed. Ralph Matlaw (New York: Norton, 1976).

39. Rufus E. Miles, *Awakening from the American Dream: The Social and Political Limits to Growth* (New York: Universe Books, 1976), p. 224.

40. See Christopher Lasch, *The Culture of Narcissism: American Life in an Age of Diminishing Expectations* (New York: Norton, 1979). The "me generation" epithet is a creation of journalist Tom Wolfe.

41. The president as "high priest" is discussed in Miller, *Democratic Dictatorship.*

42. Theodore J. Lowi, *The End of Liberalism: Ideology, Policy, and the Crisis of Public Authority,* 2nd ed. (New York: Norton, 1979).

43. Thomas E. Cronin, *The State of the Presidency* (Boston: Little, Brown, 1975).

44. Chief Justice Earl Warren candidly acknowledged this in his valedictory. See 395 U.S. vii (1969).

45. See Arthur S. Miller and Jerome A. Barron, "The Supreme Court, the Adversary System, and the Flow of Information to the Justices: A Preliminary Inquiry," *Virginia Law Review* 61 (October 1975):1187-1245; Charles M. Lamb, "Judicial Policy-Making and Information Flow to the Supreme Court," *Vanderbilt Law Review* 29 (January 1976): 45-124.

46. 301 U.S. 1 (1937).

47. 300 U.S. 379 (1937). *Parrish* set forth a new theory of liberty under the due process clause. See Arthur S. Miller, *Social Change and Fundamental Law: America's Evolving Constitution* (Westport, Conn.: Greenwood Press, 1979), chap. 4.

48. Ibid.

49. *Missouri ex rel. Gaines v. Canada,* 305 U.S. 337 (1938).

50. *Screws v. United States,* 325 U.S. 91 (1945); *United States v. Classic,* 313 U.S. 299 (1941).

51. *Smith v. Allwright,* 231 U.S. 649 (1944).

52. 334 U.S. 1 (1948). See also *Barrows v. Jackson,* 346 U.S. 249 (1953).

53. *Brown v. Board of Education,* 347 U.S. 483 (1954); *Baker v. Carr,* 369 U.S. 186 (1962); *Miranda v. Arizona,* 384 U.S. 486 (1966); *Roe v. Wade,* 410 U.S. 113 (1973).

54. John A.G. Griffith, *The Politics of the Judiciary* (London: Fontana, 1977), p. 213.

55. Berger, *Government by Judiciary.*

56. Nathan Glazer, "Towards an Imperial Judiciary?" *The Public Interest* 41 (Fall 1975):104-123.

57. Adolf A. Berle, *Power* (New York: Harcourt, Brace and World, 1969).

58. Alexander H. Pekelis, *Law and Social Action* (Ithaca: Cornell University Press, 1950).

59. See Learned Hand, "Mr. Justice Holmes," in *The Spirit of Liberty,* ed. Irving Dillard (New York: Vintage, 1953), p. 62.

60. Jacob W. Landynski, "The Making of Constitutional Law," *Social Research* 31 (March 1964):44. Landynski does not suggest how those "deepest feelings" can be identified, or how to deal with the possibility that, when identified, they may indeed be contradictory to and perhaps contrary to concepts of decency and human dignity. On the latter point see Ely, "On Discovering Fundamental Values."

61. *United Steelworkers v. Weber,* 443 U.S. 193 (1979); *Regents of the University of California v. Bakke,* 438 U.S. 265 (1978); *San Antonio School District v. Rodriguez,* 411 U.S. 1 (1973).

62. See Robert A. Horn, *Groups and the Constitution* (Stanford: Stanford University Press, 1956); Michael J. Phillips, "Thomas Hill Green, Positive Freedom and the United States Supreme Court," *Emory Law Journal* 25 (Winter 1976):63-114.

63. An immense literature exists on the coming "age of frugality," although not all of it speaks in those terms. For discussion and bibliography see Edward Cornish, *The Study of the Future* (Washington: The World Future Society, 1977).

64. Arthur F. Bentley, *The Process of Government* (Chicago: University of Chicago Press, 1908), p. 268.

65. See Arthur S. Miller, "Toward Constitutionalizing the Corporation: A Speculative Essay," *West Virginia Law Review* 80 (Winter 1978):187-208.

66. See *Amalgamated Food Employees Union v. Logan Valley Plaza,* 391 U.S. 308 (1968); *Marsh v. Alabama,* 326 U.S. 501 (1946).

67. Leicester C. Webb, *Legal Personality and Political Pluralism* (Carlton: Melbourne University Press, 1958), p. 194.

68. See Miller, "Toward Constitutionalizing the Corporation." Just as the antitrust laws permit private actions for antitrust violations, so too should the Court by extending the Fourteenth Amendment.

69. See Arthur S. Miller and Lewis D. Solomon, "Constitutional Chains for the Corporate Beast," *Business and Society Review* 27 (Fall 1978):15-19.

70. See Miller, *The Supreme Court,* p. 186, note 11. See also Sir William Blackstone, *Commentaries on the Laws of England,* quoted in Walter F. Murphy and C. Herman Pritchett, *Courts, Judges, and Politics: An Introduction to the Judicial Process,* 3d ed. (New York: Random House, 1979), p. 14: The judge is "sworn to determine, not according to his own private judgment, but according to the known laws and customs of the land; not delegated to pronounce a new law, but to maintain and expound the old."

71. The problem for the Court is to bring the Constitution into consonance with Federick Jackson Turner's observation: "Behind institutions, behind constitutional forms and modifications, lie the vital forces that call these organs into life and shape them to meet changing conditions." Frederick Jackson Turner, *The Frontier in American History* (New York: Holt, 1920), p. 2.

72. This theme will be developed in detail in Arthur S. Miller, "Oracle in the Marble Palace: Politics and the Supreme Court," (in preparation).

73. *Warth v. Seldin,* 422 U.S. 490, 519 (1975) (dissenting opinion). The majority denied standing to plaintiffs to contest exclusionary zoning ordinances.

74. Ronald G. Downing, "Judicial Ethics and the Political Role of Courts," *Law and Contemporary Problems* 35 (Winter 1970):106-107.

75. See the introduction to U.S., Senate, Special Commission on National Emergencies and Delegated Emergency Powers, *A Brief History of Emergency Powers in the United States* (Washington, D.C.: Government Printing Office, 1974).

76. 90 Stat. 1257 (1976).

77. Miller, "Constitutional Law."

78. James Q. Wilson, "The Rise of the Bureaucratic State," *The Public Interest* 41 (Fall 1975):77.

79. See Amaury de Riencourt, *The Coming Caesars* (New York: Coward-McCann, 1957).

80. As previous justices have done, without fail, throughout American history, although at times they have chosen to duck ruling on the merits.

81. See William Ophuls, *Ecology and the Politics of Scarcity: Prologue to a Political Theory of the Steady State* (San Francisco: W.H. Freeman, 1977).

82. *Brown v. Allen,* 344 U.S. 443 (1953).

83. See Miller, *The Supreme Court,* chap. 5.

84. See Abram Chayes, "The Role of the Judge in Public Law Litigation," *Harvard Law Review* 89 (May 1976):1281.

85. Nathan Glazer, "Should Judges Administer Social Services?," *The Public Interest* 50 (Winter 1978):64-80.

86. 62 N.J. 473 (1973).

87. This question has been little discussed in the literature, even though it is commonly accepted that Article III judges do have limits on their powers. But see Chayes, "The Role of the Judge in Public Law Litigation;" Robert F. Nagel, "Separation of Powers and the Scope of Federal Equitable Remedies," *Stanford Law Review* 30 (April 1978):661-724.

88. 402 U.S. 137 (1971); 422 U.S. 490 (1975); 418 U.S. 717 (1974); 411 U.S. 1 (1973).

89. *Rizzo v. Goode,* 423 U.S. 362 (1976); *Paul v. Davis,* 424 U.S. 693 (1977); *National League of Cities v. Usery,* 426 U.S. 833 (1976).

90. *Laird v. Tatum,* 408 U.S. 1 (1972); *United States v. Richardson,* 418 U.S. 166 (1974).

91. Learned Hand, "Sources of Tolerance," *University of Pennsylvania Law Review* 79 (November 1930):12.

92. *Ibid.*

93. See Felix S. Cohen, *Ethical Systems and Legal Ideals* (Westport, Conn.: Greenwood Press, 1976); Wright, "Professor Bickel, the Scholarly Tradition, and the Supreme Court."

94. Paul A. Freund, *The Supreme Court of the United States: Its Business, Purposes, and Performance* (Cleveland: Meridian, 1961), p. 181.

95. Alfred North Whitehead, *Symbolism: Its Meaning and Effect* (New York: Macmillan, 1927), p. 88.

96. Wright, "Professor Bickel, the Scholarly Tradition, and the Supreme Court."

97. Bickel, *The Supreme Court and the Idea of Progress;* Laurence Tribe, "Seven Pluralist Fallacies: In Defense of the Adversary Process," *University of Miami Law Review* 33 (November 1978):43-57.

Line-Drawing between Judicial Activism and Restraint: A "Centrist" Approach and Analysis

Henry J. Abraham

To locate and draw an identifiable, let alone a viable, line between what, for want of a more descriptively accurate appellation, may appropriately be called "judicial activism" and "judicial restraint," is arguably at best vexatious and at worst impossible. Indeed, I have pressed the latter point of view on a number of occasions.[1] Yet, notwithstanding the myriad normative considerations that inform the syndrome, "impossible" is at once too strong and too defeatist a characterization—provided one is prepared to stipulate a number of a priori basic postulates of our system of government and politics. While some, or even all, of these postulates may well be controversial in their application to the governmental process, they do represent facts and facets of its existence. Without endeavoring to be exhaustive, and without any attempt to rank-order them, they comprise the following:

1. Ours is a system of separation of powers that envisages degrees of institutional independence, subject to checks and balances that are constitutionally both explicit and implicit. Independence is thus checked by interdependence and by restraints specifically delineated by the basic law of the land. Applied interpretations of the power and authority of each branch differ, but their separate existences are generically and developmentally self-evident. While it is possible to identify periods of our history in which one of the three branches dominated one or even both of the others,[2] and while the dominant branch has but rarely been the judiciary—exceptions being the heyday of John Marshall's chief justiceship, portions of Fuller's and of Hughes's, and, to some degree, Warren's—the judicial branch *is* endowed with tools which enable it to influence and at times direct the sociogovernmental *vie quotidienne.*

2. The ultimate judicial club-in-the-closet is the power of judicial review. Although some academic argument still occasionally surfaces as to its literal justification in terms of the Constitution's language, the argument over judicial review has, in fact, been settled by history. The judiciary's power to say both yes and no to the other branches of the national government and to the constituent states is really beyond dispute. Even such pronounced contemporary critics of the judicial role as Raoul Berger do not challenge the presence and authenticity of judicial review per se; rather, they challenge its application in specific categories and instances.[3] Nor is there any basic argument as to the legitimacy of the

judiciary's penultimate power, the power of statutory interpretation or construction, a power called upon far more frequently, and far more comfortably, than the power of judicial review. What is of the essence of the underlying argument, however, is the elusive line between appropriately applied judicial review or judicial interpretation and prescriptive policymaking—which, of course, lies at the heart of the difficult assignment of distinguishing between judicial activism and judicial restraint.

3. Our system of government was designed neither as a pure democracy nor as one to be dominated by "Platonic guardians" or some other elite group, but as a system characterized by representative democracy, popular sovereignty, majoritarianism, duly limited by observance of minority rights, a federal structure, a written Constitution capable of growth or contraction, and separation of powers. Under that system the national legislative function was assigned to the people's representatives in Congress, and, by the tenor and implications of the Tenth Amendment, to the state legislatures in their appropriate spheres. The governing document, that superbly elastic product of compromise born of both experience and theory, thus emphatically vested the legislative function in the people's representatives. It did not vest it in the executive branch—other than in certain supportive manifestations outlined specifically in the document—and it certainly did not vest it in the judicial branch. It did assign crucial jurisdictional authority to that branch in the governmental process, and, as I have argued, it unquestionably implied the presence of the power of judicial review, but the Constitution reserved the fundamental power to legislate to the legislature. The Constitution did not, for it could not, mandate legislative wisdom; it did not, for it could not, mandate legislative productivity; it did not, for it could not, mandate legislative fairness, sensitivity, or even "democracy." It *did* mandate legislative authority and power, duly limited by constituional parameters and by the applicable checks and balances of the other branches of the government.

Thus, for better or for worse—and it is not infrequently for the latter—laws are designed to be fashioned and framed by the people's representatives in the national legislature and in those of the fifty states. Whatever one may think of the merits of their performances—and they rarely receive a high mark from their sovereigns, the people who sent them there—legislators are replaceable via the electoral process, a process that has been vastly, albeit not without controversy, "democratized" by the judiciary. In extremis, the legislatures' role, even the very institution of the legislative branch itself, is subject to change by constitutional amendment, although this requires genuine toil and trouble. In other words, while the Constitution requires adherence to its explicit and implicit terms and commands, that Constitution cannot and does not require legislative wisdom. All it can and does mandate is that legislative actions be performed in accordance with constitutional authority. "We fully understand . . . the very powerful argument that can be made against the wisdom of this legislation, but on that point we have no concern," was the clipped language of one of Justice Holmes's opinions for the Court.[4] And, in more colorful fashion, Holmes elaborated this constitutional and judicial philosophy to the then sixty-one-year-old Justice Stone: "Young man, about 75 years ago I learned that I was not God. And so, when the people . . . want to do something I can't find anything in the Constitution expressly forbidding them to do, I say, whether I like it or not, 'Goddamit, let'em do it.' "[5] Or, as Holmes said to famed constitutional lawyer John W. Davis on another occasion: "Of course I know, and every other sensible man knows, that the Sherman law [the Sherman Antitrust Act of 1890] is damned nonsense, but if my country wants to go to hell, I am here to help it."[6] Holmes's adoring disciple, Felix Frankfurter, who would inherit the master's chair in 1938—after its magnificent, though all-too-brief, occupancy by Cardozo—and who would become one of the most ardent and consistent advocates of judicial restraint (notwithstanding his unquestionable lifelong personal commitment to civil rights and civil liberties), well articulated the heart of the matter long before he ascended to the bench when he wrote: "Even the most rampant worshipper of judicial supremacy admits that wisdom and justice are not the tests of constitutionality"[7]—although one wonders whether Justice Douglas, for one, especially in his later years on the Court, would have accepted that statement as to "justice." Once on the Court, Frankfurter time and again lectured his colleagues and his countrymen in the same vein, as when he dissented vigorously from the Court majority's declaration of unconstitutionality of a section of the Immigration and Nationality Act of 1940:

> It is not easy to stand aloof and allow want of wisdom to prevail, to disregard one's own strongly held view of what is wise in the conduct of affairs. *But it is not the business of this Court to pronounce policy.* It must observe a fastidious regard for limitations on its own power, and this precludes the Court's giving effect to its own notions of what is wise or politic. That self-restraint is of the essence in the observance of the judicial oath, for the Constitution has not authorized the judges to sit in judgment on the wisdom of what Congress and the Executive Branch do.[8]

In what is probably his most famous exhortation of judicial abstention, he veritably cried out in the minority in the historic *West Virginia Flag Salute Case* of 1943:

> One who belongs to the most vilified and persecuted minority in history [the Jews] is not likely to be insensible to the freedoms guaranteed by our Constitution. Were my purely personal attitude relevant I should wholeheartedly associated myself with the general libertarian views in the Court's opinion [that West Virginia's compulsory flag salute by public school children violated their First and Fourteenth Amendment rights], representing as they do the thought and action of a lifetime. But as judges we are neither Jew nor Gentile, neither Catholic nor agnostic. We owe equal attachment to the Constitution and are equally

bound by our judicial obligations whether we derive our citizenship from the earliest or the latest immigrants to these shores. *As a member of this Court I am not justified in writing my private notions of policy into the Constitution, no matter how mischievous I may deem their disregard* . . . . Most unwillingly, therefore, I must differ from my brethren with regard to legislation like this. I cannot bring my mind to believe that the word "liberty" secured by the Due Process [of Law] Clause [of the Fourteenth Amendment] gives this Court authority to deny to the State of West Virginia the attainment of that which we all recognize as a legitimate legislative end, namely the promotion of good citizenship, by employment of the means here chosen.[9]

Philip Elman, then Frankfurter's law clerk, attempted to dissuade his Justice from that opinion, but "F.F." snapped: "This is my opinion, not yours."[10] To side, as I do, with Elman, does not vitiate, however, the fundamental justification of Frankfurter's jurisprudential posture—which is inexorably central to an approach to a viable line between judicial activism and judicial restraint.

4. Although it is self-evident, it must be recognized and ever reiterated that the individuals who comprise the members of the judiciary are, after all, human. Being human, they respond to human reactions. "Judges are men, not disembodied spirits; as men they respond to human situations," in Frankfurter's words.[11] They do not reside in a vacuum. They are not "dummies, unspotted by human emotions," as the demonstrably emotional Justice McReynolds put it.[12] "Our judges," wrote Chief Justice Warren early in his career on the Court, "are not monks or scientists, but participants in the living stream of our national life, steering the law between the dangers of rigidity on the one hand and formlessness on the other."[13] Similarly, in the realistic words of Justice John H. Clarke: "I have never known any judges, no matter how austere of manner, who discharged their judicial duties in an atmosphere of pure, unadulterated reason. Alas! We are all 'the common growth of Mother Earth,'—even those of us who wear the long robe."[14] And the great Cardozo spoke elegantly of the "cardiac promptings of the moment," musing that the "great tides and currents which engulf the rest of men do not turn aside in their course and pass the judges by."[15] These are honest, eloquent, realistic assessments and explanations of the facts of life of the judicial role. But they are *explanations*—not justifications per se for a conscious or subconscious failure to observe that elusive line between judicial activism and restraint. There is, quite naturally, an explanation for everything we do. But an explanation is by no means a justification. Certainly an explanation does not absolve us from the quest for the, or a line.

* * * * *

Whether the articulator of a putative line between judicial activism and judicial restraint be a participant in the judicial process, an observer, a student, or a professional cirtic, any such "line" must be articulated, no matter how slippery its definition or application. To their credit, members of the bench as well as outside commentators have often, and at times carefully, outlined their efforts to articulate the line between activism and restraint. Before endeavoring to suggest a "centrist" approach, some of these proposals or postures deserve examination. Without attempting to cite or examine each of them, they have included, but have not been confined to, the following:

1. *The frank resort to judicial activism based on personal philosophical commitments to policy goals.* It would be fair to conclude that Justice Douglas's jurisprudence throughout his record tenure of more than thirty six years on the Supreme Court of the United States is a vivid testimonial to this kind of commitment. Certainly in the realm of civil rights and civil liberties one may contend that the justice's noble heart embraced a policy of attaining "justice at any cost" rather than the emblematic "equal justice under law." An obvious illustration of such judicial reaching-out in the absence of demonstrable linguistic constitutional warrant is his now famous (or infamous) opinion for the Court in *Griswold* v. *Connecticut,*[16] in which he frankly invoked "penumbras," "radiations," and "emanations" from six different provisions of the Bill of Rights in order to declare unconstitutional Connecticut's admittedly absurd and obviously unenforceable anticontraceptive statute. But was that ridiculous statute really unconstitutional rather than absurd, or was it, as Justice Stewart put it in dissent, merely "uncommonly silly?" Should we quarantine our elected legislators against silliness or asininity? Justice Black, that towering champion of freedom, also in dissent in *Griswold,* did not think so.

2. *Reasoned endeavors to live by the basic tenets of judicial restraint.* On this point it would be natural to quote some of Justice Frankfurter's often preachy exhortations. Yet he hardly stood alone. Equally committed was his colleague and disciple on the Court, Justice John Marshall Harlan, who, although somewhat more flexible than "F.F.," often articulated the theme of restraint. He did so memorably in dissenting from the "one-person-one-vote" ruling by the Court in *Reynolds* v. *Sims,* [17] which held that the Constitution of the United States required *both* houses of state legislatures to be apportioned solely on the basis of population. Harlan admonished the Court and country that the "Constitution is not a panacea for every blot upon the public welfare; nor should this Court, ordained as a judicial body, be thought of as a general haven for reform movements."[18] Other more recent illustrations are the dissenting opinions by Justices John Paul Stevens and William H. Rehnquist in *Regents of the University of California* v. *Bakke*[19] and *Steelworkers* v. *Weber,*[20] respectively, in which they pointed to what in all fairness would appear to be crystal clear language in Title VI of the Civil Rights Act of 1964 (in the first case) and in Title VII (in the second), *forbidding* in so many words what the five-member majority in each of the two cases contended was *not* forbidden.

3. *An avowed pragmatism about the "felt necessities of the time."* This famed Holmesian phrase, used initially on the very first page of his 1881 work, *The Common Law,*[21] has ironically been used and applied as an instrument for both judicial activism and restraint. Holmes in effect saw it as the latter in the sense that he wished to admonish the judicial branch to be deferential to ongoing legislative enactments that plowed new public policy furrows, that seemed to give vent to contemporary popular aims and aspirations, as interpreted by the legislative branch, rather than as license for the courts to write their own contemporary notions of "felt necessities" into law. As he once observed to one of his early law clerks, Francis Biddle, that "feeling" of the "necessities of the time" was to be done by legislators, not by judges. Absent such legislative "feeling," the Court unanimously embraced the obvious "felt necessities of the time" in its *Brown* I and II public school desegregation decisions of 1954 and 1955.[22] There it resorted to the burgeoning spirit, rather than to the history of the equal protection of the laws clause of the Fourteenth Amendment in order to strike down governmentally mandated segregation in the public schools of state and nation. As the Court indeed did in those two historic decisions, although hardly without controversy, it must, of course, be able to hinge the "felt necessities" upon constitutional warrant. Without such warrant, however, those "necessities" must be left to legislative judgment, no matter how approbative the members of the judiciary may or may not be as members of the American body politic.

4. *A perceived obligation to embrace "the mores of the day."* More or less related to the "felt necessities," but still more wide-lensed, this perception by the judiciary raises even more questions as to the propriety and authority of its role. For who is to pronounce those mores, and how they are perceived by the sovereign people? This vexatious issue is painfully illustrated by the Court's so far unsuccessful quest to draw a line, at once predictable and acceptable, on the frontiers of the ubiquitous problem of obscenity—where judicial formulae upon judicial formulae have proved to be unworkable in the long run, if not always in the short.[23] The basic issue is drawing a viable line between the First and Fourteenth Amendment exhortations for freedom of expression and the state's, or rather society's, right to regulate morals. Given the breadth and vagueness of the constitutional injunctions of "speech and press" and "due process," judicial solutions become arguably acceptable or rejectable in the face of dubiously valid legislative responses. Yet when a constitutional provision specifically permits legislative action, as in the recently much-litigated realm of capital punishment— that is, the Fifth and Fourteenth Amendment provisions that render such punishment feasible, given the presence of "due process of law"—notions of "the mores of the day," even if judicially expressed, may not replace the legislative authority, provided the latter stays within the limits of constitutional bounds. Still, dissenting in *Gregg* v. *Georgia,*[24] Justice Brennan tried to justify his vote on the grounds that "evolving standards of decency" in effect required a holding that the death penalty constitutes a "cruel and unusual punishment" that is

proscribed by the Eighth Amendment.[25] He advanced that contention, notwith-standing the fact that the Fourteenth Amendment, which permits deprivation of life *with* due process of law, was enacted fully seventy six years after the Eighth! Nonetheless, he not only found an ally in Justice Thurgood Marshall, but Marshall went so far as to urge a declaration of unconstitutionality not only on the ground suggested by Brennan, but also because of the failure of the citizenry to be intelligently informed.[26] Whatever one's feeling about the wisdom, nature, and effect of capital punishment may be, it *is* constitutionally permissible in the presence of "due process of law," assuming legislative enactment therof. Judicial interposition on the basis of "evolving standards of decency" and/or "the mores of the day" represent the rankest kind of impermissible judicial activism.

5. *Attempts to hew to an interpretative course based strictly upon a "literal" reading of the Constitution.* This course of action is a priori appealing since it seems to provide a yardstick to assure a modicum of certainty and even predictability; but is is nevertheless deceptive. Although the "literalist" ap-proach was carefully articulated and embraced by Justice Hugo L. Black throughout his distinguished, lengthy tenure on the Court (most notably in his conceptualization of the commands of the First Amendment), it is fraught with considerably more difficulty than meets the eye. Justice Black himself recog-nized that fact with his distinction between "expression" (which he viewed as an absolute, unabridgable constitutional guarantee) and "conduct" (which he viewed as abridgable in the presence of due process of law). Although he was remarkably faithful to his absolutist-literalist approach, he consequently en-countered difficulties in his dichotomous application of "expression" and "con-duct," leading him to conclude wrongly that the wearing of black armbands by public school children in protest against the Vietnam War did not constitute protected symbolic freedom of expression.[27] Moreover, how does one "literal-ize" due process of law and equal protection of the laws? And what does one do with adjectives such as "unreasonable," as in the Fourth Amendment barrier against "unreasonable" searches and seizures—but, presumably not, and as Justice Black often so ruled,[28] against "reasonable" ones? As Justice Black put his faith and his creed on more than one occasion, valiantly striving to be consis-tently literalist:

> I will not distort the words of the [Constitution] in order to "keep the Constitution up to date" or "to bring it into harmony with the times." It was never meant for this Court to have such power, which in effect would make us a continuously functioning constitutional conven-tion.[29]

It is difficult to argue with so principled a contention, yet it is neither an unfail-ing nor a final answer to the problem at hand.

6. *Protestations in favor of embracing a "sliding scale of values" or a "spec-trum of standards."* Closely related to the third and fourth solutions suggested

by various protagonists in the quest for the line-drawing prize, this stance has recently been most consistently associated with the jurisprudential commitments of Justices Brennan and Marshall, especially the latter. Thus, dissenting in *San Antonio Independent School District* v. *Rodriguez*,[30] in which the Court narrowly upheld the Texas system of financing public education by property tax assessments, Marshall stated:

> A principled reading of what this Court has done reveals that it has applied a spectrum of standards in reviewing discrimination allegedly violative of the Equal Protection Clause. This spectrum clearly comprehends variations in the degree of care with which the Court will scrutinize particular classifications, *depending, I believe, on the constitutional and societal importance of the interest adversely affected* and the recognized invidiousness of the basis upon which the particular classification is drawn.[31]

Indubitably an extreme manifestation of judicial activism, the "sliding scale of values" or "spectrum of standards" classification approach has in fact commanded shifting majorities on the Court of late. What it has done is to create a model of triple standards or "tiers" of review under which, by dint of majoritarian judicial classification, certain legislative or executive actions are accorded a stricter judicial scrutiny than others. Thus, economic-proprietarian legislation is given the lowest standard of scrutiny, with the Court merely asking whether the legislature had a "rational" basis for enacting it.[32] The next level, which is accorded closer scrutiny than the former group, but not as close as the one to follow, includes those political processes, such as voting and election processes, that were indentified in Justice Stone's famous 1938 footnote in *United States* v. *Carolene Products Corporation*[33] as deserving of "more exacting judicial review," since they were and are viewed as "preferred freedoms." The group entitled to the highest degree of scrutiny, calling upon government to demonstrate a "compelling state interest" in order to achieve judicial approval, is that composed of what Stone identified as "discrete and insular minorities,"[34] also referred to as "suspect categories," such as race, alienage, and nationality.[35] The realm of sex or gender appears to be lodged somewhere between the highest and next-to-highest judicial categories in terms of the degree of scrutiny.[36] It is not at all impossible to defend the creation and application of such judicially applied "double standards," or even "triple standards." And, as I have attempted to show in other writings,[37] the children and grandchildren of the Cardozo "fundamental rights" dichotomy established in *Palko* v. *Connecticut*[38] in 1937 are *de minimis* explainable and justifiable. That these tiered rights represent a prima facie example of demonstrable judicial activism is beyond argument, however.

   7. *A course of judicial response based upon the notion of whether or not an action by government "shocks the conscience."* This is Frankfurter's well-known

and controversial test,[39] which was put less delicately by Justice Holmes in an exchange with his colleague Stone, in which the latter inquired as to the Holmes test for the presence of a violation of "due process of law," with Holmes responding, "when it makes me vomit."[40] These tests place a premium on individual perceptions, as was equally true, for example, of Justice Potter Stewart's response to the question of when an alleged instance of "hard core pornography" could be proscribed without violating First Amendment rights; "I know it when I see it," he quipped, not at all in jest.[41] This type of judicial review obviously places too high a premium upon one's faith in individual jurists' perceptions; it renders judicial consistency unlikely; and it makes a mockery of even a modicum of reliable predictability. Attractive theoretically as a case-by-case approach, it nonetheless invites the sarcastic question by Justice Black to his colleague Frankfurter: "Whose conscience, Felix, yours or mine?"[42] Violent sick-to-stomach levels assuredly vary with physical reactions to stress. The two tests are patently subjective and constitute unacceptable exercises of judicial activism, no matter how much faith one may have in the integrity and jurisprudence of a Frankfurter or a Holmes.

8. *The much-discussed and much-touted "neutral principles" approach to the elusive line.* Here I refer to Herbert Wechsler's well-known, controversial "solution" to the activism–restraint issue. Essentially a search for transcendent, "objective" principles of constitutional law that would be both lasting and neutral in their application, the Wechsler formula, expounded in his Holmes lectures at Harvard University over two decades ago,[43] has an appealing quality. Upon close examination, however, its pitfalls become readily apparent, notwithstanding its intellectual imaginativeness and buoyant resourcefulness. What is a "principle," and what constitutes "neutrality?" Moreover, even if one were to agree on acceptable definitions for both of these nouns, might not a genuinely "principled" application of judicial "neutrality" become self-defeating or cause a constitutional stalemate? This danger and potential frustration are nicely underscored by Wechsler's most frequently urged neutral principle, that of associational freedom, which is a veritable two-edged sword. Wechsler maintains that the constitutional issue in state-enforced segregation involved not discrimination but freedom of association. Freedom of association is denied by segregation, yet he insists that integration forces association. Wechsler questioned whether there was a "basis in neutral principles for holding that the claims for association should prevail."[44] Should they? And if they do prevail, do they really constitute a viable line between judicial activism and judicial restraint on so delicate an issue as that of race, which has more frequently been laced with allegations of applications of extrajudicial power, of judicial activism, than has any other current strand of public policy.

The eight suggested formulae for the desired line between activism and restraint discussed above have thus all been found at least partly defective— which of course is not to say that some or all of them have not been embraced, partly or even wholly, by practitioners, students, and observers questing for a linear solution. The latter is naturally most easily attained for and by those who are either complete judicial activists or adherents to resolute judicial restraint. What follows, however, is a capsule attempt to establish and support a "centrist" position in the continuing controversy.

* * * * *

There is nothing particularly novel, mysterious, or cerebral about the "centrist" position I propose. Neither doctrinaire nor open-ended, based on what Thomas Reed Powell was fond of viewing as "the logic of American constitutional law," namely, "the common sense of the Supreme Court,"[45] it embraces as its foundation the four corollaries suggested earlier in this essay: (1) A firm commitment, for better or for worse, to our system of separation of powers, is necessary, modified by the attendant checks and balances, and featuring the hallmark of genuine judicial independence. (2) We must accept, philosophically as well as pragmatically, the powers of judicial review and statutory construction. Be they regarded as expressed or implied in our fundamental document, history has amply settled their presence in our governmental scheme. (3) Our Constitution entrusts the legislative power and function to the people's elected representatives in the several legislative halls. Theirs, not the judiciary's, is the responsibility of legislating. While, obviously, the latter concept raises definitional challenges and questions, an abiding respect for the judgment of the elected branches of our government (in which one must include the chief executive) is essential. Regardless of periodic efforts to "democratize" the Court, its nature is intrinsically *undemocratic*—which is precisely what the Founding Fathers intended it to be. If the public is dissatisfied with their legislative (and executive) representatives, it has the tools to effect a change constitutionally guaranteed every two, four, or six years. The judiciary is appointed, not elected; at most it is only indirectly responsible to the body politic. In the recent telling comment by Justice Lewis F. Powell, "the high court is not responsible to the public in any political sense. . . ."[46] The Judiciary, with the appellate judiciary at its apex, is charged with the monumentally significant functions of saying yes and, more significantly, no, to the elected branches. But it must resolutely shun the siren call of prescriptive policymaking. It has quite enough to do in its proper sphere of constitutional and statutory adjudication. (4) We rightfully expect the individuals who serve on our courts to be endowed with professional merit and personal integrity. Still, since they are human beings, their responses will necessarily vary and, for better or for worse, will inevitably be at least partly subjective in their approach to and interpretation of aspects of the constitutional constellation. But we have a right to expect the principled rejection of personal preference. There is quite simply no more important element in the attempted finding and drawing of a viable line between judicial activism and restraint than the resolute commitment to shun surrender to the temptations of personal preference. It represents one horn of the dilemma of judging.

With these four corollaries in mind, coupled with the octet of visible efforts described and analyzed earlier, what specific guidelines may be offered for the suggested "centrist" position? First, I view it as calling for the rejection of any "absolutist" approach to constitutional interpretation, in the absence of a clearly discernible constitutional command that proscribes any and all choice. Arguably, no such absolutist commands exist, given the elastic nature of the ever-evolving Constitution. My respect for the intellectual leadership and the towering achievements of Justice Black is boundless, yet I am not persuaded that the Constitution contains the kind of absolutes he found in it, not even in the First Amendment, which was his understandably favorite example.[47] Indeed, as outlined above, and as his jurisprudence amply illustrated, he was not beyond definitional temporizing, notwithstanding a remarkable degree of consistent commitment to his articulated absolutist principles.[48]

Second, the centrist position would represent a quasi compromise between constitutional "literalism" and justifiable judicial interpretation of constitutional language. Admittedly fraught with danger, the suggested compromise would nonetheless be based on visible and viable principles. Thus, when the Sixth Amendment guarantees "in all criminal prosecutions" the "Assistance of Counsel," it represents a clear-cut literal command; but the point at which such counsel becomes required is justifiably subject to eventual judicial judgment in line with the umbrella obligations of "due process of law."[49] Yet the Court's reading of a multifaceted, detailed code of police procedure into constitutional language in his holding in *Miranda* v. *Arizona*[50] arguably exceeded its authority, at least in part, for it demonstrably assumed aspects of the legislative function. On the other hand, the unanimous ruling in *Gideon* v. *Wainwright*[51] was an incontestably proper response to the Sixth Amedment command, duly applied to the states via the Fourteenth Amendment.

Third, in some measure the key to my perception of a centrist posture between judicial activism and restraint is the dual, interrelated judicial obligation to note and observe both the language of a legislative enactment and the measure's legislative history. If the language of a law is judicially viewed as impermissible under the Constitution, it ought to be judicially disallowed. This was properly done, for example, with such congressionally enacted bills of attainder —bills that are expressly forbidden by the Constitution[52] —as those involved in *United States* v. *Lovett*[53] and *United States* v. *Brown.*[54] And the Court took proper judicial notice of congressional refusal, spelled out in the *Congressional Record,* to clothe President Truman with the power to seize the country's steel mills, when it declared his seizure unconstitutional as a usurpation of legislative power in the historic case of *Youngstown Sheet and Tube Co.* v. *Sawyer.*[55]

On the other hand, however, the centrist position would *not* sanction the Court's holding in *Steelworkers* v. *Weber,*[56] a ruling that, however a partisan of the results may rejoice, was not only *not* justified by the terms of Title VII of

the Civil Rights Act of 1964 here at issue, but indeed was demonstrably forbidden by its language.[57] Moreover, the history of the statute's and the specific
title's adoption, as enshrined in the *Congressional Record,* points incontestably
to the fact that racial quotas and the use of racial statistics in employment were
barred as a price of the Civil Rights Act's enactment.[58] However, Justice
Brennan, in writing the Court's five-member majority opinion, while frankly
admitting the prohibitory language of the law, and acknowledging its recognition
by the two lower federal courts that had ruled in favor of plaintiff Wever, justified his ruling on the basis of the "spirit" of the statute and that of the equal
protection of the laws clause of the Fourteenth Amendment.[59] In the absence
of pertinent legislative action, it may well be justifiable to invoke the spirit of
the expansive and more or less open-ended equal protection clause and that of
the amendment's liberty component in its due process of law clause. But given
the express language and history of the law at issue in *Weber,* the Court had only
two valid choices: either declare Title VII of the Civil Rights Act unconstitutional (an absurd suggestion!) or uphold Weber's statutorily and historically
demonstrably justified contentions while urging Congress to repeal or rewrite
the law. Invocations of the "spirit" of a law or of the Constitution are justifiable
only in the absence of duly enacted contrary commands. It is not a manifestation of Neanderthal judicial restraint to abide by the language of a law; it is
simply the judiciary's duty to do so, unless, of course, the law transgresses
constitutional bounds. The sole appropriate manner to defeat Brian Weber's
entirely reasonable allegations of the presence of statutorily proscribed racial
quotas was to have Congress alter Title VII.[60] The Court's ruling to the contrary
constitutes a prima facie example of what Justice Rehnquist, dissenting in the
case, styled "raw judicial activism"[61] No centrist position can sanction it under
such circumstances.

   In other words, when the legislature has spoken in unmistakable terms, the
judiciary's duty is to defer to it, as long as there is no violation of the Constitution. The Court may of course apply its powers of statutory interpretation and
construction, as it frequently does; but it may not interpret or construe to
achieve the precise opposite of an enactment's clear purpose, as manifested by
its language and/or its history—of which the Court was patently guilty in its
1979 *Weber* holding.

   A different issue arises in the absence of legislative action or proof, when
the judiciary is confronted with questions of public law not previously amply
adjudicated. In that event, the centrist position renders a judicial leadership role
feasible. Such an opportunity presented itself in the emotion-laden realm of
abortion, with which the Court began to grapple in the early 1970s, and which
Justice Blackmun's contentious opinion for the Court endeavored to settle in
the 1973 *Abortion Cases.*[62] But, however one might applaud the results—as I
do—he and the Court missed the appropriate jurisprudential boat by rendering
an opinion that constituted the rankest kind of insupportably excessive judicial

activism. In effect, the controlling Blackmun opinion is tantamount to the legislative writing of a Federal Abortion Code, complete with chronologically delineated trimester dates—which, assuredly, is a subject for legislative, rather than for judicial, disposition.

Fourth, considerable judicial leeway is provided by the centrist position when the key constitutional clauses at the heart of the decisional process are those conveniently amorphous ones of the Fifth and Fourteenth Amendments, namely, the due process of law clauses and the equal protection of the laws clause. Since the mid-1930s and early 1940s they have been the most litigated clauses in our constitutional firmament, with the "E.P. Clause" replacing the "D.P. Clauses" as the statistical litigation leader by the early 1950s.[63] Considerably more leeway is provided by their terminology than is the case with statutes. It is thus no wonder that jurists would insist, as Justice Powell again did in the recent past, that the Court is "far freer to reverse constitutional decisions than . . . to reverse . . . statutes."[64]

Thus, the "centrist line" can support the process of "incorporation" via the "liberty" proviso of the Fourteenth Amendment or, to bow to Justice Black's preference on the matter, via the "totality" of the amendment's first section. Admittedly, there is room for argument as to the justification of this approbation, given the disputed historical record of the thrust of the debates of the enactment's framing in the thirty-ninth Congress[65]—an historical record that has lent itself to utterly opposite readings by such qualified scholars as Charles Fairman and Raoul Berger on one side of the interpretative issue and Horace Flack and J.B. James on the other,[66] and by such students of American constitutionalism as Justice Black and Rutledge again on the one side and Justices Frankfurter and Reed on the other.[67] By the same centrist approach the line-drawing process may be said to permit a due process/equal protection jurisprudential approach that has seen the embrace of the "double standard" of judicial review and interpretation between "economic-proprietarian" issues and those concerning "fundamental" civil rights and civil liberties—the latter the children of the Cardozo and Stone approaches to constitutional mandates viewed as inherent in the Bill of Rights.[68] On the other hand, the centrist line approach would have great difficulty in finding constitutional warrant for the derivative three-tiered "scrutiny" standard that the Court has been developing during the past four decades, and especially in the past two, based upon its reading of the equal protection of the laws clause of the Fourteenth Amendment, which it has admittedly "incorporated backwards" into the due process of law clause of the Fifth.[69] For, as Justice John Marshall Harlan the younger put it on the occasion of the dedication of a Bill of Rights room in New York City:

> There is no such thing in our constituted jurisprudence as a doctrine of
> civil rights at large, standing independent of other constitutional limita-
> tions or giving rise to rights born only out of the personal predilections

of judges as to what is good. And it should further be observed that our
federalism not only tolerates, but encourages, differences between federal and state protection of individual rights, so long as the differing
policies alike are founded in reason and do not run afoul of dictates
of fundamental fairness.[70]

Unlike the centrist approach urged here, Harlan did not support the "incorporation" doctrine, but both Justice Harlan and the centrist philosophy support the use of those open-ended provisions of the two embattled amendments
in order to achieve "fundamental fairness" while giving due deference to constitutionally sustainable legislative action, be that on the federal or the state level
and eschewing, à la the Brennan opinion in *Weber*,[71] the temptation to legislate
legislative language out of existence by judicial fiat.

Searching for and evaluating the inherent spirit as well as the letter of a
constitutional provision need not result in impermissible enlargement of the judicial role—no matter how tempting that may be in order to expedite reforms in,
say, the sociopolitical or socioeconomic sphere that may well be desirable in
public policy terms but which must await legislative action. Thus, a hallmark
decision such as the resolute articulation of the Sixth Amendment's guarantee
to the right to counsel in all criminal cases in the *Gideon*[72] case and its *Argersinger*[73] offspring is beyond the rational argument. But the Court, "the Nation's
ultimate judicial tribunal," should not be viewed, as Justice Frankfurter put it,
as "a super-legal aid bureau,"[74] even though aspects of *Miranda*[75] would seem
to indicate that it is one. It is judicial-role-defensible, even exhortable, for the
Court to rule crass gender discrimination, such as that inherent in the *Reed* v.
Reed case,[76] a violation of the Fourteenth Amendment's equal protection of the
laws clause. The distinction legislated by Idaho in that case constituted unquestionably an example of a clear-cut, nonrational, sexually discriminatory legislative classification. But the Court should not view itself as a "social reform
agency"—something it propounded when it wrote what, in effect, constitutes a
Federal Abortion Code in its controversial *Roe* and *Doe* decisions.[77] No matter
how much one may applaud the results of that judicial coup, it was the legislatures' task; the fact that it was a fiendishly difficult, delicate, and politically
hazardous issue was neither mandate nor excuse for judicial intervention. According to Raoul Berger's historically accurate reading of the intent of the
framers of the Fourteenth Amendment,[78] the basis and spirit for its enactment
rendered constitutionally permissible the Court's biting of the proverbial bullet
of endemic racial, governmentally mandated segregation, culminating in the historic decisions in *Brown* v. *Board of Education* I and *Brown* II in 1954 and
1955, respectively.[79] But the Court had no constitutional mandate to turn
itself, and through it the lower rungs of the judiciary, into a combination of
national school board, transportation expert, disciplinarian, employment manager, and admissions director.[80] It was constitutionally spirited and comprehen-
sible for the Court to rule justiciable the question of legislative apportionment

and redistricting based upon the letter and the spririt of the post-Civil War suffrage amendments, as it did in *Baker* v. *Carr* in 1962.[81] But it is hardly clear that the letter and spirit of these amendments justified the kind of historical reasoning that resulted in the *Wesberry*[82] opinion by Justice Black two years later, and they certainly did not justify the sort of "judicial election supervisory board" rationalizations that have prompted lower courts to throw out entire units of local government based on dubious allegations of practices of invidious discrimination.[83]

* * * * *

What, then, of a viable line? There is none, alas, in geometric terms, nor can there be one. I submit, however, that one can endeavor to draw and follow a centrist line based on the two-pronged principles of identifying institutional role commitments and meritorious Court personnel. Neither lends itself to facile articulation, yet neither is beyond ascertainable outlines. With respect to the former, the members of the judicial branch must ever be aware that the basic role of "the least dangerous branch" of the government is intended to be that of saying yes, or, more dramatically, no, to the other branches, be they on the federal or state level. It must resolutely shun prescriptive policymaking. Ours, to be sure—and fortunately—is not a "pure" democracy, nor is it characterized by Blackstonian legislative supremacy. Our system of separation of powers and checks and balances is a sound one, notwithstanding its recurrent strains and even outrages. But our constitutional democracy, based upon majoritarian rule with due regard for minority rights, does not shroud the judicial branch with the mantle of Platonic guardians. Our judicial branch, with the Supreme Court at its apex, is the greatest institutional constitutional safeguard we possess, and only those committed to libertarian suicide would sanction a transfer of the judicial guardianship of our basic civil rights and civil liberties to either the legislature or the executive or both. That does emphatically not mean, however, that the judiciary is or should be empowered to govern. It can and does serve as an arbiter, an educator, a guardian, even a teacher "in a vital [constitutional] seminar,"[84] but it must do so by embracing those boundaries of constitutional obligations that inhere in its role. The excessive literalism of the embattled Raoul Berger, for one, is not the answer; but his exhortations to hew to the text, if coupled with something Berger rejects, namely the text's spirit—which is adopted under my propounded "centrist" line approach—may bring us close to one. This will be true only, however, if the judiciary is prepared to abide by the commendable maxims of judicial restraint, so well articulated by Justice Brandeis in his concurring opinion in the *Ashwander* case[85] more than four decades ago. The Court must view its function as an abstemious, passive one, one characterized by what Louis Lusky calls the application of "tentative" judicial power.[86] Such a course assuredly does not prevent the Court from swinging its necessary constitutional club, as it did amidst all-but-universal cheers in dispatching Richard M. Nixon into resignation as a result of its holding in *United States* v. *Nixon,*[87] and as it did in such landmark rulings as those in *Youngstown Sheet and Tube Co.* v. *Sawyer*[88] and in the historic decisions in *Brown* v. *Board of Education,*[89] *Baker* v. *Carr,*[90] and *Gideon* v. *Wainwright.*[91] It is thus both obvious and appropriate that, in accordance with the authority implicit in Article III, the judiciary does periodically revise, even revolutionize, the Constitution. But it may and must do so only in the presence of appropriate letter-and-spirit constitutional authority. Natural-law-like commitments to personalized notions of "justice," without more, are barred; ad hoc conceptualizations and implementations of what may very well be desirable national or state policy aims, even if based upon national guilt complexes, are no warrant for stepping outside the proper judicial institutional role and function. In none of its components or levels is the judiciary empowered to act as a superlegislature, no matter how inviting such a course may be. The temptations are manifold and human, yet they must be eschewed lest the guardian of the Constitution find itself ultimately emasculated by hostile reaction.

Of course, the jurists who render decisions are human beings as to whom, to repeat Benjamin N. Cardozo's immortal and poignant words, "the great tides and current which engulf the rest of men do not turn aside in their course and pass . . . by."[92] Still, as the sage Alexis de Tocqueville observed in his prescient *Democracy in America,*

> federal judges . . . must not only be good citizens and men of education and integrity, qualities necessary for all magistrates, but [they] must also be statesmen; they must know how to understand the spirit of the age, to confront those obstacles that can be overcome . . . [and they must also be able] to steer out of the current when the tide threatens to carry them away, and with them the sovereignty of the union and obedience to its laws.[93]

Notes

1. For example, Henry J. Abraham, *The Judicial Process: An Introductory Analysis of the Courts of the United States, England, and France,* 4th ed. (New York: Oxford University Press, 1980) and Henry J. Abraham, *The Judiciary: The Supreme Court in the Governmental Process,* 5th ed. (Boston: Allyn and Bacon, 1980).

2. Abraham, *The Judicial Process,* chap. 8.

3. See, for example, Raoul Berger, *Government by Judiciary: The Transformation of the Fourteenth Amendment* (Cambridge: Harvard University Press, 1977).

4. *Noble State Bank v. Haskell,* 219 U.S. 575, 580 (1910).

5. Quoted in Charles G. Curtis, *Lions Under the Throne* (Boston: Houghton Mifflin, 1947), p. 281.

6. Quoted in Francis Biddle, *Justice Holmes, Natural Law and the Supreme Court* (New York: Macmillan, 1961), p. 9.

7. "Can the Supreme Court Guarantee Toleration?," *New Republic*, 43 (1925), p. 87.

8. *Trop v. Dulles,* 356 U.S. 86, 120 (1958). (Emphasis added.)

9. *West Virginia Board of Education v. Barnette,* 319 U.S. 24. (Emphasis added.)

10. Quoted in Israel Shenker, "Friends of Felix Frankfurter Reminisce at Exhibit Honoring the Justice," *New York Times,* Oct. 23, 1977, p. 34.

11. Quoted in Abraham, *The Judicial Process,* 3d ed., p. 321.

12. Ibid.

13. "The Law and the Future," *Fortune* 52 (November 1955):106.

14. Quoted in Hoyt L. Warner, *The Life of Mr. Justice Clarke* (Cleveland: Western Reserve University Press, 1959), p. 69.

15. Benjamin N. Cardozo, *The Nature of the Judicial Process* (New Haven: Yale University Press, 1921), p. 168.

16. 381 U.S. 479 (1965).

17. 377 U.S. 533 (1964).

18. Ibid., p. 624.

19. 438 U.S. 265 (1978).

20. 443 U.S. 193 (1979).

21. Oliver Wendell Holmes, *The Common Law* (Boston: Little, Brown, 1881), p. 1.

22. 347 U.S. 483 (1954) and 349 U.S. 294 (1955).

23. See the discussion in Henry J. Abraham, *Freedom and the Court: Civil Rights and Liberties in the United States,* 3d ed. (New York: Oxford University Press, 1977), pp. 207–227.

24. 428 U.S. 153 (1976).

25. Ibid., p. 227.

26. Ibid., p. 321.

27. *Tinker v. Des Moines Independent School District,* 393 U.S. 503 (1969).

28. See, for example, his dissenting opinion in *Katz v. United States,* 389 U.S. 347 (1967).

29. Ibid., p. 351.

30. 411 U.S. 1 (1973).

31. Ibid., pp. 98–99. (Emphasis added.)

32. For example, *Williamson v. Lee Optical of Oklahoma,* 348 U.S. 483 (1955).

33. 304 U.S. 144.

34. See Abraham, *Freedom and the Court,* p. 14.

35. For example, *Loving v. Virginia,* 388 U.S. 1 (1967) (for race) and *Graham v. Richardson,* 403 U.S. 365, (1971) (for alienage).

36. For example, *Frontiero v. Richardson,* 411 U.S. 677 (1973).

37. See Abraham, *Freedom and the Court,* chaps. 2–3; Abraham, *The Judiciary,* chap. 2.

38. 302 U.S. 319.

39. See his opinion for the Court in *Rochin v. California,* 342 U.S. 165 (1952).

40. See Abraham, *The Judicial Process,* p. 375.

41. *Jacobellis v. Ohio,* 378 U.S. 184, 197 (1964).

42. As told to me by Justice Frankfurter's one-time clerk, the late Alexander M. Bickel.

43. "Toward Neutral Principles of Constitutional Law," *Harvard Law Review* 73 (November 1959):1.

44. Ibid., p. 34.

45. See Abraham, *The Judicial Process,* p. 380.

46. As quoted in the (Charlottesville, Va.) *Daily Progress,* August 13, 1979.

47. See Hugo L. Black, *A Constitutional Faith* (New York: Knopf, 1968).

48. For example, his dissenting opinion in *Tinker v. Des Moines Independent School District,* 393 U.S. 503 (1969), and that in *Brown v. Louisiana,* 383 U.S. 131 (1966).

49. See Fred P. Graham, *The Self-Inflicted Wound* (New York: MacMillan, 1970).

50. 384 U.S. 436 (1966).

51. 372 U.S. 335 (1963).

52. Article I, Section 9 (federal) and 10 (states).

53. 323 U.S. 303 (1946).

54. 381 U.S. 437 (1965).

55. 343 U.S. 579 (1952).

56. 99 Sup. Ct. 2721 (1979).

57. See Title VII, Section 703 (a), (d), and (j).

58. For example, *Congressional Record* 110 (June 4, 1964):12714–12715.

59. *Steelworkers v. Weber,* 99 Sup. Ct. 2721 (1979).

60. Ibid.

61. Ibid.

62. *Roe v. Wade,* 410 U.S. 113 (1973) and *Doe v. Bolton,* 410 U.S. 179 1973).

63. See Abraham, *Freedom and the Court,* especially chaps. 1–3, 7.

64. Lewis Powell, quoted in the (Charlottesville, Va.) *Daily Progress,* August 13, 1979.

65. See the extensive account in Abraham, *Freedom and the Court,* chap. 3.

66. Ibid.

67. Compare their several opinions in *Adamson v. California,* 332 U.S. 46 (1947).

68. See Abraham, *Freedom and the Court,* chaps. 2–3. See also Abraham, *The Judiciary,* chap. 2.

69. See Mr. Chief Justice Warren's opinion in *Bolling v. Sharpe,* 347 U.S. 497 (1955) and that by Mr. Justice Brennan in *Shapiro v. Thompson,* 394 U.S. 618 (1969).

70. "The Bill of Rights and the Constitution," Sub-treasury Building, New York City, August 9, 1964. (Reprinted by the Virginia Commission on Constitutional Government, Richmond, Virginia)

71. 99 Sup. Ct. 2721 (1979).

72. *Gideon v. Wainwright,* 372 U.S. 335 (1963).

73. *Argersinger v. Hamlin,* 407 U.S. 25 (1972).

74. *Uveges v. Pennsylvania,* 335 U.S. 437 (1948), at 450.

75. *Miranda v. Arizona,* 384 U.S. 436 (1966).

76. 404 U.S. 71 (1971).

77. 410 U.S. 113 (1973), 410 U.S. 179 (1973).

78. Berger, *Government by Judiciary.*

79. 347 U.S. 483 (1954) and 349 U.S. 294 (1955).

80. For example, *Swann v. Charlotte-Mecklenburg Board of Education,* 402 U.S. 1 (1971); *Goss v. Lopez,* 419 U.S. 565 (1965); and *Regents of the University of California v. Bakke,* 438 U.S. 265 (1978).

81. 369 U.S. 186 (1962).

82. *Wesberry v. Sanders,* 376 U.S. 1 (1964).

83. For example, *Bolden v. City of Mobile,* 423 F.Supp. 384 (S.D. Ala. 1976).

84. Eugene V. Rostow, "The Democratic Character of Judicial Review," *Harvard Law Review* 66 (December 1952):195.

85. *Ashwander v. Tennessee Valley Authority,* 297 U.S. 280 (1936). For an elaboration see chap. 9, "Sixteen Great Maxims of Judicial Self-Restraint," in Abraham, *The Judicial Process.*

86. Louis Lusky, *By What Right?* (Charlottesville, Va.: Michie, 1975), *passim.*

87. 418 U.S. 683 (1974).

88. 343 U.S. 579 (1952).

89. 347 U.S. 483 (1954).

90. 369 U.S. 186 (1962).

91. 372 U.S. 335 (1963).

92. Cardozo, *The Nature of the Judicial Process,* p. 168.

93. Alexis de Tocqueville, *Democracy in America,* ed. J.P. Mayer (Garden City, N.Y.: Doubleday, 1969), 1:150.

On the Imperial Judiciary and Comparative Institutional Development and Power in America

Stephen C. Halpern

Introduction

During the 1970s there emerged an influential scholarly literature critical of the power of the American judiciary. That literature is noteworthy for several reasons. First, by concentrating on the proper role and range of power of federal courts, it raises what has traditionally been a central issue for those studying the judiciary. Second, the literature is notable because it emerged roughly a decade after the dissolution of the Warren Court. The criticism flowered notwithstanding the presence of four Nixon appointees on the Court, men who were explicitly chosen for their relatively modest conceptions of the policy-making role of the Court. Third, this literature was written by distinguished scholars. As a result of the prominence of its authors and the severity of the criticisms they lodge, the literature has received wide scholarly criculation and even some public attention.

Nathan Glazer lofted the first volley with the publication of his article, "Towards An Imperial Judiciary?" published in the tenth anniversary issue of *The Public Interest.*[1] In this chapter I focus on the article by Glazer and on four books published subsequently which expanded upon the issues he posed. The books were written by Donald Horowitz, a former Brookings scholar who is both a lawyer and a political scientist; Archibald Cox, Loeb Professor of Law at Harvard; Lino Graglia, Baker Professor of Constitutional Law at the University of Texas Law School; and Raoul Berger, former Charles Warren Fellow at the Harvard Law School.[2]

This chapter analyzes the critiques these men make of the work of the U.S. Supreme Court in constitutional adjudication. While their writings occasionally touch upon statutory interpretation and the work of lower federal courts, they focus primarily on the development of constitutional law by the Supreme Court.[3] This will be my focus, too, in analyzing the work of "the critics"—the designation by which I shall refer to these scholars.[4]

The author acknowledges the helpful comments of Charles M. Lamb and Henry Abraham, and the assistance of Stephen Krason.

I will begin by examining four relatively new criticisms of the Court and three traditional ones which appear in the work of the critics, first presenting the basic thrust of each criticism and then analyzing the arguments advanced in support of it. The last part of this chapter contains conclusions about the general significance of the five works as a whole. Obviously, all of these critics are not in agreement on each of the seven criticisms; nonetheless each of the authors does advance at least three of them. In that sense the criticisms constitute basic themes which recur in this literature. In examining these themes, I stress not subtle distinctions among the authors, but the similar perspectives and intellectual coherence of their composite work.

The purpose of this research is to identify and document the salient criticisms in these works; assess the validity of the conclusions reached with respect to each criticism; and evaluate the overall cogency and import of this body of writing.

The Criticisms

The Widened Scope of Policymaking

The critics contend that the Supreme Court addresses a far wider range of problems today than ever before. The Court, they maintain, is now reviewing and regulating a bewildering variety of public policies and actions which previously had not been subject to judicial policymaking. In a section entitled "The Expansion of Judicial Responsibility," Horowitz comments that in the past two decades courts "have been, to put it mildly, very busy laboring in unfamiliar territory."[5] They now decide matters, he concludes, which earlier would have been thought "unfit for adjudication."[6] Pressing this same point, Glazer observes that courts "now reach into the lives of the people . . . deeper than they ever have in American history."[7] "More and more of the problems of government," Archibald Cox adds, "are being presented to and handled by federal courts as questions of constitutional law."[8]

That the Court now reviews a wider range of problems than ever before is, I think, indisputable. Yet it is essential to place that development is some context to appreciate its import and assess whether one need be apprehensive about it. There are a number of factors which have produced the broadened scope of judicial policymaking. First, during the Warren years, the Court moved to narrow or eliminate procedural requirements which precluded certain issues from being raised or certain interest groups from being heard in the judicial process. Second, in the last two decades many previously quiescent groups developed the organizational capacity to pursue their goals through the political and legal process. Racial minorities, national minorities, native Americans, environmentalists, consumers, homosexuals, students, the elderly, and the handicapped are but a few examples that come to mind. By sponsoring litigation these groups manifested their heightened political consciousness and activity. Third, the movement for public interest law, which provided lawyers, the institutional basis, the financial support, and the reforming spirit for much of the legal activity of these groups, emerged during this period. Fourth, the decisions of the Warren Court, especially on racial matters, encouraged many organized groups to pursue their objectives through the Court rather than in the other branches. This was especially true of many of the groups listed above because the "political" branches were often largely unresponsive to their goals. Consequently, the leaders of these groups often chose not to spend their limited resources in conventional political lobbying which they believed was likely to be unproductive. However, such explanations miss the most important underlying, albeit obvious, cause of the Court's policymaking explorations on so many new fronts.

The widened range of judicial policymaking is primarily attributable to the enormous growth in the scope and power of American government in the last twenty-five years. The central development in American domestic politics in the last quarter century has been the vast and virtually incomprehensible growth in the range and complexity of activities regulated by government, especially the federal government. Developments since World War II have had a prodigious impact on the scale and sweep of governmental business. We need reminding that extensive federal regulation of such matters as racial and sexual discrimination, education, health care, water and air pollution, urban and consumer affairs, and national economic development, to name only a few, either did not exist or were in early developmental stages two short decades ago.[9] Theodore Lowi notes that from 1958 to 1965 alone we witnessed a period of "unprecedented expansion in governmental authority,"[10] and that, "in modern day America there is no end to governmental responsibility."[11] Reflecting on the size of contemporary governmental undertakings, Richard Neustadt writes:

> First are the social programs legislated in the Sixties. These meant a quantum jump of Federal oversight and funding for public services that have the most direct effects on private lives, services traditionally in state and local—or in private—hands now subsidized and supervised from Washington. Consider education, health care, human rehabilitation. These spheres and others suddenly were opened up to Federal aid and oversight, and on a scale approaching highways in the Fifties, or suburban housing in the Forties, or social security in the Thirties. This movement in the Sixties was the biggest jump on the domestic side of Federal undertakings since the New Deal. . . . And after this outburst of social legislation there came problems of administrative management that are hardly to be compared with anything that came before the War, except perhaps consolidating the New Deal. These problems were the fruits of substantive complexity, limited technology, tangled jurisdiction—all at once and on every hand.[12]

Our political tradition and experience suggest that the range of questions brought before courts will roughly correspond to the range of questions government itself addresses. Tocqueville long ago observed our penchant to transform political issues into legal questions. We continue to manifest that penchant; but the scope, complexity, and penetration of public regulation has expanded beyond anything de Tocqueville, the Founders, or the most ardent New Dealers could have imagined. Hence it was quite predictable that as a result of this governmental expansion we would find a much wider array of social issues presented to courts. It is not mere happenstance that the oft-bemoaned growth of judicial power in the last generation has coincided with an unparalleled burgeoning in the overall governmental enterprise. Three decades ago Clinton Rossiter counseled, "You can't go home again; the positive state is here to stay and from now on the accent will be on power, not limitations."[13] And so it has been on the Supreme Court, as elsewhere.

The widened range of matters to which the Court's power now extends was not only foreseeable, but it has salutary effects. If the "tentacles" of the federal government have penetrated in an unprecedented way into the lives of Americans, all the more reason, one might argue, to support an assertive and powerful judicial branch. The general growth of governmental authority has made more crucial than ever the unique role the Court has played in delineating the proper relationship between the individual and government[14] and between the federal and state governments. Moreover, if the concentration and penetration of governmental power is greater than ever, one might reasonably posit that the frequency and magnitude of abuses of official power may likely be greater. Hence, in the contemporary American political context, one could argue that there is greater need than ever to nourish a system in which independent political institutions aggressively check and thereby restrain one another. A weak and passive Court could not play such a role. In fact, assertive intervention by federal courts in recent years has helped curb runaway power and abuses in the White House and arbitrary administrative action by federal agencies.[15]

To summarize, the critics are correct in maintaining that courts now make policy over a wider range of questions. However, there is nothing necessarily or logically undesirable about this development. In fact, it may be quite desirable. In contemporary American government the accent is indeed on power. It would be incongruous, and even counterproductive, if that accent were not manifested in the decisions of the highest court in the land.

Affirmative Activism

Not only has the Court expanded the breadth of questions subject to its power, the critics charge, but it has also changed the character of the power it exercises. Contemporary activism, the critics argue, differs in kind from previous activism.

The Court does not merely void unconstitutional measures these days, the argument runs, but rather it specifies—sometimes in elaborate detail—the affirmative steps that are required to remedy illegalities. In so doing, the critics maintain, the Court prescribes policies or programs in a manner strikingly similar to the executive and legislative branches.

Affirmative activism may require the Court to supervise continuous actions which affect large numbers of individuals. Consequently, it often produces extensive administrative responsibilities for the Court. The justices confronted this problem, Cox explains, in the aftermath of their holding in the *Brown* case in 1954. "The question then became: what should be the remedy? The answer has been to require 'desegregation' by judicial decree. The answer requires courts to formulate controversial programmes of affirmative action requiring detailed administration for protracted periods of time under constant judicial supervision."[16] Such responsibilities raise both pragmatic and jurisprudential questions about the limits of judicial power.

In discussing affirmative activism the critics contend that the nature of the remedies courts have imposed in some cases would have been unimaginable in the past. Let us return to a passage in Horowitz's *The Courts and Social Policy:*

> In just the past few years, courts have struck down laws requiring a period of in-state residence as a condition of eligibility for welfare. . . . Federal district courts have laid down elaborate standards for food handling, hospital operations, recreation facilities, inmate employment and education, sanitation, and laundry, painting, lighting, plumbing, and renovation in some prisons; they have ordered other prisons closed. Courts have established equally comprehensive programs of care and treatment for the mentally ill confined in hospitals. They have ordered the equalization of school expenditures on teachers' salaries, established hearing procedures for public school discipline cases, decided that bilingual education must be provided for Mexican-American children, and suspended the use by school boards of the National Teacher Examination and of comparable tests for school supervisors.[17]

To a considerable extent, as Horowitz's examples make plain, affirmative activism has been directed toward particular kinds of public bureaucracies. These agencies, like the Court, are undemocratically organized and enjoy independence from the political process and from the citizens whom they ostensibly serve. They are bureaucracies which exercise wide and largely unchallenged control over a dependent and weak clientele of welfare recipients, prisoners, the mentally ill, students, and, of course, criminal suspects. Affirmative activism can be understood, in part, as an effort by the Court to redress minimally the political imbalance between bureaucrats and those who are subject to bureaucratic power but are typically impotent to reform or influence it. Yet the fundamental development which gives rise to affirmative activism runs deeper. That development derives not from a change in the judiciary, but from the changed character in the mode of power now most commonly exercised by government.

The root cause of affirmative activism is the flourishing of the positive state, or, more specifically, the ubiquity of administrative power in the positive state. Today the overwhelming proportion of governmental responsibility and power is administrative in nature. A far-flung governmental administrative apparatus, at both the federal and state levels, is a relatively recent development; yet the wide-ranging functions which public agencies now perform are considered indispensable in the modern state by citizens and politicans alike, Reaganite rhetoric to the contrary notwithstanding. Public bureaucracies impose a unique form of control over those subject to their power. Administrative power is continuous; it operates constantly and routinely through an institutionalized apparatus which remains in place. Those regulated are invariably required to perform specific affirmative tasks or behaviors. The character of administrative power determines, to a significant degree, the character of the judicial power exercised when courts find an administrative practice unconstitutional.

Perhaps an illustration will best clarify the point. Let us compare the judicial task involved in determining the constitutionality of a law stipulating the maximum number of hours that bakers in New York state could work (negative activism) and the task involved in assessing the constitutionality of a pattern of racial segregation in a city's schools (affirmative activism). When the Court finds governmental action in both instances unconstitutional, the different character of the judicial power exercised in each case does not result from the Court's assumption of new powers. Rather, it derives from the character of the power being reviewed by the Court in the first place. *Lochner* (1905),[18] and the negative activism of substantive due process, derived from review of laws in which the essence or entire substance of a governmental power was disputed. The constitutional authority of the legislature to exercise specific powers was typically at issue in those cases. The question before the Court was relatively straightforward: either the legislature had that authority constitutionally or it did not. Having decided that question, the Court's task was completed.

Judicial review of administrative policies typically requires more than a yes or no answer from the Court. Judicial regulation of racial segregation in schools or of policies in other bureaucracies requires that the Court review an administrative practice which will and must continue in one form or another. The agency's mandate, charter, and purpose are not at issue; rather, most often, a question is raised about a particular administrative method used to accomplish a larger and concededly lawful goal. In such cases the Court usually must clarify the range of permissible and impermissible means that an agency may use so that the bureaucracy may continue to pursue goals which invariably are not an issue in the litigation. If the Court voids an administrative policy, it must, for the sake of clarity and comprehensibility of decision, articulate the criteria governing permissible and impermissible exercises of administrative power. In so doing, it must of necessity suggest a range of reforms or options which would meet minimal constitutional standards. This situation obtains when the Court negates a pattern of racial segregation in schools; procedures for police interrogation; or policies for terminating welfare recipients, committing mental patients, or disciplining prison inmates. After the Court's decision, schools continue to admit children of different races, police continue to interrogate suspects, recipients continue to be expunged from welfare rolls, mental institutions continue to commit individuals, and prisons continue to imprison. The continuous character and unquestioned necessity and lawfulness of these bureaucratic responsibilities make it incumbent upon the Court, when it negates particular practices, to accompany its decision with clear and specific guidelines which perforce will impose affirmative obligations. Such guidelines enable the agency to continue to exercise its power, but in a manner comporting with the justices' reading of relevant constitutional requirements. The nature of the power being reviewed, not judicial usurpation, imposes the affirmative responsibilities.[19]

Sustained Activism

The critics contend that the widened scope and affirmative nature of the Court's power does not constitute a temporary phenomenon or problem. They emphasize rather that these developments reflect a long-term change in the role and power of the Court in our political system. No longer, Nathan Glazer opines, are we likely to see cycles of judicial activism and restraint. Rather, he suggests that the Court will assume these broadened powers routinely and consistently in the future.[20] Horowitz, in discussing *Lau* v. *Nichols* (1974)[21] and *Griggs* v. *Duke Power Co.* (1971),[22] both decisions of the Burger Court, voices this same apprehension:

> These two seminal decisions of the Burger Court, neither of which drew a single dissent, should suffice to show that judicial participation in the making of social policy is no ephemeral development. It is part of a chain of developments that can survive the vicissitudes of constitutional "activism" and "restraint." Nor does it need to be stressed that these decisions were not solely the work of judges who "view themselves as holding roving commissions as problem solvers." That they do not so regard themselves attests to the structural, enduring character of the phenomena I have been describing.[23]

In sum, the critics maintain that our conception of the Court's proper function, role, and range of powers has been substantially and, more important, permanently altered.

There are several difficulties with this argument. First, the Burger Court has on the whole manifested a rather traditional sense of self-restraint and an evident disinclination for pioneering policymaking.[24] Second, one could argue that the Court has always been an activist institution, which has throughout our history exercised an uncommon degree of influence in the resolution of major national questions.[25] Third, even if the critics' contentions about sustained activism prove to be true, it does not necessarily establish that this development is an unhealthy one.

Even if we have been witnessing the first phase of an enduring and significant change in the Court's role, it would not be the first time in our history that a major political institution experienced substantial change in its power and function in our system. Conceptions of the roles of other national political institutions and, of course, the power exercised by those institutions, have changed drastically in the past. For instance, not very long ago scholars stressed that there were two models of behavior for American chief executives: there were, supposedly, weak and strong presidents. Some presidents, it was explained, presided placidly over the American national system and governing institutions as managers. They were "strict constructionists" who interpreted their powers to be confined to provisions explicitly enumerated in the Constitution. This limited view of the presidential role was most often illustrated by reference to William Howard Taft. In contrast, there were presidents—Theodore Roosevelt was commonly cited—who initiated novel policies and aggressively pursued presidential programs of reform for the nation. These men adopted expansive conceptions of their role as "stewards," believing that their powers were limited only by express prohibitions in statutes or the Constitution. We now recognize and accept, Neustadt concludes, that occupants of the White House no longer have any choice between the two presidential roles.

> A striking feature of our recent past has been the transformation into routine practice of the actions we once treated as exceptional. A president may retain liberty, in Woodrow Wilson's phrase, "To be as big a man as he can." But nowadays he cannot be as small as he might like. . . . In instance after instance, the exceptional behavior of our earlier "strong" presidents has now been set by statute as a regular requirement . . . and what has escaped statutory recognition has mostly been accreted into presidential common law, confirmed by custom no less binding.[26]

Not only have the president's powers grown immensely since Wilson's time, but we have come to judge presidential performance in the twentieth century, in large measure, by the vigor and aggressiveness with which chief executives exercise their power. Assertive presidential stewardship is now presumed to be a prerequisite to competent performance by any chief executive. Note Samuel Huntington's observation that our "great" presidents have all been strong chief executives who have *"stretched the legal authority and political resources of the office."*[27] C. Herman Pritchett asserts that "presidents who do not use their power vigorously are condemned as weak and as failures in office."[28] And finally, Thomas Cronin suggests that "presidents are judged great, in part, because they have dominated the other branches."[29]

If the power and role of the president have changed dramatically since Wilson's day, the federal bureaucracy has undergone no less striking a transformation. In the last half-century, bureaucratic power has become omnipresent and perhaps even preeminent. The framers, of course, intended no such development. James Q. Wilson concludes that, while the Founders would understand and approve of certain features of the bureaucracy, they "surely would be dismayed at the political cost resulting from having vested vast discretionary authority in the hands of officials whose very existence—to say nothing of whose function—was not anticipated by the Constitutional Convention, and whose effective control is beyond the capacity of the governing institutions which that Convention designed."[30] The growth of the federal bureaucracy and the nature of its power, according to Peter Woll, has thrown our original constitutional scheme out of kilter and has produced "fundamental changes . . . in the American system of constitutional democracy."[31]

Not only has the power and function of the federal bureaucracy changed, but, as with the presidency, academic conceptions about administrative power have also changed. At the turn of the century there was scholarly consensus that the power public administrators exercised was, to a large extent, discretion-free. The prevailing view was that public administrators were trained professionals who objectively implemented the standards and policies established by legislators.[32] By contrast, contemporary scholars appreciate the primacy of discretion in administration and the considerable influence administrators inevitably wield over the substance of policy.[33]

Finally, the function of the United States Congress has evolved significantly since Woodrow Wilson, as scholar, assessed it to be the central American political institution. In the nineteenth century, Congressional power, priorities, and initiatives determined the public policies dealing with major national problems. That role has been assumed in this century by the president and, to a lesser extent, by the bureaucracy.[34] Moreover, there has been a revolutionary change in the constitutionally permissible range of power that Congress may delegate. The Court no longer insists that carefully delineated guidelines accompany the legislative delegation of power, and Congress rarely chooses to impose such standards voluntarily. The result has been that vast legislative power over critical national policies have been transferred by Congress to the president and bureaucracy.[35] This development has altered the overall function and eroded the overriding power that Congress once exercised.[36]

Justice Holmes once observed that we need education in the obvious, not in the esoteric. Perhaps the foregoing observations are faithful to that counsel. They suggest quite simply that we must analyze the nature and evolution of the Court's power in the context of the comparative historical development of other major national political institutions. To do otherwise is to ensure a myopic scholarly vision. A comparative institutional perspective forces us to recognize that we have experienced and accepted considerable change in the power and functions of national political institutions other than the Court. It may be that the critics are correct in arguing that we have recently experienced a dramatic and enduring transformation of the Court's role and power. Personally, I am not persuaded. But even assuming that the critics are correct, there have been, as I have indicated, corresponding changes of similar magnitude in the development of the other branches. It would be naively ahistorical and apolitical to expect or insist that the power of the Court in the last quarter of the twentieth century ought signficantly to parallel its power in the previous century. After all, for what other governmental institution is this even remotely the case?

Judicial Effectiveness

Historically, much of the scholarly debate on the proper role of the Court has turned on normative questions. Indeed, those who criticize the widened scope of judicial power and the affirmative and sustained activism of the Court typically advance conceptions as to what the proper limits of the Court's power ought to be. Reservations about judicial effectiveness, however, are fundamentally different. They are rooted, not in normative, philosophical, or constitutional grounds, but in functional considerations. The argument is that the legal process, as a practical matter, is well suited for only a limited range of questions because of its peculiar nature, organization, and powers. Consequently, several critics conclude that courts are ill equipped to produce wise policies in many of the new realms of judicial activity.[37]

A comparative institutional perspective will also bring the criticism of judicial ineffectiveness into sharper focus. The Court is clearly not the only institution in recent times which has had difficulty making wise public policies on complex and contentious national problems. Indeed, such a comparison is especially instructive because in the last twenty-five years, the Court perhaps more than the other branches has forthrightly addressed itself to our most intransigent and glaring domestic ills—problems of racial, political, and social inequality, and of individual liberties generally. As it is presently organized, the Court may not be as able to manage some of the problems it has assumed as one might like it to be. The answer is not necessarily, however, for the Court to curtail its consideration of these matters. Why not, for instance, reform some of the institutional or organizational characteristics which hamper the Court in performing its modern responsibilities? Lower federal courts have attempted to do this through procedures established for multidistrict and complex litigation. Why not, for example, restructure the adversary process so as to provide a different kind and greater breadth of information relevant to the Court's function as a policymaker?[38] Furthermore, if the Court is assuming new responsibilities and functions, perhaps it is to be expected that there may be a period of adjustment during which the justices experience frustrations in fulfilling their new role with unqualified success.

The four criticisms of the power of the Court discussed thus far are coupled with three rather traditional criticisms found in the writing of the critics. The first may be labeled "The Court as King."

The Court as King

The contention here is that the judicial power, in particular the power of the U.S. Supreme Court, is increasingly a dominant power. The power of the Court in contemporary American politics and life, the critics suggest, is not simply excessive, it is preeminent. The Court allegedly dominates its sister branches and the political process itself. The titles of the works—"The Imperial Judiciary," "Government By Judiciary," "Disaster By Decree,"—themselves suggest this criticism and pointedly convey this theme. But beyond the titles are the explicit assessments one finds about the Court's power in our system. Berger declares that the justices have "become a law unto themselves."[39] Glazer concludes "that the controls on the Court have become obsolescent."[40] Graglia sums up his conception of the power of the Court in this observation:

> The Court has intervened so frequently and decisively on so many issues affecting the essential nature of American society that it has become, arguably, in domestic affairs at least, the most important institution in American government.[41]

This criticism of the Court is, if nothing else, time-honored. It has always turned on an inflated assessment of the power of the Court in our political system. Note, as but one example, Jefferson's protest to Chief Justice Marshall shortly after the Republic's founding that were "federal judges to become the ultimate arbiter of all Constitutional questions, we would be placed under the despotism of an oligarchy."[42]

To demonstrate that the Court has substantial or even great power is not to prove that it is predominant. While power may abhor a vacuum, it is not exercised in one. It exists in context—in an environment. Here again, of course, the Court must be assessed vis-à-vis the other branches.[43] Examining the Court's power from such a perspective, the high tribunal can scarcely be depicted as the dominant national political institution. It affronts political common sense to suggest that the power of the American president, of administrative and regulatory agencies, and of the United States Congress, pale by comparison to that of the Court. In the making of foreign policy, the most crucial issues—questions of

war and peace and of survival itself—are determined without the Court's participation. Over these matters the Court exercises no power and has given no
indication that it will behave otherwise in the future. What of our most pressing
domestic issues? In dealing with problems of energy, inflation, unemployment,
the environment, taxation, health care, education, welfare, and even so closely
related an issue to courts as crime, is it accurate to assert that the Court is the
most powerful branch of government? The opposite is more nearly true. While
the Court may make decisions in each of these realms, it operates by and large
on the margins of policies established and controled by other institutions. It
does not sit at center stage. Moreover, in their calculations of the Court's influence the critics pay no attention whatever to the substantial power that
private interests may exercise over our public life and policies.[44] Finally, as the
literature on compliance with Court decisions consistently documents, there is
often a wide divergence between the "imperial" judiciary's order and the extent
to which affected individuals and institutions ultimately conform to the judicial
will.

The relative power of each of the branches has varied during different historical epochs. When the Constitution was drafted, for instance, there prevailed
an atmosphere of distrust toward legislative bodies and their powers.[45] This was
true, in large part, because state legislatures were the dominant institutions under
the Articles of Confederation. The executive branch was weak. One scholar concludes that state legislatures under the Articles "came as near to claiming omni-
potence as the British Parliament had done."[46] During our first century under
the Constitution, ours was a government dominated by Congress. Nonetheless,
there were periods of vigorous executive leadership and perhaps even executive
dominance of Congress—arguably during the presidencies of Jefferson, Jackson,
and Lincoln.[47]

The preeminence of Congress has waned in the twentieth century. The
president and federal bureaucracy, it would seem, have become the most powerful governing institutions.[48] Samuel Huntington maintains that to the extent
that our nation has been governed in this century, it is our presidents who have
done the governing. He concludes that during this period "whenever the American political system has moved systematically with respect to public policy, the
direction and initiative have come from the White House."[49] By the same token,
students of the bureaucracy emphasize the vast influence and independence that
administrative agencies have developed.[50] Peter Woll, a student of both the
judiciary and the bureaucracy, concludes that the latter has become "the most
powerful branch of government."[51] He states:

> The bureaucracy continues to run the government and often formulates
> its major policies, while the president and Congress play out the power
> game between them, *and the courts stay in the background.*[52]

In similar vein, Frances Rourke contends that bureaucracies have displaced political parties as, in his words, "the dominant theater of decision in the modern state."[53]

Whatever one's view of the power relationships between the branches at a given time, it is important to emphasize the dynamic nature of those relationships. There has been a perpetual ebb and flow of power among the branches, creating constantly evolving balances of power. And so it was intended, as Arthur Schlesinger observes:

> The result of the calculated ambiguities of the founding fathers, was to design not a machine but a battleground—to create the conditions for permanent guerilla warfare between the two branches of the national government [the president and Congress] with powers of initiative.[54]

In sharp contrast to the critics, Woll, by explicit reference to the courts, and Schlesinger, by omitting reference to them, both appear to conceive of the Supreme Court as a kind of junior partner in the competition to control major national policies. It is hard to avoid the suspicion that scholars who specialize in and focus on the work of the Supreme Court suffer a kind of intellectual occupational hazard: they are inclined to overestimate the power and importance of the institution they study. That is not to say that the Court is not an active participant in our natural political life. Rather it is to recognize that the Court's role complicates, but does not transcend or override the shifting calculus of power between national political institutions.

Ours has been a remarkably flexible political system in terms of the fluidity of power relationships among major political institutions. Even the division of functional responsibilities among the branches has evolved to a degree and altered the character of the power each branch exercises. The president's de facto war-making powers, the bureaucracy's adjudicating functions, and the Court's latitude to legislate, all illustrate that point. Yet no branch has been "King" for too long, least of all the Court. The new role that the Court has occasionally played in recent years, and the new political leverage it may have vis-à-vis other institutions, are but recent skirmishes in the long course of the warfare which Schlesinger describes.[55]

Judicial Activism and the Democratic Process

The inordinate and unbridled power of the Court is especially troubling, the critics contend, because of the undemocratic structure of the institution. Their writings emphasize that the justices are insulated from, and are not directly accountable to, the American citizenry. They contend that the vigorous exercise of the Court's power undermines the vitality of the democratic process. Resort to judicial resolution of major national problems, they admonish, has an insidious impact on the citizenry, because it atrophies citizens' energies and diminishes their willingness and capacity to act through the democratic process to resolve contentious social problems. In so doing, judicial activism weakens the commitment to and vitality of democratic governance.

This is indeed an old criticism. Nonetheless, it resurfaces in the literature examined in this chapter. For instance, Cox writes:

> [T]here is fear that excessive reliance upon courts instead of self-government may deaden a people's sense of moral and political responsibility for their own future, especially in matters of liberty, and may stunt the growth of political capacity that results from the exercise of the ultimate power of decision.[56]

Graglia expresses a similar concern. *Brown* I precipitated a social revolution, he observes. "So important a social change," Graglia concludes, "should not have been made by unelected, lifetime appointees."[57] *"In a healthy democracy,"* he avers, "social revolutions are made by elected representatives."[58] Glazer states the case even more bluntly by contending that we have increasingly witnessed courts "replacing democratic procedures with the authoritarian decisions of judges."[59]

The critics' allegations about the relationship between judicial activism and the democratic governance needs to be examined at several levels. The aggressive assertion of the Court's power does not necessarily sap the nation's democratic spirit. In many instances, I would argue, the opposite is true.

Activist decisions by the Court may invigorate the democratic process. Judicial activism may focus the attention and energies of the political branches on problems which they have either ignored or inadequately addressed. In this sense, the Court can play a vital educational role in our democracy by broadening the range of public discussion and political debate.

When the Court intervenes it can also enliven the democratic process by fostering the development and growth of interest groups. In his excellent book, *The Politics of Rights,* Stuart Scheingold emphasizes that litigation can mobilize otherwise inactive and unorganized interests so that they can participate in the democratic process.[60] The Court may stimulate the growth of political movements when its decisions are favorable to those interests, as occurred with black civil rights organizations, and when its decisions are unfavorable to those interests, as occurred with advocates of capital punishment and opponents of abortion.

Those who argue that the Court short-circuits the democratic process implicitly assume that when the Court resolves problems it does so finally and ultimately. It would be more accurate to view a decision by the Court, much as any other political decision, as one action in a long series of actions over time by different political institutions, attempting temporarily to resolve continuing and often reemerging public issues.[61]

Not only do the critics misconstrue the impact that judicial activism has on the political process, they also raise invidious comparisons between the degree of accountability in the elected branches and the Court. They grossly overstate their case. They accept unquestioningly the American myth about the democratic nature and accountable character of power in institutions other than the Court. They do not look beyond myth and formal structures and processes to the realities of the exercise of power in the so-called representative branches. Scholars of constitutional law need to probe deeper beneath the democratic rhetoric and symbolism which surrounds the Court's coordinate branches. With what rate of success, and over what range of activities, do citizens, either as individuals or as members of organized groups, control the decisions of Congress and presidents, to say nothing of public bureaucracies and independent regulatory agencies? The answer for the overwhelming number of persons and interest groups is that they only rarely attempt to intervene, that when they do they are only occasionally successful, and, that in any event, they influence only a limited range of decisions. No less an establishment personage than V.O. Key explicitly recognized the substantial degree of independence which elected leaders enjoy when he observed:

> [A]s one puzzles over the nature of interactions between government and mass opinion and ponders such empirical data as can be assembled on the matter, he can arrive only at the conclusion that a wide range of discretion exists for whatever wisdom leadership echelons can muster in the public service. The generality of public preferences, the low intensity of the opinions of sectors of the public, the tortuousness of the process of translation of disapproval of specific policies into electoral reprisal, and many other factors point to the existence of a wide latitude for the exercise of creative leadership.[62]

The uncomfortable but undeniable reality is that all our governmental institutions, notwithstanding formal democratic design, exercise vast quantities of essentially unaccountable power and discretion—or, in Key's euphemistic phrase—"creative leadership." Moreover, as some of the most thoughtful postwar political scientists have emphasized, there is a bias in the kinds of questions raised and interests served in the so-called democratic branches.[63]

In the literature on the Court and the democratic process, scholars have not sufficiently emphasized the value and virtue of a judicial power insulated from the democratic process. We are all familiar, for instance, with the extensive and circumlocutious scholarly debates attempting to reconcile judicial review and pure democracy.[64] The two are essentially irreconcilable. We ought to have the intellectual courage to admit as much. In the next breath we should recognize that this is not so damning or sinful an admission after all.

Our system was never designed to give unlimited power to elected officials or to the electorate. Furthermore, to describe an institution's power as undemocratic is merely to characterize it, not to prove it unworthy of the power. There is nothing inherently evil, corrupting, undesirable, or unwise about allocating some or even substantial power to an institution which is not directly subject to the democratic process. The Court's insulation from that process, we need reminding, builds in a greater opportunity for the justices to assume a broader, long-term perspective than elected officials typically can or do. It also makes it likely that different perspectives may appear and prevail on the Court than those which dominate in the other branches.[65] The different range of vision which may emerge on the Court because of life tenure and political insulation is of incalculable significance, for whatever substantive coloration or direction that vision assumes, it nourishes the vitality and widens the breadth of our national political discourse. This was as true, I daresay, in the 1930s, when the Court made policies with which I personally disagreed, as it was in the 1960s, when the Court made policies with which I personally found favor.

Arthur Sutherland has observed that as a people we have not been able to "say in plain terms that occasionally we have to select wise and able people and give them the constitutional function of countering the democratic process."[66] The justices have not always been wise and able; but this does not disconfirm the utility and wisdom of allocating power to an institution insulated from the electorate,[67] even as evidence of unwise and unable elected officials does not disprove the value of electoral accountability for some institutions. We ought finally, as a nation and as scholars, to come to terms with the Court's structure and power. We ought to emphasize that one of the Court's positive contributions is that it counteracts the democratic process. Were we to do so, perhaps we could be freed of the guilt and misjudgment that led even so perceptive a scholar as Alexander Bickel to refer to the Court's power as "deviant."[68]

The undemocratic nature of judicial power is exacerbated, as the critics see it, by the justices' failure to impose limits on themselves. In the next and final theme, the Court as superlegislature, we shall examine what the critics see as the unfettered personal discretion of the justices.

The Court as Superlegislature

There are three aspects to this criticism. First, the critics stress that the justices have frequently, almost unabashedly, failed to be bound by what was intended by the framers of the Constituion and its amendments.[69] Second, they argue that the Court has failed all too often to be bound by precedent.[70] Third, they believe that when the Court breaks new ground in constitutional law, its opinions are rarely characterized by compelling logic or persuasive reason.[71] Each of these shortcomings makes it crudely obvious, the critics contend, that the justices legislate.[72] In other words, these shortcomings emphasize that the justices exercise discretion and subjectivity in making constitutional law, and that they do so based on personal predilections. Ultimately, the critics warn, this kind of judicial legislation undermines the foundations of the Court's power and legitimacy.[73]

I reject, as myth, the notion that, by adhering to precedent, applying reason and logic, or searching assiduously for the intent of the framers, the justices can determine the "correct" answers to all, most, or even many of the toughest cases the Court hears. Substantial subjectivity and discretion—what Holmes called "the sovereign prerogative of choice"—is inevitable in these cases. Indeed, neither precedent, logic, nor the framers' intent could irrefutably document the constitutionality of judicial review itself—the Court's gravest power and one accepted as legitimate by even the most extreme advocates of restraint. What made judicial review a reality? What continues to sustain it and the Court's general power in American life? The answers turn on political, not legal, considerations. Simply put, the Court's power has become accepted by the American people and the Court's sister political institutions as legitimate. In discussing the Court's role, Arthur Miller touches the core of the issue when he writes:

> The basic question, from the standpoint of American constitutionalism, is to determine how much discretionary power the people are willing to consign to the judges in the making of what Frankfurter once called "sociologically wise decisions." That problem, even today, has not yet been answered after almost two centuries after the Supreme Court began to operate as an informal council of revision of the acts of the other governmental agencies.[74]

In closing their books, both Berger and Graglia urge that the role of the scholar of the Court is to reveal the truth about that institution's power and role in our system.[75]

But what is the simple truth about the Court's power? It is this: Presidents appoint individuals to the Court primarily because of the political inclinations those persons have demonstrated and out of the hope that they will manifest those predispositions in making constitutional law. Once on the Court, justices are expected to develop and articulate a "constitutional philosophy." They are given considerable personal and institutional freedom to do so. The philosophies they devolve are essentially subjective personal assessments as to what constitute the great aims and ends of the American regime and of the United States Supreme Court. The task, if not the power of the justices, is akin to that of philosopher-kings. Supreme Court justices develop American political thought and we, as a nation, are legally bound to consider that thought to be American public policy.[76]

If I am correct, then the mixture of individuals who happen to have sat as justices is a most important factor explaining the development of our constitutional law. This will not surprise political scientists. Yet there is one crucial point to add. It is the thinking of those with legal training—primarily judges and law professors—which dominates scholarly literature and perhaps public myth about the Court. Moreover, the writing of these persons, unlike that of political scientists, is influential within the Court itself. It is the legal scholars, by and large, who led the attack on the Court in the 1970s. Those who see the evolution of constitutional law as primarily a political, as opposed to a legal, phenomenon must engage the legalists in dialogue and advance the compelling arguments that can be made about the essentially political character of the Court's role in constitutional adjudication.

Conclusions

Several propositions emerge from the preceding discussion. I shall present them quickly and then press the analysis beyond the issues raised thus far. First, it is impossible to understand the role of the Supreme Court without adopting a broader sweep of vision than the critics have. The Court is one institution in a complex governmental system. To appreciate and assess properly the Court's functioning, its work must be analyzed within a framework which considers the overall character and development of American government and of each of its branches. To fail to place the Court's actions in that larger context assuredly yields a distorted perception of its performance. Second, by their professional training and traditions, political scientists and historians are in a unique position to adopt the breadth of vision which will place the Court's power in a proper historical and comparative institutional perspective. Third, students of the Court must recognize that institutional change for the high tribunal is inescapable and not necessarily undesirable. The power, function, and structure of the presidency, Congress, and federal bureaucracy have radically and continually evolved throughout our history. If anything, when compared to the other branches in this regard, the Court has remained remarkably stable. Fourth, there are turning points in the development of political institutions when their power and function is substantially changed, and new roles emerge and become institutionalized. From the vantage point of 1982 there is very little evidence to document the critics' allegation that a permanent judicial activism in major national policy issues has become an institutionalized norm on the Court. Certainly the Burger Court has not, at this writing, asserted a role and power for the Court that approaches what the critics envisioned and feared when they wrote. However, it is true that at times in the last quarter-century the Court, more overtly and consistently than before, assumed a role as an initiator of national policy. The critics describe that development and the widened range and affirmative nature of judicial responsibilities that concomitantly ensued. However, as I have suggested, a decisive issue remains. The new role the critics lament has not stuck. It has not endured as the norm for the Court—or at least by 1982 as the norm for the Burger Court. The work of the critics is perhaps best understood as a kind of scholarly lobbying to insure that it would not stick. In this sense, their writing is as much political, and perhaps polemical, as it is scholarly. Yet this is nothing new in scholarship on the Court.

For too long, I believe, commentators have failed to distinguish between their personal assessments of the wisdom of the Court's policies and their views on a larger, somewhat unrelated question—the proper range of power the Court ought to exercise in our system. There is a substantial difference, I suggest, between asking whether one believes that an institution is exercising its powers wisely and asking whether it is wise to vest those powers in the institution in the first place. Critics of the Court must take pains to distinguish their assessment of the politics of the Court's majority at a given time or on a given subject, from their assessment of the long-term function the Court should fill and the optimal range of powers it should exercise in our political system. They ought not adjust the latter, their assessment of the Court's overall role and power, so as to alter the former, the specific policies they wish the Court to advance.

Liberals who deplored the institutional power of the Court in the 1930s and then defended that very same power in the 1950s and 1960s when it happened to advance policies with which they were personally sympathetic, assume a posture which is intellectually untenable, if not downright dishonest. Ditto for conservatives who managed precisely the opposite reversal of field. Scholars delineating the nature and boundaries of the Court's "proper" powers ought to do so without considering whether they like what the Court has done to or for us lately. The failure to make that distinction is most obvious in the work of Glazer and Graglia. Both men have written stinging attacks on the Court's handling of school desegregation, arguing that the Court's policies have been illogical and unwise. As policy analysts, if you will, they make some sound observations; yet there is a considerable leap in moving, as they both do, from questions about the *wisdom* of school busing to questions about the *authority* of the Court to make such policies.

J. Skelly Wright, commenting on scholarship critical of judicial activism in the 1950s and 1960s, strikes a persuasive note when he writes: "It is useful, then, to pierce the veil of the scholarly tradition and to see its quarrel with the Warren Court for what it really is. It is, I believe, a fundamental dispute over the good society."[77] If much academic criticism is properly cast in those terms, and I think it is, then debate ought to proceed accordingly on those grounds. If academics view the Court's policies as injudicious, then their scholarship should advance persuasive argument on the need for the Court to reconsider its positions and adopt alternative, and presumably, wiser policies. Such political criticism, however, ought not ineluctably lapse into, and be disguised as, scholarly commentary on the constitutional authority of the Court to take those actions in the first place. It disserves both scholarship and the Court to continue that tradition. Questions about the substantive wisdom of certain Court decisions and questions about the constitutional authority to make them may overlap. However, where those issues are separable, as they often are, scholars must assiduously treat them as such.

When one views the Court's work in this way it is hard to avoid a certain suspicion. That suspicion should lead one, at least to explore the possibility that it was the political content of the Court's decisions, more than any other factor, which ultimately animated and explained the attacks levied against the high tribunal in the last decade—attacks exemplified in the writings discussed in this chapter. Historians will surely recognize in time that the single most important characteristic of the legal activity the critics objected to is not found in any of the seven criticisms they advanced. What is that characteristic? It is this: For a brief period—albeit in a fairly limited and ineffectual way—the Court appeared to sympathize with and advance the cause of a variety of weak and historically mistreated groups in American society. The thrust of that effort was uncharacteristic of the role that the Court and our constitutional law have historically played. Law is traditionally, if not inherently, an instrument of the powerful; constitutional law is no exception. In that sense much of the scholarly criticism, as well as the Court's willingness in recent years to return to the conservative fold, was quite predictable.

What then of the question of "proper role" posed most directly by Cox, and to a lesser extent by Berger and Horowitz? What can be said about the appropriate or constitutionally optimal range of the Court's powers? First, it needs to be emphasized that the question has assumed a scholarly prominence far out of proportion to its significance. Indeed, it is perhaps the central question scholars have asked about the Court. Students of other branches would no doubt find this bizarre. There is no literature of comparable proportion and significance on the "proper" role of Congress, the federal bureaucracy, or even the presidency. The fetish over the Court's so-called proper role no doubt derives from the legalistic bent of analysts of the Court. That legalistic orientation overemphasizes the importance and interpretation of written words establishing and granting certain powers in a document like the Constitution.

In truth, there is no immutable and definitive constitutional role for the Court which can be deduced from the Constitution or our constitutional history. The boundaries of the Court's formal powers are in many significant respects quite vague. This permits and indeed makes inescapable a latitude for each Court to evolve its own character and legacy. That latitude, while variable and imprecise, is by no means unlimited, or even necessarily broad. The most significant constraints that limit the high tribunal in this regard derive not from the requirements of the constitutional text or from other necessities of law, but rather from considerations of political power. These political considerations turn on three basic factors. The first is the range and depth of the political authority the Court enjoys and can effectively command from the other branches, elite populations, and the American populace generally. The second is the timidity or assertiveness with which the justices are willing to explore and test the boundaries of that authority. The third is the political skill, resourcefulness and guile with which they exercise their power and probe its limits. Borrowing from Samuel Huntington's characterization noted earlier, one might conclude that "great" Courts, like "great" presidents, have "stretched the legal authority and political resources of the office." Such Courts have aggressively and successfully pressed to expand their political authority and consequently the range of major national questions subject to their influence.

All of this is to suggest that, to a considerable degree, the Court has no fixed constitutional role other than that which it attempts to assign or assume for itself. Within certain limits the Court is constantly in a state of becoming. It can and has become a product of what the justices dare make it become and what the American political order permits it to become. The measure of the justices' daring ought to be judged much as we judge the labors of our other political institutions. We ought to ask whether and to what extent Court policies have, in the long term, contributed to the wise, equitable, and constructive resolution of major national problems. Is not the recognized greatness of the Marshall Court premised essentially on this sole criterion—that is, on the character of its contribution to American national development? Could there be a more fitting touchstone for the Court's work?

Notes

1. Nathan Glazer, "Towards an Imperial Judiciary?" *The Public Interest* 41 (Fall 1975):104-123.

2. Donald L. Horowitz, *The Courts and Social Policy* (Washington: The Brookings Institution, 1977); Archibald Cox, *The Role of the Supreme Court in American Government* (New York: Oxford University Press, 1976); Lino A. Graglia, *Disaster by Decree: The Supreme Court's Decisions on Race and Schools* (Ithaca: Cornell University Press, 1976); Raoul Berger, *Government by Judiciary: The Transformation of the Fourteenth-Amendment* (Cambridge: Harvard University Press, 1977).

3. The books by Cox, Berger, and Graglia deal exclusively with the interpretation of the Constitution by the Supreme Court. Of the four case studies in the book by Horowitz, two examine constitutional law decisions by the Court. Glazer's article deals significantly, but not exclusively, with decisions by the high tribunal.

4. In using this designation, I do not necessarily mean it to refer to each of the five men in all instances. In "The Criticisms," (this chapter), I attempt to delineate which of the authors address themselves to each of the seven issues I analyze. Thereafter I use "the critics" more loosely for the sake of convenience.

5. Horowitz, *The Courts and Social Policy*, p. 4.

6. Ibid., p. 5.

7. Glazer, "Towards an Imperial Judiciary?" pp. 106, 115.

8. Cox, *The Role of the Supreme Court in American Government*, p. 36.

9. Barbara Hinckley, *Stability and Change in Congress* (New York: Harper and Row, 1971), pp. 169-175, 182-185.

10. Theodore J. Lowi, *The End of Liberalism: Ideology, Policy, and the Crisis of Public Authority* (New York: Norton, 1969), p. 302.

11. Ibid., p. 68.

12. Richard E. Neustadt, *Presidential Power: The Politics of Leadership with Reflections on Johnson and Nixon,* 2nd ed (New York: Wiley, 1976), p. 23. Joseph Califano comments on the legacy of Lyndon Johnson: "Regardless of what anyone thought of the Great Society, when Lyndon Johnson left government, it was a political, social, institutional, financial and bureaucratic reality . . . Johnson inherited an executive branch that operated less than fifty domestic programs; his legacy was a central executive operating some five hundred such programs." Joseph Califano, *A Presidential Nation* (New York: Norton, 1975), p. 13. James Q. Wilson has observed that in the 1960s a "new wave of regulation" occurred with the passage of the Water Quality Act, the Truth-in-Lending Act, the National Traffic and Motor Vehicle Safety Act, various amendments to the drug laws, and the Motor Vehicle Pollution Control Act and others. James Q. Wilson, "The Rise of the Bureaucratic State," *The Public Interest* 41 (Fall 1975):96.

13. Clinton Rossiter, *Constitutional Dictatorship: Crisis Government in America* (Princeton: Princeton University Press, 1948), p. 34.

14. Harry Jones has discussed the relationship between the growth of the social welfare state and legal rights. He maintains that the identifying characteristics of the welfare state are: significant increase in the range and detail of governmental regulation of private enterprise, increased governmental ownership of enterprises which previously were or would have been privately operated, and the furnishing of services by government directly to the individual. In concluding, Jones asks:

> In an era when rights are mass-produced, can the quality of their protection against arbitrary official action be as high as the quality of protection afforded in the past to traditional legal rights less numerous and less widely dispersed among the members of society?

Harry Jones, "The Rule of Law in the Welfare State," *Columbia Law Review* 58 (February 1958):156.

For an excellent perspective on the historical role of the courts in delineating the power of government vis-à-vis individuals, see Charles McIlwain, *Constitutionalism and the Changing World* (New York: Cambridge University Press, 1939), pp. 277-278.

15. Arthur Schlesinger, Jr., *The Imperial Presidency* (Boston: Houghton Mifflin, 1973), pp. 375-380; Peter Woll, *American Bureaucracy* (New York: Norton, 1977), p. 266.

16. Cox, *The Role of the Supreme Court in American Government*, p. 77.

17. Horowitz, *The Courts and Social Policy*, p. 4.

18. *Lochner v. New York,* 198 U.S. 45 (1905).

19. Although judicial review of bureaucratic behavior may seem dramatic and influential, it is uncommon. Courts review a fraction of one percent of all bureaucratic decisions. Review by the Supreme Court is an extraordinary occurrence. See Robert Fried, *Performance in American Bureaucracy* (Boston: Little, Brown, 1976), p. 263.

20. Glazer, "Towards an Imperial Judiciary?" pp. 111, 119. See also Cox, *The Role of the Supreme Court in American Government,* pp. 54, 100, 102; Berger, *Government by Judiciary,* p. 345; and Horowitz, *The Courts and Social Policy,* p. 9.

21. 414 U.S. 563 (1974).

22. 401 U.S. 424 (1971).

23. Horowitz, *The Courts and Social Policy,* p. 17.

24. See, for instance, Wallace Mendelson, "From Warren to Burger: The Rise and Decline of Substantive Equal Protection," *American Political Science Review* 67 (December 1972):1228, 1233, Gerald Gunther, "In Search of Evolving Doctrine on a Changing Court: A Model for a Newer Equal Protection," *Harvard Law Review* 86 (November 1972):2; Richard Y. Funston, *Constitutional Counter-Revolution? The Warren Court and the Burger Court: Judicial Policy Making in Modern America* (New York: Schenkman, 1977), pp. 336, 342, and 348; Alpheus T. Mason, "The Burger Court in Historical Perspective," *Political Science Quarterly* 89 (March 1974):35; Steven L. Wasby, *Continuity and Change: From the Warren Court to the Burger* (Pacific Palisades, Calif.: Goodyear, 1975), p. 206; Robert Steamer, "Contemporary Supreme Court Directions in Civil Liberties," *Political Science Quarterly* 92 (Fall 1977):432, 442.

25. Arthur S. Miller, "Judicial Activism and American Constitutionalism: Some Notes and Reflections," in *NOMOS XX: Constitutionalism,* ed. J. Roland Pennock and John W. Chapman (New York: New York University Press, 1979), pp. 343-44; Mason, "The Burger Court in Historical Perspective," pp. 32-33; Walter F. Murphy and C. Herman Pritchett, eds., *Courts, Judges, and Politics: An Introduction to the Judicial Process,* 2d ed. (New York: Random House, 1974), p. 6.

26. Neustadt, *Presidential Power,* pp. 73-74.

27. Samuel Huntington, "The Democratic Distemper," *The Public Interest* 41 (Fall 1975):25. (Emphasis added.)

28. C. Herman Pritchett, "The President's Constitutional Position," in *The Presidency Reappraised,* ed. Thomas Cronin and Rexford Tugwell (New York: Praeger, 1977), p. 16.

29. Thomas Cronin, "The Presidency and Its Paradoxes," in Cronin and Tugwell, *The Presidency Reappraised,* pp. 193-194.

30. Wilson, "The Rise of the Bureaucratic State," p. 101.

31. Woll, *American Bureaucracy,* p. viii.

32. Frank J. Goodnow, *Politics and Administration: A Study in Government* (New York: Macmillan, 1900), p. 22; Carl J. Friedrich, "Public Policy and the Nature of Administrative Responsibility," in *Bureaucratic Power in National Politics,* ed. Frances E. Rourke (Boston: Little, Brown, 1972), pp. 317-318.

33. Woll summarizes that new conceptualization in these words:

> Another aspect of the political nature of bureaucracy lies in the fact that the functions these agencies perform involve a direct exercise of legislative, judicial, and executive power, all of which have profound consequences to the community as a whole. The bureaucracy is not merely carrying out the law; rather it is deeply involved in the determination, interpretation, and execution of law.

Woll, *American Bureaucracy,* pp. 9-10.

34. Samuel Huntington, "Congressional Responses to the Twentieth Century," in *Congress and the President: Allies and Adversaries,* ed. Ronald C. Moe (Pacific Palisades, Calif.: Goodyear, 1971), p. 23.

35. Lowi, *The End of Liberalism,* pp. 68-97; Richard Funston, *A Vital National Seminar* (Palo Alto, Calif.: Mayfield, 1978), pp. 96-101.

36. For an excellent discussion of the evolution of the legislative delegation of power in modern democracies and its impact on legislative bodies, see Georges Bardeau, "Delegation of Powers," *International Encyclopedia of the Social Sciences* (New York: Macmillan, 1968), 4:72-73.

37. See Cox, *The Role of the Supreme Court in American Government,* pp. 86-87, 95-96; Glazer, "Towards an Imperial Judiciary?" p. 118; Horowitz, *The Courts and Social Policy,* pp. 30-31, 35, 45-46.

38. Arthur S. Miller and Jerome Barron, "The Supreme Court, the Adversary System, and the Flow of Information to the Justices," *Virginia Law Review* 61 (October 1975):1187-1245; Charles M. Lamb, "Judicial Policy-Making and Information Flow to the Supreme Court," *Vanderbilt Law Review* 29 (January 1976):45-124.

39. Berger, *Government by Judiciary,* p. 408.

40. Glazer, "Towards an Imperial Judiciary?" p. 111.

41. Graglia, *Disaster by Decree,* p. 14.

42. As cited in Karl Loewenstein, *Political Power and the Governmental Process,* 2nd ed. (Chicago: University of Chicago, 1965), pp. 245-246.

43. Arthur S. Miller writes:

> Lawyers and political scientists and Court watchers generally assume that the Supreme Court has enormous power. Any assessment should place it on a continuum with other governmental institutions, public and private.

Miller, "Judicial Activism and American Constitutionalism," p. 358.

44. Ibid.

45. Woll, *American Bureaucracy,* p. 21; and *The Federalist Papers* (New York: Mentor, 1961), Numbers 48, 49, and 51 generally.

46. Friedrich Hayek, *The Constitution of Liberty* (Chicago: University of Chicago Press, 1961), p. 183; see also Wilson, "The Rise of the Bureaucratic State," p. 101.

47. Louis Koenig, *Congress and the President* (Chicago: Scott-Foresman, 1965), pp. 60-61; Schlesinger, *The Imperial Presidency,* pp. 76-82; and Robert A. Diamond, ed., *Origins and Development of Congress* (Washington: Congressional Quarterly, 1976), pp. 199-200.

48. Charles E. Jacobson, *Policy and Bureaucracy* (Princeton: Van Nostrand, 1966), p. 23.

49. Huntington, "The Democratic Distemper," pp. 23-24.

50. William Boyer writes that "[t]he outstanding legal development in this century has been the growth of governmental policies made by numerous administrative agencies," William Boyer, *Bureaucracy on Trial* (Indianapolis: Bobbs-Merrill, 1964), p. 2.

51. Woll, *American Bureaucracy,* p. viii.

52. Ibid., p. 6. (Emphasis added)

53. Frances E. Rourke, *Bureaucracy, Politics and Public Policy* (Boston: Little, Brown, 1969), pp. 152-153.

54. Schlesinger, *The Imperial Presidency,* p. 212.

55. Karl Loewenstein comments on the sharing of power in constitutionalist states:

> The constitutional state is based on the principle of shared power. Shared power exists when several independent power-holders or state organs participate in the exercise of political power and the formation of the will of the state. . . . On the degree of autonomy and interdependence of the several power-holders depends the specific pattern of government. Nor can the reciprocal interdependence of the several power-holders be completely symmetrical and perfectly matched . . . the different patterns of government within the political system of constitutionalism are distinguished by the differential weights that the Constitution and the reality of the political process assign to the various power-holders.

Loewenstein, *Political Power and the Governmental Process,* pp. 245-246.

56. Cox, *The Role of the Supreme Court in American Government,* p. 103.

57. Graglia, *Disaster by Decree,* p. 31.

58. Ibid., p. 32. (Emphasis added)

59. Glazer, "Towards an Imperial Judiciary?" p. 120. For other references to the pernicious impact judicial policymaking may have on the democratic process, see Graglia, *Disaster by Decree,* p. 282; Berger, *Government by Judiciary,* pp. 4-5, 409; and Glazer, "Towards an Imperial Judiciary?" p. 118.

60. Stuart A. Scheingold, *The Politics of Rights* (New Haven: Yale University Press, 1974).

61. Henry Abraham writes that, *"[T]he Court may have the last say, but potentially it has the last say only for a time. . . ."* Henry J. Abraham, *The Judiciary: The Supreme Court in the Governmental Process*, 3rd ed. (Boston: Allyn and Bacon, 1973), p. 41. (Abraham's emphasis)

62. V.O. Key, Jr., *Public Opinion and American Democracy* (New York: Knopf, 1961), p. 81. In this regard see also Murray Edelman, *The Symbolic Uses of Politics* (Urbana: University of Illinois Press, 1964), pp. 172–175.

63. Lowi, *The End of Liberalism;* E.E. Schattschneider, *The Semi-Sovereign People: A Realist's View of Democracy* (New York: Holt, Rinehart and Winston, 1960); Grant McConnell, *Private Power and American Democracy* (New York: Random House, 1970); and Peter Bachrach, *The Theory of Democratic Elitism* (Boston: Little, Brown, 1967).

64. The literature on the subject is voluminous. For a brief sampling of the scholarship see Leonard Levy, ed., *Judicial Review and the Supreme Court* (New York: Harper and Row, 1967).

65. The Court performed this function from the very beginning of the Republic. The Federalists tried to preserve their power by retiring into the federal judiciary and making the third branch their last stronghold in national politics. See Albert J. Beveridge, *The Life of John Marshall* (Boston: Houghton Mifflin, 1916), 1:548.

66. Sutherland, quoted in Berger, *Government by Judiciary,* pp. 312–313.

67. Lawrence Levine has observed that the classical understanding of the separation of powers did not focus on the functional division of power. Rather, he explains, it dealt with the desirability of blending or balancing monarchical, aristocratic, and democratic elements in different governmental institutions. Levine, *The Political Doctrine of Montesquieu's Esprit des Lois: Its Classical Background* (New York: Columbia University Press, 1936), p. 130.

68. Alexander M. Bickel, *The Least Dangerous Branch: The Supreme Court at the Bar of Politics* (Indianapolis: Bobbs-Merrill, 1962), p. 18.

69. Berger, *Government by Judiciary,* pp. 245, 408; Cox, *The Role of the Supreme Court in American Government,* pp. 100, 103.

70. Berger, *Government by Judiciary,* pp. 308, 314-315, 364, 370, 371, 372, 352; Cox, *The Role of the Supreme Court in American Government,* pp. 100, 109; and Graglia, *Disaster by Decree,* p. 27.

71. Berger, *Government by Judiciary,* p. 412; Cox, *The Role of the Supreme Court in American Government,* pp. 74–75, 100, 113–114; Glazer, "Towards an Imperial Judiciary?" p. 115; and Graglia, *Disaster by Decree,* pp. 20, 60, 259, 260.

72. Berger, *Government by Judiciary,* p. 245; Cox, *The Role of the Supreme Court in American Government,* p. 114; Glazer, "Towards an Imperial Judiciary?" p. 115.

73. Cox, *The Role of the Supreme Court in American Government*, pp. 74-75, 109; Berger, *Government by Judiciary*, p. 412.

74. Miller, "Judicial Activism," p. 349.

75. Berger, *Government by Judiciary*, p. 415; Graglia, *Disaster by Decree*, pp. 281-283.

76. Lowi comments: "In the United States the history of political theory since the founding of the Republic has resided in the Supreme Court. The future of political theory probably lies there too." Lowi, *The End of Liberalism*, p. 314.

77. J. Skelly Wright, "Professor Bickel, the Scholarly Tradition, and the Supreme Court," *Harvard Law Review* 84 (February 1971):803.

10 Judicial Activism as Social Engineering: A Marxist Interpretation of the Warren Court

Joan Roelofs

Contemporary left-wing critics of American institutions either ignore the Supreme Court or accept the liberal view of it. The latter view, as applied to the Court during Earl Warren's chief justiceship (1953-1969), is that the Court was benign, that it acted as a counterweight to repressive measures of the "political" branches, that it did not participate in Cold War policies, that its major decisions had nothing to do with economic developments, and that its influence has been highly progressive. Because the Warren Court has been so frequently attacked from the right, radicals have hastened to defend it. Yet the saner right-wing critics reveal a great deal about what the Court was up to, and radical scholarship can profit from their arguments.[1]

This chapter attempts to unravel several puzzles. How could the Court have been such an anomaly among elite institutions during the Cold War period? Harvard, Hollywood, and Harper's fell into line. If, as Marxists claim, government is the executive committee of the ruling class, whose interests does the Court serve? The Court occasionally overrules and generally influences the output of the political branches of government. Finally, how could such a powerful institution produce nothing but pure justice, undetermined by the economic base of the society?

To put the Court in its proper place, we should accept the notion of the Court as "progressive" and examine the implications of that designation. Before the late 1930s, the Court was generally regarded by liberal scholarship as a bulwark of capitalism in the service of the monopolistic firms of national scope. Max Lerner stated it this way:

> The Court's power is a natural outcome of the necessity for maintaining capitalist dominance under democratic forms; . . . judicial review has proved to be a very convenient channel through which the driving forces of American economic life have found expression and achieved victory. Such a view could be documented by reference to the history of the judicial power since Marshall first established it in 1803 by his decision in *Marbury* v. *Madison*. The high points in the story would be

This chapter is a revised and expanded version of my earlier work in this area. See Joan Roelofs, "The Warren Court and Corporate Capitalism," *Telos* 39 (Spring 1979): 94-112. Those portions of the chapter which appeared earlier are reprinted here with the publisher's permission.

Marshall's use of the judicial power to give enlarged scope to the doctrine of due process of law after the Civil War, and the reading of a laissez faire social philosophy into the Constitution in the decades around the turn of the century.[2]

However, after 1937, when the Court abandoned laissez faire, it did not thereby cease serving the interests of capitalism. It merely took a broader viewpoint—that of "social engineering"—in accordance with the presumed long-range interests of the dominant corporate capitalism.[3] Political scientists tend to view the Court's output as the result of the personal preferences of the individual justices; yet the Court also articulates the dominant ideology of the society. According to Theodore Lowi: "In the United States the history of political theory since the founding of the Republic has resided in the Supreme Court."[4]

The point of view that dominated the Warren Court was that of judicial activism.[5] This was a variant of social engineering derived from the Progressive Movement as well as the sociological jurisprudence of Roscoe Pound, Louis Brandeis, and Benjamin Cardozo. The Progressive Movement absorbed the simmering protest movements of the late nineteenth century, and spearheaded the rationalization and nationalization of capitalism. Laissez faire was no longer in the interest of corporate capitalism because of the long history of abuses which provoked protest and harmed the reputations of the established, hence currently "clean" operators. Laissez faire was also seen as dysfunctional after the Great Depression of the 1930s. According to the most far-seeing businessman, capitalism would require a great deal of government intervention for the promotion of stability. The economic and political repercussions of severe depressions could no longer be tolerated.

The Progressive Movement was not originally oriented to the Supreme Court. Nevertheless, on the national level the movement faced the formidable barrier of congressional politics, rife with localistic, reactionary, petty bourgeois, and even populist elements. The congressional tentacles extended deeply into the federal bureaucracy; neither social engineering nor any coherent political policy might be expected from Washington. In the 1930s, the New Deal agencies did at the outset enjoy some independence and were indeed the hope of the "technocracy" movement. They were typically staffed by young lawyers trained in the traditions of legal realism and sociological jurisprudence. However, these agencies soon became subject to the same cross-pressures of Congress, clientele and presidential politics that fragmented the work of the older parts of the administration.

The federal judiciary, on the other hand, had its share of politicians, but many of its most able and articulate members came from the ranks of the corporate bar. Many of these judges had come under the influence of sociological jurisprudence in the elite law schools. Further channels of this ideology came

from the law reviews and law clerks assigned to each federal judge. As Alexander
Bickel has observed: ". . . the clerks . . . are a conduit from the law schools to
the Court. They bring with them . . . the intellectual atmosphere from which
they are newly come."[6] Academic lawyers increasingly permeated the corporate
bar and consequently the federal judiciary. One of the most influential of the
academics was Felix Frankfurter: it was as a teacher, rather than as a judge, that
he unequivocally advocated the doctrines of social engineering and judicial activism.[7]

Judges in America were accustomed to an activist stance. Both the common
law tradition and the task of constitutional interpretation led to habitual judicial
law making. Thus judges could comfortably assume the role of Platonic guardians.[8] Furthermore, lawyers and judges had always been dominant in the ruling
elite of this country. When their task became that of "saving civilization" (and
by the Cold War years many finally became convinced of this), they were eager
to rise to the occasion.

The Court functions as a check on democracy, as was intended. This role
has become more important as other checks have been eliminated (for instance,
indirect election of Senators) and as suffrage has expanded. The growth of
political democracy has empowered many non-ruling-class elements, while
petty bourgeois and reactionary groups continue to flourish.[9] The Supreme
Court during the Marshall era and again after the Civil War served the interests
of the growing national corporations protecting them from both rear guard and
avant-garde attacks of legislatures.[10] For example, the assignment to corporations of the rights of "persons" was a revolutionary step, to which both legal
conservatives and socialists could take strong objection.

After 1937, as the New Deal, which was permeated by the interests of
corporate capitalism, itself permeated Washington, corporate interests were more
frequently expressed in legislative and executive actions. Consequently, the
Court did not have to strike down legislation and executive actions; its role,
rather, was to legitimate these new forms of intervention, protecting them
against a "backlash" of states' righters and free enterprise champions, as well as
from possible threats from a radical left. As Arthur S. Miller has expressed it:

> The Positive State exemplifies in classic style a synthesis along Hegelian
> lines: thesis-antithesis-synthesis. The *thesis:* During the nineteenth
> century the state actively encouraged, through assistance programs and
> the legal system, the growth of business enterprise. The *antithesis:* A
> trend toward egalitarianism, particularly in the post–Civil War period,
> may be seen in the Granger and Populism movements. The liberty of
> corporations, protected by law including the Supreme Court, came to
> loggerheads with the rising tide toward equality and the spread of mass
> suffrage. Something had to give; that "something" was the co-optation
> of welfare programs by the business community—the "ruling class"—in
> a *synthesis* that at once kept the "masses" quiescent and enabled the
> rich to remain rich and even to wax richer. The Supreme Court,

ultimate guardian of corporate privilege, tried for a time to stave off that synthesis, but it had to give way in the 1930's when the economic system broke down in the Great Depression.[11]

Warren Court activism was the judicial version of "progressive" social engineering. The following are the major components of this ideology:

1. Socialism must be prevented by directing social change in such a way that grievances of the masses are heeded, while the corporate elite remains dominant. Justice Louis Brandeis expressed the view of the far-sighted elite when he stated:

> There will come a revolt of the people against the capitalists, unless the aspirations of the people are given some adequate legal expression. . . . Whatever and however strong our convictions against the extension of governmental function may be, we shall inevitably be swept farther toward socialism unless we can curb the excesses of our financial magnates.[12]

2. The agents of this social engineering are to be an elite of judges and lawyers.[13]

3. Capitalism must be rationalized if it is to survive. Robber barons and naked exploitation must go. The Court's role becomes that of legitimating controls on economic activity which run counter to the average American's conception of state and local autonomy, and free private enterprise.[14]

4. Public administration must be centralized to serve the centralized economy.

5. Defects in the United States upon which international communism can "capitalize" must be eliminated.

6. Where defects cannot be remedied, symbolic reassurance should be offered. The illusion of equality, justice, and freedom can aid in social control.[15] Court decisions appearing to enhance liberty can be generously offered when most individuals are locked into a governmental or corporate structure that is intolerant of dissent.[16]

7. Potentially revolutionary American movements must be defused.

8. The Bill of Rights must be interpreted so as to remove the advocacy of communism from its protection. The Court must legitimate repression.

Two consequences of the Court's increasingly activist role in shaping the future of America will be mentioned here. First of all, it helped to accelerate the trend toward the nationalization of American politics, economy, and culture. By the time of the Warren Court, federalism was no longer seen to impose any significant limitation on Congress' commerce, taxing, and spending powers. Nationalization of the Bill of Rights proceeded apace, partly through expanded use of the concept of "substantive" due process. Broad use of the Fourteenth Amendment's equal protection clause made the Court the overseer of state legislation. This was exercised most notably in regard to race and legislative apportionment. Today, however, the Court is invited to scrutinize just about every area of state activity. Any policy can be found to violate due process or equal protection. Given our surplus of lawyers, this sort of litigation has become a national sideshow.

A second consequence of the activist Court was to further the trend toward "depoliticization." As described by Habermas:

> The depoliticization of the mass of the population and the decline of the public realm as a political institution are components of a system of domination that tends to exclude practical questions from public discussion. The bureaucratized exercise of power has its counterpart in a public realm confined to spectacles and acclamation.[17]

The Supreme Court is even more remote from the people than is the bureaucracy. When the Court deals with vital social issues, popular political institutions are not forced to confront them. Even when popular passions are aroused in matters under consideration by the Court (as in the Bakke case), discussion tends to be channeled into narrow, legalistic terms—often obviating consideration of what the best policy might be. Ordinarily, however, most people are simply unaware of Court decisions.[18]

As a result, there is increasing alienation among the American populace. This is particularly noticeable at the local level, where political participation by nonelites was formerly common. Today interest is declining in school board elections (except among vendors and the like) because local school boards have little say in any matter of importance. Unions, state education departments, professional education associations, federal law, and administrative regulations have also preempted local decision making. Nevertheless, it remains significant that courts are now involved in every area of education policy making and in some cases have assumed direct administration. [19] One symptom of this alienation is the tax protest movement which is in part a demand for participatory democracy. Why pay the piper when you cannot call the tune? Depoliticization is not necessarily an irreversible, progressive disease. It may very well lead to the creation of opposing tendencies or a new politicization of the United States.

What of the intended consequences of social engineering? Did the Warren Court succeed in channeling reform in the desired direction and protecting the long-range interests of corporate capitalism against attack from right and left? The period saw a considerable degree of rationalization of the American political and economic system, which provided a useful underpinning for the stage of extraordinary growth in size and power of U.S. corporations.

The Burger Court has by no means reversed the trend of the Warren Court. However, it is not under the same pressure to pursue rationalization as Court decisions are of lesser importance in the current era of American capitalism. The multinational corporations face great opportunities and great risks, but many of them are beyond the ken of any organ of domestic politics. Today, further rationalization is not so important; more crucial is the maintenance of a docile population, cooperative work force, and adequate buying power through wages or welfare.[20]

In order to expound a Marxist interpretation of the Warren Court's social engineering, I will go on to examine some of the Court's major lines of decision in civil rights, civil liberties, criminal justice, and reapportionment.[21]

Civil Rights

Brown v. *Board of Education* did not come out of the blue; its antecedents lay in the cases protesting unequal treatment or lack of provision for black graduate students.[22] A reversal of the *Plessy* decision could be regarded as long overdue. Nevertheless, by declaring de jure segregation per se unconstitutional, the Court was attempting to change radically the way of life in all the southern and most of the border states. The Court is not usually so anxious to interpose itself drastically on American mores.

The great pressure on the Court to reach the decision it did in *Brown* came from an urgency to promote social change.

> Indeed, the *Brown* case, as we shall see, was no fortuitous legal aberration but was instead the fruit of the collective hopes and efforts of a distinguished group of progressive jurists. Included in this group were such eminent figures as Roscoe Pound, Louis D. Brandeis, and Benjamin Cardozo, who were largely responsible for the development of the sociological school of jurisprudence, which stood for a more enlightened understanding of the nature and role of law in a rapidly changing democratic society.[23]

The litigation itself was part of the long-term effort of the NAACP to have segregation declared unconstitutional. The choice of litigation rather than grass-roots activism was based on the consideration that the courts would be more receptive than other governmental agencies to arguments for legal equality.[24] This was also the preferred strategy of the legal leadership of the NAACP, men who had themselves been trained in sociological jurisprudence and who had strong commitments to social engineering.[25]

The effort by the NAACP was elitist from the start. Reform of American race relations was to be imposed from above. The vast majority of black people were nonparticipants in their own liberation (assuming that *Brown* would be enforced and effective). In addition, the actual plaintiffs played a passive and sometimes unwilling role. The cases argued with *Brown* (which included appeals from South Carolina, Virginia, and Delaware) were chosen for strategic reasons. The leading case, against the Board of Education of Topeka, is instructive. Topeka was not selected as a test case because there was great unhappiness in its segregated schools. On the contrary, it was selected because the black schools there were about as good as the white ones, and the NAACP wanted to challenge the principle of segregation without confounding the issue with substantive inequality.

Unfortunately for this strategy, black teachers and administrators in Topeka had developed considerable pride in their school system. They were also worried about their own jobs if desegregation should occur, and they had opposed the NAACP case from the outset.[26] They were unprepared for the *Brown* decision, and like diehard segregationists elsewhere, felt themselves victims of a remote power. The elitist approach taken by the NAACP would (if successful) have required the destruction of many centers of black pride and power. Ironically, black churches, untouched by legal and constitutional requirements, have remained in the forefront of the civil rights struggle.

The blend of activism and self-restraint on the Warren Court might not have produced so sweeping or unanimous a decision as *Brown*, but the political atmosphere lent urgency. Chief Justice Warren himself was quite prepared to act in the role of a Platonic guardian, as he felt that it was entirely proper for the Court to serve as an instrument of social progress.[27] There is evidence that he applied considerable pressure to reach a unanimous decision.[28] The reports of the judicial conferences reveal that a convincing factor was the feeling that the reputation of the country was at stake.[29] Many diplomats from Third World countries were living and traveling here. They not only saw evidence of racial oppression, but they (and their children) were themselves subjected to Jim Crow laws. Since neither Congress nor the states were prepared to dismantle the edifice of segregation, the Court stepped into the breach.

This is not to impugn the humanitarianism of the justices, or to suggest that the unconstitutionality of segregation is not an entirely reasonable interpretation of the Fourteenth Amendment. What was unusual about the case was the Court's willingness to launch a revolution devoid of political or even grass-roots popular support. Its desire for results was even more evident in the decision reached in *Bolling* v. *Sharpe,* which declared school segregation in Washington, D.C. a violation of the due process clause of the Fifth Amendment. Since the federal government was not constitutionally obliged to provide equal protection of the laws, a deus ex machina had to be found.

Since the *Brown* and *Bolling* decisions were an expression of the social engineering ideology, some consideration must be given to the use of social science in these cases. There is some controversy as to whether the social science evidence cited in footnote 11 in *Brown* was the basis for the decision, or merely supported it.[30] The social science findings were essential to the grounds on which the Court based its decision. The Court might have said that segregation itself was a denial of equal protection and left it at that. However, it argued that segregation created feelings of inferiority and impaired learning ability. For these reasons, the Court concluded, equal protection was being denied in segregated school systems.

This was not a conclusion that could be derived from common sense, and consequently the scientific evidence carried a considerable burden. Common sense might well suggest that segregation was demeaning, but that it impaired learning ability was not immediately evident. Today, persons on both sides of this question, including some of the original researchers, acknowledge the sketchy quality of the scientific evidence that segregation caused feelings of inferiority and reduced intellectual potential.[31] Furthermore, we now hear allegations that sexually and racially segregated institutions may encourage competence. At the time of *Brown*, the very scene in Court might have seemed to refute the impairment of learning theory: the brightest stars of the NAACP legal staff had largely come from segregated educational institutions, such as Dunbar High School and Howard University.

The evidence, whether or not needed to support the decision, was relevant for prediction of its consequences. One of the more limited objectives of *Brown* was to promote the equal educational achievement of blacks—they ought to be getting the same quality of education as whites. The social engineering motives transcended this objective. The Court certainly wished to end the stigma of separate education. It may also have hoped to trigger the self-assertion of blacks to demand civil rights within the system. At the most abstract level, *Brown* was to provide "symbolic reassurance." Thus, if we inquire as to whether *Brown* succeeded as social engineering, the answer must be found at different levels. 1. It was a success at the symbolic level. It indicated to American blacks and the world at large that the United States had a commitment to end segregation. 2. It stimulated the civil rights movement, which led to further progress toward integration. 3. It ended de jure segregation and promoted integration in a great many school systems. The development of private schools and white flight from central cities eroded some of these gains. 4. Equal educational achievement of whites and blacks (correcting for socioeconomic level) remains elusive. The reasons for this are not clear.[32] Furthermore, interracial contact has not always promoted greater harmony and tolerance.[33] The black power movement (like the women's movement) has produced new demands for segregated institutions, which are believed to be conducive to high achievement.

There is now a general feeling that there are no easy answers. The unintended consequences of reform from above have given pause to many. Solutions based on confrontation between even the most antagonistic groups sometimes yield more workable and longer-lasting arrangements than those imposed from above. Lunch counters and public transportation are thus far more solidly integrated than schools.

In the short run, the *Brown* decision was in accordance with the interests of corporate capitalism. It was viewed as a threat only by lower-status whites and black school personnel. It announced to the world that a capitalist society could be just and concerned with human rights. Insofar as *Brown* did lead to genuine progress for blacks (both directly through better educational opportunitites and indirectly through stimulation of the civil rights movement), it brought them into the American consumer class, while dispelling any ideas of revolution that might be circulating. The New Deal had done little for blacks; the *Brown* decision supplied this part of the "conservative revolution." As to "the fire next time," who knows?

Civil Liberties

In this area, the Warren Court reiterated the doctrines of the earlier *Schenck* and *Gitlow* cases.[34] In *Schenck*, the concept of free expression was diluted to exclude advocacy of radical ideas. *Gitlow* began the nationalization of the Bill of Rights through the illogical concept of "substantive" due process, found in the Fourteenth Amendment. Thus repression was justified and legitimated, at the national and state level.

The "clear and present danger" doctrine was fictional in its original application. Schenck was spreading "dangerous" pacifist ideas with no observable effect. Gitlow's communism was hardly likely to spark a revolution: "There was no evidence of any effect resulting from the publication and circulation of the Manifesto."[35] Nevertheless, his conviction was upheld because:

> Such utterances, by their very nature, involve danger to the public peace and to the security of the state. They threaten breaches of the peace and ultimate revolution. . . . The state may . . . suppress the threatened danger in its incipiency.[36]

The repression of socialist movements and ideas in the post–World War I period was consequently legitimated by Supreme Court decisions. Similarly, in the post–World War II period, the Warren Court sustained the principle of the *Dennis* case—that suppression of Communist advocacy was legitimate.[37] When the Court upheld convictions and citations of contempt against radicals, it cited "self-preservation" as the justification.[38] However, when it reversed convictions or vetoed administrative proceedings, the Court based its decisions on the "vagueness" of laws or the violation of "due process" in their application.[39] So long as legislatures and congressional committees applies their repression in a tidy manner, no violation of freedom of speech was found.[40]

Contrary to popular mythology, the Warren Court did not enhance freedom of expression. Its social engineering took two forms. By insisting on due process before repressive acts could occur, it created an aura of freedom, which nevertheless encouraged no one to express controversial ideas. Partly this was because any liberalization that did occur (such as permitting radicals to travel abroad by allowing them passports), came after radical movements had been destroyed by other means (such as McCarthyism). Furthermore, the Court's decisions in this area were cues to governmental agencies on what sort of repressive legislation would meet the due process standard and pass the Court's muster.

Eventually, administrative agencies and the private sector took over the job of repression through harassment, intimidation, and infiltration, so that what laws said and what the Court said made little difference. Freedom of speech is illusory for most Americans who have a job, or who would like to have one. Of course, there is freedom everywhere in the world for people who merely want to support the system. Conformity is the price paid for the "security" of the corporation.

The Warren years saw increasing conformity imposed on American political views. The undemocratic practice of judicial review has often been justified by the claim that the Court upholds our liberties against repressive majorities. This is not borne out by the results. Most individuals who were in fact vindicated by the Court had their careers destroyed and their energies sapped by the litigation process. Individuals not involved in test cases have not met with a liberalized atmosphere because of such vindications.

Would our liberties have been more secure if it were not for the Supreme Court's role? Perhaps so. Leaving the matter to judges can have a lulling effect. As Justice Jackson stated:

> In this country . . . we rarely have a political issue made of any kind of invasion of civil liberty. On the contrary, district attorneys who have been rebuked by the courts are frequently promoted by the public. The attitude seems to be, leave it to the judges. Years after the event takes place, the judges make their pronouncement, often in the form of letting some admittedly guilty person go, and that ends the matter. . . . Whether the political conscience is relieved because the responsibility here is made largely a legal one, I cannot say, but of this I am sure: any court which undertakes by its legal process to enforce civil liberties needs the support of an enlightened and vigorous public opinion which will be intelligent and discriminating as to what . . . questions are involved in those cases. I do not think the American public is enlightened on this subject.[41]

The "nationalization" of civil liberties issues removes them further from the people. The Constitution, despite interpretations beginning with *Gitlow*, clearly leaves civil liberties within the states in the hands of state government, except for the requirements of the Fourteenth Amendment relating to due process and equal protection. The Court had amended the Constitution to give the federal courts scrutiny over duly enacted and enforced state laws. Were this function to return to the states, perhaps a concerned citizenry might examine state laws and executive actions with a view to maximizing liberty. Of course, there is nothing to prevent state courts from enforcing the Bill of Rights of their own state constitutions or the federal Bill of Rights, but the focus of claimants is directed elsewhere. The need to make a federal case (which takes years, money, energy, and supporters) out of every violation of liberty does not encourage a vigorous defense of rights.[42]

Criminal Justice

The Court's decisions in the area of criminal justice had a clear constitutional basis. The due process clause of the Fourteenth Amendment can logically apply to criminal procedure. It is less convincing when due process is claimed to mandate a certain level of public utility profits, prohibit state aid to religion, or require states to permit abortions, all of which have been declared elements of substantive due process. However, the Court has great latitude as a super-legislature even in this area. First, due process is a vague concept. It has been variously interpreted by Supreme Court justices to mean all the criminal justice provisions of the Bill of Rights;[43] only those "implicit in the concept of ordered liberty;"[44] and procedures, whether or not mentioned in the Bill of Rights, that ensure basic decency or fairness.[45] In practice, combinations of these positions have led to the incorporation of almost all of the Bill of Rights provisions into the due process clause of the Fourteenth Amendment. That does not end the matter, for the provisions themselves are not easy to define: cruel and unusual punishment, unreasonable search and seizure, assistance of counsel (when, and of what quality?). Appealing to time immemorial or common law conceptions does not help much when lie detectors, electronic surveillance, and other modern techniques of interrogation are in question. Consequently, frequent redefinition of these principles keeps state law enforcement agencies in a considerable state of confusion (and anger).

The Constitution is unclear about what remedy should be applied to violations of due process. The Court has argued that the only effective remedies are invalidating convictions where procedures were improper and excluding evidence unconstitutionally obtained. This has occasioned a great deal of controversy, because while it has resulted in the freeing of obviously guilty defendants, it has not served greatly to protect the innocent. Instead, it has further weakened our criminal justice system by increasing the tendency towards plea bargaining, which bypasses the many constitutional safeguards (or traps) that a trial entails. Justice based on technicalities puts a premium on legal skills, which is not uniformly distributed despite the *Gideon* rule.[46]

The Court has been under considerable political attack because of its criminal justice decisions. Unlike the segregation cases which affected the daily lives mainly of those of low status, the law enforcement decisions were regarded as a challenge by an elite group: state attorneys general, law enforcement officials, and judges. Why did the Court challenge such formidable adversaries? One commentator has suggested that it was simply that power begets power, that after the *Brown* decision the Court realized it could get away with *Miranda* v. *Arizona, Baker* v. *Carr,* and other similar cases.[47]

An approving analysis gives the Court's motives as follows:

It is to the credit of the Supreme Court that it recognized that the nation was in the midst of a social revolution before this became apparent to most of the elected representatives of the people, and that it sought to eliminate the basic defects in our system for the administration of criminal justice within our present structure. The result of this perceptive approach has been to immunize the Court from much of the alienation expressed against other institutions of our society not only by the disadvantaged, but also by large numbers of our youth, upon whom the future of the nation depends.[48]

There is no doubt that the Court was promoting the idea that justice for all could be obtained in any court in the land. This is not to question the commitment of the justices to the idea of a fair trial. It is, however, to suggest that some great urgency in the matter led the Court to take great political risks. The criminal justice decisions were in accordance with the general centralizing tendencies in American public administration. This trend was regarded as ominous by Justice Jackson:

> The Court has been drawing into the federal system more and more control by federal agencies over local police agencies. I have no doubt that the latter are often guilty of serious invasions of individual rights. But there are more fundamental questions involved in the interpretation of the antiquated, cumbersome, and vague civil rights statutes which give the Department of Justice the right to prosecute state officials. . . . I cannot say that our country could have no central police without becoming totalitarian, but I can say with great conviction that it cannot become totalitarian without a centralized national police. . . . I think in the long run the transgressions of liberty by the Federal Government, with its all-powerful organization, are much more to be feared than those of the several states, which have a greater capacity for self-correction.[49]

No doubt, in 1955 when this was published, this view may have been regarded as paranoid, right-wing, and allied to racist states' righters. Since then there has been evidence of massive violations of civil rights by federal agencies: harassment of dissidents by the IRS and the FBI, disruption of the legal activities of such groups as the Socialist Workers Party, Nixon's COINTELPRO program, Army surveillance of peaceful, legal, civilian domestic political activity as well as spying on college classrooms and lectures.

It is precisely the centralization of data, the sharing of information by different agencies of the federal government as well as with state and local police, and the easy access to this data which computers provide, that makes these operations so intimidating. The Warren Court undoubtedly was not attempting to establish a police state, but its decisions did further the nationalization of "justice." For the problem of crime, the supporters of the Court recommended federal funds for training, equipment, and better coordination of police forces throughout the nation.[50]

The Court's conception of due process was not derived from predictive social science research. Little existed to indicate which procedures were feasible, which would ensure fairness, which would reduce crime or encourage rehabilitation.[51] In the *Miranda* case, the Court supported its decision by citing a 1931 National Commission on Law Observance Report (the Wickersham Report), police manuals from several cities suggesting "effective" interrogation methods, and articles in law journals attesting to the efficacy and legality of the third degree.[52]

The Court's decisions certainly brought some improvement in police discipline. However, the imposition of a varying federal standard on state court and police procedures has been extremely difficult to enforce and has produced great confusion. Even the symbolic reassurance in this area is weak; the "alienation" previously referred to has not been dispelled. As to the fairness inherent in our current system of justice, after all the Warren era reforms, one authority observed:

> The administration of justice in America is pockmarked by systematic discrimination againt blacks, the poor, women, juveniles, and consumers. Although special rules attempt to place litigants on a more equal footing than they may claim in other portions of the political process, the administration of justice still reflects the inequalities of American society.[53]

Evasion of federal rules is common. Furthermore:

> Bargaining with defendants over their punishment rather than determining their guilt by trial is a perversion of the adversary process that developed without any explicit direction by political leaders. It represents an adaptation to the surging caseload of the courts that resulted from the growth of America's population and perhaps an increase in crime.[54]

The question of whether there is more crime today than twenty-five years ago is likely to lead to a statistical debate. However, there is certainly a great deal of crime (of all kinds). We might have expected a decrease in the crime rate with the increasing affluence and security of the post–World War II period. Never would the paranoid suggestion be made that the Warren Court decisions intended to encourage criminals. It is nevertheless interesting to note the coincidence: the Court (although committed to social engineering) seemed not greatly concerned with the problem of crime (unlike its worries about the danger of subversion); and, crime serves an important function in our economy. Burglary, for instance, gives an extra stimulus to the consumer goods industry; it is a system of private (unwilling) charity. When a television set is stolen, the former owner will buy a new one. Vandalism aids the construction industries. Arson is generally profitable all around. Capitalism requires a growing market; consumption and destruction (no matter by whom or how) create the demand.

Crime may be even more functional in our system as a provider of employment, taking up some of the slack left by the shrinking personnel needs of the corporate sector. First, there are those people who regularly earn their living from illegal or semilegal activities (accountants, pornographers, gamblers, influence peddlers, and school lunch adulterators, to name a few). Second, there is the vast array of private security services and device manufacturers, employing an increasing number of persons. As the volume of insurance increases, that industry can become even more labor-intensive. These employment schemes may create considerable inflation, but they are no great burden on large corporations. Their costs are simply passed on to the consumer as a "crime tax." Third, public employment related to social pathology, for example, in criminal justice, mental health, and welfare systems, has grown enormously; this bill is part of the regular taxes.

None of this is to suggest that the Warren Court set out to create a crime wave. It is simply interesting to note that crime is functional in our economic system. We might reflect on the old saying: "Men make their own history, but they do not make it just as they please; they do not make it under circumstances chosen by themselves."[55]

Reapportionment

A very cynical person might regard the entire reapportionment matter as a scheme for promoting the full employment of political scientists. However, as we are only mildly cynical, we will have to see other functions and motives in the Court's decisions in the area of one-person-one-vote.[56]

A critic of the Warren Court, Ward Elliott, regards the reapportionment decisions (which Warren said were the most important during his chief justiceship) as prime evidence of the "guardian ethic."[57] This he describes as the "bureaucratic, elitist ideology of action-minded intellectuals in the modern age, most of whom thought they were beyond ideology."[58] Elliott claims that what guardians were promoting was not equality in form (such as one-person-one-vote) but special privileges in substance for the experts. The actual effect of the reapportionment decisions was a shift in political power for legislatures and parties to bureaucrats, judges, and academic researchers who were henceforth engaged in drawing boundary lines determining the extent of "natural" communities, and so forth.[59] There was also, as in the other areas of the Warren Revolution, a shift in authority from state to national government.

It is particularly ironic that the decisions spurred the centralizing tendency, because in the studies that informed and influenced the Court, a major purpose of reapportionment was said to be the revitalization of state governments.[60]

A related aim was to reverse the process whereby urban governments were bypassing state governments and dealing directly with the federal government.[61] This condition was attributed to malapportioned state legislatures:

> Problems like slum clearance, urban traffic congestion, race relations, juvenile delinquency, day nurseries to aid working mothers, health and education, factory safety, workmen's compensation, and a score of others plague city people but are often unknown in rural areas. Without adequate funds and state cooperation, cities are powerless to solve these problems unaided. Yet, the rurally dominated legislatures—unfamiliar or unsympathetic to them—too often do little or nothing to help.
>
> Is further intervention by the federal government the only answer? Or can representation in the legislatures of the states be so reconstituted that the needs and views of the urban majority receive attention and get action?[62]

These studies did not show how malapportionment was related to bad policies or weak government, or what other causes might exist for urban dependency on the federal government. Furthermore, they ignored a considerable body of political science literature which indicates that issues are not decided by voters at election time.[63] Anthony Lewis, perhaps the chief guru of reapportionment, implied that political persuasion occurs through the counting of voters' ballots.[64] The "group theory" of politics seems unknown to the advocates of one-person-one-vote.[65] Studies of how state governments actually operate were plentiful at the time of the decisions. Yet the Court insisted: "Legislators represent people, not trees or acres. Legislators are elected by voters, not farms or cities or economic interests.[66]

The views of a critic of the *Baker et al.* decisions, Alfred de Grazia, were somewhat more realistic. He maintained that one-person-one-vote was, even before it had been actualized, an obsolete concept; functional representation was already taking place. This should be recognized and institutionalized, so that all important interests could be represented.[67] For example, of representatives selected on the basis of occupation, 5 percent should be housewives.[68]

Since the theory behind the reapportionment decisions bore little relation to reality, it is not surprising that the results were disappointing. There has been considerable equalization of state legislative and congressional districts, yet we have politics as usual (if not more so). Interest-group politics is more important than ever, political participation is at an all-time low, and many cities, despite federal aid, are decaying fast. Of course, the problem is not merely one of faulty political institutions. Nevertheless, the institutional changes which resulted from Court decisions, especially allocation of greater power to the federal government, and in particular to the federal judiciary, reinforced the trend toward depoliticization of the masses.

The Warren Court decisions in the other three areas have benefited some blacks, dissenters, and criminal defendants, but in the case of reapportionment it is hard to find much of an effect beyond the symbolic. To some extent (a very limited one) an illusion of political equality was created. Although Warren regarded this as the most important area of the Court's work, surely it was the most ephemeral.

Conclusion

Has the Warren Court helped to channel reform in a desired direction consonant with the interests of corporate capitalism? The centralizing and nationalizing effect of its decisions accorded with the needs of capitalism at the time. The Court's decisions helped to legitimate the New Deal and accelerate the demise of localistic, particularistic, reactionary, and radical elements in our society. The world-view of the Carnegie Corporation (which had sponsored Myrdal's *American Dilemma*), the Twentieth Century Fund (which sponsored many of the reapportionment studies), and the Ford Foundation had found a mouthpiece in the Warren Court. This view was noble and benevolent, but was notably lacking in any commitment to genuine equality and liberty. The avant-garde of capitalism, as Brandeis had advocated, was now committed to social reform, provided only those on top remained on top.[69]

Also, the Court decisions offered not only symbolic reassurance but stimulated change within the system. Perhaps the concept of "artificial negativity" is appropriate here.[70] The optimism expressed in the civil rights movement undoubtedly helped to delay the idea of revolutionary change. As long as there is some hope for peaceful, legal change, few people will take the risks associated with revolutionary action.[71] This would have been difficult anyway, as the Court legitimated postwar suppression of radical ideas, while public and private employers completed the task of effectively suppressing dissent.

Nevertheless, in the long run, the Court may have had a minimal or negative effect on the enterprise of promoting change while sustaining capitalist hegemony. First of all, handling problems on a symbolic level can discourage attempts to find better solutions.[72] It is possible that there are no real solutions, for example, to the problem of unemployment among blacks, or the prevalence of crime, under corporate capitalism. In the short run, however, creativity may be discouraged by measures more symbolic than real. While it has not been proven, I suggest that solutions imposed by remote authorities are more likely to be symbolic than those worked out through popular political activity. Furthermore, the Court's role in the enterprise of directing change from above, since it is the institution most remote from the people, has accentuated depoliticization, apathy, and alienation. The federal judiciary is now involved in so many areas of policy and administration that citizen initiative seems pointless.[73] Political activity focuses more and more on interest-group litigation efforts. Lawyers, and judges, as Brandeis wished, are the main participants. It is significant that local school board politics, at one time an introduction to political activity for the average citizen, is now constrained in every way by judicial decisions.

The present political attitude has particular significance because disaffection is occurring on the right as well as on the left. In the center, many liberals who formerly advocated social engineering are now likewise disillusioned. On all sides, rule by elites, especially distant elites, is being rejected. The tax protest movement is in part a demand for participatory democracy; it has finally dawned on the liberty bell types that "no taxation without representation" must have a substantive meaning. In addition to the ordinary taxation to support expanded education, welfare, health, and crime control functions, there is the extra expense, particularly onerous to small business, of hiring such personnel as affirmative action officers mandated by federal law. Throwing money at problems, and accepting decrees from on high, are no longer seen as viable solutions. Chief Justice Burger has rhetorically recognized that the judiciary is involved in too much legislative and administrative activity, but seems unable to reverse the trend in practice.

Must all social engineering be repressive? It is easy enough to agree that reform promoted by an elite is bound to be ephemeral and manipulative. But it is not so easy to discover how any reform—or revolution for that matter—can be anything other than repressive. This is one source of the current pessimism shared by existentialists, democratic socialists, critical theorists, and many liberals.

The association of "social science" and "socialism" is not entirely accidental. Positivism lies at the root of modern social science and Marxism. Implicit in both are the notions that a science of man is possible, that misery can be averted through human action (rather than passivity), that the course of history can be altered, and that the good life is knowable and attainable on this earth. These ideas are also in accordance with the original Greek conception of political science. If this positivist ethic is rejected, political scientists and sociologists might as well close up shop; they would have no function. Historians, mystics, journalists, and pollsters could absorb the remaining business. This might not be the greatest tragedy to befall mankind, but the instinct for self-preservation does prod. There is no simple answer to the question of whether there can be a non-repressive social (or political) science. First, a social science that assumes the existence of, or aims at the preservation of, a repressive economic system, whether it be corporate capitalism or Soviet bureaucratic communism, will only further the repression. The starting point for a liberating social science has to be a commitment to meeting basic human needs, but it is no easy task to discover what they are. Second, the fruits of such research have to be widely disseminated and applied on a local, decentralized basis by the people concerned. This rules out bureaucratically imposed reform as well as violent revolution. Such a project would require a great deal of toleration of diversity and even chaos. Third, there must be full recognition that humans are a part of nature. Some of nature's own repressiveness (such as greater austerity) might have to be accepted. Reduced domination over nature could entail less domination over other human beings (as in relinquishing the use of nuclear power).[74] The task is formidable, but what other mission is there for social scientists?

Notes

1. See, for example, Raoul Berger, *Government by Judiciary: The Transformation of the Fourteenth Amendment* (Cambridge: Harvard University Press, 1977); Alfred de Grazia, *Essay on Apportionment and Representative Government* (Washington: American Enterprise Institute for Public Policy Research, 1963); Ward E. Elliott, *The Rise of Guardian Democracy: The Supreme Court's Role in Voting Rights Disputes: 1845-1969* (Cambridge: Harvard University Press, 1974); Alexander M. Bickel, *The Supreme Court and the Idea of Progress* (New York: Harper and Row, 1970).

2. Max Lerner, "The Divine Right of Judges," in *The People, Politics and the Politician*, ed. Asher N. Christensen and Evron M. Kirkpatrick (New York: Henry Holt, 1941), p. 578.

3. See G. William Domhoff, *The Higher Circles: The Governing Class in America* (New York: Vintage, 1970), chap. 6.

4. Theodore J. Lowi, *The End of Liberalism: Ideology, Policy, and the Crisis of Public Authority* (New York: Norton, 1969), p. 314.

5. This was the case even though not all justices took this position, and all justices refrained from activism at times. See Charles M. Lamb, "Judicial Restraint on the Supreme Court," chap. 1, this volume.

6. Alexander M. Bickel, *Politics and the Warren Court* (New York: Harper and Row, 1965), p. 143.

7. Jerold S. Auerbach, *Unequal Justice: Lawyers and Social Change in Modern America* (New York: Oxford University Press, 1976), p. 171.

8. Elliott, *The Rise of Guardian Democracy*.

9. Other Western nations also have checks on democracy; for example, the socially and culturally conservative influence of the British monarchy, and the administrative elite in France.

10. Arthur S. Miller, *The Supreme Court and American Capitalism* (New York: Free Press, 1968), p. 24.

11. Arthur S. Miller, *The Modern Corporate State* (Westport, Conn.: Greenwood, 1976), p. 93.

12. Louis D. Brandeis, *Business: A Profession* (Boston: Small, Maynard, 1933), p. 320.

13. Ibid. For modern adherents of this theory see William J. Brennan, Jr., "Law and Social Sciences," in *The Supreme Court: Views from Inside,* ed. Alan F. Westin (New York: Norton, 1961), p. 149; and Arthur S. Miller, "Science Challenges Law," in *Law and Social Change,* ed. Stuart S. Nagel (Beverly Hills: Sage, 1970), p. 114.

14. For a critical view of this phenomenon see Jurgen Habermas, *Toward a Rational Society* (Boston: Beacon, 1970), p. 102.

15. Murray Edelman, *The Symbolic Uses of Politics* (Urbana: University of Illinois Press, 1964).

16. Miller, *The Supreme Court and American Capitalism,* p. 230.

17. Habermas, *Toward a Rational Scoiety,* p. 75.

18. James P. Levine and Theodore Becker, "Toward and Beyond a Theory of Supreme Court Impact," in Nagel, *Law and Social Change,* p. 88.

19. Ray Rist and Ronald Anson, *Education, Social Science and the Judicial Process* (New York: Teachers College Press, 1977), p. ix.

20. To my mind, the most humanitarian decision of the Court in its history, *Roe v. Wade,* 410 U.S. 113 (1973), is additionally of excellent service to American capitalism. The availability of abortion permits more women to remain longer in the labor force—a boon, as they are both lower paid and less rebellious than men. Furthermore, by making two-wage families the norm, the market for cars, houses, appliances, and so forth is prevented from collapsing. Another way of supporting the market in an inflationary situation is the increase of homosexual couples, who are usually childless and both working. One would expect liberalization of laws in this area at this stage of capitalism.

21. This chapter will not deal directly with the strictly economic decisions of the Court. However, it should be noted that: "In matters directly affecting business, as in labor relations, anti-trust and tax issues, the Warren Court has been simply an enunciator of the social capitalist status quo in American politics." Alan F. Westin, "When the Public Judges the Court," in *The Supreme Court Under Earl Warren,* ed. Leonard W. Levy (New York: Quadrangle, 1972), p. 56. It is also significant that the Court's fiercest application of the antitrust laws was against the Brown Shoe Company. See Theodore J. St. Antoine, "Judicial Valor and the Warren Court's Labor Decisions," in *The Warren Court: A Critical Analysis,* ed. Richard Saylor, Barry Boyer, and Robert Gooding, Jr. (New York: Chelsea House, 1968). See also Karl Klare, "Judicial Deradicalization of the Wagner Act and the Origins of Modern Legal Consciousness," *Minnesota Law Review* 62 (March 1978): 265–339.

22. *Missouri ex rel. Gaines v. Canada* 305 U.S. 337 (1938); *Sipuel v. Board of Regents,* 332 U.S. 631 (1948); *McLaurin v. Oklahoma State Regents,* 339 U.S. 637 (1950); *Sweatt v. Painter,* 339 U.S. 629 (1950).

23. Paul L. Rosen, *The Supreme Court and Social Science* (Urbana: University of Illinois Press, 1972), p. xi.

24. Richard Kluger, *Simple Justice* (New York: Knopf, 1975), p. 133.

25. Auerbach, *Unequal Justice*, p. 198.

26. Kluger, *Simple Justice*, p. 392.

27. Ibid., p. 667.

28. Ibid., p. 698.

29. Ibid.

30. The research cited in *Brown v. Board of Education* was as follows: Kenneth B. Clark, *Effect of Prejudice and Discrimination on Personality Development* (Midcentury White House Conference on Children and Youth, 1950); Helen Witmer and Ruth Kotinsky, eds., *Personality in the Making* (New York: Harper, 1952), chap. 6; Max Deutscher and Isidor Chein, "The Psychological Effects of Enforced Segregation: A Survey of Social Science Opinion," *Journal of Psychology* 26 (October 1948): 259-287; Isidor Chein, "What are the Psychological Effects of Segregation Under Conditions of Equal Facilities?" *International Journal of Opinion and Attitude Research* (1949), p. 229; Theodore Brameld, "Educational Costs" in *Discrimination and National Welfare*, ed. Robert M. MacIver (New York: Institute for Religious and Social Studies, 1949), pp. 44-48; Edward Frazier, *The Negro in the United States* (New York: Macmillan, 1949), pp. 674-681. And see generally Gunnar Myrdal, *An American Dilemma* (New York: Harper and Row, 1944).

31. David Cohen and Janet Weiss, "Social Science, Social Policy, Schools and Race," in Rist and Anson, *Education, Social Science and the Judicial Process*, p. 75.

32. Ibid.

33. Ibid., p. 77.

34. *Schenck* v. *United States*, 24947 (1919); *Gitlow v. New York*, 268 U.S. 652 (1925).

35. *Gitlow v. New York*.

36. Ibid.

37. *Dennis v. United States*, 341 U.S. 494 (1951).

38. *Ullman v. United States*, 350 U.S. 422 (1956); *Communist Party of the U.S. v. Subversive Activities Control Board*, 367 U.S. 1 (1961).

39. *Watkins v. United States*, 354 U.S. 178 (1957); *Sweezy v. New Hampshire* 354 U.S. 234 (1957); *Koningsberg* v. *State Bar* 366 U.S. 36 (1961).

40. For example, *Barenblatt* v. *United States*, 360 U.S. 109 (1959).

41. Robert H. Jackson, "The Supreme Court as a Political Institution," in Westin, *The Supreme Court: Views from Inside*, p. 170.

42. Levine and Becker, "Toward and Beyond a Theory of Supreme Court Impact."

43. See Justice Black's dissent in *Adamson v. California*, 332 U.S. 46 (1947).

44. *Palko v. Connecticut*, 302 U.S. 319 (1937).

45. *Rochin v. California*, 342 U.S. 165 (1952).

46. That lawyers must be provided in felony cases in state trials. *Gideon v. Wainwright*, 372 U.S. 335 (1963).

47. Arthur S. Miller, "Toward a Concept of Constitutional Duty," in *The Supreme Court Review*, ed. Philip B. Kurland (Chicago: University of Chicago Press, 1968), p. 231.

48. A. Kenneth Pye, "The Warren Court and Criminal Procedure," in Saylor, Boyer, and Gooding, *The Warren Court*, pp. 66-67.

49. Westin, *The Supreme Court: Views from Inside*, p. 163.

50. Pye, "The Warren Court and Criminal Procedure," p. 77.

51. Donald L. Horowitz, *The Courts and Social Policy* (Washington: The Brookings Institution, 1977), pp. 277-278.

52. *Miranda v. Arizona*, 384 U.S. 436 (1966).

53. Herbert Jacob, *Justice in America: Courts, Lawyers and the Judicial Process*, 2nd ed. (Boston: Little, Brown, 1972), p. 225.

54. Ibid., p. 226.

55. Karl Marx, "The Eighteenth Brumaire of Louis Bonaparte," in *Marx and Engels: Basic Writings on Politics and Philosophy*, ed. Lewis Feuer (Garden City, N.Y.: Doubleday, 1959), p. 320.

56. The major cases are: *Baker v. Carr*, 369 U.S. 186 (1962); *Wesberry v. Sanders*, 376 U.S. 1 (1964); *Reynolds v. Sims*, 377 U.S. 533 (1964).

57. For Warren's estimation of the importance of *Baker*, see Anthony Lewis, "A Talk with Warren on Crime, the Court, the Country," in Levy, *The Supreme Court Under Earl Warren*, p. 170.

58. Elliott, *The Rise of Guardian Democracy*, p. 2.

59. Ibid., p. viii.

60. Anthony Lewis, "Legislative Apportionment and the Federal Courts," *Harvard Law Review* 71 (April 1958): 1057-1098; Robert McKay, *Reapportionment: The Law and Politics of Equal Representation* (New York: The Twentieth Century Fund, 1965).

61. "A Report to the President by the Commission on Intergovernmental Relations," Meyer Kestnbaum, Chairman, June 1955, in *Legislative Apportionment: Key to Power*, ed. Howard D. Hamilton (New York: Harper and Row, 1964), p. 3.

62. Department of Education and Research, AFL-CIO, "Government by Minority," in ibid., p. 79.

63. This accusation was made by Alexander M. Bickel in *Politics and the Warren Court*, p. 183.

64. "Legislative Apportionment: Key to Power," in Levy, *The Supreme Court Under Earl Warren*.

65. See, for example, David Truman, *The Governmental Process* (New York: Knopf, 1951).

66. *Reynolds v. Sims*, 377 U.S. 533 (1964).

67. de Grazia, *Essay on Apportionment and Representative Government,* pp. 166–169.

68. Ibid., p. 171. He never said he was a feminist.

69. For a general discussion of this view see James Weinstein, *The Corporate Ideal and the Liberal State* (Boston: Beacon, 1968).

70. See Paul Piccone, "The Crisis of One-Dimensionality," *Telos* 35 (Spring 1978): 43.

71. Richard Flacks, "Making History vs. Making Life," *Working Papers,* (Summer 1974), pp. 56–71.

72. Edelman, *The Symbolic Uses of Politics.*

73. Berger, *Government by Judiciary.*

74. David Dinsmore Comey, "Fundamental Conflict Between Nuclear Power and Civil Liberties," *In These Times,* Oct. 25–31, 1978, p. 17.

Part III
Behavioral Perspectives

Before World War II virtually all research in the area of public law was either historical or normative. The legal realist movement, which flowered in the 1930s, rejected the theory of "mechanical jurisprudence"—the notion that judges "discover" or "find" the law.[1] Legal realists, led by such men as Jerome Frank and Karl Llewellyn, believed that judicial interpretations of the law involved a variety of considerations which stemmed largely from the personal characteristics of the judge deciding the case. The realist contribution represented a dramatic departure from the Blackstonian model which had long dominated legal thinking and writing; yet it was not without its problems. Commenting on the writings of Jerome Frank, Sheldon Goldman and Thomas P. Jahnige have noted that "[f]or Frank each judge was unique, and the variables associated with each judge's decision making were viewed as so complex that without knowledge gained from a psychoanalysis of the judge it would be impossible to predict judicial behavior."[2]

Not unitl the path-breaking research of C. Herman Pritchett in the 1940s did political scientists develop a methodological approach, built on some of the assumptions of legal realism, which enabled them to examine the behavior of judges in a systematic way.[3] The units of analysis were the votes of the justices. The basic focus explored the character of voting divisions on the Court. Pritchett's approach constituted a direct challenge to the deeply ingrained historical and normative perspectives. As Walter Murphy and Joseph Tanenhaus have observed, Pritchett's pioneering efforts reflected Lord Kelvin's dictum that "[w]hen you cannot measure, your knowledge is meager and unsatisfactory."[4]

Following Pritchett's lead, political scientists studying public law in the 1950s increasingly measured judicial voting behavior through quantitative techniques.[5] Indeed, political scientists studying judicial decision making contributed mightily to the behavioral movement which began to sweep the discipline during this period. Public law acholars pursuing behavioral research viewed judges as political officials whose actions and decisions were not unique, but were rather comparable to those of officials in other governmental institutions. Morever, unlike the legal realists, a few adventuresome political scientists attempted to predict the behavior of Supreme Court justices based on their previous voting records.

The behavioral revolution initiated by Pritchett has since been extended by literally dozens of students of the United States Supreme Court, the lower federal courts, and state court systems.[6] Yet, notwithstanding the sizable volume of behavioral research in public law and judicial process, the problem of "measuring" activism and restraint remains a troublesome one. Behavioral

271

research faces the difficulty of defining and operationalizing activism and restraint, identifying relevant and testable hypotheses concerning the concepts, and then measuring with some precision and objectivity whether, and to what degree, decisions and judges can be properly characterized by those terms.[7]

These methodological considerations are especially important because one might reasonably contend that the philosophical, scholarly, and even political biases of students of the Court have often confounded and confused explorations of judicial activism and restraint. This has led Henry J. Abraham to observe that even the most strident activists may be considered advocates of restraint in some fields of the law, depending on the personal predilections of the individual researcher.[8] Behavioral research, however, tends to avoid this pitfall. Unlike much traditional research on the Court, behavioralists typically do not advance a particular conception of the Court's proper role and power. Instead, their studies are rooted in specific hypotheses, quantitative measurement, and reproduceable methodologies. As was noted earlier, "[t]he chapters in part III demonstrate that scholars can carefully operationalize and measure [the concepts of activism and restraint] and thereby yield results of substantive and heuristic value."[9]

We recognize that the behavioral chapters in this volume define and operationalize activism and restraint in substantially different ways. Consequently, comparing findings and assessing the cumulative wisdom of these efforts becomes a formidable task. Notwithstanding this limitation, the type of research found in part III can boast certain advantages. The crucial terms—activism and restraint—are explicitly defined. They are operationalized so that when the scholar does "measure," the process of measuring occurs objectively, systematically, and on the basis of considerations which are spelled out specifically. This advances scholarly debate if only because terms, assumptions, meanings, and measurings are known and hence are more readily subject to discussion and verification. Whatever their differences in definition and measurement, these advantages apply to the forthcoming chapters.

In one such study, Harold J. Spaeth and Stuart H. Teger argue that judicial restraint is most profitably examined not in the abstract, but in the context of the particular issues with which the Supreme Court grapples. Spaeth and Teger suggest that the justices tend to defer or overturn the policies of other governmental institutions essentially for political, not legal, reasons. The justices are inclined to defer, in other words, when they approve of the content and substance of the policies under review. This assertion is empirically supported with data drawn from the Burger Court from the 1969 through the 1977 terms, in cases raising three kinds of issues: challenges to decisions of federal regulatory commissions, questions of federalism, and definitions of standing. Spaeth and Teger find that it is the personal policy considerations, not conceptions of the judicial role, which best explain the justices' votes.

Anthony Champagne and Stuart S. Nagel next study the judicial philosophies and behavior of four of the Supreme Court's most articulate spokesmen for restraint—Justices Holmes, Brandeis, Stone, and Frankfurter. The authors emphasize the methodological problems confronted in measuring the extent to which these justices, in fact, practiced the restraint philosophy which they preached. Based upon a detailed examination of the voting records of the four justices in cases where the Supreme Court nullified congressional statutes, the authors conclude that Justice Frankfurter most frquently and consistently adhered to the tenets of restraint.[10] More generally, Champagne and Nagel find that the justices tended to exercise restraint selectively, in order to benefit particular interests or ideological causes. In this regard, their conclusions clearly complement and support the basic thrust of the chapter by Spaeth and Teger.

Between the time that a case is granted review and the final decision, the issues which the Supreme Court considers to be most prominent in a case are fluid. S. Sidney Ulmer examines Issue Fluidity, thereby extending prior research.[11] He discusses how the justices' changing perceptions of the issues under consideration by the Court may relate to traditional notions of activism and restraint. Ulmer accomplishes this by examining decisions of the Burger Court in criminal cases from 1969 through 1976. He finds what he refers to as Issue Transformation, Issue Suppression, Issue Substitution, and other forms of Issue Modification. While the fluidity of issues may evolve for sound legal reasons, it may also occur for unarticulated and legally irrelevant policy considerations. Ulmer thus defines activism in this context as the shaping of an issue for legally extraneous reasons.

In chapter 14, Burton Atkins and William Taggert explore how alterations in Supreme Court definitions of standing, ripeness, political questions, abstention, mootness, and related doctrines have varied from the Warren to the Burger Courts. The authors' work is premised on the assumption that the manipulation of these definitions affects the ease within which litigants have access to the Court. In turn, the ease of access affects the range of questions considered by the justices and hence the political role that the Court plays. Atkins and Taggert compare the degree of support within the Warren and Burger Courts for definitions which would liberalize access requirements and thereby make it easier for litigants to raise their issues before the Court and have them resolved on substantive grounds. They provide an unusual perspective on this problem by examining what the justices' individual voting records over time show about their support for broadening access to the Court. Surprisingly, the data indicate that during the Burger years there has not been a significant reduction in access to the Court when compared to the Warren era. This finding complements part of the argument Marvin Schick advances in part I of this volume regarding the wide range of issues that continue to be pressed before the presumably more modest Burger Court.

In the final chapter, Bradley C. Canon makes an outstanding contribution by meticulously dissecting the core concepts addressed in this book. He asserts that scholars invariably approach the concept of judicial activism from different vantage points and without a common definition. Consequently, Canon argues that discussions of this phenomenon often proceed from different assumptions and share little common intellectual ground. Canon attempts to provide such common ground for future efforts by presenting a broadly based fromework for understanding and measuring judicial activism. He posits six substantive dimensions of activism. For each dimension he establishes three degrees of activism—Highly Activist, Somewhat Activist, or Nonactivist. By employing this framework, one can categorize and analyze individual decisions by the character and intensity of their activism. Canon uses the framework to analyze and compare fourteen major Supreme Court decisions. One of the virtues of Canon's chapter is that other scholars may employ or refine the framework which he advances as a conceptual starting point for analyzing activism and restraint in the future.

Notes

1. For a critique of this so-called slot-machine theory of judicial decision making see Roscoe Pound, "Mechanical Jurisprudence," *Columbia Law Review* 8 (December 1908): 605–623.

2. Sheldon Goldman and Thomas P. Jahnige, *The Federal Courts as a Political System,* 2d ed. (New York: Harper and Row, 1976), p. 157.

3. As examples of Pritchett's behavioral research see *Civil Liberties and the Vinson Court* (Chicago: University of Chicago Press, 1954); *The Roosevelt Court: A Study of Judicial Politics and Values, 1937-1947* (New York: Macmillan, 1948); "Divisions of Opinion Among Justices of the U.S. Supreme Court, 1939-1941," *American Political Science Review* 35 (October 1941): 890–898.

4. Walter F. Murphy and Joseph Tanenhaus, *The Study of Public Law* (New York: Random House, 1972), p. 19, quoting Lord Kelvin.

5. For a more detailed treatment of the behavioral movement in the study of courts and judges see C. Herman Pritchett, "The Development of Judicial Research," in *Frontiers of Judicial Research*, ed. Joel B. Grossman and Joseph Tanenhaus (New York: Wiley, 1969), chap. 2. For more advanced quantitative work in the 1950s see Glendon Schubert, *Quantitative Analysis of Judicial Behavior* (Glencoe, Ill.: Free Press, 1959); Robert A. Dahl, "Decision-Making in a Democracy: The Role of the Supreme Court in National Policy-Making," *Journal of Public Law* 6 (Fall 1957): 279-295; Fred Kort, "Predicting Supreme Court Decisions Mathematically: A Quantitative Analysis of the 'Right to Counsel Cases'," *American Political Science Review* 51 (March 1957): 1–12.

6. Most of this literature is surveyed in Goldman and Jahnige, *The Federal Courts as a Political System;* Henry Robert Glick and Kenneth N. Vines, *State Court Systems* (Englewood Cliffs, N.J.: Prentice-Hall, 1973); David W. Rohde and Harold J. Spaeth, *Supreme Court Decision Making* (San Francisco: W.H. Freeman, 1976); Charles H. Sheldon, *The American Judicial Process: Models and*

Approaches (New York: Harper and Row, 1974); Stephen L. Wasby, *The Supreme Court in the Federal Judicial System* (New York: Holt, Rinehart and Winston, 1978).

7. For some of the earliest behavioral research on Supreme Court activism and restraint see Harold J. Spaeth, "The Judicial Restraint of Mr. Justice Frankfurter—Myth or Reality," *Midwest Journal of Political Science* 8 (February 1964): 22–38. For an update see Harold J. Spaeth, *Supreme Court Policy Making: Explanation and Prediction* (San Francisco: W.H. Freeman, 1979), pp. 75–81.

8. Henry J. Abraham, *The Judiciary: The Supreme Court in the Governmental Process,* 5th ed. (Boston: Allyn and Bacon, 1980), pp. 198–199.

9. Charles M. Lamb, "Judicial Restraint on the Supreme Court," chap. 1, this volume.

10. Compare these findings to those of Spaeth referred to in note 7.

11. See, for example, J. Woodford Howard, Jr., "On the Fluidity of Judicial Choice," *American Political Science Review* 62 (March 1968): 43–56; Richard Richardson and Kenneth N. Vines, "Review, Dissent and the Appellate Process: A Political Model," *Journal of Politics* 29 (August 1967): 597–616.

11 Activism and Restraint: A Cloak for the Justices' Policy References

Harold J. Spaeth and Stuart H. Teger

When police officers ticket speeders they try to displace the drivers' anger by pointing out that "I don't make the laws, I only enforce them." Nameless clerks, enforcing arbitrary administrative policies, hide behind the "I'm only following orders" lament. Judges, too, have their own excuse—judicial restraint: "[T]his is an uncommonly silly law.... But we are not asked in this case to say whether we think this law is unwise, or even asinine. We are asked to hold that it violates the United States Constitution. And that I cannot do."[1]

These excuses are convenient and useful, but are not to be taken seriously. Police do have wide discretion, as James Wilson and others have shown.[2] So do clerks and judges. That discretion is useful when it serves the actors' interests; when freedom of choice leads to an uncomfortable predicament, invoking external constraint comes in handy. The myth of the neutral bureaucrat or police officer, merely administering the policies of others, has long since died. It is high time that the myth of judicial restraint join its brothers in the "heaven of legal concepts."[3]

In the name of restraint we are told that a court should not intervene to upset the judgment of the legislature (agency, state, or whatever) unless there are compelling reasons. The matter at issue must be one upon which men may not "reasonably differ;" there must be "no doubt that any reasonable mind could entertain;" it must have more than "ephemeral significance."[4] Precedent must be given "great weight" before it is overturned; even then the reasons for change must be "pretty clear."[5] The courts are not to make policy, they are only "to police the boundaries drawn in the Constitution;"[6] "judges are not unfettered glossators."[7] Weasel words! Weasel words all!

The Constitution is not self-executing; it does not apply itself. Reasonable men always differ over questions that reach the Supreme Court and how great the difference is depends on how strongly one feels. One person's outrage is another person's yawn. What shocks the conscience of a William Douglas, who was sensitive enough to share the pain of rivers and forests, may leave a Frankfurter unmoved. The reverse is true as well. One man's sacred cow is another man's beast of burden. A law limiting the rights of labor may shock the pork-chopper without displeasing the tycoon at all. Again, the reverse is also true.

Most agree that courts should not lightly upset the judgments of the other parts of government. Most also agree that the courts should not always defer

277

to the other branches; at times judicial intervention is proper. Between these two poles disagreement rages. "It is a question of proximity and degree."[8] The proper moment for judicial intervention depends on the magnitude of the threat. A law infringing the rights of privacy is no danger at all to the judge who has small regard for the right of privacy. The judge who sees free speech as the cornerstone of liberty will quickly react to the slightest limitation thereof.

In what follows we will attempt to show, empirically, that judicial restraint, if it is anything at all, is issue specific. Judges are not deferential in general, but rather they defer to the judgment of the legislature (or other body) only when they approve of that judgment. To put it another way, a judge's votes are neither predictable nor explainable by his "firm belief or relative disbelief in judicial deference."[9] In short, judicial restraint is to judicial decision making as phlogiston is to fire.

We have chosen three broad areas of Supreme Court decision making to focus on in our search for evidence of judicial restraint. The areas are: cases challenging actions of federal regulatory commissions; cases on federalism; and cases raising the question of access to the courts. In the first two areas the justices are in a position to defer either to agency expertise or to the states. Consistent deference to those authorities will support the existence of an independent notion of judicial restraint. In the third area we look for direct evidence of a restraintist or activist philosophy: consistently voting to close the doors of the Court will support the existence of a restraintist position.

Review of Regulatory Commissions

We turn first to justices' responses to the decision making of the federal regulatory commissions. When a justice votes to uphold a commission's action, that vote will be considered deferential. When he votes to overturn or modify the commission's action, deference is absent, and his vote will be considered activist.[10] For the purpose of ascertaining the degree of activism or restraint that the justices have manifested toward the federal regulatory commissions, data have been drawn from the first nine terms of the Burger Court, 1969-1977. (Comparable data for the Warren Court are set out in the notes.) We limit our focus to the Court's formally decided cases—those that are either orally argued or, if not orally argued, appear with those that are. Where a number of cases have been decided together under a single opinion, each case is counted once, unless one or more of the justices voted differently. Then such cases are counted compatibly with the smallest number that will account for the discrepant voting.[11] Because our focus is on the individual justices and their degree of activism or restraint, we restrict our analysis to the Court's nonunanimous decisions.

The data in table 11-1 show that the Burger Court supported the agencies in almost 72 percent of the cases (63 of 88). The agencies did considerably

Table 11-1
Votes and Decisions in Support of and in Opposition to Decisions of the Federal Regulatory Commissions, 1969–1977

Justice	Pro-Commission (deferential)	Anti-Commission	Percent Pro-Commission
Blackmun	27	11	71
White	30	14	68
Rehnquist	21	11	66
Marshall	27	17	61
Brennan	27	19	59
Black	4	3	57
Powell	13	14	48
Burger	21	23	48
Stewart	20	24	45
Harlan	3	4	43
Douglas	14	19	42
Stevens	4	7	36
Total Votes	211	166	56
Total Decisions	63	25	72
Unanimous	33	9	79
Nonunanimous	30	16	65

Note: Votes of the justices are reported only in nonunanimous cases.

better when the justices were unanimous[12] (78.6 percent won) than when they divided (65.2 percent won in nonunanimous cases).[13] There would seem to be a slight presumption in favor of the agencies since only 9 cases were decided unanimously against the regulatory commissions.

These figures demonstrate substantial deference to the decisions of the federal regulatory commissions; yet they tell us nothing about the voting of the justices who participated in these cases. The vote totals in table 11-1 fill this gap and, in order to sharpen differences in the justices' voting patterns, only those agency cases in which one or more of the justices dissented are included.

Although the justices of the Burger Court as a group supported the agencies more often than they voted against them, allegations that the Court was a model of restraint toward the decision making of the federal regulatory commissions are incorrect.

If one may define a judicial activist as a justice who adheres to the norm of deference in less than half his votes in nonunanimous decisions—a fair definition, we think—then fully half of the Burger Court justices may appropriately be labeled judicial activists, as far as agency cases are concerned.[14] Douglas and Stewart clearly appear to be judicial activists. Douglas's identification as an activist occasions no surprise, given his reputation. Stewart, however, does not fit the label that analysts and commentators have bestowed on him on the basis of his overall voting behavior—that of a neutral or moderate justice, very much in the middle of the road.[15] Also noteworthy is the relative absence of deference displayed by Powell and Burger—48 percent. Not only do they fall on the activist side of table 11-1, but they also are notably different from the other two Nixon nominees—Blackmun and Rehnquist—who rank first and third in deference to the regulatory commissions, at 71 and 66 percent respectively.

What explains these rather strange findings? Inasmuch as the contents of table 11-1 are a composite to two discrete areas of regulation, business and labor, it may be instructive to break this table down into agency regulation of business and agency regulation of labor unions. Because previous analyses have shown the justices to vote compatibly with their individual attitudes toward business and labor,[16] we further subdivide table 11-1 into agency decisions supportive of and opposed to business and labor. Accordingly, table 11-2 contains the votes of the Burger Court justices in the nonunanimous decisions that concerned agency regulation of business and labor.

The data in table 11-2 reveal significant information about the justices' voting behavior that is not evident in the gross figures presented in table 11-1. While the agencies are upheld in 65 percent of all nonunanimous cases, their actual success varies from a low of 53 percent, when the agency decision is prolabor (column 3) to a high of 89 percent when the National Labor Relations Board (NLRB) is antilabor (column 4). Interestingly, the agencies do almost as well when they are antibusiness (column 2) as when they are antilabor. There seems to be a noticeable preference by the justices for decisions limiting rights, regardless of whose.[17]

This preference for "anti-anybody" decisions is subordinated, however, to a more marked and policy-oriented bias. The votes of the individual justices do not perfectly parallel the decisions. There were significantly more probusiness (column 1) and prolabor (column 3) votes. (Totals are shown in columns 5 and 6.) Of the total of 363 votes cast in these cases, 55 percent (199) were probusiness and antiunion.

When we consider the votes from the point of view of deference to agency decision making, any claims that judicial activism or restraint motivate the justices' votes must fall. The justices were deferential in 63 percent of their votes when the agency decision was probusiness or antilabor; their deference toward the agencies dropped to 51 percent when the decision was prolabor or antibusiness (columns 5 and 6). These differences suggest that the justices are more concerned with whose ox gets gored than they are with who does the goring.

When we look at the individual justices, the results are even more impressive. Except Stewart, every justice shows significant variation in his deference toward agency decision making from the probusiness to the prolabor columns (columns 5 and 6). Stewart's variation is only 4 percentage points; the next most consistent justice is Blackmun, who is 11 percentage points more deferential to probusiness and antilabor decisions than he is to prolabor and antibusiness

Table 11-2
Justices' Votes in Support of and in Opposition to Federal Regulatory Commissions
(percentage)

Justices	1 Agency decision is probusiness; Justice's votes and percent proagency	2 Agency decision is antibusiness; Justice's votes and percent proagency	3 Agency decision is prolabor; Justice's votes and percent proagency	4 Agency decision is antilabor; Justice's votes and percent proagency	5 Total Votes: Probusiness Antiunion (1 + 4)	6 Total Votes Antibusiness Prounion (2 + 3)
Blackmun	8–2/80	5–1/83	8–6/57	5–2/71	13–4/76	13–7/65
White	8–2/80	5–3/63	10–6/63	7–1/88	15–3/83	15–9/62
Rehnquist	8–0/100	2–4/33	4–7/36	7–0/100	15–0/100	6–11/35
Marshall	4–7/36	8–0/100	12–4/75	3–5/38	7–12/37	20–4/83
Brennan	5–6/45	7–1/88	11–6/65	4–4/50	9–10/47	18–7/72
Black	1–0/100	1–0/100	1–3/25	1–0/100	1–0/100	2–3/40
Powell	5–1/83	0–2/0	3–8/27	4–3/57	9–4/69	3–10/23
Burger	6–3/67	3–5/38	3–14/18	8–0/100	14–3/82	6–19/24
Stewart	7–4/64	1–5/17	9–8/53	2–6/25	9–10/47	10–13/43
Harlan	1–0/100	1–0/100	0–4/0	1–0/100	1–0/100	1–4/20
Douglas	1–7/13	1–4/20	9–6/60	2–2/50	3–9/25	10–10/50
Stevens	1–2/33	0–3/0	1–0/100	2–2/50	3–4/43	1–3/25
Total Votes	53–34/61	34–28/55	71–72/50	46–25/65	99–59/63	105–100/51
Total Decisions	6–5/55	7–1/88	9–8/53	8–1/89	14–6/70	16–9/64

Note: The totals here do not match the totals in Table 1 because two agency cases could not be categorized as pro- or anti-business: 26/691 and 31/658.

decisions. The greatest variation is shown by Rehnquist, followed by Burger. (We exclude Harlan and Black because of their low participation rates.) Rehnquist and Burger are very restrained when the commissions are probusiness, but their consciences are apparently quite shocked when the agencies favor labor. Powell and Marshall are next in line; they are virtual mirror images of each other. Powell defers to probusiness decisions; Marshall to prolabor. It is worth pointing out that both Douglas and Brennan, the most liberal members of the Court, exhibit rather moderate variation—25 points each.[18]

If any of the justices are truly deferential, it is clear that they are not the ones with the large variations. Among the most consistent justices, Stewart and Stevens clearly do not qualify; they are rather activist toward all agency decisions. Only White and Blackmun offer restraintist votes more than half of the time in all the case categories. We will tentatively list them as our only advocates, in deed, not just in words, of judicial restraint.

Before leaving table 11-2, we shall look at the rank ordering of the justices along columns 5 and 6. The ordering is nearly reversed from one column to the next. If we exclude White and Blackmun from our rankings, (as well as Harlan and Black), and consider only the remaining eight justices, the permutation is quite symmetrical. Rehnquist, Burger, and Powell are first, second, and third most supportive of business; they are fifth, seventh, and eighth most supportive of labor. Marshall and Douglas are seventh and eighth on the business cases, but they are first and third on labor. Only Stevens's rank is unchanged from one column to the next.

The data presented in table 11-2 indicate quite clearly that considerations of judicial activism and restraint are subordinated to the individual justice's substantive policy orientation toward business and labor. Those who are antibusiness and prounion support the agencies when the agencies' decisions are congruent with the value of economic liberalism and oppose them where they are not. Similarly, when the agencies are probusiness and antiunion, the economic conservatives support them but cast deference aside when the agencies' decision making is counter to their economic values. Judicial restraint is, at best, a sometime thing.

Review of Federalism Questions

We turn to a second category in our search for evidence of judicial restraint—cases on federalism. As before, we consider decisions through the end of the 1977 term. The long-standing argument is that the justices should defer to the states whenever possible. The states, the time-honored argument runs, are laboratories for testing new methods of problem solving. They also possess a strong measure of sovereignty. How often and how consistently have the justices of the Burger Court deferred to the states?

Here, we have selected a large group of federalism cases, and then further subdivided them into more discrete issue areas. Our first area is state regulation of business and labor.

The summary figures in table 11-3, gross though they be, reveal a good deal about the justices on the Burger Court. Based on our criterion for a judicial activist, only four justices escape that label. Blackmun does so by a whisker with 51 percent of his votes supporting the states. Burger and Rehnquist appear to be firmly in the judicial restraint group, joined only by Black, whose 75 percent is based on a small sample. Harlan, perhaps surprisingly, only rates 33 percent overall, albeit on a reduced data set. The two justices we tentatively listed as advocates of judicial restraint, on the basis of our previous analysis, do not look very convincing now. While Blackmun did score 51 percent overall, he slid below that mark in the economic cases. White was close to the line, but from the wrong side. He supported the states in 46 percent of all the federalism cases.

Despite the rough nature of these categories, there is considerable variation between the economic and civil rights cases. While the traditionally liberal justices show the greatest change from one area to the next (Marshall at 34 points, Douglas at 28, and Brennan at 25), the more recent appointees to the Court also fluctuate a good deal. Stevens changes 24 points, Powell 21, and Rehnquist goes down 17 points from the economic column to the civil rights list.

On the basis of these figures alone, it is clear that the Burger Court is not an overwhelming exemplar of judicial restraint. As we refine our categories this conclusion will become more evident.

As compared to their performance in the agency cases, the Burger Court justices have been less deferential to state economic regulation.[19] Clearly, the Court cannot be said to exercise restraint in this regard. But unlike the agency cases, not all the liberal and conservative members of the Burger Court reverse their ranking between the two columns of table 11-4. Burger and most especially Rehnquist do appear deferential to state regulation of labor and business both, whereas Douglas and Brennan display activism regardless of whether the regulation affects business or labor. The reason for this break in the pattern observed in the agency cases results not from the state labor cases (in all but one of which the states' regulation was antiunion)[20] but rather from the business cases. In 10 of these the state's regulation was probusiness (as opposed to 26 in which it was antibusiness). Furthermore, fully half of the Burger Court decisions pertain to national supremacy, in which economic considerations are subordinate to the application of the supremacy clause, the Twenty-First Amendment, or state-imposed burdens on interstate commerce.[21] In addition, the Burger Court has ruled on state regulatory concerns dealing with the environment: zoning and the conservation of natural resources. In 6 of these 8 cases the state's regulation was probusiness.[22]

When we move to the breakdown of cases in table 11-5, the justices' support ratings show the same kinds of substantive policy biases we observed above.

Table 11-3
Votes and Decisions in Support of and in Opposition to State Action

Justice	Business and Labor Cases		Civil Rights and Liberties Cases		Total Federalism	
	Pro-State	Anti-State	Pro-State	Anti-State	Pro-State	Anti-State
Burger	25/56%	20	75/68%	36	100/64%	56
Douglas	6/35%	11	5/7%	67	11/12%	78
Brennan	16/36%	28	11/11%	92	27/18%	120
Stewart	22/50%	22	45/40%	68	67/43%	90
White	24/53%	21	48/42%	65	72/46%	86
Marshall	20/44%	25	11/10%	97	31/20%	122
Blackmun	18/46%	21	48/53%	43	66/51%	64
Powell	13/35%	24	45/55%	37	58/49%	61
Rehnquist	36/88%	5	58/71%	24	94/76%	29
Stevens	12/48%	13	7/24%	22	19/35%	35
Black	1/33%	2	20/80%	5	21/75%	7
Harlan	1/33%	2	6/24%	19	7/33%	21
Totals	194/50%	194	379/40%	575	573/43%	769
Total Decisions	21/47%	24	51/45%	62	72/46%	86

Table 11-4
Votes in Support of and in Opposition to State Action Regulatory of Business and Labor, 1969-1977 Terms (Nonunanimous Decisions Only)

Justices	Labor			Justices	Business		
	Pro-State	Anti-State	Percent Pro-State		Pro-State	Anti-State	Percent Pro-State
Rehnquist	6	0	100	Black	1	0	100
Stevens	3	0	100	Harlan	1	0	100
White	7	2	78	Rehnquist	30	5	86
Burger	6	3	67	Stewart	19	16	54
Powell	4	2	67	Burger	19	17	53
Blackmun	4	3	57	Marshall	18	18	50
Stewart	3	6	33	White	17	19	47
Douglas	2	4	33	Blackmun	14	18	44
Brennan	2	6	25	Stevens	9	13	41
Marshall	2	7	22	Brennan	14	22	39
Black	0	2	0	Douglas	4	7	36
Harlan	0	2	0	Powell	9	22	29
Total	39	37	51	Total	155	157	50

Table 11-5
Justices' Votes in Support of and in Opposition to State Regulation of Business and Labor

| Justice | Labor Cases | | Business Cases | | | |
| | | | All Cases | | Excluding National Supremacy Cases | |
	State is prolabor; Justice votes to uphold state	State is prolabor; Justice votes to uphold state	State is pro-business; Justice votes to uphold	State is anti-business; Justice votes to uphold	State is pro-business; Justice votes to uphold	State is anti-business; Justice votes to uphold
Burger	0–1	6–2/75%	7–3/70%	12–14/46%	7–0/100%	6–5/55%
Douglas		2–4/33%	1–2/33%	3–5/38%	1–1/50%	1–1/50%
Brennan		2–6/25%	1–9/10%	13–13/50%	1–6/14%	9–2/82%
Stewart	0–1	3–5/38%	7–3/70%	12–13/48%	7–0/100%	6–4/60%
White	1–0	6–2/75%	4–6/40%	13–13/50%	4–3/57%	8–3/73%
Marshall	1–0	1–7/13%	2–8/20%	16–10/62%	2–5/29%	10–1/91%
Blackmun		4–3/57%	6–3/67%	8–15/35%	6–1/86%	5–5/50%
Powell	0–1	4–1/80%	3–6/33%	6–16/27%	3–3/50%	5–4/56%
Rehnquist	1–0	5–0/100%	10–0/100%	20–5/80%	7–0/100%	7–4/64%
Stevens	1–0	2–0/100%	3–3/50%	6–10/38%	3–2/60%	4–3/57%
Black		0–2/0%		1–0/100%		
Harlan		0–2/0%		1–0/100%		
Total	4–3/57%	35–34/51%	44–43/51%	111–114/49%	41–21/66%	61–32/66%

Of the four justices who are most supportive of state probusiness decisions, three are Nixon appointees. But when the states' decisions are antibusiness, three of these four become remarkably unsupportive. Blackmun drops 32 points, to 35 percent support, Burger drops 24 points, and Stewart goes down 22 points. Conversely, Marshall and Brennan, unsupportive of the states when they favor business, become much warmer to state sovereignty when it is opposed to business. Marshall's rating improves 42 points, while Brennan goes up 40 points.

There is more consistency in these rankings than in those for the agency cases. Four justices vary 12 or fewer points from the probusiness to the antibusiness columns, though none of these four could be considered deferential. Stevens and White are virtual mirror images of each other; Stevens is 50 percent supportive of the states in probusiness cases, but drops to 38 percent in antibusiness cases. White's movement is in the opposite direction, from 40 percent to 50 percent. Powell and Douglas also complement each other, one moving from 33 percent to 38 percent, while the other goes from 33 percent to 27 percent—hardly good examples of restraintist jurisprudence.

Only Rehnquist defers to the states enough to qualify, in this instance, as an advocate of judicial restraint. But even Rehnquist reflects his conservative economic bias. His perfect score in the probusiness cases drops 20 points when the state is opposed to business.

These results are somewhat skewed by the presence of the national supremacy cases. With the single exception of Justice Rehnquist, the justices were decidedly antistate in these decisions. While Rehnquist upheld the states with 12 of his 13 votes, his colleagues collectively did so with only 22 of their 107 votes (21 percent). If the national supremacy cases are excluded from consideration, the Court as a whole appears quite deferential: 102 votes upheld state regulation, fifty-two opposed it (66 percent). This 2:1 ratio of support holds constant whether the states' business regulations were liberal or conservative.

Notwithstanding the pro-state character of these figures for the Court as a whole, the conservative and liberal justices voted in accord with their economic orientation. With the national supremacy cases excluded, most of the justices appear more deferential, but, at the same time, the variance for most of the justices, between the pro- and antibusiness columns, also increases. Thus, Burger's probusiness score increases from 70 percent to 100 percent, his antibusiness rating goes from 46 percent to 55 percent, and the difference between the two increases from 24 to 45 points. Similar relationships hold for Brennan, Stewart, White, Marshall, and Blackmun. The issue of national supremacy seems to override the economic issues; with the former cases deleted, the economic bias is more clear.

Those who do not fit the pattern just described include Rehnquist (whose support for antibusiness decisions drops, but whose variance increases), and Douglas, Powell, and Stevens. These latter three display rather even support for both categories of cases. Douglas only participated in four cases, but the data on Powell and Stevens suggest that they are what they appear to be—moderate, middle-of-the-road justices.

Our analysis of the state economic action cases reinforces the conclusion drawn from our analysis of the regulatory commission cases: judicial restraint is, at best, a sometime thing. Blackmun and White, the two justices who exercised restraint in the agency cases, are far less consistent here. On the other hand, Rehnquist, who showed great variation in the agency cases, is consistently above the 50 percent mark here. His bias still shows through but is muted. Taking all the results so far together it is clear that the justices are motivated by their substantive policy concerns—not abstract notions about judicial restraint.

Review of Civil Rights and Liberties Questions

Our analysis so far substantiates the assumption with which we began. We could quit now, instead of running the risk of beating a dead horse. But because belief in the existence of judicial activism-restraint remains an unshakable tenet in the minds of many legal scholars, we proceed to analyze other policy areas where activism-restraint, if it actually exists, ought to be operative. Accordingly, we turn now to civil rights and liberties.

To ascertain the presence of judicial restraint in the area of civil rights and liberties, we have selected the four sets of Burger Court decisions in which the federal government and the states have separately participated in enough cases to make cumulative scaling possible. These four sets are "First Amendment," "double jeopardy," "search-and-seizure," and "poverty law." All formally decided and *per curiam* decisions of the Burger Court from its inception at the beginning of the 1969 Term through March, 1979, are included. (This is a slightly different set than that used earlier.) Memorandum cases are excluded. Cases are counted rather than opinions. Accordingly, where more than one case is decided under a single opinion, the total number of such cases is counted. The number in parentheses following the citations in the notes to tables 11-7 through 11-10 specifies these cases. In order to establish comparability between the state and federal cases, we include only those decisions in which the position of the federal or state government is antithetical to the contentions of the civil liberties claimant. If the government supports the civil liberties claimant, the case is excluded. Cases to which neither the federal nor state government is party are also excluded. Each included case, then, must appear as either progovernment (state or federal)/anti–civil liberties or anti–government/pro–civil liberties. The government, here, is never pro–civil liberties.[23]

If the justices are willing to defer to state sovereignty, and willing to countenance infringements of rights which would not be allowed if done by the federal government, then the states should be upheld more than the federal government, ceteris paribus. The more restrained justices should be willing to keep out of the states' laboratories. This should hold even if the states' violation of rights are more egregious than the national government's, since the states should be given more latitude.

Thus far we have been using 50 percent support as the criterion for whether or not a justice was restraintist. Because we can no longer compare pro- and antipolicy support, that criterion will no longer suffice. Therefore we shall now utilize another simple test: is the justice's support for the states greater than his support for the federal government? If so, we will categorize him as a practitioner of judicial restraint. If the converse is true, and his support for both state and national government is less than 50 percent, we will label him an activist.

Table 11-6 collects all the votes in the unanimous as well as the nonunanimous civil liberties cases. It is quite clear that the differences in support of national and state government do not reflect a restraintist orientation. Every justice is substantially more supportive of the federal government. Indeed, the Justices whose support levels are most similar are those who are least supportive of rights violations in general (Douglas, Brennan, and Marshall). The four justices who would qualify as restraintist under our old criterion (vis-à-vis the states) average a 25 point variation across levels of government (the four Nixon justices). The average for the three liberal justices is just 10 points. Given the role of the Supreme Court in the federal scheme of government, the greater deference shown the national government does not evidence judicial restraint.

As we have done before, we now proceed to refine our categories, so as to see in a more detailed analysis if and where the justices are deferential. We accomplish this by constructing cumulative scales of the state and federal

Table 11-6
Justices' Votes in Support of and in Opposition to State and Federal Limitations on Civil Rights

	State Cases		Federal Cases		
Justice	Pro/Anti State	Pro (percent)	Pro/Anti Federal	Pro (percent)	Difference (percent)
Burger	75–36	68	85–11	89	+21
Douglas	5–67	7	7–47	13	+ 6
Brennan	11–97	10	20–73	22	+12
Stewart	45–68	40	63–34	65	+25
White	48–65	42	72–25	74	+32
Marshall	11–97	10	20–73	22	+12
Blackmun	48–43	53	80–11	88	+35
Powell	45–37	55	70–18	80	+25
Rehnquist	58–24	71	78–8	91	+20
Stevens	7–22	24	26–11	70	+46

cases within each of the four sets of civil liberties cases and comparing the rank order of the justices between the state and federal cases within each set. The results are in tables 11-7 through 11-10.[24]

Table 11-7 contains the First Amendment cases. Excluded from this set are free exercise and establishment of religion cases, as well as those concerning obscenity, commercial speech, and libel suits for defamation and invasion of privacy. The category includes the conventional sorts of issues raised in connection with speech, press, and associational rights. As compared to the federal government, the states fared poorly. The Court supported the federal government in 81 percent of its cases and the states in only 44 percent. Furthermore,

Table 11-7
Rank Order of the Burger Court Justices in State and Federal First Amendment Freedom Cases

		State Cases				Federal Cases	
Rank	Justice	Pro/Anti State	Pro (percent)	Rank	Justice	Pro/Anti U.S.	Pro (percent)
1.5	Brennan	1–23	4	1.5	Brennan	1–15	6
1.5	Marshall	1–23	4	1.5	Marshall	1–15	6
3	Douglas	1–11	8	3	Douglas	4–10	29
4	Stevens	2–8	20	4	Stewart	8–8	50
5	Stewart	7–18	28	5.5	White	12–4	75
6	Powell	9–15	38	5.5	Powell	12–2	86
7.5	White	13–12	52	7	Blackmun	16–0	100
7.5	Blackmun	12–12	50	7	Burger	15–0	100
9	Burger	15–10	60	7	Harlan	2–0	100
10	Rehnquist	17–8	68				

Justices Not Susceptible of Ranking

	Harlan	—			Stevens	1–0	100
	Black	—			Rehnquist	12–0	100
					Black	0–2	0

Decisions Pro/Anti State: 11-14 44%   Decisions Pro-Anti U.S.: 13-3 81%

$$R = \frac{124}{131} = .947 \qquad\qquad R = \frac{132}{134} = .985$$

$$\text{Combined } R = \frac{254}{265} = .958$$

Note: Scale Order of Cases (L Ed 2d):   Scale Order of Cases (L Ed 2d):
33/266, 40/224, 41/730, 49/683, 50/376,   29/822(2), 32/653, 57/1053, 41/514, 33/154,
51/355, 56/1, 58/619, 48/243, 51/752,   33/583(2), 33/626, 37/796, 36/772(4),
49/547, 35/618, 43/448, 53/96, 41/495,   47/505, 43/260.
41/770, 33/131, 33/626(2), 37/830,
57/553, 47/708, 53/629, 41/495, 50/471.

each participating justice supported the federal government with a greater proportion of his votes than he did the states. Although the coefficient of reproducibility of the scale of state cases is slightly below .950, that of the federal cases is well above it, and the combined state and federal cases produce R=.958. The rank order correlation coefficient[25] of the justices between the state and federal scale is an exceptionally high +.95. The almost perfect correlation in the ranks of the justices strongly supports a judgment that their voting behavior was motivated by their attitudes toward First Amendment freedoms rather than considerations of federalism.

The same results obtain in 11-8, which summarizes the data in double jeopardy cases. Only Justice Black, because of his single participation in a federal

Table 11-8
Rank Order of the Burger Court Justices in State and Federal Double Jeopardy Cases

		State Cases				Federal Cases	
Rank	Justice	Pro/Anti State	Pro (percent)	Rank	Justice	Pro/Anti State	Pro (percent)
1	Douglas	0–13	0	1	Douglas	1–4	20
2	Harlan	0–5	0	2.5	Brennan	7–11	39
3.5	Brennan	3–16	16	2.5	Marshall	8–11	42
3.5	Marshall	2–15	12	4	Stevens	7–6	54
5	White	6–13	32	5	Stewart	13–7	65
6.5	Stevens	1–4	20	6	White	14–6	70
6.5	Stewart	7–12	37	7	Powell	13–6	68
8	Powell	8–5	62	8	Blackmun	15–4	79
9	Rehnquist	8–4	67	9	Burger	17–3	85
10	Blackmun	10–4	71	10	Rehnquist	16–2	88
11	Burger	12–5	71				

Justices Not Susceptible of Ranking

	Black	1–4	20		Black	0–1	0
					Harlan	0–1	0

Decisions Pro/Anti State: 8–11 42%   Decisions Pro-Anti U.S.: 13–7 65%

$$R = \frac{82}{85} = .965 \qquad\qquad R = \frac{68}{70} = .971$$

$$\text{Combined } R = \frac{148}{155} = .955$$

Note: Scale Order of Cases (L Ed 2d): 25/435, 26/300, 32/798, 44/346, 53/1054, 57/15, 25/469, 30/212, 29/549, 53/187, 57/24, 36/736, 35/425, 54/717, 31/86, 35/29, 46/195, 26/262, 30/762.

Scale Order of Cases (L Ed 2d): 43/250, 57/1, 57/43, 51/642, 53/1048, 54/207, 53/168, 57/65, 27/543, 47/267, 43/232, 53/80, 43/265, 34/438, 50/1, 50/5, 50/17, 50/336, 52/651, 55/303.

case, shows himself less supportive of the federal government than of the states. (Harlan's six votes were all antigovernment.) Though the states were upheld slightly less often than in the First Amendment cases (42 percent versus 44 percent), the Court as a whole deferred to the federal government only 50 percent more often than it did to the states in double jeopardy litigation, whereas deference to the federal government was double that accorded to the states in the First Amendment cases. Still, deference to state policy on double jeopardy is weak in the Burger Court. The relatively low rank order correlation coefficient in double jeopardy cases (+.81) compared with that of the First Amendment cases (+.95) remains well beyond acceptable levels of chance association: $< .0007$.

We should also note that both the First Amendment and double jeopardy scales combine with a number of others to form what has been labeled the *value of freedom*.[26] The existence of this value lends further support to the irrelevance of considerations of federalism as a factor explaining the justices' votes. All of the cumulative scales that correlate to form this value do so because of the justices' relative support or lack of support for what may be generally described as freedom—not their degree of deference to either the state or federal governments. In tables 11-7 and 11-8 then, the higher ranked justices are such because they are liberally inclined (profreedom), while those lower ranked are conservative (antifreedom).

The pattern of behavior displayed in table 11-9 remains consistent with that of tables 11-7 and 11-8, except that the Court supported the states in search-and-seizure litigation markedly more than it did in either the First Amendment or double jeopardy cases. Indeed, the support accorded the states almost equals that achieved by the federal government (63 percent versus 68 percent). This departure from the previous cases extends to the individual justices as well. In the earlier tables, none of the regularly participating justices demonstrated greater support for the states than for the federal government. Here Brennan, Douglas, and Marshall do so. Since their support levels are so low, however, we find it hard to believe that they are evidencing judicial restraint. (Harlan also drops in his support rating, but his participation rate is very low.) The rank order correlation between the state and federal rankings of the justices is an exceptionally high +.95.

Poverty law produced the lowest level of state support of the four civil liberties sets of cases, as shown in table 11-10. Decisions favorable to the states were handed down in 38 percent of the cases. The low level of state support here is all the more dramatic because it is paired with the highest level of federal support of any of the four sets. Of the poverty law cases, 85 percent were decided in favor of the federal government. This represents the greatest difference of proportions between federal and state support in any of the four sets. (The poverty law cases exclude those concerning illegitimate children, debtors' rights, and criminal proceedings about costs of appeals.) Again, with but a

Table 11-9

Rank Order of the Burger Court Justices in State and Federal Search-and-Seizure Cases

		State Cases				Federal Cases	
Rank	Justice	Pro/Anti State	Pro (percent)	Rank	Justice	Pro/Anti U.S.	Pro (percent)
1.5	Douglas	2–13	13	1	Douglas	2–25	7
1.5	Brennan	2–19	10	2.5	Brennan	3–36	8
3	Marshall	3–21	13	2.5	Marshall	3–38	7
4	Stevens	1–7	13	4	Stevens	7–5	58
5	Stewart	10–14	42	5	Stewart	25–16	61
6	Harlan	2–4	33	6	White	29–12	71
7	White	14–10	58	7	Powell	28–8	78
8	Powell	13–5	72	8	Burger	34–7	83
9	Blackmun	16–5	76	9.5	Blackmun	33–5	87
10	Burger	19–5	79	9.5	Rehnquist	31–5	86
11	Rehnquist	15–3	83	11	Black	5–0	100
12	Black	6–0	100				

Justices Not Susceptible of Ranking

					Harlan	1–4	20

Decisions Pro-Anti State: 15–9 63%   Decisions Pro/Anti U.S.: 28–13 68%

$$R = \frac{147}{149} = .987 \qquad\qquad R = \frac{288}{292} = .986$$

$$\text{Combined } R = \frac{435}{441} = .986$$

Note: Scale Order of Cases (L Ed 2d):
43/54, 45/416, 57/290, 24/299, 56/486, 57/667, 26/409, 28/306, 49/1000, 58/387, 29/564, 37/706, 41/325, 56/525(2), 27/408, 32/612, 36/854, 38/456, 46/209, 54/331, 36/900, 26/419, 32/783.

Scale Order of Cases (L Ed 2d):
32/752, 33/308, 45/607, 45/623, 50/530, 53/538, 56/305, 29/619, 25/60, 33/179(2), 40/341, 37/596, 39/771, 40/380, 49/1046, 54/376, 28/453, 29/723, 35/67, 35/99, 38/427, 38/561, 39/225, 39/242, 39/812(3), 40/250, 50/652, 52/617, 46/598, 48/71, 49/300, 49/1116(2), 55/268, 56/168, 32/87, 25/282, 36/208.

single exception, all of the justices deferred more to the federal government than to the states. The exception here is Douglas, who supported the states with 6 percent of his votes and the federal government not at all. This is hardly a strong example of judicial restraint. Between the two scales, the rank order correlation is again an exceptionally high +.91.

Unlike the First Amendment and double jeopardy scales, poverty law and search-and-seizure associate with other scales to form the value of equality. Although search-and-seizure, from a legal and semantic standpoint, is closer to freedom than to equality, the rank order of the justices is such that it clusters with other scales, such as poverty law, which have as their common feature allegations of racial, economic, sexual, or political discrimination, either of a statutory sort or in violation of the equal protection of the laws.[27] Toward the

Table 11-10

Rank Order of the Burger Court Justices in State and Federal Poverty Law Cases

		State Cases				Federal Cases	
		Pro/Anti	*Pro*			*Pro/Anti*	*Pro*
Rank	*Justice*	*State*	*(percent)*	*Rank*	*Justice*	*State*	*(percent)*
1.5	Brennan	5–39	11	1	Brennan	9–11	45
1.5	Marshall	5–38	12	2	Marshall	8–9	47
3	Douglas	2–30	6	3.5	White	17–3	85
4	Blackmun	10–22	31	3.5	Stewart	17–3	85
5	White	15–30	33	5.5	Blackmun	16–2	89
6	Stewart	21–24	47	5.5	Powell	17–2	89
7	Powell	15–12	56	7.5	Burger	19–1	95
8	Burger	29–16	64	7.5	Rehnquist	19–1	95
9	Black	13–1	93				
10	Rehnquist	18–9	67				

Justices Not Susceptible of Ranking

	Stevens	3–3	50		Stevens	11–0	100
	Harlan	4–10	29		Douglas	0–8	0
					Black	—	
					Harlan	—	

Decisions Pro/Anti State: 17–28 38%   Decisions Pro-Anti U.S.: 17–3 85%

$$R = \frac{186}{191} = .974 \qquad\qquad R = \frac{69}{69} = 1.00$$

$$\text{Combined } R = \frac{255}{260} = .981$$

Note: Scale Order of Cases (L Ed 2d):[a]
28/666, 30/143, 30/448(2), 32/352, 34/608,
39/38, 40/120, 44/525, 45/268, 47/701,
53/534, 59/194, 44/208(2), 54/618, 25/442,
25/561, 25/644, 39/577, 43/583(2), 26/218,
25/287, 25/307, 25/592, 25/598, 26/57, 36/16,
53/448, 39/662, 28/678(2), 25/491, 32/285,
25/593, 37/688(2), 31/36, 43/469, 47/249,
54/324, 56/658(2), 59/358

Scale Order of Cases (L Ed 2d):[a]
44/525, 37/782, 37/767, 30/231, 31/151(2),
38/618, 45/522, 47/18, 55/65(2), 50/389,
50/485(2), 54/228, 55/225, 56/658(2),
58/435(2)

[a]56/658(2) is counted as both state and federal because both were involved.

value of equality, the justices' response to considerations of federalism is as irrelevant as it is toward the value of freedom. In the scales that comprise the value of equality, the justices vote compatibly with their attitudes toward more or less equality, not on the basis of deference to the states.

Accordingly, our analysis of those civil rights and liberties issues that admit of comparability between state and federal cases reveals that neither the individual justices nor the Court as a whole support the states to the extent that the federal government is supported. Note that we do not accuse the justices of being activist or restrained in these issue areas. Rather the data indicate that they are motivated by their attitudes toward the specific civil right or civil liberty allegedly infringed. Judicial restraint is still a sometime thing.

Access to Federal Courts

So far our concern has been judicial restraint qua deference. We have investigated the degree to which the justices have deferred to other participants in the governing process in the context of a particular case. The diehard fan of judicial restraint may still argue that the concept is alive and well but invisible in these cases. Restraint is operative, the argument would run, before the case comes to the decision stage. Those who advocate a reduced role for courts will act to restrict access to the courts. If a case gets to the decision stage, that is evidence that it has passed the threshold of "shockingness" and is important enough to be decided.

In our search for the ghost of judicial restraint, then, we turn to cases concerning access to the federal courts. The term *access* is generally used in two senses: to describe the narrow gate-keeping function performed by the Supreme Court at the "decision to decide" stage of its process—the Rule of Four;[28] and to specify the formal technical requirements, such as standing to sue, mootness, exhaustion of remedies, and the like, that determine who has "access" to the judicial forum at all levels of the federal system. We will limit our investigation of access to the second sense.

The relationship between access and the exercise of judicial restraint or activism is clear and direct. A posture of open access places the Court at the center of national policymaking, while closure minimizes policymaking and results in deference to the other branches of government and to the states. However, this relationship between open access and judicial activism, on the one hand, and closure and judicial restraint, on the other, only describes the effects of access policy. The reason a justice votes to open or close access may be totally irrelevant to considerations of activism and restraint. Chief Justice Burger, for example, and those of his colleagues who support his extra-Court administrative activities, may not only believe in limited access but vote to close access because they consider it as a means to administer a scarce resource. Accordingly, justices may vote to limit access merely to facilitate the handling of what they perceive to be a pressing case-load problem. Conversely, a justice may vote to limit access because his substantive policy views do not have the support of a majority of his colleagues. He may conclude that the federal administrative agencies, the lower federal courts, and the state judicial systems reflect his policy preferences more closely than his colleagues do. Therefore, in order to realize his policy goals, he stakes out an access position that provides greater finality for agency and lower court decision making and less reviewability of their decisions by the Supreme Court.

In a 1979 article, Gregory Rathjen and Harold Spaeth analyzed all formally decided access cases disposed of during the first seven terms of the Burger Court (1969-1976).[29] Their goal was to determine what factors motivated the justices in their voting choices—not just whether or not they vote to open access, but why they vote that way. Their conclusion was that the justices respond to a mixture of motivations; for some the dominant influence was administrative/legal concerns; that is, judicial restraint. Rehnquist and Stewart fit this pattern. Other justices responded to a political attitude toward access; that is, concern with the policy of the cases. The third group of justices, the bulk of the Court, were motivated by a combination of the two attitudes.[30]

It is important to emphasize that the motivation of the justice does not determine his position toward access. That is, even though both Rehnquist and Stewart were found to be motivated by administrative/legal concerns, they did not have similar positions on the degree of access to be allowed. Rehnquist was the most supportive of closure of the nine justices; Stewart was sixth most supportive.[31]

The ideal method for testing whether the justices' votes on the access question are responding to the substantive issue of the case, or to the access question alone, would be the procedure we have been following so far. That is, we could divide the cases into issue areas and then ask whether granting access would favor the "liberal" or "conservative" cause. If a justice routinely denied access to liberal litigants, but favored access for conservatives, we could conclude that the justice was voting his policy preferences, and not responding to pure notions of judicial restraint. This method is not practical here.

Most litigants urging open access are promoting liberal causes. Environmental protectionists, open-housing advocates, and minority groups generally go to court seeking redress; governments generally are brought into court where they seek to defend the status quo. Thus, in most access cases, at least during the period studied, the proaccess litigant is also the liberal. Votes to deny access are usually substantively conservative. This lack of variance makes it impossible to apply the method we have been using.

Still, this very relationship adds great weight to the one kind of circumstantial evidence that we can offer in support of the argument that voting on the access question is greatly influenced by the substantive question involved in the case. As table 11-11 demonstrates, the rank order of the justices, determined by the proportion of votes cast in favor of open access, is identical to the ordering of the justices along the liberal-conservative continuum (as determined by the justices' scale scores).[32] The probability that such a relationship occurred by chance is extremely low.

The point here is not to argue that the justices are activists, but rather to show that considerations of activism and restraint are absent from their decision making. Considerations of substantive policy control the justices' voting behavior.

Table 11-11

Justices' Rankings on Access versus Justices' Rankings on Liberalism/Conservatism

1969-1976		1969-1973			
The Justices' Ranking on Closure		The Justices' Ranking on Their Values			
Justice	Votes Pro-Access (percent)	Justice	Scale Score on Freedom	Scale Score on Equality	Scale Score on New Dealism
Douglas	74	Douglas	.75	.79	.79
Brennan	59	Brennan	.38	.50	.61
Marshall	56	Marshall	.52	.54	.34
Stewart	41	Stewart	.08	-.12	-.13
White	37	White	-.30	-.08	.16
Blackmun	37	Blackmun	-.33	-.43	-.29
Powell	29	Powell	-.32	-.38	-.48
Burger	27	Burger	-.46	-.60	-.47
Rehnquist	19	Rehnquist	-.59	-.77	-.43

Source: (closure) Gregory J. Rathjen and Harold J. Spaeth, "Access to the Federal Courts," *American Journal of Political Science* 23 (May 1979):376. (values) David W. Rohde and Harold J. Spaeth, *Supreme Court Decision Making* (San Francisco: W.H. Freeman, 1976), p. 143.

Conclusion

We have done our best to present the evidence for the existence of judicial restraint and activism as motivating forces in judicial decision making. That evidence is underwhelming. We found, at best, that judicial deference is a sometime thing.

Table 11-12 summarizes our results. Based on the conclusions advanced above, we have indicated, for each justice, for each group of cases, whether his voting is consistent with our operational definitions of restraint or activism or some other attitude. Of the 40 justice cells, 10 indicate voting influenced by activism or restraint. Only one justice is consistent through all four categories—Burger. The chief justice never voted consistently with a pro- or antideference position, and, apart from Douglas, no justice manifested activism or restraint in more than a single category.

Even the 10 cells labeled as activist or restraintist are doubtless an exaggeration. Our criteria for attributing these classifications were deliberately quite broad. We designed a net to catch anyone who looked remotely like an advocate of judicial deference or its opposite. A more finely woven net would have been both more accurate and more exclusive. It is clear, for example, that listing Douglas, Brennan, and Marshall as activists in the civil liberties-federalism cases is a mistake. The three are liberals, and their disapproval of government interference with civil rights is due to their policy orientation—not to any notions

Table 11-12
Justices' Motivations in Four Categories of Cases

Justice	Administrative Agencies	Economic Federalism	Civil Liberties Federalism	Access to Federal Courts
Burger	0	0	0	0
Douglas	0	A	A	0
Brennan	0	0	A	0
Stewart	A	0	0	0
White	R	0	0	0
Marshall	0	0	A	0
Blackmun	R	0	0	0
Powell	0	A	0	0
Rehnquist	0	R	0	0
Stevens	A	0	0	0
	cf. table 11-2	cf. table 11-5 (columns 3 & 4)	cf. table 11-6	cf. table 11-11

A = Activist
R = Restrained
0 = Motivated by Other Factors

about the proper role of the judiciary. The same can perhaps be said about the other 7 cells. However, given our stated criteria, our methods did not detect an explanation other than activism for Douglas and Powell in economic federalism and Stewart and Stevens in administrative agency cases. Similarly, a commitment to restraint explains Rehnquist in economic federalism and White and Blackmun in cases involving administrative agencies.

We should be neither surprised nor saddened to find that judicial deference has apparently so little operative force among Supreme Court justices. If not to decide is to decide (and it surely is), then even the restrained jurist is promulgating policy decisions when he defers. Can anyone of reason and conviction really believe that someone who has attained the office of Supreme Court justice is able to submerge his politics entirely in deference to vague notions of judicial restraint? One may defer, but never blindly. Justices, like most mere mortals, defer to the ideas and institutions of which they approve. We would not want them on the Supreme Court otherwise.

For those who would preserve and perpetuate the myth that judges only find, and do not make the law, judicial activism and restraint may be useful concepts. But most people who have reached adulthood no longer believe that myth anyway. It was gospel during the heyday of the legal idealists; it became a useful myth and has now gone the way of the flat earth and phlogiston. Welcome to the "heaven of legal concepts!"

Notes

1. *Griswold v. Connecticut*, 381 U.S. 479, 527 (1965) (Stewart, dissenting).

2. James Q. Wilson, *Varieties of Police Behavior* (New York: Atheneum, 1970).

3. Rudolf von Jhering, "Im Juristischen Begriffshimmel" in *Scherz und Ernst in der Jurisprudenz* (Leipzig, 1884).

4. *West Virginia State Board of Education v. Barnette*, 319 U.S. 624 (1943) (Frankfurter, dissenting).

5. Archibald Cox, *The Role of the Supreme Court in American Government* (New York: Oxford University Press, 1976), p. 111. Cox's respect for precedent does not extend to spelling; throughout his little book he identifies the current chief justice as "Berger."

6. Raoul Berger, *Government by Judiciary: The Transformation of the Fourteenth Amendment* (Cambridge: Harvard University Press, 1977), p. 2. He spells Cox correctly.

7. Felix Frankfurter, "Some Reflections on the Reading of Statutes," *Columbia Law Review* 47 (May 1947): 534.

8. *Schenck v. United States*, 249 U.S. 47, 52 (1919).

9. Fred Rodell, "For Every Justice, Judicial Deference is a Sometime Thing," *Georgetown Law Journal* 50 (Summer 1962): 702.

10. Because we focus on the votes of the justices, no attention is paid to their opinions. As a result, a dichotomy appears between the language of the justices' opinions and their voting behavior. We recognize that our analysis would be more complete if consideration were given to the reasons the justices provide for their failure to heed the canons of judicial restraint. While we do not gainsay the usefulness of analyses that focus on what the justices say, knowledge of what they do is of at least equal importance. Reasons of space, however, preclude consideration of the justices' opinions. Furthermore, general awareness of the bases of activist opinions exists: burdens on interstate commerce, agency abuse of discretion, legislative intent, the meaning of the words used in the relevant statute. For a persuasive statement of the importance of judicial opinions as a guide to the Court's decisions, see John Brigham, *Constitutional Language: An Interpretation of Judicial Decision* (Westport, Conn.: Greenwood Press, 1978). See also Wallace Mendelson, "The Untroubled World of Jurimetrics," *Journal of Politics* 26 (November 1964): 914–922; and Harold J. Spaeth, "Jurimetrics and Professor Mendelson: A Troubled Relationship," *Journal of Politics* 27 (November 1965): 875–880.

11. For example, *National Labor Relations Board v. Burns Security Services*, 32 L.Ed.2d 62 (1972), and *South Prairie Construction Co. v. IUOE*, 48 L.Ed.2d 61 (1976).

12. The unanimous proagency decisions (other than the NLRB) are: (Citations are to the Lawyers' Edition: volume (2d series) precedes slash, page

follows.) 24/700, 27/9, 27/203, 29/74, 31/170, 32/369, 32/453, 36/426, 41/72, 41/141, 43/121, 43/279, 46/156, 46/533, 47/186, 54/648, 55/460, 56/591, 56/697, 57/595. Antiagency (other than the NLRB): 24/340, 33/723, 36/620, 39/383, 48/284, 48/626, 56/148. Pro-NLRB: 26/21, 27/735, 30/312, 31/79, 34/201, 36/764, 38/388, 40/612, 42/558, 48/382, 50/494, 57/159, 57/370, Anti-NLRB: 32/61, 48/382.

13. The nonunanimous proagency decisions (other than those of the NLRB) are: (Citations are to the Lawyers' Edition: volume (2d series) precedes slash, page follows.) 25/547, 30/560, 30/600, 31/658, 32/390, 35/223, 36/772, 37/254, 43/260, 45/191, 49/14, 53/100, 56/505, 57/1073. Antiagency (other than the NLRB): 25/691, 28/367, 36/635, 37/350, 39/370, 48/495, 57/117. Pro-NLRB: 24/405, 27/398, 30/328, 32/61, 34/422, 36/752, 39/358, 42/465, 43/12, 43/171, 43/189, 51/1, 54/586, 55/96, 57/313, 57/428. Although 55/96 concerns action of the Federal Maritime Board rather than the NLRB, it is included as a pro-NLRB decision because the subject of regulation was a labor union. Anti-NLRB: 25/146, 25/805, 29/206, 30/341, 33/122, 38/495, 40/134, 41/477, 47/196.

14. Only three Warren Court justices are activists on this same criterion: Douglas, Whittaker, and Stewart. The Warren Court, by comparison, supported the agencies in 64.1 percent of all cases between 1953 and 1959. The levels of support by justices ranged from a high of 81 percent by Minton, to a low of 42 percent by Stewart. For the justices who served in both periods, the support scores are quite similar. Sixty percent of the Warren Court justices' votes were proagency, as compared to 56 percent of the Burger Court justices. For this and other data see Harold J. Spaeth, "The Judicial Restraint of Mr. Justice Frankfurter—Myth or Reality," *Midwest Journal of Political Science* 8 (February 1964): 33.

15. Glendon Schubert, *The Judicial Mind: Attitudes and Ideologies of Supreme Court Justices, 1946-1963* (Evanston: Northwestern University Press, 1965), chaps. 8 and 9; Glendon Schubert, *The Judicial Mind Revisited: Psychometric Analysis of Supreme Court Ideology* (New York: Oxford University Press, 1974), pp. 12-13, 131-134; David W. Rohde and Harold J. Spaeth, *Supreme Court Decision Making* (San Francisco: W.H. Freeman, 1976), pp. 137-145; Harold J. Spaeth, *Supreme Court Policy Making: Explanation and Prediction* (San Francisco: W.H. Freeman, 1979), pp. 128-137.

16. Harold J. Spaeth, "Warren Court Attitudes Toward Business," in *Judicial Decision Making*, ed. Glendon Schubert (New York: Free Press, 1963), pp. 79-108; Harold J. Spaeth, "An Analysis of Judicial Attitudes in the Labor Relations Decisions of the Warren Court," *Journal of Politics* 25 (May 1968): 290-311.

17. This observation does not carry over to the Warren Court. The agency support scores there are as follows: probusiness: 52 percent; antibusiness: 65 percent; prolabor: 67 percent; antilabor: 53 percent. The consistent economic liberalism of the Warren Court is evident. See note 14.

18. Comparisons with the Warren Court, here, are also impressive. The least variant justice (in the counterparts of columns 5 and 6 of table 11-2) is Minton, whose support for business is 15 points lower than his support for labor. He is followed closely by Reed and Burton; their change goes in the opposite direction. The greatest variation is shown by Black, who is 79 points more supportive of the agencies when they are prolabor. Second most variant is Whittaker, whose 69-point difference goes the other way. Frankfurter is fifth most variant, (of thirteen justices); his support for labor is 53 points lower than his 'deference' toward probusiness decisions.

Four justices are consistently above the 50 percent support level in all categories: Brennan (though his score is exactly 50 percent in three of the four categories), Reed, Burton, and Minton. Despite their relative consistency, all four vary enough to reveal their economic biases. See note 14.

19. The Warren Court also was less deferential to state economic regulation. Only 52 percent of the justices' votes supported the states. See note 14.

20. The citations to the Burger Court's state labor union decisions are: 25/240, 29/473, 30/328, 39/195, 41/745, 42/399, 49/396, 55/443, 56/209. The state prounion decision is 55/443. Because of this small one-sided sample, we cannot perform the same kind of analysis as was done in the agency cases.

21.The eighteen national supremacy cases are: 24/312, 31/620, 36/114, 36/547, 37/1, 42/195, 44/363, 44/404, 47/780, 48/555, 48/578, 50/683, 51/604, 54/199, 55/179 (counted twice as 7 to 2 pro-state and 3 to 6 antistate), 55/403, 57/475.

22. The zoning cases are: 39/797, 49/132, 52/531, and 57/631. In the last of these the state's regulation was antibusiness. The natural resources cases are: 32/257, 43/731, 57/1018, and 57/1052. In the first of these the state's regulation was antibusiness. The remaining state economic action cases are: 35/545, 43/530, 44/1, 49/220, 52/92, 54/682, 57/91, 57/187, 57/197, and 57/727.

23. In the civil liberties cases we cannot compare the justices' support for government when the government is pro- and anticivil rights. There were only five cases during this time period where the government supported the extension of a right (25/561 on poverty law; 42/196 and 43/260 on the First Amendment; 40/607 and 58/521 on search and seizure).

24. Similar scales for the business and labor cases could not be reliably produced. The number of cases per category was too small.

25. Kendall's tau corrected for tied rankings. See Sidney Siegel, *Nonparametric Statistics for the Behavioral Sciences* (New York: McGraw-Hill, 1956), pp. 213-219.

26. Rohde and Spaeth, *Supreme Court Decision Making*, pp. 118-137.

27. Spaeth, *Supreme Court Policy Making*, pp. 130-132.

28. Joseph Tanenhaus, Marvin Schick, Matthew Muraskin, and Daniel Rosen, "The Supreme Court's Certiorari Jurisdiction: Cue Theory," in Schubert, *Judicial Decision-Making*, pp. 111-132; Stuart Teger and Douglas Kosinski,

"The Cue Theory of Supreme Court Certiorari Jurisdiction: A Reconsideration," *Journal of Politics* 42 (August 1980):834–846; Stephen L. Washby, *Continuity and Change: From the Warren Court to the Burger Court,* (Pacific Palisades, Cal.: Goodyear, 1976), pp. 31–40; Lawrence Baum, "Policy Goals in Judicial Gatekeeping," *American Journal of Political Science* 21 (February 1977):13–35.

29. Gregory J. Rathjen and Harold J. Spaeth, "Access to the Federal Courts: An Analysis of Burger Court Policy Making," *American Journal of Political Science* 23 (May 1979):360–382.

30. Ibid., pp. 379–380.

31. Ibid., p. 376.

32. For a complete discussion of how the scale scores were determined, see Rohde and Spaeth, *Supreme Court Decision Making*, chaps. 4 and 7.

12

The Advocates of Restraint: Holmes, Brandeis, Stone, and Frankfurter

Anthony Champagne and
Stuart S. Nagel

Introduction

Several justices have become clearly associated with the practice of judicial restraint, though four justices stand out as leading advocates. Justices Oliver Wendell Holmes, Louis Brandeis, Harlan F. Stone, and Felix Frankfurter argued that the power of the Supreme Court to declare laws unconstitutional should be used sparingly and that justices of the Court should accord maximum respect to legislative acts. They repeatedly expressed the opinion that the political process was the best method to resolve disputes where values conflicted, and that it was a contradiction in democracy for an oligarchic court to set itself against the elected legislature or to act in its stead.[1]

In one of his early dissents Holmes summed up the essence of judicial self-restraint in propounding his "reasonable man" thesis. The Court should not nullify legislative acts, he said, "unless it can be said that a rational and fair man necessarily would admit that the statute proposed would infringe fundamental principles as they have been understood by the traditions of our people and our laws."[2]

While the concept of judicial self-restraint is one with which most judges can agree in theory, its practice is another matter. Much depends on the tilt of the judge's mind and the depth of his conviction. Judicial restraint limits the power of the judge. Some judges may find the concept too restrictive to apply it consistently to all issues and at all times during their tenure on the bench. As Justice Sutherland has argued, "Self restraint belongs in the domain of will and judgment. The check upon the judge is that imposed by his oath of office, by the Constitution and by his own conscientious and informed convictions."[3]

If Sutherland's criticism is valid, then the restrictiveness of the concept is likely to result in inconsistency in the application of judicial restraint. That is, restraint will be exercised in such a way as to benefit some interests over others. Restraint is essentially a refusal of a judge to become involved in the policy-making process; but, in refusing to become involved, a judge is in effect

We are indebted to C.J. Van Devanter, Carla Duchin, and Eddie Roush for their assistance in the coding of the data in this chapter.

affirming the policies of the other bodies. Thus, one question here addressed will be whether, through the exercise of restraint, some justices tend to affirm policy choices which benefit particular interests.

Additionally, the consistency in the exercise of restraint during the careers of the justices will be examined. If judicial restraint is inconsistently applied, that is, if it is an exercise of "will and judgment," we would not expect consistent exercise of restraint during the career of a judge. Rather, the exercise of restraint would vary not only with the issues before the Court, but also with the political interaction of the justices. Justices, for example, may influence other justices to take a position in favor of restraint. Allies on the Court may increase the self-confidence necessary for a position to be taken. Changes in the composition of the Court may increase or decrease a justice's propensity to support a restrained position.

We will quantitatively examine the following questions: Do justices support particular interests when they take a restrained position? Does support for restraint vary over a justice's tenure? Using quantitative techniques is not an absolute method for determining the degree of a justice's self-restraint, but it should help, in conjunction with greater substantive analysis of the justice's decisions than this study reflects, to assess the exercise of judicial restraint and to answer the questions.

Method

With this intent, 100 nullification cases have been randomly selected from a total of 439. These cases involved federal, state, and municipal legislation found unconstitutional during Holmes's tenure on the Supreme Court. Selected also were the 87 nullification cases decided during the period between Holmes's last participation in an opinion in 1931 and Frankfurter's appointment to the Court in 1939. Since Brandeis was appointed in 1916 and Stone in 1925, part of Holmes's tenure overlaps with these justices. For Frankfurter, there are 123 cases. These are all the nullification cases in which Frankfurter participated through the year 1960.[4] First, the overall record of restraint (dissent in nullification cases) of each justice was determined and compared with that of the average Court member by calculating the percentage of dissenting votes on the Court, exclusive of the justice studied. The calculation of the number of votes exclusive of the justice studied is based on the sometimes inaccurate assumption that the other eight members of the Court voted on every nullification case involved in this study. To further classify each record of restraint, the legislation involved has been categorized according to: source of legislation (federal versus state); interests benefited (liberal or conservative);[5] and time periods in the respective careers of the four justices.

It must be noted that the cases involved are only those which were held unconstitutional by the Supreme Court. No cases involving legislation upheld by the Court, in which Holmes, Brandeis, Stone, or Frankfurter dissented have been included in this study. It has, therefore, been impossible to compare their lack of restraint on nullified legislation of a specific type with their lack of restraint on similar cases upheld by the Court. Thus, it is possible that, though dissent may be the best measure of commitment to a particular value, the measurement of their record of restraint in this study may be only a reflection of their willingness to dissent rather than a valid measure of their restraint.[6] Danelski points out that dissent was not commonplace in routine cases until 1940 and so one should generally be cautious in conclusions based on pre-1940 levels of dissent. However, dissents before 1940 were acceptable if matters of principle were involved.[7] The issue of restraint in nullification cases would generally seem to involve such a matter of principle. It should also be noted that votes in nullification cases only measure one aspect of restraint. Restraint might also involve, for example, refraining from overruling the decisions of administrative agencies as well as legislatures.

Holmes's Record

Holmes's Overall Record of Judicial Self-Restraint

Holmes said that the Court should nullify only those statutes in which the constitutional text had been clearly violated or where democracy had so misfired that no reasonable man could support the legislation produced.[8] He also saw greater merit in the Court's power to declare state laws void than in its power to nullify federal laws. In a speech in 1913 he explained:

> I do not think the United States would come to an end if we lost our power to declare an Act of Congress void. I do think the Union would be imperiled if we could not make that declaration as to the laws of the several states. For one in my place sees how often a local policy prevails with those who are not trained to national views and how often action is taken that embodies what the Commerce Clause was meant to end.[9]

Application of this philosophy of restraint led Holmes, on the basis of the nullification cases included in this study, to vote to sustain 22 percent of the legislation declared invalid by the Court during his thirty years of service. In comparison, the average of other Court members amounted to only 10 percent. His partiality to federal legislation is clear, since he took a restrained position in 40 percent of nullification cases involving federal legislation, and he was restrained in 20 percent of state nullification cases. This strongly restraintist position in federal cases is even more impressive when compared to that of the average of his Court, which made no distinction between federal and state legislation. The average Court member was restrained in 11 percent of federal nullification cases and in 10 percent of state cases.

Interests Benefited by Holmes's Restraint

Table 12-1 is intended to measure whether Holmes displayed any conservative or liberal bias in his restraint. The 100 nullification cases have been classified into four groups: legislation beneficial to liberal interests; legislation beneficial to conservative interests; tax cases; and miscellaneous cases. The legislation beneficial to liberal interests includes statutes designed to bestow social benefits, to protect or broaden the rights of minorities and workers, and to restrict the power of business and capitalist interests. The conservative category includes those statutes intended to restrict the rights of minorities and worker groups, the freedom of press and religion, and to benefit the interests of business and propertied groups. Antisubversive and national security legislation is included in this category.

Table 12-1 vividly demonstrates that Holmes's restraint was not only greatest toward liberal legislation, but almost exclusively confined to it. In all remaining legislation he exercised restraint in only 6 percent of the cases. The average Court member also demonstrated greater restraint toward liberal legislation and little restraint in other categories, but to a much less significant degree than Holmes.

Table 12-1
The Holmes Cases Classified by the Interest Benefited

Interest Benefited	Holmes's Votes	Dissenting Votes (percentage)	Dissenting Votes for Rest of Court (percentage)	Difference Between Holmes and Rest of Court (percentage)
Liberals	61	30	13	+17
Prominority	1	—	—	—
Prolabor	10	60	20	+40
Antibusiness	50[a]	26	12	+14
Conservatives	4	—	3	−3
Antiminority	1	—	—	—
Antilabor	—	—	—	—
Probusiness	2	—	8	−8
First Amendment restriction	1	—	—	—
Antisubversive	—	—	—	—
Tax cases	14[b]	14	6	+8
Miscellaneous	18	5	4	+1

[a]Includes 12 tax cases.

[b]Does not include 12 tax cases above.

Both Holmes and his Court's record of restraint was highest toward legislation favorable to labor, amounting to 60 and 20 percent, respectively. His overall record of restraint on antibusiness legislation was also higher than his average. But on the basis of the cases involved in this study, this restraint was almost wholly exercised in his last twelve years on the Court when he registered twelve of his thirteen dissents on antibusiness legislation. Since there were thirty-two antibusiness cases between 1920 and 1931, Holmes's restraint amounted to 38 percent during those years while his restraint in all the preceding years amounted to less than 6 percent (one dissent in eighteen cases). The overall record of restraint for the average Court member rose to 13 percent during the years 1920–1931, and dropped to 10 percent between 1903 and 1919.

This disparity in Holmes's record of restraint on antibusiness legislation is partly explained by the history of the Court during his tenure. Influenced by the lead taken by President Theodore Roosevelt, the Court between 1908 and 1917—especially after the appointment of Chief Justice White in 1910— adopted a more liberal attitude toward legislation seeking to regulate business and protect labor interests, and allowed much of it to prevail. Beginning in 1917, and especially after 1921, the Court was again dominated by a conservative majority headed by Justices McReynolds, VanDevanter, Sutherland, and Butler. During the twenties it reverted to its pre-1908 orientation toward legislative efforts to regulate business and protect the worker. In the process the Court invalidated more legislation than it had during the preceding fifty years.

Holmes's dissents were therefore more numerous during the 1920s. One would expect, however, that the percentage of dissents among the other members of the Court would also have risen considerably. The fact that it did not, and that Holmes's own record of restraint in the years before 1920 was even lower than that of his Court's average, indicates that his normal exercise of judicial restraint toward nullified antibusiness legislation was much more modest than his famous dissents would suggest. It was only after the Court adopted a reactionary approach to such legislation that his restraint became marked.

The number of nullification cases involving legislation beneficial to conservative interests is so small that only the most limited conclusions can be drawn. It is of interest, however, that Holmes voted to nullify each of the four cases involved. Similarly, in the tax cases and the miscellaneous cases his restraint was minimal.

Brandeis's Record

Brandeis's Overall Record of Judicial Self-Restraint

Brandeis, though an advocate of judicial restraint, was unlike Holmes.[10] Both justices were tolerant of social change, but for very different reasons. Holmes's skepticism made him unwilling to impose his judgment of sound policy over legislative judgments. Holmes liked "to see social experiments tried, . . . I do so without enthusiasm because I believe that it is merely shifting the place of pressure. . . ."[11] Brandeis, on the other hand, was a social reformer, "a liberal out of affirmation and championed his causes not out of disinterest, but out of strong beliefs."[12]

A progressive in Brandeis's time would tend to believe in judicial restraint, if only to allow legislatures to conduct experiments in social reform. Brandeis compiled an extraordinary record of dissents in nullification cases. He dissented in 32 percent of all nullification cases: 30 percent of state cases, and 47 percent of federal cases. The Brandeis nullification dissent record compares to a rate of 11 percent for all cases by the rest of the Court. The other justices averaged a 10 percent dissent rate for state cases and 18 percent for federal cases. The high level of restraint evidenced by Brandeis in nullification cases is even more impressive when it is recalled that Brandeis made a mighty effort to maintain harmony on the Court by refusing to dissent in many cases.[13]

Interests Benefited by Brandeis's Restraint

Table 12-2 suggests the interests which benefited from the legislation in nullification cases. In Brandeis's case, there is strong support for liberal interests over conservative ones. Brandeis averaged a 42 percent dissent rate in favor of liberal interests compared to a 12 percent rate for the rest of the Court.

Table 12-2

The Brandeis Cases Classified by the Interest Benefited

Interest Benefited	Brandeis's Votes	Dissenting Votes (percentage)	Dissenting Votes for Rest of Court (percentage)	Difference Between Brandeis and Rest of Court (percentage)
Liberals	73	42	12	+30
Prominority	–	–	–	–
Prolabor	12	58	22	+36
Antibusiness	61	38	10	+28
Conservatives	12	–	14	−14
Antiminority	6	–	21	−21
Antilabor	1	–	–	–
Probusiness	1	–	–	–
First Amendment restriction	4	–	13	−13
Antisubversive	–	–	–	–
Tax cases	41	45	13	+32
Miscellaneous	33	6	6	–

His dissent rate in behalf of conservative legislation was nonexistent compared to a 14 percent rate for the rest of the Court. His dissent rate was also high in tax cases, perhaps because some of them could have been coded to fit into the liberal category. Nevertheless, the pattern from table 12-2 is clear: Brandeis dissented in nullification cases where those cases involved legislation which benefited liberal interests.

Stone's Record

Stone's Overall Record of Judicial Self-Restraint

Harlan Fiske Stone served on the Court from 1925 until his death in 1946, being chief justice for the last five of those years. During his tenure on the Court, Stone wrote more than six-hundred opinions; and while these opinions cover the entire range of judicial business, Stone is especially remembered for his work in constitutional law.[14]

In one of his more famous dissents, *U.S.* v. *Butler* (1936), he expressed the great problem with judicial review: ". . . while unconstitutional exercise of power by the executive and legislative branches of the Government is subject to judicial restraint, the only check upon our own exercise of power is our own sense of restraint."[15] One of Stone's most significant contributions to constitutional law came in a footnote to *United States* v. *Carolene Products Co.* (1938). He suggested that judicial restraint should be exercised with economic legislation; but in matters concerning personal freedom, conscience, and processes of democracy, more searching inquiry should be made into reasonableness of the legislation.[16]

The level of Stone's support for restraint in nullification cases was quite high—27 percent compared to 12 percent for the rest of the Court. As was the case with Holmes and Brandeis, the source of legislation was an important determinant of Stone's restraint. Stone was much more likely to dissent in favor of federal legislation than state legislation. His dissent rate was 44 percent for federal legislation, compared to 24 percent for state. In contrast, the other justices on the Court dissented in only 17 percent of the federal cases and 11 percent of the state cases.

Interests Benefited by Stone's Restraint

Table 12-3 indicates that liberal interests tended to benefit from Stone's restraint. Stone never dissented in favor of restraint where conservative interests benefited, though the average dissent rate for the other justices was 14 percent. However, Stone's dissent rate when liberal interests benefited was 31 percent,

Table 12–3
The Stone Cases Classified by the Interest Benefited

Interest Benefited	Stone's Votes	Dissenting Votes (percentage)	Dissenting Votes for Rest of Court (percentage)	Difference Between Stone and Rest of Court (percentage)
Liberals	50	31	13	+18
Prominority	–	–	–	–
Prolabor	5	60	23	+37
Antibusiness	45	27	11	+16
Conservatives	12	–	14	−14
Antiminority	6	–	20	−20
Antilabor	1	–	–	–
Probusiness	1	–	–	–
First Amendment restriction	4	–	13	−13
Antisubversive	–	–	–	–
Tax cases	38	43	15	+28
Miscellaneous	28	7	6	+1

compared to an average for the other justices of 13 percent. As with Brandeis, Stone's dissent rate in tax cases was high, perhaps because some of these tax cases could fit in a liberal category.

It is especially noteworthy that Stone dissented in three of the five cases where the statute benefited prolabor interests, a dissent rate far higher than the rate for the rest of the Court. Stone's dissent rate was also much higher than the rate for the rest of the Court where antibusiness legislation was involved. Stone may have been a conservative when he came on the Court. Mason, for example, suggested that Stone was indeed a conservative, but that he was changed by his association with Holmes and Brandeis.[17] A glance at his voting behavior in nullification cases compared to that of Brandeis does show great similarities. Both of their dissents strongly benefit liberal interests, especially labor interests. Both of their dissents are far above the Court dissent rate in terms of benefiting liberal interests and considerably below the Court rate in terms of benefiting conservative interests.

Frankfurter's Record

Frankfurter's Overall Record of Judicial Self-Restraint

Frankfurter argued that legislatures should be allowed to make their own mistakes. He often sought to avoid or delay constitutional issues and argued that postponement might provide the time necessary for a solution through more appropriate and competent channels.[18]

In 123 cases that the Court nullified in the period 1939 through 1960, Frankfurter voted to sustain 24 percent. The average percentage of restraint by other members of the Court was 18 percent—a much higher average than the Holmes Court maintained. It probably reflected a greater willingness on the part of justices to dissent in the past twenty years. This is partially confirmed by the fact that there were only eight single dissents (8 percent) among the Holmes cases whereas there were twenty (16 percent) among the 123 Frankfurter cases.

Frankfurter exercised somewhat greater restraint toward federal legislation than toward state and municipal legislation. Frankfurter adopted a restrained position in 30 percent of federal nullification cases and in 23 percent of state cases. The average dissent rate in favor of restraint for the other justices was 11 percent in federal cases and 16 percent in state cases. In a 1958 dissent to an opinion which nullified a congressional act, he said:

> To sustain [this legislation] is to respect the actions of the two branches of our government directly responsive to the will of the people and empowered under the Constitution to determine the wisdom of the legislation. The awesome power of this Court to invalidate such legislation, because it is bounded only by our prudence in discerning the limits of the Court's constitutional function, must be exercised with the utmost restraint. . . . The power to invalidate legislation must not be exercised as if, either in constitutional theory or in the art of government, it [the Court] stood as the sole bulwark against unwisdom or excesses of the moment.[19]

In the *Barnette* case he went to even greater lengths to state his views on the desirability of judges exercising restraint toward state legislation.[20]

Interests Benefited by Frankfurter's Restraint

The only liberal legislation nullified by the Court during Frankfurter's tenure was eleven cases involving statutes regulating or taxing business. (See table 12-4.) Ten of the eleven cases involved state or municipal legislation to regulate or tax interstate commerce. Frankfurter voted to uphold only one of these statutes. His lack of restraint in these cases does not coincide with his many expressions of support for an adequate latitude of power between the federal and state governments. He often argued that this division of power was not only healthy for democracy, but maintaining the state as a workable unit of government provided a useful area where governmental experimentation could be carried out. In 1940 he wrote: "The autonomous powers of the state are those in the Constitution and not verbal weapons imported into it."[21]

Table 12-4
The Frankfurter Cases Classified by the Interest Benefited

Interest Benefited	Frankfurter's Votes	Dissenting Votes (percentage)	Dissenting Votes for Rest of Court (percentage)	Difference Between Frankfurter and Rest of Court (percentage)
Liberals	11	18	16	+2
Prominority	–	–	–	–
Prolabor	–	–	–	–
Antibusiness	11[a]	18	16	+2
Conservatives	60	27	17	+10
Antiminority	10	–	10	–10
Antilabor	11	27	10	+17
Probusiness	7	57	25	+32
First Amendment restriction	24	33	17	+16
Antisubversive	8	12	23	–11
Tax cases	25[b]	4	19	–15
Miscellaneous	27	33	17	+16

[a]Includes four tax cases.

[b]Does not include four tax cases above.

He also urged proper recognition for the tax needs of the states. But table 12-4 shows that his record of restraint in tax cases amounted to only one case in twenty-five (4 percent). The average dissent of other members of the Court reached 19 percent. There were dissents, ranging from one to four, on seventeen of these cases.

On the other hand, his restraint on legislation beneficial to business (57 percent) was much greater than in any other category. On other legislation beneficial to conservative interests Frankfurter's record of restraint was erratic. In eleven cases involving legislation discriminating against aliens and Negroes, he showed no restraint. But in seven cases affecting the religious beliefs of minorities, specifically the Jehovah's Witnesses, he voted on two occasions to withhold nullification. Among these was the famous 1943 *Barnette* case which revoked a state statute requiring all children to salute the flag in the public schools. Since Frankfurter was a member of a religious minority, his decision surprised many. But he maintained that "man lives by symbols" and the flag salute was one of these. It was no violation of the individual's rights nor a restriction on his freedom of religion.[22] Five years later in the *McCullom* case[23] he voted with the majority to nullify an Illinois statute providing for released time for religious instruction in the schools. In the *Barnette* case he had made a strong plea for judicial restraint toward local legislation, but apparently failed to uphold this thesis in the *McCullom* case.

Frankfurter's restraint on antisubversive legislation was also minimal, holding with the Court that the federal government had generally, though not exclusively, preempted this field when state legislation was involved, or restating Holmes's thesis that a "clear and present danger" must be demonstrated. Since the English words *freedom* and *liberty* are difficult to define, Frankfurter held that the First Amendment freedoms allowed leeway for judicial interpretation and refused to acknowledge Justice Black's position that they were specific and absolute.[24] Frankfurter's record of restraint on these liberties, totaling 33 percent, conformed with these views. His restraint was particularly marked toward municipal legislation requiring organizations to obtain permits or licenses to engage in local activities. He argued that such permits had nothing to do with interference in religious matters, but were merely a protection of the general welfare.[25]

Finally, in the field of labor legislation Frankfurter agreed with all members of the recent Court that picketing is a right that warrants protection under the First and Fourteenth Amendments.[26] He also stressed, however, that the unions had duties and that freedom could not be turned into license. According to his philosophy the economic rights and responsibilities of unions were closely paralleled by those of corporations. With these views one might suspect that his record of restraint on antilabor legislation would compare with his general average and be considerably higher than that of the average member of the Supreme Court in recent years. This is confirmed by the statistical study of his voting record shown in table 12-4.

Comparisons over the Justices' Careers

Holmes and Brandeis

Much has been written about the friendship between Holmes and Brandeis.[27] One result of that friendship was a pattern of frequent Holmes-Brandeis dissents. Taft was sure that the two justices dissented together because of their radical sympathies and was also convinced that Brandeis exerted unusually powerful influence over Holmes.[28] As Taft wrote, "He [Holmes] is so completely under the control of Brother Brandeis that it gives to Brandeis two votes instead of one."[29] Holmes was encouraged by Brandeis to dissent from the opinions of the conservative Court. As Holmes wrote, "he [Brandeis] spurred me to write a dissent."[30]

While the data must be supplemented with qualitative analysis before findings can prove conclusive, it is interesting to note that Holmes dissented in only 8 percent of nullification cases before the time Brandeis joined the Court. On the other hand, Holmes dissented in 30 percent of nullification cases after Brandeis joined the Court.

In the nineteen cases in the sample where Holmes dissented after Brandeis was appointed to the Court, Brandeis also dissented. Brandeis dissented in six additional cases without Holmes. Holmes and Brandeis generally concurred with one another. They wrote separate dissents in only two of the nineteen cases.

Brandeis, of course, remained on the Court after Holmes retired. During the period between Holmes's retirement and Brandeis's retirement, Brandeis maintained a high dissent rate in nullification cases, though there was a decided drop in the rate from a 40 percent dissent rate in the sample of 63 nullification cases when Holmes was on the Court to 28 percent in the sample of 7 nullification cases between Holmes's departure and Brandeis's retirement. In part, one may explain this difference in terms of more liberal decisions by the Court in the post-Holmes period, but the Court was far from being a liberal Court or a restrained Court. It is not too far-fetched to suggest that the loss of Holmes may have affected Brandeis's propensity to dissent in nullification cases.

Associate and Chief Justice Stone

Friendship patterns may well affect the extent to which restrained dissents will be filed. Institutional factors may also influence one's propensity to dissent in nullification cases. Once Stone became chief justice, his dissent rate dropped. During the time that Stone was associate justice, his dissent rate in nullification cases was 28 percent. After becoming chief justice, that dissent rate dropped to 18 percent. A rival explanation is that the more liberal Court of Stone's chief justiceship caused Stone's interest in dissenting in nullification cases to decline. It does seem possible, however, that once Stone became chief justice, he tried to lessen his dissent rate in order to build necessary coalitions.[31]

Frankfurter's Career

Frankfurter exhibited less variability over time in propensity to dissent than did Stone, Brandeis, or Holmes. Frankfurter did not serve on the Court with any of the other justices studied here except Stone, and Frankfurter and Stone, unlike Holmes and Brandeis, were not known for their friendship. If one examines dissents in nullification cases, one finds that during the time Stone and Frankfurter were on the Court, they dissented together in only two cases, though Stone dissented six times and Frankfurter nine times.

Frankfurter's career on the bench was divided into three parts. Table 12-5 shows that division and indicates that Frankfurter's dissent rate was most consistent over these three periods. Table 12-5 does indicate, though, that Frankfurter exercised somewhat greater restraint during his first years on the Court than during the remainder of his career, and this was due mainly to the high degree of restraint he demonstrated toward conservative legislation in the first seven

Table 12-5
Frankfurter Cases Classified by Time Periods

Time Periods	Frankfurter Votes	Dissenting Votes (percentage)	Dissenting Votes for Rest of Court (percentage)	Difference Between Frankfurter and Rest of Court (percentage)
1939–1945	34	26	16	+10
Liberal legislation	2	50	31	+19
Conservative legislation	17	35	19	+16
1946–1953	50	22	18	+4
Liberal legislation	5	—	17	−17
Conservative legislation	26	23	17	+6
1954–1960	39	23	16	+7
Liberal legislation	4	25	6	+19
Conservative legislation	17	24	14	+10

years. This conflicts with the general impression that Frankfurter became increasingly conservative on the Court.[32] While this impression might be supported by a study of his dissents on legislation declared constitutional by the Court in recent years, it is not confirmed by the statistical study of his restraint on nullification cases, though a pattern might emerge if the cases were broken down into civil liberties and economic issues.

Summary and Conclusions

We have examined two questions: Through the exercise of restraint, do justices tend to affirm legislative policy choices which benefit particular interests? Does support for restraint vary over the careers of justices? Though we again emphasize that application of quantitative techniques is not an absolute method for determining the answers to these questions, our analysis indicates that both questions should be answered affirmatively.

All the justices exercised a higher degree of restraint toward congressional legislation than toward state and municipal legislation. The four also exercised greater restraint than the average member of their Court. However, Holmes, Brandeis, and Stone exercised restraint only to benefit liberal interests. Frankfurter's dissents tended to benefit conservative interests, but he also dissented in behalf of liberal interests.[33] For at least three of the justices, Sutherland's argument that restraint is an exercise of will seems valid. There is ideological content to the dissents of Holmes, Brandeis, and Stone, though their opportunities to dissent in behalf of conservative interests were admittedly limited.

Additionally, the justices were not consistent in their exercise of restraint over time. Rather than consistency in the exercise of restraint, for the most part, it seems to vary with time. Holmes showed a much greater propensity to dissent after Brandeis was appointed to the Court, Brandeis a greater propensity to dissent before Holmes retired, and Stone was more likely to dissent before he became chief justice. Restraint is thus in part related to: the ideological content of cases and changes in that content; the presence or absence of other judges who may provide encouragement for dissents in favor of restraint; and one's role on the Court—that is, whether one is chief or associate justice.

Perhaps the most significant question faced by legal scholars is the extent to which judges should make policy. Justices who dissent in nullification cases can claim that democratic theory demands that judges refrain from nullifying legislation. Such a claim has an attractive ring, though this research suggests that those ringing phrases in praise of representative government may have a hollow tone. Judicial restraint would seem to require consistency in the application of restraint. Restraint is cheapened if it is determined by coalitions on the Court, promotions to chief justice, historical patterns, or judicial career patterns. The existence of such determinants forces one to question the strength and depth of a justice's convictions. If judicial restraint is to be more than a smoke screen to mask political alliances and ideologies, restraint must be applied consistently without concern for case result. As Spaeth has concluded, "[judicial restraint] serves only to cloak the political character of the judicial process and thereby helps to preserve the traditional view that judges merely find and do not make law."[34]

Notes

1. G. Edward White, *The American Judicial Tradition* (New York: Oxford University Press, 1976), chaps. 8, 10, 14; Charles M. Lamb, chap. 1, this volume.

2. *Lochner v. New York*, 198 U.S. 45, 74 (1904).

3. *West Coast Hotel v. Parrish*, 300 U.S. 379 (1937).

4. The cases were chosen from Blaine Moore, "The Supreme Court and Unconstitutional Legislation," *Studies in History, Economics and Public Law* 54 (1913); Wilfred Charles Gilbert, *Provisions of Federal Law Held Unconstitutional by the Supreme Court of the United States* (Washington: Library of Congress Legislative Reference Service, 1936); "United States Supreme Court Cases Declaring State Laws Unconstitutional, 1912-1938," *State Law Index Special Report Number 2* (Washington: Library of Congress, 1938); Norman J. Small, *State Constitutional and Statutory Provisions and Municipal Ordinances Held Unconstitutional on Their Face or as Administered* (Washington: Library of Congress Legislative Reference Service, 1960).

5. Tables 12-1, 12-4 and tables 12-2, 12-3 are coded in a somewhat different manner in that tables 12-2 and 12-4 allow for more overlap in interests benefited than tables 12-2 and 12-3. Comparability between tables 12-1, 12-4 and 12-2, 12-3 is therefore limited, though the main point of the tables remains; that is, both coding methods show there is bias in the exercise of restraint.

6. David J. Danielski noted that, "Some of the most important expectations defining a justice's role concern public expression of disagreement." "Conflict and Its Resolution in the Supreme Court," *Journal of Conflict Resolution* 11 (March 1967): 78.

7. Ibid., p. 79.

8. White, *The American Judicial Tradition*, chap. 8.

9. Oliver Wendell Holmes, *Speeches* (Boston: Little, Brown, 1918), p. 102.

10. White, *The American Judicial Tradition*, chap. 8; Alpheus T. Mason, *Brandeis: A Free Man's Life* (New York: Viking, 1946).

11. Quoted in Alexander M. Bickel, *The Unpublished Opinions of Mr. Justice Brandeis* (Chicago: University of Chicago Press, 1967), p. 221.

12. Melvin Urofsky, *A Mind of One Piece: Brandeis and American Reform* (New York: Charles Scribner's Sons, 1971), pp. 146-147.

13. See Bickel, *The Unpublished Opinions of Mr. Justice Brandeis*.

14. See generally, Alpheus T. Mason, *Harlan Fiske Stone: Pillar of the Law* (New York: Viking, 1956).

15. *U.S. v. Butler*, 297 U.S. 1 (1936).

16. *U.S. v. Carolene Products Co.*, 304 U.S. 144 (1938).

17. Mason, *Harlan Fiske Stone*, p. 254.

18. See generally, Joseph Lash, *From the Diaries of Felix Frankfurter* (New York: Norton, 1975), pp. 3-98.

19. *Trop v. Dulles*, 356 U.S. 86 (1958).

20. *West Virginia State Board of Education v. Barnette*, 319 U.S. 624, 646 (1943).

21. *Wisconsin v. J.C. Penney Co.*, 311 U.S. 435, 444 (1940).

22. 319 U.S. 624 (1943).

23. *McCullom v. Board of Education*, 333 U.S. 203 (1948).

24. *Bridges v. California*, 314 U.S. 252 (1941).

25. *Martin v. Struthers*, 319 U.S. 141 (1943).

26. *Thornhill v. Alabama*, 310 U.S. 88 (1940).

27. Mason, *Harlan Fiske Stone*, chap. 16; White, *The American Judicial Tradition*, chap. 8; Bickel, *The Unpublished Opinions of Mr. Justice Brandeis*, chap. 10.

28. Mason, *Harlan Fiske Stone*, chap. 16.

29. Quoted in Mason, *Brandeis*, p. 571.

30. Mark Howe, ed., *Holmes-Laski Letters* (Cambridge: Harvard University Press, 1953), p. 157.

31. Mason noted that Stone did not feel a chief justice should "gloss over principle." However, Stone had "genuine concern" over the disagreements among the associate justices. Mason, *Harlan Fiske Stone*, pp. 608, 612.

32. For example, see Glendon Schubert, *Human Jurisprudence: Public Law as Political Science* (Honolulu: University Press of Hawaii, 1975), p. 102. Tanenhaus did not find changes in Frankfurter's voting consistency over time. See Joseph Tanenhaus, "Supreme Court Attitudes Toward Federal Administrative Agencies," *Vanderbilt Law Review* 14 (March 1961): 491-492. If we dichotomize Frankfurter's career into early (1939-1949) and late (1950-1960) parts, we find little change in Frankfurter's conservatism relative to the rest of the Court. Frankfurter dissented in favor of liberal legislation 33 percent of the time in the early period and only 13 percent of the time in the late period. However, his dissent rate in favor of conservative legislation also dropped considerably—from 34 percent in the early period to 18 percent in the late period. The dissent rate for the Court (excluding Frankfurter) also dropped between the early and late period—from 25 percent in favor of liberal legislation in the early period to 13 percent in the late period and from 20 percent in favor of conservative legislation in the early period to 13 percent in the late period. Thus, in the early period Frankfurter was 6 percent more conservative than the rest of the Court in his exercise of restraint. In the late period, he was 5 percent more conservative.

33. Other evidence suggests stronger ideological content in Frankfurter's restraint than is suggested in this analysis. See especially Harold J. Spaeth, "The Judicial Restraint of Mr. Justice Frankfurter—Myth or Reality," *Midwest Journal of Political Science* 8 (February 1964): 22-38.

34. Ibid., p. 38.

13 Issue Fluidity in the U.S. Supreme Court: A Conceptual Analysis

S. Sidney Ulmer

In his timely book, *The Courts and Social Policy*, Donald L. Horowitz opens his second chapter with the following observation:

> There is an undeniable attractiveness to the judicial method. In its pristine form, the adversary process puts all the arguments before the decisionmaker in a setting in which he must act. The judge must decide the case and justify his decision by reference to evidence and reasoning. In the other branches, it is relatively easy to stop a decision from being made—they often effectively say no by saying nothing. In the judicial process, questions get answers. It is difficult to prevent a judicial decision. No other private or public institution is bound to be so responsive.[1]

Without denying the very valid distinction Horowitz is seeking to make, this statement must be modified if it is to be applied to the U.S. Supreme Court, for it fails to make clear the complexity of judicial processes in that Court and the uncertainties that plague those processes from start to finish.[2]

Article III of the Constitution extends the judicial power of the United States to all cases arising under the Constitution and under federal law. As Article III was interpreted in *Marbury* v. *Madison*[3] and *Cohens* v. *Virginia,*[4] one could argue that the Court is obligated to review all cases that fall within its jurisdiction.[5] A competing view is that the Court should review only those conflicts that meet certain standards imposed by the Court itself.[6] Resolving this matter, it may still be impossible to predict not only the direction and nature of plenary rulings but also whether such rulings will be narrow or broad— whether they will hew closely to a statutory or constitutional ground or reach out and decide matters unnecessarily confronted,[7] or if necessarily decided, based on tenuous evidence or reasoning. All this is an inevitable consequence of the fact that Supreme Court justices disagree about the proper role of the Court.

The research in this chapter was supported by the National Science Foundation (Grant #SOC77-26066). The author is particularly indebted to Stephen Wasby for encouraging this research and for useful comments on an earlier draft of this paper. Appreciation is also due Robert Bradley, a doctoral candidate at the University of Kentucky, for assistance in data gathering and other aspects of this project. All shortcomings, of course, remain the sole responsibility of the author.

319

Some justices believe in close adherence to the rule of *stare decisis*, tenets of "strict construction," judicial parsimony, and other self-imposed principles of judicial restraint.[8] Others, normally labeled activists, are motivated to "do justice" or to provide policies which they think are socially desirable or, indeed, socially or morally imperative.[9] Several opinions in the case of *United Steel Workers of America* v. *Weber*[10] starkly contrast these polar positions. Stressing that "a thing may be within the letter of the statute and yet not within the statute, because not within its spirit"[11] and the "irony" of the result dictated by a literal interpretation of Title VII of the Civil Rights Act of 1964, Justice Brennan upheld a race-conscious affirmative action plan challenged by an employee of the Kaiser Steel Company. Noting the flat prohibition against racial discrimination in the statute, Rehnquist (dissenting) argued the oft-stated principle of restraint that the justices' duty is to construe rather than to rewrite legislation and accused the majority of Houdini-like practices. Justice Blackmun, somewhat sympathetic to Rehnquist's rendering of the statute, nevertheless concurred with the majority on the ground that "additional considerations, practical and equitable, only partially perceived, if perceived at all by the 88th Congress" supported the decision of the Court.[12] Chief Justice Burger, in dissent, criticized the majority's amending of the statute "to do precisely what both its sponsors and its opponents agreed the statute was *not* intended to do."[13]

One need not bother to resolve these conflicts, nor worry whether the justices taking the various positions always do so consistently. They are emphasized here only to make the point that the evidence and reasoning required for decision by the activist judge is not the same as that required by the more restrained jurist.

As for the necessity of deciding at all, something more needs to be said. In the judicial process, questions do not necessarily get answered—at least not insofar as the Supreme Court is concerned.[14] At that level, indeed, it is a simple matter to "prevent a judicial decision." The Court has as many ways of avoiding an issue as it wants or needs.[15] Justice Frankfurter once remarked that "[i]n law also the right answer usually depends on putting the right question."[16] The "right" question is always determined by the Court itself. The only questions that get answered are those the Court chooses to address. And the answers are only those that the Court wishes to provide—be they responsive or nonresponsive to the issue posed by petitioning or appealing parties, and be they restrictive or expansive in coverage.

Through control of its dockets, the Court declines to review 95 percent or more of the issues presented to it. Even after review is granted the Court may restrict itself not to the substantive issue posed by the parties but to matters of standing, ripeness, exhaustion of remedies, and other concepts of restraint by which decision "on the merits" of an issue may be avoided.[17] The Court may grant review and address a substantive issue other than that posed by the parties. It may also decline to grant plenary review unless the parties agree to pose and argue some question of interest to the Court itself. Here, again, the justices may be expected to differ, and the differences tap dimensions of activism and restraint. An activist Court deciding an unnecessary issue in order to promote some idiosyncratic or social purpose must, after all, first frame the issue to be addressed. Since the statement of an issue always influences the degree to which the evidence and reasoning underlying a response is probative, issue formulation and substantive issue response are inseparable.

Clearly, one who would understand activism and restraint on the Supreme Court must open his lens to catch the broader picture. Traditionally, discussions of Supreme Court activism have focused on selected components of decision making. One such component incorporates decisions dealing with acts of Congress, state and local policies, and presidential actions. A Court that is particularly inclined to void the actions of other public officials is likely to be labeled "activist;" a Court that is reluctant to do so—"restrained". A second component encapsulates the responses of the Court to civil liberty claims. Historically, or at least in recent history, pro-civil liberty Courts have been viewed as activist. A third component of activism is a studied willingness to accept or even invite change in constitutional law.

Objections to activism or restraint, in the main, are only partially founded on the recipients of the Court's actions. Equally fundamental is the role of the Court in the American socio-legal system. Some persons view the institution of the Court as an umpire, an interpreter of law, denying the Court a policy-making role or, if granting such a role, restricting it severely. From this perspective the focus is not on who is favored or disfavored by the Court's rulings but in the discretionary processes by which decisions are reached. Rapid change in law, a willingness to find for preferred litigants, the inviting of test cases, the dodging of issues, or the willful formulation of issues not posed by litigants or the facts of a case—these are all crucial aspects of a broader definition of judicial activism. It is in the context of this broader definition that our subject takes on added significance.

In this chapter, we shall explore activism and restraint from the standpoint of *Issue Fluidity*.[18] Our exploration will not involve the testing of a theory. The state of knowledge in this area will not permit that. Instead, the aim is to establish the significance of Issue Fluidity as a theoretical concept, to determine if it has referents in the real world, and if so, to suggest causes, factors, or conditions that might be associated with its occurrence and some possible consequences implied by various hypothesized causes.

Issue Fluidity: Forms and Frequencies

In any given year the Supreme Court is asked to review over 4,000 decisions of state and lower federal courts. These requests constitute a pool from which the Court makes up its *Plenary Case Agenda*, that is, an agenda of the cases in which decisions will be accompanied by written opinions after full briefing and oral argument. The Court is able to grant such plenary review to only about 150 cases each year. In these cases, "What is the question?" is a serious and consequence-laden inquiry.

By using the concept of Issue Fluidity, we call attention to the fact that the question(s) to which the Court will respond in any given case cannot be known with certainty until the Court's opinion in the case is announced. At first blush this assertion may seem questionable. After all, when parties petition the Supreme Court for a full hearing, they are required to specify exactly what questions or issues the Court is being asked to review. Moreover, publishers in the field are continually summarizing the facts of pending cases along with the issues they pose.[19] Publications of this sort serve to keep the media, the bar, and others informed as to issues being presented to the legal system. Nevertheless, the inquiry is necessary if we are to understand the ways in which the Court can expand, contract, suppress, or replace issues posed by the litigating parties at various points between initial issue framing and final issue resolution. Examples of such actions in the Court have been noted in the literature on occasion. But there has been no systematic discussion of the forms that Issue Fluidity may take, the frequency with which it appears, the factors possibly associated with its occurrence, or the consequences flowing therefrom. Here we suggest several ways in which Issue Fluidity manifests itself.

Issue Fluidity is evident in any case in which the Court grants full review and then proceeds to discover and decide an issue not raised by the petitioner or appellant. Issue Fluidity is also reflected in any case in which review is granted but in which the Court then suppresses and does not decide an issue posed by the petitioning or appealing party. *Issue Discovery* occurs when the Court expands and decides an issue raised by the party seeking review. *Issue Suppression* is identified when the Court ignores and does not decide an issue posed, contracts or limits the issue, or fails to confront and decide the issue by majority opinion.

Directly associated with these concepts is the fact that the Court deals with not one but three distinct agendas. At one level it is confronted by its *Jurisdictional Agenda*. This agenda is not determined by the Court but consists of applications for review of lower court decisions forwarded by losing litigants below—four to five thousand cases per term.[20] The action taken on these agenda items determines, inter alia, the *Plenary Case Agenda*, that is, the Court selects from its Jurisdictional Agenda the cases to be decided after plenary treatment. In the process of awarding jurisdiction and deciding plenary cases, the Court develops its *Issue-Action Agenda*. This consists of the issues that the Court will confront and decide authoritatively. It is generally assumed by the media that the Court composes its Issue-Action Agenda simultaneously with its Plenary Case Agenda. There is an element of truth in this, since the Court may, in granting plenary review, accept the issues posed by petitioning or appealing parties and proceed to confront and decide those issues and no more. However, this is frequently not the case, and thus the additional conceptualization is necessary.

Issue Discovery and Issue Suppression are not mutually exclusive concepts. Both may occur in the same case or in reference to the same general issue across cases. The latter consideration has a number of ramifications, but in particular it suggests that a decision of the Court represents a static or temporary event in a dynamic process. Among others this view is seen in the work of Richardson and Vines,[21] and Casper.[22] We submit, however, that *Issue Formulation* at the level of the Court itself is equally fluid and that this fluidity is reflected not only between decisions but in the processes by which decision in a single case is ultimately reached.

Does Issue Fluidity actually occur? Certain considerations would seem to discourage it. It is not at all self-evident that judges have time for discovering issues, especially since that is how lawyers earn their keep. The adversary system and predictability in the law both require that judges decide issues that have been argued by both parties to a conflict. Appellate court judges invite problems if they consistently reverse lower court decisions on issues not raised below. Lower courts implement higher court decisions. The implementation process functions more effectively when lower court judges are not treated cavalierly and when they feel that reversals from above are based on legitimate errors below. As for Issue Suppression, a court that declines to decide issues posed, particularly after review has been granted, is a court that fails to discharge its responsibility to decide. This is not to say that occasional suppression is a major misfeasance, but suppression must be limited if the judicial system is to function properly.

In spite of all this, Issue Fluidity does occur. Notorious instances of issue discovery occurred in *Erie Railroad* v. *Tompkins*,[23] *Mapp* v. *Ohio*,[24] and many other cases.[25] Yet examples do not make a case. To get some sense of the frequency of Issue Fluidity in the Supreme Court and the contours of discovery and suppression activities in actual situations, we have examined 159 of the Court's criminal cases decided in the 1969 through 1976 Terms inclusive. These cases represent those in which the Court made significant criminal justice decisions during these eight terms.[26] They are all cases in which decision was reached after full argument and briefing, and all were accompanied by written opinions. Of 159 cases examined, some indication of Issue Fluidity was detected in 52 cases, or 33 percent of the total number.

It is submitted without further argument that Issue Fluidity, as we have defined it, is appearing with sufficient frequency to justify more attention than has been given it. This is particularly true in view of the fact that Issue Discovery and Issue Suppression represent actions of the Court that are largely discretionary, yet are actions that have major significance for the making of law and social policy in the United States. We shall indicate the several forms of Issue Fluidity actually encountered in examining the 159 cases and give one or more examples of each form.

Issue Fluidity and Plenary Review

Issue Discovery with Issue Suppression

Issue Discovery and Issue Suppression occurs when the Court ignores a question raised by the petitioner or appellant but then poses and decides one or more questions of interest to the Court itself. Two cases may be used to demonstrate how the Court can engage in Issue Discovery and Issue Suppression at the same time. One involved a Fourth Amendment question in *United States* v. *Desist*;[27] the other, *United States* v. *Jackson*, involved the federal kidnapping statute.[28] In the first, petitioners were convicted in a federal district court for conspiracy to import and consume heroin. The government successfully used tape recordings of conversations among petitioners in a New York hotel room. The tapes were provided by federal officers who used a recording device that did not penetrate "physically" into the room in which the conversations were held. The tapes were crucial in convicting Sam Desist and his co-conspirators. On appeal, the federal court of appeals rejected Desist's Fourth Amendment claim which was subsequently posed to the Supreme Court as follows: Does the Fourteenth Amendment bar the use of evidence obtained as a result of a microphone placed by federal narcotics officers in an air space separating the door of the hotel room they occupied and the door of the adjoining room occupied by suspected narcotics law violators?

In the kidnapping case time was of the essence. In *United States* v. *Jackson*,[29] the Supreme Court held that the death penalty provision of the federal kidnapping statute was unconstitutional in that it permitted the death penalty only upon a jury's recommendation, thereby making the risk of death the price of a jury trial. In 1959 Bob Brady was charged with violating the statute. Being aware through his attorney that he faced a maximum penalty of death, Brady pleaded guilty and was sentenced to fifty years–later reduced to thirty. In 1967 Brady initiated a proceeding to bar his plea on the ground that it was not given voluntarily.[30] He argued that awareness of the possibility of a death penalty, coupled with pressure from his lawyer, coerced the plea. This claim failed in the federal district court, and the Court of Appeals for the Tenth Circuit affirmed. At the Supreme Court level the question posed for consideration was this: Should *United States* v. *Jackson* be applied retroactively to invalidate the 1950 federal kidnapping conviction based on a guilty plea?

Thus, we have two cases–one asking about retroactivity and the other about Fourth Amendment rights regarding search and seizure. In responding to these cases, the Court addressed the question of retroactivity in *Desist*—a case not raising the issue—but did not address it in *Brady*—a case which explicitly raised it. Thus, Issue Fluidity occurred in both cases. It is possible, by implication, to guess at the Court's position on the specific issues posed by the parties, but such a guess is no substitute for a "holding" insofar as *stare decisis* is concerned. By declining to rule on the retroactivity of *Jackson*, the Court left open the possibility that it might later interpret the rule in *Jackson* differently.

While both cases illustrate Issue Suppression, they also illustrate Issue Discovery since the Court addressed and decided the following questions not raised by petitioners in the two cases: Did *Jackson* rule out guilty pleas in federal kidnapping cases? Was an involuntary plea proved on the facts in *Brady*? Is *Katz* v. *United States*[31] to be applied retroactively? All three questions were answered negatively. It is not asserted, of course, that one or more of these inquiries should not have been raised by the parties and decided by the Court. The point is that they were not posed by the litigants, yet the Court chose to address them within its discretionary power to do so. While one may approve of the results, it is important to understand the existence of such discretionary authority and the factors associated with its use or disuse.

Issue Discovery without Issue Suppression

A most extraordinary example of Issue Discovery without Issue Suppression occurred in *Wolff* v. *McDonnell*.[32] Wolff was a prisoner in the Lincoln Correctional Complex in Lincoln, Nebraska. Nebraska statutes provide that the chief executive officer of each penal institution is responsible for the discipline of inmates under his control. As in many penal institutions, Nebraska allows time served to be reduced for good behavior—so-called "good time" credits. In Nebraska good time credit can be forfeited or withheld for flagrant or serious misconduct. When misconduct of the defined kind occurs, it must be reported to an adjustment committee made up of the associate warden, the correctional industries superintendant, and the recreation center director. The committee evaluates the reports and takes appropriate disciplinary action.

In *Wolff*, a class action maintained that the rules and procedures used at the Lincoln Complex to determine good time credit reductions and forfeitures violated due process of law. Unlike cases in which petitioners raise a single question for consideration, attorneys here posed five specific issues for resolution: (1) Under what circumstances, if any, does due process require a state to furnish counsel or permit retained counsel for inmates in prison disciplinary hearings? The Supreme Court responded in effect by saying "none," that is, inmates have no right to retain counsel in such proceedings. The Court went on to say that counsel "substitutes" (other inmates) should be provided in certain cases, but since no sure guide was furnished to identify such cases, this apparent

Issue Discovery is insignificant. (2) Should state penal authorities, rather than the federal district court, lay down minimum procedural due process requirements for disciplinary hearings in penal institutions in the first instance? The Court replied in the negative. (3) Are state prison authorities barred from opening incoming mail from attorneys, if such mail is opened in the presence of inmate addresses, for the sole purpose of inspecting contraband not otherwise discoverable? Again, the Court said no. (4) Must state penal authorities furnish legal assistance, or a reasonable alternative, to inmates to prepare civil rights actions as well as habeas corpus suits? The Court answered yes. (5) May federal courts order newly devised prison procedural requirements to be applied retroactively to prison disciplinary hearings? They may not, the Court held.

Thus the Court in effect decided all the issues posed by Wolff and his cohorts, and no Issue Suppression occurred. But in his dissent, Justice William O. Douglas accused the majority of Issue Suppression, saying "the Court once again, as earlier in *Procunier* v. *Martinez* (1974), sidesteps the issue of the First Amendment rights of prisoners to send and receive mail."[33] Yet since petitioners did not raise that issue, Issue Suppression as we have defined it cannot be attributed to such "sidestepping." Indeed, a better interpretation would be that this represents Douglas's attempt to expand the issue beyond the inquiry posed on certiorari.

While Issue Suppression is not identified in *Wolff*, numerous instances of Issue Discovery are found. The magnitude of the issue expansion which occurred in this case can be appreciated by merely stating six rulings of the Court which go beyond the questions originally framed in the case. From these holdings one can easily infer the questions added for consideration and resolution. The "discovered" rulings include the following: (1) An inmate in a disciplinary hearing to determine reduction or loss of good time credits must be given a written notice of charges at least twenty-four hours prior to appearance. (2) A written statement as to the evidence relied on and the reasons for the disciplinary hearing must be provided by the fact finders. (3) The inmate has no constitutional right to confrontation and cross examination of witnesses. (4) A lawyer desiring to correspond with a prisoner may be required to first identify himself and his client to prison officials. (5) The adjustment committee is sufficiently impartial to satisfy due process requirements. (6) Under certain circumstances, an inmate in a disciplinary hearing must be allowed to call witnesses and present evidence in his behalf.

The extent to which the discovery of issues in this case represented judicial activism pure and simple is readily appreciated when one notes that the procedures imposed on prison disciplinary hearings by the Court rulings are taken, by and large, from procedures established earlier in *Morrissey* v. *Brewer*[34] and *Gagnon* v. *Scarpelli*.[35] Had all the procedures from these two cases involving parole and probation proceedings been applied to prison disciplinary hearings, Issue Discovery would have occurred, but brute activism or law making would have been less in evidence. As it happens, however, the Court applied some of the *Morrissey* and *Scarpelli* rules but omitted others.

Most notable among those not applied was the right to confrontation and cross examination of witnesses. Reflecting its discretionary posture on this point, the Court remarked: "We agree with neither petitioner nor the Court of Appeals. The Nebraska procedures are in some respects constitutionally deficient but the Morrissey-Scarpelli procedures need not in all respects be followed in disciplinary cases in state prisons."[36] The Court so ruled in spite of the fact that a majority of states permit confrontation and cross examination in prison disciplinary hearings. But, showing some sensitivity to a dissent by Douglas, the Court toned down its action by saying: "Our conclusion that some, but not all of the procedures specified in *Morrissey* and *Scarpelli* must accompany the deprivation of good time by state prison officials is not graven in stone. As the nature of the prison disciplinary process changes in future years, circumstances may then exist which will require further consideration and reflection of this Court."[37] In short, the majority conceded that it was legislating and promised to legislate differently as conditions might warrant. In taking this stance the Court majority was not unduly arrogant and thus the cognomen, "Imperial Judiciary," may not be justified. However, it does indicate that judicial activism is not dead in the Burger Court.

Issue Suppression without Issue Discovery

In most cases reflecting Issue Fluidity, the Supreme Court responds to at least one of the questions raised in the jurisdictional briefs but ignores the remainder and refrains from adding any new issues of its own making. There are at least two forms of this: when the Court ignores one or more issues without giving reasons and with no reason apparent, and when a reason is self-evident or provided by the Court. The first may represent judicial activism, the second judicial restraint.

The distinction we make here may call for some clarification. Generally we have no difficulty in identifying judicial activism when a justice introduces novel concepts to reach a preferred conclusion, encroaches on the other branches of government in pursuing idiosyncratic preferences, or finds a "spirit" or "intent" in the law that appears as if from the hand of Mandrake the Magician. Conversely, a justice who sticks closely to a literal or narrow interpretation of Constitution and statute, who decides only those questions which "force" themselves on the Court, or who follows precedent with some consistency is easily labeled a practitioner of judicial restraint.

If a question in a case is ignored for sufficient reason—as when decision on one point moots the issues raised in additional arguments—the restrained Court is doing just what we expect it to do. Indeed, were it to do otherwise it would violate the understanding that goes with the label. Neither the restrained Court nor the restrained justice is expected to reach for questions even though to do so might enable the articulation of values otherwise left out of the parade.

The judicial activist, on the other hand, in the extreme case is looking for opportunities to decide, determine, or at least influence the allocation of preferred values in the political system and is, by definition, adept at finding such opportunities. That being the case it might be asked: Why should an activist ignore or suppress an issue when he has the option to do otherwise, when to speak to the question might increase his impact on the development of the law? And if he does so—is not this judicial restraint? Answers to these questions are best grasped by focusing on the reasons for restraint in the first place. It is generally assumed that the restrained justice is motivated by a belief that restraint is the proper posture for a Supreme Court justice—that such an approach is in the best interest of the political system and the Court. He is restrained by these beliefs even when such an approach leads to decisions counter to his preferred values. The example frequently given here is Felix Frankfurter. But for the justice pursuing his preferences at all costs, it makes little difference whether his interests are promoted via reaching out and deciding questions or by suppressing issues which have a legitimate claim to timely Court decision. The pushing of personal values can intrude in both instances. Consequently, when a legitimate legal question is ignored for no apparent reason, we may suspect that the skillful hand of the judicial activist is at work—at least on some occasions.

Examples of Issue Suppression for no apparent reason are abundant. Consider the case of *Williams* v. *United States*,[38] in which it was held that *Chimel* v. *California*[39] should not be applied retroactively. Here the Court affirmed the denial of relief below, but at the same time it failed to determine the legality of the arrest in the case, the search-and-seizure incident accompanying it and whether the jury had sufficient facts to make an intelligent judgment about the situation. In *Nelson* v. *O'Neill*,[40] the Court ignored the question of whether the doctrine of comity and the burden of habeas corpus petitions in the federal courts require state prisoners to exhaust state remedies before moving into the federal court system. Faced with two statutory questions in *Gelbard* v. *United States*,[41] the Court decided one and ignored the other. In *United States* v. *District Court*,[42] the inquiry as to whether illegally seized evidence must always be disclosed to a defendant was bypassed. And in *Schneckloth* v. *Bustamonte*,[43] the Court failed to rule on the habeas corpus question later decided in *Stone* v. *Powell*.[44]

In *Schneckloth* the Court concluded that it is unnecessary for a prosecutor proceeding on the basis of evidence "seized by consent" to prove that the consenting party has knowledge of his right to refuse such consent. Attorneys for California representing Schneckloth, the prison warden, asked whether a search-and-seizure question should be available to a state prisoner seeking to set aside his conviction via federal habeas corpus proceedings. The Court, for its part, simply ignored the issue. Justice Powell, however, in a concurring opinion joined by Burger and Rehnquist, saw the habeas corpus question as "the overriding issue briefed and argued in this case."[45] These three justices went on to hold that "collateral review of a state prisoner's Fourth Amendment claims—claims which rarely bear on innocence—should be confined solely to the question of whether the petitioner was provided a fair opportunity to raise and have adjudicated the question in state courts."[46] But three justices do not a majority make, and thus the question had to wait for another day.

Three years later in *Stone*, the Court again faced the question and decided it on Justice Powell's view in an opinion written by Powell. Was the Powell concurrence in *Schneckloth* an invitation to interested parties to raise the issue in subsequent litigation? We cannot know. But it is certainly possible that "invitations" such as this have something to do with work-load patterns in the Court. Ironically, in deciding *Stone* the Court ruled on the habeas corpus issue but failed to rule on the constitutionality of a local vagrancy statute— a question raised in the jurisdictional briefs.

A second class of situations in which the Court fails to rule on questions posed in the jurisdictional briefs consists of cases in which deciding one issue makes the decision of other issues unnecessary according to some policy internal to the Court. Also in this class are situations in which the rules of logic are determinative—as when answers to one or more questions make one or more other questions irrelevant. Examples of cases in this classification are *United States* v. *Mara*,[47] *United States* v. *Ortiz*,[48] and *Fisher* v. *United States*.[49]

In *Mara*, the Court held that a witness before a grand jury may be required to furnish specimens of his handwriting without violating Fourth Amendment protections, even though the government does not establish the reasonableness of the request. Given that holding, other questions that assume that reasonableness must be shown were no longer material and were justifiably ignored. In *Mara* two such questions were not addressed.

A different type of situation is encountered in *Ortiz*. In *Almeida-Sanchez* v. *United States*[50] the Supreme Court ruled that probable cause was necessary to justify vehicle searches by roving patrols of United States border officials near the Mexican border. In *Ortiz* the search was conducted over sixty miles from the border at a traffic checkpoint in Southern California. Ortiz maintained that such a search without a warrant and probable cause was illegal under *Almeida-Sanchez* and that his conviction for transporting aliens who were not in the country legally should be reversed. The federal court of appeals obliged, and the Supreme Court affirmed. But the United States (the petitioner) wanted to know whether, if *Almeida-Sanchez* were extended to cover checkpoint searches, the extension should apply to a search (as in *Ortiz*) made before any federal court had declared such a search illegal. Noting this question, the Court said: "We ... decline to consider this issue, which was raised for the first time in the petition for certiorari."[51] Indeed, the Court commented that it had examined the government's brief in the Ninth Circuit Court of Appeals and found that the government had argued that the ruling by the Ninth Circuit Court in *United States* v. *Bowen*[52] (in which dicta extended *Almeida-Sanchez* to cover a checkpoint search) would determine the issue in *Ortiz.*

A final example is *Fisher* v. *United States.*[53] There the Court declined to respond to a hypothetical question concerning whether a taxpayer, whose Fifth Amendment privileges are lost when he turns tax documents over to his attorney, would retain such rights if the documents remained in the tax-payer's possession. The Court had no difficulty holding that requiring the attorney to produce the documents violated neither the taxpayer's Fifth Amendment rights nor any rights accruing from the attorney-client privilege, whether or not different facts would have justified a different ruling.

The Disappearing Question: Issue Suppression
of a Different Sort

Sometimes the issue(s) posed by parties granted Supreme Court review "disappear" by the time the case is formally decided. Unlike cases of Issue Suppression in which either new issues are discovered or only some of the issues are suppressed, it is possible for the Court to decide a case without deciding any issue *qua* Court. This is precisely what happens when no rule or holding can attract a majority of the justices and is most likely to occur when a plurality opinion announces the judgment of the Court. In some such cases there may be no majority opinion, but various concurring opinions may agree with regard to some particular question. In that event issue response will have precedential value despite the absence of a majority opinion.

At point here are the capital punishment cases of 1976—*Gregg* v. *Georgia,*[54] *Jurek* v. *Texas,*[55] *Proffitt* v. *Florida,*[56] and *United States* v. *White.*[57] In the first three cases there were no majority opinions. Nevertheless, a majority of the justices agreed in each instance that the imposition of the death penalty was not a per se violation of the Eighth and Fourteenth Amendments and that the procedures employed in each of the three states met constitutional and case law requirements. Similarly, in *White*, in the absence of a majority opinion, five justices agreed that since the Court's decision in *Katz* v. *United States*[58] was not retroactive, the federal court of appeals erred in deciding *Katz.* Evaluating an electronic search and seizure by pre-*Katz* law, namely *On Lee* v. *United States,*[59] the same five agreed that no Fourth Amendment right was violated. At the same time no majority could be found to support the proposition that *On Lee* was or was not good law.

As candidates for "disappearing question" cases, one may suggest the 1970 decision in *Dutton* v. *Evans*[60] and the 1972 case of *Peters* v. *Kiff.*[61] In *Dutton,* four justices decided the case on Sixth Amendment "right to confrontation" grounds; four justices dissented; and one joined the judgment of the Court on Fifth Amendment due process grounds. In *Peters*, a habeas corpus proceeding, the petitioner contended that blacks were systematically excluded from the grand jury that indicted him and from the petit jury that handed down his conviction. Such exclusions, he charged, violated his Fourteenth Amendment rights to due process and equal protection of the law. While such a claim has not been unusual in recent years, it was a little out of the ordinary here since Peters was a white man. While six justices agreed that Peters had standing to make such a claim, only three thought the right involved due process. Three others found a right under statutory law. The remaining three could find no reason to rule for Peters. The effect in both cases was that five questions were accepted for Court review. None was decided. These five questions, in short, "disappeared" between initial framing and the final decision.

Issue Fluidity and the Jurisdictional Decision

By and large, the Supreme Court has complete discretion to make up its agenda of cases for full plenary review. Given that fact, it can and does control not only the selection of cases but the selection of issues within cases that will be reviewed. We have noted that once review of an issue is granted, that issue may disappear or undergo some other form of transformation by the time the Court's final judgment is made. But equally if not more important are the instances of Issue Discovery and Issue Suppression that occur in the interval between a request for review and the granting of the request.

For the period 1969 to 1976, twenty-six instances were identified in which the Court granted a request for review, but only after restructuring the issues to suit its tastes or needs. In most of these instances the issues chosen for review were limited to some number less than that for which review was requested. In about half of these cases the Court limited review to a single question. In a few cases the Court agreed to review the issues posed by the petitioner or appellant but then asked the party requesting review to brief and argue one additional issue.

As examples of cases in which the Court limited the questions to be addressed on the merits at the time it granted review, one may consider *Doyle* v. *Ohio* and *Wood* v. *Ohio*.[62] These cases involved Jeff Doyle and Dick Wood, both of whom were arrested and convicted of selling pot to a police informant. Upon arrest, both were given the *Miranda* warnings and chose to remain silent. At trial both claimed for the first time that they had been framed. The prosecutor, on cross examination, used the defendant's silence before trial to impeach the credibility of defendants' testimony at trial regarding the frame. Defendants' objections to these prosecutorial tactics were overruled by the trial judge; Ohio appellate courts affirmed.

In their applications to the Supreme Court for certiorari, attorneys for Doyle and Wood raised the following questions: (1) May an accused who remains silent before trial but claims innocence at trial be asked why he did not profess innocence earlier and why he forced authorities to get a search warrant to search his car? (2) May a prosecutor in such a situation argue to a jury that the defendant's silence prior to trial justified an inference regarding his credibility at trial? (3) Can a defense witness arrested and charged with the defendant be asked the same question as in 1? (4) When the prosecutor's case rests almost entirely on the testimony of a police informant seeking leniency on a charge pending against him, can a court refuse to caution the jury regarding the unreliability of such a witness? (5) Under obligatory disclosure rules, may the state withhold from the defense incriminating statements made by the defendant until after the defense has rested its case?

In granting review, the Supreme Court limited the questions to be addressed to the first three only. It went on to hold that petitioners' Fourteenth Amendment due process rights had been violated. One may speculate that in this situation the Court did not need all the questions originally posed on certiorari in order to find for the petitioner. But elimination of issues on such a basis would only be possible, from a logical standpoint, if the Court knew in advance what the outcome of the case would be. Not knowing that, one cannot be sure that the elimination of an issue on which the petitioner could win his case is the only issue on which he could prevail. To argue otherwise would be to suppose that the Court considered and decided the question eliminated "on the merits."

On the other side—instances in which the Court expanded the issues—*Wolff* v. *Rice* and *Stone* v. *Powell* are illustrative. Like the two cases discussed above, *Wolff* and *Stone* were consolidated for decision. David Rice and Loyd Powell were convicted for murder in the state of Ohio. Their convictions depended heavily on evidence seized without a warrant in the case of Powell and with a warrant in the case of Rice. Both, after losing attempts to suppress the evidence in state courts, sued out on a writ of habeas corpus to a federal district court. In each case the federal court of appeals found the seizures illegal. California and Nebraska, granted certiorari by the Supreme Court, raised nine different issues.

One might think that such a long list of questions would provide sufficient grounds for a Supreme Court decision in these cases. Some courts consider it bad practice to submit so many issues in a case. Indeed, in the Second Circuit Court of Appeals, it is now formal procedure for staff attorneys to meet with counsel to get the lawyers in a case to simplify the issues prior to oral argument. Reflecting on this, Justice Clark once remarked: "It is amazing the number of points these people raise. They raise eight and ten points in a case. Well, you know as well as I do that there are not that many points that are of a reversible nature that would require reversal. They could narrow them down."[63]

A clerk to Justice Powell has similarly written that one of the most aggravating frustrations encountered in petitions for certiorari was "where counsel, often without a single significant question to raise, would throw in six or seven frivolous ones. I felt that this was not only an abuse of the judicial process but a disservice to the client as well."[64] This has been referred to by Thomas B. Marvel as the "shotgun, buckshot, bird shot, scatter shot, or garbage can approach."[65] Marvel reports that some judges think half the issues raised on appeal should not be raised at all and that such a bird-shot approach is very unpopular with judges.

Given all this, one might expect the Supreme Court to be looking primarily for ways to reduce the number of issues. Yet in *Wolff* and *Stone*, after perusing the nine issues raised by petitioners, the Court asked the parties to brief and argue an additional issue. In *Stone* the new question was whether, in view of the facts that police had probable cause to arrest Rice for violating an ordinance that had not been declared unconstitutional at the time, and that a seized murder weapon was obtained in a search incident to an arrest, a claim that Rice's Fourth Amendment rights had been violated was cognizable under 28 U.S.C. at 2254. In *Wolff*, the new question was whether the constitutionality of the entry and search in the circumstances of the case was cognizable under the same section.

The Court's request for additional advice in these cases strongly suggests that it wished to use the cases as vehicles for a major policy innovation. Such an activist inference is particularly urged when one considers the many grounds presented for decision by petitioners, the bias of most courts against high multiple-issue arguments, and the work load of the Supreme Court itself. Moreover, by permitting the petitioners to argue orally the points raised in the petition for certiorari, the Court might have camouflaged its true intention. But given the fact that prior to *Wolff* and *Stone*, similarly situated petitioners had been allowed to proceed under 28 U.S.C. sect. 2254, one's suspicions justifiably might have been raised by the new questions posed by the Court for argument. Section 2254, as it turns out, is a federal statutory provision governing the conditions under which an application for a writ of habeas corpus, on behalf of a prisoner in state custody, may be entertained by a federal court. The statute requires exhaustion of state remedies, but in no way before *Wolff* and *Stone* was it interpreted to mean that a search-and-seizure issue is *res judicata* once decided in a state court.[66]

Double Issue Fluidity

Double Issue Fluidity refers to situations in which the Court engages in Issue Discovery or Issue Suppression when granting review and then proceeds to engage in some further *Issue Modification* in finally deciding the case. *Wolff* and *Stone* fall into this category, since the Court permitted briefing and oral argument on all the issues raised by petitioners, added a question in granting review, but then ruled on a single issue: When the state has provided a full and fair hearing on a Fourth Amendment claim, may a state prisoner be granted habeas corpus relying on the ground that evidence seized in violation of the Fourth Amendment was introduced at trial? In spite of this Double Issue Fluidity, no justice raised any question about it. This contrasts with situations in which Issue Fluidity at one or two levels leads to discussions by concurring or dissenting justices on the discrepancies or to vigorous argument on issues suppressed or ignored.[67] This suggests the possibility that objection to Issue Fluidity by concurring or dissenting justices may depend on ideological considerations and case results rather than judicial role factors involving activism and restraint.

While *Wolff* and *Stone* illustrate instances in which Issue Discovery occurred in the jurisdictional decision and Issue Suppression in decision after plenary review, other combinations are observable. In *Spinelli* v. *United States*,[68] the Court limited review to a single question. Although Spinelli thought he had three issues worthy of consideration, the Court agreed to decide only the constitutionality of a search and seizure. Having done so, the Court then went on to decide whether a search warrant was issued on probable cause. Since the Fourth Amendment requires probable cause for the issuance of a search warrant, one might infer a constitutional violation here. But the opinions by both the majority and the dissenting justices were significantly devoid of constitutional references.

A more clear-cut example may be found in *Brooks* v. *Tennessee*,[69] a case in which the Court chose two of four questions presented by petitioner Brooks and limited review to those two questions. Under Tennessee law a criminal defendant who wishes to testify must do so before any other testimony for the defense is heard. This is supposed to minimize any motivation a defendant may have to take the stand at a later stage and equivocate. Brooks was denied the right to testify at a later point in his trial and was convicted of armed robbery and associated charges. Tennessee courts affirmed, and the Supreme Court granted certiorari.

On the merits, the Court found a violation of Brooks's Fifth Amendment rights against self incrimination—one of the issues that the Court had accepted for review. At the same time it ignored a second issue it had agreed to consider—whether Tennessee law on the point violated the state constitution. This might be excused on the ground that decision on the federal constitutional question made a ruling on the Tennessee constitution superfluous insofar as the disposition of the case was concerned. However, one might ask why a deletion was not made in the limited grant of review.

Assuming that none of this represents Double Issue Fluidity, the phenomenon is still evident in *Brooks*, for the Court went on to hold that Brooks was denied his right to counsel. This is an unusually interesting ruling since Brooks had the service of counsel throughout his trial. The counsel issue was reached by reasoning that if Tennessee law determines when a defendant may testify, the defendant is deprived of acting on the tactical advice of his counsel as to when to testify. The dissenting justices pointed out that the "guiding hand of counsel" (the majority's phrase) is restricted in any number of ways at trial. Yet, they argued, such restrictions are not unconstitutional per se. The Court, they asserted, failed to distinguish the application of the rule enunciated in *Brooks* from its application in other situations. Indeed, they noted, the "unspoken basis for the Court's decision" is "that in the majority's view the Tennessee rule is invalid because it is followed presently by only two states in our federal system."[70] On balance, the dissenters saw new law being made in *Brooks*. But, be that as it may, Double Issue Fluidity is clearly evident in the case.

Factors Possibly Associated with Issue Fluidity

Up to this point we have suggested that Issue Fluidity is a significant phenomenon in Supreme Court decision making, that it takes on a number of different forms, and that it occurs with some frequency. We have not, of course, exhaustively examined the use of the Court's discretion in making up its agendas. But we hope we have shown that the Court's Issue-Action Agenda is not merely a function of selecting cases for review. The conditions under which review is granted and the fluidity of issues after case selection but before final decision must also claim our attention.

Having said all this, we have not yet explained Issue Fluidity, that is, why it does or does not occur across the cases selected for a full hearing. Nor do we propose to do so in this chapter. What we shall do is indicate several factors or conditions possibly associated with Issue Fluidity—factors one might wish to consider in constructing a theory of Issue Fluidity. It goes without saying that the mere selection of such factors implies some kind of theoretical thinking. That we do not deny. Nor do we rule out incompatible theoretical propositions at this stage of our investigation. Openness, not closure, must be the rule at this point.

Prestige of Lower Courts

It is well known that the Supreme Court does not view all courts below as equal in the quality of their judgments. This is reflected in reversal rates and in the Court's decisions to grant or deny formal review. Justice Felix Frankfurter once observed that in a given case, the view might be that "we can't do any better [with this question] than Judge Julian Mack . . . did below. He really knows more about this field of law than the rest of us."[71] Thus, review should be denied. Another aspect of prestige involves the level of the court immediately below. State courts are less prestigious than federal courts and federal district courts are less prestigious than federal courts of appeals. Relating such considerations to Issue Fluidity, the Supreme Court might be expected to modify the issues posed by litigants more or less frequently depending on whether the errors are alleged against a high or low prestige court.

Constitutional and Statutory Issues

The assumption here is that constitutional issues are more likely than statutory issues to be fluid. This follows from the fact that constitutional provisions under which issues are framed are in many cases more ambiguous, more general as reference points than state or federal statutes. The more ambiguous the reference point, the greater the leeway in framing an issue for resolution. Thus issue modification should occur more frequently in cases involving constitutional questions.

Number of Questions Raised

Other things being equal, one may suspect that the larger the number of questions posed by the parties, the more likely the Court will be to contract or suppress one or more issues. Frequently the Court needs to decide, and in fact does decide, only a single issue to dispose of a case. Attorneys are sometimes motivated to pose as many questions as possible in the hope that the Court will decide favorably on at least one of them. It is not clear, however, whether this is always the best strategy. As the number of questions increases, so does the probability that the Court will pick one issue on which it looks favorably, but the obverse may also be true. In any event, one may hypothesize that the larger the number of questions sent forward, the larger the number that will not be chosen for resolution, that is, the greater will be the degree of Issue Suppression.

Jurisdiction

We do not know just how comfortable the Court feels with Issue Fluidity. Modification of issues posed by the parties could create cognitive dissonance for the justices, psychological tension resulting from a conflict in two or more values to which the justice subscribes. Such dissonance or role discomfort may be less in certiorari cases than in cases coming up under the Court's appeals jurisdiction. This expectation is based on the fact that certiorari jurisdiction is entirely discretionary. Since Issue Modification is to some extent discretionary, to engage in it in certiorari cases may seem less like a departure from the judicial role than in appeals cases where the jurisdiction is mandated by Congress. In saying this, one should not overlook the fact that both types of jurisdiction are treated in much the same way in the modern Supreme Court. But the technical distinction may still have some meaning for the justices at a psychological level.

Litigant Status

If the Court would like to promote the interests of a client litigant, it may do so not only by granting requests for formal review emanating from such clients, but also by modifying issues in such a way as to benefit the client either at the jurisdictional or formal stage of decision. This possibility is indicated by our knowledge that in certain periods the Court has ruled more frequently for some litigant classes than for others.[72]

Issue Complexity in the Jurisdictional Agenda

Issue Complexity may be important in at least two ways. When a social question of great significance cries for resolution but no case raises the issue appropriately, an issue posed in a less satisfactory manner may be modified by the Supreme Court to suit the occasion. A related matter is *Issue Complexity* in the overall case pool. If the Court, through lack of a sufficient number of cases in a subject area, is getting less of a variety of issues than it deems essential to its function, it may use Issue Fluidity in a smaller number of cases to increase the Issue Complexity which characterizes the Jurisdictional Agenda. For example, if in a given term the Court receives twenty right-to-counsel cases and five search-and-seizure cases, Issue Complexity might be sufficient in the former but insufficient in the latter. One possible response would be to enhance Issue Complexity in search-and-seizure cases via Issue Fluidity. This can be related to the Court's role in the sociopolitical system. The Court may make a major contribution to social stability when the issues it selects for review are representative of those issues which the American public finds more than casually burdensome or in need of resolution—issues for which resolution has not been forthcoming from other branches of government. If, whatever the reasons, a fair representation of such issues does not present itself, the Court may upgrade the representativeness of the issue pool via Issue Transformation.

Propensities of Individual Justices

It is possible that Issue Fluidity is used by particular justices to reduce cognitive dissonance. We have alluded to this possibility in commenting on jurisdiction, but the matter is considerably broader than that. For instance, the mere necessity to respond to a particular question in some kind of definitive fashion may create significant cognitive dissonance. This is most likely to happen when the Court is called upon to make a choice between two sets of values—both of which it holds dear—and where the choice is of the winner-take-all variety.

A prime illustration of this kind of problem, one might argue, is a case raising questions of reverse discrimination. It is difficult in such cases for the Court to benefit both blacks and whites. Yet cognitive dissonance may be reduced through Issue Modification by declaring the issue moot, as in *DeFunis* v. *Odegaard*,[73] or by posing the issue in such a way that it is difficult to ascertain just what specific issue has been definitively addressed, as in *Regents of the University of California* v. *Bakke*.[74] Cognitive dissonance might also be reduced in such a situation by transforming the issue into one which does not raise questions of reverse discrimination.

It is also possible that the role perception of a justice toward activism or restraint will influence his willingness to depart from the issues as posed by the litigants in a case. One may find, for example, that some justices almost always respond to the issues as originally posed, while others do not. Assuming that the cognitive dissonance created by the need to respond to some issue, or role perception, varies across justices and issues, one might predict that Issue Modification will vary with Court composition.

Experience of the Court

Courts can be classified as "older" or "younger" by the average age of their justices or by the average length of service of its members. On the assumption that older Courts will be bolder in departing from a judicial role of restraint, Issue Fluidity may be observed more frequently in older than in younger Courts. The consideration here is similar to the Snyder hypothesis that new justices require some experience before developing a high degree of self-confidence.[75]

Majority Maintenance

Other things being equal, Issue Fluidity seems more likely to be observed in marginal cases, with five-to-four or four-to-three votes than in nonmarginal cases. In the marginal case the majority must be careful to maintain the support of all members in the majority. One way of doing this is to frame the issue decided so as to satisfy all. If the issue is not so framed initially, Issue Modification may be essential.

Precedent and Caseload Considerations

On occasion the Supreme Court may feel the need to establish a precedent to cover a large number of detailed questions being posed in the lower courts. Should no case coming to it present the issue in sufficiently broad terms, Issue Transformation may occur. This consideration also relates to case load in that the Court might head off large numbers of cases likely to reach it by framing and deciding an issue in such a way as to establish a broad precedent applicable to cases percolating in the lower courts or being readied for the "launching pad."

External Threats to the Court

If a president threatens to "pack" the Court or if other external threats to the Court's integrity occur, a policy turnaround may be indicated. In that event the Court may exploit Issue Fluidity to make its retreat. It would be useful to examine the cases involved in earlier Court turnarounds to see whether Issue Fluidity was evident in such cases.

Minimizing Ego Damage

No lower court judge enjoys being reversed. When the Supreme Court feels it necessary to reverse a lower court judge, it may be less bruising to the judge's ego if the reversal is based on a misperception of the issue rather than on a failure of a legal craftsman to apply facts correctly to law.

"Sound Technical Reasons"

Issue Fluidity may be observed when sound technical reasons for Issue Transformation are present. Such reasons might include the following: (1) when the issue raised in the request for review should have been but was not raised or argued in the lower court? (2) when decision on one or more grounds obviates the necessity of addressing other grounds presented; (3) when the case is decided on statutory grounds, thereby alleviating any need to address a constitutional question; (4) when the legal questions are declared moot; (5) when legal remedies in a case have not been exhausted in the lower courts; (6) when an issue is a factual one for decision at trial. These are basically reasons for Issue Suppression where the Court, for "sound technical reasons", declines to respond to an issue raised by a litigant.

"Sound Substantive Reasons"

These would be reasons for Issue Transformation or Issue Suppression where the judgment of the Court on a substantive legal question is made. They would, at the least, include the following: (1) absence of a valid statutory or constitutional claim for relief; (2) where the error below benefits the now complaining party; (3) where controlling precedents have been misperceived by the complainant; (4) to correct misperceptions in the lower court(s); (5) where other cases have addressed the issue sufficiently.

Multiple Cases

Frequently the Court will decide a mulitple set of cases with a single opinion. This usually requires some restructuring or summarizing of the questions presented. In the process, Issue Fluidity is present, and Issue Transformation occurs.

Specific Litigant Requests

When a petitioner or respondent asks for Issue Modification and convinces the Court to engage in such modification, whatever the reason, Issue Fluidity is observed.[76]

Nested Ducking

On occasion the Court may wish to sidestep an issue but nest the "ducking" in a decisional setting which obscures or does not call attention to the action. Issue Transformation is one means of such obscuration.

Misperception

Consistent with Howard's research reported earlier,[77] good faith misperception is always a possible cause of Issue Fluidity.

Justice in a Case

Roscoe Pound has written that in no legal system is justice administered "wholly by rule and without any recourse to the will of the judge and his personal sense of what should be done to achieve a just result in the case before him."[78] Certainly Issue Fluidity may be observed in situations in which the judge thinks justice is better served by responding to some modification of the issue originally framed in the case.

An Exception to Mootness

Where an issue is clearly moot, but the Court believes the issue is a recurring one, it may be decided even though not framed for resolution by the petitioning or appealing party.

Oral Argument

The Court could possibly be persuaded to address an issue not posed in the jurisdictional briefs but brought up for the first time in oral argument.[79] An attorney engaging in such a practice, however, should be prepared to take a bit of flak from the justices, since they are known to frown on such a practice. Their ire is likely to be raised to the greatest heights when the issue was available below but "saved" by the attorney in order to defeat the major assumption of the adversary process.

Plain Error

Under the so-called plain error rule, [Supreme Court Rule 34 (1)(a)], the Court may notice a plain error not presented by the parties, thereby "discovering" new issues to decide. The problem, of course, is to know when a plain error will be observed and when it will be ignored. Moreover, even when an error is plain, rebriefing or supplementary briefing could be required—thereby obviating the necessity of deciding issues not argued by the parties.

Time

Time is a possible reason for Issue Suppression. The Court may be reluctant to discover new issues given the time restraints in which it functions. On the other hand, time might be saved, on occasion, if discovering and deciding an issue not raised will discourage future litigation.

Consequences of Avoiding Issue Fluidity

Other than considerations of time, the Court might be influenced to find and decide an issue not presented by the parties or discouraged from suppressing an argued issue when the consequences for a litigant are likely to be dire. It is for that reason that Issue Fluidity is more likely to be observed in criminal than in civil cases.[80]

Some Possible Consequences of Issue Fluidity

Certain consequences may be associated with the factors previously outlined. If the level of a court in the judicial hierarchy is an operative variable in Issue Fluidity, trial and lower appellate courts may be encouraged to increase their care in framing issues for resolution. If constitutional issues are more likely than statutory ones to be fluid, litigants may be encouraged to pursue the statutory remedy where that option is available. Attorneys deciding how many questions to raise in particular cases may be encouraged to reduce the number in order to enhance the probability that the Court will address the preferred issue.

A litigating party may be motivated to frame broad or narrow questions depending on observed tendencies in the Court. Thus, if the Court seems inclined to decide civil liberty issues for claimants, such claims might be posed in the broadest possible fashion. On the other hand, should the Court seem inclined in the other direction, the claimant may decide to offer the narrowest question he can frame. This matter becomes more complex, however, if Issue Fluidity is a frequent factor in such cases. One would then have to consider not only the probable direction of the Court but also whether the Court is likely to engage in Issue Transformation. One possible set of strategies which takes both elements into account is depicted in table 13-1.

Assuming that issues of concern can be framed objectively, inflated, or deflated, table 13-1 depicts the strategies indicated under varying combinations of conditions. If the Court shows a tendency to support civil liberty claims, and to discover claims not posed, the pro-civil liberty claimant might feel safe in presenting his issues as objectively as possible. The same strategy is suggested if the Court can be relied on to confront and decide the issues as presented. On the other hand, if a pro-civil liberty Court is inclined to suppress issues with any frequency at all, the pro-civil liberty claimant would be well advised to inflate the issues of concern to improve the chances that those issues will remain viable after Issue Suppression has taken its toll.

For anti-civil liberty Courts, the pro-civil liberty claimant should follow identical strategies across the board—that is, he should deflate his issues in each case as much as possible. Any suppression at the hands of the Court can only benefit such a claimant by minimizing his losses. At the same time, party deflation of issues might reduce Issue Suppression at the hands of the Court, thereby shifting the suppression process from Court to party control.

Do parties ever behave consistently with the kinds of considerations discussed here? It is known that the American Civil Liberties Union framed broad questions for the Warren Court but is now framing issues more narrowly for the Court headed by Chief Justice Burger.[81] The difference in the chosen strategies merely takes into account the fact that the Warren Court usually supported civil liberty claims to a greater degree than the Burger Court. This speaks primarily to the breadth or narrowness of the issues presented rather

Table 13-1
Court Tendencies toward Issue Fluidity

		Tends to Discover Issue	Tends to Confront Issues as Posed	Tends to Suppress Issues
Court tendencies toward civil liberty claims	Pro	Objective Framing	Objective Framing	Inflated Framing
	Con	Deflated Framing	Deflated Framing	Deflated Framing

than to the number of issues put forward, but it also suggests that organizations frequently litigating in the Supreme Court are not insensitive to the theoretical dimensions of issue formulation.

Table 13-1, of course, does not set out all possible strategic considerations. For example, when a litigant does not merely seek support for a claim but wants validation of a rule of law at some predetermined level of generality, the level of abstraction at which an issue should be framed within the context of table 13-1 cannot be ascertained. Since a general question is made more specific by adding restricting terms and a narrow issue more general by deleting terms, any question posed which is more or less general than the rule being sought leaves open and unpredictable the specific terms the Court might add or delete.

Other system consequences have to do with increasing or decreasing confidence in the Court or respect for the legal system. If Issue Fluidity is a function of the need to increase Issue Complexity, confidence in the Court should be enhanced. Producing needed precedents via Issue Fluidity should also increase the respect for the Court among lower court judges and in the legal profession generally. Reversals via Issue Transformation may be expected to have similar effects. And if Issue Fluidity occurs for sound technical or substantive reasons, approval from the bench and the bar should be forthcoming. By comparison, should Issue Fluidity be associated with external threats to the Court, respect for the institution as an independent arbiter in the system may be undermined. Associating Issue Fluidity with the characteristics of the justices or majority maintenance might also disturb those who believe that Supreme Court justices should be black-robed automatons who give no thought to social goals and the strategies by which goals are obtained.

Issue Fluidity could, under certain conditions, lead to an increase in the work load of the Court. This seems likely where the Court is deciding multiple cases in a single opinion. In such a situation the Court may not be able to frame a general question that adequately reflects the interests of all litigants in the cases. Likewise, if one party in a case convinces the Court to modify the issues in the case, the opposing party may not feel that the modified issue serves his interest. In both instances additional litigation may result. Broadening an issue, on the other hand, could either increase or decrease litigation in the system. Should a broad precedent resolve a large number of issues developing in the system, litigation should decline. However, should the broadening of the issue affect interests not encompassed in the issue as originally framed, such interests may commence litigation, thereby increasing case load.

The suppression of issues for review could also impose unnecessary costs on the legal system. If an attorney researches and presents a question in his jurisdictional brief, and the question is not accepted for review, a poor use of legal resources has occurred. The waste is even greater, of course, if the Court accepts a question, permits it to be argued orally, but fails to place the question on its Issue-Action Agenda. Parenthetically, any such unnecessary uses of lawyer time can only increase the cost of legal services to litigants.

Finally, the consequence of dissonance reduction via Issue Fluidity, Issue Transformation, or Issue Suppression should have the effect of reducing the number of written opinions in the Court. This would be expected if, as has been argued, opinion writing is a means of reducing the cognitive dissonance associated with making decisions in Supreme Court cases.

Testing Relationships

The quantification and testing of relationships among variables has not been the aim of the conceptual analysis presented here. Yet the concepts and linkages we have suggested are susceptible to empirical assessment. By way of illustration, we offer three hypotheses—each of which is evaluated with data derived from the 159 criminal cases we have examined.

Hypothesis 1: The larger the number of questions presented by a petitioning or appealing party, the greater the probability that Issue Fluidity will be observed in a given case.

The relationship revealed in table 13-2 is perfectly consistent with Hypothesis 1 in that as the number of questions posed increases, the percentage of cases in which Issue Fluidity is found increases from a low of 17.4 percent for one-issue cases to 100 percent for five-issue cases. The array in table 13-2 is statistically significant at about .0002 using chi-square and even more significant if other measures of association are employed. We may, therefore, accept the hypothesized relationship.

Hypothesis 2: Issue Fluidity is more likely to occur in cases coming under the Supreme Court's discretionary jurisdiction (certiorari) than in cases coming under the Court's obligatory jurisdiction (appeals).

Table 13-2

Issue Fluidity as a Function of Number of Questions Posed for Review

	Number of Questions				
	1	*2*	*3*	*4*	*5*
Issue Fluidity	15	21	10	5	1
No Issue Fluidity	71	25	8	3	0

Table 13-3 is consistent with its associated hypothesis but somewhat less so than table 13-2. The probability of being in error if we accept Hypothesis 2 is less than .12. Nevertheless, at this exploratory level of analysis, we should not yet discard jurisdictional class as a possible factor in explaining Issue Fluidity.

In granting requests for plenary review, we have found that some Supreme Court justices—as well as the Court itself—distinguish parties requesting review by their sociopolitical status. Tanenhaus and his associates have shown that in certain periods the Court is more likely to grant review to the federal government than to other requesting parties.[82] In a recent paper we have established that some justices are more likely to honor the requests of sociopolitical Underdogs than the petitions of sociopolitical Upperdogs.[83] In that work, Underdogs were defined as labor unions, minority group members, employees, individuals, aliens, and criminal suspects; Upperdogs as federal, state, or local government, and business corporations. These categories were taken from earlier work by Eloise Snyder[84] showing that the Court, in deciding cases on the merits over a thirty-year period, favored "superior litigants" over "inferior litigants"—these concepts being defined in social status terms.

Hypothesis 3: The Court is more likely to transform or otherwise operate on issues posed by petitioning or appealing parties when the parties are Underdogs than when they are Upperdogs.

The array in table 13-4 is significant at the .02 level and is quite consistent with Hypothesis 3—at least insofar as the cases we have examined are concerned. These results are not couched in any single theoretical framework. They should be viewed only as evidence for the proposition that empirical testing of the kind of relationships discussed in this chapter is feasible.

Conclusions

In this chapter we have established that Issue Fluidity is a significant phenomenon frequently observed at the level of the United States Supreme Court—especially in the decisions the Court makes in composing its Plenary Case and

Table 13-3

Issue Fluidity as a Function of Jurisdictional Authority

	Certiorari	*Appeals*
Issue Fluidity	50	2
No Issue Fluidity	95	12

Table 13-4

Issue Fluidity as a Function of the Social Class of Petitioning and Appealing Parties

	Underdogs	*Upperdogs*
Issue Fluidity	36	16
No Issue Fluidity	53	54

Issue-Action Agendas. It is a phenomenon with important consequences for the institutional role of the Court and an integral part of the Court's policy-making role. Therefore, it is a matter worthy of further study.

No attempt has been made to state and test a theory since we have first sought to identify the research problem and get some sense of its contours. This exploration strongly suggests that investigation into these matters should be pursued with an eye toward theory development. Certain variables with possible explanatory power have been noted. One may wish to use one or more of these factors in theory construction, but the list is by no means exhaustive.[85] The challenge is to formulate a theory which will be subject to empirical testing. All the variables discussed in this chapter are not equally quantifiable. Some may call for information which simply cannot be obtained, but in most cases adequate quantification is feasible. The major hurdle, therefore, is of another and more difficult kind—namely, to identify a coherent set of factors that not only explain a significant portion of the variation in Issue Fluidity but also meet threshold requirements of plausibility.

It is evident that one can more effectively identify instances of activism and restraint by considering the disparities between what the Court is asked to do by the parties in a case and what it actually does. The Court is less likely to be charged with judicial activism if it accepts for review the precise and legitimate questions posed by the parties, decides those issues and nothing more. By contrast, the failure to decide one or more questions legitimately posed by the parties (Issue Suppression) or the reaching out to decide questions neither posed nor argued (Issue Discovery) are frequent indicators of judicial activism. Such activities, when observed at the level of the Jurisdictional Agenda, may also telegraph approaching policy innovations of a substantial nature. Thus, from a number of perspectives, increased attention to Issue Fluidity can only enhance our awareness and understanding of the Court's policy making role and the constantly intermingling tendencies toward activism and restraint which inform that role.

Notes

1. Donald L. Horowitz, *The Courts and Social Policy* (Washington: The Brookings Institution, 1977), p. 22.

2. See Charles M. Lamb, "Judicial Policy-Making and Information Flow to the Supreme Court," *Vanderbilt Law Review* 29 (January 1976): 45-124.

3. 1 Cranch 137 (1803).

4. 6 Wheaton 264 (1812).

5. Alexander M. Bickel, *The Least Dangerous Branch: The Supreme Court at the Bar of Politics* (Indianapolis: Bobbs-Merrill, 1962).

6. Henry J. Abraham, *The Judicial Process: An Introductory Analysis of the Courts in the United States, England, and France*, 4th ed. (New York: Oxford University Press, 1980).

7. A recent example is found in *Quern v. Jordan*, 435 U.S. 904 (1977). There, Justice Brennan accused the Court of "reaching out" to decide a question (is the state a person for purposes of the Civil Rights Act of 1871?) not necessary to decide the case. The issue was neither briefed nor argued by the parties, and thus the Court had not had the assistance of a considered presentation of the issue. Brennan and Marshall both thought this "pure judicial fiat." The Brennan-Marshall charge was supported by the fact that both parties in the case stipulated that this question was *not* the issue framed by the case.

8. See Sheldon Goldman, "In Defense of Justice: Some Thoughts on Reading Professor Mendelson's 'Mr. Justice Douglas and Government by the Judiciary'," *Journal of Politics* 39 (February 1977): 148-158.

9. See Raoul Berger, *Government by Judiciary: The Transformation of the Fourteenth Amendment* (Cambridge: Harvard University Press, 1977).

10. 47 LW 4851 (1979).

11. Ibid., p. 4853.

12. Ibid., p. 4855.

13. Ibid., p. 4857.

14. Harold J. Spaeth, *Supreme Court Policy Making: Explanation and Prediction* (San Francisco: W.H. Freeman, 1979), pp. 30-51.

15. Stephen Wasby refers to this as "skimming off" via denial of review and summary dispositions. Stephen L. Wasby, *The Supreme Court in the Federal Judicial System* (New York: Holt, Rinehart and Winston, 1978), pp. 143-158. Or as stated elsewhere, the "justices can reach or avoid issues in varying degrees with varying degrees of visibility." Stephen L. Wasby, Anthony D'Amato, and Rosemary Metrailer, *Desegregation from Brown to Alexander* (Carbondale, Ill.: Southern Illinois University Press, 1977), p. 19.

16. *Estate of Rogers v. Commission*, 320 U.S. 410, 413 (1943).

17. Gregory J. Rathjen and Harold J. Spaeth, "Access to the Federal Courts: An Analysis of Burger Court Policy Making," *American Journal of Political Science* 23 (May 1979): 360-382.

18. See S. Sidney Ulmer, "Researching the Supreme Court in a Democratic Pluralist System: Some Thoughts on New Directions," *Law and Policy Quarterly* 1 (January 1979): 53-80, S. Sidney Ulmer, "Unseen Faces of Power: Conflict Management in the U.S. Supreme Court," (ms.). See also Richard J. Richardson and Kenneth N. Vines, "Review, Dissent, and the Appellate Process: A Political Interpretation," *Journal of Politics* 29 (August 1967): 597-616; J. Woodford Howard, Jr., "On the Fluidity of Judicial Choice," *American Political Science Review* 62 (March 1968): 43-56.

19. *U.S. Law Week* is the best-known publication providing this service. *The National Law Journal* also reports such information, though not in the exhaustive fashion that characterizes the *U.S. Law Week* service.

20. For recent analyses of the way a state court deals with applications for review and some theoretical propositions with possible applicability to the U.S. Supreme Court, see Lawrence Baum, "Judicial Demand—Screening and Decisions on the Merits," *American Politics Quarterly* 7 (January 1979): 109-119; Lawrence Baum, "Policy Goals in Judicial Gatekeeping: A Proximity Model of Discretionary Justice," *American Journal of Political Science* 21 (February 1977): 13-35.

21. Richardson and Vines, "Review, Dissent, and the Appellate Process."

22. Jonathan D. Casper, "The Supreme Court and National Policy Making," *American Political Science Review* 70 (March 1976): 50-63.

23. 304 U.S. 64 (1938).

24. 367 U.S. 643 (1961).

25. Some other examples include *Parker v. Brown*, 316 U.S. 656 (1942); *Price v. Georgia*, 395 U.S. 975 (1969); *O'Shea v. Littleton*, 414 U.S. 448 (1974); *Vachon v. New Hampshire*, 414 U.S. 478 (1974); *Mayor v. League*, 415 U.S. 605 (1974); *Fuller v. Oregon*, 417 U.S. 40 (1974); *Crist v. Cline*, 46 L.W. 4639 (1977); *New Jersey v. Portash*, 47 L.W. 4271 (1979); and *Oscar Mayer v. Evans*, 47 L.W. 4569 (1979). See also the discussion of *New York Times v. Sullivan*, 376 U.S. 254 (1964), *Roe v. Wade*, 410 U.S. 113 (1973), and *Doe v. Bolton*, 410 U.S. 179 (1973) in Lamb, "Judicial Policy-Making and Information Flow to the Supreme Court," pp. 48-74.

26. Congressional Quarterly, *The Supreme Court: Justice and the Law* Washington: Congressional Quarterly Inc., 1977), pp. 68–81.

27. 394 U.S. 244 (1969).

28. 18 U.S.C. sect. 1201(a).

29. 390 U.S. 570 (1968).

30. *Brady v. United States*, 397 U.S. 742 (1970).

31. 389 U.S. 347 (1967).

32. 418 U.S. 539 (1974).

33. 418 U.S. 539, 601 (1974).

34. 408 U.S. 471 (1972).

35. 411 U.S. 778 (1973).

36. 418 U.S. 539 (1974).

37. 418 U.S. 539, 571 (1974).

38. 401 U.S. 646 (1971).

39. 395 U.S. 752 (1969).

40. 402 U.S. 622 (1971).

41. 408 U.S. 41 (1972).

42. 497 U.S. 297 (1972).

43. 412 U.S. 218 (1973).

44. 428 U.S. 465 (1976). The case of *Wolff v. Rice* was consolidated with *Stone v. Powell*.

45. 412 U.S. 218, 250 (1973).

46. Ibid.

47. 410 U.S. 19 (1973).

48. 422 U.S. 891 (1975).

49. 425 U.S. 391 (1976).

50. 413 U.S. 266 (1973).

51. 422 U.S. 891 (1975).

52. 500 F.2d 960 (1974).

53. 425 U.S. 391 (1976).

54. 428 U.S. 153 (1976).

55. 428 U.S. 262 (1976).

56. 428 U.S. 242 (1976).

57. 401 U.S. 745 (1971).

58. 389 U.S. 347 (1967).

59. 343 U.S. 747 (1952).

60. 400 U.S. 74 (1970).

61. 407 U.S. 493 (1972).

62. *Doyle* and *Wood* were consolidated as 426 U.S. 610 (1976).

63. Thomas B. Marvel, *Appellate Courts and Lawyers* (Westport, Conn.: Greenwood Press, 1978), p. 330.

64. J. Harvie Wilkinson, III, *Serving Justice: A Supreme Court Clerk's View* (New York: Charterhouse, 1974), p. 30.

65. Marvel, *Appellate Courts and Lawyers*, p. 126.

66. *Lebkowitz v. Newsome*, 420 U.S. 283 (1975); *Cardwell v. Lewis*, 417 U.S. 583 (1974); *Cady v. Dombrowski*, 413 U.S. 433 (1973).

67. See, for example, *Meachum v. Fano*, 427 U.S. 605 (1976); *Schneckloth v. Bustamonte*, 412 U.S. 218 (1973); *Williams v. United States*, 401 U.S. 646 (1971).

68. 393 U.S. 410 (1969).

69. 406 U.S. 605 (1972).

70. 406 U.S. 605, 616 (1972).

71. Abraham, *The Judicial Process*, p. 176.

72. S. Sidney Ulmer, "Researching the Supreme Court in a Democratic Pluralist System"; S. Sidney Ulmer, "Selecting Cases for Supreme Court Review: Litigant Status in the Warren and Burger Courts" in S. Sidney Ulmer, ed., *Courts, Law and Judicial Processes* (New York: The Free Press, 1981, pp. 284–298; Joseph Tanenhaus, Marvin Schick, Matthew Muraskin, and Daniel Rosen, "The Supreme Court's Certiorari Jurisdiction: Cue Theory," in *Judicial Decision-Making,* ed. Glendon Schubert (Glencoe, Ill.: Free Press, 1963), pp. 111–132.

73. 416 U.S. 312 (1974).

74. 438 U.S. 265 (1978).

75. Eloise Snyder, "A Quantitative Analysis of Supreme Court Opinions, 1921-1953: A Study of the Responses of an Institution Engaged in Resolving Social Conflict," (Ph.D. diss., Pennsylvania State University, 1956).

76. See Bruce J. Ennis, "ACLU Litigation Strategy," (unpublished ms.)

77. Howard, "On the Fluidity of Judicial Choice."

78. Kenneth C. Davis, *Discretionary Justice* (Urbana: University of Illinois Press, 1971), p. 19.

79. William Jenkins and Carol S. Greenwald have suggested to the author that oral argument is a possible source of motivating factors.

80. See generally Marvel, *Appellate Courts and Lawyers.*

81. Ennis, "ACLU Litigation Strategy."

82. Tanenhaus, Schick, Muraskin, and Rosen, "The Supreme Court's Certiorari Jurisdiction."

83. S. Sidney Ulmer, "Selecting Cases for Supreme Court Review," *American Political Science Review* 72 (September 1978): 902-910.

84. Synder, "A Quantitative Analysis of Supreme Court Opinions, 1921-1953."

85. See Gregory A. Caldeira, "The United States Supreme Court in Criminal Cases, 1935-1976: Alternative Models of Agenda Building" (Paper presented at the Annual Meeting of the Midwest Political Science Association, Chicago, Illinois, April 18-21, 1979).

14

Substantive Access Doctrines and Conflict Management in the U.S. Supreme Court: Reflections on Activism and Restraint

Burton Atkins and
William Taggart

The debate over judicial activism and restraint presented in this book conjures up one of those perennial issues that goes to the heart of what the proper scope and function of the Supreme Court should be in the American political system. Without wanting to diminish the intrinsic significance of that issue, we do feel that much can be gained by sidestepping the normative dimension of what the Court *ought* to do and examining instead how the expansion or contraction of judicial power relates more generally to models of political conflict and decision making. In part, this can be accomplished by transposing the emphasis from one which describes the Court's role in jurisprudential language to one that views the activism-restraint dichotomy as essentially posing the query: What role does the Supreme Court perform in managing conflict for the political system? By expanding the conceptual framework in this fashion, we can interpret the Court's function by reference to broader theories of politics. Bachrach and Baratz's notion of the "two faces of power,"[1] and Schattschneider's thesis that the exercise of power and control over policy outcomes are very much dependent upon the management of conflict by political elites,[2] emerge as two illustrative models which underscore how political power is dependent upon conflict management. For Bachrach and Baratz, agenda control and "non-decisions" become as important an instrument of decision making and power as are overt, formal decisions. For Schattschneider, the oscillating borders of conflict help fashion political outcomes, and in *The Semi-Sovereign People* he argues cogently that elite institutions establish conflict boundaries and manipulate the contagion of conflict for political purposes in a pluralist democratic system.

Although they focus upon different facets of power, Bachrach and Baratz, and Schattschneider share an interest in moving beyond formal decisions made by political institutions toward a variety of processes which effectively structure agenda setting. It would perhaps seem trivial to argue that all political institutions wield substantial power in agenda definition. This function, however, assumes particular importance within the Supreme Court, and thus is far from obvious, inasmuch as a considerable portion of its agenda setting occurs in secrecy. Not surprisingly, then, a number of political scientists over the years have shown keen interest in preliminary decision making.[3] Yet if we accept the implicit premise of these studies that what the Supreme Court elects *not to do* through certiorari discretion, like the motivations behind what it in fact does, are equally related to strategies of conflict management, we still would have examined but one element among several which affect how access to or denial of a judicial forum is related to the activist–restraint controversy. Among those not frequently treated, especially within an empirical paradigm are several substantive doctrines such as standing, ripeness, mootness, abstention, and political questions that impose additional impediments upon access to the Court. Taken together, these standards are subsumed within the concepts of justiciability and jurisdiction. They are sometimes referred to as self-imposed rules of judicial restraint since they have been developed substantively by the Court itself. Their importance rests upon the fact that the Court may elect not to decide a case regardless of the merits associated with the substantive issue unless proper party, forum, and issue requirements are established.

A prevailing, albeit sterile, interpretation in law textbooks seems to be that jurisdiction and justiciability criteria evidently follow from the case and controversy requirement of federal judicial power set forth in Article III of the Constitution.[4] Yet other literature more realistically recognizes that these rules functionally shield the Court from issues it is not yet prepared to confront or those for which the federal judiciary can apparently provide little or no relief.[5] As but one illustration, the Supreme Court's repeated refusal to grant certiorari to those cases raising the issue of the constitutionality of the Vietnam War hinted strongly that the issue turned not so much on the lack of a precise issue to resolve (that is, the president's war-making authority as commander in chief of the armed forces) but rather on the Court's dilemma that either way it decided on the merits, the Court itself might be irreparably damaged.[6]

Yet the notion of self-imposed restraint suggests, erroneously we think, that these doctrines impel the Court toward the restraint pole of the restraint-activism continuum. More likely, if we draw upon the work of Bachrach and Baratz, and Schattschneider, rules (formal and informal) that define the boundaries within which conflicts are to be resolved and which thus effectively set the agenda are two-edged swords which may be manipulated to regulate policy outcomes. Rules of access, in other words, be they procedural or substantive, are usually not value free in their effect, particularly when they are subjected to interpretation by policy-motivated political actors.

The Malleability of Justiciability

Individual events are not the stuff from which generalizations spring. Yet *Powell v. McCormack*,[7] a 1969 political question case, suggests how the meaning of access rules are very much dependent upon who does the interpreting. In this instance, it is particularly relevant because the initial appeal of the House of Representatives' decision to exclude Adam Clayton Powell from his seat in the Ninetieth Congress, after his successful election in 1966 as the representative of New York's Eighteenth Congressional District, was heard by the Court of Appeals in the District of Columbia. Warren Burger wrote the opinion for the unanimous three-judge panel. The juxtaposition of his interpretation of the elements of a political question against those offered by Earl Warren for the Supreme Court reveals how substantive jurisdictional rules overlap with the already confusing vagaries of the activism-restraint debate.

At issue in *Powell* in the Court of Appeals was an injunction sought by Representative Powell against House Speaker John McCormack and individual members of the House of Representatives, relating to passage of House Resolution 278. That resolution, which had been adopted by the first session of the Ninetieth Congress, stipulated that Powell had "repeatedly ignored the processes and authority of the Courts in the State of New York in legal proceedings"; that he had engaged in "contumacious conduct towards the court of that state" such that he was held in contempt of court; and for those and other reasons he had brought the House into disrepute, had engaged in behavior unworthy of a member, and that he should accordingly be excluded from the Ninetieth Congress. Powell alleged that House Resolution 278 violated Article I, sections 2 and 5, of the United States Constitution. The complexity of the analysis set forth by the Court of Appeals is irrelevant for our purposes except for Burger's opinion, which argued, in effect, that Powell's appeal raised "a classic political question" and that the federal courts could not provide a remedy for his allegation against the House of Representatives.[8] This conclusion relied upon the language set forth by Justice Brennan in *Baker* v. *Carr*.[9] In that case, Brennan had identified six criteria which were "prominent on the surface" of a political question case. Reviewing these standards, Burger found that Article I, section 5 of the Constitution provided a "textually demonstrable constitutional commitment of the issue" to Congress; that courts do not possess the requisite skills for fashioning a remedy by which to compel the House to seat Powell; that to compel his seating would express a "lack of respect due coordinate branches of government," and that conflicting judgments by the House and by the courts posed the potential for a rather obvious embarrassment of the kind Brennan had suggested were "symptomatic" of political questions.[10]

If this embarrassment is obvious, it is equally obvious that, like many legal doctrines, the political question rule means whatever one wishes it to mean. Because of inevitable linguistic imprecision, the political question doctrine, to use it as an illustration, is probably not a precise touchstone of justiciability and very likely is a useful instrument for policymaking masquerading as a formal gate-keeping mechanism. Language by itself cannot impose absolute clarity upon such a concept and, quite obviously, neither can the byzantine prose offered by Brennan in *Baker*. Therefore, where Burger saw a direct constitutional commitment for an internal congressional solution, Warren, writing for the Supreme Court, saw little more than a relatively obvious need for judicial interpretation of Article I, section 5. Similarly, what Burger feared as the potential undermining of judicial integrity, by imposing a decision upon a situation devoid of manageable standards, Warren envisioned as little more than a situation in which the Court should adhere to a traditional norm of constitutional conflict management. Indeed, the bugbear of judicial-congressional conflict was of little concern to Warren and should not, he wrote, "justify the courts' avoiding their constitutional responsibilities." In short, what Burger wanted to avoid, Warren wished to accept; where Burger thought courts should follow Frankfurter's admonition in *Colgrove* v. *Green*[11] that courts should veer away from the political thicket, Warren assumed that judicial power was necessary to resolve the ambiguity concerning the meaning of Article I, section 5.

Thus it is really an historical accident that provides us, in retrospect, a glance at how two judges, one of whom was to succeed the other as chief justice of the United States, might interpret the fluid political question doctrine consistent with their own conceptions of judicial power and public policy. Although we recognize that the political question doctrine is but one element of the larger access universe, one might nevertheless suggest the hypothesis that both chief justices reflected a pattern common to the Supreme Court during their respective tenures—Warren Court activism and Burger Court restraint. Clearly several decisions from 1953 to 1979 suggest such an appealing dichotomy. Besides *Powell*, Warren Court activism was reflected in *Dombrowski* v. *Pfister*,[12] which constricted the abstention doctrine to allow greater federal review of state court proceedings; *Flast* v. *Cohen*,[13] which provided criteria for taxpayer standing to challenge congressional spending policies; and *Moore* v. *Ogilvie*,[14] which relaxed the definition of mootness as it applied to state election rules. Burger Court restraint limiting access could be identified in *Warth* v. *Seldin*,[15] *Laird* v. *Tatum*,[16] and *United States* v. *Richardson*.[17] Obviously, numerous exceptions to each trend exist, thus making broad generalizations hazardous. Analysis is further complicated by some confusion in the literature as to how concepts of activism and restraint should be defined.[18] Even Rathjen and Spaeth's methodologically precise scale analysis, while suggesting a "pattern of retrenchment and restriction"[19] in the Burger Court away from Warren Court activism, nevertheless indicates that access decisions of individual members of the Burger Court, at least, are not explained by any single motivation. Five different attitudinal orientations were located, prompting Rathjen and Spaeth to conclude that for a coherent policy to emerge from the Burger Court, at least as it was composed in 1979, "would be nothing short of miraculous."[20]

Although perhaps for the wrong reasons, Justice William O. Douglas displayed penetrating insight when he observed that "generalizations about standing to sue are largely worthless as such."[21] To the extent that this apparent ambiguity about standing reflects a more general uncertainty with access issues,

Douglas's observation is consistent with Rathjen and Spaeth's empirical indicators of the confusion. Similarly, if one should be circumspect in generalizing about access voting, it suggests a need to examine the utility of those decision-making models that lend clarity to this crazy quilt of legal fabric. Apparently, scale models have only limited value for achieving this. Indeed, instead of a unidimensional attitude toward access among Burger Court justices, Rathjen and Spaeth found a configuration in which "the Justices, rather, march to the beat of individualized drums."[22] Their finding suggests that we look to models of decision making which closely examine voting patterns for each justice. Or, to follow Rathjen and Spaeth's analogy, we need to record not only the tempo and rhythm of the march, but also to hazard some guesses about what melodies the justices claim to hear as they step along. Theory and data are necessary, in other words, to mesh melody and percussion.

A Consistency and Change Model of Supreme Court Behavior

Although the emphasis thus far has been on Earl Warren and Warren Burger, it is more for illustration than from any desire to limit our focus to those justices. Indeed, whatever difference exists between them on an access dimension is, in fact, but one element within the broader configuration of interpersonal dynamics established by the twenty-six justices who served on the Supreme Court from 1953 to 1979. As we proceed to explore patterns of support shown by the Supreme Court for jurisdiction and justiciability claims during the Warren and Burger Court years, we will examine how these patterns relate to intuitively plausible decision-making models. We pursue this by proposing a longitudinal model of decisional consistency and change which synthesizes earlier thinking by one of the authors of this chapter[23] with that of others writing in this field who have applied social psychological theories to the study of judicial behavior.[24]

The need to formulate dynamic models of consistency and change emerges as one major concern, given certain limitations on how attitude theories have typically been applied to the study of judicial behavior. Since much of this has been debated in the literature for years we have little interest in resurrecting it all needlessly.[25] But we do need to emphasize one significant constraint, namely, that most attitude studies provide what are, in effect, "frozen" images of judges' voting patterns. In other words, most models are essentially cross-sectional in design and therefore little can be inferred concerning the longitudinal maturation, atrophy, or variability of support justices show for inferred policy dimensions. As static descriptions of judicial voting behavior, these models implicitly assume that neither environmental, nor legal, nor behavioral factors alter a justice's response pattern from one point in time to the next. In other words, unless specifically designed otherwise, cross-sectional scaling models can only indicate justices' modal patterns and do not address the issue of variation in individual behavior over time. We view this as a substantial theoretical limitation when one needs to go beyond the issue of how well justices line up unidimensionally on access, or on any issue, for that matter. Indeed, individual behavior change assumes even greater importance when, as Rathjen and Spaeth suggest, the findings are equivocal on the issue of unidimensionality.

These observations are not meant to imply that a longitudinal consistency and change model will focus narrowly on the access issue. On the contrary, the usefulness of dynamic modeling of judicial behavior is that it bridges jurisprudence on the one hand and social and behavioral sciences on the other, since language denoting consistency and change in behavior is commonplace in each school of inquiry. Legal reasoning, for example, is permeated with the maxim that judges should apply and/or develop law within a *stare decisis* paradigm and synthesize a judicial philosophy so that decisions can be anchored to an acceptable jurisprudential norm or role. Typically, this consistency is intended to bolster objectivity, restraint, and predictability in judicial decisions.[26] These norms, however, may be juxtaposed with those behavioral theories of decision making which suggest that while an individual's values and cognitions may tend toward stability, adapting to changing environmental conditions requires some degree of attitudinal and behavioral metamorphosis in order for the organism to remain in balance with its social and political environment. This notion, found in much social psychological research,[27] suggests that judges who have long tenure on the bench may deviate marginally from a strict interpretation of *stare decisis* so that their judicial philosophies do not become petrified amid a changing political universe. William O. Douglas and Hugo Black are justices whose constitutional attitude matrix had to remain resilient during the more than three tumultuous decades they sat on the Court. Surely, by most comparative standards the world of the 1930s was fundamentally different from the one Black and Douglas encountered in the 1970s.

Confronted with dramatic and fundamental shifts in their environment, it is reasonable to assume that Black and Douglas, as well as other jurists with long tenure on the bench, encountered attitude and role conflicts that other political decision makers did not necessarily find. We can also assume that the decision make must establish some degree of cognitive-policy equilibrium in order that individual/institutional/policy equilibrium be maintained. Thus, where the environment dictates change, the spirit of *stare decisis* admonishes stability. If we assume that the poles of a stability change continuum are represented by free adaption at one extreme and strict adherence to precedent at the other, we can further assume that behavior committed to one, to the exclusion of the other, would not be suitable for a Supreme Court justice. As one illustration of how dogmatic decisions amid rapid environmental change can be less than desirable, consider the fates of McReynolds, Sutherland, Butler, and Van Devanter, labeled by some as having been "failures" on the Court.[28] Although it is usually argued with good cause that their being cast into lower eschelons of judicial repute reflects their having lost a policy struggle over economic regulation during the 1930s, we can also suggest that whatever their short-term failings might have been, their more fundamental tragic flaw was their inability to adjust their conservative economic ideologies to post-Depression chaos; whatever value their laissez faire dogma had during the first three decades of this century, it was ill-suited to the political system during the fourth. Thus it was not simply the Four Horsemen's laissez faire morality that prompted a dismal appraisal by students of the Court, but their lack of vision as to what the Court's role ought to be during a time of crisis. On the horns of the stability-change dilemma, they held to stability with a vengeance. Indeed, Sutherland virtually impaled himself when he wrote: "A provision of the Constitution, it is hardly necessary to say, does not admit of two distinctly opposite interpretations. It does not mean one thing at one time and an entirely different thing at another time."[29] Within the model we are proposing, Sutherland's observation, and the Four Horsemen generally, represent an attitude structure unresponsive to dramatic shifts in the political environment.

Models of stability and change thus draw from two elements of attitude theory—one which emphasizes consistency over time, and another which incorporates a change component. Although each might be treated as an ideal type or be the focus of a research effort, it is theoretically more plausible to posit that an individual's behavior reflects elements of both, particularly within an appellate court where the judicial role imposes constraints upon whim or idiosyncratic performance. Sidney Ulmer, perhaps more than anyone, has used these concepts to link dynamic attitude theory to judicial behavior. In numerous writings, Ulmer has argued that theories of judicial behavior should devote more attention to longitudinal models. He has generated considerable evidence that Supreme Court justices' decisional patterns show change over time, and (more important for theory building) the patterns are dimensional, or occur in patterns over time.[30] In empirical language, Ulmer has shown that a parabolic (curve) rather than a linear (straight line) equation best describes the civil liberties voting behavior of a number of Supreme Court justices. These functions indicate that a shift in the justices' voting pattern occurs at some stage of their careers and that this change is not mere variation or random fluctuation but rather a patterned response to legal and/or environmental stimuli.

This finding is important for our effort here because it describes decision making in dynamic rather than static terms. While Ulmer's theory rests upon the change element, it actually develops the definition of change from a model that assumes consistency in the justices' voting behavior. In other words, the voting patterns of the sixteen justices do not represent change willy-nilly from one term to another, but linear patterns followed by a shift in direction (the change criterion) to a second linear pattern. Accordingly, the overall parabolic patterns which portray change in fact have two components—one which Ulmer would refer to as consistency, or the linear component, and a second defined as change at the breakpoint. Both components are viewed as beneficial to the organism by behavioral models and jurisprudential ones.

In their general form, those models do not conceptualize change and consistency as mutually exclusive events. Rather, they are seen as components of an organized and beneficial response pattern that oscillates between consistency and change. Attitude theory suggests that the presence of one element to the exclusion of the other would not be optimally suitable for an individual who must function within a task-oriented small group. Mutually exclusive behavior would be evidence of dogmatism at one extreme, and or whim at the other. Figure 14-1 illustrates this point. Each overlapping circle depicts a zone of a behavior system, one representing consistency, the other change. The cross-hatched area coinciding with the overlapping portion of each component defines the zone of "responsive" behavior, that is, behavior which draws upon each element to create a system characterized by stability, yet one sufficiently resilient to remain in equilibrium with the political environment. The remaining area of each circle represents behavior patterns either entirely consistent, regardless of circumstance, or entirely malleable by the environment, and hence totally unpredictable. Neither the former, which we label *dogmatic*, nor the latter, which we term *idiosyncratic*, is conducive to the kinds of bargaining, compromise, and interpersonal relations essential for task efficiency in a small group.[31] Indeed, this model is consistent with the "responsive" decision patterns which Ulmer reports for Black and Douglas.[32] We say this because for each justice the parabolic curve best representing voting on civil liberties claims is composed of two linear subsets (with marginal fluctuation around each) joined

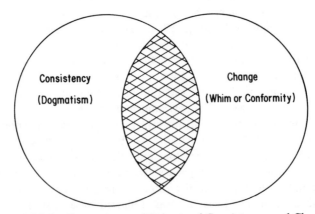

Figure 14-1. Components of Behavioral Consistency and Change

at the apex by an angle of sufficient magnitude to define a discontinuity in the response patterns. The entire set of dimensional behavior that defines change for Black and Douglas is, in fact, composed of three subsets, moving from what Ulmer defines as consistency to change and back to consistency again.

An Empirical Model of Consistency and Change

Our purpose in this chapter is to map the justices' consistency and change in jurisdiction and justiciability cases in order that we can better understand how the court collectively has managed this facet of agenda definition during the last two-and-a-half decades. We also wish to propose a method by which to assess these trends. In our model, consistency and change is empirically measured using regression equations for each Supreme Court justice. Votes are regressed along a time dimension representing the sequence of years on the Court. While our operational model draws upon the earlier work of Sidney Ulmer, our empirical definitions of consistency and change are somewhat different. Change in our model is defined as a pattern of voting behavior which produces a statistically significant equation. We define change this way because a statistically significant regression line represents a precise mathematical indicator of a voting pattern for which the modal response, the mean, would not be the best description of the trend. In figure 14-2, patterns a, b and c illustrate the types of change one might expect to find. Pattern a represents a justice who shows a linear trend toward greater support for an issue dimension over time. In b, change also occurs, but it is clearly toward less support for the dimension. While patterns a and b would obviously be best defined by a linear model, pattern c, though representative of change, would best be described by a curvilinear equation. Unlike a and b, however, change here would be made up of two components, the first showing increased support over time, the other showing decreased support. Similarly, any other nonlinear, statistically significant curve would satisfy the definition of change so long as the pattern defined by the equation was intuitively plausible.

In each of these illustrations change is operationally defined by the statistically significant regression line since it provides an objective and precise statement of those circumstances in which justices' mean support scores are not the best predicters of their pattern. "Change" thus amounts to a departure from a constant level of support for a particular issue which is statistically patterned and not random. "No change" may be represented by any of the trend lines portrayed in figure 14-3. These patterns define those circumstances in which the equation is not significant, that is, the slope coefficient is at or near zero (parallel to the x axis) and where the mean score accordingly becomes the best predicter of the justice's pattern. But as the segments of figure 14-3 indicate, a nonstatistically significant trend line still provides interpretive data about the

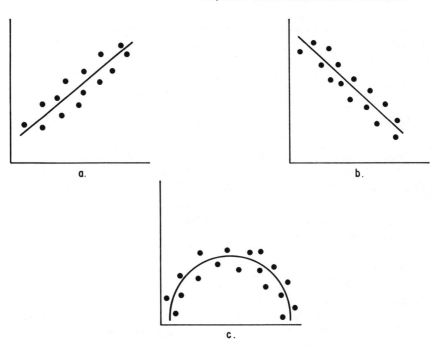

Figure 14-2.   Hypothetical Patterns of Consistency and Change among Supreme
Court Justices (A)

voting patterns. Pattern a, for example, represents what we shall define as
absolute consistency. If this pattern were to occur, all regression coefficients
would equal zero and the data would have a mean of X and a standard deviation of zero. This pattern would indicate a justice who showed invariant levels
of support for a particular issue through time. As patterns c and d show, the
intercept coefficient indicates whether the consistent level of support shown
by each justice is high or low. Typically these intercepts define a line at or
near the mean for that justice. Pattern b suggests yet another possible variation
for the no-change justice. Here the slope and regression coefficients would
also be zero, but one would be hard-pressed to call this pattern consistent.
Indeed, it may be anything but consistent and might best be referred to as
idiosyncratic, whimsical, or even random. Therefore, for those justices who show
no significant regression trend line, it is necessary to examine the variations of
scores (standard deviations), about the means in order to determine the relative
stability of their scores over time. For our purposes the coefficient of variation
(SD/X) is a useful measure since it permits a relative comparison of variability
among individual scores with means of varying magnitude. Accordingly, only
justices who show a trend line at or near zero and a relatively low coefficient of

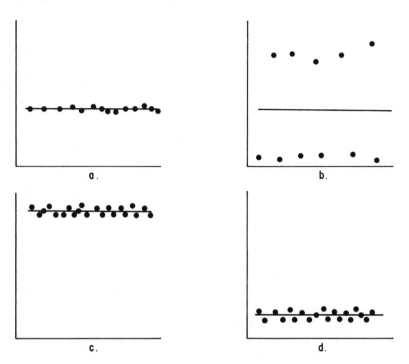

Figure 14-3. Hypothetical Patterns of Consistency and Change among Supreme Court Justices (B)

variability can be operationally defined as having a consistent voting pattern.

Individual consistency and/or change, however, are relative terms. Whatever pattern one observes must be interpreted against some standard. Thus, if Justice A shows change of degree x and the Court of which he is a part exhibits identical change, the individual's pattern is indistinguishable from that shown by the group. While this is useful information, we might be more intrigued by those justices whose patterns are at variance with the group. It is important, then, to compare each justice with the pattern found for the Court during the years he was a member. In this way, individual change can be measured against whatever change is exhibited by the group.

Aggregate Access Behavior

Our research focuses on how the justices of the Supreme Court during the 1953 to 1979 terms voted on a number of jurisdiction and justiciability claims. We decided whether or not one of these access issues was presented in a specific case by examining all formal opinions decided on the merits and determining whether or not questions concerning standing, ripeness, mootness, political questions, abstention, class action, or diversity were involved in the disposition of the case. In coding cases we adopted the following rules: cases with multiple docket numbers were counted only once; cases in which writs were dismissed as improvidently granted were not examined; where the vote was indeterminate the case was not included. This procedure produced a sample of 263 cases. Votes were coded as dichotomous—either for or against access. Table 14-1 summarizes the number and types of access issues in our final data set.

Although our primary interest is in the access voting patterns of individual justices it is instructive to examine aggregate Supreme Court trends from 1953 to 1979 to answer two important questions. First, have substantive access issues received greater or less attention through the Warren and Burger Courts? Second, how sympathetic has the Supreme Court been to expanding access to the Court during these years?

Figure 14-4 addresses the first of these questions by plotting substantive access decisions as a percentage of all decisions on the merits in each of the terms from 1953 to 1979. As one might imagine, access issues do not consume a substantial portion of the Court's attention. Nevertheless, several aspects of figure 14-4 deserve emphasis. First, the trend line plotted for the twenty-six years is statistically significant. This indicates that although the average number of cases in which access issues are raised is not large, the proportion has increased over the twenty-six terms encompassing the Warren and Burger Courts. While only about 15 percent of the Supreme Court's decisions on the merits in the last eight terms (1971-1978) raised access problems, that represents a substantial increase from the previous two decades. Indeed, one might conclude

Table 14-1
Frequency and Type of Access Issues

Issue	Number	Percent
Standing	42	15.97
Mootness	42	15.97
Ripeness	20	7.60
Political question	7	2.66
Abstention	52	19.77
Proper forum	32	12.17
Exhaustion	12	4.56
Class action	13	4.96
Federal question/jurisdiction	20	7.60
Diversity	18	6.84
Other	5	1.90
Total	263	100.00

from figure 14-4 that, apart from whether or not access doctrines had been expanded or contracted in these cases, the Burger Court has been more active than the Warren Court in making substantive decisions on access questions.

The trend is actually somewhat more complicated. The twenty-six points in figure 14-4 can actually be represented as two separate time series, one for the Warren Court (1953-1968) and another for the Burger Court (1969-1979). The data for each court are portrayed in figure 14-5 and 14-6. While overall levels of access activity obviously do not change, the trends suggested by the data are in fact different. These show that access as a substantive issue increased at a slight rate during the Warren era (figure 14-5) and has declined thus far during the Burger years (figure 14-6). The Warren Court slope is slightly greater than zero, indicating virtually no change, whereas the slope for the Burger Court is both negative and highly significant ($p < .01$). Stated in the

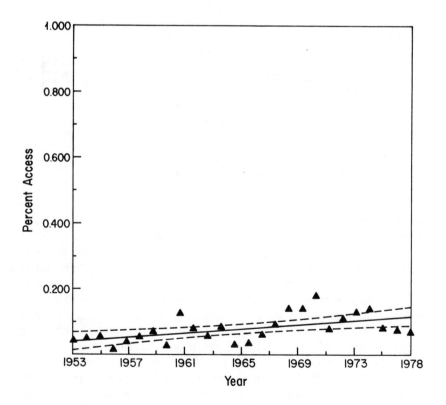

Figure 14-4. Access Cases in the Supreme Court, 1953-1979

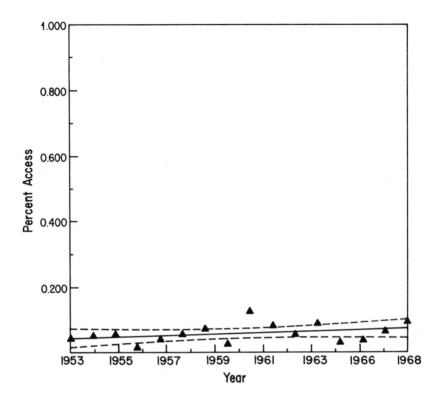

Figure 14–5. Access Cases in the Warren Court, 1953–1968

language of proportionate reduction of error, we improve our predictive capacity only 9 percent for the Warren Gourt by using a time dimension instead of the 15 year average. By contrast, we improve our estimate by 47 percent over the mean value for the Burger court data. Moreover, the direction of the patterns during the Burger Court contrasts sharply with that of the earlier period. The relatively sharp negative slope indicates that the linear trend in figure 14–4, which suggests that the Court paid greater attention to access cases after 1969 is somewhat misleading. It would be more accurate to say that while the Burger Court during the 1969 through 1972 terms followed the trend established in earlier years, by 1972 the proportion of access cases decided on the merits started to decline. It is a plausible hypothesis that the lagged reversal in the frequency of access decisions was caused by the addition of Justices Rehnquist and Powell to the Burger Court; that is certainly consistent with the data. At the very least, we can observe that to the extent that the Warren Court was devoting marginally more

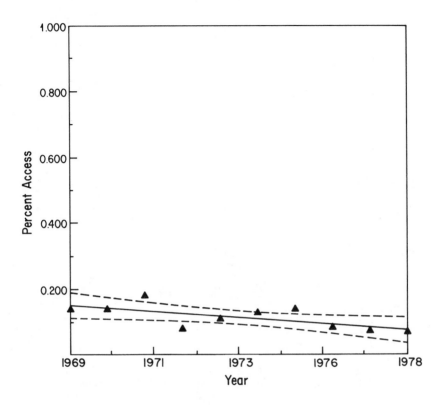

Figure 14-6. Access Cases in the Burger Court, 1969–1978

attention to access issues in the 1960s, the pattern was substantially altered in 1972 with the coincidental appointment of Powell and Rehnquist.

The proportion of decisions on the merits devoted to substantive access issues provides one indicator of its saliency in the Supreme Court. Proportions, however, indicate little about whether the Court has expanded or narrowed access. To assess this we have calculated a "proaccess" score for each Term. It is defined as the number of cases in which the Court voted to expand access divided by the total number of access decisions of the Court. These scores are then regressed over time to obtain precise descriptions of the Court's disposition of access cases.

These results, reported in figures 14-7, 14-8, and 14-9, are quite revealing. Figure 14–7 shows increasing support by the Court for access claims from 1953 to 1978. Although there is substantial variability about the least-squares line, the equation is nevertheless statistically significant. Yet the evidence does not support the hypothesis that the "activist" Warren Court showed greater support

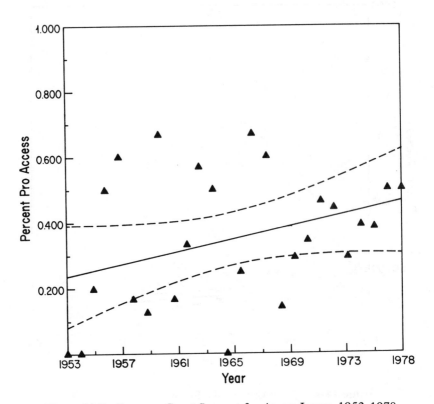

Figure 14-7. Supreme Court Support for Access Issues, 1953–1978

for access claims than the "restraintist" Burger Court. The data reported in figures 14-8 and 14-9, respectively, show that each Court has statistically significant and positive trend lines. Moreover, the data are equivocal on whether one Court supported access more than the other. True, the trend line for the Warren Court is arrayed at a marginally higher level than that of the Burger Court. But whatever inferences about greater Warren Court activism one might draw from that trend are offset by the high explained variance (.55) and a low coefficient of variability (21.2 percent), graphically presented by the tighter-fitting confidence bands for the Burger Court. Thus, while the Warren Court may have shown greater support to access claims during certain years, the overall level of proaccess decision is greater and more consistent after Earl Warren left than while he was there.[33]

These data are at variance with some current interpretations of the Supreme Court's substantive access decisions. Stephen Wasby has noted the alleged change from Warren Court activism to Burger Court restraint most broadly:

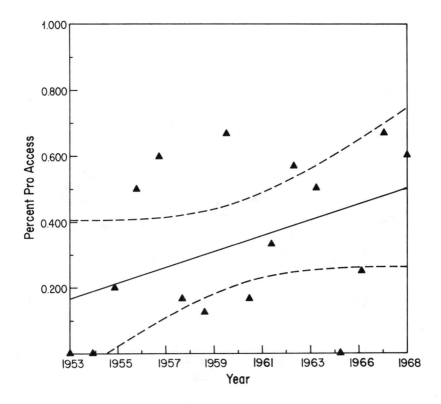

Figure 14–8. Warren Court Support for Access Issues, 1953–1968

"The Court's doctrines on access to the courts have changed over time. The Warren Court generally made access to the courts easier, while the Burger Court has been considerably more restrictive."[34] This interpretation, although stated broadly, nevertheless reflects current thinking about the Court. Arguably, *Warth* v. *Seldin*,[35] where the Court declined to decide whether exclusionary zoning ordinances violated equal protection, or *Zahn* v. *International Paper*,[36] where it ruled each litigant must satisfy the $10,000 maximum in order to satisfy the federal statutory requirement in class action suits, are only two illustrations suggesting Burger Court retrenchment. Yet the pattern of Burger Court decisions matched against the Warren Court is certainly no clearer on access issues than it is on a wide variety of other substantive matters where retrenchment against activist-liberal policies of the 1960s has only occasionally occurred. Indeed, our failure to find an abrupt change in Burger Court patterns is consistent with what has been observed by a number of commentators who have argued that there has been as much, if not more, consistency as change

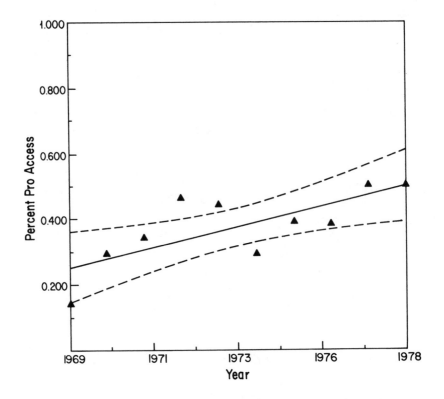

Figure 14-9. Burger Court Support for Access Issues, 1969–1978

from the Warren to the Burger era. Much of this probably reflects the lack of internal consistency within each Court. Hence, while the Burger Court indeed erected barriers to class action suits, the Warren Court established a few road-blocks of its own. Conversely, the Burger Court, which limited standing in *Warth*, broadened it in *Association of Data Processing Service Organizations* v. *Camp*.[37] At the very least, these data on aggregate access behavior suggest a decrease in the proportion of access cases decided by the Supreme Court in the 1970s but not necessarily a related inclination by the Burger Court to close access to a substantially greater extent than had the Warren Court.

Individual Patterns of Consistency and Change in Access Cases

If the differences in substantive access voting behavior between the Warren and Burger Courts are not particularly great, what of the patterns exhibited by the twenty-six justices who have served on the Supreme Court from 1953 to 1979? We begin by comparing the justices cross-sectionally by calculating their individual "proaccess" scores. These are defined as the percentage of cases in which each justice voted in favor of expanding access on standing, ripeness, mootness, political questions, class action, or abstention grounds. These scores are reported in table 14-2.

The data indicate considerable variation in the justices' scores through the Warren and Burger years.[38] More important, however, except for Minton, Reed, Burton, and especially Jackson who participated in only a few access decisions, the pattern is one consistent with what most knowledgeable Court observers would anticipate. Toward the pro-access pole of the activist-restraint dimension are most of the libertarian justices of the Warren Court era, and considerably ahead of the pack is Justice Douglas. Not far behind is Justice Black, and he in turn is followed by Fortas, Marshall, Warren, and Brennan. At the other end of the continuum are those justices to whom the appellation *restraint-oriented* is frequently applied, particularly Frankfurter, Whittaker, Clark, and Harlan. Burger and Rehnquist likewise appear toward the lower half among those justices currently serving on the Supreme Court.[39]

These patterns, though informative, indicate little about changes in the voting patterns of individual justices on access issues. In order to examine that

Table 14-2
Proaccess Scores for Supreme Court Justices, 1953–1978

Justice	Score (%)	Number of Cases
Douglas	67	203
Black	59	127
Fortas	58	26
Marshall	51	180
Warren	50	97
Brennan	48	246
Stevens	48	40
White	42	209
Blackmun	42	151
Goldberg	42	24
Powell	40	114
Stewart	36	242
Rehnquist	36	115
Burger	34	164
Clark	32	77
Harlan	31	124
Minton	29	17
Whittaker	27	33
Frankfurter	24	47
Reed	23	13
Burton	14	14
Jackson	0	3

question we calculated regression data along the lines suggested earlier. In doing this, however, we had to eliminate twelve justices who had insufficient data points. Regression data for the remaining fourteen are shown in table 14-3.[40]

To help interpret these data we present figures which portray least-squares lines and confidence bands for several justices; the direction and rate of change are vividly presented. Moreover, the relative fit of the confidence bands around the regression lines provide graphic representations of the degree to which trend data improves our statistical explanation over each justice's mean score. Figure 14-10, for example, portrays the data for Justice Douglas. It indicates, as table 14-2 had suggested, that Douglas shows a high level of support for access claims. Yet the time dimension shows that Douglas's support has not only been at a relatively high level, but was also been relatively consistent from 1953 to 1975. This is reflected by the relatively flat, nonsignificant slope (b) in table 14-3 and by the minimal variation about the mean. Still another way of describing Douglas's relatively unchanging voting pattern is to note that we improve our predictive capacity by only 1 percent using the time dimension as opposed to "guessing" his access score based upon the mean.

If Douglas illustrates highly consistent proaccess voting, Clark, by comparison, represents a pattern of relatively consistent antiaccess voting (figure 14-11). Like Douglas, Clark's decisions produce a statistically non-significant equation; yet his intercept (a) and mean score is among the lowest for the Court. The data also show that Clark had not been as consistently opposed to the proaccess claim as Douglas had been in his support of such claims. This is seen by comparing Clark's coefficient of variability with that of Douglas. The difference between the coefficients is all the more interesting since the r^2 of .01 suggests that we improve our "guessing" only 1 percent for each of them, even though their consistency through time is quite different.

Change toward greater support for access claims are represented by the patterns of Justices Marshall and Blackmun in figures 14-12 and 14-13 respectively. For both justices, a pattern toward increasing support is defined by the statistically significant trend line. These data indicate that their modal support values do not optimally portray their voting pattern in access cases; the regression coefficients provide a considerably better portrait of their voting pattern. In Marshall's case, the data are clear. While his average score is lower than Douglas's, he nevertheless showed a sharp trend toward increased support by the mid-1970s. While Blackmun's change toward greater access support is not quite as impressive as Marshall's, the summary data in table 14-3 indicate that his pattern is nevertheless a more consistent one.

Perhaps the most interesting, although not necessarily the most unexpected, finding is that Justice Black (figure 14-14), whose mean score places him second to Douglas in overall access support, shows a dramatic longitudinal shift toward the opposite pole of the access continuum. Black's mean support level shifted from 70 percent in 1953-1962 to 48 percent 1963-1971. Moreover, during

Table 14-3
Summary of Equations Regressing Supreme Court Justices Access Votes on Time, 1953-1978

Justice	Intercept (a)	Slope (b)	r^2	N Years	X	SD[a]	CV[b]
White	.38	.005	.02	17	.428	.176	.411
Court	.36	.003	.01	17	.39		
Black	.78[c]	-.021[c]	.17[c]	18	.59	.280	.474
Court	.22	.01	.07	18	.32		
Brennan	.35[c]	.01[c]	.16[c]	23	.475	.196	.412
Court	.37[c]	.001	.004	23	.38		
Blackmun	.34[c]	.02[c]	.34[c]	9	.423	.099	.234
Court	.33[c]	.018[c]	.38[c]	9	.40		
Marshall	.37[d]	.02[d]	.18[d]	13	.510	.222	.435
Court	.38[c]	.003	.00	13	.41		
Rehnquist	.31[d]	.018[d]	.27[d]	8	.373	.086	.230
Court	.37[c]	.014	.20	8	.42		
Frankfurter	.11	.031	.14	9	.238	.237	.995
Court	.12	.036	.16	9	.27		
Douglas	.62	.004	.01	23	.673	.207	.307
Court	.24[c]	.008	.07[d]	23	.33		
Harlan	.27	.004	.009	17	.311	.234	.752
Court	.28[c]	.007	.024	17	.34		
Stewart	.23[c]	.012[c]	.15[c]	21	.359	.207	.562
Court	.30[c]	.007	.06	21	.37		
Clark	.29	.004	.01	14	.32	.16	.500
Court	.21[c]	.012	.05	14	.29		
Powell	.34[c]	.018[c]	.41[c]	8	.40	.07	.175
Court	.37[c]	.014	.20	8	.42		
Warren	.46	.006	.02	16	.504	.188	.373
Court	.20	.014	.09	16	.322		
Burger	.26[c]	.016[d]	.26[d]	10	.337	.094	.278
Court	.25[c]	.027[c]	.55[c]	10	.38		

[a]Standard Deviation

[b]Coefficient of Variability

[c]$p \leqslant .05$

[d]$p < .10$

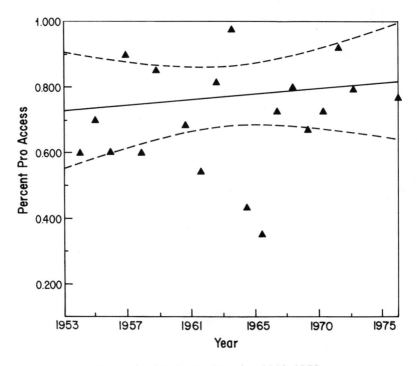

Figure 14-10. Justice Douglas, 1953-1975

three of his final six years on the Court, Black's average support rate dropped below 30 percent. Whatever remains of the myth that Black had been closely identified—along with Douglas—with the activist camp, must now be tempered with the caveat that his activism, at least as defined by substantive access voting, waned considerably during his last two decades on the Court. These data, incidentally, are consistent with those reported by others indicating that the Hugo Black of the 1960s and 1970s was a different individual, at least in terms of his voting behavior, from the activist-libertarian justice of the 1940s and 1950s.[41]

Frankfurter and Harlan's patterns, shown in figures 14-15 and 14-16, pose certain interpretive and analytic problems. In each figure we see no statistically significant departure from trend stability (as we have defined it), even though there seems to be a sharp slope in the trend line. For Frankfurter, this pattern emerges partly from the combined effects of considerable variation in scores (indeed, the largest of any member of the Court) and a relatively small N (9).

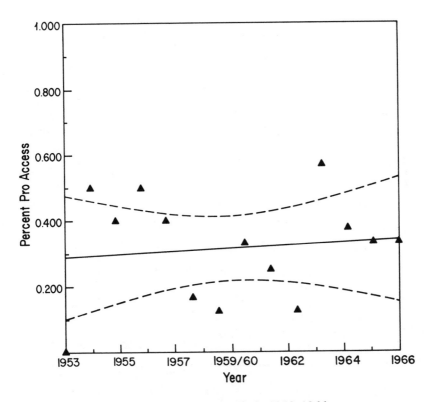

Figure 14–11. Justice Clark, 1953–1966

These factors make it difficult to obtain a significant equation for Frankfurter. The data indicate low proaccess support and little consistency. This supports the inference that Frankfurter's commitment to the norm of restraint, at least when defined as limiting substantive access, may have been something less than intense. Indeed, his commitment to denying access does not appear nearly as strong as Douglas's commitment to granting it. This is consistent with Spaeth's observation that Frankfurter's restraint was bound to the substantive issues involved in the litigation.[42] The same might be said of Frankfurter's ideological protegé, Harlan, who, like his mentor, shows relatively low levels of access support and consistency in voting in access cases.[43]

Individual-Institutional Change

The data presented graphically, as well as the remainder of the summary data reported in table 14–3, suggest a number of distinguishable voting patterns

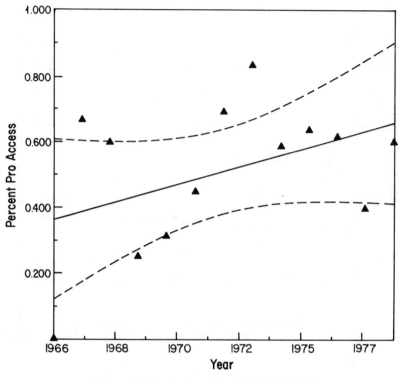

Figure 14–12. Justice Marshall, 1966–1978

in Supreme Court access cases. But change, of course, is a relative term, and obviously requires some standard against which it might be evaluated. It is useful, therefore, to compare individual change and/or consistency with the pattern for the aggregate Court. These data are in table 14–3 and the comparative results in table 14–4.

Of particular interest in table 14–4 are cells I, II, and III. In cell I are Blackmum and Burger, both of whom exhibited increasing support for access claims within a Court which also showed increasing support. Yet each of their patterns is somewhat distinct. Blackmun's regression data in table 14–3 are virtually identical to that shown for the Court on which he sat. Although our data cannot demonstrate who is leading whom, it is clear that Blackmun's movement along the access continuum is indistinguishable from that of the Court. Burger similarly shows change. However, his data indicate that his rate of change towards the proaccess pole is considerably less than that of the Court. In cell II are six justices whose individual change is empirically distinct from the aggregate

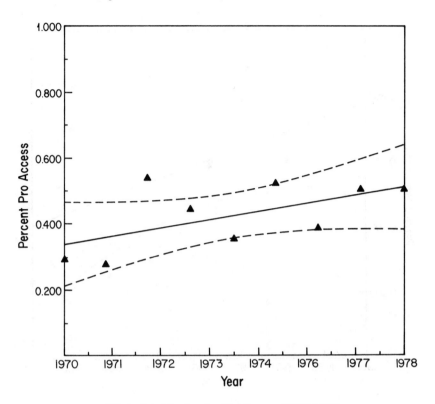

Figure 14–13. Justice Blackmun, 1970–1978

Table 14–4
Typology of Justice-Court Consistency

		Court	
		Change	*No Change*
Justice	Change	Blackmun Burger I	Black II Rehnquist Stewart Brennan Marshall Powell
	No Change	Douglas III	White IV Frankfurter Harlan Warren Clark

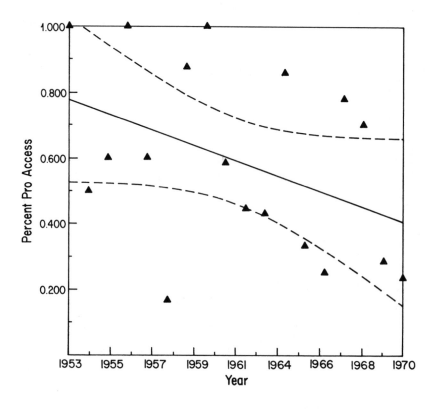

Figure 14-14. Justice Black, 1953-1970

Court. Only one of them, Hugo Black, shows a sharp departure from the pattern established by the aggregate Court. In cell III we have further evidence of Douglas's unique sustained commitment to opening access to the federal courts. Although his aggregate Court data show only marginal change, Douglas's scores suggest an intense commitment to the open access doctrine which has not diminished through the years.

Douglas's unique position in this typology suggests one more necessary refinement in our discussion of consistency. Thus far we have usually referred to consistency as the absence of a statistically significant trend line. But a second component is measured by the variance around the mean. Taking this second component into account, the data in table 14-3 show only three justices—Douglas, Warren, and White—whose access voting was highly consistent over the Warren and Burger Court years, and a fourth (Clark) who could be labeled moderately consistent. Frankfurter and Harlan, although satisfying the no-trend-line requirement, have such high coefficients of variability as to suggest that we should describe their patterns as random.

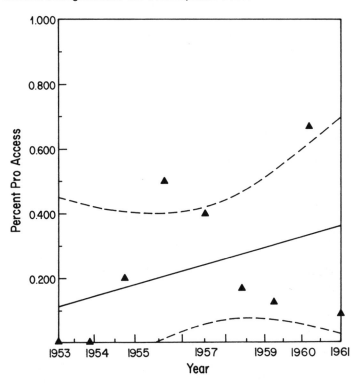

Figure 14-15. Justice Frankfurter, 1953-1961

Consistency and Change in Perspective

It is possible to interpret substantive access rules as regulating the flow of cases to the federal courts. Proper forum and party rules, and justiciability doctrines generally, represent one important set of mechanisms at the justices' disposal to accomplish that end. If erecting barriers to federal judicial power is restraint-oriented behavior, and removing the barriers is activist-oriented, the empirical question becomes: Is there a difference in how these rules were regulated and/or manipulated in the Warren and Burger Courts? To help answer this question, and in order to bridge aggregate and individual levels of analysis, we have presented a model which incorporates theoretical and empirical components designed to evaluate consistency and change at both levels. At the aggregate-macro level our data suggest greater similarities than differences between the two Courts. At the very least we do not find any overall retrenchment in Burger Court decisions as opposed to those of the Warren Court, although the data suggest that access questions consumed somewhat less of the Court's attention

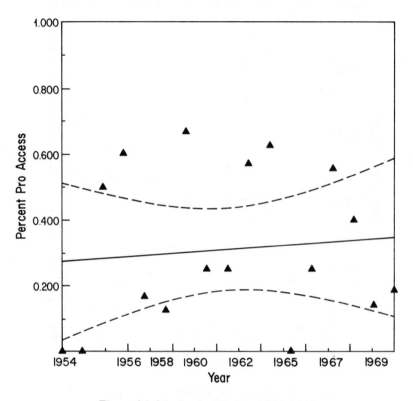

Figure 14-16. Justice Harlan, 1954–1970

after 1972 than it did in the later Warren Court years. At the very least, aggregate data do not suggest any dramatic departure in the pattern of access decisions after 1969.

Obviously, our focus has been on overall trends and patterns rather than discrete events. Accordingly, a number of exceptions to the general rule exist. For example, *United States* v. *Richardson*[44] and *Schlesinger* v. *Reservists Committee to Stop the War*[45] clearly curtailed the thrust of *Flast* v. *Cohen*[46] in which the Court liberalized the standing requirements for federal taxpayers. Undoubtedly, the substantive importance of *Schlesinger* or *Richardson*, like many other Burger Court decisions, should not be taken lightly. Nor do we wish to argue that all access cases should be given equal weight; indeed, while our measurement techniques presume their equality, the fact remains that some cases are substantively more important than others. With that caveat, our data nevertheless suggest more of a similarity than a difference in how the Warren and Burger Courts have dealt with substantive access issues.

Having said this, we should not lose sight of the rather simple but theoretically important observation that aggregate Supreme Court behavior is composed of the voting patterns of individual justices. At the individual level, our data show a variety of patterns on access voting, thus lending some support to the observations reported by Rathjen and Spaeth.[47] Consistent with our findings about aggregate patterns, the individual voting trends of the fourteen justices were not affected by changes in Court personnel. Thus much can be gained by examining individual patterns of voting behavior but we are left with the dilemma of explaining why some justices change while others are consistent, and why others display more or less random patterns.

While we can only speculate, based on the attitude consistency theory suggested earlier, we might assume that certain individuals are less resistant to attitude change than others. A complete explanation might introduce a full range of variables from personality level concepts to contextual ones, which shed light on the notion of consistency and change. It would also be advantageous to measure the intensity of commitment to the access question, since whether or not a justice is sympathetic to expanding access says little about the degree to which he is willing to support that claim. The intensity component, central to Guttman's original scale theory, has been all but neglected in most judicial attitude research.[48] To speak of intensity, however, also presumes that some issue-specific attitudes dominate, and in turn may be dominated by, other attitudes in a justice's ideological matrix. If we could come to grips with the hierarchical relationships among specific attitudes, we would enhance our ability to explain why some justices change or remain stable on any single component. Finally, attitudes toward access, or any other issue, are manifested in a collegial context. This implies an individual-group interaction in which certain persons are more likely to conform to group pressure than others.[49] Considerable research demonstrates that conformity, or susceptibility to persuasion, is personality-based.[50] This implies that attitudes manifested by voting behavior may be subservient to the satisfaction of inner psychological needs.

As we suggested at the outset, there is no theoretical justification from distinguishing access voting behavior from substantive voting behavior. In fact, evidence exists that access voting is not necessarily independent of the substantive goals of justices.[51] Accordingly, if we interpret substantive access rules as a political mechanism for conflict management and agenda definition, we can view judicial power as a tool designed to help fashion substantive policy goals. In this light, *Stone* v. *Powell,*[52] where the Court limited habeas corpus relief available to incarcerated state prisoners, did more than establish a policy affecting access to federal courts in litigation which had the single greatest percentage increase during the previous decade—it also undermined the substance of the rule set forth in *Mapp* v. *Ohio.*[53] *Stone* illustrates that the access-substance linkage is important for analyzing the activist-restraint debate inasmuch as a retrenchment in substantive access decision making does more than narrow the issue forum for the Supreme Court; as others[54] have noted, access decisions limit the ability of the Court to manipulate doctrine in tune with its collective policy preferences. Accordingly, it would have been politically unwise for the Burger Court to have dramatically departed from the patterns established by the Warren Court inasmuch as a narrow definition of proper party and forum concepts would limit the Court's power to shape public policy. Our data indicate that while important differences exist among individual justices, the Warren and Burger Courts in the aggregate exhibited considerable continuity. Conflict management in the Supreme Court, it seems, is not the exclusive domain of any single judicial ideology.

Notes

1. Peter Bachrach and Morton S. Baratz, "Two Faces of Power," *American Political Science Review* 56 (December 1962): 947-952; "Decisions and Non-decisions: An Analytic Framework," *American Political Science Review* 57 (September 1963): 632-642.

2. E.E. Schattschneider, *The Semi-Sovereign People: A Realist's View of Democracy in America* (New York: Holt, Rinehart and Winston, 1960).

3. Joseph Tanenhaus, Marvin Schick, Matthew Muraskin, and Daniel Rosen, "The Supreme Court's Certiorari Jurisdiction: Cue Theory," in *Judicial Decision-Making*, ed. Glendon Schubert (Glencoe, Ill.: Free Press, 1963), chap. 5; S. Sidney Ulmer, William Hintze, and Louise Kirklosky, "The Decision to Grant or Deny Certiorari: Further Consideration of Cue Theory," *Law and Society Review* 6 (May 1972): 637-643; S. Sidney Ulmer, "Selecting Cases for Supreme Court Review: An Underdog Model," *American Political Science Review* 72 (September 1978): 902-910.

4. See, for example, John E. Nowak, Ronald D. Rotunda, and J. Nelson Young, *Constitutional Law* (St. Paul: West, 1978).

5. See, for example, Fritz Scharpf, "Judicial Review and the Political Question: A Functional Analysis," *Yale Law Review* 75 (March 1966): 517-597; Charles M. Lamb, "Judicial Restraint on the Supreme Court," chap. 1, this volume.

6. For a suggestion that justiciability was the central issue discussed within the Supreme Court, see Justice Douglas's dissent in *Massachusetts v. Laird*, 400 U.S. 886 (1970).

7. 395 U.S. 486 (1969).

8. 395 F.2d 577 (D.C. Cir., 1968).

9. 369 U.S. 186 (1962).

10. *Powell v. McCormack*, 395 F.2d 577 (D.C. Cir., 1968).

11. 328 U.S. 549 (1946).

12. 380 U.S. 479 (1965).

13. 392 U.S. 83 (1968).

14. 394 U.S. 814 (1969).

15. 422 U.S. 490 (1975).

16. 408 U.S. 1 (1972).

17. 418 U.S. 166 (1974).

18. For a good review of the activism-restraint literature see Charles M. Lamb and Mitchell S. Lustig, "The Burger Court, Exclusionary Zoning, and the Activist-Restraint Debate," *University of Pittsburgh Law Review* 40 (Winter 1979): 169-226.

19. Gregory J. Rathjen and Harold J. Spaeth, "Access to the Federal Courts: An Analysis of Burger Court Policy-Making," *American Journal of Political Science* 23 (May 1979): 360-382.

20. Ibid., p. 380.

21. *Association of Data Processing Service Organizations v. Camp*, 397 U.S. 151 (1970).

22. Rathjen and Spaeth, "Access to the Federal Courts," p. 360.

23. A longitudinal consistency model was proposed in Burton Atkins, "Chief Justice Burger and the Criminal Offender in the United States Supreme Court; or, the Deterministic Source of Free Will Perspective," (Paper presented at the Annual Meeting of the Midwest Political Science Association, Chicago, Illinois, 1971). Consistency and change in judicial behavior has also been explored in Burton Atkins, "Judicial Behavior and Tendencies Toward Conformity in a Three Member Small Group: A Case Study of Dissent Behavior on the U.S. Court of Appeals," *Social Science Quarterly* 54 (June 1973): 41-53; and Burton Atkins, "Personality Theory and Judging: A Proposed Theory of Self-Esteem and Judicial Policy Making," *Law and Policy Quarterly* 2 (April 1980): 189-220.

24. S. Sidney Ulmer has constructed a model of longitudinal change in a number of articles and manuscripts. See particularly "Dimensionality and Change in the United States Supreme Court," in *Mathematical Applications in Political Science*, ed. James F. Herndon and Joseph L. Bernd (Charlottesville: University of Virginia Press, 1974), 7:40-67; "Parabolic Support of Civil Liberty Claims: The Case of William O. Douglas," *Journal of Politics* 41 (August 1979): 634-639; and "Parameters of Change in the Behavior of Supreme Court Justices: 1903-1973," (Paper presented at the Annual Meeting of the Southwestern Political Science Association, Fort Worth, Texas, 1979).

25. A concise review of this literature may be found in Charles Sheldon, *The American Judicial Process: Models and Approaches* (New York: Dodd, Mead, 1974), pp. 24-49.

26. See, for example, Edward H. Levi, *An Introduction to Legal Reasoning* (Chicago: University of Chicago Press, 1948).

27. Much of this is summarized in Jonathan L. Freedman, J. Merrill Carlsmith, and David O. Sears, *Social Psychology* (Englewood Cliffs N.J.: Prentice-Hall, 1974), pp. 208-381.

28. See the poll results reported by Albert P. Blaustein and Roy M. Mersky in *American Bar Association Journal* 58 (November 1972): 1183-1189.

29. Dissenting in *Home Building and Loan Association v. Blaisdell*, 290 U.S. 398 (1934).

30. See references in note 24, especially, "Parameters of Change in the Behavior of Supreme Court Justices."

31. A review of much of this literature may be found in Freedman, Carlsmith, and Sears, *Social Psychology*, pp. 138-205.

32. Change in the voting behavior of William O. Douglas and Hugo L. Black are treated in Ulmer, "Parabolic Support of Civil Liberty Claims;" and in S. Sidney Ulmer, "The Longitudinal Behavior of Hugo Lafayette Black: Parabolic Support for Civil Liberties: 1937-1971," *Florida State University Law Review* 1 (Winter 1973): 131-153.

33. These regression estimates are derived from ordinary least-squares (OLS) models. However, generalized least-squares (GLS) coefficients were obtained following Johnston's recommendation that OLS will produce efficient estimates only when autocorrelation is less than .30. The estimated autocorrelation for the Warren Court is .04, .19 for the Burger Court, and .04 for the entire 1953-1979 period. See J. Johnston, *Econometric Methods*, 2nd ed. (New York: McGraw-Hill, 1972), p. 265.

34. Stephen L. Wasby, *The Supreme Court in the Federal Judicial System* (New York: Holt, Rinehart and Winston, 1978), p. 111.

35. 422 U.S. 490 (1975).

36. 414 U.S. 291 (1973).

37. 397 U.S. 150 (1970). We wish to point out that at this stage of our research we have not calculated separate regression equations for each type of access issue. We recognize that each issue might exhibit a different pattern. Controling for case type at this point would be beyond the scope of this chapter. As to this problem our data show no substantial change in the distribution of access-type cases from the Warren to the Burger Courts.

38. Notwithstanding differences between our access coding schemes and the one used by Rathjen and Spaeth, our results closely parallel theirs. The rank order correlation of proaccess decisions for the nine justices who overlap each of our data sets is .85 (p = .02). This indicates a high degree of consistency in how our research designs tapped the access dimension.

39. However, the data for certain justices are at variance with our conventional wisdom about who were the activist leaders of the Warren Court. Goldberg, for example, typically labeled as a Warren Court activist, only moderately supports access issues, although his relatively short tenure on the Court provided little time for a pattern to emerge. Stevens, by contrast, appears at the threshold separating the six justices typically associated with Warren Court activism from the remainder who fall more toward the restraintist pole of the continuum.

40. Autocorrelation estimates for each justice are: Black (-.12); Blackmun (-.40); Brennan (.26); Burger (.00); Clark (-.04); Douglas (.08); Frankfurter (-.25); Harlan (-.01); Marshall (.04); Powell (.25); Rehnquist (-.13); Stewart (-.01); Warren (.01); and White (.09). The autocorrelation value is significant only for Blackmun. By using GLS in lieu of OLS for Blackmun obtains b = .020 < .05, and a = .344 < .05. The reader should note the similarity between these values and those presented in table 14-3; they are identical to the second decimal place.

41. See S. Sidney Ulmer, "The Longitudinal Behavior of Hugo Lafayette Black;" Glendon Schubert, *The Judicial Mind Revisited: Psychometric Analysis of Supreme Court Ideology* (New York: Oxford University Press, 1974).

43. The high degree of variability for both Frankfurter and Harlan is both troublesome and curious. By looking closely at their data plots, it might appear that a linear model would not produce optimal results and that a parabola might reduce the variance. Attempts to fit a curve to the data proved unsuccessful. For neither Frankfurter nor Harlan did a statistically significant equation emerge; nor did curvilinear equations increase the explained variance.

42. Harold J. Spaeth, "The Judicial Restraint of Mr. Justice Frankfurter—Myth or Reality," *Midwest Journal of Political Science* 8 (February 1964): 22-38.

44. 418 U.S. 166 (1974).

45. 418 U.S. 208 (1974).

46. 392 U.S. 83 (1968).

47. Rathjen and Spaeth, "Access to the Federal Courts."

48. Samuel A. Stouffer, Louis Guttman, et al., *Measurement and Prediction* (New York: John Wiley and Sons, 1966), especially chap. 7.

49. Atkins, "Judicial Behavior and Tendencies Towards Conformity."

50. See Carl Hovland and Irving Janis, *Personality and Persuasibility* (New Haven: Yale University Press, 1959), pp. 69-120.

51. S. Sidney Ulmer, "The Decision to Grant Certiorari as an Indicator of 'Decision on the Merits'," *Polity* 4 (Summer 1972): 429-447; Harold J. Spaeth, "The Judicial Restraint of Mr. Justice Frankfurter."

52. 428 U.S. 465 (1976).

53. 367 U.S. 643 (1961).

54. See Wasby, *Continuity and Change: From the Warren Court to the Burger Court*, (Pacific Palisades, Goodyear, 1976); and Matthew DeZee and William A. Taggart, "Substantive Access Doctrines: Comparative Analysis of the Warren and Burger Courts," (Paper presented at the 1981 Midwest Political Science Association Annual Meeting, Cincinnati, Ohio, 1981).

15 A Framework for the Analysis of Judicial Activism

Bradley C. Canon

This chapter seeks to set forth some commonly understood and well-structured dimensions useful to the discussion of judicial activism and restraint.[1] Such discussion is frequent, of ancient vintage, and usually more polemical than analytical. Often, however, it is not altogether clear just what the discussion is centered upon, especially if one reads the writings of several protagonists. To some extent, this is because their conceptions of activism are usually not explicitly noted or articulated, but rather are implied by the theme or context of their discussions. By way of illustration, the only volume that even vaguely compares to this one is David Forte's book, *The Supreme Court: Judicial Activism Versus Judicial Restraint,*[2] now out of print. It contains commentary by eighteen judges and scholars (including Forte). Only one author, however, presents a precise definition of judicial activism—that "the Court is activist when its decisions conflict with those of other political policy-makers."[3] Moreover, this definition was offered by Glendon Schubert who is best-noted for his many quantitative analyses of the justices' value structures rather than commentary on the virtues or follies of activism. Only a general conception of what constitutes activism can be inferred from the other writings; in none is the term assigned any framework or boundaries.

Even more frustrating, there are almost as many conceptions of judicial activism as there are commentators. Some discuss activism almost solely in terms of the Court's nullifying acts of Congress.[4] Some see activism largely in the Court's violation of its obligation of comity to the other branches of government or to the states.[5] Some contend that activism occurs when the Court abandons "neutral principles" in deciding cases.[6] In a not dissimilar vein, some see activism as the Court's unnecessary involvement in making policy or settling what are essentially political matters.[7] In fact, much scholarly discussion is implicitly ideological: activism is equated with political liberalism and restraint with conservatism. Certainly the last view is widely prevalent in the imagery of ordinary citizens who have in recent years broadly equated the Warren Court with both activist decisions and liberal results.

Another problem is that judicial activism is not a static concept. Activism now is a different phenomena than it was a generation or two ago. Classic

I wish to thank Steve Halpern, Larry Baum, and Lee Sigelman for carefully considering and commenting on an earlier draft of this chapter. The writing of this chapter was supported by a minor grant from Project '87 for which I am grateful.

discussions of activism focused on the nullification of legislation—usually liberal in nature—by conservative justices. In the Warren Court era, the focus was not dissimilar but the ideologies were reversed. More recently, however, formal conceptions of activism have been expanded. In his widely read book, Raoul Berger argues that the touchstone of activism is a failure to interpret the Constitution according to the intent of its drafters.[8] He charges the Court with gross misinterpretations of the document, especially the Fourteenth Amendment. Donald Horowitz[9] and others[10] have challenged the courts' initiation of complicated and often far-reaching policy changes which sometimes extend to the virtual day-to-day supervision of such institutions as schools, prisons, and mental hospitals. It is activism, they charge, for courts to act beyond their capacities, their expertise, and their traditional functions. Even liberals have gotten into the act by accusing the Burger Court of activism to the extent that it has blunted or dismantled many holdings of the Warren Court.[11] Those making this charge conceive of activism as a significant change in the Court's earlier jurisprudence. (Indeed, laissez faire critics of the post-1937 Court held essentially the same view.)

If commentators on the Court have numerous and somewhat dissimilar concepts of activism and do not articulate them very well, serious general usage of the concept becomes difficult if not meaningless. Overall, we receive little more than a babel of loosely connected discussion; the usefulness of any particular idea is limited. Those wanting to enter the discussion are left pretty much to their own devices.

To alleviate this situation and give a common vocabulary to commentators and debaters, I propose that discussions of judicial activism be explicitly structured on six dimensions. Basically, these dimensions are taken from the literature noted above or from similar commentary. In establishing them, I have been guided by several considerations. First, there should be a manageable number of dimensions which overlap as little as possible. Thus some conceptions noted above are not reflected in the dimensions' title, but are nonetheless in their scope. Second, the dimensions need to be operable—to have linear direction. Observers need to be able to classify court decisions as activist or nonactivist in any given dimension. Concepts such as Weschler's "neutral principles" are too abstract and directionless to meet this criterion.[12] Third, the dimensions should be universally applicable; they should not be restricted to particular jurisprudential eras or related to particular political ideologies.

The six dimensions are described briefly below—they will be spelled out in detail later.

1. Majoritarianism—the degree to which policies adopted through democratic processes are judicially negated.
2. Interpretive Stability—the degree to which earlier court decisions, doctrines, or interpretations are altered.

3. Interpretive Fidelity—the degree to which constitutional provisions are interpreted contrary to the clear intentions of their drafters or the clear implications of the language used.
4. Substance–Democratic Process Distinction—the degree to which judicial decisions make substantive policy rather than affect the preservation of the democratic process.
5. Specificity of Policy—the degree to which a judicial decision establishes policy itself as opposed to leaving discretion to other agencies or individuals.
6. Availability of an Alternate Policymaker—the degree to which a judicial decision supersedes serious consideration of the same problem by other governmental agencies.

Two basic concepts of judicial activism underlie the construction of these dimensions. One is the concept of activism as significant Court-generated change in public policy. This of course reflects the generic meaning of the term *active*. Activism as change in policy is especially found in the Majoritarianism and Interpretive Stability dimensions. When the Court strikes down laws or overrules precedents, it is almost by definition making changes in public policy. Nearly all Court decisions seen as activist make changes on at least one of these two dimensions.[13] The second concept is legitimacy. An activist decision is one which is perceived as illegitimate in terms of one or more commonly articulated beliefs about the proper role of the Supreme Court in the American political system. It is these beliefs which comprise the six dimensions. Each one measures a perception of illegitimacy.[14]

Before I go on, let me make it clear that the six dimensions are tailored to activism on the part of the Supreme Court as it develops constitutional law. Many courts alter public policy or render decisions of dubious propriety; moreover, this is accomplished not only by means of constitutional interpretation but through the construction of statutes and the development of common law or other judicial doctrines. Nonetheless, it is constitutional law which lies at the heart of the controversy over judicial activism and produces the sharpest and most memorable colloquy. Consequently, I think it best in this exploratory essay to limit the discussion and application of these six dimensions to the Supreme Court's development of constitutional law. I hope, however, that in the future these dimensions can be expanded or redefined to include activism in the nonconstitutional context.

Few constitutional law cases can be placed on every dimension. While some dimensions are fairly inclusive (keep in mind that nonactivist decisions are included at one end of a dimension), the structure of others necessarily excludes some cases. For instance, Majoritarianism will not be relevant to those decisions where the validity of legislation or regulations is not at issue, as in *Mapp* v. *Ohio*[15] or *Miranda* v. *Arizona*.[16] Or the Court may at times work from a nearly clean jurisprudential slate where the concept of Interpretive Stability is inapplicable, as in the *Income Tax* case.[17]

Moreover, some cases of constitutional importance may not be able to be placed on any dimension because it is not clear what they have accomplished.[18] This may happen where the Court's opinion has less-than-majority support or is rendered in such ambiguous terms that its policy impact is uncertain. The *Bakke* case[19] might well fall in this category. It could also happen where no policy, legally or by virtue of common practice, existed earlier and thus the decision does not change policy, as in *United States* v. *Nixon,*[20] where the Court fails to settle the main justiciable issue in a case, as in *Sierra Club* v. *Morton,*[21] or where the decision is so factually oriented or ad hoc that it does not alter policy in any general manner, as in *Jenkins* v. *Georgia*[22] (the "Carnal Knowledge" case). Reasonably free, clear, and conscious choice of policy is a key element necessary for a case to be included on the dimensions defining activism.

On some occasions the Court will have to take an activist position on one dimension as a consequence of exercising restraint on another. This will happen when the baseline policies on each dimension are diametrically opposed and one must necessarily be changed. Usually this will concern the validity of new legislation clearly in conflict with the Court's earlier precedents or doctrines. The *Jones & Laughlin* decision[23] upholding the Wagner Act and repudiating the *E.C. Knight*[24] precedent illustrates this situation; so also do the cases upholding the 1964 Civil Rights Act.[25] Such a situation does not conflict with the requirement, discussed earlier, that activism be the result of free, clear, and conscious choice of policy on the Court's part. Such choices are freely made and the policy results are eminently predictable. It is only the categorization of such decisions that is inevitably different on two or more dimensions. Fortunately, these situations are not very frequent.[26]

Usually commentators have focused upon particular Court decisions as examples of activism or restraint, and this will be the general approach here. Put in the language of social science, the unit of analysis is the decision. Occasionally, however, two or more nonsimultaneous cases involving the same policy area are discussed and analyzed together. When the Court reaches a policy position in a series of decisions just a few years apart, for instance, the court-martial jurisdiction cases,[27] or announces a change of policy in one decision and fills in the details of that change in the next few years, for example, *Baker* v. *Carr*[28] and subsequent reapportionment decisions,[29] it makes more sense to treat the cases together. This should not be carried too far, lest the whole policy becomes the unit of analysis; I would not, for example, consider the busing decisions of the late 1960s and 1970s to be mere follow-ups to the 1954 *Desegregation Decision.*[30] In this chapter, a particular decision will be the focus of discussion and categorization, but sometimes it can be useful to treat, as a group, decisions closely related in time and policy implications.

So far it has been convenient to consider the six dimensions as if they were dichotomous; decisions appropriate to them were categorized as either activist or nonactivist. Now, however, I want to introduce the notion of degrees of activism. These will reflect the fact that some Court decisions engender greater change in policy than others and that some putatively inappropriate decisions are more offensive in their illegitimacy than others.

In this essay I will categorize decisions as Highly Activist (HA), Somewhat Activist (SA) or Non-Activist (NA). The distinguishing criteria will necessarily have to differ across the dimensions, but basically they are designed to separate in the context of traditional expectations of constitutional law and the Supreme Court's role in the American political system, greater or more extreme changes in public policy from lesser ones. For example, it is a greater affront to the concept of Majoritarianism for the Court to nullify congressional legislation than that passed by state legislatures.

As I review the six dimensions, I will set forth the criteria that delineates the three levels. Presumably, most decisions can be categorized as within a particular level by consensus. The categorization of some decisions, however, will undoubtedly be subjective. This will occur when commentators disagree over the precise nature of the holding or when the criteria dividing the levels are expressed too broadly or crudely to establish an exact or precise demarcation and the case at issue falls in a twilight zone. Yet these are not crippling flaws. What is important is that different categorizations be discussed against the background of a common dimension and ordinal levels of activism. Although differences of opinion may not be resolved, an audience can draw its own conclusions based upon the common background. Thus the debate over judicial activism can be elevated by making it more rigorous, systematic, and meaningful.

We now have a framework of six dimensions, each with three ordinal categories, illustrated in figure 15-1. With the framework, we can analyze and compare the breadth and depth of activism for particular Court cases on a crude basis. We can even make some comparisons about the nature of activism in different eras. This will be illustrated later. At this point, however, I want to make it clear that it is not necessary to consider all the dimensions as equally important. My purpose in writing this essay is to tie together the several dimensions of activism found in the vast literature on the subject. Without a comprehensive treatment, discussions of activism will continue to be ad hoc or particularistic, and commentators will often be talking past one another. It does not follow, however, that those dealing with the subject have to treat all dimensions as equally important components of activism. It is certainly defensible to argue, for instance, that decisions violating the Majoritarianism criterion constitute a more serious manifestation of activism than do those violating the Interpretive Stability dimension. The important thing is that we recognize that there are several dimensions to the phenomenon we call judicial activism and that discussions should be based upon a common understanding of these dimensions and their characteristics. In this way, debates as to which dimensions, if any, are the more important components of activism will be structured and meaningful to both the debaters and the audience.

Dimensions

Ordinal Levels of Activism	Majoritarianism	Interpretive Stability	Interpretive Fidelity	Substance-Democratic Process	Specificity of Policy	Availability of Alternate Policymaker
Highly Activist						
Somewhat Activist						
Non-Activist						

Figure 15-1. A Depiction of the Analytical Framework

The Six Dimensions

I will now discuss in detail the six dimensions noted above and advance criteria for distinguishing between the HA, SA, and NA categories within each dimension. This discussion gives substance to the framework outlined in figure 15-1, developing it as a workable basis for considering systematically the concepts of activism and restraint. Nonetheless, I want to emphasize that this is an exploratory essay. If others find this framework of heuristic value, I hope they will assist in refining it further by noting particular problems and offering suggestions. Only through common endeavor will the framework be made more useful.

Majoritarianism

Majoritarianism is probably the most frequent criterion used in assessing Supreme Court activism. When the Court exercises judicial review, it substitutes its own public policy preferences for those enacted by elected representatives in Congress, state legislatures, or city councils. Such action certainly constitutes a change in public policy and is often seen as illegitimate from the perspective of democratic theory.

The violation of majoritarianism is most pronounced when the Court declares an act of Congress unconstitutional. Elected by the entire nation, Congress constitutes a coordinate branch of the federal government. Thus it seems reasonable to categorize such nullifications as Highly Activist. The justices have voided congressional legislation on an average of once a year since the Civil War, with the average approaching twice a year in the last two decades. Of course, some such decisions strike down acts having only local application or little real importance to policy, but numerous major congressional policies have also been voided by the Court. Indeed, the *Dred Scott*[31] decision and the several decisions striking down New Deal policies in the 1930s provoked constitutional crises of the first magnitude. Three voidings generated amendments to the Constitution.[32] Two other nullifications of congressional legislation induced a serious attempt to write an overruling amendment into the Constitution.[33] Beyond these cases, it is easy to point to a number of others which have voided acts of Congress and which subsequently received widespread public and scholarly criticism.[34]

A related situation occurs when the Court construes a federal statute in a manner clearly contrary to the plain meaning of its wording and/or the intentions of its drafters in order to preserve its constitutionality. In such cases, for all practical purposes the Court has nullified the statute, although it is not recorded as having done so. Interpretive nullification is less objectively determinable than straight-out voiding of a statute and probably happens less frequently. The "gutting" of the Smith Act[35] and the negation of Congress's attempt to draft nonsectarian conscientious objectors during the Vietnam War[36] come to mind. Thus while statutory interpretation ordinarily falls outside the coverage of this essay, interpretive nullifications will be considered constitutional law cases and be placed in the HA category.

Most Supreme Court invalidations affect a state or local law (including state constitutional provisions). While contrary to the majoritarian principle, such voidings are less offensive to it than when acts of Congress are negated. Obviously a federal system requires some mechanism (although not necessarily a judicial one) to review local legislation if national supremacy in specified areas is to be viable. Also, of course, the majorities nullified in such cases are local and not national. Despite these caveats, local nullifications are contrary to the letter and often the spirit of the majoritarianist perspective. The Court after all is overturning policies adopted by elected representatives, policies which are often not obviously unconstitutional and arguably ought to be protected by the principle of federalism. Moreover, the voiding of some local enactments as in the *Abortion Decision*[37] has undoubted nationwide impact. Consequently, I will place Court decisions finding state laws, city ordinances or other local legislation unconstitutional in the Somewhat Activist category.[38]

Court nullification of administrative regulations on constitutional grounds is also a part of the Majoritarianism dimension. The linkage is that the promulgating agencies are responsible to an elected official—the president in the case of the federal government.[39] Moreover, these regulations are authorized by and issued at the behest of a legislative body. On the other hand, presidential interest in most administrative regulation is quite peripheral and congressional mandates are often quite vague. In fact, although administrative law cases are frequently before the Court, such regulations are only infrequently voided on constitutional grounds; statutory or procedural deficiencies or the legality of particular agency actions not sanctioned by regulation are far more often at the crux of the decision. Nonetheless, the Court occasionally makes important public policy decisions which hinge on the constitutional deficiencies of administrative regulations, for example, *Ex parte Endo*[40] or *Procunier* v. *Martinez*,[41] and I will categorize these cases as SA.

The Non-Activist (NA) category is composed of those cases in which a statute, ordinance, or administrative regulation is challenged and its constitutionality is totally or substantially sustained. Put otherwise, it consists of cases which, had they been decided in the opposite manner, would have received HA or SA categorizations. As a rule, it is easy to identify and categorize such cases. Excluded from the majoritarian dimension are those cases coming before the Court where the constitutionality of a statute, etc., is not at issue.

Interpretive Stability

This dimension measures the degree to which a Supreme Court decision either retains or abandons precedent or existing judicial doctrine. Interpretive Stability is an important element in the debate over the merits of activism, although it is often only vaguely recognized as such and its component parts are often poorly articulated or given little attention. Indeed, discussion of the Court's activism under Chief Justice Earl Warren focused as much on the frequency and scope of its radical alterations of prior jurisprudence as upon the anti-majoritarian nature of its decisions. Many of its most memorable cases, *Mapp* v. *Ohio*, *Miranda* v. *Arizona*, and *New York Times* v. *Sullivan*,[42] to name a few, nullified no statute or ordinance but simply overturned precedent, common law doctrine, or ancient understandings about the scope of constitutional provisions. Moreover, some decisions which do void legislation are subject to even greater criticism because in addition they overrule precedent: *Baker* v. *Carr* and the *Desegregation Decision* are cases in point. Nor is the Warren Court the sole exemplar of interpretive instability. The Burger Court is sometimes criticized on much the same ground for its decisions restricting or overturning Warren Court doctrines.[43] And the post-1937 Court was seen as activist by many for its decisions legitimizing New Deal legislation by overruling or emasculating the doctrines of freedom of contract, substantive due process, and dual federalism.[44]

In part, the equation of activism with the alteration of jurisprudence stems from the ancient view of "the law" as an immanent and constant entity which judges merely "discover." To abandon long-standing precedent or doctrine was seen as an act of lese majesty or perhaps even a dangerous tampering with nature's immutable laws. Few subscribe to this hoary perspective today, but it still retains a subconscious strength. Beyond that, a major purpose of the law is the provision of a stable, predictable legal environment so that fear of personal disruption or financial loss can be minimized. The principle of *stare decisis* is of vital importance to the work of lawyers and judges; as Chief Justice Taft once put it, "it is better to have the law certain than to have it settled either way."[45] No wonder many see the unsettling of previously settled law as judicial activism.

The most visible and dramatic instance of interpretive instability occurs when the Court explicitly overrules one of its own earlier decisions. I will categorize such cases as HA. Sometimes the Court is quite straightforward about what it is accomplishing: "Our conclusion is that the case of *Adkins* v. *Children's Hospital, supra,* should be, and it is, overruled."[46] At other times it is semantically less explicit, as in the *Desegregation Decision's* phrasing, "any language in *Plessy* v. *Ferguson* contrary to this finding is rejected."[47] Few failed, however, to appreciate that *Plessy*[48] had been overruled. In general, it is not difficult to ascertain overruling decisions. However, there can be an occasional disputed situation, such as the free speech at shopping center cases.[49]

A lesser form of interpretive instability occurs when the Court drastically weakens a precedent without formally overruling it. Of course, over time we expect that future decisions may well put some limitations on a precedent's applicability. The clarification and development of precedent are the woof and warp of judicial business, and such cases hardly constitute activism. But when a precedent is drastically weakened by a subsequent decision which greatly restricts its scope or seriously compromises its logic, the ideal of interpretive stability is weakened. For example, *Gertz* v. *Welch*[50] significantly altered the concept of a "public person" as set forth in *Rosenbloom* v. *Metromedia*,[51] and the *Reidel*[52] and *Twelve Reels*[53] cases almost totally undermined the logic and practical utility of *Stanley* v. *Georgia.*[54] I will put such cases in the SA category.

Precedent can be enhanced as well as restricted. Again, some growth in scope and reasoning naturally occurs. However, on occasion the Court will expand precedent by a virtual quantum leap—by applying it to a new legal area or giving it hitherto unforeseen or rejected implications, such as *Frontiero's*[55] reliance on *Bolling* v. *Sharpe*[56] or *Collector* v. *Day*[57] as a new application of *McCulloch* v. *Maryland.*[58] Such radical enhancement of precedent will be categorized as SA.

Interpretive stability need not be measured against precedent. Another baseline is what I will term "ongoing interpretation" of the Constitution. Ongoing interpretation is an inferential interpretation of constitutional meaning drawn from long-standing and/or widespread laws or practices. No specific Supreme Court precedents directly support such an interpretation (although such support may exist at other levels). For instance, from 1791 forward virtually everyone assumed that obscenity was not protected by the First Amendment and acted accordingly; the assumption that tax exemptions for ecclesiastically owned property did not violate the "establishment" clause is similarly ancient. Only after a century and a half of ongoing interpretation did the Court affirm these assumptions.[59] However, the constitutionality of such practice is not always affirmed. Recently the Court has deemed unconstitutional some long-standing practices such as the "spoils system"[60] and state-enforced restrictions on advertising by members of professions,[61] to say nothing of its decisions in the *School Prayer*[62] and *Abortion* cases. In the latter case, Justice Rehnquist in dissent pointedly noted that laws against abortion had been on the books in virtually every state in the union for over a century without provoking a constitutional challenge.[63]

Some decisions overturning ongoing interpretation of the Constitution may well provide greater offense to the ideal of interpretive stability than do decisions overruling specific precedent. Nonetheless, I will put the former type of case in the SA category. I do so because to alter a clearly fixed precedent in the case law generally constitutes a more explicit and dramatic judicial reversal than does a change in practice or interpretation derived from tradition, without a firm footing in case doctrine.

Obviously those decisions where the Court adheres to precedent (or makes only modest adjustments) or ongoing interpretation fall into the Non-Activist category.

The Interpretive Stability dimension is not applicable to those decisions in which the viability of a Supreme Court precedent or an ongoing interpretation is not drawn into question.

Interpretive Fidelity

The Interpretive Fidelity dimension measures activism in the Court's actual or inferential construction of particular provisions of the Constitution. Activism occurs when an interpretation does not accord with the ordinary meaning of the wording of the provision and/or with the known, consensual intentions or goals of its drafters.

As every schoolboy knows, the Supreme Court has primary responsibility for interpreting the Constitution's provisions. How then, we might wonder, can the Court misconstrue that document? It is analogous to asking whether the Pope can espouse heresy. Without trying to answer the former question—indeed, I doubt it can be answered very well unless one views the Constitution as having an ultimately correct metaphysical interpretation—it is nonetheless possible to measure the interpretive fidelity of some Court decisions. Words and phrases, after all, do have some meaning and drafters of constitutional provisions did have intentions and goals. When these appear to be transgressed, dissenting justices and legal scholars often protest vigorously and engage in considerable semantic analysis or historical research. Sometimes the issue is not easily resolvable, but at times the consensual weight of interpretive hindsight joins in condemnation of what I will term *interpretive infidelity*, as in the *Japanese Relocation Cases*.[64]

The arguments surrounding judicial activism on this dimension are similar to those relating to Interpretive Stability except that the focus is on the nature and purpose of the Constitution rather than on legal predictability. While conceding the necessity for discretion in the application of vague phrases to particular situations, critics of activism here argue that the Constitution is not a constitution generically if it can be significantly altered at the will of nine (or five) justices in the course of a particular lawsuit. Although it is a "Constitution intended to endure for ages to come,"[65] it does not follow that the Court can ignore the very words of the document. Article V provides an amending process if particular provisions prove unpopular or dysfunctional. Those unworried about activism here argue essentially that the Court's main function is the smooth application of an eighteenth-century document to twentieth-century problems which may sometimes require new constructions of old provisions. It is the spirit of the document, they argue, rather than the exact wording or the framers' time-bound intentions that is important. At any rate, Interpretive Fidelity is clearly seen as a dimension of judicial activism and warrants discussion in any overall treatment of the phenomena.

Let me discuss the two considerations separately. With regard to wording, I categorize as Highly Activist any decision which appears to be in clear contradiction to one or more constitutional provisions in terms of the ordinary meaning of their wording or which is contrary to the logical implications of two or more provisions considered together. The *Minnesota Moratorium Case*[66] is illustrative. The Court upheld a state law impairing contracts despite the explicit prohibition against such legislation found in Article I, Section 10. The *Harper*[67] decision which declared state poll taxes unconstitutional provides a more complex example. The Twenty-Fourth Amendment, adopted two years previously, banned poll taxes in federal elections *only*. Had the participants in the amending process—the ultimate sovereign—intended to ban poll taxes in state elections as well, there is little doubt they would have done so explicitly. It is also clear that the ultimate sovereign did not believe that the equal protection clause rendered state taxes unconstitutional, for had it been of this belief the amendment would have been superfluous. The Court, in short, amended the Constitution in a manner that the participants in the amending process deliberately chose not to do just two years earlier.[68]

I will also place in the HA category those decisions which in effect create new constitutional provisions by reading them into existing provisions by virtue of a strained or illogical interpretation of language. A prime example lies in the creation of the so-called equal protection component of the Fifth Amendment.[69] It is difficult to derive such an interpretation from an ordinary reading of the words "nor shall any person . . . be deprived of life, liberty or property without due process of law." Moreover, if the words had been historically understood to convey such a meaning, the equal protection clause of the Fourteenth Amendment would have been unnecessary as the Amendment already contained a due process clause.

Constitutional history contains other important "additions." For instance, the method by which the Court extended the Fourteenth Amendment's due process clause from persons to corporations is perhaps well known but hardly well reasoned.[70] And the transformation of the same clause to constrain state "establishment" of religion (for instance, aid to parochial schools) is neither well known nor well understood.[71]

As an aside, it is interesting to note that some such "amendments" generate little controversy. There has been little debate over adding an equal protection component to the Fifth Amendment or over imposing the establishment clause upon the states. Apparently these actions go with the flow. It would be anomalous to forbid states to engage in racial discrimination but have the federal government do so. Corporations were the obvious progenitors of economic progress in the late nineteenth century, and the contract clause did not provide sufficient protection against potentially devastating government regulation. In sum, many Court "amendments" are welcome ones, but they are no less Highly Activist for that.

Some decisions overtly make policy by giving a constitutional provision a new interpretation which, while not contrary to its wording or implications, add on another and perhaps controversial meaning. The key word here is *new*. The interpretation is not inconsistent with the provision's wording, but it is one which had heretofore been rejected or ignored. Such decisions will be categorized as Somewhat Activist. The *Miranda* requirement that suspects be informed of their rights before interrogation is illustrative. This is certainly not inconsistent with the wording of the Fifth Amendment's prohibition against self-incrimination, but it by no means inexorably follows from that wording either, and the Court had never previously required the exclusion of statements obtained without such warnings. Or consider the *Gannett* decision[72] allowing the public to be excluded from pretrial hearings in some circumstances. Non-public trials are not contradictory to the literal phrasing of the Sixth Amendment, as the majority opinion demonstrates, but the wording had previously never been construed so narrowly.

In considering the intent of a provision's drafters, I will categorize as Highly Activist those decisions interpreting a provision contrary to the reasonably clear and consensual intentions of its writers. I will also place in the HA category those decisions applying a provision to a situation existing at the time of its adoption to which it is clear the drafters did not intend it to apply. Decisions flying in the face of the framers' intentions are infrequent, but do occur. Again the *Minnesota Moratorium Case* comes to mind. The clear purpose of the contract clause was to prevent states from altering repayment schedules as some had been doing in the hard times of the 1780s. Yet this was exactly what the Minnesota law did, and the Court upheld it.

Decisions applying a provision to a situation known to its drafters punctuate constitutional history. The Founding Fathers, for instance, were or would have been quite surprised to learn that the contract clause forbade states from altering the terms of corporate charters they granted, as the *Dartmouth College Case*[73] held. Antiabortion laws were prevalent when the Fourteenth Amendment was adopted, but no one suggested that the due process clause would render them unconstitutional.

I am not going to suggest a category of cases for the Somewhat Activist label insofar as the drafters' intentions are concerned. I think that if these intentions are not substantially clear or if there is a conflict in the evidence about what a specific provision was expected to accomplish, the justices cannot be faulted for adopting an interpretation for which there is a reasonable evidentiary basis. Indeed, in cases such as the *Desegregation Decision* where historical evidence concerning intentions can be adduced to support both sides of the coin (not necessarily in equal proportions), the Court would be damned to activism no matter which way it decided. The essence of the drafters' intentions criterion is that they have substantial clarity.

Those decisions which either fairly clearly accord with the wording of one or more provisions of the Constitution, such as the *Pentagon Papers Case*,[74] or which reject proposed new constructions of such provisions, such as *San Antonio School District* v. *Rodriguez*,[75] will be placed in the Non-Activist category. So will those which accord with the intentions of the drafters of relevant provisions, such as *United States* v. *U.S. District Court*.[76] Basically, NA decisions are those which if decided in the opposite manner would constitute activist ones.

Decisions which do not directly involve the interpretation of constitutional language or the discerning of the intentions of the drafters of its provisions are excluded from the Interpretive Fidelity dimension. By definition, of course, all constitutional law cases involve an interpretation of the Constitution. In most of them, however, this is accomplished indirectly, either by expanding, contracting, or otherwise refining a precedent; or by discussing the spirit of a constitutional provision rather than focusing on its semantic or historical meaning. In all likelihood, only a handful of cases per term will be applicable to this dimension. Also excluded are those decisions which apply a provision to a situation not known or easily imagined by the provision's authors. It would be difficult to argue, for example, that the drafters of the Fourth Amendment would have not included wiretapping or other electronic eavesdropping equipment within its scope had such devices then existed. This is not to say that the drafters would have done so; it is simply to assert that the application of the Constitution's provisions to technological or institutional developments clearly beyond the ken of the framers cannot be considered either activism or non-activism and are not part of the dimension. Finally, I will exclude from the dimension those (probably few) cases which are categorizable as activist by one criterion and nonactivist by the other. For example, *Roth* v. *United States*,[77] upholding the exclusion of obscene material from the limits of the First Amendment seems quite contradictory to the Amendment's literal wording ("Congress shall make no law . . . "), but it is also rather clear that the drafters, who were familiar with common-law constraints upon obscene publications, did not intend to provide protection for them.

Substance–Democratic Process Distinction

It is often argued that there is greater justification for the Court's engaging in policymaking in some areas than in others. The classic identification of those areas came in Justice Stone's famous Footnote Four in the *Carolene Products* case: "legislation which restricts those political processes which can ordinarily be expected to bring about repeal of undesirable legislation" and "[legislation] which tends seriously to curtail the operation of those political processes ordinarily to be relied upon to protect [what Stone had earlier termed] discrete and insular minorities."[78]

In the wake of this famous footnote, the Court for about a decade followed the so-called preferred position doctrine which subjected laws impinging upon the political process to greater judicial scrutiny. While the Court has abandoned preferred position as formal doctrine, it still uses reasoning and rhetoric reminiscent of it, and many civil libertarians continue to harken to it as a rationale for judicial activism in the area of their primary interest. Not all agree, of course; many see little distinction between Court policymaking concerning freedom of expression and that affecting more substantive policy areas. Indeed, it is this dispute which renders the substance-process distinction an important element in a discussion of activism. Thus while I will refine it to some extent, the Footnote Four philosophy serves as the genesis of the Substance–Democratic Process Distinction dimension.[79]

As refined, the crucial distinction is between those Court decisions which relate to the integrity of the democratic political processes and those which do not. It is a fundamental tenet of our constitutional system that political minorities have an opportunity through an open, democratic process to become a majority. Court decisions protecting or enhancing these processes can be accounted as more justified than decisions affecting other types of public policy.

I categorize decisions developing or altering policies affecting the political processes as Somewhat Activist. Basically, these involve freedom of expression, the franchise, conduct of elections, and the nature of representation. Such decisions do not directly affect substantive policies. Rather they relate to citizens' opportunities for input into the policymaking system. The Court has made many such decisions upholding, widening, and equalizing these opportunities in the past half-century; *Hague* v. *CIO*,[80] *South Carolina* v. *Katzenbach*[81] and *Baker* v. *Carr* are three important ones that come to mind.[82]

I will place in the HA category those decisions which make economic policy, regulate the non-political-process activities of institutions or groups, or impinge upon people's careers, lifestyles, or moral or religious values. Obviously the scope of this category is broad. It includes the infamous "substantive due process" decisions running from *Lochner*[83] to *Nebbia*[84] as well as the "new due process," the outstanding example of which is the *Abortion Decision*. Note also, however, that the substantive area includes the *Desegregation Decision* and many other race relations cases (but not those involving the right to vote or the legality of sit-ins or other forms of protest). Blacks clearly constitute a "discrete and insular minority," but on balance I do not see legislation directly governing race relations as affecting the political processes so much as it affects everyday life and community relations.[85]

Obviously the Non-Activist category consists of decisions of an opposite nature—those which produce no alteration in substantive policy or have no impact on political processes.

Some classes of decisions are inapplicable to the Substance–Democratic Process Distinction dimension. Those altering civil or criminal procedure are probably the largest such group. These decisions are ordinarily directed at the behavior of trial judges or lawyers. While they affect the judicial process, they have little if any impact on substantive policies or those relating to the political process. However, when such decisions are basically aimed at the behavior of groups outside the courtroom—for example, the police as they are affected by the *Mapp* and *Miranda* decisions—it can be argued that substantive policy is as much involved as the judicial process.

Specificity of Policy

Traditionally, judicial incursions into public policy were of a negative kind. A plaintiff challenged the legitimacy of some law or government policy and the court, if it agreed, voided the law or enjoined the policy. Such a decision often left legislators or administrators free to pursue another approach in their efforts to handle a problem. While nullification is still a prominent characteristic of judicial activism, in recent years courts have increasingly become positive policymakers as well. That is, they have begun to command governmental agencies to undertake certain policies, sometimes in minute detail. In some celebrated cases, courts have gone so far as virtually to take over the management of school systems, prisons, and hospitals.[86] Positive policymaking by the judiciary could be the wave of the future, but it will not arrive without considerable criticism. Courts may have the right to nullify constitutionally improper policies, critics argue, but they have no warrant to behave like a legislative or administrative body. Proponents of positive policymaking reply that the Constitution contains commands as well as prohibitions and that courts are obligated to enforce the former when other agencies cannot or will not do so. Here is another, somewhat more recent, facet of the debate over activism. I will call it the Specificity of Policy dimension.

Positive policymaking is most properly categorized as Highly Activist. It consists of those decisions which, in effect, declare or develop new policy, sometimes with attention to detail, or which specify in detail particular behavior governmental agencies need to follow in pursuit of an existing policy. Examples are not hard to find. The *Abortion Case* did more than strike down state abortion laws; it rewrote them, chapter and verse. The *Swann* case[87] resulted in the establishment of complicated programs of cross-town busing to achieve particular standards of racial integration. In *Miller* v. *California*[88] an explicit obscenity code was developed. *Miranda* told the police in no uncertain terms what they must do before interrogating a suspect, while *Gideon*[89] and Argersinger[90] have effectively commandeered on behalf of criminal defendants a considerable portion of the legal profession's energies.

The more traditional negative policymaking falls in the Somewhat Activist category. Such decisions usually compel a return to the status quo ante. This of course was the hallmark of the Court's many pre-1937 decisions overturning government regulation of the economy. It also describes such recent cases as *Usery*,[91] voiding Congress's imposition of minimum wages on state employees, and the *Lemon*[92] and *Nyquist*[93] cases nullifying state attempts to give financial assistance to parochial schools or their students. At times, however, the Court itself is not enamored with the status quo ante and will invite policymakers to try again with a less sweeping or constitutionally offensive policy as in the *Berger* and *Katz* decisions on wiretapping,[94] or Justice Powell's opinion for the Court in *Bakke*.

Many Court decisions make neither positive nor negative policy, but rather what I will term *permissive* policy. Such decisions say, in effect, "you can do this if you want to, but you are not constitutionally required to do it." *Rodriguez* is a good example. The Court did not require states to equalize tax bases across school districts, but it did not forbid such a policy either (and in fact more than a dozen states adopted such a policy subsequent to *Rodriguez*). Probably the great majority of Court decisions fall in the permissive category. I will categorize such decisions as Non-Activist.

There will be some Court decisions possessing aspects of two or even all three types of policy. Common sense and context will have to be applied to their classification. The *Abortion Case* and *Miller* v. *California*, for instance, have a permissive component in the sense that states are free to have no laws whatsoever governing abortion or obscenity. However, few states have chosen this option and, moreover, the option's existence was not the crucial question to the Court's decision in either case (as it was in *Rodriguez*). The *Abortion Case* also has a negative component in that it rendered unconstitutional then existing laws prohibiting or severely limiting abortions. Had that been all the Court did, a negative classification would have been appropriate; however, the Court's promulgation of its own trimester policy here clearly warrants a positive classification for the case.

The Court generally makes constitutional policy by directing the actions of government agencies vis-à-vis how they would otherwise act. However, in those cases where constitutional decisions do not directly involve government agencies, it is often difficult to categorize a decision as making positive, negative, or permissive policy. Such cases will be excluded from the Specificity of Policy dimension.[95]

Availability of an Alternate Policymaker

"Courts," Justice Stone reminded his brethren in 1936, "are not the only agency of government that must be presumed to have the capacity to govern."[96] The propriety of the Supreme Court's exercising self-restraint in the face of other agencies' attempts to develop policies for the solution of pressing problems is a frequently echoed theme.[97] There is, of course, an element of protest against judicial usurpation in this position. But it is not an objection against *all* usurpation of another agency's legal prerogatives. Rather it is an objection to courts making policy when another agency is engaged or is soon likely to be engaged in meaningful action to meet the problem. Moreover, beyond the usurpation issue, such protest usually takes into account how well courts are equipped vis-à-vis legislatures or administrative agencies to make intelligent policy in any given area.

Thus the final way of measuring judicial activism is on what I will term the Availability of an Alternate Policymaker dimension. The central question here is: to what extent could another agency make policy similar to that found in the Court's decision? Two factors shape the answer. First, does another agency have the authority to make policy and, if so, is it politically or practically feasible for it to do so? Second, is another agency better positioned in terms of expertise and access to information to make policy than is the Supreme Court?

Sometimes prior Court decisions or ongoing interpretation will leave a potential alternate policymaker dubious of its legal authority. In the era of substantive due process and dual federalism, Congress was clearly inhibited in the extent to which it could regulate labor conditions around the nation. Similarly, even integrationists mistrusted Congress's authority to desegregate schools before 1954 because the Court's *Plessy* decision had explicitly upheld the constitutionality of separate facilities. More often, however, lack of authority is not the inhibiting factor. Legislatures have always had the authority to pass laws prohibiting prayer in schools, require busing for the achievement of racial balance in schools, or even mandate *Miranda*-like warnings before the interrogation of suspects. The crucial question is usually the political or practical likelihood of another agency taking such action.

The phrase *political or practical likelihood* of action does not mean that the alternate policymaker necessarily has to arrive at the same policy as that embodied in the Court's decision. This would imply the inevitability or absolute correctness of the policy, in which case it would make little difference who promulgated it. Policymaking is a matter of choice. But it is to some extent reasoned and genuine choice—one where two or more policies (one encompassing the Court's decision) are seen as possible to probable outcomes as the issue is subject to debate and political pressures. In short, there does have to be a reasonable likelihood that an alternate policymaker could have come to the Court's position.

Quite often this is not the case. Occasionally the decisional structure effectively precludes such a choice. It would be quixotic to expect rurally dominated legislatures in urban states to reapportion themselves along the lines set forth in the *Lucas*[98] and *Sims*[99] cases. More often, intense political pressures make any real consideration of alternative policies unlikely. The word *intense* here is intended to delineate a situation going beyond mere majority opposition to the Court's policy. It implies a communal divisiveness or a strong antipathy toward minority political, religious, or cultural positions. During the 1950s, for example, no one would have expected Southern legislatures to enact desegregation laws and few legislative bodies of any region or level could resist proposed anti-Communist laws.

Beyond problems of structure and intensity, action may be precluded by indifference. Lawmakers are simply not interested in some mundane or complex issues, for example, copyright or admiralty matters, and the Court comes to make policy more or less by default.[100] The refusal of other agencies to act can also stem from a desire to pass the political buck; Congress in the 1970s, for instance, avoided choice in the affirmative action area, presumably seeing it as a no-win situation politically, leaving policymaking to administrators and judges.

Judges can lay claim to no particular expertise in substantive policy areas. Few have acquired any specialized knowledge through prior legislative experience or administrative service, and judicial dockets are always broad in scope. More important, judges lack a specialized staff to research the nonlegal aspects of the issues posed in many cases. Indeed, by comparison to other agencies, courts have virtually no staff at all. Moreover, the information processing system accompanying judicial decision making is not conducive to informed policymaking. The focus is usually upon a particular event or situation which may or may not be representative of the policy dilemma generally. Little if any attention is given by courts to the decision's impact. Briefs and oral arguments are developed by lawyers schooled in and encouraged to stress precedent and analogy rather than facts illuminating the social consequences of alternate policy choices.[101] The Brandeis Brief is so memorable because it is so rare.

Not all judicial decisions, however, call for expertise or complex data. Sometimes the information needed is simple, and the crucial question is the bottom-line choice of values. Judges are as competent as anyone else to make such choices. Statistical analyses might inform the details of a reapportionment decision, but they are irrelevant to the fundamental philosophical issue. Impact analyses would do little to enlighten a decision about the wisdom, constitutional or otherwise, or prayer in the public schools. Indeed, where the focus is on a facet of the judicial process itself (did the appellant receive due process?) the judge's expertise is paramount.

I will categorize as Highly Activist Court decisions which *both* establish policy in situations where there was a reasonable likelihood that an alternate policy-making agency would have adopted a similar policy in the foreseeable future (including situations where the Court restores the status quo ante by nullifying a recently adopted legislative or administrative policy), *and* the nature of the policy is such that choices are better informed by data or expertise not normally available in the judicial process. Once again the *Abortion Case* serves as an illustration. The policy at issue was—as Blackmun's opinion conceded—illuminated by physiology and medical technology, subjects normally beyond the ken of Supreme Court justices. Moreover, several state legislatures had already adopted policies similar in spirit if not in detail to the Court's, and public opinion polls manifested majority support for liberalized abortion policies; clearly the status quo was not frozen here.

The Somewhat Activist category is composed of decisions in which *either* the policy is one that another agency might reasonably have come to, but where the Court is just as capable of choosing in terms of expertise or availability of information, *or* an alternate policymaker is or can be better informed, but there is no realistic possibility of its adopting the Court's policy. *Gideon* v. *Wainwright* is an example of the former. There was considerable discussion of the merits and logistics of providing counsel for indigent felony defendants at the time of the decision, and many legislatures had taken steps to that effect. However, judges were certainly as knowledgeable as legislators in making policy so close to their own realm of experience. *Yates* v. *United States*[102] illustrates the latter. Congress and the Justice Department were certainly more knowledgeable about the Communist Party and subversive activities, but given the temper of the times, the Smith Act was not going to be softened and prosecutions were not going to cease.

The nonactivist category covers those decisions where the court declines to overturn or significantly alter policies established by an alternate policymaker or to impose a policy when an alternate policymaker has not done so. Excluded from this dimension are those cases where no alternate policymaker is available. For the present, I use the term to mean nonjudicial governmental bodies. Moreover, such a body's authority to make the policy in question must be plausible. Policies made by private groups or institutions do not fit the dimension.

There will be a fair amount of room for subjectivity in categorizing decisions on the Alternate Policymaker dimension. Disagreement can arise on both the authority and practical likelihood of another agency making policy. Similarly, the amount of expertise and data needed for informed policymaking can be subject to dispute. While twilight zones may be wider here than on some other dimensions, they will not be unmanageable, and their width can be reduced through future refinement.

Illustrative Comparisons

The analytical framework which is summarized in figure 15-2 has a secondary as well as a primary use—it can facilitate the comparison of the degree of activism in various Court decisions. Such a comparison may be useful to those who wish to validate or refute an argument that Case A is a more (or less) extreme example of activism than Case B or that the Supreme Court's leading decisions in one era (say the Warren Court) were more activist than those in another era (say the Court that precipitated the constitutional crisis of 1937).

	Majoritarianism	Interpretive Stability	Interpretive Fidelity	Substance-Democratic Process Distinction	Specificity of Policy	Availability of Alternate P-M
HA	– Nullification of acts of Congress – Statutory emasculation to preserve constitutionality	– Overruling of prior decisions	– Decision contrary to clear meaning or logical implication of constitutional provisions. – "Creation" of new constitutional provisions – Decision contrary to reasonably clear and consensual intent of provisions' drafters	– Decisions making substantive policy	– Positive decisions	– Alternate agency has authority and reasonable political likelihood of coming to Court's policy *and* its expertise and data are more appropriate than Court's
SA	– Nullification of state and local laws – Nullification of administrative regulations	– Radical weakening or enhancement of prior precedent – Reversal of "ongoing interpretation" of Constitution	– Dramatic new application of constitutional provision to situation known to drafters	– Decisions making policy affecting the political processes	– Negative decisions	– Alt. agency might reasonably come to policy, but Court is just as capable in terms of expertise – Alt. agency has superior expertise, but there is no reasonable likelihood it will arrive at Court's policy
NA	– Upholds constitutionality of laws or regulations	– Adherence to prior precedent, "ongoing interpretation" or minor alterations in scope of precedent	– Decisions in accord with provision's wording, logical implications or drafters' intent	– Decisions not making policy	– Permissive decisions	– Decisions not making policy

Ordinal Levels of Activism

Figure 15–2. A Summary of the Analytical Framework

Of course, such comparisons are dependent upon a mutual or common agreement about the weights to be assigned to the six dimensions. Some commentators may well believe that some dimensions are more central or essential to the concept of judicial activism than are other dimensions. If discussants agree, for example, that the Availability of an Alternate Policymaker is twice as important a component of activism as is Specificity of Policy, they can proceed to make comparisons accordingly. They can even agree that one or more dimensions are not components of activism in their judgment and should be eliminated from the comparison. So long as there is agreement as to the dimensions of activism and the weight to be given to each, comparisons between cases can be made systematically.

Similarly, comparison is dependent upon a mutual or common agreement as to the relative importance of the HA, SA, NA levels. Presumably all could agree on giving NA a value of zero and HA a value of one. Thus the only problem would be assigning a value to SA. Some may feel that activism is activism—that little differentiation should be made between the HA and SA levels, suggesting perhaps a ratio of 1.0 to .67 to 0. Others may feel that the decisions encompassed by the SA category are not manifestations of activism in anything like the degree HA categorizations are, and suggest a ratio of perhaps 1.0 to .33 to 0. Moreover, there would be nothing impermissible about arriving at different HA-SA-NA ratios for different dimensions.

Obviously disagreements on the assignments of weights and values can be compromised, especially if the parties are not too far apart. For example, a person believing Majoritarianism to be the essence of activism in colloquy with one believing that Interpretive Fidelity is the most crucial element in activism might agree to give both dimensions twice the weight of the other four dimensions. Similarly, persons approaching the HA-SA-NA ratios from the perspectives noted in the preceding paragraph might well compromise on a 1.0 to .5 to 0 ratio.

One important advantage of the framework here proposed is that it can be used numerically to integrate, contrast, or compromise various definitions of and perspectives upon judicial activism. This will be illustrated in tables 15-1 through 15-4 and discussed in the accompanying text.

Table 15-1 is the base table, and here I assign an equal weight to all six dimensions and use a HA-SA-NA ratio of 1 to .5 to 0. The values for each dimension are then summed and divided by the number of applicable dimensions. This produces a Case Activism Score (CAS).

Table 15-1 illustrates a comparison of the degrees of activism of fourteen twentieth-century Supreme Court cases. The first ten are prominent cases which are frequently portrayed or cited as exemplars of judicial activism. They were chosen to represent different judicial eras—three from the Burger Court, four from the Warren Court, two from the days of substantive due process, and one from the time of World War II. Seven of them are decisions that might

Table 15-1
Numerical Categorization of Selected Cases on Six Dimensions

	Dimension						
Case	Maj	IS	IF	S-DP	Spec	APM	CAS
Abortion Case	.5*	.5*	1.0	1.0*	1.0*	1.0*	.83
Baker v. *Carr/Reynolds* v. *Sims*	.5ᵃ	1.0	1.0	.5*	1.0	.5*	.75
Lochner v. *New York*	.5	.5ᵇ	1.0	1.0*	.5	1.0	.75
League v. *Usery*	1.0	1.0	0.	1.0	.5*	1.0	.75
Desegregation Decision	.5	1.0*	−*	1.0*	.5	.5*	.70
Miranda v. *Arizona*	−	.5	.5*	1.0*	1.0	.5	.70
United States v. *Butler*	1.0	.5	0.	1.0	.5	1.0	.67
Swann v. *Charlotte*	.5	.5	.5ᶜ	1.0	1.0*	.5	.67
School Prayer Decision	.5	.5*	0.ᵈ	1.0	.5	1.0ᵉ	.62
West Virginia v. *Barnette*	.5	1.0ᶠ	−	.5	.5	.5	.60
Miami Herald v. *Tornillo*	.5	−	0.ᵍ	.5	.5	.5	.40
Argersinger v. *Hamlin*	.5	0.ʰ	−	−	.5*	.5	.37
South Carolina v. *Katzenbach*	0.	.5	0.	.5*	0.	0.	.17
San Antonio v. *Rodriguez*	0.	0.	0.*	0.	0.	0.	.00

Weights: HA = 1.0; SA = .5; NA = 0

Letters a–h indicate categorizations discussed in the text.

Asterisks indicate cases discussed in the text.

loosely be considered liberal and three (*Lochner, Usery* and *Butler*)[103] can be considered conservative. All end up with a CAS of .60 or more. The bottom four cases are probably less prominent and do not generally possess reputations as examples of activism. They were chosen for contrast, and their CASs range from .40 to zero.

Deciding the applicability of the six dimensions to these cases and their categorization as HA, SA, or NA reflects, of course, my own judgment. It would be too time-consuming to explain each of the eighty-four entries; those designated by an asterisk have been discussed at least briefly, and most of the others are fairly obvious. A few decisions, however, posed some difficulty for me; others might come to different conclusions about them. They are designated by small letters in table 15-1. They deserve a brief explanation, and such discussion will serve to illustrate some of the categorization problems inherent in my framework.

The Baker and Sims Cases: It is supremely ironic to categorize *Baker* and *Sims* as violating Majoritarianism. The fundamental challenge to malapportionment is that the legislative process is controlled by representatives of only a small minority of the populace. Thus in the generic sense of the term, voiding malapportioned districting laws hardly offends the concept of majority rule. Nonetheless, it would generally be difficult if not impossible to determine whether legislation involved in Supreme Court litigation had majority approval among the population or not. Consequently, I will consider the enactment of laws to be a manifestation of such support.

Lochner v. New York: While the Court had earlier looked favorably upon the "liberty of contract" doctrine, as in *Mugler v. Kansas*[104] and *Holden v. Hardy,*[105] *Lochner* is the earliest case in which state legislation was voided upon this ground. It is, moreover, considered the classic promulgation of the doctrine.

The Swann Decision: While the IF dimension is not applicable to the *Desegregation Decision* because of considerable uncertainty about the intentions of the drafters of the Fourteenth Amendment concerning segregation, it seems rather clear that the drafters never envisioned an interpretation of the Amendment which would require busing or other positive modes of racial balancing.

Prayer/IF: In my judgment, a decision approving of prayers written or adopted by the state for mandatory use in public schools would violate the wording of the establishment clause of the First Amendment. Of course, the establishment clause did not originally apply to the states, and the wording of the Fourteenth Amendment cannot easily be read to render it applicable. I have not considered this point, however, because the *School Prayer Decisions* occurred some time after the establishment clause had been effectively "incorporated" into the Fourteenth Amendment through *Everson v. Board of Education.*[106]

Prayer/APM: In some areas there was little likelihood that legislatures or school boards would repeal provisions requiring schoolhouse prayer, but the issue was quite viable in other areas. A few states, in fact, had laws prohibiting prayer in schools. It is not clear, moreover, that the issue was divisive on religious or other easily identifiable grounds. Hence, on balance, I see this as an issue where there was a reasonable possibility of action by an alternate policymaker.

The Barnette Case:[107] *Barnette* overruled *Gobitis,*[108] a decision of only three years standing. It could be argued that the two cases really manifested one decision in which the justices' thought processes and maneuverings were done publicly rather than in conference and that no long-standing precedent or doctrine was overruled. Be that as it may, *Barnette* did overrule a precedent and certainly constituted a form of interpretative instability. It does not seem very useful, at least at this exploratory stage, to try to distinguish between recent and not-so-recent overrulings. In any event, *Barnette* was seen as an example of activism par excellence by Justice Frankfurter and his ideological followers. Frankfurter's dissent in this case is considered the classic argument for judicial restraint. Ironically, had there been no *Gobitis* to overrule, *Barnette* would obtain a CAS of only .40.

The Tornillo Decision:[109] It seem clear to me that had *Tornillo* upheld what amounted to "equal time" legislation for newspapers, it would have been contrary to the intentions of the drafters of the First Amendment.

Argersinger v. Hamlin: Whether *Argersinger* constitutes a radical enhancement of *Gideon* v. *Wainwright* is a close question—one illustrating the twilight zone between the SA and NA classifications on the Interpretative Stability dimension. I do not think that *Argersinger* expanded *Gideon* in sufficient measure to warrant placement in the SA category.

Table 15-1 illustrates some aspects of the comparative framework which are not easily conveyed by words. For one thing, few if any cases are likely to obtain HA categorizations across the board. Cases in which the CAS is in the neighborhood of .70 must be considered as Highly Activist decisions if that term is going to have a more general application (beyond being used for particular dimensions). On the other side of the coin, while large numbers of cases which merely affirm existing policy one way or another will have a CAS of zero, probably only a handful of cases will fall between zero and .25. This is because most constitutional law cases signifying alterations in public policy will likely be categorized as at least SA (.50) on several dimensions. The exceptions will likely parallel the *Katzenbach* case which while altering long-standing jurisprudence did so to uphold a change mandated by legislation. Put otherwise, the great majority of Court decisions containing any elements of activism will obtain CASs ranging from .25 to .75.

It is also worth noting that most of the cases historically or reputationally viewed as activist are categorized this way to some degree on both the Majoritarianism and Interpretive Stability dimensions. This implies that many cases seen as exemplary activist decisions by commentators or the American public are so classified because they seem to defy the ideals of both majority rule and that of an unchanging Constitution. Of course, this is not universally the case, as *Miranda* attests, but it is activist on only one dimension because the other does not apply to it. In the three cases where both dimensions are applicable but activism occurs on only one, the CASs are below .50.

Table 15-2 demonstrates changes in the CASs when the HA–SA–NA ratios are shifted to 1. to .33 to 0 and to 1. to .67 to 0. Cases having several SA categorizations show greater shifts in CASs than do those with few such categorizations, for instance, *Tornillo* with *Usery*. (Of course, were there a case without an SA categorization, its CAS would remain constant regardless of ratio alterations.) These shifts are sufficient to cause some change in the rank order of the cases. For example, *Usery* falls from 4.0 to 6.5 when the SA is valued at .67 while *Barnette* moves up from tenth to eighth place. Overall, however, the rank

Table 15-2

CAS and Rank for Selected Cases When SA Values Are Changed

Case	SA = .33	SA = .50	SA = .67
Abortion	.77 (1)	.83 (1)	.89 (1)
Baker/Sims	.67 (3.5)	.75 (3)	.83 (2.5)
Lochner	.67 (3.5)	.75 (3)	.83 (2.5)
Usery	.72 (2)	.75 (3)	.78 (6.5)
Desegregation	.60 (6.5)	.70 (5)	.80 (4.5)
Miranda	.60 (6.5)	.70 (5)	.80 (4.5)
Butler	.61 (5)	.67 (7)	.72 (9)
Swann	.55 (8)	.67 (7)	.78 (6.5)
Prayer	.50 (9)	.62 (9)	.67 (10)
Barnette	.47 (10)	.60 (10)	.73 (8)
Tornillo	.27 (11)	.40 (11)	.53 (11)
Argersinger	.25 (12)	.37 (12)	.50 (12)
Katzenbach	.11 (13)	.17 (13)	.22 (13)
Rodriguez	.00 (14)	.00 (14)	.00 (14)

order changes are modest. The assignment of different values to the SA categorization is not likely to make a radical difference in any comparison of activism across cases.

Table 15-3 illustrates the assignment of different weights to one or several dimensions. All sorts of possibilities exist, and only a few are portrayed here. The first column shows the CASs when all dimensions have equal weight. The second column illustrates the changes that would occur if those who felt that Majoritarianism constitutes a more important or severe form of activism agreed to assign it twice the weight of the other dimensions. Operationally, a case's score for Majoritarianism is doubled, and the CAS is obtained by dividing the sum of dimension scores by the number of applicable dimensions plus one (seven if no dimensions are inapplicable). The effect is to give those decisions categorized as HA (nullifying congressional legislation) higher CASs. Those cases in the SA category will have slightly altered CASs, the direction and magnitude of which are determined by how far the original CAS is from .50. New CASs for cases in the NA category will always be lower (unless already zero) and those for cases where Majoritarianism is inapplicable will always remain the same. In consequence, note that the two HA cases, *Usery* and *Butler*, move up in rank order of overall activism from 3.0 to 1.5 and 7.0 to 4.0 respectively.

In the third column of table 15-3, I have accorded the Interpretive Fidelity dimension double weight, reflecting to some extent Raoul Berger's position. Note here that there is a considerable shuffle in the rank order of the cases vis-à-vis the original largely because several decisions with activist CASs are in the NA category on this dimension. The realignment would be even greater did not all the HA cases on this dimension already have the highest CASs.

Table 15-3
CAS and Rank for Selected Cases When Some Dimension Weights Are Changed

Case	All Dimensions Equal	Double Weight for Maj	Double Weight for IF	Double Weight for Spec	Double Weight for Maj, IF, and Spec
Abortion	.83 (1)	.79 (1.5)	.86 (1)	.86 (1)	.83 (1)
Baker/Sims	.75 (3)	.71 (4)	.79 (2.5)	.79 (2)	.78 (2)
Lochner	.75 (3)	.71 (4)	.79 (2.5)	.71 (5)	.72 (3)
Usery	.75 (3)	.79 (1.5)	.64 (6.5)	.71 (5)	.67 (5.5)
Desegregation	.70 (5)	.67 (7)	.70 (4)	.67 (7)	.64 (7)
Miranda	.70 (5)	.70 (6)	.67 (5)	.75 (3)	.71 (4)
Butler	.67 (7)	.71 (4)	.57 (9)	.64 (8)	.61 (8)
Swann	.67 (7)	.64 (8)	.64 (6.5)	.71 (5)	.67 (5.5)
Prayer	.62 (9)	.57 (10)	.50 (10)	.57 (10)	.50 (10)
Barnette	.60 (10)	.58 (9)	.60 (8)	.58 (9)	.57 (9)
Tornillo	.40 (11)	.42 (11)	.33 (12)	.42 (11)	.38 (12)
Argersinger	.37 (12)	.40 (12)	.37 (11)	.40 (12)	.42 (11)
Katzenbach	.17 (13)	.14 (13)	.14 (13)	.14 (13)	.11 (13)
Rodriguez	.00 (14)	.00 (14)	.00 (14)	.00 (14)	.00 (14)

The fourth column gives the Specificity dimension double weight, responding to some extent to the concerns of Horowitz. HA decisions, particularly *Miranda* and *Swann*, move up in rank.

The last column in table 15-3 shows what happens when all three of the above dimensions are assigned a double weight. The divisor is now nine for cases where all dimensions are applicable. A couple of cases, most notably *Swann* and *Usery*, show a considerable shift in rank order, and the *Prayer Case* shows a considerable slippage in CAS. In the main, however, the ranks and CASs are not greatly different from what they are when all dimensions are treated equally.

In sum, varying the relative weights of the dimensions will alter the comparative rankings of decisions. However, such variations, unless the weights assigned are extreme ones, are not likely to change our fundamental perspective concerning them, that is, activist cases will not be viewed as nonactivist and vice versa. Thus disagreement by commentators over the weight to be assigned one or more dimensions is not as important as it might seem at first blush. While weighting changes to make effective or compromise various positions will affect precise comparison of cases having CASs within close range of one another when dimensions are treated equally, they are less crucial to comparison of cases with more widely separated CASs or to comparison where there is less concern for numerical precision.

Finally, table 15-4 makes comparisons between varying periods in the Court's history. I have taken those cases with CASs exceeding .50, excluding *Barnette* which is not easily linked chronologically with the others, and divided

Table 15-4
Dimension Scores and CASs for Three "Courts" Using Cases
from Preceding Tables

Court	Dimension						
	MAJ	IS	IF	S-DP	SPEC	APM	CAS
Burger	.67	.67	.50	1.00	.83	.83	.75
Warren	.50	.75	.50	.88	.75	.63	.69
Pre–New Deal	.75	.50	.50	1.00	.50	1.00	.71

them into three groups: Burger Court cases, Warren Court cases, and the pre-1937 economic regulation cases. Obviously table 15–4 is illustrative only; serious comparison across Courts or eras would require a larger number of cases for each period. Presumably, moreover, they would be selected in a reasonably systematic fashion, perhaps by a panel of constitutional lawyers or historians choosing the dozen most activist cases for a period, or the two most activist cases for each term in the period. For that matter, one might want to compare periods in terms of total output and systematically enter into the calculations important nonactivist cases as well.

Nonetheless, some observations concerning table 15–4 are slightly revealing and may whet the appetite for further longitudinal comparison of activism. Note that the average CASs for the three periods are rather similar. It is interesting to see that the Warren Court actually has the lowest CAS. On the Interpretive Stability dimension, however, the Warren Court was the most activist of the three; its activism apparently manifested itself primarily through jurisprudential changes. The pre-1937 Court, by contrast, was most activist on the Majoritarianism dimension and also usurped the prerogatives of Alternate Policymakers to a greater extent than did other Courts. The Burger Court tends to be at the middle level on most dimensions, but is highest on the Specificity dimension, presumably reflecting the modern trend of courts to make positive and detailed policies. All three score equally on the Interpretive Fidelity dimension, perhaps implying that no era has a special corner on abiding by or violating the particular wording of constitutional provisions or intentions of their drafters.

It should be emphasized that numerical comparisons as shown here have a narrow usefulness. They do provide a handy device by which summary contrasts of activism between cases can be drawn, but numerical comparison is no more than a heuristic tool. The assignment of values is arbitrary, and thus the numerical precision in the results cannot be given serious attention for its own sake. The numbers illustrate the comparisons, but they do not measure those comparisons.

Conclusion

Judicial activism is a central if not well-understood feature of the American political system. As such it has long been subject to both political polemics and scholarly analyses (although sometimes it is not easy to separate the two). Most such attention, however, has been particularistic or at least lacking in a well-articulated approach to the phenomena generally. Thus the concept of judicial activism has had little common meaning; it has encompassed whatever a given writer—or reader—conveyed or inferred. To reiterate the point made at the beginning, the primary purpose of this essay is to establish and articulate a framework facilitating common discussion and analysis of activism.

In constructing this framework, I have been constrained by the perspectives of others. With regard to the dimensions, I have structured them to accommodate the major conceptions or perspectives taken by commentators on activism even though I might not agree that some of them are important or even constitute activism. I have been similarly constrained in developing and describing the levels of activism on each dimension. In other words, the framework has a synthetic quality—it reflects the several conceptions of activism that have scholarly standing. In the absence of such a synthesis, however, the framework would have the same disability that characterized many other discussions: it would present an incomplete, personal perspective on activism. Because of the necessity of synthesis, the framework may not be as succinct or logical as anyone might desire; it can, however, be put to flexible use.

Despite the synthesis, this essay is more than a cut-and-paste amalgamation of everyone else's conceptions of judicial activism. I have tried to give unity to the framework by basing it on the underlying concepts of change in public policy and legitimacy. In doing this, I have tried to remove or minimize the polemical or ideological components or motivations accompanying various definitions of or approaches to activism. In my framework, judicial activism is conceived of as a multidirectional phenomena. Policy change can be liberal or conservative, libertarian or statist, good, bad, or indifferent; similarly assertions that a judicial decision is illegitimate can be motivated by a variety of ideological perspectives or none at all.

Additionally, I have depicted activism as something more than a dichotomous phenomenon. No one has attempted this before, although it is vaguely implied in some of the literature. If one component of activism consists of judicially mandated change in public policy, it follows that some changes are more unusual, significant, or otherwise notable than are others—that there are different levels of activism. Likewise, some Court violations of perceived role constraints are more serious than others. My use of two ordinal levels (Highly Activist and Somewhat Activist) may reflect such differentiation only crudely, but it is a first step in giving some analytical depth to these concepts. And while I have been limited to some extent by institutional arrangements and doctrinal positions in developing the two levels, their makeup reflects in good part my own views on the nature and depths of judicial activism.

What this essay offers, then, is a synthesis of others' approaches meshed into my own structure. It is an initial, not a final effort; it is open to and, indeed, cries out for further refinement. The basic usefulness of the framework lies in the provision of a common set of measures by which to analyze a Supreme Court decision, a line of decisions, a justice's judicial philosophy as reflected by his decisions, or even various judicial eras. The primary usefulness of the framework is that it facilitates analysis and possesses heuristic value. It requires a recognition that there are several dimensions to judicial activism and that it can be perceived as more than a dichotomous variable. One need not accept particular dimensions or levels, but the framework provides a basis for the discussion of these matters. Indeed, unless we use a common conceptual framework, all our analyses or commentary concerning judicial activism will continue to be unintegrated intellectual exercises.

Notes

1. Because this chapter approaches activism as a dimensional rather than a dichotomous phenomena, the term *nonactivism* will be employed for restraint.

2. David Forte, *The Supreme Court: Judicial Activism Versus Judicial Restraint* (Lexington, Mass.: D.C. Heath, 1972).

3. Ibid., p. 17.

4. For example, Robert H. Jackson, *The Struggle for Judicial Supremacy: A Study of Crisis in American Power Politics* (New York: Knopf, 1941); Henry Steele Commager, *Majority Rule and Minority Rights* (New York: Oxford University Press, 1943); Learned Hand, *The Bill of Rights* (Cambridge: Harvard University Press, 1958).

5. For example, Wallace Mendelson, *The Supreme Court: Law and Discretion* (Indianapolis: Bobbs-Merrill, 1967); Alexander M. Bickel, *The Least Dangerous Branch: The Supreme Court at the Bar of Politics* (Indianapolis: Bobbs-Merrill, 1962).

6. Herbert Wechsler, "Toward Neutral Principles of Constitutional Law," *Harvard Law Review* 73 (November 1959): 1-35; and Louis Henkin, "Some Reflections on Current Constitutional Controversies," *University of Pennsylvania Law Review* 109 (March 1961): 637-662.

7. For example, Alexander M. Bickel, *The Supreme Court and the Idea of Progress* (New York: Harper and Row, 1970); Philip B. Kurland, *Politics, the Constitution and the Warren Court* (Chicago: University of Chicago Press, 1970); and Robert G. McCloskey, *The Modern Supreme Court* (Cambridge: Harvard University Press, 1972).

8. Raoul Berger, *Government by Judiciary: The Transformation of the Fourteenth Amendment* (Cambridge: Harvard University Press, 1977).

9. Donald L. Horowitz, *The Courts and Social Policy* (Washington: The Brookings Institution, 1977).

10. For example, Lino A. Graglia, *Disaster by Decree: The Supreme Court's Decisions on Race and Schools* (Ithaca: Cornell University Press, 1976); Ward E. Elliott, *The Rise of Guardian Democracy: The Supreme Court's Role in Voting Rights Disputes, 1845-1969* (Cambridge: Harvard University Press, 1974).

11. See, for instance, James F. Simon, *In His Own Image: The Supreme Court in Richard Nixon's America* (New York: David McKay, 1973); Sheldon Goldman, "In Defense of Justice: Some Thoughts on Reading Professor Mendelson's 'Mr. Justice Douglas and Government by Judiciary,'" *Journal of Politics* 39 (February 1977): 148-158.

12. See Arthur S. Miller and Ronald F. Howell, "The Myth of Neutrality in Constitutional Adjudication," *University of Chicago Law Review* 27 (Summer 1960): 661-691.

13. There are a few exceptions. Cases such as *Home Building and Loan Association v. Blaisdell*, 290 U.S. 398 (1934) (the *Minnesota Moratorium Case*) and *Korematsu v. U.S.*, 323 U.S. 214 (1944), did not change public policy but could be classified as activist on the Interpretive Fidelity dimension.

14. I have not constructed dimensions of activism which directly reflect either the impact decisions have upon society or the controversy which surrounds them. These factors parallel to some degree the underlying conceptions of change in policy and legitimacy, but they are not the same thing. Significant change in policy, for instance, may have little real impact upon society. Consider the *School Prayer Case*, 374 U.S. 203 (1963), in this respect. And controversy may be provoked by the substance as well as the legitimacy of a decision. The *Desegregation Decision*, 347 U.S. 483 (1954), exemplifies this.

15. 367 U.S. 643 (1962).

16. 384 U.S. 436 (1966).

17. *Pollock v. Farmer's Loan and Trust Co.*, 157 U.S. 429 (1895).

18. I use *accomplish* in the legal and not the empirical sense. Recent research has demonstrated that constitutional decisions do not always produce appropriate behavioral changes and, even when compliance occurs, the impact on society may be slight. In this essay, questions of actual compliance and impact are ignored. The debate over activism focuses largely upon the Court's decisions themselves rather than upon others' reactions to them.

19. *University of California v. Bakke*, 438 U.S. 265 (1978).

20. 418 U.S. 683 (1974).

21. 405 U.S. 727 (1972).

22. 418 U.S. 153 (1974).

23. *NLRB v. Jones & Laughlin Steel Corp.*, 301 U.S. 1 (1937).

24. *U.S. v. E.C. Knight Co.*, 156 U.S. 1 (1895).

25. *Heart of Atlanta Motel v. United States*, 379 U.S. 241 (1964); *Katzenbach v. McClung*, 379 U.S. 294 (1964).

26. Another baseline policy problem may arise when the Court resolves a conflict between two existing policies within the same dimension, for example, an act of Congress conflicts with a state law or with an executive order or a

case is governed by two seemingly appropriate precedents which dictate opposite outcomes. Most such issues will be determined by statutory interpretation or other nonconstitutional canons of interpretation, but a few can involve constitutional issues, as in *Myers v. United States,* 272 U.S. 52 (1926). If it is clear what policy actually prevails at the time the case is decided, it will be the base-line policy; otherwise such cases will not be categorized on the dimension in question.

27. *Reid v. Covert,* 354 U.S. 1 (1957) and *McElroy v. United States ex rel. Guagliardo,* 361 U.S. 281 (1960).

28. 369 U.S. 186 (1962).

29. For example, *Reynolds v. Sims,* 377 U.S. 533 (1964) and *Lucas v. Colorado General Assembly,* 377 U.S. 713 (1964).

30. *Brown v. Board of Education,* 347 U.S. 483 (1954).

31. *Dred Scott v. Sandford,* 19 Howard 393 (1857).

32. *Dred Scott* was repudiated by the Fourteenth Amendment, *The Income Tax Case* was overturned by the Sixteenth Amendment, and *Oregon v. Mitchell,* 400 U.S. 112 (1970), led to the Twenty-Sixth Amendment setting the minimum voting age at 18.

33. *Hammer v. Dagenhart,* 247 U.S. 251 (1918), and *Bailey v. Drexel Furniture Co.,* 259 U.S. 20 (1922), led Congress to pass the Child Labor Amendment in 1924, but it was never ratified by three-fourths of the states.

34. For example, *The Civil Rights Cases,* 109 U.S. 3 (1883); *Adair v. United States,* 208 U.S. 61 (1908); *Adkins v. Children's Hospital,* 261 U.S. 525 (1923); and *United States v. Robel,* 389 U.S. 258 (1967).

35. *Yates v. United States,* 354 U.S. 298 (1957).

36. *Welsh v. United States,* 398 U.S. 333 (1970).

37. *Roe v. Wade,* 410 U.S. 113 (1973).

38. This of course makes no distinction between the voiding of a law unique to one state and one such as the *Abortion Decision* which affected virtually every state in the union. Consideration of a decision's geographical scope might be a useful future refinement of the classification process.

39. There are some exceptions to this generalization, such as the so-called independent regulatory commissions, but they constitute a relatively small part of the world of regulation.

40. 323 U.S. 283 (1944).

41. 416 U.S. 496 (1974).

42. 376 U.S. 254 (1964).

43. See Goldman, "In Defense of Justice," pp. 148–58, for a criticism of "backtracking" by the "new conservative activist majority."

44. Federal District Judge Dozier DeVane, as a guest speaker in a constitutional law class I took as an undergraduate, vigorously denounced the Supreme Court's "activism" for not adhering to precedent. His position is outlined in "A Federal Judge Starts a Crusade," *U.S. News & World Report,* December 12, 1958, p. 88.

45. Quoted in Walter Murphy, *Elements of Judicial Strategy* (Chicago: University of Chicago Press, 1964), p. 61.

46. *West Coast Hotel Co. v. Parrish*, 300 U.S. 379, at 400 (1937).

47. 347 U.S. 483, at 494–495 (1954).

48. *Plessy v. Ferguson*, 163 U.S. 537 (1896).

49. In *Hudgins v. NLRB*, 424 U.S. 507 (1976), the justices openly debated whether *Lloyd Center Corp. v. Tanner*, 407 U.S. 551 (1972), had overruled *Amalgamated Food Employees Union v. Logan Valley Plaza*, 391 U.S. 308 (1968).

50. 418 U.S. 323 (1974).

51. 403 U.S. 29 (1971).

52. *United States v. Reidel*, 402 U.S. 351 (1971).

53. *United States v. Twelve 200-Foot Reels*, 413 U.S. 123 (1973).

54. 394 U.S. 557 (1969).

55. *Frontiero v. Richardson*, 411 U.S. 677 (1973).

56. 347 U.S. 497 (1954).

57. 11 Wallace 113 (1871).

58. 4 Wheaton 316 (1819).

59. *Roth v. United States*, 354 U.S. 476 (1957), and *Walz v. Tax Commission*, 397 U.S. 664 (1970), respectively.

60. *Elrod v. Burns*, 427 U.S. 347 (1976).

61. *Bates v. State Bar of Arizona*, 433 U.S. 350 (1977).

62. *Abington School District v. Schempp*, 374 U.S. 203 (1963).

63. 410 U.S. 113, at 174–177 (1973).

64. *Hirabayashi v. United States*, 320 U.S. 81 (1943), and *Korematsu v. United States*, 323 U.S. 214 (1944).

65. *McCulloch v. Maryland*, 4 Wheaton 316, at 408, 415 (1819).

66. *Home Building and Loan Association v. Blaisdell*, 290 U.S. 398 (1934).

67. *Harper v. Virginia Board of Elections*, 383 U.S. 663 (1966).

68. Had the Court declared the death penalty unconstitutional as it almost did in *Furman v. Georgia*, 408 U.S. 238 (1972), the action would have flown in the face of the clear implication of the Fifth and Fourteenth Amendments acknowledging the legitimacy of capital punishment.

69. *Bolling v. Sharpe*, 347 U.S. 497 (1954); *Frontiero v. Richardson*, 411 U.S. 677 (1973).

70. *Santa Clara County v. Southern Pacific R. Co.*, 118 U.S. 394 (1886). At the beginning of the case, Chief Justice Waite announced that the Court did not wish to hear argument on the question as all justices were of the opinion that the Fourteenth Amendment applied to corporations.

71. The first such case is *Everson v. Board of Education of Ewing Township*, 330 U.S. 1 (1947).

72. *Gannett Co. v. DePasquele*, 443 U.S. 368, 99 S. Ct. 2898 (1979). The vitality of Gannett was subsequently put into question by *Richmond Newspaper Inc. v. Virginia*, 65 L. Ed. 2nd. 973 (1980).

73. *Dartmouth College v. Woodward*, 4 Wheaton 518 (1819).

74. *New York Times Co. v. United States*, 403 U.S. 713 (1971).

75. 411 U.S. 1 (1973).

76. 407 U.S. 297 (1972).

77. 354 U.S. 476 (1957).

78. *United States v. Carolene Products Co.*, 304 U.S. 144, at 152–153 (1938).

79. While the substance-process distinction has become an important element in the debate over judicial activism since the *Carolene Products* case, the distinction is not time-bound in any philosophical sense.

80. 307 U.S. 496 (1939).

81. 383 U.S. 301 (1964).

82. Theoretically, Court decisions which contract access to the franchise, the scope of free expression, and so forth, also fall into the SA category. As a practical matter, however, the Court has developed virtually no such constitutional policies (as opposed to sustaining legislative policies already in operation) in recent years.

83. *Lochner v. New York*, 198 U.S. 45 (1905).

84. *Nebbia v. New York*, 291 U.S. 502 (1934).

85. Some religious freedom cases, e.g., *Wisconsin v. Yoder*, 406 U.S. 205 (1972), can involve small and/or unpopular if not discrete and insular minorities.

86. *E.g., Wolfish v. Bell*, 439 F. Supp. 114 (S.D.N.Y., 1977); *Wyatt v. Stickney*, 344 F.Supp. 387 (M.D. Ala., 1972).

87. *Swann v. Charlotte-Mecklenberg Board of Education*, 402 U.S. 1 (1971).

88. 413 U.S. 15 (1973).

89. *Gideon v. Wainwright*, 372 U.S. 335 (1963).

90. *Argersinger v. Hamlin*, 407 U.S. 25 (1972).

91. *National League of Cities v. Usery*, 426 U.S. 833 (1976).

92. *Lemon v. Kurtzman*, 403 U.S. 602 (1971).

93. *Committee for Public Education v. Nyquist*, 413 U.S. 756 (1973).

94. *Berger v. New York*, 388 U.S. 41 (1967), and *Katz v. United States,* 389 U.S. 347 (1967), followed by the wiretapping provisions of the Omnibus Crime Control Act of 1968.

95. In *Lloyd Center v. Tanner*, 407 U.S. 551 (1972), for instance, the policy was negative in relation to those who would distribute pamphlets in shopping centers, but permissive toward the owners of the centers.

96. *United States v. Butler*, 297 U.S. 1, at 87 (1936) (dissenting opinion). See also Justice Sutherland's reply in *West Coast Hotel Co. v. Parrish*, 300 U.S. 379, at 401–402 (1937) (dissenting opinion). Sutherland's spirit, if not his ideology, lives today in the arguments of those who believe constitutional policies are too important to be left to their chances in legislative or administrative arenas.

97. My debt to Lief Carter should be obvious to all familiar with his "When Courts Should Make Policy: An Institutional Approach," in *Public Law and Public Policy*, ed. John Gardiner (New York: Praeger, 1977).

98. *Lucas v. Colorado General Assembly*, 377 U.S. 713 (1964).

99. *Reynolds v. Sims*, 377 U.S. 533 (1964).

100. See, for example, *United States v. Reliable Transfer Co.*, 421 U.S. 397 (1975) and the analysis by Harold J. Spaeth, *Supreme Court Policy Making: Explanation and Prediction* (San Francisco: W.H. Freeman, 1979), pp. 61-62.

101. See Arthur S. Miller and Jerome Barron, "The Supreme Court, the Adversary System and the Flow of Information to the Justices: A Preliminary Inquiry," *Virginia Law Review* 61 (October 1975): 1187-1245, and Charles M. Lamb, "Judicial Policy-Making and Information Flow to the Supreme Court," *Vanderbilt Law Review* 29 (January 1976): 45-124.

102. 354 U.S. 298 (1957).

103. *United States v. Butler*, 297 U.S. 1 (1936).

104. 123 U.S. 623 (1887).

105. 169 U.S. 366 (1898).

106. 330 U.S. 1 (1947).

107. *West Virginia Board of Education v. Barnette*, 319 U.S. 624 (1943).

108. *Minersville School District v. Gobitis*, 310 U.S. 546 (1940).

109. *Miami Herald Publishing Co. v. Tornillo*, 418 U.S. 241 (1974).

Indexes

Index of Names

420

47-49, 60, 113, 120, 123, 140, 181, 196, 204, 249, 255, 269, 353-355, 369, 371, 375-376, 383, 393
Wasby, Stephen L., 13, 23, 31, 33-35, 243, 275, 301, 348, 366, 382-383
Washington, George, 21, 38, 61, 65
Webb, Leicester, 183
Webster, Daniel, 97
Wechsler, Herbert, 4, 132, 209, 414
Weinstein, Allen, 163
Weinstein, James, 270
Weiss, Janet, 268
West, Rebecca, 163
Westin, Alan F., 267, 269
White, Justice Byron, 90, 113, 123, 282-283,

286, 297, 307, 369, 371, 375-376, 383
Whitehead, Alfred North, 192
Whittaker, Justice Charles E., 299-300, 369
Wilkinson, J. Harvie, III, 349
Wilson, James Q., 229, 242-245, 277, 298
Witmer, Helen, 268
Woll, Peter, 229, 232-233, 243-245
Wilson, Woodrow, 167, 190, 193, 228-229
Woodward, Bob, 24, 34-35
Wright, Benjamin F., 76, 82, 100, 132
Wright, J. Skelly, 30, 132, 175, 177, 192, 195, 198-199, 239

Young, J. Nelson, 380

Index of Cases

Index of Subjects

About the Contributors

Henry J. Abraham, James Hart Professor of Government and Foreign Affairs, University of Virginia

Burton Atkins, Professor of Political Science, Florida State University

Gregory A. Caldeira, Assistant Professor of Political Science, University of Iowa

Bradley C. Canon, Professor of Political Science, University of Kentucky

Anthony Champagne, Associate Professor of Political Science, University of Texas at Dallas

Lino A. Graglia, Rex G. Baker and Edna Heflin Baker Professor of Constitutional Law, University of Texas School of Law

Donald J. McCrone, Professor of Political Science, University of Washington

Wallace Mendelson, Professor of Political Science, University of Texas

Arthur S. Miller, Professor Emeritus of Law, George Washington University

Stuart S. Nagel, Professor of Political Science, University of Illinois

Daniel Novak, formerly Assistant Professor of Political Science, State University of New York at Buffalo

Joan Roelofs, Assistant Professor of Political Science, Keene State College, New Hampshire

Marvin Schick, formerly Professor of Political Science, New School for Social Research

Harold J. Spaeth, Professor of Political Science, Michigan State University

William Taggart, Ph.D. candidate, Florida State University

Stuart H. Teger, formerly Assistant Professor of Political Science, Michigan State University

S. Sidney Ulmer, Alumni Professor of Political Science, University of Kentucky

About the Editors

Stephen C. Halpern is associate professor of political science at the State University of New York at Buffalo. He received the Ph.D. in political science from The Johns Hopkins University. Professor Halpern has written primarily on questions of American civil rights and civil liberties and the role of the U.S. Supreme Court in the American political system. He is the author of *Police Association and Department Leaders* (1974) and editor of *The Future of Our Liberties: Perspectives on the Bill of Rights* (1982). He has been a Fellow at the Institute in Behavioral Science and Law, associate editor of the *Law and Society Review,* and a Fulbright Scholar at the University of Utrecht, the Netherlands. At present he is a candidate for the J.D. degree at the School of Law, State University of New York at Buffalo and is completing a book on school desegregation.

Charles M. Lamb is assistant professor of political science at the State University of New York at Buffalo. He received the Ph.D. in political science from the University of Alabama. He served on the staff of George Washington University from 1973 to 1975 and the U.S. Commission on Civil Rights from 1975 to 1977. Professor Lamb has published mainly in the areas of judicial philosophy, process, and behavior; and civil rights. His forthcoming books include *The Federal Government and Fair Housing* and *Implementation of Civil Rights Policy* (coedited with Charles S. Bullock III).